ALSO BY STACY SCHIFF

Saint-Exupéry: A Biography

Véra

(MRS. VLADIMIR NABOKOV)

STACY SCHIFF

RANDOM HOUSE NEW YORK

Véra

(MRS. VLADIMIR NABOKOV)

RANDOM HOUSE and colophon are registered trademarks of Random House, Inc.

Library of Congress Cataloging-in-Publication Data
Schiff, Stacy.
Véra (Mrs. Vladimir Nabokov) : portrait of a marriage / Stacy Schiff.
p.   cm.
Includes bibliographical references and index.
Romanized record.
ISBN 0-679-44790-3 (hc.)
1. Nabokov, Véra.   2. Nabokov, Vladimir Vladimirovich, 1899–1977—Relations
with women.   3. Spouses of authors—Russia—Biography.   4. Authors, Russian—
20th century—Biography.   I. Title.   II. Title: Mrs. Vladimir Nabokov.
PG3476.N3Z8626   1999
813'.54—dc21
[B]   98-48957

Website address: www.atrandom.com

Printed in the United States of America on acid-free paper

2 4 6 8 9 7 5 3

Book design by Caroline Cunningham

For Marc

CONTENTS

INTRODUCTION

INTERVIEWER: *Could you say how important your wife has been as a collaborator in your work?*
NABOKOV: *No, I could not.*

—*THE LISTENER,* OCTOBER 23, 1969

This is the story of a woman, a man, and a marriage, a threesome that adds up any number of ways. For Véra and Vladimir Nabokov the arithmetic was simple: The elements amounted to a single entity. "There is only one real number: One," argues a doubly fictional character at the center of Nabokov's first English-language novel. Other writers came in pairs, recalls a long-term publisher, but none with the Nabokovs' intensity. They were the ultimate portmanteau couple. "It was as close a marriage as I was ever present at," remembers William Maxwell, speaking for countless others. Even her detractors held that Véra Nabokov participated in her husband's work to an unprecedented degree. And that was in the Russian league, in which the competition is fierce.

The Nabokovs came—and went—as a couple. Most people never saw him without her. Not only were they inseparable but their sentences fused, on the page and in person. They shared a datebook. Their handwritings invade each other's notebooks; he would begin from one end, she from the other. Three years into the marriage Vladimir apologized to his mother for writing her in pencil; Véra was in the next room correcting proofs, with what was presumably the couple's only pen. Thirty-five years later Véra lodged the same complaint. She was writing in pencil because her pen always seemed to be in use somewhere. Only as she came to the end of her letter did her husband return it to her. They did the biographer no favors: They spent very little time apart. Why could they not be like Louise Colet and Flaubert, one hundred letters and only six visits in over a year and a half? The Nabokovs' struck many as one of the great love stories.

Who was she? "She was just a wife," remembered a publisher with whom she corresponded, on her husband's behalf, for three decades. "She was the international champion in the Wife-of-Writer Competition, adding intelligence to the usual equation," recalled a friend. "She was the Saint Sebastian of wives," concluded another. Whoever she was, when it came to self-display she favored the negative comparison. She was not a Russian aristocrat. She was not her husband's first fiancée. She was decidedly not—on this point she was emphatic—a lady driver. She was no Dark Lady of the Sonnets; she neither wrote the books nor starred in them. She appears in only one credited cameo in the fiction. Appropriately, she makes her entrance attempting to coax a black cat out of hiding. Lolita was always Dolores on the dotted line; Véra Nabokov *was* the dotted line, a walking ellipsis. "She was a Polish princess, wasn't she?" asked a translator who worked with her closely. One publisher was under the impression that she was French. Several of her husband's students knew her to be a German countess. A fair number of her correspondents got her patronymic wrong. Her husband's chroniclers, working in her lifetime, had no choice but to write around her.

Nabokov thought he would be remembered for two works—his *Eugene Onegin* translation, and *Lolita*—one of which Véra had suggested, the other of which she had salvaged. The two projects that meant the most to him in the later years were a Russian translation of *Lolita* and the revised edition of *Speak, Memory*. Véra collaborated on the first and contributed to the second. The original Nabokovian, she was a full creative partner in everything her husband did. She had a need to do something great with her life. And as he made clear from the start, Nabokov had a very great need of her. Lawyers, publishers, relatives, colleagues, friends, agreed on one point: "He would have been nowhere without her." Her marriage put her in the spotlight; her nature made her drift toward the shadows. As did some of her responsibilities, which demanded silence. Nabokov spoke fondly of having composed in the car, "the only place in America with no noise and no draft." Véra was the one who parked him there, under a tree, in the remote western outposts he so loved. And then obligingly disappeared from the picture.

To one person she remained always hugely visible. Nabokov was supremely conscious of her presence. He lit up around his wife; he played off of her. The two comported themselves as if they shared a secret. With visitors later in life they resembled nothing so much as two children plotting, in code, about how much they dared tell the adults. One Cornell colleague went so far as to use the "u" word: "He was the most uxorious man I have ever met."

Nabokov thought his wife discerning, wise, whimsical, and much else as well. In 1949 he registered his disapproval of the object of a student's affection, whom he did not consider a raving beauty. But beauty isn't everything, protested the Cornellian. "Mr. Keegan, Mr. Keegan, that's just a conceit we carry on with. Beauty *is* everything," Professor Nabokov assured him. An American admirer sought out the couple in Italy during the summer of 1967. They were walking down a mountain trail, butterfly nets in hand. Nabokov was jubilant. Earlier in the day, he had sighted a rare species, precisely the one he had been looking for. He had gone back for his wife of forty-two years. He wanted her to be with him when he made his capture.

His image was flattering, but so was the image he saw reflected back at him. One of the discarded titles within the works was "Portrait of the Artist in a Mirror"; in Nabokov's case, the mirror was to be found in his wife's brilliant blue eyes. The illusion stands prominently at the center of the highly refractive literature, as it does at the center of the marriage. Nabokov reveled in being a figment of Véra's imagination, which is no wonder, given who she thought he was. When she met him she felt that he was the greatest writer of his generation; to that single truth she held strong for sixty-eight years, as if to compensate for all the loss and the turmoil, the accidents of history. She did all in her power to see to it that he existed not in time, only in art, thus sparing him the fate of so many of his characters, imprisoned by their various passions. The genius went into the work, not the life—something Véra Nabokov had to explain regularly to family members, whose letters to her husband were turned over to her to be answered. This resulted in understandable confusion about authorship, which grew worse over the years.

It has been said that the Nabokovs "refined their marriage to a work of art." Both partners wrung an immense amount of creative mileage from it. In singular ways this was as true in Berlin in the 1920s as it was in upstate New York in the 1950s and Switzerland in the 1970s. After the advent of *Lolita,* the public Nabokov, the voice of Nabokov, was Véra's. We are accustomed to husbands silencing wives, but here was a wife silencing, editing, speaking for, *creating,* her husband. In many ways, the distant, unapproachable, irreproachable "VN" was her construct. To begin to pry the couple apart is to see what lay beneath the monument, the figure in the carpet.

Véra Nabokov—she added the accent when she arrived in America, so that the name would be pronounced to rhyme with "dare ah"—was an eminent woman because she was married to an eminent man, more exactly a man whom she helped to achieve eminence. She is important for what she reveals about her husband. Which is a very great deal; the marriage was at the heart of his existence. It defined them both. It shaped his work. The keen-eyed Saul Steinberg may have put it best: "It would be difficult to write about Véra without mentioning Vladimir. But it would be impossible to write about Vladimir without mentioning Véra." Hers was a life lived in the margins, but then—as Nabokov teaches us—sometimes the commentary *is* the story.

This volume is not one of literary criticism. From the earliest years to the final days, Véra Nabokov's was a life steeped in literature, for which she had a supremely sensitive ear, a prodigious memory, and a near-religious appreciation. But she was not a writer. She was just a wife.

Véra

(MRS. VLADIMIR NABOKOV)

PETERSBURG 3848

The crudest curriculum vitae crows and flaps its wings in a style peculiar to the undersigner. I doubt whether you can even give your telephone number without giving something of yourself.

—Nabokov, *Nikolai Gogol*

1

Véra Nabokov neither wrote her memoirs nor considered doing so. Even at the end of her long life, she remained the world's least likely candidate to set down the confessions of a white widowed female. (She did keep a diary of one girl's fortunes, but the girl was Lolita.) When asked how she had met the man to whom she had been married for fifty-two years she begged the question, with varying degrees of geniality. "I don't remember" was the stock response, a perfectly transparent statement coming from the woman who could recite volumes of her husband's verse by heart. At another time she parried with: "Who are you, the KGB?" One of the few trusted scholars cornered her. Here is your husband's account of the events of May 8, 1923; do you care to elaborate? "No," shot back Mrs. Nabokov. In the biographer's ears rang the sound of the portcullis crashing down. For all anyone knew she had been *born* Mrs. Nabokov.

Which she had not. Vladimir Nabokov's version, delivered more or less consistently, was that he had met the last of his fiancées in Germany.* "I met

* His wife always hastened to point out that she had been the third, if not the fourth, near–Mrs. Nabokov, before becoming the sole Mrs. Nabokov.

my wife, Véra Slonim, at one of the émigré charity balls in Berlin at which it
was fashionable for Russian young ladies to sell punch, books, flowers, and
toys," he stated plainly. When a biographer noted as much, adding that
Nabokov left shortly thereafter for the south of France, Mrs. Nabokov went
to work in the margins. "All this is rot," she offered by way of corrective. Of
Nabokov's 1923 trip to France another scholar observed: "While there he
wrote once to a girl named Véra Slonim whom he had met at a charity ball
before leaving." Coolly Mrs. Nabokov announced that this single sentence
bulged with three untruths, which she made no effort to identify.

In all likelihood the ball was a " 'reminiscence' . . . born many years later"
on the part of Nabokov, who anointed May 8 as the day on which he had met
his wife-to-be. A lavish dance *was* held in Berlin—one of those "organized by
society ladies and attended by the German elite and numerous members of
the diplomatic corps," in Véra's more glamorous description, and which both
future Nabokovs were in the habit of attending—but on May 9. These balls
took place with regular succession; Nabokov had met a previous fiancée at
one such benefit.* Ultimately we are left to weigh his expert fumbling of
dates against Véra's equally expert denial of what may in truth very well have
happened; the scale tips in neither direction. Between the husband's burnish-
ing of facts and the wife's sweeping of those facts under the carpet, much is
possible. "But without these fairy tales the world would not be real," proclaimed Nabokov, who could not resist the later temptation to confide in a
visiting publisher that he and Véra had met and fallen instantly in love when
they were thirteen or fourteen and summering with their families in Switzerland. (He was writing *Ada* at the time of the confession.)

However it happened, in the beginning were two people and a mask. Véra
Slonim made a dramatic entrance into the life of Vladimir Nabokov late on
a spring Berlin evening, on a bridge, over a chestnut-lined canal. Either to
confuse her identity or to confirm it—it is possible the two had glimpsed each
other at a ball earlier in the year, or that she had taken her cue from something he had published†—she wore a black satin mask. Nabokov would have

---

* One event that did take place on Tuesday, May 8, 1923, was a poet's reading of his Pushkin translations,
at a bookstore. It is very possible that both Nabokov and Véra Slonim attended.
† The two had certainly been in a room together on at least one previous occasion, if not more regularly.
Fellow émigré Alexander Brailow remembered a series of literary evenings at which the promising poet
was surrounded by young women, "many of whom were quite obviously interested in Nabokov. Among
them was Véra Slonim, whom Vladimir eventually married." It is nearly as difficult for us to patch together the events that introduced Véra and Vladimir as Nabokov felt it had been for Fate to do so in the
first place.

been able to discern little more than a pair of wide, sparkling blue eyes, the "tender lips" about which he was soon to write, a mane of light, wavy hair. She was thin and fine-boned, with translucent skin and an entirely regal bearing. He may not even have known her name, though it is certain that she knew his. There is some evidence that Véra had been the one to initiate the meeting, as Nabokov later told his sister had been the case. He had by 1923 come to enjoy some recognition for his poetry, which he wrote under the name V. Sirin,* and which he published regularly in *Rul (The Rudder)*, the leading Russian paper of the emigration. He had given a public reading as recently as a month earlier. Moreover he cut a dashing figure. "He was, as a young man, extremely beautiful" was the closest Véra Nabokov came to acknowledging as much.

Russian Berlin was a small town, small enough that she may also have known the young poet's heart had been broken in January, when his fiancée had called off their engagement. Véra Nabokov rarely divulged personal details under anything less than duress. But if she had been the one to pursue Nabokov—as word in the émigré community had it later[†]—there was all the more reason for her silence. She did not remove the mask in the course of the initial conversation, either because she feared her looks would distract from her conversation (as has been suggested), or (as seems more consistent with female logic) because she feared they might not. There was little cause for alarm; she knew a surefire way of turning a writer's head. She recited his verse for him. Her delivery was exquisite; Nabokov always marveled over a "certain unusual refinement" in her speech. The effect was instantaneous. As important to a man who believed in remembered futures and prophetic dreams, there was something oddly familiar about Véra Slonim. Asked in his seventies if he had known instantly that this woman represented his future, he replied, "I suppose one could say so," and looked to his wife with a smile. There would have been a good deal familiar to her about him. "I know practically by heart every one of his poems from 1922 on," she asserted much later. She had attended his readings; her earliest album of Sirin clippings opens with several pieces from 1921 and 1922, clippings which show no signs of having been pasted in after the fact. The disguise—it retroconsciously became "a dear, dear mask"—was evidently still in place when the two parted that evening, on the Hohenzollernplatz in Wilmersdorf. They could not have seen each other more than a few times before Nabokov's departure for

---

* Nabokov chose the pseudonym in part so as not to be confused with his father, Vladimir Dmitrievich Nabokov, an eminent jurist and statesman, and a founder of the Constitutional Democratic party.
† The rumor on the street was that Véra had written Vladimir in advance, asking that he meet her, at which meeting she appeared masked. The Nabokovs' son never learned how his parents first met.

France, yet within weeks he had written her that a moth had flown into his ear, reminding him of her.

From France, where he went as a farmhand to recover from his broken engagement, Nabokov wrote two letters at the end of May. The first he dispatched on the twenty-fifth, to eighteen-year-old Svetlana Siewert, the former fiancée. He realized he should not be writing but—liberated by geography—permitted himself the luxury. He had clearly been reprimanded for his persistence before. While he had told friends he could never forgive Svetlana, he could not help himself; she would simply have to hear the tender things he had to say. He had spent months composing despondent verse, convinced that his life was over. Svetlana and her family, he claimed, were "linked in my memory to the greatest happiness I ever had or will have." He remained stubbornly in love with her, saw her everywhere he looked. He had traveled through Dresden, Strasbourg, Lyon, and Nice, and felt no differently anywhere. He planned to continue on to North Africa, "and if I find someplace on the planet where neither you, nor your shadow can be found, then I will settle there forever."

Two days later he wrote to Véra Slonim. She had already written him at least three times; he admitted that he had been coy and had awaited another letter before responding. He may have needed a little convincing: It is the only time in their correspondence he hesitates before setting pen to paper, and one of the few in which he has no need to chide her to write more often. Was he still too preoccupied with Svetlana? He does not sound so in his first letter to Véra:

> I won't hide it: I am so unused to the idea of people, well, understanding me—so unused to it that in the very first minutes of our meeting it seemed to me that this was a joke, a masquerade deception. . . . There are just some things that are difficult to talk about—one brushes off their wondrous pollen by touching them with words. . . . Yes, I need you, my fairy tale. For you are the only person I can talk to—about the hue of a cloud, about the singing of a thought, and about the fact that when I went out to work today and looked each sunflower in the face, they all smiled back at me with their seeds.

Suddenly Africa sounds less enticing. Forty-eight hours after telling Svetlana he will be changing continents, the young poet felt compelled to return to Berlin, in part for his mother's sake, in part because of a secret, one "I desperately want to let out."

How much did Véra know of Svetlana? Probably a good deal, directly or indirectly. Nabokov and Svetlana Siewert had been engaged since 1922, just after the March 28 assassination of Nabokov's father at a Berlin political meeting.* Vladimir had been in love with Svetlana, one of the acknowledged beauties of the emigration, since she was sixteen. She had agreed to the engagement only after the murder, so distraught was her friend in the weeks following his father's death: "He was a poet, and I, I was a child." She had pitied him but did not truly love him. While her parents had been concerned about his liberal politics and his ability to support their daughter, they had welcomed him as a member of the family. After his graduation from Cambridge University in 1922 Nabokov summered with the well-off Siewerts in Germany; he spent every evening with them in Berlin. Many of his first published poems were dedicated to Svetlana. These she read with great pleasure. With very different emotions she read the diary he foisted upon her, in which he had described his previous love affairs. (In the neat summary of his biographer, Brian Boyd, Nabokov's had been "a youth of energetic sexual adventure.") Svetlana was so offended by his descriptions that she threw the journal across the room. Nabokov was an ardent man, which made her nervous. She took to calling him Tiger because of his abundant energy; she was a little afraid of him, put off by his intoxicated talk of passion. With relief, on January 9, 1923—weeks after her fiancé had published a volume of verse in part dedicated to her—Svetlana broke off the engagement. She cried; he cried; everyone cried. She assured him she could not provide him with what he needed. Her parents explained they worried that he could not provide her with what she needed; he would remember them with particular emnity.[†] The two removed the gold rings they had worn, which were melted down and incorporated into religious icons. The results of the breakup can be read in Nabokov's poems of that winter, all of them recopied neatly into a notebook, by Véra.

She who had appeared disguised at the first meeting believed in full candor; it may have been one of her least winning characteristics. Many years later she allowed that it had taken her husband several months to get over Svetlana, although she also suggested that the matter had been settled before she entered the picture, which was not entirely true. Nabokov made no secret of his anguish in the poems he composed in mid-1923. "But sorrow not yet quite cried out / Perturbed our starry hour" qualifies as an open admission; he wondered if it was perhaps "romantic pity" that allowed her to under-

---

* Vladimir Dmitrievich Nabokov was killed by a bullet intended for a political opponent, whom he attempted to shield with his body.
[†] Decades later in his notes to *Eugene Onegin,* he wrote with feeling about "a rejected suitor's unquenchable exasperation with an unforgettable girl and her Philistine parents."

stand his verse so well. By November he was writing transparently of renaissance, of the rebirth of his "rickety" soul. She knew precisely where she stood soon enough. On January 8, 1924, Nabokov would write Véra Slonim: "My happiness, you know tomorrow it will have been exactly one year since I left my fiancée. Do I have any regrets? No. That had to happen, so that I could meet you."

From France Nabokov mailed his summer 1923 verse back to Berlin. On June 24 Véra Slonim would have opened her copy of *Rul* to a poem that struck familiar chords. There could be no doubt in her mind about the identity of the person to whom "The Encounter" was addressed: "And night flowed, and silent there floated / into its satin streams / that black mask's wolf-like profile / and those tender lips of yours." Aloud Nabokov wondered if the two of them were meant for each other. "I wander and strain to hear / the movement of the stars above our encounter / And what if you are to be my fate . . ." The verse spoke for itself but its epigraph was equally forthcoming. From Alexsandr Blok's celebrated "The Stranger" Nabokov had borrowed half a line, the other half of which makes reference to an unknown woman's "dark veil," much-needed distraction to the poet, who has been left by the woman he loves. It was a discreet but all the same public seduction.

Much can be gleaned from reading *Rul* that spring and summer, when Véra Slonim wrote Sirin-Nabokov with regularity. An article about the memorial service for his father—one of the paper's founding editors, and a pillar of the émigré community—had run in April, as had a piece by Nabokov's uncle Konstantin, on the death of Sarah Bernhardt. In and among the ads for pawnshops, for the tailors who could transform military uniforms into evening wear, for magical weight-gaining powders, the ads reminding readers that *Rul* could be purchased even in Estonia and Japan,* were a series of Sirin chess problems, finally a two-act play by Sirin, who spent the summer focusing on verse dramas. On June 6 Véra Slonim published her first translation, of a parable by the Bulgarian writer Nicholas Rainov, from a section of the *Bogomil Legends* called "The Book of Riddles." Bulgarian is decipherable to a Russian speaker, and Véra had spent several weeks in Sofia, where she had picked up something of the language. Nabokov probably had no hand in placing the translations, although he was one of *Rul*'s favorite sons; through her family Véra was already acquainted with at least two of the paper's editors. The pieces may have been done on assignment, given that she

---

* Noting the addresses from which *Rul* subscriptions came in, editor Iosef Hessen asked: "Is there a place on earth to which Russian émigrés were not swept?"

was already working as a paid translator. Whatever the case, she had a busy summer—four installments of the Rainov appeared in June—and a very different one from that of the young poet whose hands were worn from picking fruit in the south of France. It was courtship by literature in a number of ways. On Sunday, July 29, Véra Slonim's first translation from the English appeared, a Russian version of Edgar Allan Poe's "Silence," a cryptic masterpiece of prose poetry. The Poe shared the page with a Sirin poem penned ten days earlier, in Toulon. "Song" is a plaintive tribute to Russia, to which its author remains convinced they will all one day return, a conviction it was just barely possible still to hold at the end of 1923. The lines of its first and last stanzas are deliberately, rather awkwardly, constructed around two syllables, the Russian word for faith, or "*vera.*"

Véra Slonim published three additional translations in 1923, one in July—she was away from Berlin on vacation in August—and two in September. The last was Poe's "The Shadow," another rhapsodic, biblically styled parable, and a companion piece to "Silence." Financial necessity may have accounted for her prodigious translating that summer, the summer of the "witches' sabbath" of inflation. The *Rul* subscription that had cost 100,000 marks a month in July was no longer available in September, when the weekly price had risen to 30 million marks; by early December, a single copy of the paper sold for 200 billion marks. By that time the Ullstein presses that had been turning out *Rul* were requisitioned to turn out money, nearly worthless by the time it was printed. The price of a streetcar ride from the Russian suburbs into the heart of Berlin had risen to the millions; in the three months between the time Véra Slonim and Vladimir Nabokov met and the time they were reunited, the cost of a ticket rose seven-hundred-fold. By the time the crisis began to be tamed, by the time the Reichsbank had again begun to print currency on both sides of the paper, Véra Slonim's signature was no longer to be found in *Rul.* It would virtually disappear from the published page, save from the front matter of her husband's books.

2
———

Nearly a half million Russians had settled in Berlin over the previous three years, when the ruble went a long way and the city was cheaper for those fleeing the Revolution than any other. Its suburbs, where residence permits could be obtained easily, proved especially welcoming. There were émigré Russian everythings: Russian hairdressers, Russian grocers, Russian pawnshops, Russian antique stores, Russian foreign-exchange speculators, Russian

orchestras. There were two Russian soccer teams. To some it seemed as if the
Russians had taken over Berlin; these were not downtrodden, frightened
refugees but a sophisticated, vibrant community of professionals and aristocrats. *Rul* was one of 150 Russian-language newspapers and journals; by 1923
Berlin outshone Petrograd and Moscow as the center of Russian book publishing. Eighty-six Russian publishing firms were founded in Berlin, one of
them by Evsei Slonim, Véra's father. He and a partner briefly opened a firm
called Orbis. Véra worked in the office during the days, evidently in order to
earn the money for horseback riding in the Tiergarten. All of this would
change with the inflation; the next years of exile were to be substantially
leaner. By 1924, the center of the Russian emigration would shift to Paris. But
for a few more months Russian cultural life burned on brightly in Berlin,
with a slate of readings and festive gatherings each evening.

With Nabokov's return, the romance continued through the fall of 1923
on the sidewalks of Berlin, in the southwest suburbs of the city. In their me-
andering the two were hardly alone. The poet Nina Berberova, who had yet
to meet either Véra or Vladimir, remembered that "all of us sleepless Russians wandered these streets until dawn." The critic Vladislav Khodasevich,
with whom Berberova lived for a decade, remembered a sea of "clinging
couples like statues"; those lovers were to be frozen in every doorway
in Nabokov's *Glory,* in whispering mid-embrace. In October Nabokov's sisters and younger brother moved with their mother to Prague, where she
could claim a Czech government pension. Vladimir accompanied the family,
whom he surprised with the precipitate announcement that he was returning
to Berlin, for reasons that became clear only later. Véra helped him to retain
a room at a boardinghouse; she lived with her family a fifteen-minute walk
away. Their assignations—arranged by note or telephone—took place on
street corners, near railway bridges, in the Grunewald. Nabokov's winter
poems are saturated in images of Véra, a slender shadow detaching itself
from the velvety darkness, poised to explore the black magic of the Berlin
streets. The world may have been falling apart around them, but the poetry
is full of enchantment and rebirth, as eight months before it had been full of
self-pity and despair. Nabokov was yet to coin the phrase, but there is everywhere proof that he had found in Véra a companion who could devise a harlequin: "Divining, you notice all / all night's silhouetted games / I start to
talk—you answer, / as if rounding off a line of verse." Acutely aware that he
was in the company of a translator, he felt impelled to choose his words with
an invigorating exactitude. He sensed that with Véra one had to speak
"amazingly." He cursed the telephone, over which everything came out so
wretchedly. He feared bruising her with an "inept endearment." At once he

seized upon something a later admirer was to describe thusly: "With her for a reader, the classics would reveal themselves like paintings liberated from layers of carelessly applied varnish." He felt she spoke with enormous distinction. Never has any woman received so many tributes to her vowels.

It is clear that the two slipped quickly into a relationship; by November Nabokov was swearing that he loved as never before, with an infinite tenderness, that he regretted every minute of the past he had not shared with Véra. The ease with which the two fell together is clearer still if we allow ourselves a glimpse at the thematic shadows the Berlin nights cast on the fictions, which is a little like saying we shall now base our idea of female anatomy on the work of Picasso. This both was and was not the case; the image is more refraction than reflection. But the trails are there all the same. During a November separation Nabokov had written Véra: "You came into my life and not the way a casual visitor might (you know, 'without removing one's hat') but as one enters a kingdom, where all the rivers have waited for your reflection, all the roads for your footfall." A month later he returned to the same image:

> Have you ever thought about how strangely, how easily our lives came together? And this is probably that God, bored up in heaven, experienced a passion he doesn't often have. It's as if in your soul there is a preprepared spot for every one of my thoughts. When Monte Cristo came to the Palace he had purchased, he saw on the table, among other things, a lacquered box, and he said to his major domo who had arrived earlier to set everything up, "My gloves should be here." The latter beamed and opened this otherwise unexceptional lacquered box, and indeed: the gloves.

"In everything from fables there is a grain of truth," he concluded, before asking her to telephone his old apartment very late at night, so as to be certain to disturb his ex-neighbors.

When the muckraking "biograffitist" comes along in the 1974 *Look at the Harlequins!* to ask how Vadim Vadimovich N. met the woman who turned his life around, our narrator shuts the door in his face—but not before referring him to *See under Real,* a novel written thirty-five years earlier, in English. *See under Real*'s actual and phonetic counterpart is *The Real Life of Sebastian Knight,* written thirty-five years earlier, in English. It is almost impossible to separate Véra from the fictional Clare in that novel, who "entered his life without knocking, as one might step into the wrong room because of its vague resemblance to one's own. She stayed there forgetting the way out and quietly getting used to the strange creatures she found there and petted despite their amazing shapes." From the original manuscript Nabokov had deleted a line, which followed the passage about how well Clare fitted into Sebastian's life: "They became lovers in such a speedy manner that for anyone who did not know them, she might have passed for a fast girl or he for a vulgar seducer." Events move with the same lightning speed in *The Gift,* for wholly nonfictional reasons: "Despite the complexity of her mind, a most convincing simplicity was natural to her, so that she could permit herself much that others would be unable to get away with, and the very speed of their coming together seemed to Fyodor completely natural in the sharp light of her directness."

Between Véra and her fictional shadows there is plenty of room for distortion—"They're all Picassos, not one is Dora Maar," Dora Maar grumbled, dismissing nearly a decade of portraits—but Nabokov did indulge in a certain amount of autoplagiarism. His early letters to Véra sound familiar to readers of *The Gift;* his enchantment with her was precisely that of the preordained variety Fyodor feels for Zina, who had in turn been clipping the young poet's work two years before she meets him. Nabokov perfectly summarized the correspondence in that novel:

> What was it about her that fascinated him most of all? Her perfect understanding, the absolute pitch of her instinct for everything that he himself loved? In talking to her one could get along without any bridges, and he would barely have time to notice some amusing feature of the night before she would point it out. And not only was Zina cleverly and elegantly made to measure for him by a very painstaking fate, but both of them, forming a single shadow, were made to the measure of something not quite comprehensible, but wonderful and benevolent and continuously surrounding them.

In 1924 he had written Véra along very much the same lines, declaring: "You and I are entirely special; such wonders as we know, no one else knows, and nobody loves the *way* we love." Despite her perfect understanding, Véra Nabokov was always quick to deny all resemblance between Zina and herself. She shares even that elusiveness with her fictional counterpart. When Fyodor suggests to Zina that their romance will be the very theme of his book, Zina—a character in someone else's book to begin with—shudders. But then the result will be autobiographical!

The self-effacement predated the literature. In the last months that Nabokov lived with his mother in Berlin, Véra did not meet his family, as

Svetlana had often done. When she telephoned and wrote to him in Prague in the fall and again over the winter she did so under an assumed name. When Nabokov's sisters asked who was calling, Véra replied "Madame Bertrand." Already Vladimir complained that she was not holding up her side of the correspondence; he kept expecting one of his sisters to dash in excitedly, bearing an envelope from "Madame Bertrand." This masquerade continued until 1924. Why the deliberate camouflage? In part Véra seemed determined to tread with the silent but firm footfall Nabokov found so appealing, entering "as if gliding across glass," "airborne and unexpected," as he had it in two November 1923 poems. She had little aptitude for drama, for which—as she may have suspected—Nabokov's two younger sisters had a more highly developed taste; Elena Nabokov Sikorski fondly recalled having listened in on her brother's amorous conversations. (She understood even at the time that Madame Bertrand and Véra were one and the same.) Véra may have been aware too of a need for delicacy at Nabokov's end. A Jewish name has a certain ring to aristocratic Russian ears, and while she would have known that Nabokov's father had championed all sorts of unpopular causes—democracy and Jewish emancipation among them—she may have been unwilling to run any risks with his mother. To a German they appeared to be two attractive Russian émigrés of about the same age; to some Russian eyes the couple did not look so eminently well-matched. It is possible too that Véra kept her name to herself simply out of what would later be revealed to be a hypertrophied sense of discretion.

And the mask? With its whirl of charity balls, Russian Berlin was full of masks. Nabokov's literature is a veritable carnival of them, in which—cleverly and infuriatingly—the crucial piece of information is often disguised, a ruse Nabokov much admired in Gogol. "Is 'mask' the keyword?" asks Humbert in *Lolita*. Certainly it matters more than the charity ball, or who pursued whom. Even before she met him, Véra Slonim knew her man, counted on his being able to recognize the "delight in the semitranslucent mystery." She sensed—was it something he had written, or something she had heard said of him?—that he would agree that "a little obscurity here throws in relief the clarity of the rest." And she knew how to hide behind her words, which became something of a family specialty. Certainly the veils did nothing to detract from her allure as far as her husband-to-be was concerned. In his most personal apotheosis of a mask, Nabokov wrote Véra a year after their 1925 marriage: "My sweet, today I sense especially vividly that since that very day when you came to me in the mask that I have been unbelievably happy, that the golden age of my soul has begun." He referred to his own use of disguises as "the little silk mask of an additional pen name." Conversely,

there were plenty of reasons why at twenty-one, in Berlin, Véra Slonim
would be exquisitely attuned to the risk of exposing herself, above and beyond her taste in gnomic prose poems. One scrap of evidence suggests that
she generally fostered a taste for camouflage, a happy weakness for a translator to have. In a 1924 letter Nabokov had asked her to describe what she was
wearing. He was pleased by her response; he could picture her perfectly, so
well that he was impatient to remove several items. Furthermore she had included an unnecessary accessory in her description. "But you really wouldn't
dare wear a mask," chided Nabokov, when the two had known each other
for precisely eight months. "You are *my* mask."

3

Véra Evseevna Slonim—to return to Mrs. Nabokov her given name—was
born in St. Petersburg on January 5, 1902. She was the second of what were
to be three Slonim daughters; her birth followed by eighteen months that of
her sister Helene, called Lena. Rabbinical records indicate that her parents
had married on April 16, 1899. It was a second marriage for Véra's father and
late for the bride as well: He was thirty-four, she was twenty-eight. Both
were from the Mogilev area, in the Byelorussian Pale of Settlement, about
four hundred miles from Petersburg but by all other measures several uni-
verses away. Byelorussia had the highest concentration of Jewish residents
anywhere in the Empire; Mogilev was a city of forty thousand people, over
half of whom were Jewish. A thriving, Europeanized, industrial center of
a million inhabitants, Petersburg was the cultural and economic capital of
Russia.

Véra's father, Evsei Lazarevich Slonim, had been born on January 30,
1865, in the predominately Jewish village of Shklov, outside of Mogilev. His
father, Lazar Zalmanovich, was a member of the petty bourgeoisie, a low-
ranking tier on Russia's all-important social hierarchy. Neither he nor the
family's friends were wealthy, though Véra's grandfather did briefly prosper,
long enough to ascend for several years to the Mogilev Merchantry and to see
that his son attend university. Evsei Lazarevich Slonim completed his gymnasium studies with honors in 1884. He was nearly two years older than his
classmates, not entirely unusual given the stringent admission standards for
Jewish children, for whom Russian was not a native language. In the fall of
1884 he matriculated as a law student at St. Petersburg University, thereby
circumventing his military service, scheduled for the following year.

Slonim passed his law exams brilliantly—he figured in the top 15 percent of his class—in May 1890. He was no prodigy in completing the mandatory dissertation, but also worked throughout the eighteen months in which he prepared the paper, as other classmates did not. After four years as a barrister's assistant he moved on, for what under the best of circumstances may have been financial reasons. The system did not favor apprentice lawyers, who were paid irregularly and poorly; nearly half supplemented their income with outside work or with family monies. At the time of his marriage, in 1899, Evsei Slonim left the law for the tile business. Over the next years he changed profession repeatedly, prospering with each move; generally these were years of unprecedented economic growth in Russia. Of Slava Borisovna Feigin, Véra's mother, born in Mogilev on August 26, 1872, we know virtually nothing. Her family—which would play a crucial role in the Nabokovs' lives—were merchants in the city of Minsk, most likely in the grain business, of more modest means than the Slonims. The Feigins were less assimilated, or at least more often had recourse to Yiddish, otherwise absent from Véra Slonim's childhood, although it had been both parents' first language. In photos Slava Borisovna appears less often than her husband, who is always impeccably dressed, whose light-gray eyes sparkle, and who carries himself with distinction. She was a large woman with a wide jaw, dark-haired and dark-skinned, less the obvious beauty than her three daughters would be. In the rare portraits Véra Nabokov drew of her early years, the mother is nowhere to be found.*

At the time of Véra Evseevna's birth the Slonims made their home on Bassejnaya Street, in a predominately Jewish Petersburg neighborhood. The habit of nomadism was instilled early: They moved three times over the next years before settling at Furstadtskaya 9, probably just before the birth of Véra's younger sister, Sonia, in November 1908. Four blocks from the Neva, the Furstadtskaya apartment was easily the family's most impressive address, and their last before the Revolution. Next door to the handsome building is Saint Ann's Lutheran Church, a little green-and-white-columned Palladian gem; it was from the church that the Slonims rented their second-floor apartment, although by that time Evsei Lazarevich was the owner of a four-story building, in a less desirable part of town. Catherine the Great's Tauride Palace, the Duma's meeting place, stands at the end of the street; on Véra Evseevna's sixteenth birthday the Constituent Assembly would meet there for the first and last time. An eighteenth-century garden—a beautifully

---

* Elena Nabokov Sikorski, Véra's sister-in-law, cannot recall her ever having spoken of her mother, about whose patronymic there is even question.

landscaped field of rolling hills and winding paths—surrounded the structure. In winter a high wooden tower was constructed in the garden and
flooded with buckets of water, for tobogganers; as a child Véra flew down the
silvery slopes in the Tavrechesky Gardens on an upholstered sled. Some of
the most prominent members of the Jewish community lived in the neighborhood, populated mostly by professionals.*

Nabokov reminds us of the obligation of all literary biographers to establish at the outset that "the little boy was a glutton for books." So were
some little girls, nowhere more so than in cultured, logocentric Petersburg, in
a country in which one dueled over literature. Véra Evseevna remembered
having read a newspaper at the age of three. At the time the newspaper was
probably not what a Jewish three-year-old ought best to have been reading,
filled as it was with news of the 1905 pogroms, pogroms that brought to the
Jewish community a fear it had not known since the Middle Ages. She could
remember a poem for life after two readings, a talent that would serve her
well in her chosen occupation, though not an unusual one for a Petersburger,
nearly every one of whom could cite his share of Pushkin. She admitted she
had been a highly precocious child, perhaps as much so as her highly precocious husband; she recalled moments from her first year of life. Mostly it is
telling that she felt that the child had had gifts the mature woman did not
share. It was as if she were speaking of someone else; she was always better
able to applaud the talents of others.

For the most part she was educated at home with her sister Lena, although it is unclear if this was done because her health demanded it, because
her parents found it fashionable (or convenient, with two girls of nearly the
same age), or because she was Jewish and, like many Jewish young men, she
was instructed at home and sent to school only to submit to the annual exams.
Russia was in any event a country in which, well in advance of the rest of Europe, girls were educated, none more so than three daughters of a successful
Petersburg lawyer, in particular one without a son on whom to settle the
mantle of intellectual heir. Nina Berberova, born a few months before Véra
Slonim and a few blocks from Vladimir Nabokov, early on wrote down for
herself a list of professions, "completely disregarding the fact that I was not a
boy." Like Véra, she was capable of discussing the relative merits of the Social Democrats versus the Social Revolutionaries long before she was old
enough to cast a vote. Young women routinely went to law school; half the

---

* Luzhin's father's mistress, the chess-playing "aunt" of *The Defense,* would have been a neighbor.
Nabokov nearly was one, having lived at a rented home on Sergievskaya Street for the two years ending
with the fall of 1908, when the Slonims arrived.

medical faculty in prerevolutionary times were women, as were a quarter of economics students. Oddly, even when the anti-Semitic decrees had made legal careers inaccessible to Jews, government schools for girls remained open to Jewish girls.

The tradition of educating upper-class women dated back to the nine-teenth century, and the upper classes still being infected by the Francophilia of those years, the language in which girls were educated was French. It was a prerequisite at the Princess Obolensky Academy, which Véra and Lena Slonim attended, sporadically, between 1912 and 1917. The school was not necessarily the most elite of the private schools for girls in Petersburg, but it was one of the most expensive. Petersburg was a cosmopolitan city—its wealthy inhabitants subscribed to the London *Times* and to the *Saturday Evening Post*—and German was also taught at the Obolensky, although Véra Evseevna felt she mastered the language mostly in Berlin. For the time and place the Slonim girls were perfectly normal quadrilingual children. At home French was their first language (Véra's was accentless); from her eleventh year, English was the language of play; Russian essentially qualified as a third tongue. When Lena and Sonia Slonim left Petersburg they claimed to be fluent in five languages. Véra's fourth was German and she does not appear to have had a fifth, unless, as has been suggested, it was telepathy.

Our only glimpse of Véra Slonim's academic record is her Obolensky report from the end of her sixth form, the equivalent of an advanced placement year. She submitted to the examinations in the spring of 1917, which supports her assertion that she had begun her studies uncommonly early. At least three years younger than her classmates, she entered school only after special permission had been obtained from the Ministry of Education. She was fifteen, and at the time reading the Russian edition of William James's *The Principles of Psychology*. Her strengths were more in languages and mathematics than in the sciences, and she excelled—her grade here surpassed even those in French and German—at algebra. Her passion for engineering and all things mechanical may already have been born at the time.

At home the girls, at least the older girls, were entrusted to a governess. Véra Slonim remembered having asked when she would be free of her chaperone and having received the disappointing response "When you are married." Years later Lena Slonim would tell Véra how shocked she was by her own son's independence after the close surveillance of their Russian childhoods. Most of their time was spent in the company of those hired to teach them; a whole corps of people was recruited for instruction in ballet, piano, and tennis, and to see to it that the girls were properly steeped in the classics. Dickens, Byron, Tolstoy, Maupassant, and the English poets constituted a large part of the fare. Tutors, like all help, were easy to find and could be had for abysmally low wages; even the relatively poor in Petersburg could afford to keep servants. Véra's time with her parents was limited to Fridays, when the family came together in the evenings, presumably out of a religious instinct if not for a traditionally observant Sabbath. The household was not a hugely social one, although the Slonims did vacation with relatives. In the summer, when Petersburg is hot and fetid and unlivable, the family decamped, as did everyone who could afford to; large portions of the city were deserted through the silver-skied months. The Slonims shared the Russian taste for Finland, just over the border from Petersburg; the summer resorts of which were packed with Russians. Véra passed her childhood summers on the sand and the little wooden walkways at Terioki, where games were organized for the children; on the exquisite beaches along the Bothnian coast; and at least once in Territet, Switzerland, a few miles from the Montreux Palace Hotel, where her sixty-two years of nomadism would at last come to an end.* From this or another Swiss trip she returned to Petersburg in 1914, the blinds of the railway car drawn along the way, although they were some distance from the front. Photos reveal an intent, ravishing, blonde, with her paternal grandmother's and her father's light eyes, otherwise a fair version of her darker, round-faced older sister, who appears more willing to smile for the camera. The two are perfectly groomed and impeccably dressed, often in identical outfits. As a relative later reminded Véra, hers was a luxurious childhood, though this was not a matter on which the Slonim girls were invited to dwell. Evsei Lazarevich raised his daughters to understand that while they should never think it a disadvantage to belong to a good family, they should never assume it to be an advantage either.

Much has been said of the unreality of St. Petersburg, a splendid stage set of a city built on a swamp in the world's most inhospitable climate. Its colors are Scandinavian. Its buildings are plagiarized from Venice and Amsterdam by architects born in Italy, France, and Scotland. Its pink granite embankments were originally Finnish. Its aspirations were highly un-Russian, something not lost on the rest of the Empire, to which it scarcely seemed to belong; its paper mills and shipyards and steelworks were British-, Dutch-, and German-owned. This Venice-inspired mirage would grow wildly, from a population of 1.5 million in the year of Véra Evseevna's birth to 2.5 million in 1917. On all levels, a city of Petersburg's stature at Petersburg's latitude—that of south-

---

* And where she might well have fallen in love with her future husband, as he would assert, had they only met.

ern Alaska—represented a triumph of reason over realism. Its impressive statuary waited out the blizzards under makeshift wooden pyramids; its residents braced themselves for floods every autumn; spring announced itself with the crash of massive blocks of ice breaking up on the Neva. (For Véra Evseevna, the scratch-scratch, rasp-rasp of the servants sweeping snow from the roofs registered as a particularly festive sound; it signaled that the thaw was near.) In the dead of winter, when the ice storms raged, it could be dark for as many as nineteen hours a day. The only city where the wind blows from four directions, as Gogol had it, Petersburg was at the same time a capital that was meant to appear imposing, while behind its gorgeous Palladian façades all was decidedly more precarious. Even the stones themselves were counterfeit: There is no quarry remotely near Petersburg, much of which was constructed of plaster over brick, beautifully doctored to appear majestic, permanent. Small wonder Petersburgers clung to those certainties they could. "One cannon shot was heard at exactly 12 o'clock," remembered Véra Nabokov, "and all of Petersburg adjusted their watches."

For Véra's family little was as reassuringly certain as that midday explosion. The Slonims were Jewish at a time and in a place where their last name colored their every move. The words "Russian" and "Jew" had come together only in about the middle of the nineteenth century, at the time of Véra Evseevna's grandparents, and hung together uneasily, more awkwardly even than did "liberal aristocrat" for Nabokov's father. In one historian's phrasing, the words "Russian Jew" still constituted "less a description than an aspiration." Only in 1861 was a Jew with a university degree officially awarded the right to live outside of the Pale of Settlement; eighteen years later that right was reluctantly extended to Jewish graduates of all institutions of higher learning. At that time most St. Petersburg Jews were still unable to read Russian. In Jewish families living in the most elite Petersburg neighborhoods at the turn of the century—and the Slonims were not yet doing so—about half still spoke Yiddish at home. A tiny and wary minority, they both felt and were made to feel alien. The risk of expulsion followed them everywhere. Jews of the Pale were dismissed as Jews of the provinces, but even Petersburg Jews, even an assimilated family like the Slonims in their native country, were said to belong to a "colony."*

And that colony was engaged, between the judicial reforms of the 1860s and the Revolution, in what must have seemed like a colossal, rigged game of

---

* As an English visitor exclaimed at the time of Véra Evseevna's birth: "I would rather be treated as a swindler, a forger, or a vulgar assassin, than as a respectable Russian Jew!"

Simon Says. A few rights were granted the Jews; it was understood that every right not expressly granted was denied. The Jewish statutes of 1914 ran to nearly a thousand pages, all of them ripe with complications and contradictions. Even someone who had read them all could remain in doubt as to what exactly was permitted and what was not. This left one in a constant state of possible infraction. Furthermore, the rules were subject to change at any time. The Jews could be expelled from the city one minute, invited to stay the next. A Jewish law graduate could practice diligently as an apprentice, or he might be pressured to leave the city, as without having passed the bar he had no right to residency. If he asked to submit to his law boards so as to secure his right to residency, he might be told there were no vacancies in the Jewish quota for testing. And if he was lucky enough to find a place despite the odds, he might, after passing the bar, learn he could not practice in Petersburg as a new percent rule had recently taken effect. A Jew could serve on a jury, but not as a foreman. A Jew could play in a military band but not lead one. A Jewish soldier could pass through Petersburg on leave but was required to spend his furlough outside of the city. There were quotas for how many Jews could be admitted to hospitals. Jews could die, but only in specified numbers. It was a source of outrage that—in flagrant disregard for the law—Jews continued to compete for cemetery space in quota-defying numbers. For the right to reside in Petersburg countless professionals registered as domestic servants, including the greatest historian of Russian Jewry, several renowned artists, and one future president of Israel. The case that most seized the public imagination was that of a young woman who registered as a prostitute in order to attend university; she was expelled when it was discovered that she was not practicing her trade. Nor were the city's most privileged Jews unaffected by these restrictions. When the "Railroad King" Simon Poliakov donated a dormitory to St. Petersburg University, Jews were specifically barred from living in it.

Through these mine-infested waters Evsei Lazarevich cut a careful if confident path. His career was marked on all sides by the on-again, off-again game of acculturation: When he had come to Petersburg—and he appears to have been the first in his family to have done so—his name was Gamshey Leizerovich.* Under that name he earned his legal degree, which secured his

---

* Jews commonly changed their names, both to assimilate and to disappear; often they created a multitude of spellings in order to throw Russian civil servants off their trail. Zalman Aronovich Slonim, evidently Evsei Slonim's cousin, arrived in Petersburg under that name in 1900. The following year he became Semyon Aronovich. By 1902 he had revised his transparently Jewish patronymic and was known as Semyon Arkadievich.

right to settle in Petersburg. Each semester he secured residency papers, renewed with each return from a visit to Mogilev, and extended when necessary. He was part of a huge wave of Jewish law students that greatly alarmed the State; by 1890 nearly half the Empire's apprentice lawyers were Jewish. The release of these statistics set off a furor. Within a matter of years it was next to impossible to do what Evsei Lazarevich had dreamed of doing in 1884. Between 1889 and 1896 no Jews were admitted to the bar anywhere in the Empire. Over the next eight years—when Evsei Lazarevich would himself have relinquished the idea of sitting for his law boards—only fifteen Jewish candidates were approved. Jewish lawyers represented a particular embarrassment to the State because they were able to argue against the laws that had been promulgated to keep them in their places.

And this was, in part, what Evsei Lazarevich spent the next years doing. His actual legal career was short-lived: He worked as an apprentice for the four years following his graduation, for two Jewish barristers, the second of whom had an established practice and appears to have arranged for his lodging. Almost certainly because of the new restrictions—this was the year he should have passed the bar—he moved house and changed professions; the year of his marriage found him working for a large tile business, evidently owned by the Jewish family of a law school classmate. Possibly with the help of his wife's dowry, he opened a kitchen tile company in 1900, which he ran for several years. The business entitled him to a trade certificate but did not automatically confer on him the rights of a merchant of the second guild. Whatever he did immediately afterward proved profitable, as he was able to buy a building in 1907 and to obtain his first telephone number. Other members of the family joined him in the capital: a brother, Iser Lazarevich, practiced dentistry and lived with his family in Slonim's building, into which a cousin, an engineer, moved a few years later. An older brother, David Lazarevich, appears to have moved to Petersburg with or just before Evsei Lazarevich, but not to have stayed in the city. An uncle enjoyed some prominence in business circles.

Véra Nabokov remembered her father as a lumber merchant. He was "a born pioneer in the truest sense, having taught himself forestry and priding himself on never allowing a tree to be felled without having one planted in replacement. He also built a little railway, a kind of feeder line, on one of the estates to bring timber close to the bank of Zapadnaya Dvina, down which river it was floated to Riga, tied up into enormous rafts by skilled peasants." At least after 1909, he did so in conjunction with a Dutchman named Leo Peltenburg, a man who became a close friend and who would be instrumental in helping Slonim to transfer his assets abroad at the time of the Revolution. Also the father of three daughters, Peltenburg was a kindhearted man, quick to dispense wisdom and good cheer. Véra reserved a soft spot for him in her heart; she corresponded with him all her life. Leo Peltenburg ran a one-man firm, with agents throughout Russia and Germany; he traveled often to Petersburg, along with his daughters. For Evsei Slonim there were more than the usual advantages in having a foreign partner. What Véra Nabokov left unsaid in her impressive report on her father is that the timber trade—Russia's second-largest export business at the time—was a predominately Jewish one. And as such additional regulations applied. The Jewish lumber merchant could not freely fell timber. He could not build or operate sawmills. He was obliged to ship his timber abroad in log form, which was less profitable than shipping lumber. He could ship only through specified ports (Petersburg was not among them); he could not lease land from the railroads in order to store his inventory. Of this Véra made no mention. There was every reason, however, why she would have a natural ear for a narrative technique later described as a "system wherein a second (main) story is woven into, or placed behind, the superficial semitransparent one."

Slonim put his legal training to good use over these years. In a number of court petitions he represented Pavel Vladimirovich Rodzianko, an eminent industrialist—his brother was chairman of the Duma—engaged in a number of gold-mining operations. Slonim negotiated for the exploration rights in several mountain ranges in eastern Russia, government concessions of which were elaborate affairs. He would have received a quick education in securing timber rights from his court work on Rodzianko's behalf. The relationship appears to have been a close and mutually satisfactory one; from 1913 until the Revolution Slonim served as the chief estate manager for Pavel Vladimirovich's daughter, a neighbor on Furstadtskaya Street. Maria Pavlovna Rodzianko and her brother controlled a colossal fortune, including a great deal of Petersburg real estate. The finances were in a fabulously tangled state when they entrusted them to Evsei Slonim, who remained in place when Maria Pavlovna and her husband separated. The Rodzianko work constituted a prestigious position—a mere sideline according to Véra, but a time-consuming one, judging from the court appearances and the petitions filed regularly on Pavel Vladimirovich's behalf—and one that suggests that Slonim's politics may not have been as left-wing as could otherwise be expected of a Jewish non-barrister practicing in Petersburg. He voted with the Kadets, as did most of the intelligentsia, but the family was less radical politically than the liberal Nabokovs.

Evsei Lazarevich's longest-running legal concern had nothing to do with his aristocratic neighbors. In 1900 he filed a petition for the right to enter the second guild of the St. Petersburg Merchantry, which may explain the detour he had made into the tile business the previous year. Rank mattered more than wealth in prerevolutionary Russia, and entry into the second guild would have assured Slonim of the closest thing a Jew could claim to an inalienable right: The secure privilege of residency in Petersburg. In particular he made the case for his right to hire a Jewish clerk from the Pale of Settlement in his home. He appears to have had in mind his brother Iser, then a member of the Mogilev petty bourgeoisie. The matter was tightly regulated, as the government feared a kind of Trojan horse invasion of the capital. In a case that reads like a collaboration between Sholom Aleichem and Joseph Heller, Slonim's petition wound its way from ministry to ministry. Briefly he had been a member of the second guild of merchants' sons in Mogilev; he argued that by virtue of his law degree, his trade, and his present residence he should be admitted to that guild in Petersburg. In 1900 the courts ruled that he must first obtain the right to unrestricted residency in the Empire, a right conferred by the very rank he was seeking. Whether Slonim fought the verdict as he did for the sake of his daughters, whose right to reside in Petersburg was contingent on his standing; whether he fought purely for the fate of his brother; whether he fought for the additional rights for himself; or whether he fought for principle's sake is unclear. He was known for his selflessness; legal precedent may well have been his interest. He proved uncommonly persistent. He pursued the matter for thirteen years, in which time Iser secured his right to live in Petersburg by virtue of his medical degree, and in which time the petition wound its way to the Senate. The request Evsei Lazarevich filed in October 1900 was ultimately denied in November 1913.

Both Véra Evseevna and her future husband were quick to stress the primacy of childhood impressions. To his first biographer, Andrew Field, Nabokov confessed his belief that the "specific gravity" of childhood fixes the character of a Russian even more so than it does the character of other nationalities. Speaking for Martin in *Glory* and as himself in *Speak, Memory,* he held that prerevolutionary Russian children had a sort of genius for recollection, that their memories were somehow rendered more indelible by a destiny who knew what she was about to deprive them of. Independently Véra made the same observation in 1958: "An average Russian child of the beginning of this century can ordinarily record a total of reminiscences which appears stagger-

ing even to an exceptionally gifted American."* She was by no means inclined to dwell on these recollections; everything in her history but little in
her temperament could have made her a full-time nostalgic. She appeared
almost frighteningly detached from her past. When asked about her Petersburg childhood and that of her husband, Véra Nabokov confined herself to
lines like "Both of our sets of parents were extremely intelligent people." In
her eighties, she declined an offer of photos of the Furstadtskaya Street
home. Her sister Lena told her son that she had been taught to look forward,
never back; she spoke of wanting to put the past in a box and turn the key,
twice. Véra effectively did as much, without seeming to realize that the key
hung heavily on her delicate wrist. Evsei Lazarevich plainly took misfortune
in stride and forged on, a habit he imparted, with some variation, to his
daughters. From the opposite angle Slava Borisovna's demeanor may have
worked the same effect. She was a high-strung woman, enough so to have
produced an unflappable daughter, one with no taste for any kind of unnecessary hand-wringing. As one of her closest relatives wrote Véra many years
later, "Judging by your letter, you're in a good mood, but then again, you
know how to make a good mood." The Slonim girls, living in straitened circumstances in Berlin ten years after the Russian Revolution, could not have
been less similar to the more famous three sisters in Russian literature. They
were taught to be proud and capable and supremely rational, to rise above
and, perhaps most of all to expect, adversity. In their sixty years of correspondence the past is rarely mentioned; there were no plaintive wails for St.
Petersburg.

Some things were to be insisted upon, on the other hand. Véra Slonim
learned a great number of lessons from her father, only one of which was
how to hold a thirteen-year-grudge, a lesson she would put to good use.
"They were raised to be perfect," reports Lena Slonim's son, who knew his
mother and aunts were pushed hard to excel academically. They were incul-
cated with a firm sense of noblesse oblige, as with a respect for hierarchy; the
Slonim girls knew well how to decode a social situation, and what they could
rightfully expect from one.† In part these seemed to be survival tactics for living in an uncertain climate; the lessons Véra Slonim learned were exactly the
reverse of those her future husband learned in the incunabula of his first
pampered eighteen years. "One is always at home in one's past," Nabokov
would write, certainly not in reference to his wife. Evsei Lazarevich passed

---

* The exceptionally gifted American she had in mind was Edmund Wilson.
† Lena Slonim Massalsky was conscious enough of rank—and of her own worth—to leave a dinner if she
did not think she had been well seated.

his lofty sense of responsibility on to his middle daughter, whom he clearly encouraged. As she recalled later:

> A few years before the Revolution my father bought up the greater part of a small town in Southern Russia which he had planned to develop into a model little city, complete with modern canalisation and streetcar transportation, and somehow that plan so enchanted me that I was promised I would be allowed to take a hand at it when I grew up.

As precarious as the world may have been around them, Evsei Slonim had a taste for adventure, one he fostered in his daughters. He wrote off a neighbor's child with the remark that the child was "calm, but uninteresting." When slandered in a newspaper—during the war he was cited by name as an exploitative apartment owner, after he had actually waived his rent for soldiers' wives—he lost no time in challenging the paper's editor to a duel. He received an apology instead.

"As a little bit of musk fills an entire house, so the least influence of Judaism overflows all of one's life," observed the poet Osip Mandelstam, who had already embarked on his literary career in Petersburg when Véra Slonim was a child, but whose background was in many respects similar. Véra Evseevna remained as areligious all her life as her family appeared to be in Russia, but knew well that her existence was predicated on a hard-won—and flimsy—right. She offered only one view of her distant ancestors, asserting that her father "traced his descent in direct line from a celebrated though abstruse commentator of the Talmud who flourished in Spain in the XVII century, and who traced *his* descent in direct line from the Ancient Judean Kings." None of this can be documented, though Véra Nabokov's was neither an unlikely nor an unusual claim. The most telling thing about it may be her simple assertion of the fact. It is what she believed, or what she wanted believed, or—at best—both. It is also not something she might have asserted in quite the same way in Petersburg. It was possible to feel affluent, even, to an extent, acculturated, but never entirely at ease. Mandelstam wrote of the Jewish tutor who first introduced him to the concept of Jewish pride and whom he failed to believe, as he could see the tutor put that pride away as soon as he set foot again in the street.

This vulnerability turned, on steely principle, to a point of honor, which Véra Evseevna handled decades later with show-stopping directness. In mid-conversation—in the south of France, in Switzerland, in New York—she would ask her interlocuter, often someone she had known for years, if he was aware that she was Jewish. She tossed this query out as if throwing down a glove. It was as if she needed the air-clearing before the conversation could proceed; honesty very nearly constituted a religious principle for her.* She believed in full candor, which was not the same as full disclosure. At one tender point she warned her sister Lena that her religious identity had better be made perfectly clear, "since for me no relationship would be possible unless based on complete truth and sincerity." The pro-Semitism of her future husband and his father is well documented (it could be termed philo-Semitism in the case of Vladimir Nabokov, whose previous conquests included a disproportionate number of Jewish girlfriends), but the matter was clearly much more personal for Véra. Great numbers of inaccurate things were written about her over the years but the single one she found it incumbent upon herself to correct was a line in the *New York Post* that made her a Russian aristocrat. "In your article you describe me as an émigré of the *Russian* aristocratic class. I am very proud of my ancestry which actually is Jewish," she alerted the paper in 1958. Asked if she was Russian her reply was simple, "Yes, Russian and Jewish."

There were lessons in deportment as well to be drawn from the years in a booby-trapped world. Evsei Slonim appears not to have dignified the obstacles by acknowledging their existence, a quality he shared with his daughter. Calmly, quietly, he went his own way. His name shows up nowhere among the lists of those who were lobbying for reform, for Jewish emancipation. It was Nabokov's father who—in a speech condemning the 1903 pogroms—made the point that the Jews of Russia amounted to a caste of pariahs. In a notebook she could not have expected anyone ever to read, fifty-six-year-old Véra Nabokov remonstrated: "I loathe people who push themselves and to see Jews do this disgusts me even more—for we owe it to our honor not to give support to the slander that this is a Jewish trait. God knows, I have seen many, many Jews who were dignified, and proud, and modest—but who takes notice of them?" At no point in her life would she make an entrance that could be described as anything other than "gliding across glass."

4

The Petersburg of Véra Slonim's childhood was a mythical city, and like all mythical cities this shimmering, culturally prodigious metropolis had an obligation to melt away. It began to do so in 1914, when its name changed to

---

* Mandelstam knew something of this straight-spined tradition as well: "My father often spoke of my grandfather's honesty as of some lofty spiritual quality. For a Jew, honesty is wisdom and almost holiness."

Petrograd; "St. Petersburg" disappeared from maps for the next seventy-seven years. The first rumblings of revolution had made themselves felt in those same newspapers Véra had been reading as a three-year-old. January 1905 brought the greatest strike Russia had yet witnessed; life in Petersburg essentially came to a standstill. The situation deteriorated as the year wore on; the government manifesto issued in response to the unrest provoked violence and pogroms throughout the Empire. A sense of dislocation and apprehension accompanied the next years, years in which the Slonim girls learned to hold fiercely to their own opinions, something in which few Russians stand in need of supplementary coaching. There was already about Véra Slonim the kind of "intellectual arrogance" of which Diana Trilling wrote in her autobiography, linking it back to her father's deep confidence in her. Discontent hung heavily in the air, and certain precautions were taken: If Véra Slonim learned about the French Revolution, she did so at home, not at school, where it vanished from the curriculum after 1914.

In 1916, as she was sitting for her Obolensky A levels, the inflation that had set in the previous year rose to crisis levels. The war with Germany had ruined the Russian economy. Already the breadlines stretched the lengths of streets. By the fall prices had quadrupled, and Petrograd—the city at the greatest remove from the food-growing areas—braced itself for a miserable winter. The blizzards came but the supplies did not; only about a quarter of the trains that normally serviced the city arrived. Lines formed everywhere, for everything. Laid-off workers scuffled in the streets. The hunger quickly transformed itself into discontent with the monarchy; the frustrating course of the war did not help, nor did an especially savage winter. The rest of the country continued calmly on its way, but in the cities, and in Petrograd in particular, the feel of violence was palpable. The trouble exploded a little over a mile from Furstadtskaya Street, when the weather broke in February. Within days what had begun as a large-scale hunger riot billowed into a full-blown revolution. On February 27 the troops that had been sent in to quell the violence mutinied; the bark of machine guns could be heard through the night. By early March Tsar Nicholas II had been convinced to abdicate. He was replaced by a liberal Provisional Government, in which Nabokov's father was named Minister of Justice, and of which he wrote probably the most succinct epithet: "I primarily remember an atmosphere in which everything seemed unreal." Too hastily, this transfer of power was heralded as the Great Bloodless Revolution. The stage was set for the arrival of Lenin, whom the Germans covertly returned to Russia with the hope that he would topple the new democracy, thereby extracting it from the war. Lenin emerged from his train at the Finland Station on April 16 to the tune of "La Marseillaise," an anthem that must have rung uneasily in Véra Evseevna's ears; it had been sung by demonstrators all spring. The Slonims were for the most part on Furstadtskaya Street, where they appear to have stayed through the coup d'état of October, when Lenin's troops stormed the Winter Palace, overturning the aptly named Provisional Government, and into 1918, when Petrograd looked less like the legendary Venice of the North than like an armed encampment. Anything that could vaguely be construed as edible was consumed. No one bothered to clear the snow that winter, when groups of Red Guards huddled around bonfires in the streets, interrogating anyone who passed. By the summer of 1918 the Bolsheviks had instituted a one-party system. What had begun as an idealistic, liberal uprising had ended in totalitarianism. Véra Slonim's nineteen-year-old husband-to-be, whom she had yet to meet, had fled with his family to the Crimea the previous November, where he was carrying on a succession of romances, and denouncing the work of Dostoyevsky for the first recorded time.

Evsei Slonim would have seen himself as a member of the intelligentsia, a classless class whose features Nabokov described as "the spirit of self-sacrifice, intense participation in political causes or political thought, intense sympathy for the underdog of any nationality, fanatical integrity, tragic inability to sink to compromise, true spirit of international responsibility." As such he was probably not greatly sympathetic to the Tsar, said to pronounce the word "intelligentsia" in much the same humor he pronounced the word "syphilis." (Most professionals and academics belonged to the Kadet party, the party of Nabokov's father, a center faction that had been striving toward a truly constitutional monarchy. The party of the Rodziankos—or at least of Duma chairman Mikhail Rodzianko—was the Octobrist party, to the right of the Kadets.) Véra Nabokov could not object strenuously enough to the assertion that the intelligentsia had failed to oppose the Bolsheviks at the outset of the Revolution. This had not been the case in her household, or later, in the emigration, when a number of White officers figured among family friends. We know little of her active sympathies during this crucial year, a year when all was dangerous, when public transportation and electricity functioned sporadically, when looting and murder were the order of the day, but we know a certain amount of the disorder she witnessed. Upon seizing power in October the Bolsheviks made their first victims the liberals who had preceded them; the terror spread quickly and indiscriminately. Any well-to-do citizen of any political stripe was at risk. Iosef Hessen, the esteemed writer and publisher who was friendly with both the Slonims and the Nabokovs, recalled that every move, every decision, was made with heightened consciousness. A wrong step in the street could result in an ambush. More than seventy years later, Véra Nabokov wrote to a member of the Rodzianko family, a few years older than she: "I remember vividly how we waited in line in front of the prison when we were trying to find where M. P. [Rodzianko] had been jailed. I also remember that, there being no candy, you had in your pocket several lumps of sugar, several of which you offered me." For Jews matters were more complicated yet. The Revolution brought with it a new wave of pogroms, far more extensive than anything of the tsarist years. By late 1919 even the liberal parties would be infected by anti-Semitism, as the Jews were credited with having turned Russia upside down. Through these events an equation was forged between Communism and Jewry, an equation that explained Véra Slonim's future politics more than she herself ever would. After the escape from Bolshevik Russia, there remained always something revolutionary in her spirit, never in her fiercely held political views. She would rather cancel a vacation than spend one in a country whose foreign policy she deemed pro-Communist. A mail strike was enough to send her running in the opposite direction.

Along with nearly all else, her schooling was interrupted by the civil war. For at least six months after the October Revolution the Slonims lived in Moscow, where Véra did not attend class. She was back at the Obolensky Academy for a month or so before leaving Petrograd for good, a departure the family made in haste. The differing personalities of the three Slonim girls are neatly displayed in their depictions of the events that preceded their exodus, events that took place at a time when everyone had come to fear the squeal of automobile tires beneath his windows, all the cars in Russia having been requisitioned by the Bolshevik authorities. Sonia Slonim, who would have been about eight, reported that her father was arrested, then sentenced to death, from which sentence he was narrowly saved.* Lena Slonim, then about eighteen, and who at least in the eyes of her sisters would adopt an indifference bordering on ambivalence about her background, made no reference whatever to any such events, dramatic or otherwise. Véra, a year younger and afflicted with a pathological addiction to literalism, often at the expense of truth, recalled that the family "not so much decided to flee as had to do so after a long nocturnal search by a band of soldiers who had come to arrest my father (who was not sleeping at home in anticipation of arrest)."

Slonim traveled immediately to Kiev. The women in the family, along with a servant, escaped aboard a freight train to Véra's maternal uncle's home in Byelorussia, then held—it was the end of World War I—by the Germans. This was easier said than done. The trains had no fixed destinations; they

---

* If such a thing happened, no one else in the family was aware of it.

might stop for a day or more without warning. When they did no one knew
where they were, much less in whose territory they stood politically. Although the Slonims' papers were perfectly valid, they were stopped and held
at the Byelorussian border. They could do nothing but sit in the car and avoid
attracting attention, which they did, nervously, well into the night. Finally
the train began moving, slowly at first; it was unclear whether they were
heading forward or back. After a mile or two they looked out with relief to
see German helmets, then an emblem of order. A German officer befriended
Véra and Lena and saw to it that their papers were properly stamped, for
which service he was rewarded with a hugely welcome bar of soap. When the
Bolsheviks arrived the women again fled south, to Odessa.

The nightmarish journey to Odessa represented one moment of her life
in which Véra Slonim cast herself as the heroine of the tale. This was a story
she could be persuaded to tell. The Slonim women and their forty-three suitcases boarded what she described as one of the last trains for the Crimea; certainly none followed directly behind it, as both Véra and Lena remembered
the rail ties being pulled up for fuel. In their freight car they were joined by
followers of Simon Petliura, the Ukrainian nationalist leader and a notorious
anti-Semite. The pogroms of 1919 were at their height in the Ukraine that
fall, claiming somewhere between fifty thousand and two hundred thousand
fatalities, for which Petliura's troops—who did not distinguish between Bolsheviks and Jews—have generally received credit. Asleep on her bags on the
floor, Véra was awoken by the sound of a militiaman roundly insulting a Jew,
whom he threatened to throw from the train. When the delicate seventeen-
year-old girl spoke up in her fellow traveler's defense, the separatists were so
taken aback they changed their approach completely. Politely they escorted
the Slonim women through their next series of adventures. Along the way
through the Ukraine the train stopped at an inn run by a Jewish family, the
bar of which was overrun by returning White troops, uneasy allies of the
Petliurists. Concerned that the travelers would be disturbed in the expected
ruckus, the innkeeper sent his thirteen-year-old son to a brothel to secure
some legitimate distraction for the men. At dawn the hotel porter threw sand
at their windows to wake the Slonims, who escaped with their friends the
Ukrainian separatists. It was the soldiers as well who advised the women to
avoid Kiev, where they had hoped to rejoin Evsei Slonim; the separatists
knew the city was about to be taken. While Véra and her family traveled on
to Odessa, Petliura's men delivered word of the detour to Slonim. On the
train through the Ukraine the soldiers broke into song; when one noticed
that Véra took an interest in their music, he sang her what sounded like a bal-

lad several times over. Véra Nabokov had the words in her head all her life. She could sing the ballad still in her eighties, in Ukrainian.*

Evsei Slonim rejoined his family in Odessa, a city in which chaos reigned well before the arrival of the Bolsheviks. "No one knew who would be arrested tomorrow, whose portrait it was best to hang on the wall and whose to hide, which currency to accept and which to try to pass on to some simpleton" was one appraisal of the situation. At the end of 1919 the family managed to move on toward the Crimea, where they spent more than six months in a villa in Yalta, the last piece of Russian soil to be held by the Whites. Probably in November, at the bitter end of the civil war, the Slonims fled, on a Canadian boat whose captain agreed to ferry passengers across the Black Sea. (He accepted passengers when he discovered there were no valuables to be acquired cheaply in Yalta, the war's victims having lost virtually everything by the time they reached the southern port.) One photo survives from the journey; in it Véra looks like a character from *Oliver Twist*—a stylish one, but a Dickensian waif all the same. Her eyes are enormous and meet the photographer's with great weariness; the rest of the face is as much that of an eight-year-old as of an eighteen-year-old. The reality of Véra's departure from Russia is embedded in Martin's departure in *Glory,* a turbulent crossing to Istanbul. Certainly the description of the bewildered passengers "sailing as if by chance" fit the actual picture; the "rashly chartered" Canadian freighter proved more salubrious than the filthy vessel on which the Nabokovs had crossed the same sea a year earlier. On board ship the captain befriended Véra and Lena, allowing the girls the use of his cabin while he was on deck, a great luxury in the overcrowded vessel. (For a woman who was to be remembered for being unapproachable and fiercely independent, this first escape was one unremitting proof of the kindness of strangers.) In a novelized version of the life, the unsteady trip across the Black Sea would creak like a heavy-handed piece of foreshadowing. To Véra it could have felt like nothing of the kind. The fictional Martin could not grasp the danger of his situation. Véra Slonim—who since 1918 would have been accustomed to danger on all sides—could not have grasped the finality of hers.

The family was delayed by rail strikes, first in Istanbul and again in Sofia, where Véra learned the Bulgarian she put to use in her Rainov translations. After four weeks in Sofia, Evsei Lazarevich arranged with some French soldiers for a private carriage for his family and for a special rail per-

---

* Véra Nabokov's speaking proudly of these events did not preclude her quibbling with every detail of the account when they were set in print by others. Doubtless she would find fault with this one as well.

mit. On beds of hay they traveled to Vienna—Véra found the city architec-
turally glorious and greatly reminiscent of Petersburg—where they checked
into a good hotel, and normal life resumed. Other émigrés traveling the same
route were struck in particular by the sight of white bread and well-fed
horses, something they had not seen in Russia for three years; the first weeks
abroad must have felt dreamlike. Early in 1921 the family settled in Berlin.
Historically Germany had been tolerant of political refugees. Furthermore,
life there was cheap; it seemed the perfect place to wait out the storm. With
the assistance of Peltenburg, his Dutch associate, Evsei Slonim managed
to sell his Russian properties to a speculator willing to gamble that a Bolshevik regime could not last. Soon after his arrival, and having made some contacts in Bulgaria, he set up an import-export business, specializing in farm
machinery.

Despite the plain facts of the dislocation—the Russian language has no
word that rings with the joyous, elective sound of "expatriate"—the first
years of exile were comfortable. They were so especially if Véra Nabokov's
account of them can be believed. She remembered that her father had "made
much money through the sale of Russian estates, his own, and those of some
business acquaintances for whom he acted as broker." She had very smart
clothes, and happily attended all of the best dances, including plenty of charity balls. The general mood in the Russian community, which swelled that
fall to over a half million members, has been described as one of defiance
rather than despair. Véra's disposition over the crises of the next years was no
different. (She was constitutionally incapable of self-pity, even of self-
dramatization. Her letters suffer as a result.) It was assumed that, in her
words, "everybody was going back in a year, or two, or ten." She was eighteen years old; she went stunt flying; she hoped to learn to pilot an airplane.
She rode sidesaddle in the Tiergarten. She learned to shoot an automatic in a
basement firing range, among a group of former White Army officers, at
least a few of whom must have paid special attention to the wisp of a girl with
the crystalline laugh and the impeccable posture and the ice-blue eyes. She
talked, and argued, more about politics than about literature. She did not like
to see the Berlin stay "deprived of its high adventure"; she shared the taste for
exploit with which her future husband would infuse *Glory,* the novel that on
a perfectly literal level most closely resembles his autobiography. "We went to
automobile races, and boxing matches, and the celebrated Berlin variety
show, Scala," Véra recalled. She did not adhere to the "welter of vodka and
tears" school of description.

On the family's arrival in Germany, Sonia was sent to boarding school
near Lausanne, to complete her grade school education. She later returned to

Berlin to attend a Russian gymnasium, and for dramatic training. Lena—who had received the highest possible grades at the Obolensky Academy and a gold medal along with them—went to Paris. At the Sorbonne she earned a degree in modern languages, returning to Berlin two years later. Véra was discouraged in her plans to attend university. She had been prone to respiratory infections, and her father voted against her attending Berlin's Technische Hochschule, as she had hoped to. She did not qualify for admission without supplementary course work, a strain he thought inadvisable. That she could have been so easily convinced seems odd, given what we know about her resolve; it may be a tribute to her father's authority, or it may qualify as a tiny grain of defensiveness about her lack of higher education. In any event the degree in architectural engineering never materialized, though even without it she was to engage in much bridge-building—and throw the occasional stick of dynamite. Save for a stenography course in 1928, her formal schooling had come to an end. She went to work in her father's import-export firm, probably in 1922. At about the same time Véra spent two months teaching herself to type, first by memorizing the keyboard, then by taking dictation from whomever she could enlist.

At his office address on Neue Bayreuther Strasse, Evsei Slonim backed an established Moscow publisher in a literary venture. Orbis's dual mission was to translate Western literature for Russians, and to translate the Russian classics into English, for export to America. Beginning in 1922 Véra worked in that office as well, writing and translating, both for her father and for Orbis, occasionally freelancing for the automobile firm in the building. She handled all but the German correspondence, which was entrusted to a young German woman. The Orbis office would be gone by the following year, a casualty of the inflation, but it survives as the scene of one of the few certain non-encounters between Vladimir Nabokov and Véra Slonim. Nabokov fondly remembered having climbed the stairs to Evsei Slonim's office, debating with his university friend Gleb Struve the fair price to ask for the Dostoyevsky translation they were contemplating. He met with his future father-in-law, and he left the office. Fate is merciful in some ways, a tasteless, prankish, absentminded, clumsy, uncooperative cheat in others. She did not introduce Vladimir Nabokov to Véra Slonim that day. But neither did she saddle him with a Dostoyevsky translation, for which he might never have been paid.

It is highly improbable that anyone ever placed a telephone call from Petersburg 3848, the Slonim home on Furstadtskaya, to Petersburg 2443, two miles away, where the Nabokovs' doorman would have answered. This did not prevent Vladimir from contemplating the long history of his and Véra's near-encounters. In Russia they had had mutual friends—both knew different members of the same prominent families—but they did not meet. Nonetheless Nabokov took it upon himself to divulge that he and his future wife had been strolled by their governesses side by side in a Petersburg garden. "They could have met many times when they were children; at dancing class, perhaps; it bothers them, and they go over it," a visitor reported, in the 1960s. By some accounts the two had acted as extras in the same Berlin movies. Véra had twice summered near his family's country estate. Nabokov positively contorted himself in his attempts to glimpse the workings of the Fate that had finally bent his and Véra's roughly parallel paths; repeatedly he "directed the searchlight of backthought into that maze of the past," just as Van would later do in *Ada*.

What would have happened had there been no Russian Revolution? Andrew Field asked Véra. Two sentences into her answer she was interrupted by her husband: "You would have met me in Petersburg, and we would have married and been living more or less as we are now!" he asserted peremptorily. For the two not to have met and married remained wholly unimaginable to the man with the protean imagination: He held an almost religious conviction about the stubborn inevitability of their union. He who had been so much buffeted about by history—who having lost his country, his father, and his fiancée, had every reason to believe, as he did, that Fate was ill-inclined toward him—preferred to see coincidence as a marvelous artist. Fate holds a place of honor in Russian literature and Nabokov did nothing to dethrone her; her combinational moves are to be seen in every one of his novels, a body of work often said to be distinctly un-Russian. As Brian Boyd has made clear, destiny's contortions in bringing together Véra Slonim and Nabokov—or at least Nabokov's view of those contortions—lends a thematic design to a whole catalogue of fictions.*

In front of others Véra Nabokov was happy to indulge her husband's insistence on destiny's near-misses in Petersburg and final, foreign triumph. She herself spoke of Fate's devious ways. She shared her husband's retrospective capacity and had at least as robust a visual memory. But she did not share her husband's obsession with reconfiguring the near-misses and the uncanny parallels of the past. It was the uncertain past that concerned him, the uncertain future that concerned her. She did not believe Fate as painstaking as her husband; she was more inclined to take matters into her own hands.

---

* And as W. W. Rowe has demonstrated, Nabokov is frequently at work in the background, quietly arranging patterns, from Quilty's appearances in *Lolita* to the benevolent squirrels in *Pnin*.

She had ample reason for doing so. For a Jew in Russia to be a fatalist was tantamount to inviting disaster. Nabokov trusted in a thematic design which could not have looked quite so dazzling, so sure-handed, to someone who was in the habit of gingerly tiptoeing one step ahead of destiny. Véra made only one small acknowledgment to predestination, many years later. When a publisher asked for a publicity photo of her husband, she sent one of him in his infancy. "If you look carefully into the baby's eyes," she advised, "you can see all of my husband's books." Of this she seemed herself perfectly convinced in 1923, although predestination was perhaps not the word for it. "Oh, I have a thousand plans for you," cries Zina in *The Gift*.

If indeed Fate meant finally to allow Nabokov "the upper hand in his dealings with destiny," she threw one last curveball. He missed Véra dreadfully during their January 1924 separation, when he was again in Prague with his mother and siblings. He had never imagined he could pine for Berlin, which suddenly seemed to him an earthly paradise. He was bored without her. He counted the days until their reunion. He spoke repeatedly of their soon-to-be-realized happiness. Already he was dreaming prophetically that he was seated at a piano, with Véra turning the pages of his score. But then—with the return imminent—a small domestic disaster struck. On the morning he read of Lenin's death, he wrote Véra sheepishly: "Something has happened (only don't be angry). I can't remember (for God's sake, don't be angry!) I can't remember (promise that you won't be angry), I can't remember your telephone number." He knew it had a seven in it, but the rest had entirely escaped him.

✳ 2 ✳

THE ROMANTIC AGE

Oh my joy, when will we live together, in a beautiful place, with a mountain view, with a dog yapping outside the window? I need so little: a bottle of ink, and a spot of sunshine on the floor—oh, and you. But the last isn't a small thing at all.

— Nabokov to Véra Slonim, August 19, 1924

1
———

Here is what she must have known by the time she married him: That he was the most gifted Russian writer of his generation. That he was a man of titanic self-absorption. That he had a certain knack for falling in love. That he had an equivalent lack of ability for taming the practical world. How much of this she knew when she fell in love with him is unclear. On only one aspect of the appeal did she offer comment: "Don't you think it was more his verse than his face that attracted?" she asked rhetorically. That the verse could have eclipsed the rest of the package says a good deal about Véra Slonim's commitment to literature; twenty-four-year-old Nabokov, lithe and still dapper and aristocratic-looking, left an impression. Women flocked to him. In the minutes that had elapsed between Svetlana's retreat from the scene and Véra Slonim's appearance on it, at least three women had laid claim to his time, if not his heart. Those names did not figure on the list of conquests he drew up for Véra in the early days of their courtship, a list on which twenty-eight names precede Svetlana's.* (The roll call is composed on a piece

———

* Both Nabokovs maintained that the list was offered up not as exposition but as imitation, of Pushkin. Nabokov's inventory very nearly rivals that of the Master, who listed sixteen serious infatuations

of Evsei Slonim's letterhead.) He felt he could tell her everything, and appears to have done so, with happier results than those he had achieved with Svetlana Siewert. At no time was Nabokov shy about his string of overlapping conquests, explaining in 1970 why he did not want two stressed in particular: "I've had many more love affairs (before my marriage) than suspected by my biographers." He regretted, though, the artistic energy those adventures may have cost him, especially in light of the emotional return. Of Véra Slonim's prior romantic history we know nothing, save that—if she arranged to meet a man alone on a dark street for what were plainly extraliterary reasons—there presumably was one.

She was not particularly happy in 1923, and may have been entirely miserable. Her discontent reverberates throughout Nabokov's letters. In the same missive in which he wrote that he could not commit a word to the page without hearing how she would pronounce it, he swore that what he most wanted was to provide her with a sense of well-being, "hardly an ordinary happiness." There was reason for her to be dispirited at home, though even later in life Véra Nabokov asserted that she had a tendency to focus on the negative side of things. That habit was obvious in the first months of the relationship, when Vladimir asked her not to deprive him of his faith in their future together, repeatedly assured her that their separations were not enjoyable for him, begged her not to resent his absences or second-guess his feelings. At times his fascination with her prickliness—he had written that she was made of "tiny, sharp arrows" and that he loved each one of them—wore thin. Was she trying to make him fall out of love with her? If she had fallen out of love with him he wished she would say so directly: "Sincerity above all!" he swore. "At first I decided to just send you a blank sheet of paper with little question marks in the middle, but then I didn't feel like wasting the stamp," he wrote from Prague, puzzled and a little hurt by her silence. She tortured herself and consequently tortured him. Did she not understand that life without her was unbearable? He acutely felt her "sharp corners," which he found difficult to navigate. "I feel pain from your corners / Love me without hesitation / Without these numerous torments / Do not abbreviate the encounters / Or dream up any separations," he entreated, in an untitled and unpublished poem.

Possibly Véra was taking a page from the international handbook of intellectual coquetry. Had she had any inkling of what lay ahead for the woman who was to marry V. Sirin, she might well have hesitated for a mo-

---

and eighteen light romances. The practice was not an uncommon one; Khodasevich compiled a list for Berberova as well.

ment now. One thing is certain: She did not share her future husband's
genius for happiness. Her evasions wrought rhapsodic tributes from him:
"You see," he averred, "I am speaking with you like King Solomon." Only in
these protests of devotion can we read of Véra's hesitation; at some indeterminate point between 1925 and her death she destroyed her letters to
Nabokov. Discretion does not seem to have been at issue so much as merit.
His words, even the private ones, had a value for posterity. She felt strongly
that hers did not. She disowned her literary work as well, shrugging off the
Rul pieces as juvenilia. The woman who saved every shred of her husband's
published work kept no copies of her own translations. She was certain she
would disapprove of them if ever she reread them, which she did not. (They
are exact, but not inspired.)

Nabokov made no secret of his feelings about women writers—a symptom of provincial literature, he asserted—and Véra may have been sensitive
to this prejudice.* She was neither the first nor the last woman to renounce
her literary aspirations on falling in love with a writer. Boyd feels she could
have been a writer of talent had she chosen to be, but believed so fervently in
Nabokov's gift that she felt she could accomplish more by assisting him than
she might have on her own. Nabokov's 1924 description, written on a day
when he was overjoyed not to have to chastise Véra for her silence and could
instead acknowledge a "stellar" communication, reveals all we know of her
letters of the 1920s: "You know, we are awfully like one another. In letters,
for example: We both love to (1) unobtrusively insert foreign words, (2) quote
from our favorite books, (3) translate our impressions from one sense (sense
of sight, for example) into the impressions of another sense (sense of taste, for
example), (4) ask forgiveness at the end for some imaginary nonsense, and in
many other ways."

Véra Slonim's ability to transfer the observations of one sense into the
vocabulary of another—what is properly known as synesthesia and often
manifests itself as "colored hearing"—must have delighted her future husband. The synesthetic cannot help seeing the world differently; for both
Nabokovs, letters on the page, words in midair, appeared in Technicolor instead of black and white. The ability can be a burden as much as a luxury:
Two people gifted with synesthesia fall into each other's arms as two people
with photographic memories might, or two young heirs to legendary for-

---

* In the 1950s, a few Cornell students recoiled when their professor announced unselfconsciously that
"Austen is a kitten, and Dickens, Dickens is a great big dog." He read Austen with more than the usual
preconceptions; Russia has not yet produced a great female novelist. On a more personal level, he did
nothing to encourage the aspirations of his sister Elena, who wrote to say that she too suffered from the
"family disease." She yearned to publish something of her own, and never would.

tunes, or—in Berlin of the early 1920s—two people who believed the recent earthquake in Japan to be the result of the Jewish/Masonic conspiracy. Two synesthetics might have a thorny discussion over breakfast as to the color of Monday, the taste of E-flat. They might commit a poem to memory chromatically; they might recognize the silhouettes of numbers. The trait is genetic—Nabokov had inherited it from his mother, from whom Véra felt his artistic sensibility generally derived—and the couple passed it on to their own son, although it predominates in females. Nabokov was fascinated to discover that while his palette differed from Véra's, nature occasionally blended colors. His "m," for example, was pink (pink flannel, to be exact); Véra's was blue; their son's pinkish-blue.

Or so he liked to believe. Sharing this information decades later with a visitor, he was interrupted by Véra, who gently attempted to set the record straight. Her "m" was strawberry-colored. "She spoils everything by saying she sees it in strawberry," grumbled her husband, demonstrating another truth about synesthetics: Their recall is so perfect that its defects tend to be those of perception rather than of fact. Nothing is lost on the synesthetic, for whom reality—and in Véra Slonim's case, the printed page—bears an added dimension.* For the Nabokovs it amounted to their own private *son et lumière*. Musical notes appear to have had no optical effect on Véra, however, as they do on many gifted with colored hearing and as they would on her son, for whom the key of a piece of music adds a shade as well. (Véra did enjoy music although her husband did not, chromatically or on any other level.) But she was well equipped to appreciate the hues of her husband's supersaturated prose. She would have understood perfectly Clare Bishop's insistence in *Sebastian Knight* that a title "must convey the colour of the book—not its subject." For his part Nabokov delighted in the luminosity of Véra's handwriting, her voice, her walk, tinted like the sky at dawn. Explaining the halos he and his wife saw on the page, he noted that Véra's differed from his own. "She has different colors. And I don't think they are quite as bright as mine. Or are they?" he asked. "You don't want them to be," she needled him. As quick as she may have been to efface herself on most fronts, the one thing she could not make disappear was her pride. Often it was the only thing she left behind; it was this Cheshire Cat's smile.

From the start Nabokov extolled Véra's acuity, her intuition. No trifle escaped her attention. Like Clare, with whom she shares other qualities, Véra "possessed, too, that real sense of beauty which has far less to do with art

---

* In light of the literature, it is interesting to note that while synesthetics are generally gifted with superior memories, they often suffer from difficulties with spatial navigation.

than with the constant readiness to discern the halo round a frying-pan or the likeness between a weeping-willow and a Skye terrier." Nabokov marveled over her later analysis of their American neighborhood: "Véra says that the top of the west face of the Hopkins' house, corner of our street and Quarry St., ressembles [*sic*] a skull (quite easy to see, the dormer is the snub nose, the windows on both sides are the sockets, and old Hopkins is eighty) and that the front of the Millers' house is strikingly like James Joyce . . . well it's hard to explain, but it's there." She was a stickler for detail; no one who has read her husband can underestimate what that was worth. This "capacity to wonder at trifles" was for Nabokov the mark of a kind of genius, as much as was the ability to discern the connections between things. Véra was the kind of woman who came back from the hairdresser to report that sitting under the dryer had been like watching a silent movie. She was the most demanding kind of reader. If the historians of the Weimar years, eager to convey the sense of chaos that backed the artistically efflorescent life in Berlin, were to mention a general strike on page 20, then a streetcar had better not be said to be running on page 22. "All seemed on verge of collapse," declared one scholar, commenting on these Berlin years, when the country had recovered from the hyperinflation but when its society still lay in tatters. Véra corrected him. "It now seems as if everything then seemed . . . ," she scrawled in his margin.

Of his literary gift Nabokov was not always as certain as he would later claim—Véra acknowledged privately that there had been doubts and failures and griefs along the way—but he had no quibbles with himself. He was the eldest and favorite of a family of three boys and two girls; his parents were said by some to have coddled him, by others to have deified him. He had been raised to believe that he stood at the center of an exquisitely opulent universe (his was the brand of prerevolutionary childhood in which it was possible to speak of "the smallest and oldest of our gardeners"), and that pride was something that he carried with him long after both that universe and its opulence had vanished. He had what can only be termed an entirely robust sense of self. "All Nabokovs are selfish," explains his sister Elena Sikorski, who recognized her brother's privileged position without rancor, but acknowledges that it cost others in the family dearly. He might just as well have been speaking of himself when he wrote of a minor character: "He loved himself with a passionate and completely reciprocated love."

Véra Slonim was not nearly so much at ease with herself, but Nabokov would have had a difficult time finding in Berlin another woman who was as fiercely wed to her opinions. This confidence was a great attraction; nothing was frightening when he was with her. In Véra he found the odd combination of feminine grace and unfeminine determination that Fyodor so admires in Zina in *The Gift*. Not only was she unwavering in her convictions, but Véra's convictions were not always of the commonsensical kind. In mid-1924, Vladimir wrote of having visited his father's grave with Véra. He was still deeply affected by his loss and missed his father deeply: "When we were last at the cemetery, I felt it so piercingly and clearly: You know everything, you know what will happen after death, you know it utterly, plainly, and calmly, just as a bird knows, having sprung from its branch, that it will fly and not fall. And that is why I am so happy with you, my love." We have no sense of what she might have told him that day, or later; we know only that neither Nabokov thought death entirely final. Véra Slonim may have been the first to have settled on that conviction; her translation work indicates an interest in the otherworldly. If Poe and Rainov have one thing in common it is a fascination with the underweave of life, a realm of substantial shadows that lies beyond that of illusory existence. For someone who appeared relentlessly literal-minded, they represented an odd choice of texts.

A number of critics have linked Nabokov's first successful attempts at locating a reality beyond the human world to his marriage. In his 1924 play, *The Tragedy of Mr. Morn,* for the first time in Nabokov's work, a character moves from one world, one consciousness, to another. The word "metempsychosis"—the passing of a soul from one body to another after death—appears in *Mary,* his first novel. He later told Véra with satisfaction that his family had understood, on hearing him read *The Eye,* that the hero dies and his soul is transferred into Smurov. And in 1925, on the eve of the anniversary of his father's death, he adopted a new tone in his letter to his mother: "I am so certain, my love, that we will see him again, in an unexpected but completely natural heaven, in a realm where all is radiance and delight." The work is filled with characters handicapped by various mental tics: Vadim Vadimovich N. in *Look at the Harlequins!* suffers from an inability to turn in space as we are unable to turn in time. The narrator of "Lance" cannot approach a dream landscape head-on. (In much the same way, Nabokov complained he was afflicted by total recall, an affliction of which he could be miraculously cured by the presence of a biographer.) After Véra's entrance into his life, he began to grapple with the idea that while space may be finite, time is not. The works teem with "ex-mortals," with hints and glimpses of something beyond our immediate existence. This "serene superknowledge" which permeates so much of the fiction appears to have been either a direct import from Véra or a simultaneous one.

More explicitly, he thanked her for having taught him something of reason. Almost reflexively, since the age of six, he had written poetry. As a seventeen-year-old he had looked upon these poems as small miracles, 100 percent inspiration. "Now I truly do know that in art reason is the negative particle and inspiration is the positive particle, but only through the secret union of them is born that white flash, the electric trepidation of creating the perfect," he wrote Véra in January 1924. He was spending seventeen hours a day on thirty lines of *Morn*. "In winding ways," she had been the one to instill the drama in him. He had always recognized the value of intuition, but now grasped that of precision. The man who would make American amphitheaters thunder with the news that literature was to be approached with the precision of an artist and the passion of a scientist himself came to that realization when he was older than the undergraduates in those auditoriums, after he had met a woman who was the first to denounce "circumlocutions, those hangnails of speech." Decades later he credited Véra with keeping his prose as exact as possible. "Writing is all that is dear and important to me now," Nabokov had written Svetlana Siewert in his last letter, as a kind of renunciation. With a very different emotion, he repeated his conviction to Véra Slonim. "I am prepared to undergo Chinese torture for the discovery of a single epithet," he claimed, exhausted by his labors on *Morn*.

From Prague he returned to Berlin with a near-complete manuscript in his bag. He knew the pages would not be lost on Véra. Already he had written that she was among the three people who understand his every comma, and one of those was now dead.* Relatedly or not, he loved her "savagely, endlessly," "to the point of fainting." The January reunion must have been sweet, but the rest of the winter was a stressful time for Véra, still working for her father. This was the winter when the economy took its toll, claiming what remained of Slonim's assets. He withdrew from Orbis at the end of the year; by 1925 he was entirely ruined. Probably at his office Véra typed *The Tragedy of Mr. Morn*; her days of translating for publication had come to an end, a fact that suggests that she had not undertaken the assignments purely for financial reasons. If anything she would have been in greater need of the income now.

Throughout 1923 and midway into 1924, Véra lived with her parents on Landhausstrasse. There was trouble on the home front that year, a probable cause of the distress to which Nabokov's letters allude. Lena, returned from the Sorbonne, had taken a room with the family of *Rul* editor Iosef Hessen. At some point in 1924 Véra's parents went their separate ways; Evsei Slonim set up house around the corner with Anna Lazarevna Feigin, twenty-five

---

* The second was his mother, who had until Véra's arrival on the scene copied out nearly everything her son wrote.

years his junior. "Aniuta" Feigin was the daughter of his wife's brother, which from a no less complicated angle made her Véra's cousin. Véra and Anna had known each other since childhood. An energetic and enterprising woman who had graduated from gymnasium in Minsk and conservatory in Petersburg, Anna Feigin had arrived in Berlin two years after the Slonims. In Germany she studied both bookkeeping and music theory; through Evsei Slonim's good offices, she went to work as a representative for Leo Peltenburg.*

Slava and Evsei Slonim appear not to have reconciled; they were living apart at the time of their deaths. And the repercussions were felt, quite strongly, along party lines. Véra and Sonia, whatever their sympathies with their mother, remained close to Anna Feigin, whose advice Véra actively sought over the next five decades. Véra dutifully accompanied her mother on a sanitarium visit at the time of the separation, as she would the following summer, but she did so sullenly. Lena distanced herself from the family, with whom her relations were to remain troubled. Anna Feigin felt she had treated Evsei Slonim's eldest daughter impeccably, but that Lena "has always had a capacity for unexpected idiocy." Lena held a lifelong grudge against Anna Feigin, for reasons which had more to do with her own marriage than with Anna Feigin's involvement with her father. The three sisters—all of whom made their careers working with language—were to have a fiendishly difficult time communicating with one another. Even the events of the next twenty years would not be enough to heal the wounds.

The family as Véra had known it in Russia ceased to exist after 1924. She searched for a room in August; most likely it was around this time that she began to tutor language students. Vladimir suggested she take a room in his boardinghouse—he felt he should be seeing her forty-eight hours a day—which she did not do. The romance was by 1924 quite serious; it had long before been physically consummated, and by midsummer the two considered themselves engaged. Nabokov was pleased to report to his sisters that when he walked down the streets of Russian Berlin he left a gratifying rustle of "That's Vladimir Sirin" in his wake. He had to beat the girls away with a stick. On the other hand he felt ready to settle down, and with his letter he included a photo of his intended. In other ways, too, the relationship matured. Véra's involvement in her father's affairs diminished—Orbis closed without having published a single title—but she had plenty of new responsibilities.

---

* Here again Véra could not have been more generously unforthcoming. In response to a scholar's query, she explained: "Anna Feigin was my cousin, niece of my mother. We have always been in very close relations with her. She was born in 1890. In the early fourties [*sic*] she joined us in New York, and in 1968 she joined us again." She omitted only all mention of the 1920s, which is to say the heart of the matter.

Nabokov was supporting himself, as it sometimes seems was half the emigration, tutoring English. (He referred to Véra as his only serious competition as an English teacher in Berlin; she worked at improving her vocabulary in her spare time.) From Prague that July he asked Véra to find him a few additional lessons. And would she mind recopying the enclosed poems, and submitting them both to *Rul*? He missed the rustle of her eyelashes against his cheek, but he did not appear to miss any literary ambition she might herself have once entertained, if indeed he knew of any. She could have had no doubt about his feelings on this subject. Seemingly apropos of nothing, in the same letter to his family in which he announced his intention to marry, he added: "The sharpest jealousy of all is that between one woman and another, and that between one littérateur and another. But when a woman envies a littérateur, that can amount to H_2SO_4 [sulfuric acid]."

2

Véra Evseevna Slonim, of Berlin-Schöneberg, and Vladimir Vladimirovich Nabokoff, of Berlin-Wilmersdorf, married at the Wilmersdorf Rathaus on April 15, 1925. They had known each other for just under two years; they were unable later to agree on how long they had been engaged. The signal event that was to inform Véra Slonim's next seventy-seven years could not have taken place more anticlimactically. Their witnesses at the town hall ceremony were two of their more distant acquaintances, chosen by virtue of their being precisely that. There are no photos of blushing brides, beaming grooms; there are no photos at all. Even the rhapsodic Nabokov could not coax poetry out of the early days of the marriage. "We were ridiculously poor, her father was ruined, my widowed mother subsisted on an insufficient pension, my wife and I lived in gloomy rooms which we rented in Berlin West, in the lean bosoms of German military families," he recalled later. The lean German bosoms had to wait a little; it was several weeks before the newlyweds managed to live at the same address. On the evening of April 15 they broke the news over dinner to Véra's family, in one of its configurations. "By the way, we got married this morning," Véra said. A wedding announcement was printed, in French, and ostensibly mailed, but not very scientifically. Gleb Struve, then in Paris and in regular touch with Vladimir, was surprised not to have been told of the marriage, which he learned about from mutual friends. Struve counted among Nabokov's closest friends at the time. There are some hints that Nabokov feared disapproval. He admitted to Véra that he feared his friends would not understand the most divine thing in his life, that they would launch "a predatory campaign."

Nabokov's mother learned the news after the fact as well, when she visited Berlin in May. She was not surprised—she and her daughters had assumed Véra and Vladimir would marry—and embraced Véra warmly. No discomfort whatever materialized. Nabokov's grandmother had but one question concerning the new addition to the family, a reason Vladimir may have feared a "predatory campaign": "Of what religion is she?" On Véra's side matters were doubtless more complicated. It may be a matter of simple coincidence that the dissolution of the Slonims' marriage directly preceded Véra's entering into a union of her own. Her father would have been preoccupied at the time, however. Slava Slonim's reaction is not known, but there is every reason to assume that Véra's approach to the matter conformed to that of Luzhin's fiancée, in *The Defense*. When her mother tells her that Luzhin has asked for her hand in marriage, the daughter replies, "I'm sorry he told you. . . . It concerns only him and me." Discretion was to Véra Nabokov the greater part of valor. The more emotionally raw the issue, the more opaque she found it desirable to be on the subject.

Her opacity allowed her detractors plenty of room. Perhaps because Nabokov's romantic past was so variegated, the assumption in the émigré community was that Véra had somehow coerced him into marriage. One report had her showing up at his room, pointing a pistol at his chest, and threatening, "Marry me, or I'll kill you." She was considered difficult, blunt, "*imariable*." Since not everyone was as charmed by her "idiosyncratic form of directness" as her new husband, the marriage seemed altogether inexplicable, especially to the anti-Semites, which was to say a fair (and growing) proportion of the Russian community. That her father had been an estate manager impressed no one among the pedigree-conscious, who saw Nabokov as marrying down. Even Jewish friends were left with the sense that she had been the prime mover: Contrasting Véra to Sirin's flock of female readers, an admiring acquaintance recalled: "The one who finally got Nabokov to marry her was Véra Slonim . . . thin and slight, blond." Perhaps it was not so much Véra who seemed *imariable* but, in the English sense of the word, Nabokov who did not seem the marrying kind.

Of their emotional commitment at the time more can be said. In his fiction Nabokov was killing off wives well before his marriage: The books are full of dead wives, fickle wives, lost wives, dim-witted, vulgar, slatternly, ineffectual, scheming wives. Even Mrs. Luzhin, who has in common with Véra her marriage to a master, a man tormented by his genius, cannot save her fictional husband from his demons. The same holds true for Mme. Perov, the unfortunate fate-mate of the pianist in "Bachmann," who in her devotion more closely resembles Véra. Alone among Nabokov's couples, *The Gift*'s Fyodor and Zina make out well—or will once they find the keys to the apartment. The narrator of *Look at the Harlequins!* finds his "You," but only on the fifth try; Sebastian Knight leaves his Véra-like Clare, with disastrous results. Boyd has made a case that many of these marriages and women are related to Véra in that they are highly imaginative inversions of her. Certainly in the fiction we more often meet her antithesis than Véra herself; in his books Nabokov would hold distorting mirrors up to his own marriage, there where Véra would habitually hold a "No Trespassing" sign. Here was an author able to write an autobiography in which his marriage seems nowhere to figure, even while that marriage—as Boyd has persuasively argued—would play a significant role in shaping his fictions.

Behind all the inversions and elisions and contortions were, however, a man and a woman ardently, uncomplicatedly in love. Nabokov's letters of 1925 are deliriously passionate ones, more so even than those written prior to the wedding. To his sister Elena, about a year after his marriage, he offered some wisdom:

> The most important thing in love is complete, radiant truthfulness—so that there won't be any of the petty deceptions, those quick lies that are in all other human relationships—and no posing before yourself, nor before the one you love: that is the true purity of love. And in love you must be Siamese twins, where one sneezes when the other sniffs tobacco. And then you must remember that the greatest love is the simplest love, just as the best verse is that written most simply.*

Véra had a chance as well to share her convictions. She had a little more experience when she did so, having been Mrs. Vladimir Nabokov for fifty years when she wrote: "Things that are precious, honesty, tenderness, broadmindedness, life in art, and true, unselfish, touching attachment, are the greater

---

* Did the way Nabokov approached *Anna Karenin(a)* have anything to do with his marriage? He taught the book as if its real moral message was that loveless marriages of the Karenins' kind constitute a crime against human nature; to his mind, Kitty and Levin represent the "Milky Way" of the book. He talked about Kitty and Levin's "brain-bridge" and "tender telepathy" in the same way that, in interviews, he wondered after Véra's capacity for "domestic telepathy," or described Fyodor's ability to communicate with Zina "without any bridges." For Kitty and Levin, "the brain-bridge is a light and luminous and lovely structure leading towards vistas of tenderness and fond duties and profound bliss."

values by far." She could not stress enough to her correspondent the value of a good woman who loves "in a pure, unselfish way," one capable "occasionally of sacrificing her own desires and pleasures in life to what you would rather do." Have you been happy in love? Véra asked a young poet who came to visit in the 1960s. "We think that is all it takes," she advised.

The evidence points to Véra's having attributed the breakup of her parents' household to her mother; the partnership her father enjoyed with Anna Feigin may have impressed another definition of marriage upon her. It is almost impossible to believe Véra could have enjoyed much of a relationship with her mother, given her proximity and loyalty to the woman for whom her father left Slava Borisovna. The Nabokovs spent a good deal of time with Slonim and Anna Feigin in 1925, consulting with them on most decisions. When Vladimir envisioned a vacation in Biarritz, he sought out Slonim's advice on the subject; would the climate be good for his daughter? (The answer was no; the seaside vacation never took place.) He was entirely taken with his stately and cultivated father-in-law, who much enjoyed his prose, and whom he regularly met over a chessboard. Triumphantly he wrote his mother that Evsei Lazarevich "understands so well that the most important thing for me in life, and the only thing of which I'm capable, is to write." Although he was nearly out of funds—perhaps precisely because he was—Slonim continued to dream. He told his new son-in-law he hoped to buy farms in France for his three daughters.

The newlyweds were separated for nearly two months in the summer of 1926, when Véra—whose health was also fragile at the time—accompanied her mother to a sanitarium. She left her husband a bouquet of roses, a box of candies, and a numbered notepad, on which he might write her daily. He did so, religiously. She was less obliging. Early on Nabokov complained that if they were to publish an anthology of their letters she would be able to take credit only for 20 percent. He urged her to catch up. In a more despairing mood he chastised her: "My pet, I am the only Russian émigré in Berlin who writes to his wife every day." He missed her terribly, and dined nearly every evening with her father and Anna Feigin, from whom he also regularly borrowed money. He sent Véra his new poems (on the back of one letter can be read her attempts to commit the fresh verse to memory), accounts of *Mary*'s first reviews, word games; he reported on the activities of their stuffed animals. The puzzles and acrostics were less appreciated than the statements as to how much he missed her. She was miserable, homesick, and cold, and in her few letters complained bitterly. He offered to write her twice daily, if his doing so might in any way boost her spirits.

More successful were the summer trips the two made together, late that

July and in 1927, to Binz, an island resort that afforded Véra a view of the
Baltic Sea of her childhood, from the opposite shore. The Nabokovs were
chaperones the first summer for Joseph and Abraham Bromberg, ages eleven
and thirteen, whose tennis games Vladimir was hired to improve. Anna
Feigin had arranged the trip; she was a cousin of the boys' father, whom she
had persuaded to offer Nabokov the job. The owner of a thriving fur-trading
business, Herman Bromberg had been happy to oblige. Plans do not appear
to have been made in advance, and on the 1927 excursion the Nabokovs and
their wards arrived at the resort to find that no rooms were available. In
the bar a "flushed fellow" offered to share a bed with Véra; Nabokov responded—as one of his charges looked on—with "a hook on the man's jaw,
flooding himself and the drunk with the latter's sticky liquor."* They stayed
elsewhere, but the image tangled itself up with two others. In *King, Queen,
Knave,* a novel begun shortly after the trip and in part conceived on the
Baltic, two tanned, self-satisfied foreigners dance in the Siren Café at a resort
on the same bay. They appear entirely lost in each other. They also happen to
reveal a little about how the Nabokovs were seen, at least by Nabokov:

> The foreign girl in the blue dress danced with a remarkably handsome
> man in an old-fashioned dinner jacket. Franz had long since noticed
> this couple; they had appeared to him in fleeting glimpses, like a recur-
> rent dream image or a subtle leitmotiv—now at the beach, now in a
> café, now on the promenade. Sometimes the man carried a butterfly
> net. The girl had a delicately painted mouth and tender gray-blue eyes
> and her fiancé or husband, slender, elegantly balding, contemptuous of
> everything on earth but her, was looking at her with pride; and Franz
> felt envious of that unusual pair.

They are quite unforgivably happy, busily speaking their incomprehensible
tongue, and clearly privy to every little thing about Franz. Decades later,
Vladimir dreamed of dancing with Véra. In his 1964 diary he noted:

> Her open dress, oddly speckled and summery. A man kisses her in pass-
> ing. I clutch him by the head and bang his face with such vicious force
> against the wall that he almost gets meat-hooked on some fixtures on

---

* Véra remembered the offer being followed by a slightly less violent sequence than did her husband:
"VN splashed the man's drink into his face and all over him."

the walls (gleaming metal suggestive of ship). Detaches himself with face all bloody and stumbles away.

3

"As I was saying every name has its responsibilities," Nabokov proclaimed on the first page of his first novel. He could not have devised a better introduction to a literary marriage had he had his new wife in mind. Their match truly was alliterative, a fact that could not have been lost on the man who would compose a small treatise on Flaubert's ingenious Emma Bovary nomenclature.* The two quite reciprocally exchanged monograms in 1925: Véra Slonim married Vladimir Sirin and got Vladimir Nabokov; Sirin married Véra Slonim and wound up with Véra Nabokov. More than most couples, they transformed themselves in the process. It is not overstating the case to say that "Vladimir Nabokov" was the literary child of their marriage, as George Eliot has been said to be that of the union of Marian Evans and George Henry Lewes; "VN" certainly was such a construct. (So disassociated was Vladimir from his family name after his years as Sirin that when first he saw Nabokov in print he read it as "Nobody." His second thought was that he was reading an obituary.)

Véra assumed her married name almost as a stage name; rarely has matrimony so much represented a profession. It was one of the ironies of the life that—born at a time and place where women could and did lay claim to all kinds of ambitions—she should elevate the role of wife to a high art. (Then again the talented Russian poet whom she married would make his name as an English-language novelist.) Traditionally a man changes his name and braces himself for fame; a woman changes hers and passes into oblivion. This was not to be Véra's case, although she did gather her married name around her like a cloak, which she occasionally opened to startling effect. She would never be forced to make a woman's historic choice between love and work. Nor would Verochka, as Vladimir called her, squander any of her professional training, though as it happened her husband would be the direct (and sole) beneficiary of that expertise.

The consensus holds that the watershed year in Nabokov's art was

---

* Nor could Nabokov have failed to notice that his wife shared her initials with the woman we know as Tamara and Mary, and whom he had loved between 1915 and 1916 as Valentina Evgenievna Shulgin. Oddly, Valentina worked all her life as a typist.

1924–1925; that he could have written neither the title story of his first collection nor *Mary,* a more sophisticated work, before his marriage. That novel—which Nabokov recalled having begun "soon after my marriage in the spring of 1925"—is dedicated to his wife. It can be read as the story of a man liberated from a crippling burden of nostalgia; its émigré protagonist finds himself suddenly able to walk away from the past, which is about to pay an unsettling call. Its author was now a serious prose writer, no longer an emotionally unripe poet trafficking in fairy-tale imagery.* Véra is nowhere in the book, but neither is the title character; both women cast long shadows, one toward the past, the other over the future. Every émigré paper reviewed the novel on its 1926 publication, for the most part glowingly. On hearing excerpts from *Mary* read aloud at a literary gathering, *Rul'*'s literary critic Yuly Aikhenvald declared that a new Turgenev had appeared. The new Turgenev continued to write as often as he could, while crossing Berlin regularly by streetcar on his way from one student to the next. He had already noticed that he was for the most part oblivious to his lessons, which he gave practically unconsciously.

Quickly Véra came to the rescue in his battle with the practical, the world that seems to conspire against the artist at every step. There is no evidence that—like Nora Joyce, like Sonya Tolstoy, like Emily Tennyson, who wound up a semi-invalid—she ever evaded secretarial duty. She seems to have embraced it; her sister-in-law Elena felt she lived for it. She insisted on assuming all the wage-earning responsibilities that could be rerouted in her direction. The hours could be grueling and the work enough for two; on one occasion Nabokov reported that he and Véra had put in an eight-hour marathon session, and had two ten-hour days still ahead of them.† For some time in 1927 the two translated into English the miserable dispatches of a London paper's Russian correspondent, work that kept them up half the night as they raced to meet the journalist's deadlines. There was money to be made as well in translating personal letters. Véra ultimately relieved her husband of this brand of drudgery; she teamed up with an English professor to rework a series of political articles. Regular employment for a foreigner— and in many cases these were highly overqualified foreigners—was spectacularly difficult to secure. Many of the young émigrés were acquainted with a Russian-German publisher named Jakow Trachtenberg, the compiler of a Russian-language textbook for Germans. Véra contributed to this project,

---

* Russian writers commonly come to prose from poetry. As Nabokov would observe in a few pointed examples, that would be the undoing of some.
† The captivating dance of the pronouns in the Nabokovs' correspondence begins here. What he wrote was: "I am working on a big translation, and yesterday Véra and I worked for 8 hours . . ."

work which Vladimir had begun; she collaborated as well on a Russian/
French and Russian/German dictionary. Reminded of her grammatical
labors years later she panicked, then performed her disappearing act: "He
[Vladimir] never took it seriously, it was just hack work, most of it done by
me. It does not exist." The primer has survived, but Véra had nothing to fear.
Neither her name nor her husband's figures in it.

To her capacity to wonder at trifles, Véra joined an ability to deal with
them, a gift she did not share with her husband. The phone number forgotten in Prague had caused Nabokov the anguish it had because the alternate
means of communication bordered on the unthinkable. "After all, I'm afraid
of the post office!!!" he yelped, partly in jest, partly in tribute to learned
helplessness. Forty years later his list of favorite hates included "everything
connected with the post: stamps, envelopes, finding the right address." Telephone numbers proved delusions in his hands. Objects had a tendency to run
for their lives in his presence. The man who was afflicted by perfect recall of
his own past proved constitutionally incapable of remembering the name of
someone to whom he had been introduced on repeated occasions weeks before. In America he might just as easily get off a train at Newark as in New
York, might lavish on Mr. Auden praise intended for Mr. Aiken.* He lent his
own list of tortures, nearly verbatim, to Van Veen in *Ada*: "The obstructive
behavior of stupid, inimical things—the wrong pocket, the ruptured shoe-
string, the idle hanger toppling with a shrug and a hingle-tingle in the darkness of a wardrobe . . ."† From the list of the things Nabokov bragged about
never having learned to do—type, drive, speak German, retrieve a lost
object, fold an umbrella, answer the phone, cut a book's pages, give the time
of day to a philistine—it is easy to deduce what Véra was to spend her life
doing. She never compiled a list of favorite dislikes, at least on paper. Had she
done so her catalogue would have included at least some of the following:
cooking; housework; untruths; cruelty to animals, even in fiction; her husband's inertia; snakes; ineptitude in all forms, but particularly in publishers'
royalty departments; all ambiguities not confined to fiction; talking about
herself; giving the time of day to a philistine.

At the top of Nabokov's list, of course, came the typing. With Clare in
Sebastian Knight, Véra was virtually alone in seeing "the uncouth manuscript

---

* "I understand now the wild look that passed in his eyes. Stupid, but has happened to me before," he confided after the misadventure.
† As he worded it on his own behalf in a 1970 interview with an Israeli journalist, the catalogue consisted
of: "Stupid, inimical things: the spectacles case that gets lost; the clothes hanger that topples down in the
closet; the wrong pocket. Folding an umbrella, not finding its secret button. Uncut pages, knots in
shoelaces."

flaunting its imperfections." Nabokov was an ardent corrector, and Véra typed and typed, beginning with the short stories in the fall of 1923, on to *Mary* in 1924, by way of stories, plays, and poems, to *King, Queen, Knave* in 1928, nearly every page her husband wrote until 1961. She worked from his dictation, setting down the works, in their final form, in triplicate. How complicit was she in the actual writing? She was more than a typist, less than a collaborator. "She presided as adviser and judge over the making of my first fiction in the early twenties. I have read to her all my stories and novels at least twice; and she has reread them all when typing them," Nabokov asserted later. Small wonder she knew the bulk of them by heart. The words were entirely his, but she was their first reader, smoothing the prose when it was "still warm and wet." When scholars questioned the arrangement she shrugged off any active involvement, even when the handwriting is on the page. She could only have been transcribing her husband's comments, she insisted. On a mechanical level she corrected his spelling and usage; as she put it, he "was very absentminded in what concerned grammar" when composing a book.

It is all the same difficult not to picture Véra as *Sebastian Knight*'s Clare, lifting the edge of a page in the typewriter and declaring, " 'No, my dear. You can't say it so in English.' . . . 'There is no other way of expressing it,' he would mutter at last. 'And if for instance,' she would say—and then an exact suggestion would follow." It is even more difficult to separate Clare from Véra when Véra's other close fictional counterpart can be heard in a Berlin café, eyes lowered, head propped on an elbow, listening to what Fyodor has written that day: " 'Wonderful, but I'm not sure you can say it like that in Russian,' said Zina sometimes, and after an argument he would correct the expression she had questioned."* Zina shares with Véra the same precision in her use of language; she officiates equally "as a regulator, if not a guide." It is perhaps not necessary to extricate Véra from Zina and Clare at all when some thirty years later, as if quoting from his own fiction, Nabokov described his wife's role in his literary life in nearly identical words.†

Did Véra appear in the work, each Nabokov was asked at different

---

* This would have mandated unusual powers of persuasion. Iosef Hessen remembered assigning twenty-year-old Nabokov a translation into the Russian of Romain Rolland's *Colas Breugnon* for *Rul*. Hessen made a few suggestions on the proofs before passing them on to Nabokov's father. When the proofs returned to Hessen, Nabokov Senior smiled indulgently and admitted that his son had erased all of Hessen's corrections.

† In 1965 he told an interviewer, "Well, after that my very kind and patient wife, she sits down at her typewriter and I, I dictate, I dictate off the [index] cards to her, making some changes and very often, very often, discussing this or that. She might say, 'Oh you can't say that, you can't say that.' 'Well, let's see, perhaps I can change it.' "

times? "Most of my works have been dedicated to my wife and her picture has often been reproduced by some mysterious means of reflected color in the inner mirrors of my books," declared Vladimir. He said refractions, she said they're fictions; so far as Véra was concerned, no trace of her likeness was to be found anywhere in her husband's pages. In "Sounds," a short story of September 1923, Nabokov introduces for the first time a radiant, delicate, thin-wristed woman with pale, dusty-looking eyes, translucent, blue-veined skin, and hair that melts in the sunlight. (The story is autobiographical, but the woman on whom it is based—a brown-haired cousin of Nabokov's named Tatiana Segelkranz—does not answer to that description.) That physical description applies as well to Zina, into whose surname Nabokov built some of the shimmer he associated with his wife. And it applies equally to the Véra of Nabokov's letters. Aside from the acknowledged cameo appearance in *King, Queen, Knave* (in which the Véra double has gray-blue eyes and pale hair and speaks with animation)—and a little premonition of that appearance, in "A Nursery Tale," a story Nabokov read aloud to her father—Véra makes no entrances as herself in the work. Ultimately it is not her image but her influence that hovers over the page; she was more muse than model. The fictional description of the early years that truly conjures up Véra is that of the reader gifted with perfect understanding:

> And Clare, who had not composed a single line of imaginative prose or poetry in her life, understood so well (and that was her private miracle) every detail of Sebastian's struggle, that the words she typed were to her not so much the conveyors of their natural sense, but the curves and gaps and zigzags showing Sebastian's groping along a certain ideal of expression.

It was most prominently in this respect that she left her mark on the fiction. She fully participated in the making of the literature in that the one highly discriminating person on the receiving end became a part of the tale for Nabokov; Véra was in this sense a little bit a character in search of an author. "She and I are my best audience," Nabokov declared with a rolling chuckle in 1966. "I should say my main audience." Friends felt she was the only audience he needed.

In the early days Véra constituted a large portion of her husband's entire audience. By the early 1930s, when his star as a prose writer had risen, the Russian community in Berlin had dwindled to about thirty thousand people. It was virtually impossible for most young writers to make a living, much less to do so while attending to their talent. For those who continued to write, the rewards were few, the infighting proportionately great. Accusations of illiteracy abounded. The clamoring to publish remained keen, so much so that even the innately generous littérateur might find his virtue sorely tested: "To get into literature is like squeezing into an overcrowded trolley car. And once inside, you do your best to push off any new arrival who tries to hang on," complained one compatriot, who displayed a sharp set of elbows where Nabokov was concerned. This is to some extent always true, but it was spectacularly so in the emigration; communities in exile are not renowned for their generosity of spirit. And in this case the desperation, the bitterness, was enhanced by the fact that the usual compensations of publishing were missing. The writers were in Europe, the readers in Soviet Russia. As V. S. Yanovsky noted, "Reviews were considered the ultimate reward, since the higher authority, the reader, was missing!" Books were issued in printings of eight hundred to fifteen hundred copies, though the latter figure was generally reserved only for Ivan Bunin, who enjoyed Olympian stature among the émigrés well before he claimed his Nobel Prize. The total print run of *Sovremennye Zapiski* (*Contemporary Annals*), the best émigré review, in Paris, was no more than a thousand copies. Nor were things much better in Soviet Russia. One writer calculated that in order to survive in Petrograd at the time, Shakespeare would have had to turn out three plays a month. At least there a Russian writer would have had an audience.

Nabokov insisted that he had never expected writing to be a source of income; given the climate in which he began his career, this amounted to nothing so much as a glorious concession to reality. Furthermore the Nabokovs fell into a cultural bind. The more Europeanized Russians acutely felt their Russianness in Germany; at the same time they felt anything but Soviet. On a good day Vladimir praised this state of affairs. He claimed to keep his distance from the despicable spirit of the emigration, reveling in his "almost idyllic isolation." He described his world as one of discomfort, loneliness, and "quiet, inner merriment." Later he based his qualified admiration for Emily Dickinson on the fact that she had managed to create in double isolation: once from people, again from the ideas of her time. Véra said nothing about discomfort or loneliness or merriment. But for her it became a point of honor that her husband's gift had developed in a near-vacuum. She essentially congratulated those who recognized as much.

Nabokov was so huge and protean a presence on the page that he left little room for those who might attach themselves to the literature. He never tired of telling his reader how he was to be read; the man who believed in the supremacy of the individual was a benevolent (sometimes not so benevolent) dictator in his prefaces. He insinuated himself everywhere. He could occupy the footnotes (*Pale Fire*); supply his own review (the long-unpublished last chapter of *Speak, Memory*); parody his flap copy (*Ada*); affix a fictional foreword (*Lolita*); respond to his editor's qualms in an afterword (*Nikolai Gogol*); offer up a misleading genealogical tree (*Ada* again); displace even the well-meaning editor who might affix a list of his previous titles to the front matter of a novel (*Look at the Harlequins!*). There was no textual apparatus from which he failed merrily to swing. By definition, only an intrepid reader was going to be able to meet him on his own ground. Here Véra's pluck, her proud sense of intellectual independence, served her well. "The people I invite to my feasts must have stomachs as strong as wineskins, and not ask for a glass of Beaujolais when I offer them a barrel of Château Latour d'Ivoire," the older Nabokov boasted. The younger Nabokov was not quite so self-assured in regard to his art—he was more sensitive both to praise and criticism than he liked later to admit—but knew already that he was looking for an intrepid reader. Of Clare he would write: "She had imagination—the muscle of the soul—and her image was of a particularly strong, almost masculine quality." He evidently feared Véra would have difficulty stomaching only one small selection of his work, a collection of erotic poems, few of which he shared with her. Otherwise she brought to the literary front the nerves of steel she had brought to that train in the Ukraine.

Her audacity was soon legendary in the Russian community, in no way diminished by the fact that she carried a pistol in Berlin. Most likely it was a Browning 1900. This was not entirely unusual at the time—the city was overrun by snipers and pickpockets in the wake of the hyperinflation—but Véra had acquired the pistol earlier, and had fully intended to use it.* "Were you really practicing shooting in order to kill Trotsky?" asked a friend, years later. "Well, yes, I'm afraid I was," confessed an amused Mrs. Nabokov, who was not yet Mrs. Nabokov at the time. She was proud to admit she was a crack shot; she claimed to be every bit as fine a marksman as her teacher, a Berlin champion. To select interviewers she confirmed that in the early 1920s she had been involved in an assassination plot, which most understood to have been aimed at Trotsky, a few to have been focused on the Soviet ambassador. She may have been inspired by—in any case she was not daunted by—the suicide mission of Fannie Kaplan, a fearless young Russian Jew who had fired her Browning three times at the well-protected Lenin in 1918, and who had been executed for the attempt. There can be little question that Véra Slonim har-

---

* Handguns are everywhere in the novels. Brownings turn up in the plays *The Man from the USSR* and *The Event,* though neither gun—introduced in the fourth act and the second act respectively—will go off in the last.

bored similar aspirations, which found their way into a poem Nabokov composed months after meeting her: "I know, with certainty / that in that lacquered purse of yours / —nestled against powder case and mirror / sleeps a black stone; seven deaths."* He went on to imagine her waiting silently in a doorway for her victim to emerge, buttoning his coat. Poetically his concern is not that the assassin exposes herself to a grave danger but that her mortal business might induce her to forget him and "all these, my idle songs."

There was little cause for alarm. Within the next four years a very different tribute was written to Véra's derring-do. Yuly Aikhenvald, one of the elder statesmen in the emigration, was quick to applaud Nabokov's talent; he recommended the young Sirin to both Nina Berberova and Vladislav Khodasevich. A gentle and much respected man, Aikhenvald was equally quick to notice Sirin's valorous second. In the first years of the Nabokovs' marriage, he composed a poem titled "Véra:" "Fragile, tender and precious, / like human porcelain / But the strength of her will is undeniable / And stern are her judgements against the base." Under her "tranquil shroud" he could sense the stirrings of a sacrificial deed. The one he had in mind was not on the order of an assassination attempt, or even of the senseless feat that Martin performs in *Glory,* the sort of mission of which Nabokov admitted he dreamed during these years, when "The Romantic Age" seemed an appropriate title for that novel. This act of heroism was equally self-immolating. Aikhenvald saw Véra as a fearless guide to Vladimir on "the poetic path." She was on every count his champion. The wife of another émigré writer phrased it differently: "Everyone in the Russian community knew who and what you meant when you said 'Verochka.' It meant a boxer who went into the fight and hit and hit."

4
_____

Véra's resourcefulness stood her in good stead in 1928, when her husband was at work on his second novel. Late in 1927 her father had fallen ill with what he believed after a few months to be malaria. Vladimir was "in the full bloom of my literary strengths" in the spring, turning out manuscript pages at a steady clip. Véra fortified him with a special concoction of eggs, cocoa, orange juice, and red wine, but could do little for Evsei Slonim, whose health continued to deteriorate. Eleven chapters into *King, Queen, Knave,* Nabokov

---

* The detachable magazine of the Browning held seven rounds.

grumbled that "the typewriter doesn't function without Véra," who was exhausted from caring for her father. Sixty-three-year-old Slonim was installed in a sanitarium, where Véra appears to have been the daughter elected to look after him. She spent every other evening at his bedside. His health did not improve, and he died—of sepsis resulting from bronchopneumonia—on the afternoon of June 28, 1928. Véra, who somehow wound up on the death records as his wife, was responsible for the burial. (Sonia was living and working in Paris. A technical translator for a steel concern, Lena was in Berlin, but the arrangements fell to Véra.) Two days later an obituary ran in *Rul,* which—even allowing for the exaggerated tone of Russian obituaries—draws a picture consistent with the rest of the evidence, of a man of great personal dignity, distinguished by "his readiness to ignore his own needs for the sake of others, to deny himself anything in order to make others happy." Nabokov was busy putting the finishing touches on *King, Queen, Knave,* a chilly, beautifully observed novel about an ill-fated love triangle; Véra was distracted in her grief by her mother, who had spent a certain amount of time at sanitariums and was ill throughout much of the year. On August 17, a week shy of her fifty-sixth birthday and after a brief hospital stay, Slava Slonim too died, of a heart attack. Five days later she was buried in the Jewish cemetery, alongside the husband from whom she had been separated. Anna Feigin signed for the burial.

Whatever emotional effect the dual losses had on Véra, the financial fallout made itself most immediately felt. She claimed that she went to work at this time to pay the expenses incurred in her father's illness; she made no mention of her mother's expenses, which could not have been negligible. That year she attended stenography school; she was already an accomplished enough typist to have been coaching friends. On the recommendation of a friend, she took a clerical position in the office of the commercial attaché of the French consulate, located a streetcar ride from the Nabokovs' rooms on Passauer Strasse. She owed the job to Raisa Tatarinov, a Jewish émigré who had organized a loose-limbed literary group, one of the two which Nabokov regularly attended. (It was at a 1926 reading held by this group that Aikhenvald had made the Turgenev comparison; if Véra and Vladimir met before the masked evening in 1923, they did so at the Tatarinovs'.) Véra had more dignified work than many of her compatriots; the aristocrats famously drove taxis, but the émigré intelligentsia supported itself in any way it could. Raisa Tatarinov, who held a law degree from the Sorbonne, also worked as a secretary. Nina Berberova strung beads and addressed thousands of Christmas cards. Elsa Triolet designed jewelry. Those whose German was good paid the rent composing articles like "How to Organize Your Kitchen." A very great deal of cross-stitching and cigarette-rolling got done. Nabokov coached tennis; he and Iosef Hessen's son, George, organized an exhibition match to attract boxing pupils. He continued to give English lessons, an occupation that provided free meals as well as travel benefits.

October 1928 brought welcome news: Ullstein offered 7,500 marks for the German rights in *King, Queen, Knave*. This was several times what the publisher had paid for *Mary* and a fortune compared with what Vladimir was earning as a tutor. Much to the consternation of her boss at the consulate, Véra quit her job early in the winter. Her husband was eager to indulge his childhood passion for butterfly collecting; an expedition was planned for the southern Pyrenees, of which he had been dreaming for some time. It is almost impossible to believe that Véra did not experience some misgivings about the plan, much though she later reported on her desertion with glee; her husband reproached her more than once for being "hysterical over all sorts of utterly foolish, practical thoughts." Even he admitted that their financial situation was not altogether rosy. Moreover, unemployment was on the rise in Berlin. One incentive for the 1929 trip was to meet with Gleb Struve, in the hope that Nabokov's friend and early champion might arrange for meetings with French publishers and translators. That dinner took place early in February during the Nabokovs' two-day stay in Paris. Several days later Véra was hunting her first butterflies and mastering her husband's system for killing his catches; she was careful always to see that he did so in the most humane way possible. From the Pyrenees Vladimir groused that he was spending more time with his butterflies than with his pen, but Véra managed to photograph him at his makeshift desk, at work on the first pages of what became *The Defense*.* The photo reveals that the four-volume *Dahl*—the Russian equivalent of the *OED* and a volume that Nabokov claimed to have read from cover to cover at least four times—had made the trip to France with the couple. Vladimir had originally hoped to stay in France until August but by late June, probably for financial reasons, the Nabokovs were back in Berlin.

Vladimir would say that Russian Berlin "was nothing more than a furnished room, rented out by a crude and malodorous German woman." Beyond that stood a crude stage set of a corner of the world they had left behind. All seemed, and much was, counterfeit. Very little of the country wore off on the couple, who—with the exception of a few months in 1932, when they had enough money for only one room—generally took two rooms, one for each of them, and used a communal bath. (For better or worse these were years

---

* Nabokov lent the Roussillon outpost to another artist furiously composing a masterwork: Hermann at the end of *Despair*.

when the economy had made boarders something of the rule; the middle-class family without a lodger raised suspicions.) Both Véra and Vladimir caught the new German craze for sunbathing; they spent a certain amount of time lounging in the less than spectacularly clean Grunewald, where, as Nabokov famously remembered, "only the squirrels and certain caterpillars kept their coats on." They remained lifelong sun worshipers, Vladimir bronzing to a deep orange, Véra to a pinkish brown. The Weimar passion for calisthenics also made an impression. Nabokov reported to his mother months after the marriage that regardless of the weather, he and Véra exercised with the windows open, stark naked, every morning. Dealings with the rest of the world fell to Véra, who assumed the lion's share of negotiating with landlords, often a delicate process in the couple's case; she could have written her own account of the appropriated overcoat. In the tradition of the Jewish scholar's wife as she had existed two or three generations before, Véra was the one familiar with the marketplace. It was she who had a better command of the local language than the learned author with whom she lived.

Nabokov insisted on his lack of German, but it should be stressed that his definition of linguistic competence differed from most people's. (Véra's version of this was categorical: "Personally, my husband had no contacts with any Germans at all and never learned, or tried to learn, the German language.") He was perfectly able to understand a movie in German; he and Véra went every few weeks to the cheap neighborhood cinema, not only for foreign films. He communicated with the Bromberg boys, who had forgotten their Russian, in German. The German translation of *The Defense* was read aloud to him, for his approval. Later he would say that his German was only good enough to allow him to read entomological journals, which is roughly equivalent to saying that one's English is only accomplished enough to enable one to practice medicine. It was strong enough—or something was—to enable him to rewrite the English translation of Kafka. He clearly made some attempt at speaking the language, not only because it would have been quite impossible for him not to, but because he admitted to mangling it. His summer charges laughed at his efforts. The point was less linguistic than philosophical; he wanted no part of this never-adopted country, which he had long disliked.* And the isolation suited him. As the tide of the Russian emigration ebbed, leaving the Nabokovs increasingly alone in Berlin,

* The confusion over the language issue was partially of Nabokov's own making. In his 1944 *Nikolai Gogol,* he claimed to know "three European languages," a collection that could only have included German. For his 1947 Guggenheim application, he had acquired a "fair knowledge of German." By 1975, he could read but not write the language. What survives of his attempts to write in that language vigorously supports his claim that his German was execrable.

Vladimir confessed that he was happier in a country in which his Russian stood in no danger of corruption, as it might have in France.

The language barrier was but one of several, constructed on both sides. For two very different sets of reasons the Nabokovs had lived outside the norms in Russia. Now another whole set of conventions failed to apply. Véra herself could not stress how little they cared to be part of Germany. "Who wanted assimilation?" she challenged one historian. In no way was she, as he had asserted, "in search of citizenship." This was fortunate, as the couple's situation was irregular from the start. In June 1925 they obtained Nansen passports, soon enough demoted to "Nansen-sical" passports. Green Nansen documents were issued as of 1922 to the stateless, who enjoyed few legal rights, and who, with the papers in hand, were condemned to interminable bureaucratic deliberations each time they hoped to travel or work; the documents proved more effective in closing doors than in opening borders.* Nabokov later railed brilliantly against these humiliations, recalling with a sweet sense of revenge the insults a few émigrés managed to hurl at the "rat-whiskered" functionaries who controlled their fates. Their statelessness in these years would have as much to do with the Nabokovs' later obsession with rights and privileges as did the stateliness of their childhoods. All the same, when Vladimir cursed the German zeal for imposing forms and regulations on foreigners—for treating them like "criminals on parole"—he did not seem aware that his wife had already had a full dress rehearsal for this state of affairs. She was well accustomed to belonging to a colony. The criminal treatment may have seemed to her unjust, but would also have felt familiar.

Despite their feelings about Germany, the Nabokovs cast a vote in 1929 for prolonging their stay. On the return from France they purchased a modest slice of lakeside property in Kolberg, an hour southeast of Berlin. Covered by pines and birches, the parcel abutted a little beach, dotted with waterlilies. On the land they envisioned a small cottage, to be shared with Anna Feigin. They spent a fair part of the summer on the isolated property, in the primitive splendor of a mailman's shack, swimming, swatting away horseflies, picnicking with visitors. They had as many friends in Berlin, and were as social, as they would have or be anywhere again. Vladimir reported to his mother that he was giving his wife tennis lessons—she had played as a child, but could not have had much practice since—and that her game was progressing beautifully. For her part Véra had more momentous news to share with her mother-in-law. Her son had been working consistently and well, and had

---

* It was a cruel irony that the documents took their name from Fridtjof Nansen, the polar explorer.

already completed about half of a new novel. Everything about it set it apart from his previous books. "Russian literature," asserted Véra, "has not seen its like."

Vladimir finished *The Defense*—a novel in which a wife, with all the good intentions in the world, squelches her husband's erratic genius—before the year was out. By that time the Nabokovs were installed in two rooms on Luitpoldstrasse, for the second time. The stock market crash in New York had disastrous effects on the German economy, the prosperity of which had been assured by a wave of foreign investment. That tide now ebbed; sawdust sausage was invented. Again the couple were forced to tighten their belts. The dream of building the house at Kolberg evaporated; Nabokov managed to set a murder scene but never a house on the property. They relinquished the land, and Véra went back to work. In April 1930, on the recommendation of the commercial attaché of the French consulate, she took a secretarial job with a law firm that acted for the French. Her monthly income was slightly less than what she had earned in her previous position, but the day was shorter as well, and the Weil, Gans & Dieckmann office was only a fifteen-minute walk from Luitpoldstrasse. For five hours a day she devoted herself to French and German stenography, French and English translation. Additionally she worked overtime when the situation demanded it. In particular she remembered Bruno Weil's involvement in the purchase of a German factory by Renault: "I at that time not only spent an entire Sunday at one of the big hotels where our French subcontractor was staying, interpreting during negotiations and later spending countless hours reworking the French text of the agreement, but I spent a lot of time working on it at home as well, until the deal could be cut." Throughout the 1930s she continued to give English lessons, as did Vladimir, and worked sporadically for an American agency as a tourist guide. Her principal source of supplementary income was stenography assignments, for which she was paid on a handsome hourly basis. Her clientele varied: Véra had something of an established relationship with the representative of a French perfume concern. She recorded the proceedings of an international convention on eliminating slums. Without holding what could legally be considered full-time employment, she managed to produce an income of RM 3,000 to RM 3,300 a year, or a little over half of what a well-placed banker earned at the time.

All the same Nabokov resented his wife's job, which claimed so much of her time and energy. He especially disliked the fact that she was required to get up early; morning was not Véra's shining hour at the best of times. (Vladimir said it all when he referred to her affectionately as "my morning blind girl.") And she put in such a mercilessly long day! Nor was her husband the only one to rail against her commitments. German unemployment hovered around five million in 1930, when industrial wages were lower than they had been in 1914 and many families found themselves in financial straits. A married woman who accepted a job opened herself to criticism as a *Doppelverdiener,* or second wage earner. In 1932, by the end of which year the unemployed numbered over seven million, out of a workforce of about thirty million, a law was passed permitting the government to dismiss women who were second wage earners from public service. In any event, Véra's schedule amply supports her later assertion that—no matter how spare the Berlin years—"we always had the possibility of earning more money, had we wanted to put more of our time into earning it." It also to a very great extent explained Nabokov's proud assertion of 1935: Despite having to support himself with tennis, boxing, and language lessons, he had managed in ten years to turn out seven novels and a fair selection of poems. (He did not mention the thirty-odd short stories.)

Véra must have concurred with her husband about the long hours and the early mornings. Neither prevented her from returning home to hear, and to type, what he had written between lessons in the course of his day. In the decade following the marriage he wrote in a white heat: most of *The Eye* in the first two months of 1930; *Glory* between May and the end of the year; *Laughter in the Dark* (then *Camera Obscura*) in a matter of months immediately afterward; stories and poems for *Rul* until its October 1931 demise; a draft of *Despair* between June and September 1932. For Véra this added up to a great mountain of pages, sublimely different from those she spent her days transcribing.* Nabokov reported that he held his novels in his head, already formed, fully developed film ready to be printed, but he indulged all the same in the usual orgies of corrections. There is a reason why his books are filled with paeans to smart typists. There were paeans on Véra's side— retrospective paeans anyway—to the arrangements of the early 1930s as well. She made a virtue of necessity, as her father had done in floating timber to Riga on ingeniously constructed rafts, not because it was the best way, but because it was the best way for a Jew to do so while observing the letter of the law. She saw to it that her husband benefited from his cultural isolation. In this she was exactly the reverse of *The Defense*'s Mrs. Luzhin, eager to saturate her husband in the real world so as to spare him the painful, lonely communion with his own obsessive genius. Without mentioning quite how he had managed the feat, Véra boasted of Nabokov's "having developed his tal-

---

* She may well have looked forward to the pages at home. Anna Dostoyevsky remembered the hours in which she took down her husband's dictation as among the happiest in her life.

ent to a luxurious blooming virtually in a vacuum," of his having lived "a life within and practically outside of a milieu of strangers." Others found this to be a description of a living hell; there was a rash of émigré suicides. Véra made of their disenfranchisement an exalted thing.

Nabokov was to pay a price for this creative independence among the émigré community. Especially as his star rose in the 1930s, that community was happy to point out how un-Russian were his works, how "foreign" (read: Jewish) was the company he kept. Even one of his then-admirers wrote that *King, Queen, Knave* read like a beautiful translation from the German; that *The Defense* took place in outer space; that *Glory* was wholly devoid of Russian atmosphere. The more the critics attempted to tie him to his Russian roots, the more he, the consummate escape artist, attempted to confound them; much of his later resistance to the idea of literary schools and influences could be explained by these years, when his readers were few and their need to claim him great. Though the uncertainty clearly took its toll on Véra, she maintained later that the artistic considerations alone had value, that the financial considerations were not merely secondary but unreal. Which made them her department, along with other apparitions like landlords and grammar books and postage stamps. When an aspiring Paris-based writer gracelessly imposed on Nabokov in the 1960s for advice and perhaps something a little more concrete, Véra responded for her husband. Bluntly she explained that he was unsympathetic to his correspondent's plight: "As a young author, he too could not make a living with writing alone but gave lessons (English and tennis) and made innumerable and very dull translations for businessmen and journalists." She recommended this approach to the craft as the best one—it was the key to independence—though she might more honestly have suggested the young man find a wife.

Véra conceded that a great many isolated moments of her past surfaced in her husband's novels, and the offices of Weil, Gans made the transition intact. Musically rechristened Traum, Baum & Käsebier, the firm comes to us as the corporate victims of Margot's crank calls in *Laughter in the Dark*. These they well earned, based on the description of the firm of the same name in *The Gift*. Zina's accounts are so vivid that Fyodor is able to describe the offices down to its resident wildlife, its distressed furniture, the carbon paper wilting in the heat. The shamelessly self-promoting Weil has been transformed into the shamelessly self-promoting Traum, who advises the French embassy instead of the French consulate. A generous layer of grime covers everything in sight; Zina's officemate reeks of carrion; her work consists of shorthand depositions for divorce cases, such as that of the man who has accused his wife of sexual congress with a Great Dane. The place reminds

Fyodor of Dickens "in a German paraphrase," but that is only because Fyodor cannot himself identify it as pure and vintage Nabokov, with its hilarious and unflinching attention to the grotesque, the tasteless, the self-important.

Alexis Goldenweiser, a highly esteemed attorney from a prominent Kiev family, wrote Nabokov on reading these pages of *The Gift* in newspaper form in 1938. He had often paid visits to Traum, Baum & Käsebier; the firm was then called Weil, Gans & Dieckmann. He delighted in the accuracy of Nabokov's depiction; he knew well the decrepit staircase that led to the opulent suites. And he could confirm that Bruno Weil's pronounced Francophilia was born of energetic rainmaking, as is that of his fictional counterpart. In *The Gift,* Nabokov has the lead partner writing popular biographies of figures like Sarah Bernhardt in his desire to cozy up to his French clientele. Weil wrote on Dreyfus, to the same end. In an odd twist of fate, it would be Alexis Goldenweiser, twenty years later and on another continent, who—insofar as anyone ever succeeded in doing so—would induce Véra to document these years. He elicited from her all we know of her chimerical days at Weil, Gans & Dieckmann, in order to file her reparations claim against the German government.

Otherwise Véra admitted to little deprivation, citing only the "high adventure" of these years, the same words her husband uses in describing Martin's oblique triumph in *Glory,* which Nabokov thought his happiest work. The emigration, the couple's limited finances, the dispersal of his family, allowed Vladimir to live a little bit outside the world. Véra did the rest. She had the marketable skills, as did her sisters, both of whom were working as secretaries and interpreters at the time. (During the brief period of the 1930s when all three Slonim sisters were married, they were also all three supporting their husbands.) She was perfectly at ease with both facets of the observation her father had made of her new husband: Writing was indeed the most important thing in the world to him, as well as the one thing of which he was supremely capable. She was the family's primary wage earner throughout these years, yet she never acknowledged as much, occasionally displaying her own loose grasp of reality. (In 1934, when Véra was out of work, Nabokov alone brought in a third of what she had been earning between 1930 and 1933.) She flatly denied that she had supported her husband, in one visitor's opinion because admitting she had done so might reflect poorly on Vladimir. He was on this count entirely happy to embrace reality. When a Russian-Jewish friend felt the chill in the air and decided it was time to leave Germany, he asked if the Nabokovs would be doing so as well. Vladimir answered that they could not because of Véra's job.

5

Increasingly those political winds made themselves felt. In June 1932, the Reichstag was dissolved and the ban on the SA and SS lifted. Communists and Nazis scuffled in the streets. By the end of the summer an unofficial civil war was brewing. For many the elections of 1933 would be the cue to leave Germany. Food shortages had already begun to make themselves felt; bombs and grenades exploded in the streets. Soon enough the Nabokovs' correspondence began to resound with a chorus of "When are you fleeing Berlin?" The couple focused in this case more on the smaller than on the larger picture. They set their sights on their August move from their single room to two large rooms offered them in Anna Feigin's apartment on Nestorstrasse, and on Véra's September vacation. For reasons of economy, they elected to spend the vacation in a French village outside of Strasbourg, to which they had been invited by Vladimir's cousin. The Kolbsheim cottage had been lent to Nicholas Nabokov. His wife, Natalie; her sister, Zinaida Shakhovskoy; and their mother, Princess Anna Shakhovskoy, were vacationing in France at the time. While in Kolbsheim Vladimir's career was discussed at some length; Princess Shakhovskoy proposed that he offer some readings to the émigré communities in France or Belgium. While admitting that he was "in somewhat of a dead-end situation," the writer haggled a little over the terms. All the same, after Véra returned to Berlin, her husband left Kolbsheim for Paris, where he explored the possibilities of resettling. In France as well Véra was treated to a little preview of things to come. On the Russian Orthodox calendar the celebration of the Greek martyr-sister Véra—to the Orthodox a saint's day is more important than a Russian's actual birth date—falls on September 30. When Princess Shakhovskoy came down for breakfast that morning in 1932 she congratulated Véra warmly on the occasion. Evidently with some indignation, Véra responded, "I'm Jewish, Princess!" What may have been a simple correction was heard by some in the room as a battle cry. It would come back to haunt Véra later.

In Paris Vladimir saw a good deal of his new friend, the poet Nina Berberova, and fell quickly into the welcoming arms of Ilya and Amalia Fondaminsky, wealthy patron saints of the emigration, whom the Nabokovs had met in Berlin.* Fondaminsky, a onetime Socialist Revolutionary commissar, was now publishing *Contemporary Annals*. Eternally optimistic, fi-

---

* On their return to France in 1931, the Fondaminskys had reported that Sirin-Nabokov "lives in two rooms with his wife, a very fine and delicate woman."

nancially secure, he was one of the few in a position to transcend all émigré squabbles. By the end of the month Vladimir had moved in with the couple, and Madame Fondaminsky was to be found at her typewriter, transcribing pages of *Despair* for the author. (Vladimir warned Véra that she would need to redo the text all the same.) During the stay he wrote her nearly every day, with news, to pass on compliments, for opinions, for advice. At least two kinds of directives followed from Véra's end. He had made all the calls she suggested, to publishers and translators; he had written his letters. And yes, in accordance with her request, he promised to be careful crossing the streets of Paris. He submitted *Despair* around; he reported on a long, debauched evening from which he had awoken at two-thirty the following afternoon; he toyed with the idea of writing something in French. He reported on a conversation he had had with Mark Aldanov, one of the best of the older generation of émigré critics, who despite advanced degrees in three fields could not fathom the younger novelist's humor. His confusion is understandable. "I said to Aldanov, 'Without my wife, I wouldn't have written a single novel,' " Vladimir reported. Aldanov replied that news of Véra's heroic assistance had already reached Paris. It is impossible to tell if Vladimir was surprised that a statement he made sincerely was shrugged off by Aldanov, or if he made the statement in jest and was astonished when Aldanov took it seriously. Generally he was pleased with his visit—his prodigious output of the last years had secured his reputation as the best writer in the emigration, though the epithet made some sputter—and convinced they should move immediately. Véra was less sanguine, especially as she would be unable to work legally in France. She did not agree with her husband that they could survive otherwise. Partly as a consequence, neither Nabokov was in Paris on December 10, 1932, when Véra's younger sister, Sonia, married an Austrian-Jewish engineer. It would be five years before Véra would again set foot in France, and by then the circumstances would be far different.

On January 30, 1933, Hitler was named Chancellor, and the loudspeakers began to blare; at the end of February the Reichstag burned. Within weeks Jews were being paraded barefoot through the streets by Nazi youth. In its German edition, *Laughter in the Dark* sold precisely 172 copies that year, when another Russian import of the 1920s began to sell briskly: It was the *Protocols of the Elders of Zion*. Volumes of *Mein Kampf* sailed out of bookstores all over the city. In the spring the first Jewish laws were promulgated; the Weil, Gans offices closed, without warning. (The firm reopened for a short time later, with a skeleton staff.) Still, despite her husband's pull to Paris, despite the brown-uniformed SA teams tramping throughout the Grunewald, the assaults on Jewish lawyers, the mass rallies, Véra remained rooted in Berlin.

With her light hair she was a less obvious target than some. And she was by no means alone in her stubbornness. Her sister Lena, married to a titled Russian named Massalsky, remained in the city as well. Plenty of Berliners had left, but plenty stayed; Jewish emigration between 1934 and 1937 dropped off considerably. Véra Nabokov did not precisely keep a low profile, as has been suggested. With relish she told the story of having been advised by her former consulate boss to call the office of a German minister then organizing an international congress, for a stenography assignment. "I said 'they won't engage me, don't forget I'm Jewish.' But he only laughed and said 'they will. They have been unable to get anyone else.' I did as I was told, and was accepted with alacrity, whereupon I said to the German to whom I was talking 'but are you sure you want me? I'm Jewish.' . . . 'Oh,' he said, 'but it does not make *any* difference to us. We pay no attention to such things. Who told you we did?' " The wool producers' convention was to begin the next day; she got the job. Dutifully she copied down the speeches of four Nazi ministers.

By that time swastikas hung in every street. Uniformed Nazis had begun to make the rounds of cafés, soliciting donations to the party. It was not wise to refuse them. Véra Nabokov cannot be imagined tipping a coin into one of those metal boxes; she can only have avoided cafés. The newspapers were filled with new rules—they were said to resemble nothing so much as a school magazine—but only one Nabokov was reading them anyway.* The first boycott of Jewish businesses was held on April 1, when storm troopers were posted at the doors of all establishments. Véra witnessed firsthand the destruction of a culture in May 1933 when she stumbled upon a book-burning on her way home. It was twilight; she stayed long enough to hear the crowd burst into patriotic song but hurried on before the storm troopers began to prance around their bonfire. Tens of thousands of volumes went up in flames; though Nabokov would set his own little conflagrations under Marx and Freud, the sight of Berlin youths doing the same must have sent chills down the spine. By the fall, it was considered seditious to buy those authors' books.

Why did they stay? The Nabokovs had long thought the city a miserable dead end; the year after their marriage Vladimir had written Véra that hearing German made him sick, and that the cuisine did little more for him. He would prefer almost any provincial outpost to Berlin, a city he vowed, in a draft of *Speak, Memory,* that they had both disliked.† Initially Véra had ad-

---

* As Véra remembered of her husband: "He did not have enough German to read a novel, and did not read the German newspapers."
† By 1939, for added reasons, it had become "thrice-damned Germany." The line was later deleted from the last chapter of *Speak, Memory.*

mired Germany for its democratic institutions, an affection she could no longer feel. She did not frighten easily, if at all; her father had also waited until the bitter end to leave Russia. Mostly they had no place to go. Berberova's description of the face of the continent at the time goes some way toward explaining their inertia: "On the map of Europe were England, France, Germany, and Russia. In the first, imbeciles reigned, in the second living corpses, in the third villains, and in the fourth villains and bureaucrats." Zinaida Shakhovskoy visited the Nabokovs on Nestorstrasse in 1932 or 1933 and was surprised to find them every bit as disgusted by Russia and Russians as they were by the situation in Germany. (She pointed out to them that in their blanket condemnations they were guilty of the same kind of racism as the Germans.) They were comfortably settled with Anna Feigin, the only relative to whom Véra felt close; the arrangement reduced their living expenses considerably and provided them the great luxury of domestic help. Véra continued to work freelance assignments and to offer language lessons; her students included their great friend George Hessen, also still in Berlin. Nabokov did not find politics in any way broke his literary stride. Writers should "occupy themselves only with their own meaningless, innocent, intoxications," he announced in 1934. "I am writing my novel. I do not read the papers."

Years later he offered another explanation: "We were always sluggish. Gracefully sluggish in the case of my wife, terribly sluggish in my case." He repeatedly wrote down the prolonged stay in Berlin to laziness, although when it came to dillydallying, Nabokov talked a better game than he played. He had begun to research and write *The Gift*; the French translation of *The Defense* was enjoying gratifying reviews. He heard often of his growing stature in Paris. In 1933 for the first time a far-off, tinny echo of his name sounded in America, not yet loud enough to qualify as a Sirin call. As if dwarfed by the events around the couple, the biographical record thins at this point. Ivan Bunin passed through Berlin in December 1933, having become the first Russian to claim the Nobel Prize. Both Nabokovs attended the reception held for him by the much reduced émigré community. By that time anti-Semitism had greatly increased among the city's Russians, many of them monarchists who welcomed Hitler with open arms. (The irony of Hitler's attributing his anti-Jewish policies to the danger of Bolshevik agitation could not have been lost on Véra.) The Russian proprietor of one of Berlin's largest garages warned Iosef Hessen that his drivers had decided that he and Sirin— "the kike and the half-kike"—should not speak at the Bunin banquet, at any cost. Nabokov and Hessen delivered their speeches all the same, during what must have been, for every possible reason, a nerve-racking evening for Véra.

Her father-in-law had been murdered, by a monarchist, at a public meeting, where a scandal had been expected; Hessen had been the one to telephone the Nabokov home with the news. The picture is otherwise blurry for the next months, the latter half of 1933 and the first of 1934, which is precisely as Véra intended it to be. In her attempts to make these prolific years look effortless she obscured one other small detail.

She reemerges on May 9, 1934—nearly nine years to the day she had met her husband—at Anna Feigin's well-furnished apartment on Nestor-strasse. Nabokov and George Hessen's half-brother are on that evening hunched over a chessboard. Quietly Anna Feigin escorts Véra out the door. No one other than the four people in the room, on a leafy street near the Hohenzollerndamm station in southwest Berlin, knows where she is going. Presumably by taxi the two women make the mile trip east to Berchtes-gadener Strasse, where at eleven A.M., in a private clinic, after an evening's labor and a difficult delivery, Véra will give birth to a large baby boy, *"ein kleiner russischer"* in the words of the attending physician. After some delib-eration, the child was named Dmitri.

Everyone was startled by the news, some to the point of disbelief. Within days Vladimir had announced the baby's arrival by (handwritten) letter to Natalie Nabokov and to Khodasevich in Paris, to Struve in London. When no congratulations were forthcoming from the latter, Nabokov wrote again: "I've been somewhat preoccupied by the appearance of my son Dmitri (I wrote to you about it, but you apparently took it for a joke)." His mother's re-action was a little more gratifying: The shock had been enormous but also delicious. She was astounded by the news, highly solicitous of Véra's health. The word "pregnant" had never been pronounced, save in the presence of the Hessens and Anna Feigin (and presumably some medical personnel); Véra had continued on her usual lesson-giving rounds, had held to her flawless posture, and had dressed with phenomenal discretion. She took some plea-sure in having made an appearance at the Bunin evening without anyone's being the wiser about her condition. Her husband wrote this down to the Russian powers of nonobservation, but failed to give credit where credit was due: Concealing a five-months-pregnant belly requires some skill. It is possi-ble that this was neither a first nor a last pregnancy; there is some hint of a miscarriage earlier, and there was very likely another pregnancy in the sum-mer of 1936. Superstition aside, why the secrecy? So much did Véra insist on emotional reserve that she admired it in Dmitri as a baby. The pregnancy, like the marriage, concerned only her husband and herself. And, too, nothing is quite so platitudinous as childbirth and childrearing. It takes a Nabokov to write rapturously of diapers and stroller, to locate poetry in a "postlactic all-clear signal." The very concept of ordinariness was foreign to Véra, who had no desire for her experience to be contaminated by anyone else's. And yet as Richard Holmes has written of Mary Wollstonecraft at a similar juncture 140 years earlier, as the guillotines clattered away outside and inside the Gallic air was thick with domestic bliss, "This extraordinary and exceptional woman had become a mother—just like any other." Nabokov's sister Elena shrugs when asked about the clandestine pregnancy: "That was pure Véra."

Once the secret was out it was loudly broadcast; the new father reported endless phone calls, flowers, telegrams. Véra stayed at the Schöneberg clinic for two weeks, where Vladimir visited twice daily. At home she was quickly exhausted by the "heavenly labor" involved in washing out clothing and diapers. On June 10 she was back at the typewriter, explaining her husband's silence to his French publisher. A week later she typed a long letter to the agent who had been negotiating with that publisher; her husband was frustrated in his attempts to settle on terms for translation rights in *The Defense*. He was not exactly getting rich, was rather in desperate need of money. Much of the rest of the summer and fall were devoted to the transcription of *Invitation to a Beheading,* a first draft of which Vladimir had written in a lightning two weeks, on Véra's return from the clinic. To his dismay the typing seemed to be taking an inordinate amount of time; in November an exhausted Véra was at the machine night and day. From outside the third-floor apartment, recalled Nabokov, "we heard Hitler's voice from rooftop loudspeakers." Inside the typewriter clattered away, setting down the account of Cincinnatus's life in prison, rich in mental adventures, the only kind, Véra would remind us, that matter.

THROUGH THE
LOOKING GLASS

Yes, the mirror reflection is always there.

—NABOKOV TO MARC SZEFTEL

1

"Véra was a pale blonde when I met her, but it didn't take me long to turn her hair white," Nabokov chuckled to a journalist. Atypically, an entire chromatic age was lost on him. Early in the marriage, slate streaks appeared in the hair that melted in the sunlight. Véra reported with pride that it had begun to turn when she was twenty-five. As a new mother in her early thirties, she was grayer (and thinner) yet; she looks as wan as she reportedly felt. In a few years she would be almost entirely pearl-gray. By her mid-forties, the opalescent bob paled to a radiant cloud of white. (Lena Massalsky's hair did the same at the same age, although the sisters would not discover this until later.) Véra expressed a desire even to hurry it along. "I wish it would go all white," she sighed in 1948, when it was very nearly there. "People will think I married an older woman," her husband protested, to which, without blinking, Véra replied, "Not if they look at you." She would be as striking in the late 1940s, with the pearly hair and the alabaster skin—the discrepancy between the hair and her young face was particularly dramatic—as she had been in the mask-wearing 1920s. She took great pride in the white halo, which seemed somehow to match her refinement, her agelessness; it removed her from all categories. It lent her an air of divinity. With delight she shared one hairdresser's amazement: Her color could not be reproduced artificially. Hers alone was the genuine article. Well before then she was very aware of her looks; the reflections in her husband's fiction were not the only ones she thought distorted. "The camera and I have been at odds since I was a child," she grumbled. The statement reveals a certain vanity and, too, a loose grasp of the truth. Véra Nabokov was beautiful, and she photographed beautifully.

She was highly conscious of presentation and appeared always impeccably dressed and coiffed, even when the Nabokovs had nothing. It is easy to imagine her standing before a mirror, less easy to imagine her meeting her own reflection there. Already she had eyes mostly for her husband. It was his portrait—the portrait of an artist—she saw in the looking glass. He knew enough about the makers of literature to realize how much he benefited from that attention. In 1931 he had written Struve:

> People of the writing variety—homo scribo or scribblingus—are extremely conceited and vain, and resemble in that way certain women who immediately seek themselves out in a summertime group photograph, can't get enough of themselves, and always return, through the entire album, to that photo, though they pretend to be looking at their neighbors and not themselves.

Véra saw her husband always before her; he saw her image of him. This optics-defying arrangement sustained them at a time and in a place when little else did; it was the first in what was to be a repertoire of deceptive techniques, for which the couple had only begun their magic act. Already Vladimir had acquired a reputation for being impenetrable, almost impossible to get to know. "The thoughts and feelings of the other person rebounded from him as from a mirror," observed another émigré. This was a cardinal sin among Russians, for whom it is a virtue to be "open-souled," among whom one speaks not "one on one," not "*en tête-à-tête*," but "soul to soul."* Among the many who found Sirin brilliant, brittle, and impenetrable was the man before the looking glass, who cut from *Speak, Memory* a reference to "the mirrory quality of his [Sirin's] personality." (The ever-charitable Aldanov held that watching Nabokov and Bunin talk was like watching two movie cameras trained on each other.) Véra so much existed in Vladimir's achievements, and in her pride in those achievements, that conversation with her could prove equally flattering. When she called the British embassy in

---

* Decades later, his Russian colleagues at Cornell wondered if he had a soul, and if so, why he took such pains to hide it.

search of a translator "who would be an experienced man of letters with fine style," she heard nothing facetious in the suggestion that perhaps H. G. Wells might be capable of tackling the job. Her sense of humor—usually quite lively, and one of the qualities Nabokov professed to admire most about her—failed her utterly at such moments.

Why her self-effacement? The vanity was there, in ample supply. The desire, or the ability, to look herself in the eye was not. She was most comfortable in a mask, most herself when reflecting light elsewhere. This moon was no thief. She informed a biographer that she panicked every time she saw her name in his footnotes. Her sisters took a different approach, gravitating toward the spotlight, even if that meant creating one of their own. They had no trouble discoursing at length about themselves. Meanwhile Véra developed a passion for secrecy. She had both the good and the ill fortune to recognize another's gift; her devotion to it allowed her to exempt herself from her own life while founding a very solid existence on that very selflessness. (Her father may well have shared this disposition, but the cloak of invisibility falls differently on a woman.) She was at once a model of solicitude and sincerity; on the one hand she was difficult to please, and on the other her husband could do no wrong. Nabokov's work had always been fostered by women, all of whom had copied out his verse, but few brought to it Véra's critical faculty. She affixed to it her own (and Zina's) ambition, while on the page—as she would later, in a more convoluted arrangement—she assumed the passive role, allowing her husband to speak through her. Her whole being was to constitute a mask.

For all her evasions, she was not unaware of the importance of what she publicly demoted to mere assistance and what detractors identified as her spell, or domination. She acknowledged a greater role with at least one friend. Years later Leo Peltenburg's middle daughter reminded her: "Back in Berlin, you said that someone should write a book on the influence a woman bears on her husband, in other words on stimulation, and inspiration." Véra and her husband shared an admiration for Musset's "La Nuit de Mai," ten stanzas in which the patient but demanding muse urges a subject upon the despondent poet. Noted Nabokov in his 1951 diary: "V[éra] says that if Musset had been writing his 'Nuits' today, the conversation would have been between the poet and his secretary." When Véra's father had asked after Nabokov's work in Berlin he had habitually inquired after "their work," implicating his daughter in the process, and perhaps revealing something of his own feelings on the subject. Véra never objected to the assertion that she had been her husband's muse.

In October 1930 she typed a letter for her husband, to Struve: "My wife

and I are still trying to move to Paris—at a somewhat upbeat tempo."
Nabokov was not at his best with music and confused adagio with allegro:
After the Paris trip of 1932, France was regularly discussed. In March 1933
the couple were granted visas, although they stayed put, possibly because of
the pregnancy that fall. Vladimir claimed in August that they expected to
move over the winter; the following spring they were entirely distracted by
the birth of Dmitri. Véra asserted later that "from the moment Hitler seized
power we began to prepare our departure," a departure over which she repeatedly hesitated, even at a time when only a few thousand Russians remained in Berlin. The employment prospects remained a consideration:
Early in 1935 she took a position handling foreign correspondence for an engineering firm called Ruthspeicher, manufacturers of heavy machinery, for
whom she worked primarily in English. She had done a great deal of technical translating and was hired in part for that expertise. Before or just after the
birth of Dmitri, she had gone so far as to design and attempt to patent a
lateral parking device for cars, a retractable wheel affixed laterally to the
chassis of a car. Connected to the engine, the wheel could be lowered on command, to maneuver the vehicle into position. From Berlin she submitted her
design to Packard. The marvel is not that she took the initiative of doing so
but that she designed the parking system when she had not yet learned
to drive.

Nabokov's memories of having accompanied Dmitri to the Grunewald
date in part from that time; he was looking after their son while Véra was at
the office. "As before, Véra doesn't have a free minute; I help out as best I
can," he wrote his mother. The Ruthspeicher position proved short-lived, as
the Nazis forced out the firm's Jewish owners, and all Jewish employees with
them, four months after Véra's arrival. More than ever now the Nabokovs
were struggling financially. "I'm rather sick of being so hard up," Vladimir
sighed in May 1935, just after the couple's tenth wedding anniversary. He
and Véra were perfectly exhausted, though continually delighted by Dmitri,
whom they were deceiving into walking on his own. He would do so only by
grasping at trees and bushes as he moved; they fixed a branch in his hand,
and off he went. At eight months Véra began to teach him the names of
plants and trees, always to remain a test of literacy in the Nabokov family. At
about the same time she sacrificed something more than her job to the new
government. As the Nazis had established strict rules about gun ownership,
Véra arranged to send her pistol to Paris, with an embassy friend. The transfer proved harrowing. At lunchtime she crossed Berlin to deliver the handgun to the embassy; her taxi was immobilized by a Nazi procession. As the
demonstrators passed they knocked on the car windows, rattling their cans of

collection monies, demanding contributions. The pistol hidden under her clothing, Véra sat impassively, pretending she heard nothing.

The nature of the Nabokovs' poverty has been the subject of some dispute. Véra objected heatedly to one depiction of it: "The point of émigré life was that even people who were much worse off than we, never allowed the financial considerations to occupy even one tenth part of their consciousness." She held that her father did not discuss his financial woes, even after having been utterly ruined. They may never have discussed it, but the Nabokovs' was alternately genteel poverty, proud poverty, golden poverty, dire poverty. One thing it was not was unusual poverty. Few other émigrés were any more fortunate. In Paris many were already starving. (Again Nabokov's definition was different. "I, you understand, need comforts not for the sake of comforts, but for the sake of not thinking about them," he had explained to Véra in the early days of the relationship.) And his star seemed to wax as his fortune waned. It was all very well and good that Albert Parry had proclaimed of him in *The New York Times* that "our age has been enriched by the appearance of a great writer," but it was nonetheless true that he did not own a single decent pair of pants. And Véra had seen the last of her steady jobs. Her work permit was revoked on religious grounds, not long after the Ruthspeicher job. The bleakest years were yet to come.

At many times, but especially in the first six years of his life, when their finances were as delicate as they would ever be, Dmitri represented the couple's only luxury. In Hitler's Berlin, Véra and Vladimir spun a Russian-speaking cocoon around their son, who grew up in as sheltered a context as had his mother, in a fair approximation of the silken comfort of his father. Bundled in furs, Dmitri rolled about Berlin in the Rolls-Royce of prams, on loan from a taxi-driving poet. Few mothers have enjoyed such elegant tributes as does Véra in her husband's autobiography; Nabokov eulogized the scrupulous care with which she attended to their son's diet and general hygiene, the patience with which she indulged his passions. (In *Speak, Memory,* that unlikely how-to book, he offers one crucial piece of advice: "I appeal to parents: never, never say, 'Hurry up,' to a child.") Dmitri grew quickly, to the point where at twenty months he was mistaken in a photo for a five-year-old. A more silent tribute yet to Véra is woven into *Speak, Memory,* in which her name figures nowhere in the text. Before composing his pages on Dmitri's early years, Nabokov asked his wife to set down her impressions. Aside from a few phrases, none of those recollections found its way directly into the final manuscript. But if anyone has ever wondered how Nabokov knew what Véra felt on a windy railroad bridge near Nestorstrasse, it is because she described for him the long waits for trains to pass below, Dmitri in his lamb-

skin, she in her black cloth coat, "my feet hurting with the cold, my hands
only kept from going numb by holding his in my right, then in my left (that
incredible amount of heat his big baby body generated!)" Nabokov made
the memory his own, confirming their cup-half-empty, cup-half-full world-
views: ". . . and the fervency of his faith kept him glowing, and kept *you*
warm too, since all you had to do to prevent your delicate fingers from freez-
ing was to hold one of his hands alternately in your right and left, switching
every minute or so, and marveling at the incredible amount of heat generated
by a big baby's body."

From Véra's pages on Dmitri's childhood, written when he was sixteen,
we know a great deal about what mattered to her. Her first lines afford no
surprise, coming from the would-be Trotsky assassin: "He was always so
brave. In every new experience he would exhibit a degree of courage unexpected in one so small." Victory mattered, as did the right weapons: "He
often got the worst in an exchange of physical arguments but always got his
little victory in the verbal skirmishes." She delighted in his perceptions of
color, his innate gentleness, his neologizing, his discretion, his fascination
with the technical, his strengths as a storyteller. (These indicate that he was
not impervious to the world around him. This three-year-old's invented hero
walked to the Italian frontier, where he was sent back for want of a visa.) In
June 1936 Véra and Dmitri spent ten days in Leipzig, where they stayed with
Anna Feigin in the Brombergs' spacious apartment. In Berlin Vladimir
missed them terribly; it was the second separation of the year, as he had been
on a triumphant reading tour in France and Belgium in January. Véra took
Dmitri to a sort of petting zoo in the city, but as she observed, the "sudden
exposure to nature had an unexpected result. A baby who loved to run
around (and a fast runner he was) suddenly became a little lap-baby." He refused to return to the ground, and for the next few days insisted on being carried, exclusively by an exhausted—he was "a big baby, a heavy armful of a
baby"—Véra. Vladimir was fascinated to learn that his son should be afraid
of squirrels, but doubtless worried, too: Véra appears to have been pregnant
during this trip. As exhausted as her husband knew her to be with Dmitri, he
advised her to remain motionless as much as possible. He wrote a little wistfully of a secretarial job about which a friend had called Véra, but which he
knew she could not accept.

While in Paris and Brussels in January, Nabokov had begun a full-scale
campaign, a search for the person, the publishing contract, that might expe-
dite their move to Paris. "My fate" had taken on a new connotation; he had
done his best to interest as many friends and acquaintances in it as possible.
He met masses of people, everyone from France's Edmond Jaloux to Franz

Hellens, Belgium's foremost writer. ("You would really like Hellens!" he wrote Véra. "He's the premier writer of Belgium, and his books *don't bring him a thing*!") It was far more difficult to pull up stakes now than it would have been in 1931 or 1932, when Vladimir was still joking about the suitcase-dusting that went on in the émigré community each time word leaked out of an all-night meeting of the government. He and Véra had had a little tussle over the English edition of *Despair*; the novel had been sold to Hutchinson in London, but the author had been desperately unhappy about their translation and had asked to have a hand at it himself. Vladimir asked Véra to send his revised version; she had balked, of the opinion that it was not yet entirely polished. He attempted to reason with her: Its imperfections were no more numerous than the "birthmarks" on any of his Russian-language manuscripts. Four months later, when Véra was in Leipzig, Vladimir reported that the British publisher was not exactly convinced by the revision. What should he answer?* The better his work got, the more difficult it seemed to be to get it translated, and the more dire the family's financial straits. In May he wrote the historian Mikhail Karpovich, who was to play a great role on the other side of the looking glass, in America, and whom he had met briefly, to ask if perhaps some sort of teaching position might be arranged. Was there any hope? "I am not afraid of living in the American boondocks," swore Vladimir. "I could, in addition to an elementary Russian course, teach one on the side on French literature." By November he conceded that he was at his wits' ends, that his position was "desperate in the extreme." Was there work anywhere, if not in Great Britain or North America, then in India or South Africa?

In the fall of 1936, his "fate" became what Véra feared might more accurately be labeled his "plight." The monarchist politician General Biskupsky—one of the most reviled figures in the emigration, a man of so many schemes it was impossible to say where, if anywhere, his loyalties lay—had been named head of Hitler's Department of Émigré Affairs in May. As his undersecretary he appointed Sergei Taboritsky, who had been convicted for the 1922 murder of Nabokov's father. (Véra was careful to say that Taboritsky was not simply a Monarchist—"there were decent people among the Monarchists"—but a true Russian fascist.) According to Véra, Taboritsky's mandate was "ferreting out Russian Jews and maintaining a corps of Russian fascist translators and intelligence agents to interrogate prisoners of war."

---

* *Despair* enjoyed the distinction of having been the sole work to be accepted in Russian and very nearly rejected in the author's English. Nabokov admitted later he was not entirely pleased with his translation, which he thought flattened the novel into "a half-baked thriller."

Her first concern was for her husband, especially in September, when Biskupsky began to register all Russians in Berlin.

Vladimir continued to issue all-points bulletins but found the fates curiously indifferent to his distress signals. "We're slowly dying of hunger and nobody cares," he wrote Zinaida Shakhovskoy. She had already proved a guardian angel and did again now, quickly arranging for him to read in Brussels, from which city he would continue on to France. By January 19, 1937, Nabokov was on Belgian soil, never to return to Germany. Later Véra explained: "My husband was abroad before I was because I insisted on his departure as soon as Taboritsky was released from prison and appointed a member of the commission for managing the Russian refugees in Germany."* She had remained behind to prepare for their definite emigration. In the ensuing correspondence—once again "allegro" would be the wrong tempo for the final exodus from Berlin, where the anti-Semitic laws had been extended, and a true ethnic cleansing had begun—there is no hint that life in Berlin might have been uncomfortable for her. That both Taboritsky and the head of the Foreign Policy Office believed the evil in the world to be the single-handed work of Jews appeared to have made no impression on her at all.

2

Between January 18, 1937, when she put him on a train for Belgium, and May 22, when they were reunited, Véra received a letter from her husband every day, sometimes twice a day. In those four tense months he did everything he could to advance his career, with the possible exception of write. His Brussels reading was beautifully arranged by Shakhovskoy and provides a clearer sense of Nabokov's definition of linguistic fluency, from which the geography of the next years derived. Excusing himself for *"son pauvre français*

---

* Biskupsky did manage to wreak havoc with Véra's family, but not on the front she had anticipated. Lena's husband, Prince Nicolai Massalsky, was a Russian scholar, no friend of the fascists. Biskupsky's committee supplied a passport in Massalsky's name to a White Russian officer, who in that guise participated in all sorts of anti-Semitic activities, beautifully sullying Massalsky's reputation. (It was a peculiarly Nabokovian twist, this creation of the "disreputable namesake," sounding like something out of the short story "Conversation Piece, 1945"—or like the kind of wizardry Golyadkin believes to be practiced on him in Dostoyevsky's *The Double*.) That incident—and the generally anti-Semitic behavior of the Russians who remained in Berlin under Hitler—forever soured Lena on her countrymen. "I don't know a single Russian, White, Red, Green, or of any other color, and I avoid them like the plague," she wrote Véra in 1960, from Sweden. Véra learned of Biskupsky's treachery years after the fact. So far as the Nabokov family went, Biskupsky did nothing when Vladimir's brother Sergei was arrested much later by the Gestapo, assuring family members there was no cause for concern.

d'étranger," he went on to lecture on Pushkin in faultless French. The real triumph was the Parisian evening, which was sold out in advance; the appearance represented something of the return of the prodigal poet. Nabokov was introduced by Khodasevich, who observed, among other things, that Sirin's heroes are all of them artists, even when art is not exactly their métier. To an overfilled auditorium Vladimir read for over an hour and a half from his novel-in-progress, *The Gift.* The applause was deafening. The most captious thing that could be said of the evening was said by the large-hearted Aldanov: "I will refrain from saying whether one need write the way Sirin does. But at present, he alone can write that way." The accolades accumulated over the next week, as Nabokov began a whirlwind tour of the French and Russian salons. He was toasted everywhere, introduced to everyone, to the French writers who might be able to arrange for translations of his work, the editors who might help him place stories. "I'm the toast of the town, I'm surrounded by hundreds of the kindest people," he informed his wife, moving from lunch to café to reception. As a Nansen passport holder, he could obtain no French working papers; his ability to settle in France depended on these connections. Despite the compliments, despite the bravura performance at the January reading, this made for exhausting work. In the same February letter in which he described for Véra his greatest triumph to date—a reading James Joyce had attended, after which the two had chatted, mostly about Joyce's eyesight—he wrote of his first visit to Gallimard, an interview he had had some difficulty arranging. Having been told by the publisher's receptionist that Gaston Gallimard was occupied with another caller, he installed himself in the waiting room. Eventually the receptionist went to lunch, leaving him alone. An hour after the agreed-upon meeting time he wandered back to where he assumed Gallimard's office to be; the publisher too had left for lunch. Twenty years later—after Gallimard had published *Despair* but rejected *Invitation to a Beheading, Bend Sinister,* and *Speak, Memory*—the firm again became Nabokov's publisher. The reception would be dramatically different.

He continued on his social rounds in February in London, with two readings and a great number of dinners. He inquired after lecturing possibilities in England but was not overly optimistic. He had begun a version of an autobiography, in which he tried to interest publishers; fragments of it would be folded into *Sebastian Knight.* He saw scores of people, including his nontranslator H. G. Wells. By comparison the days in Paris seemed like a vacation. He was universally charming, as only a writer in pursuit of a publisher can be. He kept a very un-Nabokovian list of all those to whom he was introduced. This effort took its toll. After two weeks he reported that he was exhausted from all the sherry, from the constant strain of being cheerful, from the serial introductions. Between each appointment he spent unaccountable amounts of time in the London subway, which depleted him further. "I am rather fed up with the whole business, and I so desperately want some peace, you and the muse," he wrote Véra. All the same the London prospects began to burn brighter. By the end of the month letters were flying in all directions on his behalf. The country was expensive but he felt the food was good; he could easily see his family installing themselves in London. He thought they could realistically manage as much, after a summer in the south of France. He counted on a reunion by mid-March, at the latest. "I have never loved you as I love you now," Vladimir swore, worried that his wife was tired and lonely. He reminded her of the Peltenburgs' insistence that she visit them in Holland; perhaps she should go now? She should keep in mind that she at least had Dmitri. He had no such consolation, and missed them both dreadfully. He longed for her. He was counting the days until March 15.

He returned to Paris early in March, buoyant, but all the same painfully aware that his fate hung in a delicate balance. The strain of living with that uncertainty can be read in the letters to Berlin; it took its toll as well on his health. He had suffered from psoriasis in the past, and in Paris the condition—aggravated by stress—deteriorated. The wild itching kept him from sleep and greatly affected his mood; the disease spread even to his face. (His condition was not much helped by the fact that this was a particularly cold and rainy spring in Paris.) He felt as if in constant torment, especially as he hesitated to use the ointment he had been prescribed for fear of ruining the sheets at Ilya Fondaminsky's, where he was again a houseguest.* He could not wait to get to the Riviera, where the sun would offer some relief. In the meantime, he worried for his sanity. He was itching in other ways too; he felt he would burst if he did not get back to *The Gift*. He could not be more sick of his "society lifestyle." He continued to write Véra of the admiration his work and his person evoked, not always in the most comforting terms. In England he made a less than prepossessing entrance: "My hat (which lost any and all shape after the first Parisian rain) elicits surprise and laughter, and my scarf dangles along the sidewalk, having been flattened in the process." In Paris he left a different impression, one that was no more reassuring to his wife: "I have been encountering two breeds of ladies here," he related early in March. "Those who quote to me excerpts from my books, and those who

---

* But in a different apartment, this time on the avenue de Versailles; Amalia Fondaminsky had died in 1935. The earlier apartment, on the rue Chernoviz, made its way into the final chapter of *Pnin*.

ponder the question of whether my eyes are green or yellow."* He had found
a French-English translating job, but was waiting for answers from all kinds
of journals and publishers. In March, in another piquant example of the future shimmering through the past, Putnam's turned down the pages they had
seen of the English-language autobiography. He wanted only to write; there
was too much noise at the Fondaminsky apartment for him to do so.

To make matters worse, in February Véra began to balk at the idea of the
move. "Tell yourself that our Berlin life is over—and please, get ready to go,"
her husband implored her as he raced about breathlessly, attempting to establish some kind of base for the family, in France or England. But from
Berlin Véra began to raise all kinds of nettlesome objections. For the next
two months they sang a painfully atonal duet: He said March, she insisted
on April. He said France, she said Belgium. He said France, she said Italy.
He said France, she said Austria. She developed a sudden obsession with
Vladimir's mother, who had been promised a glimpse of the grandson she
had not yet met; she insisted they not move west without first venturing east,
as a family, to Prague. And while in Czechoslovakia, Véra hoped to spend
some time at a Franzenbad sanitarium, taking the cure for rheumatism.
Nabokov railed at this proposal. After all he had done to secure a foothold in
London and Paris, was he really to be hauled off to the backwaters of eastern
Europe, far from all opportunity? He felt he had depleted himself reaching
this other, more promising, shore, and "that after your letter I truly feel like
a swimmer who is being torn from a rock he has reached by some whim of
Neptune, a wave of unknown origin, a sudden wind or some such thing."
This time common sense was surely on his side, he argued. Stubbornly Véra
proposed that she and Dmitri make the Prague trip and meet him later, an
idea to which her husband objected as well. He did not want to put off their
reunion for another month. He could not believe his mother's equilibrium
depended on their visit. As for Véra's rheumatism, the south of France would
prove just as salubrious. It would also be free of doctors insisting she stay forever. A Czech sanitarium would not.

"The Eastern side of my every minute is already colored by the light of
our impending meeting," Nabokov assured his wife, imploring her not to be
jealous of his life in Paris, or of his female admirers, all of whom were powerless in comparison with her. He continued to solicit her advice on all publishing matters—What should he tell Putnam's? Did she agree that various
pages were ready for submission? Did she have a title for him?—but also

---

* Véra grappled with the same riddle. "His eyes were not actually hazel, but somewhere between hazel
and green," she concluded later.

could not refrain from telling her that everyone with whom he had spoken found her Prague plans foolhardy. Meanwhile the middle of March came and went. He was expecting to make a second short trip to London at the end of April; Véra wrote waspishly that she did not see the point in her joining him in France before then. He was incensed; she was effectively delaying their meeting for an entire month. Why was she so dragging her heels when they could meet before the London trip? Forced to choose for the first time between his work and his wife, Vladimir wrote that he would rather cancel that trip than go without seeing her for another four weeks. He could not assure her enough of his love—nor could he desist from reminding her that her plan was sheer insanity. Everyone agreed: The visas alone that would be required for the three of them to travel to Prague and back amounted to a lifetime's labor. If all she needed was a rest, he would assume round-the-clock care of Dmitri, in France. She remained adamant, citing what she viewed as the ironclad obligation to his mother. At last Vladimir relented, on the condition that Véra settle on the ever-sacred May 8—the anniversary of their first meeting—as a firm date for their reunion. To his consent she responded by again changing her tune, writing anew of Italy and Belgium. And in what must have irritated even more, she left him without a letter on March 28, the anniversary of his father's murder, a date to which he was highly sensitive. He knew her to be overwhelmed—before April 1 she and Anna Feigin had emptied the Nestorstrasse apartment and moved to temporary quarters a few blocks away—but this was inexcusable. It was hardly the selfless behavior of the woman who had proved the impeccable "helpmeet, on the poetic path."

On insult she heaped injury. The supremely capable Véra had neglected to obtain hard currency for the Prague trip. Her husband exploded: How could she accuse *him* of carelessness? If she had only listened to him they would already be together in France. On April 6 she wrote vaguely that she would make a final decision about Prague in the days to come. Quite accurately, her husband observed that she appeared not to be reading his letters. "What is the problem, what is it about this plan that evokes in you such confusion, while the most complicated and most awkward (as it turns out) traipsing across Czechoslovakia seems to you easily accomplishable?" He was frantic. "Without that air that comes from you I can neither think nor write nor do anything else," he swore. He wanted only to get back to *The Gift*. The separation was unbearable; her waffling made it infinitely worse. He strove to control his considerable anger but she did not make this easy. It was as if every time he mentioned a minor triumph that might propel them west, she found a frivolous reason to steer east. He suspected that his wife was exhausted, but she was exhausting him, too.

In mid-April Véra began in a different vein. On or just after their twelfth wedding anniversary, she wrote her husband that she had been told he was having an affair, with a Russian woman whom she named. He replied that the slander did not surprise him in the least. He had heard similar rumors himself, though according to the scuttlebutt in Paris, the affair was not with the acquaintance Véra mentioned, but with Nina Berberova. The truth was that every one of his moves was noted and remarked upon, maliciously, in the émigré community. In those circles his lack of politics raised eyebrows, as did his lack of religious conviction; his nonobservance of Orthodox Easter was providing a fresh source of tongue-wagging. It had been noted that he drank hot chocolate, not Pernod, like an honest writer. Mostly though it was his talent that won him enemies. With Fondaminsky he puzzled over his relationship with Bunin; the very mention of Nabokov's name was said to send the Nobelist into a fit. "Of course he doesn't like you," Fondaminsky agreed. "You spread it all around that you're the best Russian writer." Vladimir challenged him. "What do you mean I spread it around?" "Well, you write," Fondaminsky sputtered. The situation was more ridiculous yet in Vladimir's eyes: Bunin envied not his literary talent, but " 'the success with women' with which shallow gossip rewards me." He counseled his wife to summon as much contempt for these rumors as did he. He always told her everything, and would continue to do so. There was no call for hysterics, which she had displayed. And again he begged her to stick to their new itinerary. He would meet her in Toulon, after her trip to Prague.

While her husband was doing his best to be patient with her, Véra suddenly lost all patience with Berlin. Before Vladimir could even reassure her of his fidelity she had hatched a new plan. She would fly to Paris immediately, lodging in her sister Sonia's hotel room, with Dmitri. Something had evidently rattled her, which was not difficult to imagine in a country where Jewish doctoral students were barred from exams, where signs reading "Jews Not Admitted" hung in bakeries and butcher shops. Surely by 1937 Véra had seen enough red flags in her life. (She could not have been particularly reassured by a visit with Zinaida Shakhovskoy's brother, Ioann, a future Orthodox archbishop of San Francisco. He stopped by at about this time, noting that the Nabokovs appeared to be leaving Germany. Véra explained that it was not healthy for Jews to stay, to which Shakhovskoy replied that they ought instead to stay and suffer.) Vladimir deemed Véra's sudden Parisian plan a costly and awkward alternative. Should she not bypass Paris altogether? He wholly sympathized with the torments of living "among the rascals," however, and—if she felt she had the courage—suggested she leave immediately for the Riviera. They went another round, he sketching the cottage he had found for them and outlining their living expenses, at least half of which would be his responsibility; she writing again of Prague. Twelve weeks after Véra had sent him off from Berlin, Vladimir surrendered, in a letter written in a blind fury. "I lack the strength to draw out this long-distance chess game," he conceded, promising that if she would leave immediately for his mother's he would apply for a visa and meet her there. At least that way they would be together on May 8, if in Prague. Meanwhile the second chapter of *The Gift* had come together in his mind, commas and all. Shortly after receiving this letter Véra and Dmitri left for Prague, arriving on May 6. Véra breathed a deep sigh of relief as they crossed the border.

On the cardinal eighth—the only May 8 the couple would spend apart—Nabokov was still writing from Paris. He was a helpless victim of bureaucratic torture. No amount of beating his head against the wall at the Czech consulate would produce the required visa. (His predicament was complicated by the fact that his Nansen passport was about to expire.) He needed for Véra to apply pressure at the Prague end. Under no circumstances should she come to France, or he would never obtain the necessary papers. He begged her to arrange things for him; she wrote indignantly that he was not making a serious effort to join her. Never in his life had he been so wretched. In his mind's eye he could barely see her clearly; he worried that Dmitri would fail to recognize him. Their correspondence had disintegrated into "a series of petty bureaucratic reports," and he knew all he needed to know of the situation in Prague from what she had written of her adventures with a bedbug. He begged her not to add to his torment by writing of her anxiety about the wait. If he had not committed suicide in February, when the psoriasis had driven him to the brink, it had only been because of her. After a last-minute relay among consulates and embassies, more in debt than ever, his affairs in perfect disarray but with a new story in mind, he boarded an eastbound train on May 20. Two days later the couple was reunited. This was the trip that was to be described years later, without inflection, as the visit to Prague, "to which we journeyed to show our child to my mother in the spring in 1937."

Nabokov found his wife perfectly miserable and in poor health. The stay in Prague was short and bittersweet; he may have suspected when he said good-bye to his mother that year that he was doing so for the last time. (He could not have known that he would never see his sister Olga again, and that twenty-two years would elapse before he would see his favored sister, Elena.) After a few days the family decamped for Franzenbad, where Véra submitted to a series of mudbaths. During her treatments Vladimir journeyed back to Prague, for a reading, and to visit with his mother. Véra moved south to Marienbad, where Anna Feigin met her; Nabokov arrived days later—and several days later than expected—bearing volumes of Kipling and the poet Léon-Paul Fargue for his wife. He had resisted the idea of meeting in Marienbad but made good use of his stay, writing "Cloud, Castle, Lake," one of his favorite stories, and his only short story of 1937. At the end of June the family pushed on to Paris, where Vladimir again lodged at Fondaminsky's. Véra and Dmitri were invited to stay at the Brombergs', on the rue Massenet, where there was a spare bedroom. Briefly they visited the International Exposition, which was drawing record crowds to Paris; the immense swastika at the top of Albert Speer's German pavilion spoke more to the future than did the brilliant displays of colored light. On July 7 the Nabokovs left for Cannes, where they settled in a modest hotel several minutes from the beach. Finally Vladimir could bask in the sun, as he had longed to do throughout the Parisian months. By this time he was well acquainted with an odd property of the clear light of day, one he articulated later in the year: "Sunlight is good in the degree that it heightens the value of shade." And he discovered as well the reason for his wife's irritability, her indecision, her sudden love affair with eastern Europe.

3
———

A week after the arrival in Cannes, Vladimir confessed what Véra had long suspected. He was in the midst of a delirious love affair. The woman was the one named in Véra's letter, Irina Yurievna Guadanini. He was still very much in the "delicious daze of adultery." He could not shake his infatuation, and thought he would have to leave Véra. She avowed that her response was simple: "I suggested that he ought to join the lady if he was in love." In truth her response appears to have been less antiseptic, much more in keeping with the heartfelt advice she offered a young poet later: "You should never give up what you love." Nabokov wrote his mistress that Véra was not going to release him from the marriage. At the same time he could not think of living without Irina. He did not see how he could return to his former life; he pleaded now for Irina's patience, as he had pleaded for Véra's months earlier. He reported that the evening of the revelation—it was probably Bastille Day 1937—had been, save for the evening of his father's murder, the most horrible night of his life. For Véra it could only have been the most horrible, without exception.

She could often be blinded by her confidence in human reason—as was said of a vigorous woman of an earlier century, "She was not more reasonable, in the last resort, than the rest of humanity. She paid in full and stoically,

the penalty of supposing herself to be so"—but where her husband was concerned her instincts were infallible. Although Vladimir had written openly
of having spent time with Irina Guadanini, Véra had had her suspicions, as
early as mid-February. She knew from her father that men left women; the
emigration, and the dislocations of Berlin in the 1920s, had in no way reinforced the bonds of matrimony. She had always been one of her husband's
most astute readers; the daily correspondence had been—exactly as Nabokov
would later observe of Sirin's sentences—"clear but weirdly misleading."
Who better to ferret out the truth from between his lines? All of the urgent
requests that she join him immediately had elucidated one striking detail:
Vladimir did not want his wife anywhere near Paris. The fears of which she
had written her husband had been confirmed in a detailed, unsigned four-
page letter that arrived in mid-April, just as the Paris-Prague tug-of-war intensified. Véra was certain that Irina's mother had sent the letter, presumably
to speed the disintegration of the marriage. Others speculated it had been
Fondaminsky, with whom Véra was in touch, and who was well disposed
toward her. The author of the anonymous missive—it was in French, but
patently written by a Russian—reported at length on Vladimir's infatuation
with Irina, "a pretty woman, blonde and neurasthenic like him," adding that
Nabokov had accumulated a great number of enemies in the literary community. This does not sound like Fondaminsky, or in general like the work
of a well-wisher.

Nabokov was an instinctive flirt.* He had met both Irina Guadanini and
her mother, Vera Kokoshkin, during his 1936 trip to Paris, after which he
had written them jointly. Madame Kokoshkin had been less won over than
her daughter. The older woman found the writer brilliant—she agreed he
was a "20th century miracle"—but frightening. Vladimir had begun seeing
Irina romantically early in February; her head full of his poetry, she had attended the January 1937 reading, and he had called on her three times the
following week. Three years younger than Véra, Irina was a vivacious and
highly emotional blonde, briefly married, now divorced. Her laugh was musical; she had a lively sense of humor; she took great joy in playing with
words. Once again Nabokov was seduced by a fine memory for verse. Her
Petersburg background was not dissimilar from his. In and around Paris
Irina Yurievna eked out a living as a dog groomer. She had a reputation, only
enhanced by the involvement with Nabokov, as a siren. Nabokov's allure was
established fact as well; when a friend's twenty-one-year-old daughter tele-

---

* And an irresistible one. Introduced to a particularly striking woman at a Paris reading in 1940, the first
two words out of his mouth were "Anna Karenin!"

phoned Fondaminsky to ask if he might arrange for her to meet his illustrious houseguest, Fondaminsky laughed. He was not surprised by the request, assuring his caller that all women, regardless of age, fell under Sirin's charm. He also invited her to a private reading the writer was to give at his apartment two days later, of the English autobiography. This would have been in late February or early March. Already Vladimir was surrounded by admirers but smiling only at the blue-eyed blonde at his elbow. Mark Aldanov pointed her out, "the *femme fatale,* the breaker of hearts." When Vladimir spoke of the disintegrating state of affairs in Germany, noting that "the novelist was God's translator" at reading the writing on walls, tears glittered in Irina's eyes. "How beautiful!" she swooned. She did not leave his side that evening, or any more often than was necessary that spring. He had called her immediately upon his arrival in London in February. It was the *coup de foudre*; she worshiped the imprint his head left on her pillow, his abandoned cigarette butt in the ashtray. With tears streaming down his face, he professed to her mother his perfect inability to live without her. The closest the relationship came to earth appears to have been the games of hangman the two played in Irina's notebook.

It was inevitable that Véra should have learned of the affair; it was not conducted with any great discretion. Probably it would have raised few eyebrows had it not been for Véra's reputation as her husband's second, or had Vladimir been better liked. Few believed him capable of living without his wife. Blind passion was one thing, all-knowing intimacy a rarer commodity. Marc Slonim, an émigré editor in Paris at the time and a distant relative of Véra's, commented that very few women aside from Véra would be able to tolerate Nabokov's monomaniacal approach to literature. "Were his hands to be cut off, he would learn to write with his mouth," Slonim quoted him as having boasted. How many women would allow someone else's obsession to dominate their lives? This truth was hardly lost on Vladimir, for whom it now constituted an indescribable torture. He could not live without Irina—the longing for her was unlike anything he had ever known—but at the same time his fourteen years with Véra had been utterly "cloudless." He wrote Irina in June that he and Véra knew each other's faintest nuances. A week later he celebrated the splendid rapport he enjoyed with his lover. He could not live without her, felt it beyond his strength to swear off her. The choice he had to make seemed to him impossible, especially given Dmitri. This letter he mailed unsigned. The strain was such that he felt he was going out of his mind.

As if leaving a trail of breadcrumbs in the forest, he had passed through Czechoslovakia in May sending furtive signals back to Paris. He arranged for Irina to write him at a post office address in Prague, under his grand-mother's maiden name.* The Czech weeks had been weeks of perfect du-plicity. It was agony pretending to Véra that all was on the former secure footing. On the other hand, he was delighted to inform Irina that Fate had provided them with a lovely ruse: Gallimard had bought *Despair*, and he would be able to claim he needed to meet with his French publisher alone. He posted an anodyne letter to Irina and Madame Kokochkin, clearly a smokescreen. He slipped outside to write of his longing; it was "indescrib-able, unprecedented." He stole a few minutes at the post office, at the sta-tionery store, addresses he did not normally frequent. He wrote from a park bench in Franzenbad and carried his letter "around like a bomb in his jacket until he could post it." He dragged his heels about leaving for Marienbad, where he had been expected days earlier. (It was something of a miracle that he could write a short story under the circumstances, which he did in forty-eight hours at Marienbad. Then again, "Cloud, Castle, Lake" is very much the story of a man wedged between two realities, a pleasure trip that proves a torture, and a happiness that, once sighted, cannot be grasped.) Meanwhile he denied over and over to Véra what was true. He felt terrible deceiving her, especially since her health was poor. On one pretext or another she inquired after Irina daily. "You always have something derisive to say about everyone else, why not about Irina?" she chided. Nabokov reported on these interro-gations to Irina, who noted in her diary that Véra was tormenting her lover. There were plenty of additional questions. He could not shake off his sordid sense of deceit, the vulgar banality of his situation. It would be years before he uttered the phrase, but he was discovering firsthand what Emma Bovary appeared to have taught him later: Adultery was a perfectly conventional way of rising above the conventional. He could not condone his behavior, could not forgive himself for having sullied what he saw as his fourteen im-peccable years with Véra. He was a great distance away from his 1920s en-dorsement of "radiant truthfulness." Never had he sounded so much like one of his characters, brought down by his passion, unable to escape his own pri-vate abyss, heartrendingly separated from his own self-image. He resembled himself—or at least his idea of himself—about as much as Felix does Her-mann in *Despair*, that portrait of the artist in a cracked mirror.

What was to be done? In the immediate very little, save for Vladimir to lead a double life and for Véra to continue to probe. During their four-day stopover in Paris he conducted an extraordinary amount of business with

---

* As it happened, he chose the name of the paternal great-grandmother, Baroness Nina von Korff. The Baroness had married her daughter off to her lover, so that she could continue her affair in peace.

Gallimard. After a month's separation, the reunion with Irina was electrifying. Nabokov felt that he had never waited for anyone as he had waited for her on July 1. He had been paralyzed by fear that she might not appear at their late-night rendezvous. "I love you more than anything on earth," he wrote in her notebook, having stopped by to see her when she was out. When he headed for the Riviera with Véra and Dmitri he left Irina with a notepad on which she could cross off the days until his return, exactly as Véra had done for him in the past. Generally the letters sound painfully like those he had written his wife fourteen years earlier. He wrote of preordained compatability; he marveled over the commonality of their impressions; he felt his lover's handling of him flawless. (For the more mortal among us there is cold comfort in the idea that even Nabokov could not coax two entire vocabularies out of reckless passion.) Ten days later Véra exacted her confession, which in no way put an end to the love letters. If anything, Nabokov yearned for Irina even more desperately than he had in Czechoslovakia. Nothing slaked his desire. He begged her to be faithful to him, though he realized this was not entirely fair. He pleaded for longer letters. He promised they would be together early in the fall. As if to prove his point, he had left a change of clothes at her apartment.

Véra's response to the affair was to blame herself. She felt she had neglected her husband because of the daunting task of caring for a child and on account of the unbearably difficult material conditions under which they had lived in Berlin. Vladimir explained as much to Irina, reporting that his wife was now doing all she could to make up for her inattention. "Her smile kills me," he declared miserably, late in July. Nor did Véra so much as mention Irina after the confession. "I know what she is thinking," Vladimir brooded. "She is convincing herself and me (without words) that you are a hallucination." It was a familiar strategy: Vigorous denial was at times Véra's only form of acknowledgment. Irina's mother was not surprised; days earlier she had predicted that Véra would "bamboozle her husband and not let him go." Her calm was true to her nature but also constituted an apt torture. In a Paris-bound letter, Vladimir wrote that the situation was all the more frightening because relations with Véra appeared perfectly even-keeled. He feared he was forgetting Irina. Late in July the Nabokovs moved to a two-room apartment across from their hotel, from which they followed a tunnel to the beach. From the woods above Cannes Vladimir confessed that he thought his wife probably knew of his continued correspondence, but that he felt so madly sorry for her that he did not dare conduct it openly. In this he was well advised, as he had promised to terminate the exchange.

In August, presumably when Véra discovered that her husband was still writing his lover—Irina received four letters in the first ten days of the month—storms broke out on the home front. Vladimir described such tempests that he feared he would end in the madhouse. Véra vehemently denied later that these battles had ever raged. She offered to prove under oath that these scenes—which her husband deplored, and which Irina and her mother duly recorded in their diaries—had never taken place. Vladimir had nothing to gain from inventing such things, and was brutally honest in his letters to Paris. Had he wanted to break with Irina, he could have done so without eliciting her sympathy; it is unimaginable that voices were not raised. There is powerful evidence as well that Véra threatened to take Dmitri from his father. One quality was more dear to her even than her devotion to truth, however. Her husband's undignified behavior was one thing, her own quite another. She was far too proud to admit that most of August passed in a spasm of violent arguments.

Irina countered by offering to go away somewhere, anywhere, with Vladimir. When next she heard from him he announced that Véra had forced him to end the affair. He would not be writing again. This put Irina on the first train to Cannes, on or about September 9. On the morning of her arrival she headed directly to the Nabokovs' apartment and waited outside until she was able to intercept Vladimir on his way to the beach with Dmitri. He made a date to meet her later in the day, in a public garden.* As they strolled toward the port that afternoon, he explained that he loved her but could not bring himself to slam the door on the rest of his life. He begged her to be patient but remained noncommittal. Irina left the following day for Italy, brokenhearted, near-suicidal, convinced that Véra had somehow hoodwinked Vladimir back into the marriage. She attended a reading he gave in Paris at the end of the following year, but never saw him again.

She did not disappear as quietly as Vladimir (and Véra) might have hoped, however. She never entirely recovered from the affair; Nabokov remained the great love of her life.† She predicted that he would deceive again, as soon as he had the chance, all the while protesting that his marriage was impeccable. She wrote poems to their star-crossed love for the next four decades; she kept an extensive notebook of Nabokov clippings, parallel to the one kept by Véra. In the 1960s she wrote a flagrantly autobiographical short

---

* The scene is eerily prefigured in Nabokov's 1927 poem "The Snapshot." In it an "accidental spy" is captured lurking in a beach shot taken by the photographer of his wife and son. Oddly, Irina had copied the poem into her 1937 diary. As it happened, Véra arrived an hour after Irina. She learned later that her rival had remained on the beach, watching her.

† In her devotion she was initially encouraged by her mother. "If he loves you, then even later you can take him away from her," she advised Irina, just after the Cannes fiasco.

story about the relationship and the meetings in Cannes, called "The Tunnel." It is liberally sprinkled with quotes from Vladimir's 1937 letters; its epigraphs are taken in part from Sirin's poetry. The lovers know from the start that their affair is doomed; the hero of the story refers to his passion as the "shipwreck of his entire life." He begs for his lover's patience while he attempts to extricate himself from his marriage, which, on leaving the city for the Riviera, he is unable to do. His mistress meanwhile worships the imprint his head has left on her pillow, the abandoned cigarette butt in the ashtray. "Gradually something alien, foreign began to penetrate his letters," which arrive less and less frequently. On the Riviera the heroine accosts her lover, on the beach, with his little girl. He makes a date to meet her later in the day in a public garden. As they stroll toward the port that afternoon, he explains that he loves her but cannot bring himself to slam the door on the rest of his life. He begs her to be patient but remains noncommittal; somehow they will manage to see each other again in the fall. At nightfall the heroine passes by his house, where she feels she should call to demand her happiness. A woman's shadow deters her. At the entrance to the train tunnel she throws herself on the tracks.

"The Tunnel" was not the only piece of literature to follow this debacle. For the latter half of 1937 Nabokov was at work on Chapters 3 and 5 of *The Gift,* a novel that has been described as his ode to fidelity. The story of an artist as a young man, the book reads like a hymn of gratitude to a woman who in nearly every imaginable way resembles Véra. Zina is easily the single most appealing woman in his fiction; even Véra, who spent her time distancing herself from Zina, defended the character's purity and moral authority.* Vladimir appears to have been perfectly aware of the chasm that separated the reality of his fiction from the fiction of his reality. In June he had told Irina that he had written foolishly about faithfulness. Later he reported that he was finishing a chapter, but assured his lover it was not the one about Zina, instead the one on his hero's biographical labors. Véra was battling a figure who was dangerously, splendidly flesh and blood, but Irina was playing a far more arduous game, having to run competition with a rival who existed partly in prose.

The Nabokovs spent a quiet winter, in Cannes and in Menton, with Vladimir writing furiously. On the financial front they had received a reprieve in September, when news arrived that Bobbs-Merrill had offered six hundred dollars for *Laughter in the Dark.* The Indianapolis textbook firm was to be Nabokov's first American publisher. For the second time he put

---

* Of course I am not Zina, she would say dismissively. Zina is only half-Jewish, and I am entirely Jewish.

The Gift aside to rework a book; this one he simultaneously translated and reworked, rendering it more commercial.* Véra could not have been in any
hurry to return to Paris, where her husband's deception was common knowledge in the Russian community. She spent time alone with her Berlin friend
Lisbet Thompson and her scientist-husband Bertrand in Menton that summer; there is no indication that she mentioned the affair. Whether she spoke
of it or not—and the evidence points to her having had an admirable ability
to face the truth, even if she kept that truth to herself—she could not have
helped developing a new vigilance. She had learned one lesson, and may have
learned substantially more. To Irina, Vladimir had confessed that he had had
a series of fleeting affairs—a German girl met by chance in the Grunewald;
a French girl for four nights in 1933; a tragic woman with exquisite eyes; a
former student who had propositioned him; and three or four other meaningless encounters. He listed these to prove to Irina that she was in a category
of her own. He does not appear to have mentioned the earlier transgressions
to Véra.† As with all things she had a firm sense of priorities; among the fiancées only one caused her any dismay, the one with whom she had the most
in common. She asked a biographer to omit from his inventory of ex-fiancées
only the name of Eva Lubrzynska, the fashionable and highly accomplished
Polish Jew whom fate threw several times in Vladimir's direction, and with
whom he had resumed his affair after a chance encounter at a charity ball in
1919 or 1920. Véra bristled visibly when Eva's activities—she married the son
of the architect Sir Edward Luytens—were reported on later. The Irina
Guadanini affair proved Véra's rule of thumb, a lesson her husband had
learned from Gogol: Leave out only the crucial parts. Until confronted with
the fact that her husband's 1937 letters to Irina had survived, she was ready to
deny that any such affair had ever taken place. And she went further, in her
clear but misleading way. When asked to choose several personal letters from
her husband for a volume of published correspondence, she selected four
adoring missives, all dating from the months of the Guadanini affair—a bold,
unblinking strike on all other versions of their story.

   Nabokov worked steadily on *The Gift* through the winter. It was to be
the novel from whose autobiographical tones he had the most difficult time

---

* He succeeded. The Bobbs-Merrill reader, reviewing the novel for a second time, hailed it as "light, popular fiction," the last time anyone would say as much of a work by Nabokov.
† The only hints of philandering in the correspondence appear in letters of the thirties, to Gleb Struve
from Prague, which Nabokov several times assured his friend was filled as ever with girls, and to Khodasevich, from Berlin, in 1934: "Berlin is very fine right now, thanks to the spring, which is particularly juicy
this year, and I, like a dog, am driven wild by all sorts of interesting scents."

extricating himself. (In 1938 he admitted to having lent his hero a few of his own traits. Over the years they became fewer.) On its American publication in 1963 the book was hailed by Stephen Spender as "autobiography thinly disguised, and repudiated (of course) by the author." A sumptuous weave of fiction, memory, and biography, the work manages to defy not only novelistic form but novelistic dimension as well; it is a gorgeously textured Möbius strip of a book, which would remain one of both Véra and Vladimir's favorites.* While it has been read as an acknowledgment by Nabokov of his enormous debt to Véra, it is equally possible that he wrote of Fyodor and Zina's perfect rapport, of her confidence and unerring support for his talent, as a way of reminding himself of what the marriage represented. Toward the end of the book a young girl who rouses in Fyodor a familiar brand of "hopeless desire" makes a fleeting appearance. He recognizes in her something of Zina's golden presence; he also watches her walk off. Nabokov's portrait of an artist concludes with a crescendo of emotion—an affirmation of melting happiness—that happens to coincide exactly with what would have been a renewed commitment to the marriage. As he was finishing the book, he wrote to Irina to ask that she return his letters. He claimed—in this Irina's mother felt Véra was dictating—that they contained mostly fictions.[†]

Does Zina mirror Véra, or did Véra begin to mirror Zina? It is true that Véra wrote her mother-in-law of Nabokov's work just as Zina articulates her ambitions for Fyodor; that Véra's relief at her husband's not speaking his mind about his contemporaries sounds like Zina's fears plagiarized. Zina shudders with indignation at the attacks of Fyodor's critics, just as Véra did. And while Véra never recognized herself in Zina—or ever admitted doing so—she naturally enough assumed her place. When a critic presented his reading of the novel's last page, Véra responded with a long protest, a disclaimer that only demonstrated how entangled she was with Zina's time and place. In the emigration it hardly mattered whether life imitated art or art imitated life: People reacted to Véra Nabokov as if she *were* Zina Mertz, that "alien, sullen young lady," a girl with character, who "looked down her nose at everything." "Everyone lived in fear of her temperament," one of the Nabokovs' good friends admitted, though it is unclear if that friend was

---

* Nabokov had been happy to write off *Orlando*—which he read with the rest of Woolf in 1933—as first-rate drivel. Were anyone strong-stomached enough to venture closer, something surely could be said about Woolf's version of time-travel, the visions of Persian markets superimposed on 1920s London, and *The Gift,* begun at the time. In any event Nabokov knew when he began *The Gift* that he was not the first to attempt a hybrid of fiction and history; *Orlando* is a novel with an index, one with a mind of its own.
† One cannot help but think of Humbert Humbert and the "fragments of a novel" he defends to Charlotte.

speaking of the real woman or of the counterfeit version. It was as if Nabokov wrote Véra back into his life. Perhaps he was not so much assuaging his wife's fears as convincing himself. The last chapter of *The Gift* was written in January 1938. A letter went out to Irina in February. She did not open it.

4

Véra spent part of the difficult summer of 1937 translating *Invitation to a Beheading* into English. This was done at the request of Altagracia de Jannelli, a New York literary agent who had taken an interest in Nabokov's work and who was responsible for the September sale of *Laughter in the Dark*. As for the rough translation Véra was making, "I want this at once," Jannelli urged. The saucy redhead—whom Vladimir addressed as "Mr." for the first three years of their association—rivaled Véra when it came to her devotion to Vladimir's work. A small volume of Nabokov rejection letters had accumulated in her files before Bobbs-Merrill took on *Laughter*; Jannelli expected at least sixty publishers to writhe when the novel was published, in the spring of 1938. So tenacious was she that she often made repeated assaults on the same house. While she flogged Nabokov in New York, she served as a one-woman advertisement for America, writing spirited hymns to the openness of American society, the wonders of air-conditioning, the efficiency with which business matters were concluded. Moreover, America was the only country in which an author stood to make any kind of real money. She was frustrated that her talented client did not see her point, beside herself when she learned he had left Paris for the wilderness of southern France, where cables barely penetrated. She prayed he would not write her next from Abyssinia. (In the meantime, she must have had the time of her life drafting a cover letter to accompany the Bobbs-Merrill author's questionnaire Vladimir returned that fall. To the question: "What is your favorite book?" he named in first place, "The book I shall write some day.") The Nabokovs were in no danger of leaving for Abyssinia. As Vladimir observed late that summer, "Our situation is particularly disgusting now, we've never been so broke before, and this slow death doesn't seem to upset or even worry anyone." In the spring the composer Sergei Rachmaninoff responded to a dire SOS with a generous twenty-five hundred francs, repayable whenever fortune permitted.

Years later, in reconstructing the happier moments of the fall, Vladimir worked in part again from Véra's memories. She recalled Dmitri's fascination with the treasures amassed on the Cannes beach, at midday:

The smooth bits of glass licked by the sea to translucence, sometimes to complete transparency, green mostly, though some pink, and one (the gem of the collection) a beautiful dark amethyst. That collection comprised too bits of patterned pottery, and once in a while chance would have a complete little pattern preserved on a small chip, smoothed out to roundness and silkiness by the sea water. And sometimes you would help chance and complete the design.

She had no idea how far her husband would carry that idea. Tumbled through Nabokov's imagination the stones emerged brighter still:

And among the candy-like blobs of sea-licked glass—lemon, cherry, peppermint—and the banded pebbles, and the little fluted shells with lustered insides, sometimes small bits of pottery, still beautiful in glaze and color, turned up. . . . I do not doubt that among those slightly convex chips of majolica ware found by our child there was one whose border of scrollwork fitted exactly, and continued, the pattern of a fragment I had found in 1903 on the same shore . . .

The weather was glorious; Vladimir reported that nude sunbathing was possible as late as November. He and Véra appeared very much back on their earlier footing. In January, as he was putting the finishing touches on *The Gift,* they both fell sick. Vladimir wrote Jannelli that he had had bronchitis for a month "and now it is my wife's turn." They sounded again like the Siamese twins he had described to his sister in 1925.

They moved around a great deal after the New Year, from Menton, where they were settled when the Germans marched into Austria; to Moulinet, in the hills high above Menton; west to Cap d'Antibes, in August. Rooms were not easy to come by, and Véra spent much time writing hotels about vacancies. She was delighted to be in the mountains at Moulinet, noting rather whimsically that the fields were dotted as much with flowers as with little military tents.* Nabokov wrote prodigiously—two plays, *The Event* and *The Waltz Invention* date from 1938—but continued to pour nearly as much of his energies into the campaign to land a steady job as into the campaign to write the book he had described in his Bobbs-Merrill author's questionnaire. At no time was the family's future as uncertain as it was now, even before it became clear that France would not qualify as a long-term home.

---

* On this ridge, at Dmitri's age, Humbert Humbert would lose his mother to lightning.

It has been noted that Nabokov might just as easily have become a major French writer as a major English-language one.* In the previous two years he had written a much-praised article on Pushkin as well as the story "Mademoiselle O," in French; one of the greatest Russian-language novels of the century; shards of an autobiography in English. He later documented the fantastic congealing of Hyde inside Jekyll for his students; his own partial metamorphosis of 1938 would have been infinitely more difficult to chart. And the family's hold on the planet was so tenuous that a gust could have pushed them in any direction. Jannelli was agitating for a move to America, pressuring Bobbs-Merrill into writing a letter for Nabokov in April, to help him gain entry into the United States.† This birthday present—affidavits were worth their weight in gold at the time—went unacknowledged; throughout 1938, his sights remained trained on London. Perhaps sensitive to the perception that her husband had somehow evaded active military service, Véra held later that the migration to America had been planned before the outbreak of war, but the path was in truth more circuitous. Nabokov might well have become a French writer, but in 1938 and 1939 he devoted more of his energies to becoming a British academic.

On Bastille Day, 1938, from a shabby mountain hotel in Moulinet, he found himself conjuring with a different set of tribulations than he had the previous year. Bobbs-Merrill's reader had not taken to *The Gift,* deeming it "dazzlingly brilliant" and therefore entirely without promise for the American market. Jannelli had forwarded the report to the Riviera, where her author rose energetically to his own defense. He could not believe that an astute reader could fail to notice the inherent logic to the book. And how could a publisher's representative have missed the fact that the entire story was "threaded on my hero's love romance (Fate's underground work being shown)"? He swatted away Jannelli's suggestion that he write a book with some human interest, just as a year earlier he had swatted away an editor's suggestion that he open himself up emotionally on the page. If Véra disagreed with him on either count she said nothing; she would object frankly enough to ideas for novels or stories—none of which was ever to be written—but those vetoes were immune to market conditions. In May she had partly translated and typed a letter to Jannelli from her husband's dictation: "I schall [*sic*] never, never, never write novels solving 'modern problems' or

---

* Speaking of himself in the third person, he offered up this assessment of the only thing he had in common with Joseph Conrad: "both men might have chosen French as readily as English."
† Angus Cameron at Bobbs-Merrill gave Jannelli permission to write whatever she liked in his name, if only because he never again wanted to face the convoluted copyright and translation situation the firm had tackled with *Laughter.*

picturing 'the world unrest.' I am neither Upton Sinclair nor Sinclair Lewis." Meanwhile they were slowly starving. Fyodor asks Zina to put her trust in fantasy alone; it made for a thinning diet. Nabokov proved unrepentant when he learned over the summer that Bobbs-Merrill had passed on their option to translate his other titles. By this time *Laughter*—for which its author had had high cinematic hopes—had been rejected by every major Hollywood studio as well.

Only in August did he obtain a *carte d'identité,* legalizing his stay in France, though not granting him the right to work; the vast German migration of the mid-1930s had severely taxed the French sympathy for foreigners. It was some weeks still before the family was able to head to Paris, where the publishing contacts were. The city did not look as scenic in 1938 as it had two years earlier, when Vladimir had written Véra of the great esteem in which his work was held, of the "Eiffel Tower standing in its lace pantaloons with ants of light scurrying up and down its spine." Nor was it anything more than a way station. Mournfully Vladimir concluded that they were in Paris for an indeterminate period of time "because there is nowhere else to go (and more importantly, no means by which to go there)." They settled in a studio apartment on the rue de Saigon, steps from the Bois de Boulogne. This put them near the edge of Russian Paris; the neighboring sixteenth arrondissement was, as Véra put it, "the residence of most Russian refugees—at least, of the greater part of the intelligentsia." In that apartment, on the edge of one world perched precariously on the edge of another, her husband began his first English-language novel. He had spoken English as a child; he had been schooled at Cambridge. When it came to writing in English he had practiced on himself, setting aside *The Gift* to translate *Despair* for Hutchinson, again to rewrite *Laughter* for Bobbs-Merrill. Whatever country the family were to settle in, the lucrative market was clearly not the Russian one. The conversion seems to have come about naturally, although on one occasion Nabokov told a reliable witness that Véra had encouraged him to make the leap. Her handwriting can be found all over the manuscript of *Sebastian Knight,* but for all their merit these corrections cannot be said to render her husband's English more fluid.

For the next decade he would complain bitterly, humorously, of the handicap he suffered writing in English, "a champion figure skater switching to roller skates." Véra put it differently. Not only had her husband "switched from a very special and complex brand of Russian, all his own, which he had perfected over the years into something unique and peculiar to him, a true 'thing of beauty,' " he had embraced "an English which he then proceeded to wield and bend to his will until it, too, became under his pen something it had never been before in its melody and flexibility." She concluded that what he had done was to have substituted for his passionate affair with the Russian language *un mariage de raison* which "as it sometimes happens with a *mariage de raison*—became in turn a tender love affair." (Dismissing the meanings she well knew would be read into her analysis, she warned, "This phrase does *not*—repeat *not*—apply to VN's and my marriage." *Sebastian Knight* is doubtless the greatest English-language novel to have been written on a bidet, a statement that says as much about the discomfort of Nabokov's nationally fragmented selves—here was his spanking new English hammered into shape on a suitcase laid across that ultimately European fixture—as it did about the family's material situation.* Vladimir would have been unaware that in at least one technical respect he fell into an exile's tradition. On the other side of Paris twenty years earlier, James Joyce had finished *Ulysses,* on a suitcase balanced across an armchair.

Whatever handicap his second language proved, Nabokov's English did nothing to slow him down. He wrote *The Real Life of Sebastian Knight*—an ingeniously constructed novel and as *The Gift* had been, another play on the art of biography—in two months, completing it at the end of January 1939. The narrator's search for the truth about his dead half brother, the writer Sebastian Knight, the novel is resplendent not so much in its language as in its reflections and deceptions and illusions.[†] The work bears no hints of the family's material distress, of the gathering clouds of war; it is one of Nabokov's most playful books. Boyd has located a shadow of Irina Guadanini lurking in its corners, those corners the fictional biographee does not want explored. Certainly Sebastian Knight ventures where Nabokov did not, leaving his Véra-like Clare for the Other Woman, with predictable results. Sebastian's brother can think of no other author so eager to blind his reader with the harsh light of personal truth in the prismatic lens of the novel; readers of *Sebastian Knight* can name one. It is notable, though not enough so to call in the Viennese delegation, that all refracting aside, the two most focused pictures of Véra in her husband's art come to us back to back, in *The Gift* and *Sebastian Knight,* just after the only time in the marriage he considered leaving her. As for more concrete halls of mirrors, Véra typed in 1938 the lines about Clare's life having been subsumed, fourteen years earlier,

---

* Fondaminsky put a less romantic and slightly inaccurate spin on it. "You must realize," he told others in the emigration, "he lives with his wife and child in one room. In order to create, he locks himself in a tiny toilet, sits there like an eagle and types."
† Nabokov did not feel so confident of his English as to forgo having it checked by a native speaker, as was the case with his next few books. Lucie Léon Noel reviewed it with him, paragraph by paragraph. Her husband was working simultaneously with Joyce.

by the "pages slipped into the slit and rolled out again alive with black and violet words." In those violet words her husband bestowed on Clare one of his
wife's favorites, the poetry of Donne.* For Christmas, 1938, he bestowed on
Véra a handsome, hardcover edition of *The Love Poems of John Donne.*

A darker shadow lurking in the corners of the novel may be that cast by
Nabokov's own brother Sergei.[†] Ten and a half months younger than
Nabokov, Sergei had suffered as much from his parents' inattention as
Vladimir had profited from the same parents' adulation. Sergei was a great
number of things his brother could not easily abide: a stutterer, a music lover,
a homosexual, and, as of 1926, a practicing Catholic.[‡] Although they had
been at Cambridge together the two were not close. Only in Paris did they see
each other regularly, and that contact was tempered by hesitation on both
sides. Sergei was of the small school who continued to regret that Vladimir
had not married the splendid Svetlana.[§] He reported a great deal of squab-
bling in the Nabokov household; he found Véra prickly, the visits awkward.
Generally he believed Véra to have been an unfortunate, and domineering,
influence on his brother. Sergei may have tipped his hand a little, proving
that in life as in fiction there are limits to the truths one brother can posit
about another: To his eye Dmitri was not only spoiled, but frightfully Jewish-
looking. "Thank God that they got out of Germany," he confided in Elena.
"They would have had a difficult time, and right now it would be utterly
ghastly."

Familial relations exhibited signs of strain on the other side as well. Véra's
sister Sonia was in Paris, as she had been since the late 1920s. She held a lucrative job as a secretary and translator, in seven languages. (She had managed to
obtain elusive working papers in years when they were more readily available,
and with the help of her eventual employer.) Both Nabokovs found Sonia tir-
ing—she had an elevated sense of self-importance—and spent a minimal
amount of time with her. She could be either perfectly charming or immensely difficult. Her 1932 marriage had lasted eight months, after which her
husband—lucratively employed at the time of the courtship but by 1935 a
member of the *Normandie's* kitchen staff—had left her. Sonia divorced him
and never remarried, although she was, in Véra's understated phrase, "always

---

* The two women share this taste with *Pale Fire's* Sybil Shade, who translates Donne into French, as Véra
did as well.
† With his brother Kirill, twelve years his junior, relations were at once more simple and more distant.
‡ In a letter about his brother's conversion, the very mention of Catholicism conjures in Vladimir's mind the
depictions of the suffering Saint Sebastian. The name is generally not an upper-class Russian one.
§ "Why couldn't you have married him?" Sergei implored Svetlana in the late 1930s. "He would never
have turned out so badly."

a good dresser," and rarely lacked for company. Lena had remained in Berlin, where, having converted to Catholicism, she had been able to work until being stripped of her papers in 1937. Her 1930 marriage to Prince Nikolai Massalsky also proved unhappy, and she had left her husband before their son Michaël was born, in July of 1938. She was consequently alone in Germany, and although she appeared to be Princess Elena Massalsky, she was equally well a Jew with no citizenship. Hounded by friends of Nabokov's father's assassin, she was twice interrogated by the Gestapo. At some time after November of 1938, when the Jewish shopwindows shattered so loudly in Berlin, the Nabokovs appealed to Zinaida Shakhovskoy, in Brussels. Somewhat abashed, Vladimir wrote to plead Lena's case: Could Shakhovskoy help in any way to get his sister-in-law out of Germany? There was little she could do; ultimately Lena managed to escape to Finland. (Through the fall of 1938 Véra swapped herbal cures with Shakhovskoy, whom she recruited as well for some matchmaking. She also thanked her profusely for the hand-me-down dress. It was gorgeous. Sounding like a woman few would meet, Véra wrote: "Now I feel like going to a ball—I haven't been for so long!") Of greater immediate concern to the couple, Vladimir's mother was sick and penniless in Prague. Hitler's advances made a visit impossible. In March Nabokov sent a cry for assistance to Alexandra Tolstoy, the novelist's youngest daughter and head of a New York–based refugee organization. His financial situation having gone from wretched to catastrophic, he could do nothing for his mother, who was suffering from pleurisy. Could the Tolstoy Foundation lend a hand? With Hitler's annexation of Czechoslovakia that month she lost her pension, her only source of income. At the end of March her condition worsened. She was taken to a hospital, which no one in the family could afford.

With an eye on lectureships that were said to be available that year at Leeds and at Sheffield, Vladimir traveled twice to London in the spring of 1939. For months before his April departure Véra had been searching for a two-room apartment in Paris; until London the three of them shared a cramped room at the not very aptly named Hotel Royal Versailles, a run-down institution that lent its lobby to a 1939 short story. Vladimir's quarters in London were infinitely more congenial; he lodged with the family of a former Russian diplomat, whose bathtub and butler he could not stop exclaiming over. He lobbied all the right parties for teaching positions, collecting letters of reference as he made his way around town. Bitterly he complained to Véra that he had no talent for this kind of self-promotion, an assessment with which she agreed. He papered London with copies of *Sebastian Knight*. He called on his Cambridge mentors for advice. He made an effort to sparkle as much as he could socially, but this was decidedly not his sport. He felt as if he were idiotically feeling his way in the dark.

Véra's side of the correspondence can be read clearly in her husband's responses. "No—emphatically, I'm NOT a man about town," he fumed on April 17, after he had written one too many times about his tennis games, the trips to the British Museum's entomological division, the butler-administered breakfasts in bed. There was a limit to how much business could be conducted on a Sunday morning in London. He collared people ceaselessly; there was no cause for his wife's alarm. He had spoken with everyone she suggested and had even been in touch with her old friends the Rodziankos, though he was less optimistic than she that they could help. Her concern for their future was crystal clear. He agreed entirely that on his return and in anticipation of a teaching position he would do nothing but write in English about Russian literature. He was doing all in his power, to the best of his capabilities. At the same time, he wrote on their fourteenth wedding anniversary, he was prepared to face a possible disappointment, and wanted her to be as well. He was vexed by her dark hints about the future, though whatever anger he felt when he began a letter generally dissipated—in Véra's case anyway—by the third paragraph. She was disturbed by and envious of his social rounds; she did not believe he was really making much of an effort. As she had not been earlier, she was now entirely powerless herself to support the family. And in his correspondences of the last few years her husband had been complaining of having become "criminally absent-minded"; she shuddered to think he might prove so now, when so much was at stake. Hers was the frustration of the capable, the brand Diana Trilling described as that of the woman with the fine sense of direction who must "yield to the male navigator determined to drive us a hundred miles out of our way."

One thing Véra was determined to avoid was another summer of 1937. She seeded her husband's belongings with little notes; he was delighted to have worn his tuxedo on a night he might not otherwise have done so, as he found a message from Véra in the pocket. And she was forthright about her fears, much to her husband's dismay. Surely she had to believe that "our love, and everything, is NOW always and absolutely safe." As a result he garlanded the name of every woman he met with unflattering adjectives. An actress friend of his host's was "old and fat—I'm pointing that out just in case—although if she were young and thin it wouldn't change things." He had eyes, he insisted, only for Véra. During these two trips, in April and June, he spent a good deal of time with Eva Luytens and her family. For the most part he managed the reports on his visits with his ex-fiancée tactfully. Eva was not attractive, she was not up to her husband's caliber. He repeated an observation Eva had made: In the end she—Jewish, and five years his senior—had married a non-Jew six years her junior. Her ex-fiancé had married a Jew. Fate had had its way all the same. If Véra did not bristle when she read that her husband had borrowed money from Eva she must have done so when she heard that Eva had produced a leatherbound volume of Vladimir's verse, much of it about her. (Worse, their author deemed some of it good.) She could not have been happy to have read that her husband had considered Eva's offer of hand-me-down dresses.

Vladimir was back in Paris on May 2, 1939, the day his mother died, in Prague. For want of a visa, he did not attend the funeral. A few days earlier the Nabokovs had moved to the two-room apartment for which they had so long waited, on the rue Boileau. It was practically empty, and remained so. From the rue Boileau Véra began to dispatch letters to foreign publishers on her husband's behalf; she called on directors to inquire after the fate of his plays. Vladimir returned to London for his second round of "telephonadas" (" 'telephone' + 'armadas,' " he explained), none of which yielded any sign of a long-term prospect. This did not dim his roseate confidence in the future. In the course of the June trip he assured Véra that even if nothing were to come of the teaching positions, they could certainly count on some income from *Sebastian Knight* in the fall. He suggested she give up the rue Boileau apartment. With the security deposit they would spend the summer in the south and establish a base in London afterward, no matter what. At the same time, he picked up a translating assignment, a scientific treatise on the bone structure of mice. He felt he had acquitted himself well of his responsibilities but was painfully aware that no applause seemed to be coming from across the Channel. He was back in Paris by mid-month, and for the summer the Nabokovs again moved to the Riviera, the key to the rue Boileau still in their pockets; after the time it had taken Véra to find the apartment, she had strong feelings about relinquishing it. No teaching positions, nor any admiring reader for *Sebastian Knight,* materialized. "What do you expect me to do? I am a good hypnotist, but I cannot hypnotise the publishers," cursed Jannelli, explaining her frustration at not being able to sell *Mary, The Defense, King, Queen, Knave,* or *Glory* in New York. In a way that had happened before, Nabokov's fate was dangled before him years before it would materialize. From Mikhail Karpovich at Harvard came the first of several letters that summer describing a position teaching Russian at Cornell University. Nothing came of it. On July 1, from Fréjus, Nabokov queried the Tolstoy Foundation about the possibilities of obtaining an American visa. It cannot have been an easy summer. Still, Véra would complain later that the Riviera had lost all the charm it had held in the 1930s.

The family returned to Paris the day before the declaration of war. In the flush of those first harried minutes after September 3, when the gas masks were handed out, when the air-raid alarms sounded nightly, they did what Vladimir's mother had done when the first rumblings of Revolution had been felt in Russia: They sent their son off, in this case with Anna Feigin to Deauville, where Dmitri remained until mid-December. They missed him, but knew the separation to be necessary. Meanwhile Vladimir redoubled his efforts to obtain American visas. He began his own blitzkrieg campaign—so different in tone and tempo from the *drôle de guerre* around him—bombarding the Tolstoy Foundation, Mikhail Karpovich, his cousin Nicholas, now teaching music at Wells College, with urgent requests for help. He fretted that no one understood how utterly dire was his situation. The ever-loyal Jannelli gathered precious affidavits in New York; Vladimir left her and the Tolstoy Foundation with the alarmed impression that he would be mobilized were he not to leave the country before December 10.* To his agent he dictated the kind of letter he hoped Bobbs-Merrill would submit on his behalf to the American consul. His desperation can be read in its final line: "And, please, make it quite clear to Bobbs-Merrill that, once in New York, I shall certainly write for them *the novel* they expect from me." (Had she known of them, Véra would doubtless have found distressingly familiar the lengths to which Alexandra Tolstoy went for the family. To one refugee coordinator, Tolstoy suggested that if nothing could be done for Mr. Nabokov, certainly someone would be willing to offer his wife an affidavit for domestic service. The appeal echoed the thirteen-year campaign Evsei Lazarevich Slonim had waged to bring his brother to St. Petersburg.) The Bobbs-Merrill letter went out punctually, along the lines Vladimir had requested, as did an affidavit from Serge Koussevitzky, the conductor of the Boston Symphony Orchestra. For a few weeks the Nabokovs—more penniless than ever, all émigré publishing having come to a standstill—held out hope that they might leave in December, but what they were to remember as the dimmest, most miserable period of their lives lasted five months longer.

Since September the family had been accepting monthly thousand-franc loans from a friend who owned a Parisian cinema; Nabokov went back to giving English lessons that winter. Among his three students was Maria Marinel, the eldest sister of a conservatory-trained harp-playing trio, all of whom became devoted family friends. Maria's younger sister, Elisaveta, of-

---

* By law he was required either to leave the country or to answer the call for mobilization within a time limit. At Véra's urging, he did not answer the call. He was of the same mind, recalling afterward "the nightmarish feeling that accompanied the thought of French barracks."

fered a portrait of Véra at the time, hardly the serene Vermeer that would suffice for the years to come: Slim and lovely, Véra leaned over a bathtub, washing the family's sheets. (On another occasion when the Nabokovs gave a small party, Véra could be heard holding forth at great length on Proust. Maria Marinel was glad to have the excuse of entertaining a disruptive Dmitri in the next room, as she felt the discussion was over her head.) Berberova provided a correspondingly bleak picture of Vladimir, whom she found lying in bed in January, ashen and destitute, after a bout with influenza. The apartment was practically free of furniture. She claimed to have brought the family a chicken, which Véra immediately set out to cook, a statement Véra later found offensive, more offensive than she could possibly have found a chicken in the winter of 1940. The family's circumstances were not lost on Dmitri, who informed Maria Marinel, "We have a very hard life." Véra did all in her power to shelter him from his reality. When he spent the night at Anna Feigin's, his mother announced grandly to friends, "Tonight my son is dining out." And his father was forthright about his desire for Dmitri to have all that of which the Revolution had deprived him. Over the winter Véra and Vladimir together prepared a series of lectures on Russian literature; by April Nabokov reported that the course was nearly ready, but that he was delivering it to the walls. At the end of 1939 he had also written a novella called "The Enchanter." He read it, one night during the blue-out, to three friends and the woman doctor who had treated his psoriasis. Word of its unusual subject spread quickly, stories of forty-year-old seducers of prepubescent girls not being in great supply at the time. It was unpublishable and, unlike the two thousand pages of lecture notes, would do nothing to put its author on that boat to America. On the other hand the novel into which it blossomed, in another language, on another continent, would twenty years later allow the American writer Nabokov to realize precisely the reverse of what the Russian writer Sirin now dreamed. It would send Véra and Vladimir sailing back to Europe.

A few less enduring fictions helped speed the departure. Nabokov urged the Tolstoy Foundation to assign him an invented series of well-remunerated lectures. It went without saying that this arrangement would remain purely "metaphysical." Similar letters went out to friends, who were to assure the authorities that they would lodge the family on their arrival. The visas came through in February 1940, but the Nabokovs still lacked the $650 they needed for three steamer tickets. Nicholas Nabokov was among those who suggested that his cousin sail alone and send for his family later, when he could afford to do so. It is easy to imagine how this idea would have sat with Véra. Having had a closer view of the Nazis than most in Paris, she can have had no great desire to meet up with them again; while few in Paris that spring believed a German would ever march into the city, she would have belonged to that small minority. She had already spent much of the fall running desperately from office to office, in search of the requisite visas. Vladimir appears to have considered the idea of sailing alone, or at least was remembered by many as having been in such a panic to leave that he contemplated doing so. Véra's determination to leave can be read in her having compromised her unassailable ethics by offering a 200-franc bribe in exchange for exit permits. In April a Jewish rescue organization headed by a former associate of Vladimir's father offered the family half-fare tickets on a crossing. A second agency, committed to assisting non-Jews who had been victims of the Nazis' racial policies, supplied additional funds.*

In all of Nabokov's work there is barely a clock that functions properly, and yet now, abruptly, in the nick of time, everything came together. The monies arrived the morning after the Germans had invaded the Netherlands, Belgium, and Luxembourg, when the thunder of antiaircraft guns could be heard outside Paris. By the time the Nabokovs sailed, nine days later, the files at the Quai d'Orsay had been burned by the best-dressed cadre of arsonists in history; traffic police patrolled with rifles; the city had begun to fill with bewildered refugees from Belgium and northern France. The scene at the Gare Montparnasse was chaotic; the Germans were barely seventy miles from Paris. The Marinel-assisted departure was made in haste, amid great chaos and with some concern for Dmitri, who was running a 104-degree fever and who was plied with sulfamides all the way to the embarkation. On the same day Winston Churchill delivered his first radio address as Prime Minister, an address in which he acknowledged that the Maginot Line had been penetrated. If good-byes were said they were not extended to Sergei, who may have been left "to stutter his astonishment to an indifferent concierge," as Vladimir later surmised, with oddly phrased contrition. Véra had listed Sergei (and not Sonia) as her nearest relative on her application for immigration; she also borrowed Ilya Fondaminsky's avenue de Versailles address, which sounded—and was—statelier than the rue Boileau. She saw neither her brother-in-law nor Fondaminsky again. Both men were to perish in concentration camps.

A crossing on the French Lines' *Champlain* was not without drama at the best of times. Christopher Isherwood had sailed to America on the same vessel the previous year and noted that it seemed very small, "slithering down

---

* As Nabokov assured the American Committee for Christian Refugees, "I have sound reasons to believe that I shall be able to make good in America."

the long grey Atlantic slopes." Compared with the Canadian cargo ship on which Véra had sailed from Yalta it must have felt luxurious, however, especially as a benevolent French Lines agent took it upon himself to assign the family to a first-class cabin. Certainly perfect comfort would have been the impression Véra conveyed. As Elisaveta Marinel wrote, given the fear of U-boat attack and Dmitri's illness, the crossing must have been difficult, "but you, Véra Evseevna, are superhuman, and if you had the strength to get out despite the odds, then you probably arrived better than anyone else under the same circumstances."

Véra Nabokov left no record of what she thought as she sailed into New York harbor on May 27, 1940, but a few scraps of evidence can be assembled. She had been turned back at borders before, when in possession of a regular passport. Under more pacific circumstances, Isherwood had looked out from the same deck to find New York terrifying, visibly pulsing with New World energy. That Véra may have been flustered is confirmed by Dmitri's recollection that his mother lost her composure precisely once in her life, and that before a bureaucratic ordeal at the Port of New York. At customs the keys to the Nabokovs' trunk failed to materialize, turning up later in her pocket. (The trunk was opened with a firm blow of a hammer—then immediately and accidentally closed again, either by the porter or by Vladimir.) The family looked miserably lost, and very poor; the trip across Manhattan and to the Upper East Side felt interminable. In the taxi from the pier there was a comic fumble with the unfamiliar currency, when Véra attempted to bestow a hundred-dollar bill on an honest driver to whom the Nabokovs actually owed ninety-nine cents.

There was plenty of cause for concern. For the third time a mythical, flourishing world had collapsed behind the Nabokovs, who escaped as if through a trapdoor. This one came banging down behind them. It was not literally true that they had made their way "out of the cell, which in fact was no longer there." Despite what Vladimir liked later to claim, the building at 59, rue Boileau was not obliterated by a bomb. The Germans were in Paris on June 14, however; the *Champlain* hit a mine and sank on its next westbound crossing. And among the many borders they had traversed the Nabokovs had this time crossed a truly semantic divide. In Berlin and Paris a Russian counted as an émigré. In America, she was a refugee.

THE PERSON IN QUESTION

Anyone can create the future, but only a wise man can create the past.
— NABOKOV, *BEND SINISTER*

1

"I speak fluently English, French, and German," Véra had written on her immigration documents, a claim that speaks for itself. Linguistically this third dislocation was the most jarring. She who had worked in English throughout the Berlin years was far from entirely at ease with the language; unlike her husband, she had never set foot in—much less studied or conducted business in—an Anglophone country. A full year after the arrival in New York she would recall, "I find it difficult to follow many-pronged conversations in English." The handicap must have been all the more acutely felt in the company of academics, with whom she would spend the summer of 1941. There was every reason why those who met her in the first American years should have been struck primarily by Véra Nabokov's silence.

Vladimir had known Véra Slonim for a matter of months when he first invited her to settle in America with him. As unrealizable as that dream had seemed in 1923, the reality proved vastly more complicated now. Nabokov had been penniless when the two married, but he had been penniless and celebrated. For the first time his reputation had not preceded him. The family had fled together, but they had done so precipitately, amid (as Vladimir had it) "the panic-stricken, gaping suitcases and the whirlwind of old newspapers," to say nothing of the advancing Germans. All of Véra's papers, and most of her husband's early editions, were stashed in Ilya Fondaminsky's basement, from which only a small portion would be recovered. Véra was thirty-eight years old, with a six-year-old son,* savings of just under one hundred dollars, and a husband with no long-term job prospects. None of these impediments—it remains to be seen if this made Véra's life more or less pleasant—could blunt Vladimir's essential optimism. "A miracle has occurred: My wife, my son and I have managed to repeat Columbus's feat," he wrote an eminent scholar, who he hoped might help him find a university position.

The taxi driver whose integrity cost him the tip of a lifetime deposited the Nabokovs at the apartment of Natalie Nabokov on May 27, 1940. Nicholas Nabokov's first wife did all in her power to make the new arrivals comfortable, arranging for them to occupy the flat across the hall in her East Sixty-first Street brownstone until the Tolstoy Foundation located a summer sublet on upper Madison Avenue. The irrepressible Altagracia de Jannelli was on the doorstep immediately. Within days of his arrival she escorted her client to Bobbs-Merrill's New York office; she made certain that he paid a second call at the beginning of July, when the firm's Indianapolis-based president was in town. From these visits Vladimir concluded that the book his onetime publisher would most welcome from him was a mystery story, which, at least initially, he set out to write. By early August he had begun to rail against the publisher's attempts to dictate length, theme, and content of the work; a Russian friend to whom he mentioned these conversations expressed surprise that anyone would have been so bold with the notoriously defiant Sirin. By the end of the summer, even while Bobbs-Merrill held out hope that Nabokov might produce a novel for their spring list, he had begun to snicker about the "genteel book, with agreeable protagonists and moral landscapes" that Jannelli expected from him, a recipe on which he would produce a startling variant later. "What I am composing now will hardly satisfy her," he confessed of the agent, who forbade him to write in Russian, a ban he repeatedly broke. Ultimately Véra was the only beneficiary of Jannelli's resolve. In the fall the agent reassured Bobbs-Merrill that she knew how to wring the tardy manuscript from their author. She was providing him with a typewriter, "so that his wife may whip it into reading shape." What Véra did with the shiny new Royal was to keep Jannelli off the doorstep; she found her husband's dogged representative a perfect nuisance. In mid-November Véra used the newly acquired machine to report to Jan-

---

* Dmitri provided an additional cause for concern. Raised tri- and quadrilingually, Vladimir and Véra had done all they could in the emigration to shelter their son from French and German for the sake of his Russian. He arrived in America speaking no English.

nelli that her husband was making some progress in his work, but that the obligations of earning a living were rather slowing his pace. Jannelli never made another sale for Nabokov. The Royal served Véra for the next twenty-five years.

More than simply literary agents were kept at bay over the summer months. As the New York heat and humidity disagreed with Véra and Dmitri, the family decamped for the Vermont farm of Harvard historian Mikhail Karpovich, their base until mid-September. The Karpoviches' 250-acre property—Nabokov described it affectionately as "a ram-chakal farmhouse haunted by great sulky porcupines, song-of-Bernadette-smelling skunks, fireflies and a number of good moths"—amounted to a lively Russian colony set amid the mountains of southern Vermont. The hospitality of the learned Karpovich and his huge-hearted wife, Tatiana, was unrivaled; the sprawling farmhouse and its outlying buildings were filled perpetually with visitors, often distinguished ones. As the Karpoviches had elected not to install electricity, running water, or a telephone line, there were no luxuries about the Vermont property beyond the essential ones: animated discussion, the commotion of children, incessant tea-drinking, wild raspberries. Vladimir continued to think of his future "with a certain horror," but the operative feeling that summer was one of immense relief. He profited from the moment of repose to commune with the local butterflies. Karpovich's eleven-year-old son, Sergei, remembered the new arrival running about the area with his net, clad only in a pair of shorts; the half-naked Russian made quite an impression on the local farmers. At least some of Véra's day was claimed by the gaggle of children, her own and others'. "Vladimir Vladimirovich" proved a mouthful for the Karpovich offspring, who took to calling her husband by his patronymic alone. Véra spent her time correcting them. Had they no idea whom they were addressing so carelessly?

From their summer idyll the Nabokovs were gently summoned back to New York by Alexandra Tolstoy. She had spent these months, as she would much of the fall, dispatching letters in all directions on the family's behalf, to those who might offer Vladimir work as well as to those who might advance funds. By September she had arranged for an interview with Nicholas Wreden, the Russian-born manager of the Scribner's Bookstore. Vladimir had promised Alexandra Tolstoy that he "would be glad to take any work that would give me and my family a chance for existence," but returned from Scribner's with a markedly different attitude. Wreden, who proved the immediate salvation to a number of refugees, had proposed that he begin by wrapping packages, from nine to six. The pay was sixty-eight dollars a month. With more amusement than indignation the man whom Tolstoy had been describing in her letters as the contemporary Russian writer of the greatest promise declared, "One of the few things that I decidedly do not know how to do is to wrap anything." Furthermore, the family could not live on sixty-eight dollars a month, especially if he had no time in which to earn additional funds. At the end of a restorative summer he felt doubly besieged, by flu and by anxiety.

In New York the Nabokovs settled at 35 West Eighty-seventh Street, in what Véra remembered as "a dreadful little flat." They had two rooms in the brownstone; their telephone was a few flights of stairs away in the doorman's quarters. Daily Véra walked Dmitri to the private school at which Natalie Nabokov had arranged for him to enroll at full scholarship. His English came quickly; Véra was proud to observe that within months of entering the first grade he was "promoted" to the second. Vladimir began tutoring three older women studying at Columbia, with whom he was pleased. Great lovers of Russia all, they appeared to him to "brilliantly debunk the émigré preconception of the lacquered emptiness of the American mind." He volunteered as well at the Museum of Natural History, arranging the Old World Lepidoptera collections. Soon the Tolstoy Foundation's efforts, along with his own, began to bear fruit. He was commissioned to write his first English book reviews; arrangements were made for a series of guest lectures. In December he received an invitation he qualified as his "first success." A ten-week summer position at Stanford University that Aldanov had dangled before his eyes the previous year in Paris was offered to him for 1941. Dorothy Leuthold, one of the three Columbia students, volunteered to drive the family cross-country, in her new Pontiac.

Early in October Vladimir misplaced a phone number with which his cousin Nicholas had supplied him, further proof, if proof were needed, that telephone numbers proved delusions in his hands. His first meeting with Edmund Wilson was arranged by note. "Dear Mr. Wilson," he began, "I would have telephoned myself, but cannot find your number." The first years in America were more about livelihood than about literature; it was Edmund Wilson more than anyone who helped Nabokov to connect the two. By December the eminent American critic was suggesting—the idea could not have been more comical in retrospect—that the two collaborate on a translation of Pushkin's verse play *Mozart and Salieri,* a translation that would be published in *The New Republic* the following spring. At the same time Véra invited Wilson and his then-wife, Mary McCarthy, to a small party, to be thrown not at the Nabokovs' apartment but at the more comfortable hotel lodgings of their Berlin friends Bertrand and Lisbet Thompson, who had emigrated earlier. The end-of-the-year celebration would be canceled, but the Nabokov-Wilson correspondence was off and running. Over the next years it proved one as rich in strong opinion, from Nabokov's end, as it was in trade secrets, from Wilson's: How to give your publisher the slip. How to avoid having to review a novel by Thomas Mann. When to wriggle free of an option clause. How to secure a Guggenheim. Where poetry could be made to pay. How to extort an extra one hundred dollars from an editor. How to circumvent "a man named Ross" who persisted in editing people at *The New Yorker.* Nabokov's immediate concerns were not yet so delicious; 1940 was one of the few literature-free years of his life. At the same time he had never worked as hard as he did that winter, preparing his Stanford classes, writing reviews, filling in at the museum, angling for a position as a guest lecturer.

With Dmitri at school, Véra was free to work again, at least part-time. In this respect the swelled immigrant community in New York proved helpful. In January the lawyer Alexis Goldenweiser put her in touch with a Russian colleague who needed assistance with his foreign correspondence. He offered Véra a nine-to-seven job, which she explained was not feasible. The attorney proposed that she handle his French correspondence only, for which he offered a paltry sum. While she was grateful to Goldenweiser for his recommendation, she made it clear that this remuneration was insufficient. One of her greatest attributes—independent of, but in tandem with, her husband—was her sense of her own worth. For all of the selfless devotion, Véra could never be said to underestimate herself. She should not be working for forty cents an hour, just as her husband should not be writing a mystery novel. In 1941 she was saved by her unwillingness to compromise. Almost immediately a better position turned up, at a Free French newspaper, the only job other than that for her husband to which she affixed the adjective "fabulous." Probably she began work at the paper at the end of January.

She would have been highly conspicuous on West Eighty-seventh Street. Well before she opened her mouth, no one would have mistaken Véra Nabokov for an American. Neither of the elder Nabokovs appeared remotely well fed, a look that Véra wore better than her gaunt husband. (When he arrived at Wellesley College for a guest lecture in March, Vladimir overheard a cafeteria cook swear, "We are going to put some fat on the bones of that man," a promise on which, indirectly, Wellesley made good. In the eyes of a friend's daughter, Véra looked as if she were about to blow away.) In a long black dress and a long black coat, Véra introduced Dmitri to the Statue of Liberty, the Fulton Street fishmarket, the Bronx Zoo, the Staten Island Ferry. She was for him a part of those enchantments. In those rounds she looked decidedly foreign, and would the more so the farther she ventured from New York. Nor could Dmitri—despite the "American" in which he was soon chattering away fluently—be mistaken for a native. Nicholas Nabokov and his second wife dined with the new arrivals at the Russian Tea Room just before Christmas 1940. The more recent Mrs. Nabokov—Nicholas would leave behind four of them, whose activities were routinely conflated with Véra's—remembered Dmitri spectacularly bundled in fur, a picturesque and decidedly exotic sight. The following summer the seven-year-old left an indelible impression while exploring the upper reaches of a Stanford amphitheater in shorts resembling lederhosen, a felt hat with a feather jauntily perched on his head. In Berlin and Paris a Russian accent was a Russian accent; in New York it was simply, and distinctly, foreign. The alienation must have been fierce, at a time when America was not yet at war and not yet much concerned with the messy world beyond its shores. As Nabokov reminds us, "*Stranger* always rhymes with *danger.*"

It had never been much in Véra's power to bow to the local mores, and after three migrations she was all the more unwilling to do so. There was generally less suppleness to her persona than to that of her husband, who took to America as he took to most things, with a bantering, inquisitive enthusiasm. Véra's memory of Dmitri and the fur reveals something of her unyielding approach to the New World that winter:

> On walks through Central Park, D., aged 6 and wearing his furcoat brought over from Europe, would be approached one by one by 6, 8 or 10 little and not so little boys to be teasingly asked "Are you a boy or a girl?" and would patiently reply to each "No, I am a boy, and this kind of coat is worn by boys where I come from," which, at times, so much astonished the interrogators that the bantering beginning would result in a long and friendly talk.

She lamented that this gentleness would be bred out of her son by American schools.

Her husband, a quick-change artist by nature, began almost immediately, consciously and not, to toy with the local idiom. His wardrobe told an interesting tale, especially about a man whose work is so rich in lived illusions. Almost as if in a fable, he met in quick succession a series of individuals who counted among his staunchest supporters in his new world. Chief among them were Harry Levin, then a promising junior instructor in Harvard's English Department, and his Russian wife, Elena, from a liberal background similar to Vladimir's. The young couple had spent their 1939 honeymoon at the Karpoviches' farm, at which time Levin had abandoned his cast-off tweed blazer in a closet. When the Levins were introduced to the

Nabokovs in the fall of 1940, the Nabokovs were returning from Vermont; Vladimir sported the retired blazer, to whose provenance he remained oblivious.* Over that summer Karpovich had passed on to Vladimir an ultramarine suit of which Nabokov was fond and in which he delivered his 1941 Stanford lectures. Additional hand-me-downs came his way from Serge Koussevitzky. It is not surprising that prior to George Hessen's immigration Nabokov prepped him by advising that he must "play the real American." Early on the couple appear to have realized that for Vladimir's professional survival they could not too much align themselves with the Russian community, a decision that would cost them later.

Véra engaged in none of this molting; generally she was less interested in costumes than disguises. Willingly or not, she was engaged in a new game, in a new language, in which the rules were ill defined for newcomers. The possibilities for ridicule were enormous, especially for someone with a heightened sensitivity to propriety, an investment in remaining inconspicuous. At half her age her father had effected a similar transformation: His move from a Yiddish-speaking shtetl to a Petersburg university was a move from the religious to the secular world, from one class to another, but it must have been less traumatic than was his thirty-eight-year-old daughter's in 1940. The "rapid acculturation and abiding separateness" that was said to describe the life of the St. Petersburg Jew equally well described these first refugee years in America, where so much was possible and at the same time so much was alien. Véra recognized the difficulties inherent in the enterprise. She spoke eloquently about the "pathetic attempt of a very small and bewildered individual to throw an anchor of his own amidst the incomprehensible, tossing, perhaps frightening element around him," although when she did so she was speaking of Dmitri on the arrival in America. She seems to have had little interest in reinventing herself, only in inventing an American writer where there had been a gifted Russian one, in seeing that the twice-deposed king with whom she traveled recover his scepter.

In March 1941 Nabokov arrived in Wellesley for a two-week guest lectureship, which he owed indirectly to Karpovich. Véra was in bed with a crippling case of sciatica, an illness that cost her the newspaper job. In sixteen days Vladimir wrote her no fewer than eight times. Almost immediately he did so with good news: Edward Weeks had bought "Cloud, Castle, Lake" for

---

* The blazer had never looked better. "Everything looked elegant on him," remembers Elena Levin, who was meeting someone she had regarded as a master since the publication of *Mary*. The *Atlantic*'s Edward Weeks made a similar observation: "He just had to walk into the room and the girls looked around—the clothes didn't make any difference."

The Atlantic, a deal the two men sealed over breakfast that week. Vladimir solicited his wife's advice as to what he should do next. Was it wiser to attempt something in English, or write a piece in Russian and then translate it?* Even at this delicate moment in his metamorphosis he made light of his predicament, citing an invented text that would be written in 2074 about the linguistic travails of Vladimir Sirin. He reveled in his attempts at deciphering Americans. "I'll be so bold as to assume that when they say, 'It will be a tragedy when you go away,' that that is the simplest American politeness," he asserted. But in confidence he admitted that he was bored and longed to come home; when he feared he could not fill fifty minutes he dragged out his lecture by covering the blackboard with the names of Russian writers. He punctuated his letters with comments clearly aimed at dissipating any jealousy his wife might be harboring. At Véra's end fidelity was doubtless less at issue than were finances. She failed to place a section of *The Gift* in a Russian anthology in which Vladimir had hoped it might appear; she had no money; she was rapidly piling up debts. Further she was unwell. Lisbet Thompson and one of Nabokov's Columbia students checked on her daily and accompanied Dmitri to the park. The doctor paid regular calls. Vladimir had himself been borrowing money during his trip; he came home via the Chekhov Theatre in Ridgefield, Connecticut, for which he had proposed to work up a stage adaptation of *Don Quixote,* but found on March 28 that he lacked the funds to return to New York. (He lodged in the actors' dorm but took care to specify that it was the *male* actors' dorm.) Véra might have worried that quixoticism could be contagious when her trainfare-less husband was offered, and rejected, a permanent position in Ridgefield: "It's true, it is quaint here, but all the trees have been chemically treated, so there probably aren't many butterflies."

She had not recovered her health on his return, and was in great pain throughout April, when it seemed the California trip might have to be canceled on her account. Nabokov had been pleased with the visit to Wellesley and Wellesley had been no less pleased with him; in mid-May he received an invitation to join the faculty for a one-year appointment, at a salary of three thousand dollars. He was to be "an interdepartmental visitor," a title that— with its overtones of outer space—seemed perfectly to describe his situation. It was neither a permanent position nor a munificent sum, but the Wellesley offer allowed the Nabokovs to set out for California with the future a little less undecided than it had been. Véra was evidently well enough to pack

---

* He was not yet his own translator: "Cloud, Castle, Lake" was rendered into English by Peter Pertzov, whom Altagracia de Jannelli had located years earlier.

up the apartment on Eighty-seventh Street and pile into a car—along with the dictionary, the typewriter, Dmitri, three butterfly nets, and Dorothy Leuthold, pupil and chauffeur—for two weeks. It would be another year before her frustration with their state of affairs would seep into her correspondence. Bitterly she remarked in mid-1942, "Yes, Russia is *en vogue* right now, but as far as a position is concerned, that hasn't helped my husband yet." (Vladimir vented the same frustration at the same time but in radically different terms: "Funny—to know Russian better than any living person—in America at least,—and more English than any Russian in America,—and to experience such difficulty in getting a university job. I am getting rather jittery about next year.") Later she alluded to grave difficulties in getting reestablished. Despite the overt stalwartness, her chagrin with their hand-to-mouth existence, with the familiar set of uncertainties in an unfamiliar world, plainly exacted a toll. In the 1950s she privately attributed her departure from the newspaper position to "illness which resulted from all the migrations and anxieties."

2

She caught some of her first American butterflies that summer, as Leuthold chauffeured the family to California, from motor court to motor court, through Tennessee, Arkansas, Texas, New Mexico, and Arizona, a trip Véra hugely enjoyed. Some of this collecting she did in a knee-length black dress with a lace collar, a garment she could hardly have purchased with this kind of expedition in mind. She still looked unwell, her skin more ashen than translucent, her cheeks sunken. On a crystalline morning in early June, on the south rim of the Grand Canyon, both Nabokovs triumphed lepidopterologically, each in his own way. Vladimir set off with Dorothy Leuthold down a mule trail, where after a short walk he netted two specimens of what he recognized to be an undocumented *Neonympha*. When he returned to the Pontiac, where Véra and Dmitri were attempting to warm themselves, he discovered "that right beside the car Véra had herself caught two specimens, sluggish with the cold, with nothing but her fingers." Nabokov named his capture after Leuthold; he commemorated his success in "A Discovery," a poem that appeared in *The New Yorker* in 1943. Véra's parallel find went undocumented. A certain competitiveness crept into their collecting, for which the passion was primarily Vladimir's. "I've had wonderful luck. I've gotten many things he didn't get," Véra interrupted her husband to tell his first biographer. "And I once saw a butterfly that he wanted very much, and he wouldn't believe me, that I had seen it," she continued. "Yes, that's right, that's right," agreed Nabokov. "And on the side of the path you saw snakes actually jumping into the air." She entered into the collecting, which would occupy a fair portion of the remainder of her American summers, with enthusiasm, and spoke of her finds with pride.* (When her husband was not there to pique her modesty, she was more retiring on the subject. After fifty years of collecting she demurred, "I am not a trained lepidopterist. All I know about butterflies I have learned from my husband.") If anyone was to acknowledge the cost of these expeditions it was not to be Véra. "I bungled my family's vacation but got what I wanted," Vladimir reported, after a summer detour to Telluride, Colorado.

The Nabokovs very quickly took the measure of America, "a cultured country of endless variety," as Vladimir initially described it. America would be longer in taking theirs. In the first weeks a New York City barber sized up his client in a glance, pronouncing him an Englishman, a recent arrival, and a journalist. Flabbergasted, Nabokov asked how the barber had arrived at his conclusions. "Because you have an English accent, you haven't yet had time to remove your European shoes, and you have the high forehead and the face of a newspaperman." "You're a real Sherlock Holmes," conceded Vladimir, to which the sleuth with the shears replied, "Who's Sherlock Holmes?" During the cross-country excursion Véra took Dmitri for a haircut and heard a less assertive investigator west of the Mississippi ask her seven-year-old son where he made his home. "I don't have a home," replied the child, who had lived at twenty-one addresses in the previous three years. "Where do you live then?" inquired the astonished barber. "In little houses by the road," Dmitri replied, a comment by which his mother was charmed. As Dmitri sees, looking back, "It was a real drifter's life."

In Palo Alto the Nabokovs settled into a comfortable Spanish-style bungalow at 230 Sequoia Avenue, a brisk twenty-minute walk from the heart of the lusciously landscaped campus. Véra spent her time with Dmitri, or running the house. She was disappointed not to be able to attend her husband's lectures, which were enjoying great success despite the modest audience.†

---

* Of a collecting trip in Wyoming's Bridger-Teton National Forest in 1952, Nabokov reported: "On a slope near Togwotee Pass at timberline I had the pleasure of discovering a strain of *C. meadi* with albinic females. The species was anything but common there, but of the dozen females or so seen or caught as many as three were albinic. Of these my wife and I took two, hers a dull white similar to *hecla 'pallida'*, mine slightly tinged with peach." Véra's version of the story was a little different. "I also caught a white female of *Colias meadi*, which nobody seems to have taken before me, and the existence of which most lepidopterists doubted or denied. My husband also took a whitish female, but mine is all white," she advised friends.

† Only a handful of students registered for Nabokov's courses, although a number of interested faculty and auditors from the community attended as well.

Nabokov taught two courses, of which that on Modern Russian Literature proved to be the more labor-intensive; the bulk of the writing he did that summer was a rewriting of Gogol, Pushkin, Lermontov. "My husband is working much and gets rather tired, not so much from the lectures (7 a week) as from preparing for each one: Not finding any decent translations of the Russian classics, he translates them himself for his students. . . . And so teaching Russian literature is, of course, very exhausting," Véra explained.* This was the summer when she lamented the state of her English. They attended a great number of parties, which she found "very 'formal' (and genteel)." Many evenings were spent in the company of Henry Lanz—the Finn who had offered Aldanov, and Nabokov, the Stanford position—and his chessboard. In the course of the summer the two managed to play 214 matches. "He kept score, being a pedant," added Vladimir, who could not help but note that the presumed nonpedant had prevailed 205 times.† Even after 214 matches, he was never to know that Lanz had forfeited his own summer salary in order to bring him to Stanford, just as he was never to know that he was lecturing in Harry Levin's jacket. No one is so much a character in someone else's drama as the new immigrant. And at this early stage it was difficult to determine who was starring in whose fiction: America in the Nabokovs', or the Nabokovs in America's. Neither had a vaguely accurate idea of the real life of the other. It is easy enough to fathom how Véra was perceived in the false reflection she left behind. One student vividly remembered her serving tea from a gleaming, silver samovar, while explaining the rituals of Russian tea service. When she read of this later she offered only one comment: "I wonder where Véra could have obtained a samovar, large or small." It was not the first thing a three-time refugee packed.

In July the happy but not particularly profitable word reached the Nabokovs that James Laughlin, the publisher of New Directions, proposed to buy *Sebastian Knight* for $150. It was a paltry advance, but for a manuscript that had been written three years earlier and been rejected on two continents innumerable times since, it was a welcome one. Reversing a well-established tradition, Véra arranged to send a third of Laughlin's advance to Anna Feigin, still in unoccupied France. Over the next years and whenever possible,

---

* Translation was never a subject on which Nabokov minced words—or liked to see words minced. Of the available edition of Gogol's "The Overcoat" he declared: "The existing translation is vileness and an embarrassment." His work on Pushkin, Lermontov, and Tyutchev did not go unacknowledged; much of it was published in 1944 as *Three Russian Poets*.

† This was not everyone's recollection. Cyril Bryner, Emeritus Professor of Slavonic Studies and a young teacher in the department in 1941, remembered that "Nabokov lost as many as he won, and was not a happy loser."

the Nabokovs dispatched money abroad, to a multitude of addresses. The awareness of old friends and relatives still in Europe—the Marinel sisters, George and Iosef Hessen, Anna Feigin, all of Véra's and Vladimir's siblings—held the difficulties of the first American years in check; both Nabokovs mentioned at various junctures their chagrin at having had the good fortune to escape when they had, especially in light of the "Neanderthal hardships" their loved ones were now suffering. There was much scrambling to make ends meet, and much weariness (Vladimir claimed he was so tired over the summer of 1941 that he could barely detach himself from his lawn chair), but Véra concluded, "Despite this, we're very happy that we're able to exist." Laughlin emerged as the direct beneficiary of their fatigue. By the time the New Directions contract was signed, the agreement included an option for Nabokov's next three books.

The task of reviewing the galleys of *Sebastian Knight* fell to Agnes Perkins, the head of the Department of English Composition at Wellesley, to which the Nabokovs traveled by train in mid-September, arriving with monstrous colds. Vladimir's English in 1941 was not yet entirely without quirks, quirks which might be termed ungrammatical as easily as they might be termed stunningly original. All of the stories he published that year were stories he had written in Russian and that—with and without assistance—he had rendered into English; he was less an author himself than he was Sirin's translator. With *Sebastian Knight* he began to break out of the Sirin chrysalis, although not all of the critics who read the novel on its publication that winter agreed. *The New York Times*'s Sunday reviewer found the work silly, the author's English "interesting in a Walt Disney sort of way." "All of this might sound nice in another language,"* he suggested. Probably Véra took these words more to heart than did the book's author, who was not so much indifferent to criticism, as he liked to protest, as he was invigorated by it.† He openly admitted that writing in English was a handicap to him. A year after *Sebastian* was published he moaned that his English was still not on a par with his Russian; even when it was, he had something in mind other than conventionally correct English. No one who had grown up having to render "Cap d'Antibes" into Cyrillic could help playing with words; with satisfac-

---

* Such snipes were to persist long after 1941. So foreign was Nabokov's English to the tried-and-true stuff that Vita Sackville-West would sniff of *Lolita*: "I don't know what language it was originally written in. . . . it is not even bad American and certainly is not good English."
† The novel, published officially on December 12, 1941, went out with a long endorsement from Wilson comparing Nabokov with Proust, Max Beerbohm, Virginia Woolf, Kafka, and Gogol—and yet terming him a true original. Kay Boyle, in *The New Republic,* welcomed the book more warmly than had the *Times,* pronouncing it "a delight to read."

tion Nabokov noted that his next book, his highly personal biography of Gogol, sparkled with "a dewy multitude of charming little solecisms." Those solecisms were not as universally admired as he might have liked. In 1945, Katharine White at *The New Yorker* expressed concern for his taste for obsolete language; she inferred that he had learned his English directly from the *OED*. Among the pieces on which she was at work at the time, she described "Double Talk" as "a very long and very badly written but funny and bitter one by Nabokov who does not want me to edit it except for a word or two whereas it has to be turned by me into English and cut and transferred from the past to the present." (Véra professed great sympathy for White, for having to put up with her husband's exigencies.) For good reason Harold Ross swore he would cut his own throat if Vladimir Nabokov were to become a professor of English.*

Ross had a while still to live. Véra settled the Interdepartmental Visitor and Dmitri into a furnished apartment near the Wellesley campus, but Nabokov did not teach English—or for that matter any regular course—in 1941. Other than frequent meals with students and six lectures a year, he had few campus obligations; in their comfortable, clapboard home he felt his family was living in "splendid solitude." The awkward honeymoon with America continued all the same. He was forcing himself to write in English, a torment he both did and did not want to admit to. He lived with fierce, constant tempation, to which he occasionally succumbed; he wrote some of his most memorable Russian verse at the time. It was a perfectly visceral discomfort. "At night I have belching spells from Anglo-Saxon lentils," he railed. Meanwhile Véra was making vast efforts of her own: She was daunted by the prodigious industry—she used the word "heroism"—of the American housewife. "I am not a good cook," she cheerfully admitted (it was not something she had been raised to do) and she had no qualms about saying that she did all in her power to stay out of the kitchen as much as she possibly could. Later she was to be teased about the fact that scrambled eggs constituted half her repertoire; the new arrivals substituted primarily on deli food, Campbell's soups, canned vegetables, fruit, and eggs. Throughout much of the Wellesley period this woman who believed that the world of the imagination was the only one that mattered waged a halfhearted war on Massachusetts dustballs. "All of my time is spent on housekeeping (which I can't stand—I'm a terrible housewife)," she grumbled. "As a housekeeper

---

* The general feeling at *The New Yorker* was that Nabokov had learned his English from reading a dictionary. After the publication of *Lolita*, he delighted in telling an interviewer that his English came to him direct from *Webster's*.

I'm not bad but disgusting," she later clarified, rather overstating the case, and at the same time damning America's multitude of so-called conveniences.* As if further proof were needed of the indecipherable ways of Americans—or, for that matter, of the exoticism of the Nabokovs—Véra and Vladimir left Dmitri with a baby-sitter on the evening of October 31, 1941, while they attended a faculty function. "Why is no one taking you trick-or-treating?" asked the blond Wellesley student on duty, who proceeded to paint the seven-year-old's face with watercolors and parade him around the neighborhood in the Indian headdress purchased in Santa Fe that summer. His mother was abashed on her return.

America's entry into the war in December did little to help the newly published *Sebastian Knight,* but the Nabokovs' immediate concern was how to survive once the Wellesley appointment was over. Nine days after Pearl Harbor Vladimir wrote a series of the letters at which he had become such a reluctant master over the previous decade. He was to solicit help from so many parties in these years that he could entirely forget having done so, a periodic cause of unpleasantness later.† The field of Slavic Studies had not yet begun to bloom; with the war and the consequent budget cuts, academic positions became scarcer still. As the Wellesley year wore on and no new prospects emerged, he joked that he would probably soon be commanding a squadron anyway. Several days after his forty-third birthday he announced that he did not find the prospect of being drafted altogether unappealing.

The real battle was one waged closer to home. Over the course of the Wellesley year—Nabokov's last public lecture took place in mid-March—he gravitated increasingly toward Harvard's Museum of Comparative Zoology. He had lost no time in finding his way to the MCZ, where by the end of the year he was volunteering twice a week. The butterfly work did not interfere with his academic responsibilities, but as Vladimir—and Véra—were very aware, the science interfered with the writing. Véra knew well the force of her husband's passion: During a similar period she grumbled, "To talk with him you have to 'wake' him not from sleeping, but from butterflies." The addiction got worse before it got better, which could not have made everyone happy; even the Marinel sisters chided Vladimir for having devoted his first

---

* In this torture she was far from alone. When Isabel Stephens, a Wellesley Education professor who was the Nabokovs' neighbor in Cambridge, filled out her 1946 faculty questionnaire, she listed three occupations under "Special projects carried on outside of the department": "Marketing, washing, ironing." Under "Interesting plans for the future," Stephens wrote: "Hoping to get a cleaning woman two days a week."

† Having been peremptorily denied a meeting with Nabokov twenty-eight years later, one potential benefactor indignantly produced Vladimir's letter of December 16, 1941, so as to refresh his "phenomenal memory."

two American years to lepidoptera. It is impossible to say whether Véra was more concerned with the financial or the artistic repercussions of her husband's scientific passion: She sounded neither relieved nor regretful to report in midyear that Vladimir had been appointed a Research Fellow at the Museum, a post that would bring in a small sum but claim only half his day. "We're hoping that he'll earn a bit extra with literature," she offered. In a desultory fashion her husband was at work on his biography of Gogol, for Laughlin, and on a new novel.

"Why is it so difficult to imagine oneself at forty?" one of Nabokov's eternally youthful characters wonders. To the young Véra and to the older one, Véra at forty, Véra the resident alien, would have seemed a near-fictional creation. Her world had always been predicated on a certain uneasiness, but was now supremely precarious. She who had always had an ear for the subtlety of language was without an ability to express it; the world in which she moved was oblivious to the genius of the man with whom she lived; her child was beginning to prefer Superman to Gogol.* In 1942 she had lived as long in the emigration as she had in Russia; the splendor of Petersburg was a long way off. She had invested all of her energy in a literary career that had already once been deprived of an audience but was now deprived of its very substance. Moreover, its practitioner had developed a new rapport with a microscope. Never someone who would have been good at recognizing herself, she probably least conformed to her own self-image now. If anyone had told her as a young woman that she might one day live in America, she might well have believed them. That she was again contending with blackouts and food and fuel shortages only reinforced her conception of the world and its permanent state of turmoil. Had she heard that in the peculiar new alliance between her adopted country and her native one her sympathies would lie entirely with the former she might have been surprised. But at the thought that her datebook for 1943—one she and Vladimir shared, as was their habit—would open with recipes for oatmeal cookies, sugar cookies, and Sand Tartes she would have been incredulous.

Véra would never be able (or willing) to camouflage the person who had lived through two major inflations; there would be a dollop of refugee anxiety in much that she did. But those who knew her later were never to glimpse a bewildered—or demoralized—refugee. The poverty, the isolation, the uncertainty, never seemed to matter, not because she was an optimist by nature, which she was not, but because she made certain that the

---

* Briefly her husband caught the fever too, composing a poem, now lost, on the Man of Steel's wedding night.

pedestrian concerns never showed. Or as Maria Marinel gushed shortly after the Nabokovs arrived in America, "Véra Evseevna, you will always be twenty years old! . . . life has not yet managed to soil you. And knowing your life, your troubles, and your sense of responsibility, I find that stunning and beautiful." The worst indignity for someone like Véra may have been the only one to leave a mark. She must have felt, as had Madame Luzhin before her, at a Berlin dance, "depressed that everyone was looking at these movie people, at the singer and at the consul, and nobody seemed to know that a chess genius was present at the ball, a man whose name had been in millions of newspapers and whose games had already been called immortal."*

Publicly, she remained stoic about the family's situation. Her only comments on the bleakness of their prospects went to Goldenweiser, with whom she could be perfectly blunt. "As before, we have no 'perspectives' for the fall, except for the perspective from the window of our little flat here," she sighed as the 1941–42 academic year wound down. The second semester had been difficult for all kinds of reasons: Dmitri had attended three schools, none of them satisfactory, had been sick throughout the winter, and had recently submitted to a tonsillectomy. She herself had persistently been unwell. Vladimir was, with good reason, nervous about the year to come. His literary luck was not all good, as he discovered when "Spring in Fialta" proved, on the first attempts at publication, to belong to "the boomerang variety of manuscript." The salary he accepted at the MCZ was a third of what the family had lived on at Wellesley. Véra was rattled, and, as she had been in Berlin, often dispirited. "Try to be cheerful when I get back," Vladimir begged later in the year, "but I love you gloomy too." He was less fond of what he termed her "little economic wailings."

The bulk of the summer of 1942 was spent at the Karpoviches', a vacation Véra enjoyed less than she had the previous stay. Almost certainly the cause was a falling-out with Tatiana Karpovich over how to discipline the boisterous Dmitri. The youngest Nabokov that year composed a story about a mother who "was so kind that when she had to spank her child she gave him some laughing-gas first," a tale which does a fair job of conveying Véra and Vladimir's attitude toward parental discipline, one which caused some dismay among their friends. Véra left Vermont early, and alone, to hunt for an apartment in Cambridge. She was under strict instructions to find one

---

* The phenomenon had a literary parallel, articulated by Nabokov: "Vinteuil is accepted by everybody in this provincial town of Combray as a vague crank dabbling in music, and neither Swann nor the boy Marcel realizes that in reality the music is tremendously famous in Paris. . . . As already remarked, Proust is intensely interested in the various masks under which the same person appears to various other persons." And, too, Ada will prickle at "the insufficiency of her brother's fame."

with a room in which her husband could work undisturbed, which she did, renting a third-floor apartment in a large brick building on Craigie Circle, a twenty-minute walk from the museum. For one hundred dollars she acquired the furniture of the previous tenant, a professor with execrable taste. The cramped headquarters proved the Nabokovs' longest-lived American address; with Véra and Dmitri sharing a narrow, twin-bedded room so that Vladimir could write at night in the room next door, they would remain at Craigie Circle until mid-1948. Mary McCarthy was a long time in recovering from the décor when she visited; others remembered only Vladimir's bed, strewn with index cards. Isabel Stephens, a neighbor and Wellesley colleague, was led to believe that he littered the floor with his cards, which Véra collected and put in order for him. (She did find her day's typing on the floor when she woke in the morning.) While in Cambridge Véra learned that Anna Feigin had arrived safely in Baltimore, with her brother, Ilya. Both Nabokovs were distraught to find that the Hessens had not sailed on the same ship; they left France finally at the end of the year. "Now this gigantic stone has rolled off of my chest, with its tiny swastika, and it is easier to breathe," Vladimir wrote, welcoming them.

In the spring Véra had typed her husband's curriculum vitae and a list of eight topics on which he could speak; financial necessity made him a traveling lecturer that winter. He set off early in October 1942 for two months of speaking engagements that took him from Georgia to Minnesota. This made Véra a de facto curator of Lepidoptera at the MCZ. From the South her husband instructed her which butterflies to pin into the sliding glass cases, and in which order. "Good Girl," he applauded from the train to Atlanta, "for doing so many trays." While all in Cambridge appeared on an even keel, his trip was one rich in the Pninian moment with which his life—especially his life apart from Véra—was so rich. He had long vaunted his absentmindedness, his ineptitude, the "dilly-dallying [which] has always been my specialty."* His encounter with the American South was enhanced by the adventure of the renegade cufflinks (a replacement set materialized out of thin air and was affixed to his overstarched cuffs by a well-meaning female guest, decidedly "not the best-looking of them"); the case of the wrong lecture in the jacket pocket; the case of the mistaken identity. (After a long wait for his ride to campus, he realized that the college had been "expecting a gentleman with Dostoyevsky's beard, Stalin's mustache, Chekhov's pince-nez, and Tolstoy's tunic," a gentleman who was no other than himself.)

---

* "Then again, only *humans* are capable of absentmindedness," we are reminded in *The Enchanter*.

All of this information was transmitted to Cambridge in daily dispatches, to which Véra responded with equal frequency. Nabokov challenged his wife to determine telepathically which paintings hung on his hotel room wall; he wrote of his delight in their shared life. He hastened to banish any specters of jealousy that might be arising at her end. Lounging on his bed, naked, he assured her that he missed her on all counts. Intermittently he was putting the finishing touches on the Gogol biography—he promised Laughlin that it would take him ten days to dictate the thing to Véra—even while he battled the impulse to write in Russian. From Cambridge Véra sent him a partially completed form he might submit to the Guggenheim Foundation for a fellowship. She suggested that he write Agnes Perkins and Amy Kelly at Wellesley, to remind them how much he would like to return to some kind of position there, an appeal that would bear fruit the following spring. Nabokov's tour as a traveling salesman in literature proved the couple's last long separation; they would never again be apart for more than a matter of days.

When he returned to Cambridge on December 12, Vladimir found Véra in Mount Auburn Hospital with pneumonia. She stayed for several weeks, into the new year. To her husband's relief, Anna Feigin was at the apartment, sleeping on what was euphemistically termed the sunporch. Were it not for his wife's cousin, Vladimir felt, he and Dmitri would have disappeared completely. As a result of the illness the typing of the Gogol book did not begin until nearly mid-January, however. "She still cannot manage more than five pages per day," Vladimir wrote Laughlin apologetically of his wife, "but this rate will improve steadily." Progress on the manuscript was slower than expected, as—doubtless relatedly—was the recovery. More than typing appears to have been at issue: By March only 130 pages were ready, which indicates a certain amount of rewriting. For Véra the scene must have been reminiscent of *Invitation to a Beheading,* which she had also typed while convalescing, on a different keyboard. There was every reason in the world why Vladimir, congratulating his publisher on his upcoming nuptials, should have written that year of marriage: "It is a very pleasant state as far as my own experience goes."

We do not know if—frail as she was, well-acquainted with her husband as she was—the woman who "presided as adviser and judge over" Nabokov's first fictions offered comment on the Gogol pages as she typed. Other early readers did. Neither Karpovich nor Wilson approved entirely of one of the most eccentric biographies ever written, a book that begins with the death and ends with the birth of its subject, visiting every one of its author's pet peeves along the way. Laughlin asked if Nabokov could not see his way to supplying the plots of Gogol's works; the author responded not by doing so but by writing Laughlin's admonishment into the book. In the slim volume Nabokov takes issue not only with the existing translations but with *Roget's Thesaurus* as well; he manages to include a subtle plug for one of his own future works. Is it truly necessary, pleaded Karpovich, for you to grind every one of your personal axes at Gogol's expense? Wilson thought his Russian friend overindulged in puns; the cleverness threatened to overwhelm the book. Véra had the advantage of knowing her husband better than did either Wilson or Karpovich; he was not capable of holding up a mirror to Gogol that did not include his own reflection as well. Above all the biography amounted to a primer on reading Nabokov. Véra also had some experience of the matters of which he spoke. "Gogol was a strange creature, but genius is always strange," Nabokov declares of his subject. To Laughlin he explained that the real plots hid always behind the visible plots. Twenty years later Véra advised a friend mystified by a young relative's behavior: "Artists are unusual people, and their reactions may sometimes appear disappointing. Most of the time the truth is different from the way things look."

3

The appeals Véra had advised to Professors Kelly and Perkins paid off in the winter of 1943, when Vladimir was invited back to Wellesley to teach two noncredit courses in Russian. (There was sad irony in the fact that his deliverance came courtesy of the pro-Soviet sympathies that began to blossom all over America.) Again his title reflected his irregular status: According to the September 1944 faculty questionnaire that Véra completed for him, he was now "Extracurricular Instructor in Russian."* In the simple disguise of a language professor he traveled from Cambridge to Wellesley, by wartime car pool, for semiweekly meetings of his courses. The commitment required more of his time than he had anticipated, not because of his enchantment with his students but because of his disenchantment with the teaching tools at hand. He could not help but blaze his own trail. "I invent my own phonetics and rules for I am just created in such a way that I am utterly incapable of taking advantage of the work of others, no matter how substantive that work might be," he explained. His "real life" was located not at Wellesley, and not even with his literature—he felt as if the person who had been writing in

---

* Only in the fall of 1944, when a department would be formed of which Nabokov was chairman and sole member, would he be known officially as "Lecturer in Russian."

English under his name was but a construct, "as if it's not myself in fact who composes"—but at the Museum of Comparative Zoology. So disassociated was he from Professor Nabokov that he told a student interviewer he would laugh to hear himself lecture.

"Wars pass, bugs stay," Vladimir announced that winter, making no question of his priorities, much less where the Wellesley classes fit in the scheme of things. He took the museum work altogether seriously, spreading, pinning, and labeling specimens for the collection, focusing on his favorite "Blues" of the Lycaenidae family, for which he had devised a novel taxonomy. He maintained his reputation as an original even at the highly original MCZ, where he was generally regarded as a gifted amateur, not only because of his lack of a graduate degree. This could not have disturbed the man who had written his mother from the other Cambridge more than twenty years earlier: "I love to play the eccentric."* He was no less quick to report on his follies than were his colleagues, one of whom noticed that his hallway greetings boomed in inverse proportion to how clearly Vladimir recognized the person he was addressing. In 1944 he acquired an assistant who would become a trusted friend, seventeen-year-old Phyllis Smith, then a Simmons College freshman. Nabokov delighted in sharing with her the tales of his American mishaps, the misunderstandings that seemed to accrue to someone unfamiliar with the local mores. His recurrent question seemed to be "Is this really the way they do things in America?," the implication, "Do you think this as absurd as we do?" So much of his and Véra's experience had been that of his characters: breaking out. Now for the first and only time they struggled with getting in.

Despite the butterflies, Nabokov finished writing—and Véra finished typing—the Gogol manuscript in May. That spring Véra began to submit her husband's work to magazines, as she had done in Europe, a sign that she felt more confident of her English (or of that of her husband, who had just received the first of two Guggenheim Fellowships). She had by this time also assumed her husband's correspondence with publishers, Laughlin chief among them. Hearing of their interest in the American West, the independently wealthy Laughlin invited the Nabokovs for a summer stay at his ski lodge in Alta, Utah. It proved a restorative vacation, though Véra was disappointed by the weather; a cold wind seemed to howl constantly through the

---

* As with most things, Nabokov's definition was his own. "An eccentric," he wrote, "is a person whose mind and senses are excited by things that the average citizen does not even notice." By this definition he was married to an eccentric and the father of one as well.

Wasatch Range canyon. (For someone born in St. Petersburg she was un-commonly sensitive to cold. Her husband was sturdier, but quick to conclude that America's climatic conditions were "not quite normal.") Nor was she won over by Laughlin or his wife, which may explain why the publisher re-membered her primarily for her glacial charms. In Alta as later, Laughlin sensed that Véra feared he might somehow lead her husband astray. Her concern proved misdirected, but well-founded: She was visibly unenthusias-tic when Vladimir proposed to their host that they climb to the top of 13,000-foot Lone Peak in search of a rare butterfly. After an eight-hour ascent, the two nearly perished on the way down, as they slipped through a steep snow-field at the edge of a cliff, over which Nabokov nearly lost his publisher. They were due back at the lodge at four; at six Véra called the sheriff's office, which sent out a car. A sheriff returned with the men several hours later. There were no histrionics on their return. Vladimir seemed more rattled by his wife's systematically defeating him at Chinese checkers, to which the two devoted a good deal of time over the summer.

Despite himself, Vladimir made a new friend in July, on a mountain road outside of Alta. Leaving his overheated truck behind, a coal-dusted young man hailed Nabokov, who should by 1943 have learned not to judge anyone by his attire. He glowered silently at the truck driver but did not stop. John Downey was unwilling to be shaken off so easily and pursued the lepidopterist with a volley of questions. Pointing to the left and right with his net, Nabokov administered an ambulatory Latin exam before he was willing to believe that the seventeen-year-old shared his highly recondite passion. When Downey passed with flying colors, the older man stopped in his tracks. "Vladimir Nabokov," he offered, extending his hand. A few years later Downey's wife and Véra joined their husbands for a collecting trip, just before the erstwhile truck driver began his master's in entomology. Véra applied a little litmus test of her own. "Tell me, Norine," she asked Mrs. Downey, over a picnic table near Salt Lake City, "does your husband understand my husband's work?" "I'm sure he does, because he uses it all the time," responded Norine Downey, referring to the lepidopterological papers. "That's good, because many people don't," sighed Véra, referring to the fiction.

Mrs. Downey was understandably misled by the question. In Cambridge Nabokov returned to the magic world of his microscope; if Véra disapproved she waited some time to intervene. It had not been long since she had typed a line stating that Gogol had become a great artist when "he really let himself go and pottered happily on the brink of his private abyss." The letters are studded with wails about the difficulty of changing languages, of keeping the Sirin inside at bay, of the clumsiness of feeling his way in English.* The butterfly work must have been doubly appealing, once as passion, again as refuge: The language of science is beautifully constant. The discipline was an all-consuming one, however. Nabokov later admitted that after the MCZ he was never to touch a microscope, "knowing that if I did, I would drown again in its bright well." Véra threw out a lifeline just after the New Year. On January 3, 1944, her husband wrote Wilson: "Véra has had a serious conversation with me in regard to my novel. Having sulkily pulled it out from under my butterfly manuscripts I discovered two things, first it was good, and second that the beginning some twenty pages at least could be typed and submitted." He promised that this would be done quickly and it was: "I, or rather Véra, have-has typed out already ten pages of *The Person from Porlock*," he reported days later. By mid-month thirty-seven pages of what was to become *Bend Sinister* went off to Wilson.

Progress on the novel slowed after the initial burst. The teaching schedule interfered, but mostly the butterflies were to blame. Nabokov knew his habit was costing his family, too. "I am devoting too much time to entomology (up to 14 hours per day) and although I am doing in this line something of far-reaching scientific importance I sometimes feel like a drunkard who in his moments of lucidity realizes that he is missing all sorts of wonderful opportunities," he admitted. On account of his passion he had grossly neglected his finances.† The jovial comments did not fall on deaf ears; a Russian writers' bureau arranged for several hundred dollars to be advanced him that spring. He talked about retiring from the MCZ, something he would not do until the fall of 1947. Meanwhile a sort of compromise was worked out, one Vladimir described to Hessen on the twenty-first anniversary of meeting Véra: "It's Sunday today, and as usual on this day, I am staying in bed since I know—and Véra knows—that if I get up I will stealthily make my way to the Museum. It's particularly pleasant working there on Sundays." Cambridge friends who remembered Véra waiting on her husband while he sat propped up in bed remarked on her humble devotion. At those times she appears, however, to have had him precisely where she wanted him.

She succeeded less well in keeping the financial anxiety at bay than she

---

* "The urge to write is sometimes terrific, but as I cannot do it in Russian I do not do it at all," Nabokov grumbled in November 1945. Only in 1946 did he report that he had begun to feel "acclimated" to the English language.

† He knew that the scientific work made him unpopular for other reasons. "I have long since grown accustomed to the repulsive, slippery smile that runs across the faces of my Russian friends in New York when the conversation turns to entomology. In their conceptions, any fool who has written a 'work' on history or economics is a 'scholar,' " he griped.

did the bill collector. (The rent on Craigie Circle alone was sixty dollars a
month, or three-fourths of Nabokov's museum salary.) Shortly after the
move to Cambridge Véra began to give private language lessons, as she did
intermittently over the next years. One of her less willing victims was the
eleven-year-old daughter of Wellesley professor Isabel Stephens, eager to
help the family financially. In 1944 Dmitri was enrolled at the Dexter School,
in Brookline, for which he had a partial scholarship; Véra paid off a portion
of the private school tuition with secretarial work. That year she took a position in the Department of Romance Languages at Harvard, where she assisted a French and a German professor on a part-time basis. Again the job
proved short-lived, either because the permanent secretary returned from
leave, as Véra asserted later, or, more likely, as she wrote at the time, because
the position "was incompatible with everything else, since V. is busy all day
and needs a lot done for him and he needs help with a lot of things." By 1947,
when a Harvard library position was offered her, she would not even pause
before responding that she was unqualified for the job. By that time she had
found full-time work, at home.

Her job expanded in 1945, when Wellesley suggested that Nabokov
teach a course in Russian literature in translation. From the Stanford summer he knew how much preparation this would entail; he had no trouble resisting the offer. Véra prevailed upon him to accept it, promising to write the
lectures herself. Sparing her husband the necessity of looking up dates or biographical details, which she knew he found tedious, she compiled a concise
history of Russian literature. Together the two rewrote some thirty lectures,
which Nabokov delivered twice a week at Wellesley; these proved part of the
repertoire for nearly fifteen years, ultimately part of the published repertoire.
At the top of a talk on romanticism, Véra queried: "Volodia, would it be too
involved to say . . . that, while during the Middle Ages every facet of human
nature was dulled and all the contents of it kept frozen like a Bird's Eye
peach, it took roughly speaking four centuries to defreeze it?" She wrote a
great number of pages on the Russian poets, all subsumed in Vladimir's lectures. "A little tartly," she acknowledged that her husband had reworked the
lectures so many times that not a word of her original texts remained.

Finances kept the Nabokovs close to Cambridge between 1943 and the
summer of 1947, when they were able again to head west, to Colorado. During those years Vladimir pursued a number of avenues to supplement—or
replace—his Wellesley wages. He asked to be sent on a second lecturing tour
at the end of the 1944 academic year; he flirted with film work. Véra made
his Hollywood ambitions perfectly clear in a 1947 letter to an agent interested
in the rights to *Bend Sinister*: "My husband wishes me to add, however, that,

being a novelist and not a picture man, he is more interested in the financial side of a possible sale than in the quality of a possible picture." Nabokov continued to hope that Harvard might notice his presence in their backyard and exploded with frustration when they did not; Wellesley car-poolers remembered him fulminating about this injustice from the backseat. (Both he and Véra were vocal about their disdain for the Slavists at Harvard and Yale, which did nothing to improve his chances at either institution.) In 1946 he was briefly considered for a vacancy at the head of Vassar's Russian program, but was rejected, allegedly on the grounds that he was a prima donna. He energetically pursued the possibility of heading up a Russian unit for the newly created Voice of America, a position his cousin Nicholas mentioned initially, and ultimately took for himself.* Nothing came of any of these opportunities, although Vladimir was put under contract at *The New Yorker* in June of 1944. That summer found the family vacationing in Wellesley, taking their meals at a private home near campus. Rationing only accentuated the deprivations they already felt. A Wellesley physics professor who joined them at mealtimes remembered Vladimir's ill humor—he was decidedly not where he wanted to be in August, when *Bend Sinister* failed to convince an early reader—but mostly the professor remembered Véra's unease. She seemed poised to anticipate her husband's displeasure. Certainly she knew how to tone down his attacks. In a letter that went out over her name, Véra alerted a magazine editor to her husband's low, and frank, opinion of Soviet poets. After a fair amount of vitriol was spilled, she stepped out from behind the typewriter: "I think he would have used milder expressions if he were not down with the flu." This was wishful thinking, as other letters on the subject attest. More often she did not temper her husband's remarks, and the thunderbolts sailed.†

She had already begun to serve as his emissary. At the end of 1943, she had traveled to New York for the day; Vladimir had sent her to see Wilson, with whom she discussed her husband's fraying relationship with Laughlin.‡

---

* Confusion between the cousins continued. The rumor around the VOA office was that the personnel office had intended to offer the post to Vladimir and hired the wrong Nabokov. The FBI could not keep the two Russians straight. Nicholas's photo ran even with Vladimir's obituary.
† To Philip Vaudrin, at Oxford University Press in 1947: "Since you are asking me what I think of these translations, I believe that what you want is my frank opinion. Here it is. These translations are absolutely terrible. I cannot imagine how a firm of your standing could have been induced to publish such trash. They are caricatures of the originals, couched in execrable English, with all the clichés typical of graphomania. Moreover, the author does not always understand the sense of the Russian lines. Last but not least, his choice of pieces is in the worst taste." The book in question was an anthology of poetry, *The Wagon of Life,* Sir Cecil Kisch, translator.
‡ Even after this encounter Wilson got Véra's name wrong, sending love to "Sonya." Probably he was thinking of the wife of their mutual friend, Roman Grynberg.

By early 1945, she had begun to teach in her husband's stead at Wellesley when he was not well enough to do so. A less endearing habit was Vladimir's tendency to slough off other people's enthusiasms on his wife. If someone began to effuse about a new novel or play, Nabokov sidestepped their accounts with a cursory, "Tell it to Véra." He did not feel he needed to be burdened with other people's impressions. In an arrangement that evidently suited both partners in the marriage and clearly amused at least one, Véra began to lend her husband something more valuable than a willing ear. In May of 1944 Nabokov visited Cornell University for the first time, not yet aware that his American odyssey was to end in Ithaca, New York. From the train home he wrote George and Sonia Hessen. He was alone, but the letter bears a postscript, ostensibly from Véra. In his wife's hand Nabokov had added: "Véra sends you both sincere regards. (I have long been imitating Véra's handwriting!)"

After a burst of enthusiasm, Knopf rejected the new novel in 1945. By that year Véra had assumed Vladimir's correspondence with the interested editor, beginning her first letter as she would countless others, "My husband has turned over to me your letter for an answer." The missive reporting that she would send on the novel's first chapters before the end of the week is signed "Mrs. V. Nabokov"—but in Vladimir's hand. This reverse mitosis was not always perfectly neat; occasionally the two tripped over each other on the page. Véra wrote a foreign agent about a contract her husband had signed and had asked her to return; Vladimir accidentally signed the letter himself. She had by now found an English-language voice, but seemed still reluctant to step out from the wings. The self-effacement was extreme enough to be telling—and to be recounting a very different story. In the fall of 1946 Edmund Wilson was in Cambridge and took the Nabokovs to dinner, after which the three paid the Levins a visit. Wilson reported on the evening to Elena Thornton, about to become his fourth wife: "Véra is wonderful with Volodya: she writes all his lectures, types his manuscripts, and handles all his publishing arrangements. She also echoes all his opinions—something which would end by making me rather uncomfortable but which seems to suit Nabokov perfectly."

Why would a strong-willed, independent-minded woman now in comfortable command of the English language—she soon noticed that Anglicisms were creeping into her French—second all of her husband's opinions? She did so only more passionately as the years went by; in the late 1950s a colleague spoke with Véra at a crowded faculty party about Auden, then crossed the room to hear Vladimir expound the same (dim) views, in precisely the same terms. In no course that Nabokov taught did Dostoyevsky ever earn a grade above a C minus; he fared no better with Véra. The only person who argued more violently than Nabokov for the novel for art's sake was his wife. Most of the time Véra believed simply that he was right. She had lived with his arguments for a long time; the two had similar tastes from the beginning. (She could disagree, vociferously, but only with company before whom it was safe to do so. Véra detested the work of George Eliot, which her husband defended on a private occasion. "Now why did I marry you?" wailed Véra. He was no more indulgent than she when their judgments failed to coincide. "Good Heavens, how could you like *that*?" he would cry.) With Wilson there was a certain amount of circling the wagons. Wilson was as tenacious a debator as Nabokov, happy to agree provisionally, only to reopen the discussion hours later; early on Nabokov compared him affectionately to the psoriasis on his elbow. Véra was no less obstinate. In some cases the beliefs were initially hers, seconded by her husband. Nabokov would dismiss *Dr. Zhivago,* applaud the works of Robbe-Grillet, register perfect indifference to Robert Musil, based on his wife's evaluations. Her heightened sense of dignity had some bearing as well on the undivided front. So too did her confidence in her husband's genius. When Wilson found he could not muster for *Bend Sinister* the enthusiasm he had felt for Nabokov's earlier work, it was to Véra he apologized. He hoped she would forgive him. If anything, she made a stronger case for her husband than he did himself. So convinced was Nabokov of his enormous talent he did a less than enticing job promoting it. He insisted he was squeamish about selling himself, incapable of arranging his own affairs. This was not entirely true, but it was a convenient case to make. Véra, who had as much conviction but a different stake, willingly stepped in.

The Nabokovs' views—strong opinions in Vladimir's case, nearly religious convictions in Véra's—were not the prevailing ones in America, or in Cambridge, in the early 1940s. At Wellesley Nabokov could not find a kind word for the art produced by the Soviet state, America's ally at the time; he was asked to tone down his remarks. He made no secret of his belief that one ought to learn Russian not to understand what Stalin thought of war but what Tolstoy did. He evinced no enthusiasm for "Uncle Joe," no sympathy for America's allies on the Eastern Front. Neither Nabokov hesitated to express unfashionable views about the USSR, which shocked people; Vladimir and Edmund Wilson fought like cocks on the subject.* A degree of subtlety

---

* Having heard enough sympathy for the Bolsheviks, Nabokov divided the Russian emigration into five easy categories: (1) those still crying over the lost furniture, (2) the anti-Semites, (3) idiots, (4) philistines and profiteers, (5) decent and freedom-loving people, or what remained of the tattered Russian intelligentsia.

was required to understand that the Nabokovs' disdain had nothing to do with sterling silver samovars and everything to do with art and freedom; that subtlety was not in great supply in the 1940s, when the couple were as often as not cast as White Russians. It was difficult for an American—it was difficult even for Wilson—to fathom that a Russian could be neither for the Soviets nor for the Tsar.

For good but not always comprehensible reasons, the Nabokovs took the unpopular stand after the war that helping Germany back to its feet should not constitute an American priority. In December 1945, Dmitri's school made a collection of used clothing to be sent to German children. Vladimir explained why his son would not be allowed to participate in the clothing drive: "When I have to choose between giving for a Greek, Czech, French, Belgian, Chinese, Dutch, Norwegian, Russian, Jewish or German child, I shall not choose the latter one," he proclaimed, in a statement that shows every sign of having been drafted by Véra. At no time could forgiveness be counted as one of her fortes, and it certainly was not as word of the fates of family and friends left in Europe began to filter back to Cambridge. That news had a vast effect on the totalitarian hell depicted in *Bend*, a novel that Nabokov described as being related in tone to *Invitation*, though "even more catastrophic and ebullient." Into its skewed world he had folded many of the nightmarish frustrations, and much of the pain, of the previous decade. He hoped to portray in the book the defiant vigor of the free mind even in the midst of oppression; as if to pry open the cage, the author—a representative of divine power—subtly intervenes at the end of the novel. Unlike *Invitation to a Beheading, Bend Sinister* is permeated with a sense of vulnerability, of the fragility of life and love. Ilya Fondaminsky and Sergei Nabokov had perished; Véra's sister Sonia had made a harrowing, last-minute escape from France via North Africa; Vladimir's younger brother, Kirill Nabokov, had been arrested but had talked himself free; friends had spent years in labor camps. Nabokov swore that if his hate for the Germans could increase it would, but that it had already reached its limit. Véra went further: "I don't understand for the life of me why everyone is suddenly in a rush to help the 'poor' Germans, without whom Europe supposedly can't survive: Oh, it would, and how!"*

None of the reports from Europe lessened Vladimir's deep-seated revul-

---

* To Colonel Joseph I. Greene, who was arranging for a German translation of *Bend Sinister* in 1948 as part of an educational program, she wrote that she hoped the book might prove instructive but confided her belief that "knowing the Germans as we do, we cannot help entertaining some doubts as to their susceptibility to re-education."

sion for anti-Semitism, a prejudice to which he was more sensitive than his wife. Véra took the slurs in stride, or at least on a rational level; Vladimir was always ready to call a duel. He had a sophisticated radar for the faintest glimmer of prejudice, as much out of deference to the ideals of his liberal father as to his Jewish wife. Since the arrival in America he had been fascinated by the hotels that advertised "restricted colonies" or "exclusive clientele" in the pages of *The New Yorker*. No manifestation of anti-Semitism was too small to irk him. He leveled charges of racism even against Alexandra Tolstoy, to whom he and his family owed so much. The miserable summer of 1946, spent in Bristol, New Hampshire, to which the Nabokovs traveled by taxi, was memorable for one such episode. The accommodations were not promising; the lake was filthy, the resort backed on to a highway, the butterflies were poor. Fried-clam fumes from the local Howard Johnson's wafted across the area. After sitting down in a local restaurant the Nabokovs noticed a sign, "We welcome strictly Christian clientele." Vladimir wasted no time. "And what would happen if little old bearded Jesus Christ drove up, in an old Ford, with his mother (black scarf, Polish accent)? That, and other questions, so intrigued me that I took apart the restaurant's manager, leaving him and those present in an indescribable tizzy," he recounted afterward. He had just finished *Bend Sinister* and was said by his doctors to be suffering from nervous exhaustion as a result; it is doubtful that the reaction would have been different at a more tranquil time.

Véra did no such jostling on her own behalf; her elbows were reserved for her husband. These were years when she more often hid behind him than he behind her, a configuration that gradually reversed itself. During the Wellesley years she was a picture of good-natured grace, or at least was to those who saw her. The Nabokovs socialized little during these years, counting among their friends Amy Kelly and Agnes Perkins, both older women.* Those who knew Véra well—Phyllis Smith, Vladimir's much-liked assistant at the museum; Isabel Stephens, his car-pool colleague; Sylvia Berkman, who helped him to smooth his prose—assumed her to be terribly lonely. Lonely she may have been but sentimental she was not: "We had a few close ties with 2 or 3 old ladies at Wellesley—dead now" was how she later described some of these intimates. She felt that their work precluded any social life in Cambridge.

---

* Kelly had been fascinated by Vladimir from the start. "She treated him like royalty," recalled a student in Kelly's 1941 dorm, who had reason to remember him: The Claflin Hall girls had not been allowed to be seated at dinner until Nabokov arrived at the faculty table, which he generally did less than promptly.

According to a little investigation the FBI conducted in 1948, the Nabokovs had virtually no contact with their neighbors, though there was endless Craigie Circle speculation about them.* For his sister in Geneva, Vladimir drew a picture of the morning routine in Cambridge in the fall of 1945, much of it centered on getting Dmitri out the door for his 8:40 bus: "Véra and I watch through the window . . . and see him striding toward the corner, a lanky, little boy, in a grey uniform with a reddish jockey's cap and a green bag (for books) slung over his shoulder." At 9:30 he headed off himself, with his Véra-supplied thermos of milk and his two sandwiches. Sylvia Berkman was invited in for dinner from time to time on the Wellesley afternoons, and sensed Véra was very grateful for the company. "She had so little companionship" was how she, the closest of the Wellesley friends, phrased it. Isabel Stephens assumed she must be downright miserable. Elena Levin, arguably the friend with the most in common with Véra during the American years, saw things differently. "She was much too busy—and much too proud—to be lonely. She would have been happy to have been on a desert island with Vladimir."

Certainly her time was much in demand. In 1945 she made some inquiries into printing *The Gift* privately; it is telling that neither she nor Vladimir thought of her translating the novel in the 1940s. She could not yet "slice, chop, twist, volley, smash, kill, drive, half-volley, lob and place perfectly every word," as her husband described the ideal translator's abilities. When an editor like Edward Weeks of *The Atlantic* called, he spoke with Véra about which poems her husband should like to publish. After the war, when the French agent who had handled Nabokov's works in Paris visited Cambridge, it fell to Véra to present her with the Gogol book and talk up the collection of short stories that followed. For a translator-friend in Italy she painstakingly recopied Vladimir's plays, all drafts save one having been lost in the war. Nicholas Nabokov hired his cousin to translate a piece of Pushkin's he had set to music; Véra reviewed the voice part with Vladimir, who fit his work to Nicholas's composition. When Vladimir needed the word for the black accordion-like partitions that separate train cars, he called the Stephenses. They were of no help. He called Berkman, who was equally mystified. In the end Véra headed off to Harvard's Widener Library, where she consulted every available book on railroads. She could find no word for the partitions, which appear in *Speak, Memory* as "intervestibular connecting curtains." By January 1946 she was, against her will, in charge of Vladimir's

---

* The FBI also found no reason to believe them anything other than perfectly loyal Americans.

correspondence. In this she brought upon herself the curse of the conscien-
tious; her husband's dilatoriness weighed not on his mind but on hers. To this
she combined the curse of the capable. Hundreds of letters went out beginning with apologies. The choice was either a letter from her or no letter at all.
By 1949 she felt that there were not enough hours in a day for the correspondence. She was at the time walking the Dutch translator through the hidden
meanings in *Bend Sinister,* levels of meaning which—she could have been describing herself—were not to enter his text, but which which he would need
to penetrate in order to do the novel justice.*

Not all of the editorial help went to her husband. In 1950 Harvard University Press published Amy Kelly's scholarly biography of Eleanor of
Aquitaine, which went on to become a surprise bestseller. Véra is thanked in
the acknowledgments. She managed always to read copiously, mostly fiction
in the 1940s. More often than not she was disappointed, returning her books
to the Cambridge public library without finishing them. To a friend in Italy
she strongly recommended F. Scott Fitzgerald's work, especially *Tender Is the
Night, The Great Gatsby,* and *The Crack-Up.* (Wilson was very likely responsible for fostering this taste, although he was less successful introducing Véra
to Faulkner, whose work was lost on her.) She was a great fan of Evelyn
Waugh, whose novels she thought splendid, especially *A Handful of Dust,
Scoop,* and *Vile Bodies.* She spoke highly of Laura Hobson's *Gentleman's
Agreement,* although she noted disapprovingly that the work, which was gen-
erating much excitement, was *un roman à these.* Assiduously she reviewed
Dmitri's schoolwork, helping him with his Latin, coaching him on both sides
of the Roosevelt/Dewey debate, reading him Gogol and Poe. Both Nabokovs
consulted with Wilson about reading lists for Dmitri, who Wilson thought
would be much enamored of Twain. Véra's reaction to the idea shocked
Wilson in 1946, and would have shocked him all the more were he to have remembered it a decade later. "She won't let her 14-year-old son [Dmitri was
12] read *Tom Sawyer,* because she thinks it is an immoral book that teaches
bad behavior and suggests to little boys the idea of taking an interest in little
girls too young," he marveled.

Véra's life was made no more agreeable when Vladimir determined to
give up his four-pack-a-day cigarette habit in the summer of 1945. On few
subjects was he as comic—or as nostalgic—as on this one. In his suffering he
took to following a colleague around the museum so as to inhale his scent; he

---

* The actual words were: "I hope this helps. It is only meant, of course, to help you penetrate the actual
words of the passage and find an equivalent for them. Otherwise it is all my own and my husband would
not want it, I think, to enter your text."

came as close as he could to embracing the man, who smelled divine. He waxed rhapsodic on the glories of his former habit, as he was still doing thirty years later. And yet he would not allow himself to touch the packet of Old Golds he kept in the bedside table in case of emergency. "We shall fight in the hills. We shall never surrender," he vowed, but he felt wretched, especially when, at virtually the same time, Harold Ross was so bold as to edit him at *The New Yorker.* "Nothing like it has ever happened to me in my life," he growled to Wilson, who managed to call off the pencils but could do nothing about the nicotine withdrawal. Nabokov's personal calvary coincided with a case of chicken pox for Dmitri; Véra must have been beside herself. She had had a dress rehearsal for this double torture the previous summer, when Vladimir had been hospitalized with a serious case of food poisoning in Cambridge while she was in New York with Dmitri, whose appendix was being removed. Acknowledging a certain protectiveness on his wife's part, Nabokov had appealed to Wilson to alert Véra without allowing her to rush back to Cambridge. He knew the unanswered telephone would torment her.*

The arrangement—Véra serving as Vladimir's first lieutenant, as Sylvia Berkman described it—was not without its lapses. Nabokov traveled to Providence, Rhode Island, in March of 1947 to deliver a talk to a woman's club there. (He still could not afford to turn down extracurricular work, although did not sell himself short either. Véra had begun to alert editors soliciting reviews that their rates were unacceptable to her husband. "In fact he does not remember having ever been offered anything so absurd as $5 for a review," she castigated one such offender.) In Providence Vladimir did Pnin one better; he delivered the wrong lecture. Mrs. Pnin assumed responsibility for the misunderstanding: "I am afraid, I am the one to blame: at the time we made the original arrangement I was sick and omitted writing down your selection of the subject," Véra explained to the club's president, who registered a sharp complaint. (The subject had been chosen by Vladimir and clearly indicated in the club's letter confirming the talk.) Her husband would be willing to return to Providence to deliver the expected lecture at no charge. Still, prompted either by an inner sense of justice or by an external voice, Véra could not help adding: "He also thinks that to some extent you got even with him by misspelling his name on your program."

She had clearly already acquainted herself with an area with which she would become expert, with what her husband termed in *Bend Sinister* the

---

* Original even in his less alluring moments, Nabokov wrote Wilson, "Incidentally I vomited into the telephone which I think has never been done before." The account of the hospital stay constitutes in itself a small masterpiece.

"devices of shadography." Hers was not a visible role, but it was a vast one. As if in acknowledgment, she began to swell to New World proportions. America had a curious, Carrollian effect on both Nabokovs: Within weeks of his last cigarette, Vladimir had gained forty pounds. The Wellesley girls were astounded by the transformation. By December 1945 the 124-pound émigré weighed in at just under 200 pounds, a mark he soon exceeded. Véra noted he somehow even grew taller in the process. As she reported disapprovingly: "Volodya is always bumping into the furniture because he cannot remember his new dimensions. He claims that 'his belly is all in bruises.' " He was clearly a very good deal heavier than she would have liked. She too grew to new dimensions, though not yet to her full stature. On July 12, 1945, two months after the Germans surrendered and a month before the Japanese were to do so, the couple submitted to their American citizenship tests in Boston. They had dutifully memorized the Bill of Rights; Amy Kelly and Mikhail Karpovich went along as witnesses. It was easy enough to explain how blond, 106-pound Véra Nabokoff became on her naturalization certificate gray, 120-pound Véra Nabokov. For once something was gained in translation as well: On her Parisian papers she had been 5 feet 6 inches tall. By some quirk of calculation she was 5 foot 10 by the time the American formalities were over. Meanwhile Dmitri grew and grew, and at twelve was just under six feet tall. (With good reason, Nabokov remembered Craigie Circle as the "shrunken dwarf apartment.") "When he and Véra walk along the street she seems tiny," Vladimir observed. At the same time she began to loom larger and larger. She must have felt like Alice, attempting to introduce herself to the Caterpillar: "At least I know who I *was* when I got up this morning, but I think I must have changed several times since then." There was every reason in the world why Amy Kelly should fervently congratulate the couple on having been "literally born again to a new life of happiness and prosperity."

4
———

Nabokov had been brought to Wellesley to serve in a "generally inspirational capacity." That he did, but not entirely as the administration had intended. "I spent most of my time studying French, Russian, *and* Mr. Nabokov," remembered one student. "I know I always used to put on mascara when I went to his class," recalled a second. He was as much a subject of fascination to the college girls as were the MCZ specimens to him; in 1945 you could make quite an impression in Wellesley, Massachusetts, by kissing hands. "We were all madly in love with him," a third alumna reported. For many of the girls he was the first European; he tallied perfectly with the romantic conception of the Continental, bohemian artist. Best of all, he seemed fragile, in dire need of being taken care of. For all of his charm and erudition he appeared—and often was—lost. The college paper reported that the first meeting of the fall, 1946, Russian Literature class was delayed by ten minutes, while the students waited eagerly for their professor to arrive. At last "they noticed a face peering through the window frantically demanding, 'Where does one get in this place?' " If the girls were not yet entirely aware of how heterodox were their professor's opinions, they recognized immediately that there was something unorthodox about his person. "He was the only man I'd seen in my life who wore pastel shirts, pink shirts," observed a student. He made a practice of annihilating translators.* He announced that he had heard from another faculty member that it was time to give exams. Could he trouble the class to memorize a poem, as proof of their effort? Merrily he informed an attractive blonde he intended to use her in a book one day. He seemed terrifically miscast as a Russian instructor; he talked openly about the fact that he was not a good teacher. Everything about him spoke of another world, a distant realm of Old World sophistication and erudition, a world— far from the seas of Peter Pan collars and saddle shoes and bobby sox—that occasionally followed him to class. One day in a classroom under the eaves at Green Hall a butterfly flew in the open window. Nabokov stopped short, nimbly caught the creature by the wings between his thumb and index finger, mumbled its Latin name, then, slouching his way toward the window, set the insect free and returned to the lesson.

Few of the girls believed his heart to be in the rudiments of Russian grammar. A few knew better where it was. A great number of his students watched him adoringly; nearly as many noticed that his attention was reserved for the best-looking girls in the class. If he was not outright flirtatious he was uncommonly attentive. "Ah, Miss Rogers, I see something new has been added," he commented when the mascara-wearer, a perceived favorite, returned from spring vacation with an engagement ring on her hand. "He

---

* Generally the body count in Nabokov's classrooms was high. He took pleasure in slaughtering Gorki and Hemingway at Wellesley; he wrote later of killing off Emma Bovary and Anna Karenina. Occasionally a student proved a casualty, as was the case with one 1944 Wellesley freshman. On hearing her name on the first day of class Nabokov began jumping about the room, waving his arms madly. "Do you have any idea what that *means?*" he asked, scrawling it on the board, analyzing its composite pieces, making buzzing circles in the air, and thoroughly humiliating the student in the process. "I think he forgot there was a person there," remembered the Wellesley alumna, who never went back to class. Her name means "mosquito" in Russian.

definitely flirted, but always with the dumbbells," remembered one alumna, who was as aware as others of the eyes sliding past her. Inevitably overtures were made. "I took a course in Russian, and I got sidetracked on a course on Vladimir Nabokov," recalled Katherine Reese Peebles, a junior who interviewed the new professor for the school paper in 1943 and who was as well placed as anyone to testify: "He did like young girls. Just not *little* girls." That fall the two began taking long walks across campus together, hand in hand, exchanging kisses. A Memphis-born belle with an exuberant mind and an irreverent streak, Peebles was well versed in the art of flirtation; the inherent beauty of a wartime blackout was not lost on her. "I was a perceptive young woman, and men were my study. I liked this one because I couldn't read him," she recalls of the mutual seduction. Nabokov quickly discovered that his student knew *Alice in Wonderland* cold; the two began reciting passages to each other as they traipsed around campus, "stumbling and bumbling" through the winter dark, traveling the longest possible distance between cups of coffee, at the student union and in town. The relationship entailed a fair amount of kissing and fondling; campus affairs were at the time as difficult to consummate spatially as they would have been socially. There was no question that Nabokov was eager to make more of this one, which Peebles happily encouraged, to her friends' consternation. Since Stanford, those who knew him had commented that Nabokov poked around campus like an "avid eavesdropping anthropologist"; Peebles caught him seizing on her American slang, snapping up the unfamiliar terms. She also saw shadows of the winter of 1943 in his later fiction. Nabokov wrapped his long, padded overcoat around the two of them as they stumbled across campus together; the image would find its way into *Look at the Harlequins!* much later.* Matters came to a conclusion late in the winter, when Nabokov's avidity began to make Peebles skittish. After class one day she commented on the halfheartedness with which her professor erased the blackboard. At least one layer of Cyrillic always shone through the next. "Then can you read this?" Nabokov asked, scrawling three words on the board and just as quickly erasing them. He had written "I love you," in Russian. Peebles dropped the course, and the professor.

Later overtures met with less enthusiastic responses, not for any lack of persistence on Nabokov's part. A student who sculpted a bust of him and at whom he made a number of passes deflected his attentions with news of her boyfriend. At the same time she felt great affection for him, charmed by his

---

* Images that Peebles thought born of the campus romance indeed appeared later, but also preceded it. A similar cloak-wrapping turns up in a 1934 poem, "How I Love You."

apparent helplessness. Nabokov remained playful and was not angry to have been rebuffed. Others found him highly flirtatious but in their innocence made little of his attentions. Once while walking into Green Hall he suggested to a student that they sit in the main reception area so as to study a set of murals commemorating "America the Beautiful" together. "Do you realize how wonderful this is?" Nabokov rhapsodized, ostensibly over the art. He and his student were seated close together on a narrow couch; the enthusiasm seemed genuine at the time, a transparent ploy in retrospect. Only a few of the girls knew their professor to be married. Those who had set eyes on Véra thought her stunning, "with long, thick, glossy white hair falling almost to her shoulders and very smooth, radiant pink-white skin." In the mid-1940s, Nabokov gave a reading of his poetry, at which Véra sat in the middle of the front row. One student remembered the debut of an act to be perfected later: "I could see the back of the head of her to whom his love poems were addressed—and from time to time between poems I could hear the shuffle of papers and the sounds of their two voices as he bent forward to discuss something briefly."

Véra surely noticed the general swooning; any woman would have been sensitive to her husband's appreciation of it. Nothing in her behavior indicated that she knew anything further. Certainly she would have been under the impression that Vladimir found the Wellesley girls callow, sheltered, uneducated, as, among other things, he did. "I have given my damsels exercises to do, and they sit having bowed their fair, blonde, dark (and absolutely empty) little heads ever so low, and they write," he declared, from the classroom. (They were not unaware of this. One alumna fondly noted Nabokov's "gentle dismay" toward the lot of them, "a bemused acceptance of what fate had dealt him: American college girls.") Doubtless Véra did not need to wait for the September 1947 *Mademoiselle,* in which her husband was profiled, identified as the sort of professor "who is more than a clichéd campus crush." Confronted with accounts of his misdemeanors of the Wellesley years later she categorically denied all. She was more vested in clearing his name than in sparing her feelings. At the same time she knew well that her husband enjoyed women. His letters are too frequently punctuated with reassurances of his love to believe she did not experience jealousy, even where there was no cause. Some of those bulletins were written at this time, when he left Massachusetts to lecture elsewhere. She liked to believe that his willpower was as great as her own, which it was not; the last dalliance was not that with Irina Guadanini in 1937 any more than the last cigarette was that of 1945. And obscuring the truth with the literal worked well for someone as compulsively candid as Véra. Nabokov was vocal in his admiration for Katherine Peebles's lithe, long-legged body. Boldly he had informed her, "I like small-breasted women." In a more innocuous context Andrew Field repeated that comment in his 1984 biography, where some forty years after the fact it fell before Véra's eyes. She did not quibble with the circumstances that might have led her husband to unleash the remark. In her outrage she went the baby-out-with-the-bathwater route. "I like small-breasted women!" Nabokov declares to a dinner table of students in Field's book. "No, never!" Véra remonstrated in the margin. "Impossible for a Russian."

The enchantment the Wellesley girls felt for the exotic professor of Russian was not equaled by the administration. Nabokov had long felt he was underpaid; moreover, he worried about the security of his position, a year-to-year appointment. In October 1947, months after *Bend Sinister* was published to tepid reviews, he traveled to Cornell to discuss an opening there. Véra substituted for him in Wellesley. On his return he wrote Wellesley's president to ask if she might be able to predict whether a permanent appointment might appear anywhere in his future. The answer was not encouraging, for reasons Véra gathered to be political; she concluded that her husband's frank anti-communism cost him a permanent appointment.* Having received and accepted an offer to join the Cornell faculty as associate professor of Russian Literature, Nabokov submitted his Wellesley resignation on November 30, 1947.† He felt that it would be "quite a wrench" to leave and was in fact very reluctant to do so, but in the end the strain was in greater part Véra's. Early in the winter Vladimir began coughing up blood, an illness that was misdiagnosed first as tuberculosis, then as cancer. Her anxiety was immeasurable, especially in light of the new appointment. The couple entreated friends to be discreet, terrified that the Cornell position might slip from their grasp.‡ Throughout the ordeal Véra commuted to Wellesley on Mondays, Wednesdays, and Fridays, by bus and trolley, to teach her husband's three courses. "I

---

* She was correct to a degree. Mrs. Horton later recollected that Nabokov refused to offer an introduction to modern Russian literature and drama, which he wrote off as Bolshevik nonsense. Other members of the faculty felt this material deserved a place in the curriculum. There is evidence as well that Nabokov rather frightened the dean with whom he had the most frequent dealings, who did not know what to make of him. Which was not unusual; he made some of the most eminent people in his field uncomfortable. He acknowledged as much in *Ada*, in which another V.V. notes that plodding academic administrations tend to prefer "the safe drabness of an academic mediocrity to the suspect sparkle of a V.V."
† Believer in overt destiny though Nabokov was, Cornell had to knock a few times before attracting his attention. The offer was not his first from the university. In November 1943 he had been asked "to help prepare Army Trainees by instructing them on various themes in Russian history," an idea he found unappealing. Various foreglimmers had preceded this, in 1939, 1941, and 1942. He had read at Cornell in May of 1944.
‡ One person who was not so alarmed was Wilson, who wrote a mutual friend of Vladimir's illness: "I did not take it so seriously at that time as he wanted us to believe because I know him to be a hypochondriac."

didn't receive any money for it, but my work there saved his [Vladimir's] salary," she reported later of his final semester, three months of which were entirely hers. There were hints that the Wellesley administration looked askance at this arrangement, but they had no reason to object to the substitution. Véra was a better teacher of language than her husband, more organized, less invested in originality. "She made me disciplined, which he never did," was one student's recollection. Véra read Vladimir's lectures carefully, with attention to her audience. There was every reason in the world why she should write the Marinels that what with all the illnesses, with Dmitri's spring vacation from the Dexter School, and with all else—curiously she did not mention the Wellesley routine—"my head is spinning." She fell behind in her correspondence, begging the indulgence of a foreign agent, to whom she explained that she "had been compelled to put aside all those things that could wait and some of those that could not." Her husband spent much of his last Wellesley semester in bed, with what proved a tenacious case of bronchitis. His mood was not improved by the realization that there would be no western butterfly expeditions that summer because of the move to Ithaca.

Bed was of course one of Nabokov's preferred studios. Despite or because of the convalescence, these proved prolific months. He had been toying again with an autobiography, a project he had described to a Doubleday editor in 1946 as an unusual one: "It will be a sequence of short essay-like bits, which suddenly gathering momentum will form something weird and dynamic: innocent-looking ingredients of a quite unexpected brew." The provisional title was "The Person in Question." The first of these "essay-like bits" to be composed directly in English appeared in *The New Yorker* in January 1948; the Wellesley administration doubtless chafed at the enthusiastic response to them. Nor were the pieces of what would become *Speak, Memory* Nabokov's only project in the last Wellesley year. He had submitted the first completed chapter of the memoir from Estes Park, Colorado, in the course of a trip Véra hugely enjoyed, despite the fact that she had been irritated not to be able to find a copy of the *Saturday Review* anywhere in the region. Also in Estes Park her husband was busily at work on "a short novel about a man who liked little girls."

Over these months a little tug-of-war went on with the Cornell administrators, eager to put their new recruit to the greatest possible use. Speaking for the search committee, the Russian historian Marc Szeftel attempted—as had others before him—to lasso Nabokov into teaching a survey course in literature. He did so in vain. (Although it had been part of the original employment proposal, Nabokov would nearly have to be blackmailed into teaching it later.) He proved equally unavailable when asked to assist with

the preparation of Russian-language teaching materials before the fall semester. Instead he attempted to direct a little lassoing of his own: "Possibly
my wife, who is also a teacher of Russian, can be of help to you," he suggested
to Milton Cowan, the director of Cornell's Division of Modern Languages, in
a letter Véra edited, tempering her husband's fierce reaction to what would
have amounted to a lucrative few hours' work. Vladimir made a series of
efforts to find a Russian position for her at the university. Whether Véra
wanted a job is unclear; generally she had an enormous capacity but no great
ambition for work. If she took a job they made more money, and if their finances were healthier Vladimir could write more, and if Vladimir could
write more, they were both happier. Meanwhile at Cornell others were making more far-fetched claims for Véra's talents. The housing situation in
Ithaca was tight; with difficulty, Morris Bishop, who had been partly responsible for the Cornell appointment, located a spacious, simple home on an acre
of land for his new colleague. He testified to its owners that "scrubbing was
Mrs. Nabokov's joy." Privately he suggested to his new friends that they find
a cleaning lady.

"The horrible packing process is beginning," Vladimir moaned in mid-
June. "Don't know whether we will take our furniture with us, or whether
we will burn it," he added, perfectly enunciating the couple's relationship to
the material world. (Apart from the upright piano on which Véra played
simple arrangements of arias for Dmitri, the unloved furniture remained in
Cambridge.) Vladimir attempted to assist with the process but proved so useless he was chased from the house by an exasperated Véra, who rang Sylvia
Berkman at about ten in the morning and asked if she might entrust her husband to her. "I will never get this place cleaned out if he stays here," she
sighed. Vladimir turned up at Berkman's address with a carton of butterflies,
which he hoped she might store for him, as she did. Having solved this wor-
risome problem to his satisfaction, he called Véra. He called her again about
fifteen minutes later, "to see how she was getting on"; after another fifteen
minutes he called again, to ask if she needed help. Finally Véra asked that her
husband be kept from the telephone. He was entrusted to Berkman's sofa,
where he sat talking, confiding that he divided literature into two familiar
categories: "the books I wish I had written, and the books I have written."
Before the departure—fate curiously mimicking itself, or *The Gift*—Véra realized that she had misplaced the key to the Ithaca house. "Do you think I
should tell Vladimir about it?" she pressed Berkman, in a state of some agitation. Berkman counseled her against doing so; it would do no good for
Vladimir to worry for ten hours about something he could not remedy. Véra
held on to her uncomfortable secret. Once again she was heading toward a

door that she alone believed—with reason—to be closed. None of her dis-
quiet showed. Apart from the incident at the Port of New York, Dmitri
Nabokov does not remember his mother ever having been bewildered. We
never know what will happen beyond the skyline of the last page of *The Gift,*
how Zina and Fyodor will grasp the happiness for which Fyodor has for so
many pages been priming himself, to which a missing set of keys bars his
way. We do know how Vladimir and Véra Nabokov arrived in Ithaca, the secure post on which they had so long set their sights. Breaking and entering,
they eased into 957 East State Street as they might have in a fictional version:
by locating an open window, through which one of them climbed.

✳ 5 ✳

NABOKOV 101

One thing is essential: Whenever talented people approach art with the sole idea of serving it sincerely to the utmost measure of their ability, the result is always gratifying.

—NABOKOV, *LECTURES ON RUSSIAN LITERATURE*

1

Nearly all of the characters for which Nabokov is best remembered—Lolita and Humbert, Pnin, Shade and Kinbote, the Vladimir Nabokov of *Speak, Memory*—were born or partially bred in Ithaca. The same is true of the character he was to create for and with his wife, and by which she was in large part to be remembered.* She would return the compliment later, constructing a persona who was neither Vladimir Vladimirovich Nabokov, nor V. Sirin, nor Professor Nabokov, nor the author of *Lolita,* but "VN," a monument unto itself, the supreme designation in a lifetime of anagrammatic pseudonyms. The real life of Mrs. Vladimir Nabokov—or someone who conducted her correspondence as Mrs. Vladimir Nabokov, a formula Véra arrived at only gradually—begins on the other side of that obliging window on East State Street. It began as do all American lives, with driving lessons.

Within days of the arrival in Ithaca, Véra found her way to Burton Jacoby, a colorful and enterprising mechanic at the W. T. Pritchard Garage. Jacoby offered driving instruction, a sideline that allowed him an occasional

---

* The two facts are related. Véra's having assumed the role she did in Ithaca allowed her husband the time to write as he had not done since the first years of their marriage.

Véra Nabokov's mother, Slava Borisovna Feigin, at the time of her marriage in 1899.

Evsei Lazarevich Slonim, in his student days, St. Petersburg.

Evsei Slonim with his daughters Véra (left) and Lena, on a summer estate, probably near Riga, about 1904.

Slonim with his daughters, Véra (left) and Lena, c. 1909.

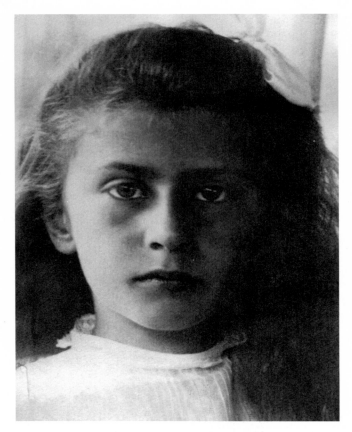

Véra Evseevna Slonim, c. 1909.

Véra and Lena Slonim on the beach at Sestroretsk, on the Gulf of Finland, c. 1909.

The extended family, on a summer holiday, about 1909. Véra's maternal grandmother sits in the middle row, far left. Véra's mother is at her side, next to Lena and Véra. Evsei Slonim stands behind his parents, Lazar and Bela Slonim, at right.

Lena (left) and Véra in Italian folk costume, 1911.

Véra in Constantinople, April 18, 1920. Six months earlier she had made the trip across the Black Sea that her husband would borrow for the hero of *Glory*. She never saw Russia again.

Vladimir Nabokov, c. 1923.

Svetlana Siewert, a year before her engagement to Nabokov.

Véra Slonim in Berlin's Tiergarten, probably several months after having met her future husband, 1923.

The Nabokovs on vacation in Krummhübel, in the mountains along what is today the Polish-Czech border, Christmas 1925. "I went flying on skis," Vladimir reported afterward. Never having skied before, Véra fared less well, lending a fall— along with the photographer's narrow shadow, and the beige dress (left)—to *King, Queen, Knave.*

Véra at Saint Blasien, 1926.

The Nabokovs on the beach, probably July 1926.

Portrait of the artist's wife in a mirror, Berlin, mid-1930s.

Vladimir and Dmitri in Menton, France, December 1937, the month Nabokov asked Irina Guadanini to return his love letters. They contained mostly fictions, he claimed.

Irina Guadanini.

Sonia Slonim, 1930s.

Lena Slonim Massalsky, 1930s.

Zinaida Shakhovskoy with the Nabokovs, Menton, France, 1938.

AMERICA

Véra and Vladimir on their first trip across America, summer 1941.

Véra and Dmitri in Yosemite National Park with Lisbet and Bertrand Thompson, 1941. The Studebaker is the one in which the Thompsons had chauffeured the Nabokovs around the Riviera in the late 1930s.

Craigie Circle, Cambridge, c. 1942.

A Wellesley College tea, Phi Sigma House, 1942.

Katherine Reese Peebles, splendidly positioned to testify of her Russian professor, "He did like young girls. Just not little girls."

Véra and Dmitri along Trail Ridge Road, Colorado, 1947.

Nantucket, 1945.

On Ithaca's East Seneca Street, in the yard in which *Lolita* was nearly destroyed, c. 1951.

Véra Nabokov's permit to carry a .38. To the authorities she submitted a simple reason for carrying the handgun: "For protection while travelling in isolated parts of the country in the course of entomological research."

Ithaca, September 1958. Paraphrasing the narrator of *Sebastian Knight,* Nabokov explained the latter part of his composition process: "Well, after that my very kind and patient wife, she sits down at her typewriter and I, I dictate, I dictate off the cards to her, making some changes and very often, very often, discussing this or that. She might say, 'Oh you can't say that, you can't say that.' 'Well, let's see, perhaps I can change it.'"

Ithaca, September 1958. "I don't like to be photographed (might have enjoyed it if it all had happened some 15 years ago, at least), but it is even more of a nuisance to refuse unless the refusal is accepted at once," Véra grumbled that fall.

The author of *Lolita* and his wife arrive in Paris in October 1959 with their ten bags. "Madame Nabokov is 38 Years Older than the Nymphet Lolita," screeched the headlines.

London, 1959, the day after Weidenfeld's triumphant *Lolita* reception.

The Mondadori reception for *Lolita,* Milan, December 1959.

Filippa Rolf, the Swedish poet whom the Nabokovs took under their wing for two weeks in 1961, a visit that would haunt them all later. "They are mating like butterflies behind any bush right in the middle of the conversation, and they separate so quickly that one doesn't notice until later," Rolf observed of the couple during her stay.

The Nabokovs photographed by Rolf, the flash in the mirror, Nice, 1961. "She is a fine decoration in an armchair," concluded Rolf of Mrs. Nabokov.

Véra with twenty-seven-year-old Dmitri, Villars, Switzerland, summer 1961.

Véra as Dmitri remembers her, Villars, 1961.

Véra preparing Vladimir for a photo shoot, 1964.

Champex, Switzerland. With or without their equipment, the Nabokovs' routine elicited frequent tennis metaphors. "It was almost as if they played verbal tennis with each other. He hit the ball—and back it flew," recalled Robert Boyle.

Véra in her *Lolita* glasses, poolside at the Montreux Palace, 1966.

March 1976, Vevey, Switzerland.

Montreux Palace, 1964. Nabokov's appraisal: "Most of my works have been dedicated to my wife and her picture has often been reproduced by some mysterious means of reflected color in the inner mirrors of my books."

commission on the sale of a car. By mid-July Véra was the proud owner of a beige 1940 Plymouth, a four-door sedan that was by all accounts nearing the end of its useful life when she purchased it, on the installment plan. Behind the wheel she proved a quick study: Jacoby found her an outstanding pupil, "always so kind and gracious." He was not alone in commending her new talent; Vladimir announced in September that Véra had bought a car and learned to drive in a remarkably short time. Self-interest may have brightened his admiration: Cornell's sumptuous campus sits at the top of a steep hill, cut through with gorges and streams and waterfalls. Its scenery is spectacular, but the grade can be steep. On their arrival in hilly Ithaca it had been decided that a car would be a necessity, despite the excellent public buses. "One of us had better learn to drive," went the thinking; Vladimir appears to have been relieved that it was not he. Véra knew her husband's peccadilloes as well as his capabilities—when he provided an address it was almost guaranteed to be an approximate or an obsolete one—and she continued to worry about his health through the fall. She had looked into driving instruction in New York; she appears to have been eager to take the wheel.

Over the course of the first year in Ithaca, Véra nonetheless encouraged Vladimir in a few halfhearted attempts to master this American sport. "It's not very hard," she assured him. Practically speaking they would both need to drive if they were to head west on a long trip together. The task of teaching Nabokov fell to one of his students, a highly articulate senior named Dick Keegan, whom he immediately befriended, either for his own considerable charms or for those of his gray Dodge coupe. Keegan discovered that driving was not difficult for Nabokov. It was virtually impossible for him. He had very little interest in focusing on the road; he insisted that he was terrified of sliding behind the wheel. He distrusted cars, unsurprising in a man who claimed to be intimidated by electrical pencil sharpeners but odd all the same for the author of the most original road novel ever written. Keegan noticed that even in the passenger seat his student professor had a tendency to forget he had requested a destination as soon as he was delivered to it. This did not prevent Nabokov from announcing annually, long after the move from Ithaca, that this year, at last, he planned to learn to drive. He never did.*

By choice and by default, Véra became the designated driver. For a variety of reasons the task was not simple. As Nabokov described it just after the beginning of the fall semester, Véra "carts around her non-driving but advice-

---

* Nor did this prevent him from entering into a spirited exchange with Wilson as to where the accent falls in the word "automobile," metrically speaking.

giving husband." He wondered mischievously why she resented his sitting at her side, offering up various suggestions at street corners; he seemed only dimly aware that marriages have foundered on less. Having spent a disappointing year at St. Mark's, fourteen-year-old Dmitri was enrolled in the Holderness School for the fall of 1948. As a new driver, Véra felt uneasy making the four-hundred-mile trip to and from Plymouth, New Hampshire, alone. She also felt uneasy leaving Dmitri, whose absences weighed heavily on both parents. Burton Jacoby accompanied her so as to share the driving; Vladimir stayed home. For the next few summers intermittently successful attempts were made to recruit a friend or a student to join the family on its western excursions. Accustomed to advertisements for himself, Nabokov's students grew accustomed to his advertisements for a pinch-hitting driver. In June 1949, at the end of his junior year, Richard Buxbaum accompanied the family to Salt Lake City, where Vladimir had been invited to lecture at a writers' conference. The trip got off to a terrifying start. In western New York State Véra drove into the dead-man's lane in the middle of the highway to pass, but found herself facing a truck carrying a combine, the chute of which extended into the lane. Buxbaum reflexively reached for the steering wheel; the vehicles missed each other by a matter of inches. Chilled, Véra pulled over. She suggested quietly that it might be better if Buxbaum drove.*

Parking was never her strong suit. Early in the 1948 fall semester the couple moved from their summer lodgings to a handsome home with a beautifully groomed lawn on East Seneca Street. In the newly refurbished attic apartment lived a law student and his young wife, who may have had some idea of Mrs. Nabokov's confidence behind the wheel when Véra asked if Gert Croghan might accompany her on a Boston trip. This did not prepare Harold Croghan for the sight that greeted him when he looked out his third-floor window one sunny afternoon that winter. The house stood on a steep double lot at the corner of Quarry and Seneca streets; Véra had managed to maneuver the Plymouth into an awkward position on the hill, essentially blocking all four corners of the intersection. He watched the curious scene for a few minutes before making his way downstairs. "Why don't you call the police?" he suggested, refusing Véra's invitation to take the wheel. Twenty-four-year-old Croghan had been a Marine platoon commander; he did not

---

* Again this summer the Nabokovs were unwitting characters in someone else's drama. Having spent part of August at a Jackson Hole, Wyoming, guest ranch that was under government surveillance, they made a walk-on role in FBI reports as "an elderly man and his wife, both of whom spoke with a pronounced accent." Discreet inquiries were made, in Wyoming and at Cornell, where FBI agents were assured that Nabokov's reputation was excellent, that the family did not qualify as subversives.

habitually shy from a challenge. Neither did he think it within even his powers to liberate the Plymouth from its position. "It would have taken a heli-
copter," he remembers. The lateral parking device Véra had invented in
Berlin would have come in handy now; this was one predicament she seems
to have anticipated. A neighbor on East Seneca Street recalls Véra pulling up
at the foot of the hill, which could be terrifyingly slippery in winter. In his estimation, "It looked like an uneasy truce between her and the car."

Generally however, she drove too well, which is to say with a liberal interpretation of the speed limit. "And pray, find me a Russian who does not
care for fast driving?" Gogol reminds us, not to be contradicted by Véra
Nabokov. At least one Massachusetts policeman observed as much when
Véra chauffeured her husband to Boston for extensive dental work at the
end of the 1950 spring semester. Vladimir quipped that they returned to
Ithaca "minus my teeth and the Massachusetts part of her license." "She did
not stop when a policeman in a car signaled to her and then he followed us
for ten minutes and finally, at 70 miles per hour, crowded us to the curb," he
elaborated to Wilson, who probably had an easier time than the officer
believing why this distinguished-looking white-haired woman had led a
high-speed chase to a screeching conclusion: She had not understood the
policeman wanted her to stop. This was one thing Burton Jacoby had not
thought to teach her. She was a supremely law-abiding citizen in general—
Dmitri's leisurely approach to his traffic violations would disturb her
greatly—but the speed limit did prove immoderately low. Her husband enjoyed teasing her about this. He was always happy to pronounce his wife a
demon driver.

Did she enjoy the driving, or was she again the victim of her own competence? Regularly she solicited advice about cars from friends; she engaged
in a fair amount of automotive window-shopping. For one very brief moment she cast herself as a car salesman, attempting to assist Dmitri in selling
an Italian specialty car to one of her husband's publishers. "Iso-Rivolta is not
a sports car but a very elegant sedan. It has a marvelous American motor in
combination with a beautiful Italian carrosserie, and the smoothest run I
have ever seen," she wrote glowingly. In her seventies, she asserted proudly
that she was the family driver. A visitor found that in her eighties she lit up
when he mentioned the cross-country excursions. "I *loved* driving the car,"
she told him, a smile spreading across her face. Her husband boasted that in
the course of the Cornell years his wife had driven him more than 150,000
miles, all over North America; in one letter she became "my heroic wife
who drove me through the floods and storms of Kansas" for the sake of a
butterfly specimen. Véra took a slightly different view of this heroism, or at

least did when writing to an old friend in 1962: "I have upwards of 200,000 miles under my belt, but each time I get behind the wheel I hand my soul over to God."

She genuinely did enjoy the drama of the open road, the visual thrill of the moving landscape, the moments of high adventure. Vladimir recorded a number of her casual roadside comments in his diary, offering a sense of what it was like to be in a car with Véra: "My Oldsmobile gobbles up the miles like a fakir does fire. Oh look over there, that tree is squatting on all fours." "The little flames of the autos are like one candle lighting another in the dusk." "Oh, the sunlight! I can see the ignition key reflected in the window again," she exulted, an observation that found its way directly into *Lolita*. (For that novel she compiled an inventory of services to which a car submits at a tune-up, with which to send Humbert and Lolita back on the road, from Beardsley.) With zest she described having picked their way west amid thunderstorms and tornadoes, "and a few 'dust devils' which are unpleasant little *tourbillons* of sand which are supposed occasionally to 'flip a few cars over.' " She recalled an "apocaliptic [*sic*] traffic jam" in Houston. The two-week drive to Mount Carmel, Utah, proved particularly rich in adventure. "The most exciting thing was when this young hooligan fired a cobblestone into our windshield. We were sprayed with glass dust, and the hole as the size of a fist, but the cobblestone fortunately hit below eye level and fell to my feet. The state trooper took a photo of the cobblestone, the broken windshield and of Volodya sitting behind the glass but said there was nothing he could do, because the offender was a minor," she reported animatedly, after an unscheduled stop in Missouri, where a new windshield was installed. Her capacity for dramatics could be aroused by these physical adventures where it was more often dampened elsewhere. Having dropped Dmitri off in New Hampshire after the 1950 Thanksgiving vacation, the Nabokovs drove most of the way toward Ithaca without incident. They then headed "through the grey wall of a storm, sometimes hydroplaning or fishtailing because it was so slippery," Vladimir wrote the Hessens. "There was a moment when I said to Véra, 'You're going to drive off into the ditch,' and she didn't reply." In the margin Véra took issue not with the backseat driving but with her husband's choice of words. "It wasn't a ditch," she clarified, "but a terrible ravine."

The chauffeuring around Ithaca was less theatrical, at least to the Nabokovs. To nearly everyone else it offered some degree of spectacle. At first grudgingly and soon with good humor, Dick Keegan provided much of Nabokov's transportation for the first academic year. Véra was busy settling into the Seneca Street house, a four-bedroom home she and Vladimir found uncomfortably large, even with the series of boarders they took in. For two trimesters of the 1948–49 academic year, she also taught high school French at the Cascadilla School, a private school on the edge of campus. Keegan understood that Véra might not have proved as willing as was he to transport Vladimir to the liquor store; on several occasions she cornered her husband's driver to ask if he had taken him to buy cigarettes, which, indeed, Keegan had. Nabokov was still chain-smoking, intermittently. Véra took over at the wheel after the spring of 1949, when Keegan had graduated, when she was more confident of her abilities, and when the couple rented a series of homes farther afield than East Seneca Street. The chauffeuring put her on campus more than she had been before. And so the archetypal symbol of independence—in succession a Plymouth, an Oldsmobile, a used Buick Special, a new Buick—was to involve her more closely yet in her husband's work. Rarely was Vladimir seen on campus without Véra; rarely was Véra sighted at the grocery store without Vladimir. "Inseparable, self-sufficient, they form a multitude of two," a former student and future critic remembered. The attention-getting part was the distribution of labor. More than a few heads turned when, in the supermarket parking lot, Véra set her bagged groceries down in the snow while she shuffled for her keys, then loaded the trunk. In the car her husband sat immobile, oblivious. A similar routine was observed during a move, when Nabokov made his way into a new home carrying a chess set and a small lamp. Véra followed with two bulky suitcases. The intrepid Russian woman with the queenly carriage and the halo of white hair who made heads turn all over campus soon developed a reputation for waiting on her husband hand and foot.

Generally it was a flawless performance. A student who escaped a few minutes' of a heavy snowstorm by cutting through Goldwin Smith Hall, where Nabokov kept his office and usually lectured, noted one occasion on which it was not. Inside the doors at one end of the building stood Vladimir, tapping his foot. At the other end of the north-south corridor, at the far set of doors, stood a patient Véra, a pair of her husband's galoshes in hand. On a snowy day outside of *Pale Fire*'s Parthenocissus Hall the poet John Shade waits for Mrs. Shade to fetch him. "Wives, Mr. Shade, are forgetful," Kinbote reminds Shade, luring him into his car. This one was not: Véra rarely kept her husband waiting, if only for the good reason that she was customarily with him in the first place. And when he got home it was she who kept track of his responsibilities. Keegan admired her ability to order the details of both of their lives. "Did you grade the papers you got last Tuesday?" she asked her husband on one occasion, after Keegan had delivered him from campus. Nabokov admitted that he had not. "Well, I did some of them for you," Véra conceded. On a similar occasion she asserted, "Vladimir sometimes forgets things, but we're like a good rugby team. We don't have much practice, so we just use brute strength."

A fair amount of brute strength was required on her part during the early Cornell years. The initial months were happy ones: Ithaca was gorgeous, lush and green, home even to an occasional butterfly of interest. Véra was a walker; she strolled happily through Collegetown, to Stewart Park; she admired Ithaca's crystalline gorges and waterfalls. Dmitri settled in quickly at Holderness, a relief to his mother. Nabokov's enrollments were low and his schedule far from exhausting. "This is a genuine tranquil professorship, and not some preposterous Harvard + Wellesley combination," he announced, a touch prematurely. The Nabokovs fell into the welcoming arms of Morris Bishop and his wife, Alison, who became their only close friends at Cornell. To his sister Vladimir explained the decision to send Dmitri away to school (the "hooligan element" elsewhere, and the language instruction): "We miss him, and Véra and I live quietly and very, very happily." He was able to work throughout the winter, finishing the seventh installment of his memoir early in February. One semester later the demands of academic life and of the university began to grate, especially as they appeared disproportionate to the financial rewards. Nabokov had been at Cornell for five months when he wrote the head of the Literature Division that he could not make do on his present salary, an appeal he repeated to a higher authority several months later.* As he lobbied strenuously for a raise he wrote an émigré friend in New York that teaching was, of course, his last priority. He made no secret of this on campus. Véra did a fair amount of goading, not about his work but about his university commitments. She urged her husband to attend the faculty receptions she would later deny he had ever attended. "You *must* go," she advised, insisting when he balked.† On one occasion when he decided his personal honor stood between him and a holiday reception, she went instead. Probably this was Christmas 1951. Marc Szeftel was surprised to find Mrs. Nabokov at the home of a professor whose department's policies were not to her husband's (or her) liking. "Everything has its limits," she explained. It

---

* In one of his periodic assaults on his administrators, he complained in particular of the amount Seneca Street was costing him. The rent was in the vicinity of $150 a month; Nabokov was earning $5000, or after deductions, about $4200 a year. Neither Véra nor Vladimir was spendthrift, but Dmitri's tuition claimed one third of their income, and the couple never lived on anything resembling a budget. The only expense that might have been considered an extravagance was the summer trip west, an annual rite during the Cornell years.

† He did not overextend himself fitting in at such affairs. On one occasion he turned to a visiting professor to whom he had not been introduced and asked, "Will you tell me why in the United States they bury their universities in forests?" He liked to regale friends with his story of an encounter with a plump new addition to the faculty who introduced herself with, "I am the new professor of ice-cream making."

could not have escaped her notice that her husband now held the kind of position for which he had been vying since 1936. She knew it far beneath his abilities, but she also knew it to be necessary.

They dealt with his chafing at the job—and his sense of its slim rewards—differently. Nabokov availed himself of every opportunity to find a better position elsewhere. Before the first Ithaca year was out, he received a fan letter from the wife of a Baltimore professor, who had admired his *New Yorker* pieces. "I envy you for basking in the mellow climate of Johns Hopkins. The elements here are rough and raw. Is there a Russian department at your college?" replied Vladimir, masquerading as Véra. By 1950 he was sending out confidential feelers to friends at Harvard and Stanford. He made repeated assaults on his superiors, on one occasion rehearsing his arguments in his diary. The distributor of paychecks braced himself for Nabokov's weekly requests for advances on his salary, an unorthodox request in the academic context. At the same time attempts to involve him further in the development of the curriculum proved futile. When the dean to whom he carried his salary protests inquired if he might assist Szeftel in developing Cornell's Russian Studies program his initial response was quick and blunt: "I want to warn you that I am a hopelessly poor organizer with no practical sense whatsoever so that my participation in any committee would be, I am afraid, pretty worthless. I am moreover ridiculously absent-minded and unless I am doing some research work of my own, my mind is apt to wander in a most annoying (to others) fashion." He—or Véra—toned down the response before sending it on to the dean of the College of Arts and Sciences, but the protests of helplessness kept him as far from academic committees as they did from the steering wheel of a car.

He made equally energetic efforts to have Véra hired as an instructor of Russian. These came to naught, officially because enrollments were too low to justify additions to the staff, unofficially because Véra's Russian "was deemed 'too literary' and not 'contemporary enough.' " She enjoyed only a brief career as a language instructor. Cornell's language teachers at the time were largely drill instructors, meant to impress set phrases on their students' memories. Véra had no respect for the system or its practitioners; she griped to the Russian-born Szeftel of the prominent linguist with whom she worked, "You just wait, Fairbanks . . . will transform Russian in such a way that soon you and I will cease to understand it!" Some on campus, including Milton Cowan, the head of Cornell's languages empire, credited Véra with having poisoned her husband's mind against the Division of Modern Languages and linguistics in general, a hostility that makes itself felt in *Pnin*. She did not need to poison Vladimir's mind, already poisoned against Cornell's approach, but she did voice her dissatisfaction. She may have been quite out-spoken about this. In the first few years in Ithaca she worked in both the German and French Departments, a career on which she offered no comment save to say that she left the German post after several weeks, and that "the French gave her notice." When she groused later about Cornell language instruction she employed virtually the same words as does a character in *Pnin,* who may have been taking his words out of her mouth. Both noted that the university "used whoever was at hand to teach languages provided they kept one lesson ahead of the students."

She had her work cut out for her propping up the reluctant professor. It could be argued that a man accustomed to a valet has an even greater need for a wife; one friend of the couple, commenting on Vladimir's immense charm, noted that he had a very intimate way of approaching women, as if to enchant them entirely so as to be able to ask if they might do his laundry. In Véra he had found someone who did not begrudge him the mileage he wrung out of his real and learned helplessness, the special dispensations he was accorded for claiming his hands—the same hands that could nimbly manipulate a butterfly specimen under a microscope—were "limp fools." She rose to the challenges, as relieved to be obscured in the act of doing so as she was delighted to be of service. Her husband detached himself from various responsibilities; she assumed the responsibilities, but dismissed herself. It snows with conviction in south-central New York State, enough so that a good half hour could be required to liberate a car on a midwinter morning. Or so Nabokov complained, offering up the inconvenience as a primary reason for leaving Cornell. Doing so three times a week had become too difficult for him. Véra was at once more precise—and more diffident—when Boyd described the finger-freezing ordeals. "Nabokov never scraped snow," she corrected him, omitting to volunteer who, precisely, had. The stupefied neighbors reported it had been she.

One thing she did not do on East Seneca Street was clean house. She finally got her cleaning woman, in the form of a gentle, boyishly good-looking junior who lived in the basement apartment next door, a barberry hedge away. On his landlady's recommendation, Robert Ruebman was hired for the job, at eighty-five cents an hour. On Tuesday afternoons the eighteen-year-old English major dusted and vacuumed and cleaned bathrooms, a routine that was interrupted by the snack Véra provided for him. Along with the open-faced ham sandwich, the milk and cookies, she offered occasional advertisements for her husband's courses. She did not feel he could afford to miss them. Ruebman would mow the lawn, polish the car, seal the floorboards, clean the boarder's room, cash a check at the Triangle Bookstore. Véra appears to have been very fond of him; he found her crisp but delight-ful, if, instinctively, as foreign as did the rest of the neighbors. Spontaneously, and for no particular reason, he asked in German if he could do anything else on his way out one afternoon. "*Sonst noch was?*" Véra repeated, and laughed, and said "No."

At Cornell generally she dealt with her husband's hesitations as she had with the driving. "If he had office hours, he kept them secret," recalled one student. The few who delved further into the mystery found Véra, or both Nabokovs, at the office. His mind was still on the unfinished page. So was hers, but the concern manifested itself differently. Increasingly the marriage evolved into a tale of two marriages, a port for him, a career for her. Her ca-pability was matched only by his capacity for ignoring everything that did not concern his own work. In early 1950 it was more than broadly hinted to Nabokov that his requests for a salary adjustment might fall on more sym-pathetic ears if he would consent to teach the European Literature class he had wriggled out of earlier. Against his will and with Véra's help, he braced himself for the course for which he would be best remembered, Literature 311–312, which he began teaching in September 1950. Still he railed against his wages, complaining that he earned less than a constable or the chief of a fire brigade.* His enchantment with Cornell hardly increased when he learned that, for a constable's wages, he was teaching in a fictitious depart-ment. After two years in Ithaca and having adorned his letterhead appropri-ately, he discovered that he could not be chairman of the Russian Department for the simple reason that that department was a figment of his imagination. (Cornell was under the impression—one the dean of the College of Arts and Sciences stiffly shared with Nabokov in May 1950—that they had in their employ an associate professor of Russian, a member of the Literature Divi-sion.) Partially because of this little contretemps, in the spring of 1951 he was transferred for administrative purposes to the Department of Romance Lit-erature, headed by the ebullient, highly cultivated Morris Bishop. He taught no courses in the department, where he was essentially parked because there was no place for him elsewhere, and because Bishop was delighted to have him. Afterward faculty decisions concerning Nabokov were taken with "a touch of almost amused generosity." In short the cossetting continued, which

---

* Again Véra fought truth with fact. When Field wrote that Vladimir felt "he worked for the wages of a provincial peasant," Véra riposted, "N. did not know how much a peasant earns, especially a 'provincial peasant.' " This too was certainly true.

is another way of saying that the petulance paid off.* The citizens of Ithaca could only have been relieved he was not driving on their streets.† The faculty could only have been relieved to have seen little of him at their meetings. After sitting in on a visiting scholar's French Literature course in 1949, he could barely contain his obloquy. He assured Keegan and his classmate Joyce Brothers that they had earned their degrees simply by *enduring* Professor Wolfe's lectures. At the end of the semester he marched into the dean's office and insisted that all the grades be raised by 30 points. On further thought, everyone in the course should receive a 100—minus five points for having been so dim-witted as to have sat through the class for an entire semester.

2

"It is fine that you are liking it up there, and I have heard from a number of Cornell people that you two are an enormous success," Laughlin wrote Véra in the fall of 1948. In this case, the truth was in the pronouns. Being Professor Nabokov was not a game Vladimir could have played, as he played it in Ithaca, alone. With varying degrees of resentment, family members grew accustomed to hearing from Vladimir via Véra. For a good decade her letters to her sister-in-law began with apologies that, yet again, she was in charge of answering Elena's missive. (At the end of the decade she had not stopped writing, but she had stopped apologizing.) Often this put Véra in the uncomfortable position of having to protest her husband's love for his sister, something that only a letter in his own hand could have decisively proved. In Russian Véra attempted to explain the correspondence-by-proxy to the patient Elena:

> It is foolish of you to doubt Volodya's love for and interest in you. He is very glad to receive your letters and always sincerely intends to answer them immediately, but the entire trouble is that he is a writer, that he has a passionate need to write his own literary things. In the meantime a mass of his time is wasted on university work that is tedious for him,

---

* To Katharine White after a short editorial tug-of-war Nabokov summed up his mnemonic talents, not the conventional ones for a university professor: "As you have probably noticed I often make mistakes when recalling names, titles of books, numbers; but I very seldom err when recollecting colors."
† When his student showed more interest in dreaming up names for new models of cars—Wouldn't "Avatar" be lovely?—Dick Keegan conceded defeat. "It's a good thing you don't drive; you'd end up in a ditch," he informed his pupil. "Touché, Mr. Keegan," replied Nabokov. Dmitri seconded the motion years later. "I wouldn't want to see him driving in the mountains, or worse, in the center of Milan, in a moment of artistic inspiration," he warned an Italian journalist.

and so little time remains for his writing that he is forever putting off everything else. He doesn't read business letters at all, sometimes he'll look through them; he doesn't want to give any thought to any kind of business decisions. . . . I'm the one who must answer them. Taking advantage of the fact that a typewriter has no handwriting, I often write business correspondence in his name, and he signs it. Sometimes this can be very difficult for me. He receives an enormous amount of mail. By the way, we have an entire folder of letters from "fans" whom we don't know from Adam, and occasionally [letters] from the discontented. That sort of thing is very customary here.

Zinaida Shakhovskoy, who had so often championed the Nabokovs in Europe, was less indulgent of this habit than was Elena Sikorski. After the first Cornell semester Véra thanked Shakhovskoy for her letter. Among a number of other points, Vladimir had wanted to say "1) that he was very glad to get your letter, that he lost it (together with the address) while moving . . . 2) that he is asking me to reply to you, since he is afraid that by the time he gets a free minute, your letter will again sail irretrievably into the folders of 'unanswered letters.' " The correspondence was one of the first after the war, which had been immensely difficult for the Shakhovskoy family; especially after the years of assistance, a letter from Nabokov's wife was not what Zinaida considered a proper response. Her sister Natalie, to whom the Nabokovs owed so many kindnesses in the New World, displayed more humor about the same routine. "Volodya has still never written me a letter in his life," she complained to Véra. Was he hoarding his autograph? If that was the case she promised to return the letter upon reading it. "That disgusting lazybones," she teased. "Verochka, all hope is on you."

The smart publisher—Laughlin was one—noticed early on that letters addressed directly to Véra met with responses more quickly; presumably they were spared the charade of the two in-boxes. Other friends adapted quickly to the routine, aware of the dubious authorship even of those letters signed by Nabokov. Roman Grynberg, a highly cultured publisher and businessman whom Vladimir had tutored in Paris and who lent money to the Nabokovs and the Wilsons throughout the 1940s and 1950s, knew how to get results. He dispatched an urgent envelope to Ithaca in March 1949: "Dear Véra and Volodya, I am writing you both in order to get an answer (Véra to the side: 'what a tricky man'). I really need answers." Wilson simply glided from addressing Véra to addressing Vladimir, moving by the second paragraph of one "Dear Véra" letter to an analysis of "your satire" in "The Vane Sisters." Where style is signature the closing fillip fooled no one: Véra made little attempt to sound like her husband on the page, even while he regularly masqueraded as her, a trick that could be accomplished with a little adjectival drainage. The two voices could not be more different; Véra was direct and flinty while her husband was impudent in a deeply humorous way. In no language did she share his verbal velvet on the page. One early routine involved Véra drafting a letter, Vladimir editing it, Véra typing it, Vladimir signing it. Documents that evolved in this fashion generally became more pointed as they materialized. To Harold and Gert Croghan the Nabokovs complained bitterly of the disturbances from the attic apartment. In an early Seneca Street note Vladimir commented, "I am afraid I must insist that at 11 p.m.—or at 11:30 at the latest—all loud talking, moving of furniture, etc. should cease." In a later missive, he deplored, in Véra's words, "the unfortunate sonic arrangement of this house."

Securing her insomniacal husband a decent night's sleep—or the Proustian silence he needed for composing—preoccupied Véra as much as the correspondence.* As she explained, "unsolicited sounds make him terribly nervous." The Croghans provided the whipping posts of the first Cornell years. The two lived in terror of their own footfalls; a vacuum cleaner or a Saturday afternoon opera provoked pounding from below. On a number of occasions a grim Véra appeared at the bottom of their stairs for an interrogation. The Croghans felt like "husband and wife serfs" as they stood before her to be reprimanded. (They were barely on speaking terms with the Nabokovs when Véra asked Gert Croghan if she might accompany her on a Boston trip.) One can only imagine the torments Véra must have suffered on her husband's behalf in all the motel rooms he lent to *Lolita,* with their various acrosonic intrusions. In October 1950, E. B. White appealed to Nabokov—through his wife, Katharine—for information on spiders; he was at work on a first draft of *Charlotte's Web.* Nabokov replied from Cambridge that he could not be of much help, a sentence he claimed that the hotel's plangent heating system had rudely interrupted. Ten days later Véra drove him to lecture in Toronto, where they descended at the best hotel the city had to offer. Vladimir heard only "slamming doors, shunting trains, the violent waterfall of one's neighbour's toilet." It was Humbert Humbert who noted that "There is nothing louder than an American hotel," but it was Nabokov, for whom nothing was quiet enough, who said it first. "I have no illusions about hotels in this hemisphere," he wailed from Toronto's Royal York. They were for drunken sales-

---

* In this she had a soul mate in Mrs. Thomas Carlyle. Having spent a Sisyphean day silencing the world for her husband's sake, Jane Carlyle continued to do so in her dreams.

men, "and not for the weary poet (or the weary poet's wife, says Véra)." He had yet to deliver his Chekhov lecture. Véra, on the other hand, had spent the day driving—and part of the evening fixing a flat tire in the dark, by the side of the road.

Had she not been on hand to complain that her husband was not sleeping, her presence might well have gone unnoticed. From a later Cornell address Véra wrote urgently to the home's owners, on sabbatical in Ann Arbor. Before leaving Ithaca the couple had had their dog put to sleep. His legacy had survived him. "What can I do? The fleas are bothering my husband," pleaded Véra, whose skin must have crawled a little too. Even in her kindnesses, she feigned translucence. Probably in 1950, she made an early-morning excursion across Quarry Street to the home of an English department teaching fellow, his wife, and their three-year-old child. Through an upstairs window Frances Sampson saw Mrs. Nabokov approaching the doorstep with a wooden cart of blocks, presumably once Dmitri's. The delivery was intended for their daughter, playing on the steps. As young faculty the Sampsons were supremely conscious of rank; this felt "as if royalty had just stopped by to bestow a gift on a peasant." The blocks were discreetly entrusted to the child. The doorbell never rang.

Not only had the nomadic years left their mark, but Vladimir, anyway, never considered Cornell a permanent post. He confessed to a sort of superstition about settling, the idea that the purchase of a home was more or less an invitation for an avalanche to descend.* Carrying the concept of displaced persons to new heights, the couple famously moved from sabbatic house to sabbatic house over the years in Ithaca. Locating their next address and moving their affairs was Véra's responsibility. Generally Vladimir accompanied her on the initial inspections. She made the tour with her notebook in hand, he with his hands clasped behind his back. Explanations about furnaces, lawn care, security were referred to Véra, as, on one such tour, the laws of kashruth nearly were. "Oh yes, I know all about keeping kosher," exclaimed Véra brightly, proceeding to explain how a sullied piece of silverware can be redeemed by plunging it into the earth. Otherwise, especially in the early years, she had little contact either with the faculty or the faculty wives. Neither Nabokov was remotely clubbable, a word Vladimir spelled "club-babble." Véra belonged to none of the Ithaca "book clubs, bridge clubs, babble clubs." She did not even belong to the prestigious Drama Club, an association of

---

* As is clear from his *Lolita* screenplay, it was his belief that houses are struck by lightning and burn to the ground, a conviction that, given his past, was perhaps not unreasonable. Hotels proved no less combustible in his imagination once he had settled in one.

faculty wives which met on Friday evenings so as to relieve its participants of the obligation of entertaining for their husbands.

On Seneca Street, while Véra quieted the world around him, Nabokov wrote the remaining pages of the "autobiographical thingamabob" he had begun in mid-1948. Late that year Katharine White had written to Harper's president on her author's behalf about a book contract.* She could not speak highly enough of the five pieces *The New Yorker* had published. Nabokov's grasp of the idiosyncracies of English and White's grasp of the idiosyncracies of her author had improved in tandem; the cries the two emitted regularly had given way to a fond dialogue. While White admitted that fireworks still flared occasionally when Vladimir's command of idiomatic usage was questioned, she testified that working with him was a delight.† Nabokov was encouraged to apply for a fellowship the publisher sponsored, but was not granted the award because it was felt, confidentially, that while the work was of considerable distinction, it was unlikely to attract a considerable audience.‡ All the same Harper offered a contract for the book of memoirs, a contract with which the author had enough quibbles to set off alarm bells in the publisher's office. As an earlier editor had noted, "If anybody again ever tells me that a White Russian [*sic*] is not capable of reading a contract, I shall have evidence to the contrary." Nabokov mentioned having being taught by a lawyer friend to read agreements; all evidence points to that friend having been Véra. (It would have been difficult to find an American lawyer likely to object to the wording of a reprint clause on the grounds that—for example—a war might well be declared on the book's publication day.) After a protracted correspondence, an agreement was signed, in May of 1949.

It was fitting, if inconvenient, that as Nabokov made this foray into the past, the past took a few small steps toward him. As he and Véra ironed out the Harper contract, word came from Geneva that Elena Sikorski had run

---

* Nabokov's editor for the 1947 *Bend Sinister,* Allen Tate, had left Henry Holt and Company in early 1948, having fought valiantly for the novel and—before leaving—having confidentially advised Nabokov on what terms, if any at all, he should sell Holt his next book.

† As Nabokov recounted the skirmishes in part, *The New Yorker* had a habit of eliminating a favored word or two of his prose, because they were a "family magazine," or because the magazine "pessimistically thought that an unusual term might bother some of its less brainy readers. In the latter case, Mr. Nabokov did not always give in, and this resulted in some spirited fights." This was aside from what he quaintly referred to as "the question of the corrected grammar." It was also well after an early tussle that had so disturbed him—the manuscript in question became "Portrait of My Uncle"—that he claimed he was tempted to give up writing. At one such juncture he howled that he would prefer not to be published in the magazine at all appearing in "so carefully mutilated" a form.

‡ Nabokov would doubtless not have entered into a contract had he learned as much. He was told he was denied the award because he was not exactly a "beginning" writer, for whom the fellowship had been established.

into a familiar-seeming woman at church. She approached her; the woman had taken one look at her and exclaimed, "The eyes of Vladimir!" It was Svetlana, Nabokov's ex-fiancée of 1922. The two had a lovely visit, about which Elena wrote her brother, who exploded. He chastised his sister for having based her sense of the relationship on his youthful verse instead of on the reality, which had more to do with Svetlana's family and their "amiable feelings for our father's murderer, their bourgeois crudeness in ending the romance, and much else that I will one day tell you." There was clearly still much pain, still very close to the surface. Even in Pushkin's life Nabokov drew a vivid portrait on this account, squeezing a good deal of passion into an occasional note. Svetlana herself had written him directly in 1948, a letter he had ignored. Nor, relatedly or not, was this outburst the end of Svetlana. Vladimir was still dreaming of her as late as 1967.

Most of the benevolent female characters in Nabokov are women we barely see; inside or outside the parentheses, quickly, efficiently, and often in childbirth, they die. They fail to materialize even in the works that bear their name. The faithless, treacherous, obtuse women claim their roles front and center; the literature is full of simperers, sirens, underaged, willing, and un-willing sexpots. After a crowded adolescence and early adulthood, the life was full of one smartly but simply dressed wife, whose feelings about sex will never be known to us but whose sense of propriety, of loyalty, of honesty, in-formed every aspect of her existence. In the early days she was a nearly spec-tral presence: She was everywhere present and yet nowhere—even to the offending flea—visible. In *Speak, Memory* she accomplishes a parallel feat. Pages of the book are dedicated to early courtships and erotic attachments. Véra is named only in the index, a section of the book we are informed will "please the discerning." (And that was added to a later version.) She is more evident there than in the text, a disappearing act she would manage to reprise with her husband's biographers. In 1949, while at work on what were to be-come the last pages of the memoir, Nabokov notified Katharine White that the chapter in progress was to be addressed to Véra, in the second person.* We are in fact aware that someone else is in the room with us as early as Chapter 6, when incongruously—and not again for another sixty-six pages— he addresses an offstage "you" to whom we have not been introduced.† The identity of that person becomes obvious only in the last chapter of the work,

---

* He had used the device before, in several variations. Zina is evoked several times before her appearance in *The Gift,* even included in a plural "we" well before we know who inhabits that pronoun with our nar-rator.
† In 1966 Alfred Appel pointed out this inconsistency to Nabokov, who shrugged it off. The offstage ad-dress was not yet part of the text when the pages appeared, in their early form, in a June 1948 *New Yorker.*

although we are never formally introduced. (In the memoir's 1951 incarnation we do learn—later, and in the context of Nabokov's early romantic history—that 1925 was "the year I married my present wife," an odd locution. She never amounts to anything more specific than "my dear.")* She has no voice of her own. Nabokov speaks for her ("we shall never forget, you and I"), and to her ("you know, I still feel in my wrists certain echoes of the pram-pusher's knack"), and through her ("you questioned the right of a place to call itself a forest when it was so full of refuse"), and about her ("You always considered abominably trite, and not devoid of a particular Philistine flavor, the notion that small boys, in order to be delightful, should hate to wash and love to kill"). But Véra never speaks. In fact the only part of her that so much as appears in her husband's memoir are her delicate hands, in which Dmitri's perfect newborn fingernails are displayed, his plump baby hands warmed. The sense that she was eternally on hand, looking over the author's shoulder—as the author is in so many of his works on hand, looking over his characters' shoulders—was the sense that she projected at Cornell, where she was so often to be described as "hovering." And like the shadow at Cornell, the "you" of *Speak, Memory,* the other half of that conspicuous "we," cannot be unseen once sighted; the flavor of that first intrusive "you" leaks out all over the two hundred pages that follow.

Most of all with *Speak, Memory* Véra was equal parts aide-de-camp and aide-mémoire, setting down her memories of Dmitri's childhood for her husband.[†] Fittingly, insofar as the chapter addressed to her amounts to a tribute, it is a tribute to Véra and Vladimir's mutual creativity, to the birth and early childhood of Dmitri, to the couple's joint couvade. This, too, is love of a kind. Nothing could have better agreed with Véra—who only once, when forcefully pushed, admitted she might be lurking in her husband's texts—than this oblique and semi-anonymous salute. (Another woman might have felt excluded; the other women in Nabokov's life had in common their urge to proclaim their place in his work. On reading the first half of *Lolita,* Irina Guadanini reported that it was all about her and America.) Even the more direct expression of love in an early version of the memoir's last chapter is toned down. The tender and much palpated love of which we read was at an earlier stage "this exquisite, this inexpressibly pathetic throb of mortality (the

---

* To great narrative effect another of Nabokov's women hides under her married name. Mrs. Richard F. Schiller dies on page four of *Lolita,* though hundreds of pages have to turn before the first-time reader understands why he should have retained that information.

[†] She was hardly the first woman to do so. Madame Chateaubriand performed the same service for her husband, who reworked her memories as his own. Dorothy Wordsworth's journals have been called an offering to her brother.

consciousness of my love for my son, for you).'' Not everyone would understand love to be a shared illusion as the Nabokovs understood the term. For some Véra's incorporeal presence raised suspicions. This was love not as delusion but as magic act; at Cornell there was no question as to who was doing the conjuring. Nor is there in *Speak, Memory.* "In the hush of pure memory" the magician has a coconspirator, a famulus who—at a critical juncture, their most cherished creation between them—knows precisely when to be silent. That reticence too speaks volumes. As doubtless did Nabokov's dedication page: For the first time since *Mary,* he dedicated a published volume, again to his wife. This time he cited her by name.

Véra spent the spring of 1950 typing the manuscript of the memoir, under more than the usual pressure. In April Vladimir was hospitalized for ten days with a grippe followed by intercostal neuralgia. For the month Véra—just out of bed after a bad case of bronchitis—taught his classes for him. She arranged a fall lecture for him at Smith; she solicited Wilson's advice on the soundness of Harper's publishing plans. Nabokov profited from his sick leave to put the finishing touches on the manuscript, boasting that Véra was "doing an amazing job replacing me at the university." The arrangement must have proved a relief to them both. Véra kept a strict eye on her husband, affixing a faux wax seal even to a short missive to Hessen, under which she scrawled "Seen and approved, Véra." Nabokov had hoped to finish the book no later than April so as to have it out before the Christmas book-buying season; the illness interfered with his schedule, enough so that Harper postponed publication to January 1951, to his great dismay. In the meantime his editor was in dire need of a description of the book in order to write his catalogue copy. Vladimir professed to have neither the time nor the talent to produce a synopsis, but offered to appeal to a friend in possession of both. Véra composed an anonymous two-page description of the manuscript, comparing it with Tolstoy and Proust, and praising, among other virtues, two qualities she admired above all else: the memoir's originality, and its author's "absolute lucidity of wording." With a low chuckle and without revealing the identity of its author, Nabokov wrote that he had toned down the encomium a bit. The manuscript was finished at last in May, which set Véra on an end-of-semester typing marathon. The bulk of the pages went to Harper on June 5.

Both Nabokovs were well aware that their financial future depended to a great extent on the fortunes of the memoir. To supplement his Cornell income Vladimir had agreed to translate *The Brothers Karamazov*; the April illness forced him to reconsider. Over the next few years he contemplated a number of similar projects, for financial reasons. In the fall he proposed a piece on the Soviet idea of America in plays and stories to *The New Yorker*; in January 1951 he attempted to sell to the publisher of the English edition of *Madame Bovary* his corrections to the translation. Nor was that all. "With one thing and another I have almost completed a small book on the structure of *Madame Bovary* for students. Would you be interested in publishing it?" he queried a Rinehart editor. A few years later he and Véra narrowly missed translating what they referred to as "The Old Man and the Fish" into Russian, a project to which Nabokov had agreed on the condition that his name not be attached to it. While the search for a memoir title began, Véra offered an innocent piece of advice. Her husband was teaching *Eugene Onegin* and railing against the existing translation of Pushkin's verse masterpiece. "Why don't you translate it yourself?" she suggested, perhaps the six words of encouragement she would most come to regret, culminating as they did a full decade later in five thousand index cards—three 16-inch-long shoeboxes' worth—each of which she painstakingly typed, several times. By the fall, when Nabokov was busily soliciting loans, the memoir loomed more and more significantly as their financial salvation. Véra appealed to friends: Harper had agreed to send out a number of advance copies of the book, and she and Vladimir wanted that list to be as long as possible. "Could you not send us a list of people you know (and people you don't) who would be interested in the aforementioned?" she queried Hessen, who dutifully complied. (Harper did not, balking at the long list.) A few weeks later she wrote Katharine White while her husband spent a quiet day composing in bed, between battles with midterm bluebooks. Picking up the baton in one of the few correspondences not normally hers, Véra explained, "He has never had so little time for his writing. In this respect it is probably the worst year of his life." Her husband's fatigue could be read between her lines; the typewriter was itself failing. Between February when the "p" disappeared and May, when the "h" succumbed, most of what it produced verged on the half-legible. Over the summer, when the Royal was finally sent off for repair, Véra resorted to handwritten letters.*

The title for Nabokov's memoir was longer in coming even than was the manuscript. (Late in July Nabokov sent Harper a last chapter in the form of a review of the book, about which he had mixed feelings. It was not included in the memoir, and was published only in 1999.) Véra put a good deal of energy into the title search over the winter; we can only be grateful that she did

---

* These did not always meet with satisfactory results. For her sister-in-law she had copied out Vladimir's recent poems, "but the author found that they were illegible, so it's better that I not send them, rather, I'll bang them out on the typewriter when it's fixed."

not prevail, or the magnificent piece of prose that went out into the world as *Conclusive Evidence* and metamorphosed into *Speak, Memory* might have been titled "Fluorescent Tears," "Roots," or "The Winding Way." Against the advice of both the Whites and Wilson, Nabokov settled on *Conclusive Evidence*. The two buried "v"s had a lovely ring to them; moreover, they struck him as philosophically correct. (It is tempting to think they did so because of Véra. It is equally possible that Nabokov was alluding to his own name and patronymic. When he had first contemplated a memoir, in 1936, the working title for the much-rejected pages was "It Is Me.") For all the excitement generated by *Conclusive Evidence* it might just as well have been titled "Fluorescent Tears."* While most of the reviews were stellar, a few of the loudest voices were dissenting ones. Like most of Nabokov's work, this volume failed to charm *The New York Times*'s Orville Prescott, on whom the idea of man as mirage was lost. "He is not interested in characterizing anybody," cavilled Prescott. "He does not even paint a clear picture of himself." Sales were flat, not much assisted by the fact that Nicholas Nabokov had published a different kind of musical memoir a few weeks before *Conclusive Evidence*. Even Vladimir's editor had had trouble keeping the two Russians straight. There was every reason why Nabokov—pained by the wrong-address compliments he received over the years—should have had a highly developed sense of a second, if not a tertiary, self.†

Publication month found both the couple distracted by other concerns. "In the course of five days straight, non-stop, Véra and I have from ten in the morning until two in the morning been correcting my students' compositions," Vladimir noted in February 1951, when posters advertising *Conclusive Evidence* decorated Ithaca bookstores. A warm front swept in that month, melting the ice; he studied the shadows of the drops as they fell from the eaves. In his diary he noted Véra's remark on the thaw: "The icicles are dripping, and what a display of diamonds!" In March she spent ten days typing and retyping and typing again the story into which those New York State stalactites dissolved, "The Vane Sisters," which Vladimir dictated to her, a story with which he was much pleased, far more pleased than would be *The New Yorker,* which rejected it. The same month Véra found in a trunk three French translations of her husband's early stories, which she sent to his Parisian agent. In short she forged ahead.

---

* So quiet was the publication that in speaking to the couple years later, Cass Canfield lamented that Harper had not had a chance to publish the memoir. "But you did," protested the Nabokovs.
† Well aware of his sentiments, Harry Levin added a line to his congratulatory note on the publication of *Conclusive Evidence*: "Incidentally, I glanced at your cousin's book, and found it somewhat inconclusive."

In the spring the Nabokovs sold the piano that had made the trip from Wellesley, bade an unemotional good-bye to 802 East Seneca Street, and "lightly laden," set out for the West in their aging car.

3

If ever there was a time when Véra should have discouraged her husband from working on an unsaleable manuscript, it was now. His work, for which new hopes had been raised at every juncture and in turn by three American publishers, had amounted to a series of "dismal financial flops." The strain was felt most acutely on Seneca Street in 1951. That spring Dmitri was accepted to Harvard with a partial scholarship, news in which Véra delighted but which made her more nervous yet about finances. Even Dmitri was aware of the family's precarious monetary state at the time. Vladimir felt he had come to the end of the line. Never again would he allow one of his books to be hushed up, as he felt Harper had just taken such perverse delight in doing. Forswearing a guilelessness which few associated with him in the first place, he vowed to be fierce and cunning in the future. The "Vane Sisters" rejection had stung badly, for both financial and artistic reasons. And he had no hope whatever that the book on which he was currently at work would be accepted by any magazine.

Nothing could have looked less like the answer to their difficulties than that manuscript, to which he had intermittently turned his attention since the summer of 1947. Almost parenthetically he mentioned it to a publisher for the first time in November 1951. "Moreover, I am engaged in the composition of a novel, which deals with the problems of a very moral middle-aged gentleman who falls very immorally in love with his stepdaughter, a girl of thirteen," he advised Viking's Pat Covici. The truly level-headed wife of a man in debt to friends for several thousand dollars might have counseled him to turn his attention to something more saleable; the mother who had balked at the idea of introducing her twelve-year-old son to Mark Twain might have been expected to keep her distance. But all bets were off where art was concerned, or at least where Vladimir's art was concerned.

Lolita owes her birth to Nabokov but her life to Véra; she was several times nearly incinerated in Ithaca. The manuscript came close to meeting its demise as early as the fall of 1948, when Vladimir made a trip to the trash barrel behind the Seneca Street house with his pages. Dick Keegan arrived on the scene minutes before Véra, who stepped outside to find her husband had set a fire in the galvanized can next to the back steps and was beginning to feed his papers to it. Appalled, she fished the few sheets she could from the flames. Her husband began to protest. "Get away from there!" Véra commanded, an order Vladimir obeyed as she stomped on the pages she had retrieved. "We are keeping this," she announced. On at least one other occasion, less dramatic than this bonfire manqué, she was observed filing away pages her husband deemed deficient and later published. She did so again with *Lolita*: Nabokov remembered Véra's stopping him several times in 1950 and 1951 when, "beset with technical difficulties and doubts," he had attempted to incinerate *Lolita*. As no one had yet considered the manuscript for publication, the dissatisfaction could have been only artistic. She who had traveled to Ithaca a few years earlier alone in the knowledge that they were to be shut out of their house on arrival was for these years alone in the knowledge that her husband was at work on a "time bomb," a work so inflammatory that he blacked out the research notes—on sexual deviation, on marriage with minors—in his diary. Plenty of manuscripts have burned, among them first drafts of *Jekyll and Hyde* and *Dead Souls*. A three-person brigade intervened to save *A Portrait of the Artist as a Young Man* from the flames; in *Pale Fire,* Kinbote looks on as John Shade indulges in a little backyard auto-da-fé. That *Lolita* did not meet with the same fate, in the context and climate in which Nabokov was composing in the early 1950s, is testimony to Véra's ability to—as her husband had it—keep grim common sense from the door, shoot it dead when it approached. She feared that the memory of the unfinished work would haunt him forever.

She was by no means complaisant about his plans. When Vladimir announced to colleagues that he was going to write a novel about the love life of a pair of Siamese twins, Véra put her foot down. "No, you're not!" she exhorted. We have the relatively sedate "Scenes from the Life of a Double Monster" instead. (On *Lolita*'s loud publication one uncomfortable colleague consoled himself that the damage could have been far worse. Vladimir might have forged ahead with the Siamese twin idea.) Much later Véra staunchly opposed his plan to publish a collection of his favorite Russian poems, in his translations. Moreover she was sensitive to his artistic obligations. Probably in the spring she had written Elena Sikorski, explaining why she was the author of the letter in terms her sister-in-law would immediately understand: "Right now there's a new short story 'coming out of him' and he can't do anything until he 'gets it out of his system.' It's like a sickness, you know him." With equal grace she could serve as prod and brake; Field may have best described her when he called her Vladimir's "intellectual visa checkpoint." He depended on her good, and uncommon, sense: "My wife, of course, is a wonderful adviser. She's my first and best reader," he had told a reporter just after the publication of *Bend Sinister.* In Berlin, when her husband was about to sacrifice a night's sleep to an impossible four-line palindrome, it had been she who had quietly ordered, "Go to sleep, Volodya." The palindrome remained unfinished. She made it as possible as she could for him to work without making it possible for him to overwork, something that became more and more difficult once the English language began to accommodate itself to his needs. The later letters are full of concern that she could not persuade her husband to take a much needed vacation. At times she sounds on the verge of hiding the pencils.

She could express this frustration to her sister-in-law, an ocean away. In Ithaca she had no one to whom she could speak openly about these or any other concerns, with the exception of Morris Bishop's wife, Alison. (That fondness did nothing to preclude her heading off an inquiring biographer fifteen years later with the categorical, "We had no close, really close friends at Cornell.") She confided her hopes, her qualms, her excitement about the new manuscript to no one, even while her husband boasted regularly to a colleague that he was at work on a new novel that would get him kicked out of America, as—quite differently than he imagined—was to be the case.* Véra was always circumspect, but was so especially about what she was reading in the early 1950s. These were staid times in a provincial place. Over the summer she had even less of an opportunity to share her concerns. Véra and Dmitri by turns drove Vladimir across Ohio, Indiana, Illinois, Missouri, and Kansas to Telluride, Colorado, a destination they reached on June 30. This was the family vacation Vladimir claimed he had bungled for the sake of his butterflies. At the end of July Dmitri set off on his own; his parents spent the remainder of the summer in perfect isolation, surrounded by wildlife, on a ranch in West Yellowstone, Montana. They returned to a smaller, more comfortable home in Ithaca, at 623 Highland Road. There were no regrets about the move, as the "dreadfully drafty dacha"—their landlord had returned to find Véra had stuffed all the keyholes full of cotton wads—had proved ruinously expensive. Moreover, on Highland Road there were no boarders, a breed Véra generally disliked and with which the Nabokovs had had nearly as much luck as would Charlotte Haze. Véra described three of the East Seneca Street four: "One was a professor and an inveterate drunkard, another was completely crazy (he's currently in the crazy house), and the police

---

* In 1951 or 1952 he had told Marc Szeftel, who had heard from mutual friends about "The Enchanter," that he was at work on an American version of that manuscript. Earlier he had promised Szeftel a glimpse of the novella, with the warning, "Remember, it is not for kids!" He never made good on the promise.

are looking for another of them now. He only stayed a week and passed himself off as something entirely different from what he was." It was a lineup into which Humbert Humbert could have slipped comfortably.

The fourth Ithaca winter must have felt more temperate, as the couple knew it would be an abbreviated one. Karpovich had arranged for Vladimir to replace him at Harvard for the spring semester, a move that put Véra near the close friends whom—even to the intruding biographer—she did acknowledge. In addition to the older women who had been Vladimir's Wellesley colleagues, Cambridge meant Elena Levin, the Karpoviches, the Wilsons, and ultimately a few other couples to whom the Levins introduced them. Even in those highly evolved circles Véra had no confidante, as her husband had in Wilson, no advocate like Katharine White. She was difficult to get to know, unforthcoming about herself, vociferous in her opinions, an off-putting combination. With those she did not like she did not bother with phatic conversation. She had a great deal in common with Elena Levin, eleven years her junior, a brilliant reader and a devoted faculty wife. The Levins' household gods were the Nabokovs': Joyce, Proust, Flaubert. Yet even with Elena—whom Véra saw regularly in the spring of 1952, and with whom she corresponded for the rest of her life—there was something less than a meeting of the minds. Repeatedly the Levins discovered what could be called the reverse side of Véra's obsessive devotion to Vladimir: She could be uncompromising, prickly, blinded by single-mindedness. Véra had for so long steeled herself against the world's indifference, its occasional hostility, that she seemed unequipped to respond to its welcome; the pride proved not so much a chink in the armor as a kind of armor itself. It left her, in Cambridge company, with no discernible sense of humor, seemingly self-righteous, priggish, proud. "You know, Véra, if you weren't Jewish you'd be a Fascist," one Harvard friend exploded, cringing at her intolerance. Quickly Elena Levin learned she could not invite the Nabokovs with other colleagues. He buffooned, and she was combative, overly eager to remind the assembled guests of her husband's greatness. Wilson remarked on the same quality later:

> Véra always sides with Volodya, and one seems to feel her bristling with
> hostility if, in her presence, one argues with him. . . . She so concentrates
> on Volodya that she grudges special attention to anyone else. . . . I al-
> ways enjoy seeing them—what we have are really intellectual romps,
> sometimes accompanied by mauling—but I am always afterwards left
> with a somewhat uncomfortable impression.

Even allowing for his dim view of the Nabokovs' marriage—so different in number and nature from his own—there was some truth in Wilson's statement. Véra had no particular expectations for herself but she had outsized ones for her husband. The vaulting, vicarious ambition isolated her.

Generally she had little need to confide in anyone other than her husband and, in time, Dmitri. She did not feel it necessary to set her anxieties, her disappointments, to paper; she had no inclination to dwell on these matters. She had been in irregular touch with her sister Sonia, now a United Nations translator in New York, and with her elder sister, Lena, a translator in Sweden, but for the most part those correspondences amounted to catalogues of Dmitri's and Vladimir's triumphs. When Lena offered to phone her—the two had not heard each other's voice since the mid-1930s—Véra discouraged the idea. There was so little one could say in a brief, long-distance conversation. She claimed a long, "newsy" letter would be far preferable, failing to acknowledge that she rarely had the time to write one.* To Anna Feigin she did address her monetary anxieties, as Vladimir had in the Berlin years; nearly until the time of her death, Anna Feigin remained the family's unlikely financial adviser. She now counseled the Cambridge-based Véra not to worry about their various material setbacks. They had always managed before. Somehow they would again.

So little need did Véra have of the world that the appointments in the diary she and her husband jointly kept appear to have been with Gogol, Pushkin, Fet, rather than with living persons. These were the subjects of Nabokov's Harvard lectures, the schedule for which she devised for him. He was teaching three courses: the second half of Karpovich's Modern Russian Literature course (one student thought Karpovich must be an awfully good friend to assume the soporific first years of the course and leave Nabokov the entire nineteenth century); his own course on Pushkin; and, against his will, a section of Humanities 2, Harvard's version of Cornell's European Literature course. Again he had had to be bribed and bullied into the assignment, at least in part because the reading list included *Candide* and *Don Quixote,* the latter of which he had neither read in the original nor taught.† He and John H. Finley, Jr., the eminent Greek scholar who taught the first half of the large course, went a few rounds to determine how Nabokov could make peace with the idea. The deaf ear Vladimir turned to these entreaties manifested it-

---

* Lena had taken the opposite position in proposing to call. "I would like to call you one of these days. It's expensive, but I would like to indulge myself, since one can say more by phone in two minutes than one can in 50 letters."

† He had read Cervantes in three languages, but never in Spanish. He was doubtless further handicapped by the fact that he would not be able to savage the novel's translator.

self as a blind eye; he could not seem to decipher Finley's long, handwritten response of July 23, 1951. Dutifully Véra typed out Finley's letter, so that her husband might reply to it. The classicist ultimately won his case with an assist from Harry Levin, who reminded Nabokov that he could doubtless count on at least an additional thousand dollars were he to take on Humanities 2, an amount that—with a few curricular compromises, all of them titles of Harvard's choosing—he could probably parlay into fifteen hundred.

The titles did not much matter. Nabokov's 1952 section of Humanities 2 began with an announcement along these lines: "There are two great writers in English for whom English was not the native language, the first and the lesser of whom was Joseph Conrad. The second is I."* The showmanship at times appeared a substitute for scholarship and did not universally charm the Memorial Hall audience. One student found it offensive that Nabokov presented *Don Quixote* in terms of how he would have written the book—then went on to discuss how he would improve upon it. Another disapproved of the visiting professor's devoting an entire class to a discussion of whether *Anna Karenina* should or should not be translated with the final "a" in English. And was it truly necessary for Nabokov's assistant to spell out Austen's name on the blackboard? In the Russian Literature course he greatly enjoyed teaching the work of Sirin, revealing only late in the semester that Sirin was he, or that he was Sirin. The section men who graded for him in Humanities 2 found it odd that they saw so little of him. The puns were dreadful.

Véra heard none of these grumblings and clearly liked what she did hear.† She felt a real—and well-justified—sense of triumph that spring. A little more than a decade after the arrival in America, both Dmitri and Vladimir were Harvard men. This mattered; Véra had consistently described Wellesley and Cornell as being among the finest American universities. She glowingly described her husband's Humanities 2 lectures. "V. is giving *grandiose* lectures, in an enormous auditorium," she exulted, in a letter Vladimir read before it was mailed. "540 registered students . . . intently listen and applaud after each meeting of the course. (After the lecture on *Don Quixote* applause; after the lecture on *Bleak House,* the same; on Tuesday he begins *Dead Souls.*)"‡ Her husband's pride was her own, as can be heard in this midwinter report: While Vladimir was growing tired of his lectures, "he

---

* His students were more puzzled than impressed. Thornton Wilder, a three-time Pulitzer Prize winner and bestselling author, had taught the course the previous spring. He had made no such claims.
† Generally Nabokov's lectures were better received at Cornell than at Harvard, where the campus culture was more formal.
‡ Nabokov had been told to expect an enrollment of 400, which in his memory grew to 600. Attendance may have been higher, but the official enrollment at mid-semester was 387.

is obviously taking great pleasure in the increasing glory and respect which he feels here. (In our boondock Ithaca there simply wasn't anyone capable of understanding who had joined the ranks of their 'faculty.')" She did not even bother to pretend to be speaking for him when she added that she was thrilled to be around people who knew her husband's work by heart.

After the first two Cambridge weeks the Nabokovs moved into the congenial clapboard home of May Sarton, tucked away on narrow Maynard Street, ten minutes from campus. With the house came the first in a short series of rented pets, a tiger cat named Tom Jones, rechristened "Tomsky" by the Nabokovs. (In a charming example of her slightly synthetic English, Véra remembered Tomsky as "a gutter cat.") She took great delight in the antics of the affectionate animal, who took as much delight in her husband. "When V. reads and writes while lying on the sofa he pounces on his stomach, pounds a bit with his paws, and curls up on him," Véra noted. At the end of the semester, just as the couple were beginning to set their sights on the drive West, Tomsky came home limping. He would not eat; Véra felt his nose, which was hot and dry. In detail she reported to Sarton on their trips to the hospital, first to admit Tomsky, the next day to visit him. He turned out to be suffering from several infected bites. After a three-day hospital stay the animal was discharged. "He was much thinner, very hungry and very clean, the white spots dazzling white, and he was quite recovered from his woes," Véra announced happily.* The dedication she showed Tomsky was perfectly consistent with her character, but the woman who bent down repeatedly to gauge the temperature of a cat's nose was not often in evidence. A few students inadvertently found the way to her heart. At the end of Humanities 2 one admiring senior asked her to pass on to Professor Nabokov his compliments on the course. He was rewarded with a most dazzling smile. "But you must, you *must* tell him yourself," Véra pleaded. This remained always a direct route to her affection. Later at Cornell, a colleague of Nabokov's introduced him to a student who had attended every one of his European Literature lectures although he was not enrolled in the course. Beaming, Vladimir led the student directly to Véra, for whom he made him repeat each of his kind words.

She was more reserved on the subject of her son's lectures. She took to attending William Langer's History of European Diplomacy course, a class in which Dmitri was enrolled. The two happily sat together in the large lecture hall, or did whenever possible. Langer was a punctual man; the doors to his

---

* The evidence suggests that the Nabokovs were more careful with Tomsky than with Sarton's dishes. Generally the couple were not regarded as model tenants.

classroom closed promptly at the top of the hour. On several occasions
mother and son regarded each other forlornly through the window of a
locked door. It is unclear whether Véra attended the course because its subject intrigued her—Langer's expertise was in Russian and Middle Eastern
studies, two areas about which she felt passionately—or because Dmitri's ab-
senteeism worried her. In any event, Langer's were the only lectures outside
the Literature Department she appears to have heard. At Cornell she attended a vast number of courses, but they were without exception taught by
the same professor, the one whose letters she typed, edited, and wrote, on the
letterhead of a nonexistent department.*

4
———

In a later attempt to urge his own meticulousness on an editor, Nabokov referred to "the double-dotted 'i'." Nothing could have better described the
arrangement that began in Goldwin Smith Hall late in the 1940s and continued there for nearly a decade. As early as the second Cornell semester,
throughout the Harvard interlude, and until the departure from academia in
1958, he arrived for class with his assistant in tow. The assistant trailed a few
steps behind him on campus; often she appeared at Goldwin Smith Hall on
his arm. She carried his briefcase, and opened any doors that stood in his way.
In the classroom she placed his notes on the lectern. She helped him off with
his coat before half-removing her own. In the European Literature course,
she sat either in the front row of the lecture hall or, more often, in a chair on
the dais, to the professor's left. Her eyes rarely left him.† If he dropped a piece
of chalk she retrieved it; if he needed a page number or a quotation she provided it. Otherwise she had no speaking role during the lecture. After class
she erased the blackboard. She lingered at the podium while Nabokov answered questions. When he forgot his glasses she was dispatched on a search-
and-rescue mission: The professor labored uncomfortably from memory
until her return.‡ She rarely missed a class, although she did occasionally
teach one, and she often proctored exams alone. All administrative affairs

---

* After a while Véra began to cross out the "Department of Russian Literature" when using the letterhead. Vladimir was more likely to let it stand, sometimes with a little marginal snort: "Now without Russian." The fictional department lived on through the stationery well into the 1950s.
† In the Russian Literature courses, which were smaller, she sat facing Nabokov, often in the front row,
sometimes in the last.
‡ Holding the glasses aloft she made a dramatic entrance into the lecture hall: "Oh, yes, yes, yes," exulted
Nabokov, smiling, and thanking her profusely.

were delegated to her. The man who spoke so often of his own isolation was one of the most accompanied loners of all time; at Cornell especially he was in the constant company of his assistant.

In the classroom the act was a perfectly synchronized one. Nabokov might near a certain quotation and the assistant, as if animated by some kind of "brain-bridge," would rise from her seat to offer the appropriate notes, to extend the appropriate page, to sketch the appropriate diagram. Promptly she responded to his cues. "My assistant will now move the blackboard to the other side of the room," the professor would command. "My assistant will now pass out the bluebooks." "Perhaps my assistant could find the page for me." "My assistant will now draw an oval-faced woman"—this was Emma Bovary—"on the board." And the assistant—whom Nabokov addressed as "Darling" outside of the classroom—would do so. The stage directions do not figure in the published lectures. (The routine was a little different in the Russian Literature classes, in which the assistant audibly served as prompter and aide-mémoire, and committed sophisticated diagrams—scanning matrixes for Tyutchev—to the board.) A smile played visibly on her lips when he discussed Anna Karenina's skating outfit, attire he described as having been made of "rubberized tweed." A smile must have played on her lips too when he announced that he had read *Anna Karenina* for the first time at the age of six, but that his wife had done so at the age of three.* We do not know how, if at all, she reacted when he discussed Anna and Vronski's dreaming in unison, about which he observed, "This monogrammatic interconnection of two individual brain-patterns is not unknown in so-called real life." Occasionally the assistant rerouted an errant lecture; she might cut off an off-color aside with a glance, or prompt a line with a nod. For the most part she sat straight-faced and straight-backed in her chair, a huge, unexplained, and intimidating presence. And despite her attempts to remain faceless, a face was now fitted to her by a decade's worth of Russian Literature and European Literature students. Even before the most spellbinding lecturer, a roomful of red-blooded undergraduates is sure to engage in a game of Find-What-the-Sailor-Has-Hidden. Her identity was by no means obvious. One gifted student was shocked when—having written an essay so stellar it precipitated an invitation to his professor's home—the mask dropped, and he found himself being introduced to "Mrs. Nabokov." Revolution and migration had already dissolved several identities. In the Cornell classroom a new one constituted itself, seemingly without any active participation on Véra's part.

These were the most public years of the Nabokovs' lives; Véra could not

---

* In some courses the ages got younger as the semester progressed. Was anyone out there *listening?*

have failed to realize that her presence in the classroom would be as much re-marked upon as her husband's shredding Dostoyevsky in front of two hun-dred undergraduates, his trampling Freud, his dismissal of that great realist writer "Upton Lewis," his suggestion that the Rinehart translation of *Madame Bovary* was so bad the job must have been done by the arch-philistine Homais himself. For the most part the tirades proved the stuff of enchantment; the slurs were savored long after the course was forgotten. The corrections to the translations proved more memorable than the books. Much that took place in the room was unforgettable. It was "quite a performance on her part as well," remembered a graduate student who sat in on the Euro-pean Literature course in 1958. The assistant was deemed as legendary, as mesmerizing a presence as Professor Nabokov.* "Everybody was fascinated by her," recalled Alison Bishop. And yet no one agreed on exactly what to make of her. One student winced at Professor Nabokov's treatment of his flunky, which struck her as downright exploitative. A group of Cornellians thought her so severe they referred to her as the Gray Eagle. Another class dubbed her the Countess. She was radiant, regal, elegance personified, a head-turner, "the most beautiful middle-aged woman I have ever set eyes on." She was a waif, dowdy, half-starved, the Wicked Witch of the West. She was German. She was a princess. She was a ballerina. Whoever she was, she was "mnemogenic"—as Nabokov had written of Clare in *The Real Life of Sebastian Knight*—"subtly endowed with the gift of being remembered."

What was Véra Nabokov doing in her husband's classroom, lecture after lecture? Nabokov had no graduate degree but was by inclination a master of specificity; the naturalist-professor instructed his students to dissect literature with a scientist's care. Which is precisely what they did in explicating the scene before them:

- Mrs. Nabokov was there to remind us we were in the presence of greatness, and should not abuse that privilege with our inattention.
- Nabokov had a heart condition, and she was at hand with a phial of medicine to jump up at a moment's notice.
- That wasn't his wife, that was his mother.
- She was there because Nabokov was allergic to chalk dust, and be-cause he didn't like his handwriting.
- To shoo away the coeds.

---

* One alumnus-turned-critic teased her later, when PBS planned a series with Christopher Plummer de-livering Nabokov's lectures. "But who is going to play you? If realism is to be achieved, *someone* must play 'the assistant,' " contended Alfred Appel, to whom Vanessa Redgrave seemed the obvious choice.

- Because she was his encyclopedia, if ever he forgot anything.
- Because he had no idea what was going to come out of his mouth—
  and no memory of it after it did—so she had to write it all down so
  that he would remember what to ask on the exams.
- He was blind, and she was the Seeing Eye dog, which explained why
  they always arrived arm in arm.
- She was intended as living proof that he had a fan club.
- She graded his performance, in order to review it with him in the
  evenings.
- We all knew that she was a ventriloquist.
- She had a gun in her purse, and was there to defend him.

No one was certain who marked the exams; a few students admitted that
they made a practice of smiling at Mrs. Nabokov in the hope that their geniality might register in their grades. Initially she waded through the bluebooks before her husband. Later she alone graded the examinations,
unbeknownst to the 1958 senior who could not refrain from adding a panegyric to the professor's luminous assistant to the back of his bluebook. (It was
returned without comment.) By 1951 she was remunerated for her efforts. To
his department chairman Nabokov wrote just before 1953 fall midterms: "I
estimate that I shall need at least $70 to pay my assistant for grading the pa-
pers since there are 231 students in 311 [Masters of European Literature] and
36 in 325 [Russian Literature in Translation]."* He anticipated that an additional $90 would be necessary in January, for finals. It was a little coy not to
have named names, or perhaps it was not coy in the least, as Véra wrote this
letter herself.

As the reputation of the European Literature course grew, so did its enrollment. By the spring of 1954 Professor Nabokov—or someone in his
household—was requesting that "my assistant, Mrs. V. Nabokov," be credited with 130 hours' work. That was a brutal amount of time to spend deciphering the handwritings of anxious undergraduates. Véra must have been
relieved when, toward the end of the decade, the university provided a teaching assistant for the course. She herself was terrifically exacting, but not an
ogre of a grader. Henry Steck, a graduate student in the Department of Government, took on the job in 1958. He spent five days reviewing some two
hundred bluebooks, which he evaluated according to a rigorous scale. After
reading each exam several times, he delivered the bundle to Professor

---

* This did not prevent Nabokov from complaining that he had 270 students, and therefore 270 bluebooks
to grade.

Nabokov's office, hoping finally to have a word with the great man. Mrs. Nabokov met him at the door, standing like a sentinel between Steck and her husband. She took the exams, immediately raised all the grades to the eighties, and sent Steck on his way. Another assistant met with a warmer welcome. When she graded for the course in 1957, M. Travis Lane was asked to compile a collection of student bloopers, which she was invited to share with the Nabokovs at their home, over a glass of sherry. She remembered Véra's emitting a musical laugh, as well she must have when she learned that her husband the stickler had met his match in a humorist. To the question: "What was the pattern of Anna Karenina's wallpaper?" one luminary had replied, "little railroad trains."

Even when she was not acting the sentinel at the door, Véra allowed her husband to speak in the first person plural, which seemed so much more naturally to accommodate his pronouncements. She reserved the same right for herself. The impressive student to whom a not very impressive exam was returned was told: "*We* thought you would do better than that. *We* had confidence in you." A student suffering from an eye problem returned her bluebook to Professor Nabokov's office with an apologetic, "I have written with some difficulty." Witheringly Véra replied, "And it looks as if we will read it with some difficulty." An aspiring novelist slipped his manuscript to the professor, who read a few pages and agreed to discuss the text. Véra was the one to do so, from the far end of her husband's office. As she spoke, remembered Steve Katz, sunk low in Nabokov's armchair, "he leaned over me like the tallest dentist in the world, and occasionally supported her presentation by a word or phrase."

Nabokov was a mesmerizing lecturer, but part of the charm was in the tart condescension, the well-honed insult. The students who noted this were clear-eyed. He was simply pitching "way, way over our crew-cut heads," concluded one. Nabokov provided a perfect summation of his attitude toward academe in an October 1956 letter to Hessen: "I write you while proctoring exams, the empty heads are bowed down. I see it is impossible to write; they keep asking me questions." Before him two hundred students squirmed in midterm agony as they racked their brains for wallpaper patterns. Certain things clearly felt beneath his dignity, as was suggested by Véra's habit of proctoring exams and keeping office hours. He grumbled that he did not see why Sirin should have to lecture on Joyce, a complaint to which only one other person in Ithaca, New York, would have been sympathetic. Nabokov and his assistant both felt he should be on the syllabus and not behind the podium, a sense that set them apart from the Cornell colleagues. "I am too little of an academic professor to teach subjects that I dislike," Nabokov proclaimed, which may explain why Véra prepared much of his Dostoyevsky talk for him. She wrote its first draft, at the very least. She was the one who explained how Dostoyevsky, working under constant stress and in a hurry, hired and then married his stenographer, "a woman full of devotion and practical sense. With her help he met his deadlines and gradually extricated himself from the financial mess he had been in." Much of the repertoire consisted of the pieces on which Véra had worked at Wellesley; the libretto of the Ithaca years is more clearly discernible, if only because she neglected to throw out the draft pages, in which her sizable contribution can be read. Some of her lines are embedded in the Joyce lecture as well, for which she did the library work. Only to this extent was she her husband's ventriloquist.

Nabokov did not teach literature as it had been taught in America before or as it has been taught since. For one thing he taught Gogol's "The Greatcoat," Tolstoy's *Anna Karenin,* Proust's *The Walk by Swann's Place,* Dostoyevsky's *Memoirs from a Mousehole.* He consulted his own dictionary of literary terms. There was the "parallel interruption," the "perry," the "knight's move," the "sifting agent," the "special dimple." He had no use for plot or psychology; he taught that literature was in the images, not the ideas. Very little was sacred. In this he upheld the legacy of one of his own esteemed Petersburg teachers, the Symbolist poet V. V. Hippius, who was said to teach "not literature but the far more interesting science of literary spite."* Nabokov was known, vaguely, as a writer, by the mid-1950s as the creator of *Pnin,* by the end of the decade as the author of *Lolita,* more conspicuously as the man who annually filled the Goldwin Smith amphitheater to capacity crowds when he lectured on *Madame Bovary* from the Sunday comics; who taught "The Metamorphosis" with the assistance of his favorite newspaper, the *Daily News.* The eccentricities rather than his literary reputation accounted for his legend. By the time he left Cornell, his European Literature course was among the most popular on campus.

He also taught his students how to read. More even than did the English majors, the government students, the home economics majors, the pre-meds, the mathematicians, the engineers found he was to change their lives.† "He savored words, drew vibrant word pictures, and made reading great books a joy for me and my husband to this day," remembers Supreme Court Justice

---

* One writer skewered by Hippius was the sixteen-year-old poet Vladimir Vladimirovich Nabokov, whose romantic verse Hippius memorably deconstructed before his classmates.
† The literature-loving English majors occasionally proved more immune to his charm. To several of the brightest he appeared superficial, as was perhaps to be expected of a professor who savored Tolstoy's lawn tennis game. Many were discouraged from taking his course, considered a class for dilettantes within the department.

Ruth Bader Ginsburg. What even the good readers did not entirely realize at
the time was that on Monday, Wednesday, and Friday between noon and
12:50, in the guise of teaching several hundred undergraduates how to parse
Proust, Flaubert, Tolstoy, as he filled Goldwin Smith C with his booming
baritone, he was teaching them how to read Nabokov. Caress the details, he
directed. Art is a deception; the great artist a deceiver. Read for the tingle, the
shiver up the spine. Do not read but—here he feigned a stutter—re-re-read
a book. Look at the harlequins. Véra was in that amphitheater every day
though no one needed to absorb the lesson less: She was already the world
champion Nabokov reader. Surely she must have been a little bored on hearing for the fifth or sixth time that the moral message of *Anna Karenina* lay in
the metaphysical love of Kitty and Levin, "on willingness for self-sacrifice,
on mutual respect." If she showed no signs of stirring in her chair, save to
shoot a disparaging look at the inattentive student, to reprimand the one who
had absentmindedly lit up a cigarette, it was because the lectures sounded
like something other than lectures to her. Later a Cornell colleague observed
that when Mrs. Nabokov had been obliged to teach in her husband's stead
she had altered not a word of his texts. In the margin eighty-four-year-old
Véra chastised him. But of course she had not changed a thing! Had he not
understood that her husband had been a perfectionist, that each lecture constituted a work of art? So much did she believe this that she quibbled equally
with the colleague's assessment that when teaching in her husband's stead she
delivered "as good a piece of merchandise as Nabokov the master himself."

Nabokov had no heart condition; he was not allergic to chalk dust. For
the most part at Cornell he was in robust health. To a certain extent Véra was
a Seeing Eye dog; her husband was not blind but did demonstrate an unerring capacity to get lost on his way to class, on Cornell's central Arts Quadrangle. As at Wellesley, he had difficulty locating his classroom. He was
sighted wading into the wrong lecture hall; in 1958 he was unable to show his
replacement to the classroom in which he had taught for nearly a decade. He
appeared incapable of turning on a light. In one class he did a nervous little
dance before the switch, confessing his fear of the electrical plate, which he
did his best to avoid.* On campus he could be slow to recognize colleagues;
"Of course you remember Bobby," Véra might say, prompting her husband
to affix a name to a face. He showed every sign of delighting in his role of
befuddled professor; it is less clear if Véra was comfortable with the role that

---

* When much was at stake, he could cozy up to a light switch. In Alfred Appel's fond recollection, on a
midwinter afternoon when the heads had begun bobbing the amphitheater lights burst on—for Pushkin,
for Gogol, for Chekhov—the bright spots in the Russian literary firmament. The dramatic release of the
window shade was of course reserved for Tolstoy.

afforded her. "We did not know he was an author, but we knew he was a character," recalled one student, less certain of what to make of his companion. Literary wives have traditionally provided assistance to their writing husbands; academic wives are meant to be trotted out for the occasional department tea. In the words of one former student, "Véra Nabokov was everywhere a faculty wife shouldn't be—walking with him on the quad, talking to him in the halls, laughing delightedly at some joke he had whispered to her, sitting on the stage of the lecture hall while he read in a dry dull voice."

Whether she knew the extent of her husband's Wellesley indiscretions or not, she would have realized that her presence at his side effectively did prevent straying of another kind. The Wellesley exploits remain the last recorded acts of near-adultery, to be followed only by unsubstantiated hints and a great deal of head-turning. Véra was typing drafts of *Lolita* during the first five years in Ithaca, when her husband was charting sexual maturation and studying sexual perversion, withdrawing *The Subnormal Adolescent Girl* from the library, flipping through *The Best in Teen Tales, The American Girl, Calling All Girls,* taking notes on Clearasil and Tampax, reviewing Havelock Ellis. If the first-person narrator of *Look at the Harlequins!* is to be trusted, Véra knew well not to be personally "ruffled by a too robust erotic detail"; she would have understood this research to be conducted in the service of art. More likely she was concerned with her husband's tendency to veer into the off-color anecdote. These were the mild-mannered Eisenhower years, and out of her earshot Vladimir rather pushed the envelope. When he attempted to do so in his assistant's presence he appealed to her with the look of a mischievous schoolboy. Nor did he desist from the kind of provocative comments that had secured him his reputation in Berlin, a reputation that had found its way to Cornell via convoluted émigré pathways and, to some, suggested a different reason for his wife's dancing attendance on him. At least he adopted a fresh set of similes. When he saw an attractive favorite student again in 1958 he was quick to assure her that she was looking more than ever like Audrey Hepburn.

Véra was an encyclopedia, but so was Vladimir. The seminar courses in particular were punctuated by mini-conferences between the professor and his assistant. One Russian Literature course ground to a halt when, outlining the genealogy of the princes of Kiev during his lecture on *The Song of Igor's Campaign,* Vladimir could not recall a name and date. He turned to Véra, who provided the fugitive information. When his classes were small, Nabokov arranged for them to meet in his living room, where Véra always appeared with a snack and usually remained for the duration of the hour. She was not retiring. When Professor Nabokov began extemporaneously to recite Pushkin for his students he was interrupted by a quiet voice from the far end of the room: "No, Volodya, that's not right." A protracted debate ensued, the students bemused by this head-on conflict. "Darling, you're absolutely right, you're absolutely right," Nabokov at last conceded, as in fact she was. These melees made abundantly clear to those present that the cookie-supplying Véra was also her husband's professional and intellectual partner. The final for Nabokov's fall 1952 Russian Poetry course (enrollment: six) was administered at the couple's dining room table. Véra plied the students with tea and cookies throughout.

Apart from the occasional digressions, all of which sounded as lapidary as the lectures themselves, Nabokov generally had a very firm idea of what was going to come out of his mouth. And he had an equally good idea of what he had said afterward. All of the lectures were pre-prepared, no tautology in this case: Nabokov claimed later that they had been delivered practically from memory.* Occasionally a gem would slip from his lips and—with real delight—he would stop in mid-lecture to jot it down. This was unnecessary, as someone else in the room was assiduously mopping up the bons mots. Doubtless there were discussions in the evening of the day's performance— Had he killed off Emma Bovary as brilliantly as he had the year before? Had anyone in the room caught the Hemingway swipe?—but it is unlikely that Véra's grades carried much weight with this student. He knew a happy turn of phrase when he saw one. And from the outset his flamboyant account of Pushkin's duel—as much a digression on the culture of dueling as an account of the great poet's agonizing death—had had the desired effect. One student looked to the back of the room after Pushkin's death in Ithaca in 1948. Véra, along with several colleagues and a visiting friend, were dissolved in tears. While she kept upstarts in their places she provided the same service for the lecturer. His own high entertainment was not lost on Professor Nabokov, who could collapse in laughter at the dais, tears streaming down his face. From her perch the earnest assistant would gesture to him. He was laughing so hard that no one could understand a word of what he was saying. From this behavior the inevitable conclusion presented itself: Mrs. Nabokov had no sense of humor.

The antics made for a highly picturesque classroom. One day Nabokov came to class with the wrong edition of *Anna Karenina*. He had only his Russian copy, from which he began to read aloud as planned, with great relish.

---

* That the students were unaware of this was a tribute to his delivery. Neither an architecture student who audited the course twice, nor a particularly attentive pre-med, nor a favored art student noticed. This despite Nabokov's confident assertion that the alert students knew full well he was reading.

Ten minutes into his dramatic and incomprehensible performance Mrs. Nabokov returned to the lecture hall, waving an English edition in the air. Without a word, in midsentence, he switched to the page she held open before him. There was plenty of drama in the contrast between the two performers: Professor Nabokov the buffoon, the showman, the sage, the evangelist, the classroom conjurer, "pulling," as a colleague put it, "rabbits out of textual top hats," seemed the polar twin of the stern, sphinxlike person beside him. Whereas Véra appeared always in a nondescript, monochromatic wardrobe—to most viewers it registered as a single black dress, a baggy sweater over a long, shapeless skirt—Vladimir bloomed forth in all the pageantry the American 1950s had to offer. Véra's heightened sensitivity to color seems to have had no effect on outfitting her husband. His Cornell students were startled by the salmon-colored shirts as they were by his assistant's austere elegance.* The pink shirt was matched to a blue sweater and knotted with a yellow tie, all three components struggling for supremacy under the regulation tweed blazer; he was almost the walking incarnation of the creative writer trying to break out of the professorial straitjacket.† It was assumed that she, whoever she was, was the aristocrat. The adjectives that most commonly attached themselves to her suggested as much. She was formidable, regal, stately, imperious; she reminded students of nothing more than a Borzoi. She terrified a great number of Cornellians. Which made the benevolent gesture all the more appreciated. "Once she smiled at me and made my week," recollected one student fondly.

Dmitri Nabokov has suggested three reasons why his mother attended his father's lectures: So as to be completely up-to-date in the event that she had to substitute for him; because she was a full creative partner in all he did; because he wanted her to be there. A hint of her calling can be found in "Bachmann," a short story Nabokov wrote the year after he had met Véra. Bachmann's stellar career at the piano takes off the first day his admirer Mme. Perov sits down, "very straight, smooth-haired," in the front row of one of his concerts. It ends the first night she fails to appear, when, after seating himself at the piano, Bachmann's eye catches on the empty seat in the middle of the first row. A few Cornellians seemed to appreciate Bachmann's secret in recalling the performances of Professor Nabokov. "It was as if he were giving the lectures for her," a former student mused, echoed by several

---

* Did he dress in the dark? Where did he shop? Such were the mysteries probed by one student whose attention to detail on the page was much applauded by her professor.
† Nabokov's apparel stood in distinct contrast to the pipe-and-English-tweeds look generally favored by the humanities faculty. From the first he had cut a rumpled figure, liberally interpreting Cornell's predominately tie-and-jacket dress code.

others. Another alumnus had the sense that Nabokov found lecturing for himself and his wife a more gratifying task than attempting to raise the students up by their illiterate bootstraps. Surely the person who tried to make herself the most invisible was—to the man on the stage—the most visible. And surely she knew this. For whom else could he have been speaking when he listed on the blackboard the names of the five greatest Russian poets? The name Sirin stood out for its obscurity. "Who is Sirin?" asked an intrepid graduate student, as she and a friend grew suspicious. "Ah, Sirin, I shall read from his work," Nabokov answered with a straight face and no further explanation. After class some of the students who heard these tributes raced across the quadrangle to the card catalogue. And there discovered, as Nabokov's Harvard students had, the true identity of that elusive Russian master.

His eyes lit up when his assistant was around, but the effect went further. On a particularly dim Ithaca morning Nabokov began lecturing in the dark. After a few minutes Véra left her seat in the front row to switch on the amphitheater lights. As she did so a beatific smile spread across her husband's face. "Ladies and gentlemen"—he gestured proudly from the front of the room to the back—"my assistant." The salute was a loving one; what she had done to elicit it was to flood Vladimir Nabokov in light, which, for both of them, was the desired effect. She was not meant so much to impress her husband's greatness on his students, although to many the occasional glance was interpreted as "Do you have any idea who he *is*?" The adulation was instead meant to ricochet between them. Nabokov saw in his wife's eyes the image to which he aspired; she saw before her the performer she had done so much to underwrite. She allowed him not to walk, but to talk, into his own reflection. With his assistant in the room he was able to achieve the effect he had aspired to in *Conclusive Evidence,* as he described it in the memoir's long-unpublished final chapter, which he had expected to represent the volume's most important pages, the summation and analysis of his themes. He might better have called them an account of the magician laying out his equipment. Posing as a fictitious reviewer and speaking of himself in the comfortable third person, he wrote: "But one is inclined to think that his [Mr. Nabokov's] true purpose here is to project himself, or at least his most treasured self, into the picture he paints. One is reminded of those problems of 'objectivity' that the philosophy of science brings up. An observer makes a detailed picture of the whole universe but when he has finished he realizes that it still lacks something: his own self." For this trick he needed an assistant.

What did *she* think she was doing in the classroom? A little bit of keeping her husband in line. Perhaps mopping up the bons mots; this was the woman who would compare her husband's brain to an oil well. Despite Nabokov's later blustering about how a tape recorder could have replaced him, there is evidence of real anxiety in the early days at Cornell. He was overwhelmed by Ithaca, uneasy in the classroom. Initially Véra may have been in place to ease the stage fright; long after he had left academia, Nabokov had regular nightmares that he was about to deliver a lecture but could not decipher his notes. Her attendance certainly made her husband happy, and in the simple and irreversible emotional equation that defined the Nabokovs' lives this made her happy. In his 1977 biography, Field cites Nabokov's remark that he "likes to be able to watch faces as he reads." What Vladimir had actually said, however, and what one Nabokov had excised, was that "Nabokov likes to be able to watch his wife's face as he reads." It was always a pleasure for Véra to hear Vladimir read what he had written; what music lover would object to regular performances of Callas singing "Casta Diva"? Early on the couple considered the lectures to be publishable material; this Ithaca delivery of them was the polishing of a private work-in-progress, an act at which Véra had long been present. She never thought it anything but a privilege to hear the translation of *Madame Bovary* corrected annually, much though she must occasionally have felt she should have stayed home and cleared her desk. She grumbled periodically about the blue-books, often about the correspondence, on rare occasion about the driving, never about the classroom routine. Nor did she shrink from the appellation "my assistant," which to her ears sounded like an honorific. It was the appellation she later chose for herself when on her tax return she was required to declare a profession. When the student who had been surprised to learn the identity of Nabokov's assistant wrote his former professor years later, he asked him to pass on regards to "your charming wife (your 'assistant,' I recall)." Véra answered the letter, signing off, "Mrs. Vladimir Nabokov, still V.N.'s 'assistant')."

She had a further, more personal interest in the lectures. The amphitheater lights went on over her husband, but they did so to allow him to sing the praises of the writer's best creation: his reader. It was the excellent reader who saved the artist again and again from "being destroyed by emperors, dictators, priests, puritans, philistines, political moralists, policemen, postmasters, and prigs"—as from snow shovels, department meetings, dustballs, bluebooks, lube jobs. Véra knew where she sat in her husband's private pantheon. She showed no sign of having felt oppressed, eclipsed—or, for that matter, central, indispensable, a full creative partner. At all times she appears to have believed that she stood not in her husband's shadow but in his light. The tacit participation worked two rather paradoxical effects. It established her as everywhere present in a life from which she sought—and fought—to absent herself. What one student remembered as the "quality of her presence" vividly colored her husband's classroom, a room in which he spoke eloquently about—this, too, was *Madame Bovary*—absence as a kind of "radiant presence." And because Véra worked so diligently to submerge her identity, another had to be created for her. As she would have learned from Literature 325 and from a manuscript she had typed, facts will persist in sticking to us, they "cannot be discarded by the most ardent nudist." By the time she had grown into her English-language self she had become something of a fiction, an amalgam of the sphinx, the Countess, and the Gray Eagle. She made none of the energetic attempts to wriggle free of this mask that her husband discussed when lecturing on Kafka and Gogol's fantastic worlds. Every artist's wife knows this fate, though the process is rarely so public. Erect in her chair, her coat thrown back around her shoulders, Véra sat for hours and hours for a portrait that resembled her only slightly in the end. Of all the characters conjured into being at Cornell, this one—variously and perplexedly described as disciple, bodyguard, secretary-protector, handmaiden, buffer, monitor, quotation-finder, groupie, advance man, professorial understudy, nursemaid, courtier—proved among the most original.

After 1955 she did own a pistol, but it lived in a shoebox, not in her purse. And at least as far as can be ascertained, it never went to class.

NABOKOV 102

The Doppelgänger subject is a frightful bore.

—NABOKOV, *STRONG OPINIONS*

1

For the silent partner, she could have a very loud voice. Elena Levin laughs when asked if Vladimir deferred to his wife in conversation. "No one ever had to defer to Véra, in conversation or otherwise," she contends. Outside the classroom Professor Nabokov's assistant was quick to assert herself. Wilson found Véra rerouting him to an argument about poetry "with a certain deadliness"; when she spoke directly to the world she could do so with near-brutal force. The Cornell faculty—and especially the occasional Cornell landlord— were among the first to discover as much. The fall 1952 semester was spent in a newly constructed glass-fronted home at 106 Hampton Road, a house about which Véra had a semester's worth of questions. Mercifully, there were no fleas, but what to do about the intrusive moonlight? (Professor and Mrs. Wiegandt, having only barely moved in themselves, suggested she hang curtains, or at least sheets.) Herbert Wiegandt had a few complaints of his own, which he straightforwardly presented to Vladimir in a February 10, 1953, letter, after the Nabokovs had decamped to Cambridge. Most of all he was concerned with damage that had been done to the newly laid kitchen linoleum, and with a missing carving set. By return mail he had his explanation. "We never used your silver. We know nothing about that carving set. We did not wash the tiles in your downstairs bathroom with any hard or other solution," riposted Véra, as Vladimir, adding: "And we did nothing to encourage the 'curling' of your linoleum."

What passed for conversation with most academics and their wives could, depending on the company, amount with the Nabokovs to provocation. In the spring of 1958 Professor and Mrs. William Moulton invited the couple with Eric Blackhall, a visiting professor of German Literature, and a college dean, for cocktails. Véra kicked off the afternoon by delivering a virulent attack on the Wilhelm Busch album lying on a table in the Moultons' living room, in her opinion a prime example of German cruelty. Ultimately Jenni Moulton managed to salvage the conversation, and to lead the new professor toward Véra on the davenport. She asked after his field. "Goethe," replied Blackhall. "I consider *Faust* one of the shallowest plays ever written," declared Véra, as much to the visitor's astonishment as to her husband's manifest delight. She seemed to enjoy disconcerting people. She asked a twenty-eight-year-old assistant professor how he could possibly stand those new French authors and, for that matter, how he could teach them. Indictment struck the young scholar as her modus operandi. It is impossible to say if she had learned this gauntlet-flinging from her husband, who greeted colleagues with salvos like these, delivered for the delectation of French scholar Jean-Jacques Demorest: "To your knowledge, did Stendhal ever pen a decent sentence?" "Does anyone worth reading in France still believe that that fellow Dostoevski could write?" "Do you think your country will ever again beget authors as perfect as Bossuet and Chateaubriand?" Véra knew her eristic assaults greatly amused her husband, who smiled benevolently upon them, as he did whenever an interlocutor unwittingly stumbled on the ambushes of his wife's pet peeves. She could "irritate the intelligent and puzzle the nincompoops" as well as he. (She was actually far harder on the intelligent than on the nincompoops.) And the Nabokovs could do so in concert. Not only was Auden emphatically denounced at one side of the room by Véra and later, in the same terms, by Vladimir, but the couple had a synchronized go as well at Jane Austen, whose importance, they argued from opposite ends of a dinner table, had been ridiculously inflated. Any number of nineteenth-century French writers could be counted as her equal. And this at the home of the head of Cornell's Creative Writing program.

By the early 1950s Véra's understanding of academic life, her sense of her husband's caprices were ingrained enough that—while she seems never to have voluntarily spoken for him—she did not hesitate to edit or silence him. He depended on her for this service.* As much as she admired, and shared,

---

* As the scholar Carl Proffer has pointed out, "Spousal censorship in Russia is at least as old as Dostoyevsky's second wife." She did a fine job on his diary, stopping just short of the ink Bulgakov's wife strategically spilled on her husband's more compromising pages.

her husband's sinewy convictions, she evinced periodic discomfort at their airing. On one such occasion she expressed relief that he had enjoyed himself in a public forum, "and therefore was amusing, brilliant and—thank God— did not say what he thinks of some famous contemporaries." The attacks were clearly a form of amusement to both Nabokovs, a means by which to spice up life in "udder-conscious and udderly boring Cornell," a place they felt overly tame. But Véra more carefully observed the limits.* She counseled a little mercy when her husband was too stern with an aspiring writer in his office. He administered a home botany exam to a young relative, who failed it miserably. "You know, Mitya doesn't know anything," Vladimir shrugged, in the great-nephew's presence. "Don't pay attention to him, he's an old crank," Véra assured the humiliated teenager. And she toned down her husband's ebullience, which could be as robust as her indignation, enough so to drown out even her strong voice. Clare's plucking at the sleeve of Sebastian Knight in a helpless effort to control his laughter in a London theater prefigures the same scene at Cornell. The critic Alfred Appel recalled an Ithaca viewing of *Beat the Devil*, at which half the audience was laughing at the movie, the other half laughing at Nabokov laughing. Véra "murmured '*Volodya!*' a few times, but then gave up, as it became clear that two comic fields had been established in the theater."

Both Nabokovs were quick to seize on the perceived slight. One colleague felt that Vladimir "teetered always on the thin edge of unendurable insult." Insecurity is in part the immigrant's lot, the price of deciphering a new culture; Véra had had a head start in this respect. Woe to the correspondent who hinted that she had perhaps mixed up her tsars. "I am sorry to disappoint you, but I am a Russian woman, and quite sure of the sequence of Russian Tsars and the dates of their reign," came the tart response. "I am equally well informed regarding my husband's family and its antecedents," she added, correcting her correspondent's version of Russian history, which she found deficient. No one could fire off an "Incidentally" with quite the force of Véra, who accomplished with these killer adverbs what her husband could with a pair of heart-stopping—"(picnic, lightning)"—parentheses. The inchoate sense of grievance, the grudge-holding, was something of a Slonim family trait. In the summer of 1950, Véra's older sister proposed sending some well-bred Swedish friends on a visit to Ithaca. Véra responded that she and Vladimir were insanely busy, that they had no time even to see

---

* As with much concerning the couple, this made for a baroque arrangement. When a journalist noted that Véra occasionally censored her husband's conversation—the journalist felt she was very much understating the case—Vladimir, who had approval of the text, censored out the description of his wife censoring him, thereby effectively censoring her censoring.

their own acquaintances. Additionally she asked that Lena refrain from sending her presents of any kind; the Nabokovs were straining to keep their possessions to a minimum, on account of the frequent moves. This she said directly, no more or less so than she did anything else. She suspected that Lena needed to "show off her family" and attempted to fob off the Swedes on Sonia, then in New York. Lena countered that she was only trying to do her friends a favor. She was well past the point in life where she needed to display her family; her sister's phrase proved that she knew nothing of her existence, or its hardships. And she had no interest whatever in speaking with Sonia, who had insulted Lena's husband in 1932.* Véra and Lena did not speak— or communicate—for the next nine years.

It is difficult to say which came first: Véra's serving as picador to her husband's matador, or the discomfort some Cornell faculty members felt in the couple's presence. The synchronized teaching did nothing to endear them. It was so expertly handled it appeared to have been rehearsed. Even those who admired the performance begrudged Nabokov his assistant; Szeftel noted in his journal that Véra was reading her husband's bluebooks "in another selfless show of devotion." Resentment of Véra accumulated in equal proportion to the mystique. The faculty—acutely aware that Nabokov had no Ph.D., no graduate students, few seminars, and, by the mid-fifties, enviably high enrollments—chafed at the husband-and-wife routine. When Nabokov was under consideration for a job elsewhere, a former colleague at that institution discouraged the idea. "Don't bother hiring him; *she* does all the work," he warned. Nabokov himself did nothing to check this kind of sniping. He told his students Ph.D. stood for "Department of Philistines." He treated even his own performances flippantly. When a colleague with whom he was friendly insisted on attending one of his lectures he conceded, "Well all right, if you want to be a masochist about it." Other Ithaca wives were asked point-blank why they could not be more like Véra, held up as the gold standard. This did nothing to win her friends, had she wanted them. It was felt she had no need for confidantes because she was so close to her husband; her reverence was as objectionable as his irreverence. Well before the advent of *Lolita,* Nabokov was respected but not universally liked by his colleagues; some faculty members crossed the street to avoid him. Within the department, his course was so much discouraged that one English major concluded there must be something illicit about it. There was reason to perceive slights. In the land of the

---

* Lena still did not know the fate of the husband whom she had left, but whom she valiantly defended, and who had disappeared during the war. Véra expressed no curiosity about him whatever. For reasons that are unclear but probably had to do with rumors swirling in Berlin, she seems to have shared Sonia's low opinion of Massalsky.

footnoters, as Bishop had called them, Nabokov was a man apart. Véra was from outer space.

The cultural divide was considerable. Ithaca, and Cornell, are to a great extent America. The place is scenic and civilized but also remote, tucked inaccessibly behind the Adirondacks. To the Nabokovs the university's agricultural origins were more apparent than its academic prowess. For all of its distinguished professors, Cornell was a loose-limbed institution with a model forest, a fish hatchery, a pig farm. The rail connection was poor and the air service not much better. As Véra explained to a visiting relative, "Our only airline (The Mohawk) pounces on every pretext to cancel flights—on holidays, weekends, rainy days, etc."* After all she had lived through, Ithaca's calm, its parochialism, may have been a relief, but the land of the sterling carving set, the hypersensitive linoleum, also felt unfamiliar. Nabokov reveled in his new medium. His object was to enrich the magic potion of his new language as earlier he had arranged things so as not to dilute his first one. He went out of his way to attract to his flypaper mind every nuance of American life. (To Jean Bruneau, an assistant professor of French Literature, he explained his motives differently. With a glint in his eye, he warned that publication of his new novel would scandalize America in its savage attack on the American language.) At all times the couple were aware of more than a renter's distance between them and what those around them considered the real world.† They took to showing off some of the artifacts they discovered in the rented stage sets to visitors; they appeared to be playacting at their American life. The exotica was of great use to Nabokov—who could have imagined the Mexican knickknacks, the pink toilet-cover furs?—but less charming to Véra who, in the time-honored immigrant way, could not help but being astonished, and horrified, by Americans. As for American schools, they were all poor, even the most expensive ones.

Some of the ambivalence showed. When Leo Peltenburg died in 1955, his middle daughter wrote Véra with the news. Acknowledging previous reports from Ithaca, she opined: "I think Vera your husband and your son are glad that they found a new home country in the U.S. As to you I am not so sure." Much of Véra's animus was directed not to the man in the street, but to

---

* The schedules nearly prove the undoing of Gradus in *Pale Fire,* to whom they seem the work of a practical joker.
† Their permanent address at Cornell was Goldwin Smith Hall. Partly to distinguish himself from the linguists on campus, whose headquarters were elsewhere, Nabokov went so far as to call himself a Goldwin Smith man. For once his scholarship failed him. He would hardly have done so had he known that Goldwin Smith, a British historian who had taught at Cornell between 1868 and 1871 and left the school his fortune, had written some wholly unsavory things about Russian Jews, especially about the "prosperous usurers" of the Pale.

fellow academics, who should have known better. Her litmus test of good taste was recognition of her husband's genius. So long as the owner of a roadside motel remained more impressed with a published author than did the Harvard professor who failed to hire him, her respect was reserved only for the hotelier. Lena Massalsky was to say that after twenty-six years in Sweden she could not decipher the local mores; Véra had more trouble with the tolerating than with the deciphering. While Vladimir had long noted that the non-Russian could never hope to understand the "lyrical plaintiveness that colors the Russian soul," someone like Véra could never be expected to appreciate the wide-open expansiveness of the American soul. A middle-aged man's obsession with a twelve-year-old girl was one thing. What Véra could not comprehend was the publisher's wife who, at an early encounter, blurted out the details of her messy emotional life, or the publisher who discussed his sentimental travails within a taxi driver's earshot. She addressed only two words, and an exclamation point, to this subject. "Amazing Americans!" she declared. It all seemed to her like something out of a bad novel—something by John O'Hara, or James Gould Cozzens.

Some of her strongest feelings were reserved for politics. As early as 1948 she expressed a desire to participate in local politics and wondered how to go about doing so. Was there an office of some kind she could run for, she wondered, outraged by a Town of Ithaca ruling on secondary school education. (She was teaching at the Cascadilla School at the time.) Her husband dissuaded her from getting involved, at least on the local level. "It's dangerous," he counseled, as indeed it would have been—for him. She was frustrated that she had not been able to vote in the 1948 elections; she had not lived in Ithaca for the requisite six months. She met with the same trouble in 1952, when the Harvard semester interfered with the residency requirement. Again in 1956 the lack of a permanent address worked against her, as the Nabokovs had spent a sabbatical spring in Cambridge and an itinerant summer. Véra considered these regulations unfair; she was nothing if not exquisitely sensitive to her privileges. Only in 1964, when she was no longer living in America, did she vote in a U.S. election. Vladimir never voted.

She warmed quickly to political discourse. From the Hampton Road house she fired off a letter to the *Cornell Daily Sun* on December 12, 1952. An editorial in the previous day's college paper had rallied to the defense of Professor Owen Lattimore, the prominent China expert whom McCarthy had labeled a top Soviet agent. Lattimore was something of a hero to the intellectual establishment; moreover, in twelve brutal days of testimony earlier in the year, Senator Patrick A. McCarran's Internal Security Subcommittee had been unable to establish any kind of case against the Johns Hopkins profes-

sor. Véra drew the *Sun*'s attention to Lattimore's activities from 1944 on, citing chapter and verse. She had read all of his work. To her mind the case
against the Sinologist was airtight: He had unquestionably advanced the
Soviets' hold on China. She felt "the two McSenators" were undermining
their own efforts by branding "everybody left of Thomas Dewey" as a Communist, but regretted not the sullied reputations, only the fact that the sena-
tors' zealotry allowed the Communists room to hide.* She specified that her
communication was intended to set the matter straight, not for publication.
(It did not appear in the paper.) The Cold War assumed great—if sometimes
awkward—proportions in her mind. In his 1951 diary Nabokov recorded his
wife's prediction: "She also says that if there is a war with Russia, it will start
in Alaska. We shall see those awful little maps in newspaper[s], with horribly
energetic, blackly curving arrows pointing to Whitehorse, or to Le Pas."
Given what she had lived through, she could be forgiven for too quickly
transposing the past on the future. Both Nabokovs read E. B. White's *Charlotte's Web* at the end of 1952, when the Korean War was at its height. Afterward Vladimir wrote Katharine White: "We both loved Andy's book. Véra
says she wishes he could find some relative of Charlotte and persuade her to
make a nice big web for all of us informing the silly Asians that this is a Terrific and Humble country, and not to be slaughtered and eaten."

Her anticommunism was rabid and instinctive. Milton Cowan believed
the source of her disdain (and by extension her husband's) for the Languages
Division to be her misinterpretation of Gordon Fairbanks's classroom readings. In his course materials for intermediate-level Russian Fairbanks included a copy of the USSR constitution, with which he contrasted Soviet
ideals and reality. Where he saw instruction Véra saw only propaganda; in
her take-no-prisoners approach, she found the reprinting of the document an
affront. (In truth her scorn seems to have been directed at Fairbanks for simpler reasons. When Field noted that Fairbanks spoke little Russian, Véra corrected him. In her opinion Fairbanks did not speak *any* Russian.) She had no
bones to pick with McCarthy's agenda, found every reason to believe Alger
Hiss to be lying. Arthur Schlesinger Jr.'s most vivid recollection of Véra was
an impassioned defense of McCarthy she made at Schlesinger's Cambridge
home, probably during the spring of 1953. To her mind intellectual freedom
paled in light of the Communist threat. Her explanation, her support of
McCarthy's overblown tactics, virtually amounted to a plea.

---

* Four days after Véra wrote her letter, Lattimore was indicted on seven counts of perjury. The charges
were later dismissed. Véra's enthusiasms, if ever she spoke of them, could not have endeared her to Edmund Wilson, whose *Memoirs of Hecate County* McCarthy had attacked as pro-Communist.

Even after McCarthy had fallen from favor—even after 1954, when he had been discredited—she continued to believe his overreacting preferable to what she viewed as American complacency. Her fervor on the subject resulted in a spirited exchange with Mark Vishniak, a former law professor, the Secretary General of the Constituent Assembly of 1918, and a *Contemporary Annals* editor who since 1946 had consulted on Russian affairs for *Time*. Anna Feigin, then living not far from Vishniak in New York, had written her cousin that the editor had referred to Véra as "a McCarthy fan." Véra was disturbed by the notion, evidently more by the fact that she was being spoken about in New York than by Vishniak's assessment of her politics. She wrote that she had laughed to hear herself described as a fan, prattle someone of Vishniak's stature could not possibly take seriously. But Vishniak could be forgiven his appraisal when Véra continued:

> I suppose that McCarthy is a fairly insignificant figure inflated to enormous proportions by the Bolsheviks and the Bolshevik supporters so that they could hide behind his back. And most importantly I consider that not being wholeheartedly for all sorts of men—of very dubious political probity—who speak out against McCarthy does not further mean that one is for McCarthy. I think as well that Soviet agents, and all manner of Communists, should be fished out from the Government, that this is not always done with sufficient speed or sufficient competence, and that the Hisses are more dangerous than all of the McCarthys and similar cheap demagogues.

Generally she held that firm measures were the only kind the Communists understood, an attitude that would astound academic friends later. In 1955 her concern remained the source of the rumor, however. "After all," she wrote Vishniak, "in certain American circles right now to be 'for McCarthy' is considered significantly more serious a crime than passing military secrets to Soviet agents." She worried that the allegation against her had not been as innocent as it seemed.

Vishniak was as much surprised to hear from Véra as he was by the contents of her letter. He knew her only slightly; the remark had been made in a casual conversation. He felt that she was making a mountain out of a molehill—further proof that he knew Véra Nabokov only slightly. Surely, he suggested in reply, there was some middle ground? She would not, after all, say he was a Bolshevik, and *he* found McCarthy—whose behavior he considered unconscionable—a major figure. His influence was not to be underestimated. Twenty years her elder, Vishniak had lived through the same events

as had Véra. His position was interesting: He reminded her that inconse-
quential figures often turned out to be just the opposite. He warned against
whitewashing the reckless McCarthy, as against labeling all those who opposed him Bolsheviks. Véra was unmoved by the argument—"I continue to
consider him [McCarthy] an episodical figure and the real threat to be those
horrible agents that have entrenched themselves in various institutions, even
in the most secret ones," she wrote—but was yet more bitter about Vishniak's
refusal to divulge his sources. She had no intention of reconsidering her
views, even while she felt she had been slandered.

What an émigré like Vishniak would have realized but few others did
was that for Véra principles, not people, came first. In the McCarthy exchange
the two adopted a sort of dueling code. At a certain point Vishniak asked for
her formal acknowledgment that the "incident" was now over. Grudgingly
and coyly, Véra complied. "Enough: Really *was* there an incident?" she rejoined. No habit was more to inform the combative next decade than her stubborn, procrustean dedication to principle.* In this respect she outdistanced
her husband, for whom personal honor remained always of the greatest importance, but who limited his engagement with the world to the world of literature. For Véra principle informed all. It could even vitiate truth. The
Nabokovs believed that the émigré critic Marc Slonim received monthly
checks from the Soviets. Véra always denied categorically that she and Slonim
were related. (The rest of the family disagreed.) A 1967 vacation to France was
canceled when de Gaulle withdrew militarily from NATO. One Ithaca car
dealer severely underestimated the wrath of Véra Nabokov crossed. When
Véra went to pick up the new Buick she had ordered, probably in 1957, she
did so with her check already written. The dealer who announced to his
lovely-looking client that a few additional costs had crept into the transaction
watched helplessly as she tore her check into small pieces and headed out the
door. The Buick Special was purchased elsewhere, at her price.

2

Véra spent a certain amount of time researching the gunsmiths of Paris and
the history of firearms during the sabbatical spring of 1953. "We spent two
months in Cambridge—or rather Widener," Vladimir reported, speaking
for the couple, who were delighted again to be living a stone's throw from

---

* The Russian word *printsipialnost* has been defined as "a mental habit of referring every matter, however
small, concrete, or trivial, to lofty and abstract principles."

Dmitri's dormitory. The curling linoleum was exchanged for a hotel room; work on the *Onegin* commentaries continued, with Véra serving as research assistant. She unearthed details on nineteenth-century firearms and powder-packing methods; to her fell the task of finding out what time the sun rose on the morning of Onegin and Lenski's duel. (She also attempted a March re-union with the much-loved Tomsky, who journeyed to the Ambassador Hotel by taxi one afternoon. Véra set out tea for his escorts and a dish of cut-up liver for the gutter cat, who promptly vanished under a sofa.) In mid-April, she drove Vladimir at an easy pace to Portal, Arizona. The two rented a tiny cottage in the foothills of the southeastern corner of the state, sur-rounded by blossoming cacti, sixty miles from civilization. Vladimir made the trip "on the verge of a breakdown," so debilitated was he from the five-hour days in Widener. He was at work on *Lolita,* which he was composing so furiously that his hand was cramped by evening.

Véra's more vulnerable side was revealed in Arizona that spring. At dusk one May evening the couple were walking near their back porch when Vladimir stopped his wife in her tracks; directly in front of her lay a fat rat-tlesnake. She had nearly stepped on it. With a length of pipe he dealt the creature a powerful blow; the snake still managed to spit at him when he bent down to make sure it was dead. "St. George-Vladimir is saving his trophy: a seven-piece rattle," Véra reported, with admiration for her husband's quick-witted courage. The name stuck for some time. Her affection for the desert did not survive the intruder. "Moreover, Vladimir killed a few days ago a fairsized rattle snake a few feet from our doorstep (we are saving its 7 rattles), and that settled everything so far as I am concerned," she declared, before the Nabokovs packed and headed twelve hundred miles north, to Oregon. They found refuge in the "mellow academic townlet" of Ashland, in a modest hill-side house surrounded by flowers. The destination was not chosen arbitrar-ily: Dmitri had a summer job at a construction site in the area, the collecting was new to Vladimir, and Humbert needed the additional miles. In this scenic spot Timofey Pavlovich Pnin was born, if he did not exist already.

Véra spent July and August typing *Lolita* from her husband's dictation, as the manuscript neared its final form. She mailed the first chapter of *Pnin* to *The New Yorker* on July 26; she collaborated on a Russian version of *Con-clusive Evidence,* work she later claimed she had no memory of having ac-complished. It was a vastly productive summer and a happy one; Véra far preferred the green of Ashland, and the lush garden of roses, to the desert. Dmitri was in residence, which delighted his mother more than did his job. He and his dump truck had already managed to roll over once. When he was rescued from the cab, he was found hanging upside down in the driver's seat.

Surviving their son's brushes with danger had become a staple of the Nabokovs' lives; Véra had moaned that she did not think she would ever get used to his mountaineering, and never did. Dmitri would recognize hints of the distress his ascents caused his parents in "Lance," his father's last short story. The echoes are fairly loud: In a 1940 letter, Nabokov had referred to his bicycle-riding son as "Lance"; a boisterous, adventure-loving Lance Boke turns up as well in *Pnin,* having borrowed one of Dmitri's prep school misdemeanors, as the fictional Lance borrows Dmitri's sinewy size. Nor did Vladimir venture far for his physical description of Mrs. Boke, she of the feigned cheerfulness, who produces a familiar, blurred effect: that "of melting light on one side of her misty hair." (There was a price to pay for Dmitri's having been so hugely brave, as Véra had acknowledged in her notes for *Speak, Memory*: The much-cossetted child turned out to be a daredevil. The concerns of 1953 only increased when he bought his first MG. They multiplied again, in the early 1960s, when he began to race in a Triumph TR 3A, modified for competition.* By the time he took up offshore racing his mother was beside herself.) Both parents spent the spring and the summer of 1953 worrying ceaselessly about him. After many years Véra took the tribulations in stride, or at least as a given: "A parent's job is to worry," she sighed later. But the criteria for her emotional health remained unchanged. "We like it much better here than in Arizona," she wrote her sister-in-law, from Oregon, ". . . the main thing is Volodya is writing well."

But the image of the rattlesnake—news of which made its way into every summer correspondence—clearly burned before her eyes. It unsettled her as armbands and goose-stepping did not. She would always recall that rattler, a herd of cattle, a slumbering bear, with undimmed horror.† Snakes remained for her among the greatest of depredations; she declared later that all would be well in the world if only there were no snakes in the neighborhood, no Khrushchev in the Kremlin. Relatedly, when Dmitri offered his mother an old American revolver the following spring she readily accepted, trading it at the local gun shop for a Browning .38 caliber. Dmitri was not surprised: "She liked guns. She always liked guns." She had been keen on acquiring a weapon, and was delighted by the opportunity to do so. In Decem-

---

* The Triumph was replaced by a custom-tailored Alfa Romeo TZ, in which Dmitri raced successfully in 1964 and 1965. He also twice flew off competitive tracks at top speed in the car, sustaining only minor injuries.

† In the spring of 1949, contemplating a trip to Teton National Park, Nabokov had written to a fellow lepidopterist: "My wife has some timorous questions about grizzlies." The colleague responded that Véra had nothing to fear from bears, but should know how to comport herself in the presence of a moose. (Give it a wide berth.)

ber 1955, she applied for a license to carry a pistol. Four members of the Cornell community vouched for her good character and testified to her ability to wield a firearm in a careful and reasonable manner. The Ithaca undersheriff took a full set of fingerprints. While there were generally not many fifty-three-year-old housewives in Tompkins County filing pistol applications, Véra was surely the only one in history to supply as her reason for doing so: "For protection while travelling in isolated parts of the country in the course of entomological research." The humor of that line may have been lost on her but other implications were not: She indicated that Russia was her country of birth, but stipulated that she had emigrated in 1920. The Browning was a gun she would have had difficulty firing, and which she appears never to have fired. But the automatic that never went off hung heavily over the scenes that followed, especially when it was bound up with Véra's ubiquitousness, her ferocity, her exoticism, her politics—and the explosion that was about to detonate over Ithaca when the contents of a different shoebox were revealed.

Had she been left to her own devices, Véra probably would have owned the .38 for years without anyone in Ithaca outside the county clerk's office being any the wiser. But the handgun had a habit of making an appearance, at Vladimir's urging. Jean-Jacques Demorest dined with the Nabokovs one evening, along with the Literature Department's chairman, Joseph Mazzeo. After the meal Vladimir suggested that his wife furnish the weapon; perhaps their visitors could be persuaded to fix the thing. Véra made a trip upstairs, producing the instrument from a handbag. It seemed she had not pulled the slide back forcefully enough and a cartridge had jammed. The visitors were dumbfounded, and unable to offer any assistance with the mechanism, with which they were unfamiliar. On this or another occasion—Mazzeo saw the Browning more than once—Véra explained that she had acquired the pistol so as to protect Vladimir from rattlers when he was collecting butterflies, an image that, at both ends of the zoological spectrum, fairly summed up the relationship to many. Nestled in the glove compartment of the car, the Browning traveled across the West with the Nabokovs. Jason Epstein became *Pnin*'s publisher a decade later and was also treated to a viewing of the gun. His wife very nearly fainted on the spot. The weapon was produced as an explanation for why Véra—then living in an isolated home a little bit in the Ithaca woods—was not frightened; the effect was much the opposite. Barbara Epstein left with the impression that Véra felt there were Indians outside, that the Nabokovs were at all times under siege. The conclusion was correct although the Browning had little to do with it. But word of it spread on campus, where it was said that Mrs. Nabokov was traveling to class with a handgun, where it was rumored that the couple slept with a pistol under their mattress, in the event the Bolsheviks came for them. (Epstein concluded that Véra carried the weapon—Sibyl Shade should have taken note—to guard against the likely campus assassin. Recalling the setup in the Goldwin Smith classroom, he concluded: "She really had him covered.") The point was that the accessory required little stretch of the imagination, given Véra's persona. Elena Levin never saw the weapon but was wholly unsurprised to hear of its existence.

To the 1964 Bollingen Press reception for *Eugene Onegin* Véra—who had done so much to research the circumstances of Pushkin's duel—carried a beaded evening bag with a mother-of-pearl handle. Saul Steinberg, whose grasp of images the couple thought unrivaled, attended the festivities, probably at Nabokov's request. At the end of the party, the three found themselves alone on the Upper East Side street, with Steinberg's date. "Véra, show him what you have in your handbag," Vladimir directed, with what Steinberg recognized as immense pride. Véra extracted the Browning. Slightly daintier than the handgun she had carried in Berlin, the weapon would have made a bulge in an evening bag; assuming it was loaded, it would have weighed nearly a pound and a half. To the great artist's eye the gesture was ripe with symbolism. It seemed as if Véra had been appointed the keeper of her husband's virtue. Véra would have shuddered at the mention of symbolism, but it was her husband after all who asked his students to list the contents of Anna Karenina's handbag, critical to an understanding of her character.

3

"You will perhaps be interested to learn that he is finishing a great novel, based on an idea that he believes has never been explored (at least not in the way that he has done so). It is a work of more than 400 pages, the plot of which unfolds rapidly," Véra advised the French publisher of *Gogol* in November 1953, noting that her husband had been at work on the volume for nearly four years.* After a series of hints to Viking's Pat Covici, this was the first overture to an editor on *Lolita*'s behalf. Since the September return to Ithaca Vladimir had been devoting sixteen-hour days to the manuscript; his academic duties seemed relaxing in comparison. The Russian *Conclusive Evidence* continued to hang over the Nabokovs' heads; it had been expected for January but Vladimir—who felt he was writing the book anew—found

---

* According to Nabokov's diary, it had been begun exactly five years earlier.

the project an unending one. (A final draft was submitted to Chekhov Publishing much later. In a charming slip, Véra dated her cover letter April 1, 1854.) On December 6 she sent up a triumphant salvo: "V. asks me to jot that he is *finishing* the book today," she announced, to the Hessens. Three days later she requested a personal meeting with Katharine White, for reasons she preferred not to commit to paper.

Lolita made its first trip to New York at the end of December 1953, when Véra carried the manuscript to White's East Forty-eighth Street doorstep. The bundle bore no return address. Vladimir had hesitated to mail the pages; Véra explained that the author's name would not be attached to the manuscript, which her husband intended to publish under a pseudonym, soon divulged to be "Humbert Humbert." She exacted a promise "that his incognito be respected." Most of all they wanted the thing kept from the office and, in particular, from the very proper William Shawn. From the start both Nabokovs recognized the manuscript as "a time bomb."* "In an atmosphere of great secrecy," Vladimir had promised Wilson a glimpse of the pages earlier in the year. If Véra had as strong a taste for anything as she did for literature, it may well have been for complot: The stately middle-aged woman carrying to East Forty-eighth Street the 459 subversive pages of a manuscript that she and her husband alone were convinced was a work of genius—demanding guarantees of secrecy from another distinguished woman generally described as "formidable"—seemed precisely the role for which the years of silence, exile, and cunning had prepared her. (For various reasons White did not read the manuscript until much later. She had five granddaughters; she told Vladimir she would be lying if she did not say she had been disturbed by the book. Furthermore, she didn't have a thing for psychopaths.)†

What Véra thought of the manuscript burning the hole in that bag is perfectly clear. She had steered her husband away from poetry; she had headed off the Siamese twins. She chastised herself for *Eugene Onegin*: "I can't believe I let him take up this project," she berated herself, as she often would regarding her husband's translation work, which she felt cost him a few titles of his own. About *Lolita* she had no such qualms. This did not mean she was unaware of the dangers of her husband's publishing—and of the public's misreading—the sexually explicit confessions of a middle-aged

---

* The situation was a delicate one. Nabokov had an obligation to show the magazine the work, which he knew they could not publish but which he needed for them to refuse—secretly if possible—before he could submit it elsewhere.

† "Would we like our sons to marry Emma Rouault, Becky Sharp, or *La belle dame sans merci*?" Vladimir retorted.

European's obsessive pursuit of a prepubescent girl.* She presented the matter firmly but delicately to her sister-in-law, to whom a copy was sent on first publication: "In any case don't judge it until you've read it all the way through. It's not pornography at all but an incredible, most subtle probe to the depths of a horrible maniac and explores the tragic fate of a defenseless young girl. (V. studied the law on the protection of orphans, and there is no law that would have prevented this turn of events.)" A few weeks later, having heard nothing from Geneva, she wrote again. "V is afraid that Lolita *has stunned you* and that that's why you're so silent. Don't judge it until you reach the end. It's frightening. *But it is a great book.*" As much as she claimed to think it ridiculous that the novel might run into publishing difficulties, she understood very well what the book represented to 1950s America. She had heard firsthand of Wilson's woes with *Memoirs of Hecate County,* a collection of stories and a novella that had been withdrawn from sale and prosecuted for obscenity in 1946. (That year she professed admiration for that book. "I am very fond of Wilbur!" she had assured Wilson, naming the hero of the volume's third story. After relations with Wilson soured, she backtracked, insisting that the Wilbur to whom she had referred was the poet Richard Wilbur. She was indeed fond of Richard Wilbur, but she had not yet met him in 1946. Privately she remarked that *Hecate County* left her indifferent.) As much as she believed in the sanctity of art, she remained entirely the mother who thought her twelve-year-old too young to be exposed to Mark Twain. "*But it is a great book,*" she reminded her sister-in-law. In her next breath she added, "And hide it from your son." She had already once warned that *Lolita* was not a book for children. Elena was not to leave it lying around.

Pat Covici, the first publisher to read the novel, did not think *Lolita* even a book for adults. At least not for adults unwilling to serve jail sentences; he advised Nabokov strongly against publishing the novel, and felt that bringing it out anonymously was in particular an open invitation for a court case. The manuscript had arrived at his office unsigned; Nabokov had submitted it only after exacting a written promise, "legally binding you and any person connected with your firm, not to divulge the author's true identity under any circumstances, unless I give a formal authorization for doing so." Covici's

---

* Cursing the public's naïve inability to distinguish author from protagonist, she acknowledged that the conflation could result in some "unpleasantness." She thought this naïveté a particularly American trait. In Sweden her sister railed against her new countrymen for the same reason. Carl Proffer made the same observation about the Russian mind, secure in its conviction that "reality always lies just under the surface of fiction." Even Nadezhda Mandelstam would assure Proffer that "in her mind there was no doubt that the man who wrote *Lolita* could not have done so unless he had in his soul those same disgraceful feelings for little girls."

news reached the Nabokovs on Irving Place, during Véra's January bluebook blizzard, while Vladimir was at work on the adventures of another middle-aged European boarder, with which he replaced *Lolita* on the editor's desk two weeks later. The first and favored child was returned by express mail, with no indication of an author's name anywhere on the package. The same day Vladimir attempted to interest New Directions in his time bomb, but discovered that Laughlin was out of the country. In March Simon & Schuster's learned Wallace Brockway paid a call on the couple to discuss a new edition of *Anna Karenina,* for which Vladimir was to provide the critical apparatus. Nabokov profited from the meeting to discuss another girl who meets an early and tragic demise; in two black springbinders, the manuscript went to Simon & Schuster on a highly confidential basis on March 18.* Vladimir had his hands entirely full throughout the semester (as Véra later put it, he "was up to his chin in Pnin"), when he was simultaneously at work on the Tolstoy annotations.† Initially he had hoped to finish *Pnin* by June; he was to be off by a year, although Covici offered a contract for the book based on the first chapters. Ten weeks after sending Brockway the manuscript, Véra took the liberty of nudging him—at his home address—about "the novel about H.H. and L." At the end of June Brockway had to admit that his colleagues could see the book only as sheer pornography. He suggested Barney Rosset's Grove Press. Nabokov was undeterred, although he had come to realize that an agent might be necessary in placing the novel. He would be willing to surrender a princely 25 percent commission. Probably because Laughlin was still away, the manuscript spent the remainder of the summer in Ithaca, locked in a drawer. Its author made a note to himself, so as to remember where he had stored the keys.

It was Véra who followed up on the idea, presumably at Covici's suggestion, that the novel stood some chance of publication abroad. On August 6, 1954, from Taos, New Mexico, she wrote to Doussia Ergaz, the resourceful Russian literary agent who had long handled Nabokov's work in France. To a series of housekeeping matters Véra affixed a last question: "My husband has written a novel of extreme originality, which—because of straightlaced morality—could not be published here. What possibility is there for publication (in English) in Europe?" She begged for a speedy reply, providing the Taos address where she expected to be until the end of the month. The sum-

---

* Brockway seemed the perfect reader. He was something of the in-house pundit at Simon & Schuster but worked primarily out-of-house, as a freelance editor, and would therefore have been less likely to share the manuscript with the wrong readers. He proved very discreet indeed.
† They were never published as such.

mer had been a disappointing one. Financially the summers were always difficult, and that of 1954 had been especially lean. *Pnin* would not truly begin
to earn his keep until the following year, and *Lolita* was proving a most uncooperative child. Dmitri had not been much better: He had spent the last
part of the spring semester on probation for throwing firecrackers—the occasion was his twentieth birthday—and Véra was even more alarmed that
with one year of university left, his plans for the future had not yet begun to
cohere. Vladimir was despondent about the whole *Lolita* "fiasco." The novel
had cost him nearly five years, and was by far his best work in English. Nor
were the three Nabokovs finding their accommodations outside Taos, which
they had rented by mail, to be as scenic as they had hoped. As Véra wrote the
adobe home's owner later, they had "never found a description to differ so
much from reality." The woman profoundly attuned to the elasticity of
words now cursed those very powers:

> We expected to find a small house in "three acres of orchard and gar-
> den." We found a house by the road with a narrow and almost impass-
> able strip of kitchen garden in the back. There was no place to walk, or
> even sit outside, for the patio offered no privacy with the Martinez fam-
> ily constantly circulating back and forth from the side gate. Moreover, if
> the wind came from the south, the smell of the sewer pervaded the patio
> and invaded the house. . . . The "rushing mountain river" proved to be
> an irrigation ditch. There was dust and sand constantly falling down
> from the ceiling, there were flies coming in through the doors and the
> falty [*sic*] screens, there were mice littering shelves and drawers with
> their droppings. When we first arrived, we decided to leave at once,
> then decided to try and stay.

With her sister-in-law she abandoned all euphemisms, describing a yard
overrun by chickens, and the objectionable Martinez clan.

Taos failed to charm the Nabokovs as well. The town struck Véra as "a
second-rate Greenwich village";* she was delighted that ten miles separated
her from it. Her disappointment, if not Vladimir's, was much on display
from the start. When a friend of the home's owner attempted to help the
Nabokovs settle in, he found Véra chilly and unforthcoming. As the house
had no phone, he was obliged to call on the family in person. Véra resisted his
overtures, barely enduring the elaborate picnic he had arranged, excusing

---

* Taos "is a dismal hole full of third-rate painters and faded pansies," her husband apprised Wilson.

herself early from a tea to which he invited the visitors. Delighted that this loyal *New Yorker* reader knew his work, Vladimir proved more receptive to the westerner's attentions. He asked to meet Frieda Lawrence, an introduction their substitute host said he would be happy to arrange. Véra vetoed the plan: "She's a dreadful, awful woman and I don't want to meet her. I don't want to go, and I don't want you to go without me" was the reaction. She entirely disapproved of the writer's famously plate-throwing widow, could not have felt any more fond of her domestic arrangements, and may at the time have been suffering from her own: Early in August, two chipmunks drowned in the cistern from which the Nabokovs' drinking water was drawn. The animals were discovered only after the entire family had fallen ill.

The unsavory neighbors, the chipmunk corpses, the boomerang manuscript, and the financial strains all paled in light of a single August moment, however, when Véra discovered a hard lump in her breast. On Tuesday, August 10, a doctor at Albuquerque's Lovelace Clinic diagnosed the growth as cancerous. The next day Véra cabled her sister Sonia in New York, asking her to arrange for immediate surgery, which was done, a family doctor having agreed to cancel his weekend plans. The three Nabokovs made a precipitate departure from New Mexico, or at least departed as precipitately as they could: A general airline strike loomed. On Thursday Dmitri drove his mother to the Superchief Train, which made a whistle-stop along the highway between Taos and Santa Fe. If she lost her composure she did not do so in front of her family. For his part Vladimir was hysterical. About his own illnesses he was generally cavalier, but the possibility of losing Véra left him panic-stricken. Dmitri never saw his father so much on the edge as he was the following day, when the two raced the train cross-country, "hurtling in pursuit, tires popping, in the family Buick." Dmitri attempted to distract him with levity: "How can you say that when your mother is dying of cancer?" Vladimir reprimanded him. He was put out of his misery in New York, where the growth had been removed at Mount Sinai Hospital immediately upon Véra's Saturday arrival. It proved benign.

This was hardly Véra's first race across a continent with calamitous news ringing in her ears. After the Ukraine, and the crossing of Germany in 1937, and the mad dash to Saint-Nazaire, she could have been forgiven had she developed a railroad phobia, which she did not. When Lisbet Thompson suffered a similar scare in 1961 Véra recommended her favored corrective: a hearty dose of mental discipline. "Keep track of all your symptoms, consult a good specialist, but do not allow those upsetting thoughts to preoccupy you. These thoughts occur to every person alive. But the only way to keep sane

and well is to combat them with all the power of will you have," she counseled her friend. She had concluded as much in the midst of the 1954 misadventure, upon being told with great certainty that she had breast cancer.
"One just *must* train oneself not to indulge these thoughts," she assured Lisbet. (The only casualty of the repeated misdiagnoses was Véra's confidence in
American medicine, which she concluded to be a brew of improbable reasoning and black magic.) While friends were told of a brush with ill health,
Véra's indisposition was typically described as gallbladder or liver trouble.
Without elaboration, she reported that she was recovering quickly. She was
well enough by August 23 to write to the New Mexico landlord, from Anna
Feigin's apartment in New York. Gently she suggested that further rent
should be forgiven. Despite the circumstances this was a godsend; after the
hospital expenses, the Nabokovs were unable even to send their monthly
check abroad to Vladimir's family. They returned to Ithaca "in a pitiful state
of destitution and debt." A few days after they had done so, Doussia Ergaz's
response to Véra's August 6 letter arrived in Taos. It was some time in catching up with the couple. Ergaz knew just the publisher for *Lolita*. She would
love to see the manuscript in question.

On October 1 *Lolita* made a fourth trip to New York, with an unsigned
letter; Laughlin read the novel promptly and just as promptly rejected it. He
too advised against publication, which he deemed an act of self-destruction
for both author and publisher. Undaunted, Nabokov directed Laughlin to
forward the manuscript to Roger Straus at Farrar, Straus & Young, taking
care to avoid using the postal service—the first line of censorship, as the
Comstock Act had made it a crime to distribute obscenity by the mails—in
doing so.* Straus was longer with the novel, but reluctantly concluded on
November 11 that the work could not be introduced to America without a
court battle, which he did not believe could be won.† Moreover no publisher
"in his right mind" would consider doing so for an anonymous author.
Nabokov had no intention of attaching his name even to a proposed excerpt,
allowing only that he might feel differently in a year's time.

It was Véra who replied to Straus's letter. The rejection was less trou-
bling than was the fact that the publisher had mentioned that Vladimir
might have heard of Straus's reading "from various of our mutual friends."
This line set off alarm bells in Ithaca. Who exactly did Straus have in mind?

---

* Five years later, *Lady Chatterley's Lover* would fall victim to the U.S. Post. In 1953 a Cornell literary magazine had been deemed unsuitable for mailing and confiscated.
† In the course of these months Straus had, on his lawyers' advice, also resisted Wilson's campaign to reis-
sue *Hecate*. The fates of the two novels were to remain curiously tangled.

queried Véra. He admitted that he had discussed the manuscript with Edmund and Elena Wilson, as well as with Mary McCarthy and her husband Bowden Broadwater.* This news seemed to mollify Véra, though those friends' reactions would not have. With the exception of Elena Wilson, who shared her high opinion of the work, the consensus was that its author had lost his mind. "The poor darling had clearly flipped," was the reaction at the McCarthy-Broadwater household. At Wilson's suggestion, Jason Epstein asked to see the manuscript. He did not add that Wilson had already offered him a preview of sorts, or how Wilson had billed the two black spring-binders. "It's repulsive," Nabokov's early and most energetic American advocate had advised Epstein, words he toned down only slightly when writing the author himself.† In truth the book temporarily soured him on Nabokov: "Did you read his *Lolita* by the way? Thought it was so repulsive that it rather put me off him," Wilson griped the following year. (Elena Levin suspected he found the novel particularly tasteless for the same reason White had resisted it: Wilson had a very young daughter. Harry and Elena Levin had no such problems with the novel, which they found admirable and hugely erotic. They did however come to understand their friend's sudden, earlier interest in their prepubescent daughter, whom Vladimir had taken to interviewing exhaustively.) Early in December Nabokov mailed Epstein the manuscript, exacting the usual promises about incognitos.

At the end of 1954, one year after Pat Covici had done so, Epstein read and rejected *Lolita* for Doubleday. The report he submitted to the firm's editor in chief is a masterpiece of good sense. Epstein too found Humbert's obsession, and Nabokov's exhaustive, intimate account of it, repulsive; in its plot the book was strained at best. But he recognized the author's pursuit of conscience behind Humbert's self-destruction. "That the passion should be such a sordid one is the mark of the author's perversity—and he is a remarkably perverse man—but it doesn't deprive the novel of the merits that it does have," he wrote, voting against the work on the grounds of "its outlandish

---

* At times in 1955 it seemed that everyone in New York had read or was reading the manuscript. Which may explain why the August 27, 1955, *New Yorker* carried a Dorothy Parker short story about another widow, her maiden daughter, that daughter's suitor, and the romance that blossomed in the suitor's car. The story has nothing more in common with Nabokov's—in fact it is almost antithetical to the tale he forged from the same elements—save for one curious detail: It takes its title from the name of its heroine, Lolita. Vladimir noted as much with "a yelp of distress." White firmly reassured him that his suspicions were unjustified. She further assured him that as his book was to appear soon, and as everyone knows books are long in preparation, at least no one would think *he* had lifted the title from Parker. Nothing could have been further from his mind.

† It had been eight years since Nabokov had failed to grasp the merits of *Memoirs of Hecate County,* into which Wilson had even inserted an allusion to his Russian friend. He told Wilson he thought the work a failed tribute to *Fanny Hill*; Wilson would say the same of *Lolita*.

perverseness," but advocating a few more readings. "Without suggesting any qualitative comparisons, it would be fair to say that he has, in effect, written *Swann's Way* as if he had been James Joyce," Epstein concluded, the first to recognize what Véra and Elena Wilson alone believed. Viking, Simon & Schuster, New Directions, Farrar, Straus, and Doubleday were then "the four American publishers, W, X, Y, Z"—they should of course have been "the five American publishers, V, W, X, Y, Z"—whom Nabokov was to describe as having seen the book early on. None of them appears in any shape or form to have suggested the author transform his twelve-year-old into a boy, or Humbert into a farmer, as Nabokov later claimed.* But none of them offered to publish the thing either.

4

"If only everything would fall into place soon," Véra griped in January 1955, bemoaning sons and their careless studies, financial difficulties that were that winter as acute as they were chronic, and her own health. She had been unwell for an entire year with one thing or another, and was bored of it. She made no mention of the rejection letters that had been piling up in her files, or of the week she had spent teaching in her husband's stead. (Her attitude toward the rejections is clear from her advice to Sylvia Berkman, who had trouble placing a short story at the time. Véra counseled patience and the long view: "Just think of all the rejections received by people who got tremendously famous later on so that the same publishers who had kept snubbing them before clamored for MSS.," she wrote, choosing as an example Sinclair Lewis, whose work her husband had been deriding for years.) Ultimately things did fall into place, although the interim months proved draining. In February *Lolita* sailed off across the ocean. Vladimir had no illusions about where he was sending the manuscript. "I suppose it will be finally published by some shady firm with a Viennese-Dream name—eg 'Silo,' " he predicted.† Nor was there any delay about sending *Lolita* off. The manuscript returned from Doubleday and went to Doussia Ergaz within the week, which suggests that the couple had by now decisively voted to abandon

---

* Doubtless this was the same fictional publisher who suggested Nabokov salvage *The Defense* by transforming the chess-playing Luzhin into a demented violinist.
† He had at least one clue. Ergaz had written that the house she had in mind for the manuscript was one that published works that "one would not dare publish" in England.

hopes for American publication and determined to try their luck abroad. Generally their correspondence fell off dramatically at this time. Even the Karpoviches wondered about them.

The year was in large part consumed by *Pnin,* although so many projects littered the Stewart Avenue apartment that Nabokov had every reason to apply for a sabbatical. (He was granted leave for the spring 1956 semester only.) This was the winter that the "Old Man and the Fish" translation had been expected, a project that was almost certainly to have been Véra's. Nabokov had written Chekhov Publishing in the first person plural to indicate that the novel was awaited, and earlier had proposed: "I do have a first-rate translator for you, and that is my wife, Véra Nabokov. She has translated a good deal for me during our thirty years' association, and I can highly recommend her." With a new book under way it was unlikely he would have agreed to translate anything, much less Hemingway. While the project never materialized, Nabokov did convince Jason Epstein to commission a translation of Mikhail Lermontov's *A Hero of Our Time,* a work on which Véra would collaborate. All the Stewart Avenue industry bore fruit toward springtime: *The New Yorker* bought "Pnin's Day," which ran in April, the week of Vladimir's fifty-sixth birthday, and the same week that Doussia Ergaz reported that she had read and loved *Lolita.* She planned the following day to share it with the publisher of *Histoire d'O.*

The agent of providence assumed an unlikely form. Maurice Girodias, the colorful publisher of *The Whip Angels, Memoirs of a Woman of Pleasure,* and a host of other classics, took to *Lolita* immediately.* "I felt I had the obvious, immediate duty to publish the book," he remembered, far more impressed by the novel than he had been by Ergaz's delicate description of it, which had left him expecting scholarly pomposity or, worse, something "frighteningly respectable." His second and third readers were equally awed. Girodias's only condition—even before reading the manuscript—was that its author attach his name to the work. "If the publisher were to propose very favorable terms, I would be tempted to permit the book to be published under my name," Vladimir conceded, warning Doussia Ergaz that cuts in the novel were, however, out of the question. He must have felt tired of being asked to sign the thing, and more comfortable doing so for a publisher an ocean away.

---

* Girodias's ability to summon such masterpieces into existence was ingeniously simple. He would presell the volumes to a select clientele, lured with titles and blurbs of his invention, for works like *White Thighs, The Sexual Life of Robinson Crusoe,* etc. Once the orders arrived he advanced funds to his authors, who "hastened to turn in manuscripts which more or less fitted the descriptions."

He knew well how distant those writers' reputations remained.* An advance
of four hundred thousand francs, or about a thousand dollars, was agreed
upon, to which Vladimir telegraphed his assent. The sum was twice as much
as Girodias had previously paid for a book. Ergaz drew up a simple twelve-
clause agreement granting Girodias world English-language rights, which
Vladimir signed before an Ithaca notary on June 20.† These constituted the
two pages Véra most often parsed in the next decade; she must have known
them by heart. Girodias's Olympia Press immediately set about preparing the
edition so as to take advantage of the fall tourist trade. After the long wait,
Lolita was rushed into print.

Shortly after agreeing to the Paris publication, the Nabokovs shared the
good news with Morris Bishop, who admitted to feeling more unsettled than
celebratory. Bishop was as capable as the next Jaguar-driving polymath of
composing a dirty limerick, but was all the same alarmed by Vladimir's report. "I queried him on the scabrous subject," he confided in his wife. "It is
about a man who loves little girls, a subject which (rightly I think) is absolutely taboo in this country. He says there is not an indecent word in it, and
it is really a tragic and terrible story. Well, I hope it doesn't make a real scandal." His admonitions were not what either Nabokov wanted to hear. Their
delight that this misfit of a child had finally found a home must have com-
mingled with their concern; it may explain why Bishop felt his friend defended the novel as one would one's idiot child. Vladimir knew the work to
be provocative well aside from its subject matter—he sent excerpted pages to
twenty-two-year-old Dmitri, boasting, "It's full of pepper and gun powder"—but this time around more was at stake: America, and Cornell, represented refuges for which the Nabokovs had fought long and hard. Véra
shared her fears with Alison Bishop, who found her beside herself with
worry. Her husband was fifty-six years old. How would he find another job?
She later denied having harbored any such apprehensions, with the same vehemence that she would deny that her husband had attempted to publish the
novel under a pseudonym, an act that seemed as incriminating in retrospect

---

* He appears to have felt differently about affixing his name to the novel in 1955 than he had in 1954,
when he regularly claimed that he might well change his mind in a year's time. Aside from his frustration
level, the only factor that may have played a role in his decision was Dmitri's law school application, which
would have been pending in the winter/spring of 1954–55. Dmitri disagrees that his application would in
any way have influenced his father's actions.
† Neither author nor publisher considered three small matters at the time the contract was drafted: that
the novel had any commercial potential whatever; that it might ever be published in America; that its film
rights were of any value. Girodias braced himself to lose a fortune, convinced the novel was far too beautiful, too subtle, to sell.

as not having done so felt criminal at the time. On both these points Véra did protest too much.* Furthermore, her sentiments were almost inevitably aligned with those of her husband, who expressed concern with what might happen after publication at Cornell, where one could be dismissed for "moral turpitude." As a result, he conceded Girodias use of his name but made great efforts to ensure that Cornell's not be revealed. One of the great ironies of *Lolita*'s publication was the extent to which its author went to protect the academic position from which the novel was at long last to liberate him.

The second triumph of 1955 was Dmitri's graduation from Harvard. The ceremony itself was a source of great pleasure, with the caps and gowns, the celebratory lunch afterward on the lawn. As Véra reported to Berkman after the June festivities: "He was happy, V. was happy, and 'cum laude' was an unexpected blessing." To his parents' initial dismay, Dmitri had expressed an interest in pursuing an operatic career. As much as they had proved expert at scrambling financially, they wished no such insecurity on their son; the tribulations of an artistic career were too vivid to them both. While soliciting friends' opinions about Dmitri's passion for singing, they strongly urged him to consider law school, to which he was accepted. There were other plans for him as well. As early as January 1955, Vladimir was flogging his son the translator on Covici, as he would later on Epstein, as he had earlier flogged Véra on the Chekhov editors. (This was a very special offer, Vladimir informed Covici, as he did not customarily check others' work for free.) The Lermontov translation was entrusted to Dmitri. This left Véra with an additional responsibility over the summer, when "for Pnin's sake" the couple remained in Ithaca, despite the "nostalgic longing" she felt for the West every spring. She labored to impress her considerable work ethic on her son.

Hers were hardly sentimental letters to a young poet. Véra advised Dmitri immediately to obtain the existing translations, "which you will need for consultation but not for plagiary." He could count on invaluable—and free—assistance at their end, with difficult and obsolete phrasings. On his end he should devote as much as an hour and a half to a page, proceeding at a pace of three to four pages a day. He was to work every day, without vacations. "It is very enjoyable work but it is also quite exacting and above all it has to be followed up with the utmost perseverance because there will be a

---

* When the Olympia edition went on display at the Ithaca Public Library, Véra called Alison Bishop in a panic; Morris must have them remove it at once, at least until the book was proved to be great art. As both Bishops were in bed with pneumonia, neither was able to rise to her assistance.

time limit," his mother advised. Moreover, as the contract was yet to be signed, she advised total discretion. Did he feel up to the task? If so she could promise that a more ambitious project would follow. "I want a quick reaction *by mail,*" Véra signed off, making it clear that the first dollars of Dmitri's advance were not to be applied to a long-distance call. The severity of her tone may be explained by a letter she had written a few days earlier on the translator's behalf. The admissions secretary at the Harvard Law School had wondered when the school might receive Dmitri's acceptance deposit. The task of explaining that he would be devoting a year to musical training and should thus like to defer the Law School's offer fell to his mother, who apologized for her son's silence. She was preoccupied with his future that summer, and worried too about his grasp of practical matters, in which she felt him sadly deficient; she was aware of how utterly independent she had been at her son's age. Berkman knew how difficult the career decision had been for the Nabokovs, but felt in the end they had done the right thing for all concerned. "If anyone wants a chance as much as he wanted that one, it does seem that he ought not to be denied," she reassured the future basso's mother.

The Lermontov project was tackled over the next year behind a thicket of pronouns. Véra grappled with the contract; she devoted some of her summer to the 1839 text, the first major prose novel in Russian, and a work to which Tolstoy's style has been traced. A year later, as the text neared completion, Nabokov mentioned that Dmitri "has assisted Véra and me very ably in our Lermontov translation." A month afterward he apprised Levin: "I have finished (with Dmitri's able assistance) the Lermontov book and sent it to Doubleday." At the same time Véra described the project thusly: "Last year Dmitri began a translation for Doubleday, and this summer, in Utah, V. finished it. I had my share, too." She was not always so modest. At the end of June 1956 she wrote with relief to Elena Levin, in a dazzling display of unparallel pronouns: "We have just completed a lot of work (translation), which took up all of my time, and finally I have some time for myself." She had been forthright about the division of labor with Dmitri, to whom she had initially made it clear that the less time he asked of his father, the better he acquitted himself of the task. Earlier in June she had chastised him: "Instead of taking a good rest, your father and I have been working all this time on the 'Hero,' and shall be saddled with this job to the end of our vacation. Is this fair?" In the fall of 1957 Vladimir was too busy to offer up suggestions for flap copy, which Véra supplied. Much later Dmitri credited his parents with polishing the Lermontov translation, for which father and son are credited in the published edition. At the end of 1955 Nabokov complained that he was doing three jobs, "each of which is really made for a whole man." This was true—what with *Onegin, Pnin,* Lermontov, and the teaching he could have said four—but the support staff was superb.

A month before *Lolita* was published in Paris Wilson visited the Nabokovs in Ithaca. He had never seen them so cheerful; later he theorized that the difficulties with *Lolita* had had a stimulating effect on Vladimir. The couple appeared to him to be flourishing, though they were more bound up in Dmitri and his exploits than Wilson might have liked; with horror and pride, Vladimir held forth on the sexual habits of the younger generation. The visit was even more of a success than his hosts would have realized. Wilson happily confided in a mutual friend afterward that having been thoroughly repelled by *Lolita,* he was delighted to be reminded of how much he liked the novel's author. Dismayed by her loyalty, he was as comfortable as he ever was with Véra. He could not suppress a snideness about her assistance in administering her husband's exams, even while he admired the couple's sacrosanct family relations. The two butted heads openly about the French definition of a word, which rather appropriately happened to be "fastidious." Véra held that it meant "hard to please," while Wilson insisted—dictionary citations traveled back and forth over the next weeks—that it meant "tiresome." (Vladimir sided with his wife.) Fastidious as she was, Véra conceded defeat only grudgingly, although when she read of the argument much later she scrawled "My mistake" next to the account.

Just before she disappeared again behind the typewriter, she sent up another quiet flare of self-assertion. Perhaps because she was writing to a woman who published, and who had enjoyed a rich academic career, she closed her summer letter to Berkman:

> The only thing to report about myself is that I hate humid heat, that our apartment is pretty hot in hot weather (we shall have a house in August), and that though I am not doing anything of value of my own, I am kept busy by my men, at this time Vladimir especially (*all* his letters and much other paper work).

This was the long letter that had begun with the report of Dmitri's graduation, a missive from which she at first appeared to have exempted herself. It is not the first instance of Véra distancing herself from the enterprise at home, but it is the first that hints at some kind of personal accomplishment. The words "value of my own" rustle loudly on the page, and with a certain poignancy. They prove but a glimmer. Within days she was subsumed by the typing of *Pnin,* and by the move to the small cottage she had found for the fall semester. She spent the first week on Hanshaw Road alone, as Vladimir was hospitalized with a severe attack of lumbago, a misadventure that nearly resulted in a chapter called "Pnin at the Hospital."

Girodias published *Lolita* in September, nearly before his author realized he had done so; Véra and Vladimir held the book's two volumes in their hands for the first time on October 8, 1955. The novel's early days were quiet ones. Both Nabokovs were more distracted by the fortunes of *Pnin,* not being so much cosseted in New York, where Pat Covici was finding the manuscript a collection of sketches and not a full-fledged novel. "My Poor Pnin" proved more deserving of his original title than its author intended; after months of deliberation, Covici rejected the book. (The editor to whom Nabokov had first mentioned *Lolita* and who had been the first to contract for *Pnin,* Covici published neither novel in the end.) A measure of Vladimir's desperation can be read in the fact that he turned next to Harper, whose publication of *Conclusive Evidence* he had so much maligned. *Pnin* would remain homeless until mid-1956, when Epstein finally made an offer for the book, no less concerned about its marketing than Covici had been. Speaking for his Doubleday colleagues, Epstein allowed: "As one of us has said, it's the kind of book that the customer will have to read in advance before taking it home with him." If Vladimir was discouraged about *Pnin*'s fate, as he should have been, if Véra had qualms about *Lolita*—and it is impossible to think she could not have, when Bishop had estimated that there was a better than average chance her husband would be fired, and they were financially stable for the first time in thirty years—then Graham Greene delivered the Nabokovs a Christmas present at the end of 1955 disproportionate to any they had or would ever receive. Asked by the (London) *Sunday Times* to name the three best books of 1955, he included an English-language novel of which no one had heard, available neither in America nor in Great Britain, but that could be purchased, in a two-volume, light-green edition, in Paris.

The forces Greene set in motion in London were some time in making themselves felt in America. For the spring sabbatical Elena Levin had found a quiet, first-floor apartment with kitchenette for the Nabokovs at the Continental Hotel in Cambridge, where they arrived on February 3, 1956, after a valiant battle with icy roads. They settled in for a three-month stay, spent primarily at Widener. It was at the Continental that they read, in Harvey Breit's February 26 *Times Book Review* column, that a work called *Lolita*—"a long French novel about nymphets," author unnamed—was causing a minor scandal in London. Having been named by one paper a best book of 1955, it was denounced in another as one of the filthiest. (The Nabokovs' real debt was less to Greene than to *The Sunday Express*'s conservative editor in chief,

John Gordon, who led the countercharge.* Together Greene and Gordon worked their combinational magic.) Two weeks later Breit elaborated on the mysterious French work, revealing the name of its author, and quoting Harry Levin's uncredited assessment of the book a sort of cross between *Daisy Miller* and *The Possessed.* Gallimard promptly acquired French translation rights.[†]

From the room at the Continental Véra responded to an immediate volley of publishers' queries. Gently she assured the editors at Indiana University Press that while her husband applauded their spirit of adventure, this was not a book for them; there was a reason she had sent it to a Paris agent in the first place. She composed in part or in whole a reassuring letter to the devoted Pat Covici, who worried for Vladimir's reputation: *Lolita* could in no way be said to be "lewd and libertine." The novel was a tragedy, and the tragic and the obscene were mutually exclusive.[‡] At the beginning of May, the couple set off by way of the Grand Canyon for Utah, where they had rented a lovely cottage amid five acres of sage and cedar with a glorious view of Mount Carmel, accommodations that proved as satisfactory as those in Arizona had proved unsatisfactory.[§] Here Véra, or Vladimir, or—as Véra was once half-seriously to refer to them later, "V & V Inc."—finished the Lermontov translation. Nabokov continued with his *Onegin* commentaries, which he hoped to complete by Christmas. Mount Carmel was lovely until late June, when a snake attempted to pay Véra a visit, from a windowsill. Shortly afterward she drove Vladimir north, collecting along the way.

In Ithaca the Nabokovs settled into a new house, at 425 Hanshaw Road. Véra braced herself for the familiar academic drill. "Another busy year. Another *dreadful* Ithaca winter," she moaned, well before the snow had begun to fall. "The winters here *are* dreadful, cold, dark, icy, complicated by driving over icy steep hill streets. We have no garage this year and shall probably have to shovel out our car to drive to college in the morning for the best part

---

* John Gordon's words, in part: "Sheer unrestrained pornography . . . The entire book is devoted to an exhaustive, uninhibited, and utterly disgusting description of his [Humbert's] pursuits and successes. It is published in France. Anyone who published or sold it here would certainly go to prison." A whole echo chamber of ironies surrounded *Lolita*'s introduction to America, not the least resonant of which sounded with Harvey Breit's influential voice: He had himself written pornography for a dollar a page.

[†] It was Raymond Queneau, future father of *Zazie dans le métro,* who convinced the firm to do so.

[‡] On this count the Nabokovs were mistaken. In the eyes of the court, comedy and tragedy made no difference. Literary merit was—or was hoped to be—the only defense.

[§] The cabin was perfectly isolated, but the Nabokovs entertained at least one visitor this summer, a washing machine repairman who did nothing to alter Véra's opinion of those amazing Americans. He told the couple of his visits with the people in the flying saucers, who would not show their hands when they talked. "What language did they speak?" demanded Vladimir.

of two or three months."* Despite the academic duties, despite Pushkin, Vladimir was attempting work on a new novel. He was exhausted by his efforts; Véra sounds exhausted by him. "Since he is working all day and all night and has completely tortured himself I am looking forward to the end of this book. Although I do know that having finished one thing he immediately grasps for the next," she wrote her sister-in-law in a letter that began with the assurance that Vladimir had been planning to write her for some time. Two months later he claimed to be on the brink of doing so, though when Véra reminded him of his promise she met inevitably with the same response: "Yes, of course, but today I am too tired." She suggested Elena blame *Onegin*. She herself did, and yet knew this to be her own fault. A year later, when *Onegin* was still not finished, she grumbled that she was beginning to hate Pushkin, who had for so long kept her husband from a new book. The Master stood quite literally in Nabokov's way; by April 1957, when Véra had begun to type out Canto One of the annotated translation, the manuscript had grown to waist height.† In Paris, *Lolita* had been banned at the request of the British Home Office, who did not want copies of the filthy green volume floating across the Channel. So long as her husband's position was not threatened Véra did not shy from controversy. The woman who was capable of holding up her end of a nine-year silence noted with satisfaction that the novel was creating "a lovely row in the French press."

For every one of his friends who weighed in with misgivings about *Lolita* in the course of 1956, there was a publisher somewhere in the world who wrote to express interest. Between vetting *Pnin* proofs and co-proctoring her husband's exams, Véra fielded these queries. Late in the summer, the Danes commissioned the book. At the same time Jason Epstein arranged for *The Anchor Review* to carry a long excerpt from the novel, a move calculated to pave the way toward U.S. publication. Véra drove Vladimir to New York in mid-October to confer with the magazine's editors, at the Epsteins' apartment. At the meeting Nabokov was asked how he happened to know so much about little girls; Véra explained that her husband had sat on the Ithaca buses with a notepad and listened carefully. He had also haunted playgrounds, until his doing so had become awkward. There were otherwise no little girls in his life. The second matter of business the Nabokovs had hoped

---

* She was not alone in this habit. "How persistently our poet evokes images of winter in the beginning of a poem which he started composing on a balmy summer night!" exclaims Kinbote in *Pale Fire*.
† Its publishing history too proved complicated, partly because of Vladimir's demands, partly on account of the manuscript's girth. Cornell University Press could not settle on terms that would prove both financially viable and acceptable to the author. The labor of love was published finally by the Bollingen Series which, as Morris Bishop dryly observed, "loves to lose money."

to conduct in New York—a contribution to a Festschrift being prepared for Aldanov—went unattended. In a lovely instance of the Old World falling prey to the New, the Buick was towed, and the half day meant for Aldanov was devoted instead to recovering the car.

As much as *Lolita*'s various misfortunes claimed Véra's time throughout the winter, her attention was diverted by the domestic front. (In a neat carbonic tribute to the double life, a sheet of paper survives on which she inadvertently superimposed a letter about *Pnin*'s motion picture rights on one to an Ithaca lawyer who seemed to feel the Nabokovs had not paid a dishwasher repair bill at their new address.) She arranged for Anna Feigin's brother Ilya, partially paralyzed after a stroke, to move to an Ithaca nursing home, where she might look after him; within the Slonim family as well she paid the price of the capable. By ambulance her cousin traveled to Ithaca's Oak Hill Manor, where Véra visited him regularly until his death. For some reason the second Hanshaw Road home—larger than the Nabokovs had liked, but modern and comfortable—had proved unsuitable; in February 1957 Véra packed the family up again. She may well have shared in the strain she described on her husband's part, as the winter was particularly brutal. "I wonder if you New-York-Citiers can imagine the amount of snow we are having?" she queried Epstein before the move. Perhaps because of the allocation of labor, she did not find midwinter Ithaca as scenic as her husband. Nabokov saw the junipers as "albino camels." Véra heard only a symphony of complaining car engines, of whining tires up and down the street.

Mercifully the new house had a garage, but one fixture at the Highland Road address proved less welcome. Under some duress the Nabokovs had agreed to care for their landlords' Siamese cat, to whom Vladimir spoke in Russian. All began swimmingly. By the end of the first month of cohabitation he was disgusted by the animal, who would not offer him a moment's peace. Bandit seemed willing enough to believe Véra was Mrs. Sharp but could not fathom why the new Mr. Sharp would not allow him in his study. The animal was unrelenting, and pressed his case by offering up home trophies, with which he played mouse-tennis against the office door. Véra's distress can be imagined; the Royal York's plumbing was nothing compared with this. She wrote the Sharps in South Africa but found the mails distressingly slow. "Do you think this letter will reach Leopoldville by air mail in two weeks?" she asked one of Nabokov's seminar students hopefully, having explained the Bandit-induced anguish. (The cat, like his *Pale Fire* counterpart, was farmed out, to friends of the home's owners.) At their new rental at 880 Highland Road Véra and Vladimir entertained Ivan Obolensky, the first American publisher to come calling about *Lolita*. He arrived on March 4, days before *Pnin* was published to rave reviews, Nabokov's first success in America.

Pnin's publication provided a reprieve from the *Lolita*-defending in which the couple had been engaged since friends had begun to read—and in Wilson's and Bishop's cases, failed to finish—the book. The consensus was that he had settled on a most distasteful subject; the book seemed a monstrous frivolity. Bishop intentionally avoided the novel, which allowed him, if asked, to shrug it off as a peccadillo, as something his friend and esteemed colleague had done in far-off Paris and of no consequence to the university. He believed nothing of the kind and fretted over the subject, as deeply worried for his friends as he was disapproving of the book. "I would not like to have to defend him in that," he confided in Szeftel, anticipating a scandal. "Would you?"* Szeftel was one colleague who had read the book. He was not shocked, but did think the publication of a volume on such a "salacious topic" could lead to trouble at a coeducational institution. We know less of what Szeftel thought on reading *Pnin,* the bumbling hero of which was rumored to have been—and has recently been demonstrated to have been—based on him, a claim Nabokov did not always deny. Even Mrs. Szeftel had noted the resemblance to her husband on reading Pnin's adventures in *The New Yorker.* The borrowed biography in no way interfered with the success of the novel, which went into its second printing two weeks after publication.† It was among the ten finalists for the 1958 National Book Award.‡

By the end of the spring of 1957, *Lolita* had publishers in Italy, France, and Germany. Obolensky was not alone in pursuing American rights in the novel for his own firm; Epstein was doing all he could to convince Doubleday to publish the book, especially as his author kept him apprised of every one of Obolensky's moves. Nor did Vladimir desist from a little strategic nudging: "Lolita is young, and I am old," he reminded his editor. At Doubleday Epstein had his work cut out for him. The firm's head was Douglas Black, who had sunk a small fortune into the failed defense of *Hecate County.*

---

* When finally in 1957 he did read the book, Bishop resisted its charms. "Nabokov's *Pnin* is a shimmering delight. His *Lolita* is not," he concluded.
† The real-life echoes appear to have enhanced Vladimir's enjoyment of that acclaim. In October 1957 the Nabokovs had a drink with Colgate College's Albert Parry, who had been the lone voice in America to place a bet on a distant dark horse named V. Sirin in 1933. By 1957 all had come full circle; his prediction had been amply fulfilled. Are you angry with me about *Pnin?* Nabokov asked Parry at the time. The Colgate professor looked puzzled. "Oh, well, every Russian who teaches Russian subjects in America sees himself in Pnin and is even quite cross with me," Vladimir explained. When Parry said he had no such illusions and was not angry, the novelist looked crestfallen.
‡ John Cheever won, for *The Wapshot Chronicle.* Nabokov was one of two St. Petersburg natives on the shortlist; Ayn Rand was also nominated, for *Atlas Shrugged.*

As editor in chief and *Lolita*-supporter Ken McCormick remembered it, the Doubleday lawyers' 1957 reasoning went like this: Having robbed a bank once and been prosecuted for it, the firm should do its best not to be caught standing around on the corner while a second crime was in progress. They would only receive a stiffer sentence for *Lolita*, construed as a second offense.* At Simon & Schuster, senior editor Maria Leiper thought the novel brilliant and wrote a delirious report. She suggested Brockway read behind her. She was startled when he confessed he had already read the novel, which he had not much liked. Her colleagues were universally horror-struck; the head of the editorial department deemed the book "repulsive." A Harper & Row imprint distinguished itself by shunning *Lolita* not on legal or ethical but on artistic grounds. Most of these editors read copies of the novel that had been imported discreetly in the bottoms of suitcases, in the great *Ulysses–Lady Chatterley* tradition. (Anaïs Nin claimed she had made a tidy profit reselling copies of *Lolita* in America at a considerable markup.) At Random House William Styron made an eloquent case for the novel, which he was tempted to publish privately; Hiram Haydn, Styron's editor and the firm's newly named editor in chief, could only sputter in response. Surely Styron knew he had an adolescent daughter? The loathsome book would be published over his dead body. In reading the novel Haydn was "revolted to the point of nausea," so entirely did Humbert and Nabokov merge in his mind. Lambasted by his peers, he held his ground even as the novel raced up the bestseller list a year later. All of this wrangling went on very much behind the scenes. But even at his birth poor Pnin's virtues were shadowed by that of his nubile cousin. *Time* reviewed *Pnin* glowingly, but devoted nearly as much space to the sotto voce scandal the novel's author had occasioned in Europe with another book.

Véra planted flowers that spring in the Highland Road yard, for the first time in her life. This was the yard in which pheasants left their *Pale Fire* tracks, from which the Nabokovs' laughter rang out over the neighborhood as they played twilight games of horseshoes. The pieces had finally begun to fall into place. At this pivotal moment one additional piece of the past, too, fell into place. That summer, most of which was spent typing *Onegin*, for which Dmitri was preparing the index, Véra learned from Anna Feigin that she could file a restitutions claim in Berlin. "Well then, if that is indeed the case, then forcing the Germans to pay could only be pleasurable," she wrote Goldenweiser, who offered to represent her. Her case was presented on the

---

* There was huge and sad irony in the fact that Wilson, who had done so much for Nabokov's publishing history, should now prove inadvertently to be standing in his friend's way.

grounds that on the arrival in New York she did not have enough English to secure a job in America. She filed her claim as the greatest English-language novel written by a non-native-speaker climbed the bestseller list.

5

Speaking for her husband in 1952, Véra had written a Houghton Mifflin editor: "The question of mimicry is one that has passionately interested him all his life and one of his pet projects has always been the compilation of a work that would comprise *all* known examples of mimicry in the animal kingdom." She warned that the results could be massive, though if a truly serious work on the subject was what Houghton had in mind, "Vladimir is your man." Vladimir never tackled the subject; Véra instead wrote the book on mimicry, though never between hard covers. The word "copyist" takes on new meaning in the Nabokovs' correspondence, especially as that correspondence evolved in the 1950s. In August 1951 Véra wrote an editor at the newly founded Chekhov Publishing House about *The Gift* (*Dar*), a Russian-language edition of which the house was considering. The draft is in her hand, but Vladimir's voice. Nabokov then recopied the document, which he signed and sent. Answering this missive was simpler than would be answering some of those that followed. With the novel under submission, the couple began to relay each other in the correspondence. In October a Chekhov editor found herself thanking Vladimir for his wife's letter. The arrangement entailed a certain degree of contortionism on all sides. The same month Véra composed a letter for Vladimir inquiring after "a letter my wife wrote in my behalf this fall."

She amiably embraced these awkward poses, at which, by nature, or by force of practice, she was expert. Chekhov accepted *The Gift*; seventeen years after it had been written, the novel was published in Russian.* The Chekhov staff needed a summary of the book, something Vladimir had his usual aversion to composing. In the guise of an impartial reader, Véra wrote of Fyodor and Zina's "nightly roamings on the spellbound moonlit streets . . . full of magic and poetry." She submitted the unsigned précis to Chekhov with the line, "I have finally managed to get one of the 'good' readers to make a synopsis of DAR." It was an appropriate ruse for a work in which her husband

---

* It bears a dedication to "The memory of my mother," but cannot precisely be said to be the only work dedicated to someone other than Véra, to whom the English-language edition is dedicated.

described nature's cunning and seemingly frivolous use of disguise, in which he discoursed "about those magic masks of mimicry; about the enormous moth which in a state of repose assumes the image of a snake looking at you."

In the early 1950s those letters to which Véra did lend her signature as well as her voice went out from "Véra Nabokov" or from a more neutral "V. Nabokov." As Véra Nabokov she might write, for example, to ask if a publisher might consider adding a reprint edition of *Bend Sinister* to its list. As the paper piled up over the Cornell years she searched for a formula that would serve all of her epistolary purposes. By 1956, when she had begun a testy exchange with Maurice Girodias about perceived violations of the *Lolita* contract, she settled on a signature that seemed to correspond to her identity, or nonidentity. From these years, and just in time, emerged "Mrs. Vladimir Nabokov," who in her formal Old World script would sign "Véra Nabokov" above her married name, which she typed, in parentheses, as if to mute the potency of the alias. The formula allowed her to speak for Vladimir without clumsy explanation and without a circuitous round of excuses. In and just after 1957, when further camouflage was in order, she wrote as "J. G. Smith," a fictional Cornell secretary who shared her handwriting and her cadences, and who could be even more terse than Véra. It was J. G. Smith who composed waspish letters of non-recommendation on Professor Nabokov's behalf. He had only the vaguest memory of the candidate in question, whose grasp of the Russian language "is as sketchy as that of any average college graduate who studied 'linguistics.' "*

Signatures aside, there was little question as to who stood behind Véra's words. On occasions when her letter failed to achieve the desired effect, Vladimir weighed in, referring back to "my letter, signed by my wife." Véra did not object to these assertions. One can hear her, though, attempting to convince her husband that a word from him—one she would if necessary compose—was required. The protracted history of securing *Lolita* a Paris publication was recast by Vladimir in the first person ("On August 6 of that year, from Taos, New Mexico, I wrote Madame Ergaz. . . . I now asked her to find somebody in Europe who would publish *Lolita* . . . and next spring I got in touch with Madame Ergaz again . . ."), when nearly the entire correspondence had been conducted by Véra, who knew well that the natural end of mimicry is concealment. She herself made no secret of her role, telling reporters later she had been the one to pursue European publication. But on paper she made the same claims as her husband, referring even to her own

---

* As "Mrs. Véra Nabokov" she more gently suggested to another student that he would be doing himself a favor by appealing to a different instructor for a reference letter.

letters as his. As sometimes they were, having been composed by him, with a request that they go out over her name.

It was one thing to enjoy complete freedom in their epistolary pas de deux, quite another to admit to it. Véra's grumbling that the business matters fell to her did not prevent her from writing crossly to a correspondent who suggested she was speaking for her husband: "Allow me to clear up one misunderstanding: I am certainly not 'protecting' my husband. He always makes his own decisions." After some trouble between Gallimard and Girodias, Vladimir drafted a letter to the Gallimard editor: "I have no way of judging if a rumor that reaches me from Paris is true or false. My wife does not make herself the 'echo' of anything; she merely is kind enough to jot down my queries and apprehensions." In the happy days with Andrew Field, Véra was disappointed to hear that her letter had inadvertently offended. The biographer needed to bear in mind that she simply typed what her husband dictated, word for word. (In truth, Nabokov did very little dictating after *Lolita*.) To one steely letter she affixed a disclaimer: "Personally I would appreciate your explaining to the gentleman that I never answer my husband's letters otherwise than he asks me to do." For his part Nabokov never disclaimed Véra's words, though he did at times ask her to add something to a letter she had mailed off earlier in the day, occasioning a second, or third, communication on the same afternoon.

Véra took little pride in the correspondence, which had already, in advance of *Lolita,* threatened to overwhelm her. In one of the dozens of letters to Elena Sikorski in which Véra apologized for her authorship, she begs that Vladimir be forgiven: "He simply does not know how to write sloppily and in a rush." The implication was that she did. The happy valiance with which she appeared to conduct the business affairs was in truth not so simple for her. She felt that her English was second-rate, that she was "a bad letter-writer," that she was ill at ease in business, that she had trouble reading contracts, that her arithmetic was lame. In some of these protests a certain pragmatic disguise was in use. She was comfortable with the masquerade; the routine worked best if the expectations of her were low.

Similarly she shrank from the idea that she was the protective and adoring wife, a slavish follower of all people surnamed Nabokov. She railed against the assertion that she was "fiercely protective of her man." She assured agent Swifty Lazar that *Ada* was a remarkable, a sensational, book, an evaluation that had nothing to do with her being the author's wife. When a Rutgers professor asked Nabokov to name the great untranslated titles of European fiction, Véra replied. Professor William Lamont pursued the matter, enclosing a preliminary list of his selections. Véra weighed in about Bely and Bulgakov before adding, "And, as you can well imagine, I consider *Zashchita Luzhina* [*The Defense*] by Nabokov as one of the best novels ever written in Russian." When Lamont acknowledged that at her suggestion he had put "your talented boy friend's novel on the list" she could barely contain her fury. (The phrase "boy friend" had not helped.) Lamont had asked her candid opinion, which she had supplied. "In doing so, I acted as a person well at home in Russian literature, by no means as a 'loyal and devoted wife.' " She invited Lamont to ignore her suggestions completely, so intent was she on not being thought—despite all the assistance, the impersonations, the assumptions of his responsibilities—her husband's flack.

With intimates there was no smokescreen about the smokescreens. In October 1956 Véra advised Sylvia Berkman, "V. was asked to suggest a candidate for [a Guggenheim] and I think I composed a very adequate letter listing your high qualifications. V. signed the letter, of course, and [the] reaction was enthusiastic." (There was no question as to who the active force was. "Let us push now," Véra added.)* She was always embarrassed to have to hold up her husband's end of the Sikorski correspondence, all the more so when she was asked to impart harsh words. "I'm sorry for this unpleasant letter. Be angry with Volodya for it," she begged her sister-in-law. As it was, Vladimir had expressed himself far more severely, "but I refuse to repeat it." With friends the dual, or delegated, authorship made itself felt clearly. Letters came addressed to all sorts of entities: "Dear VVs, Dear VerVolodya, Dear Author and Mrs. Nabokov." "Dear V. & V.," wrote the ever-astute Morris Bishop in 1959, "How happy is the English language in its second person plural! I need not specify if I speak to one or both of you; you blend or separate at will!" The language was as useful as it was happy. With two voices at their disposal the Nabokovs could work all kinds of effects. They could badger more tenaciously. Véra could render Vladimir more distant, his judgments more divine. "My husband asks me to say that he thinks ULYSSES by far the greatest English novel of the century but detests FINNEGANS WAKE," she enlightened one scholar. Some of the greatest advantages of this tango, or tangle, of pronouns would be realized only in the decades to come, when the arrangement would be refined to high art. In the 1950s, the mimetic disguise was largely a matter of convenience. For reasons of efficiency, Véra fronted for Vladimir, the man behind whom she had walked on campus for a decade.

---

* The Guggenheim letter, reprinted in *Vladimir Nabokov: Selected Letters 1940–1977,* is signed "Vladimir Nabokov." He is almost certainly responsible for its second half, in which he wondered after his eligibility for a third fellowship.

By the time it was necessary to write Maurice Girodias—and Doussia Ergaz about Girodias—"Mrs. Vladimir Nabokov" was firmly in the saddle. The relationship with Girodias began to sour almost upon the book's publication. "Véra Nabokov" began to reason with Ergaz in November of 1956 about why the Olympia contract should be considered null and void; over the next years "Mrs. Vladimir Nabokov" wrote and signed a plump anthology of missives explaining which clause of the agreement Girodias was presently in violation of. The essential problem was not so much what was in the agreement as what was not. Girodias had bought world English-language rights in the novel; the Nabokovs were willing to fight for some share of the American rights, which they had plainly signed away. By the time U.S. publication began to look like a possibility, by the time Simon & Schuster and Random House were considering the novel, relations with Olympia had curdled. The novel had been banned in France; Nabokov had opted not to join Olympia in its litigation. Not unreasonably, Girodias felt that given his early advocacy of an unpopular cause, he deserved something for his efforts. Nabokov felt that given his publisher's dilatoriness, his casual accounting procedures—and probably too the fact that *The Whip Angels* and *Memoirs of a Woman of Pleasure* made for compromising company—Girodias was overreaching himself. He wanted only to end their association. The situation was complicated by the ad interim copyright under which the novel was protected. If more than 1,500 copies of the book were imported into the United States, or if more than five years were to elapse without the book's being published in America, its copyright protection lapsed. The deadline was September 1960. Agreeing on a U.S. publisher for *Lolita* became not so much a luxury as a necessity. And agreeing on terms with Girodias was the first—and as it turned out the most difficult—of the mythic labors involved in publishing it.

The division of responsibility in arranging for *Lolita*'s American life, while not entirely neat, was nonetheless interesting. The letters to *Lolita*'s American suitors—Ivan Obolensky, Epstein, ultimately Putnam's Walter Minton—were composed and signed by Vladimir. The threatening, cajoling, demanding letters—those warning about "the sacred figure" of 1,500 copies, that the publisher who added the book to his list would have to be one with the resources to take the litigation as far as the Supreme Court—were composed and signed by Véra. When a particularly firm hand was called for with Girodias, Vladimir stepped in; when a housekeeping matter arose, Véra stepped in. As the paper accumulated the lines blurred, and with them, in a perfectly Nabokovian way, the identities on the page. Increasingly, letters opened like this 1957 one to Epstein: "Vladimir started this letter but had to switch to something else in a hurry, and asked me to continue on my own."

The epistolary two-step served everyone's purposes. It also gave way to an off-putting confusion about authorship. The correspondent was left to fashion a response that would mollify, tantalize, charm two parties, a game that involved some subtle guesswork as well as some delicate phrasing. Many of the hallmarks of Nabokov's fiction—the doppelgängers, the impersonators, the Siamese twins, the mirror images, the distorted mirror images, the reflections in the windowpane, the parodies of self—manifested themselves in the routine the couple developed for dealing with the world, a routine that could leave a correspondent feeling as the books can: humbled by one knotty, magnificent inside joke.

Only on the telephone did Véra's flutey, lightly accented voice ring loud and clear—and unaccompanied. Whenever possible Vladimir shunned that instrument, delegating the foggy realm of "space spooks" to his wife. He found long-distance calls particularly abhorrent. He informed an editor that while he enjoyed their telephonic visits, he instantly forgot half of what the editor said and seven-eighths of what he himself said. Especially as his words became more sought after and the need to chose them carefully that much greater, the solution was to entrust all space-spook scuffling to Véra. "V hates the telephone—so I had to call," she noted flatly, when the first *Lolita*-related query arrived from Hollywood. Later, when Vladimir wanted information on the film of the novel, he asked Stanley Kubrick if he would mind terribly talking to him by phone through Véra. He promised he would remain at her side throughout the conversation. When William Maxwell telephoned the Nabokovs in Switzerland from *The New Yorker*'s offices, Véra was put in charge of explaining to him that her husband's "communicatory neurosis" had prevented him from taking the call. The same neurosis would not interfere with his dictating to his wife a letter about the publication of *Eugene Onegin,* which she wrote out longhand, from a hospital room thirty-five miles away.

Increasingly Véra began to step out from behind the typewriter. She was by now perfectly at ease on the page in English, though her English was always a little stiff, and Russian remained the language she spoke with her husband. All of the publishers who attempted to pry *Lolita*'s American rights from Girodias's clutches discovered that Vladimir conferred with her on every detail. She was active in the negotiating; just after Christmas 1957, Minton announced that he was "making one last appeal to M. Gerodias [*sic*], along the lines that Mrs. Nabokov suggested." (This did not prove the winning strategy, which Minton has described as having been far simpler: "I just lied my head off to both of them."* Girodias was insisting on half the pro-

---

* Reminded of this later, Minton revised his statement to: "I didn't lie. I just did not tell them all the details."

ceeds; Nabokov was insisting on a 10 percent royalty. Minton offered a 17½ percent royalty and simply failed to reveal to either party the other's share.) He would conclude that Véra was to blame for most of the difficulties with Girodias. "She is a lovely lady of a very actively suspicious turn of mind which just complements her husband's," he warned the Parisian publisher, when the disposition of British rights in the book created additional friction. (Girodias had already concluded that Véra was a force to be reckoned with, and that the couple lived in a state of complete osmosis.) It was true that Véra had begun, even semiprivately, to refer to the French publisher as Girodias the Gangster. It is also true that what looked dubious from one angle was instinctively sound from another. But Nabokov's wife was not Caesar's: She was never above suspicion. Ivan Obolensky was persuaded that Véra had single-handedly botched his negotiation.

Slowly she had been coaxed out of the wings—by the pressure of work, by her devotion, by the demands of an exceptional novel. Inadvertently, "Mrs. Vladimir Nabokov" had made a name for herself. Not that this spelled an end to the counterfeit letters, which she continued to issue, the disguise becoming more and more artful. Even in the late 1950s something more variegated yet could be produced. The correspondence with Dmitri—over these years to consist largely of one long, heartfelt plea to spend less, drive more slowly, translate more quickly, and above all spend less—fell to Véra. On one occasion she yielded her pen to, or forced it upon, Vladimir, who dispensed the habitual wisdoms. "Mama is angry and doesn't want to write," he explained at the end of the missive, typed by the person who had not wanted to set words to paper. This was Véra affording herself a great luxury, which she rarely did. In February 1958, as the Nabokovs settled into their last Ithaca house, as Minton cabled Girodias that he had reached an agreement with all parties, as the French Minister of the Interior lifted its ban on the novel, as the Lermontov translation appeared in Ithaca bookstores, she who had for so long been hovering "beneath the word, above the syllable" was now very much in evidence. She was just as often misunderstood—Obolensky was as certain she was French as some Cornellians had been that she was a German princess—but she was at least now the shadowy figure in the foreground. She had emerged just in time for the arrival of Hurricane Lolita, which would have flushed her out anyway.

�֍ 7 �֍

PAST PERFECT

*We did not expect that, amid the whirling masks, one mask would turn out
to be a real face, or at least the place where that face ought to be.*
— NABOKOV, *LECTURES ON RUSSIAN LITERATURE*

1

What possesses a person to start a diary? Véra Nabokov began what amounted
to one in a recycled 1951 datebook. She was fifty-six years old; *Lolita* was a
newborn. As with most other demonstrations of self, she came to this one
obliquely, if not accidentally; the exercise may well have belonged to the my-
husband-started-but-had-to-switch-to-something-else-in-a-hurry school. The
datebook began its second life on Tuesday, May 20, 1958. Its first entry is in
Vladimir's hand, though not entirely in his words: "Long distance has always a
bracing effect, says Véra. A call from Jason Epstein, Doubleday, at 10 AM asking if [I] would undertake a translation of Tolstoy's short novels—*Hadji-Murad*
etc. Véra answered I would think it over." The pages continue in a collabora-
tive fashion, as only the Nabokovs could devise one; it is almost impossible to
believe that the two were not sitting next to each other that May Tuesday. The
next line is again Vladimir's: "Véra went to look for a dress around noon." In a
different hand the paragraph continues: "Véra came back without dress. Shopping in Ithaca a disaster. A NY firm (Best) displayed a mediocre collection in
one half of dingy restaurant hired for this purpose. No sales ladies. No trying-
on rooms. No attractive dresses." The addition is Véra's, in the third person, a
character in someone else's book.

For the next few pages the couple's comments alternate, in a desultory fashion. The datebook seems to have migrated between them, as a single pair of eyeglasses later would. Dmitri has called in raptures about an audition (says Véra); Jason Epstein has called in despair (says Vladimir), having missed out on the opportunity to publish *Lolita*. ("Literally wailed," reports Vladimir.) What Epstein *was* publishing was a collection of thirteen stories—*Nabokov's Dozen*—a copyright taxonomy for which Véra prepared while her husband sorted Wyoming, Oregon, and New Mexico butterflies. Vladimir reported on the letter he had written Harry Levin about *Onegin*, then on submission to Cornell University Press. He had alerted Levin that the press might well turn to him for a reading of the three-thousand-page manuscript. Here it is diary as dialogue: "(you forgot to mention the main object of the letter to Harry, which was to ask him for utmost discretion—nay, secrecy!—in handling the MS)," Véra added, interrupting her husband in mid-sentence. She is correct about the intent of the Levin letter, no enormous surprise as she was its author. Writing Bishop in the guise of her husband, she had implored: "Should they send you the MS would you do me the very great favor of not showing or mentioning it to anyone at all. Under no circumstances would I want Karpovich or Jakobson, or any other Slavist to glimpse it."

Following this bit of in-house conversation Nabokov cedes the pen entirely to his wife, after which the tussles are not with her husband but with the world and her conscience. Nabokov's first cousin Peter de Peterson was in America on business that May, when he proposed a Memorial Day visit to Ithaca. Air connections being what they were, Véra realized that Peterson would need either to leave Newark at 7:30 A.M. or to arrive in Ithaca at 7:30 P.M. Her anguish on the subject indicates that even in the small matters she had not entirely left the well-ordered universe of prerevolutionary Russia behind. "Query: what is less inhospitable," she wondered, "to oblige a man to get up at 5 A.M. or to tell him to come here only in time for dinner?" Her remarks fall off here, interrupted on the page by the entries Vladimir had made in the datebook seven years earlier, in the life by the summer departure from Ithaca. The preceding weeks had been devoted less to the diary than to three other volumes. In mid-May Minton had sent on page proofs of *Lolita*, which Véra had vetted, followed by their author. Together the two also read through the proofs of the story collection, scheduled to be published a month after the novel. Most of all Véra was distracted by the demands of *Onegin*, out of the house but not entirely off her desk. "The very thought of the proofs appals me: there is so much that will have to be checked on every page, some of it in different languages," she groaned, having mailed off the two previous bundles.

Meanwhile the French translator of *Lolita*—who happened to be Maurice Girodias's younger brother, thirty-two-year-old Eric Kahane—was in constant touch, primarily with Vladimir. As every translator of Nabokov before or since has discovered, Kahane was involved in a debilitating act of lacemaking. "Some days I barely manage 8 or 10 lines and feel like murdering you. Other times, I get 2 or 3 pages done but am dead to the world the morning after," he cursed in a letter to the author. Perhaps more than anyone in the spring of 1958, Kahane was attuned to the exquisite richness of the language, the sinuous humor of the lines that the novel's subject had for the most part obscured. The details were endless, as were the arguments, which provide some sense of what Véra faced on a daily basis. Kahane suggested an original phrasing; Nabokov offered an alternative. "That's a beautiful word—but it does not exist," Kahane objected, to which Nabokov countered, "Yes it does," citing as his source the *Grande Larousse* of 1895. "It was bloody Alcatraz" is Kahane's summary of the experience.

Gallimard had no great expectations for the book, or at least had none when they acquired rights to the novel in 1956. By the time Kahane, holed up with the manuscript in a gardener's toolshed on the Riviera, began to grasp that he might well be remembered as the worst-remunerated translator in history, by the time the Nabokovs pushed off from Ithaca for Glacier National Park, Véra and Vladimir understood that everything about their lives was to change. On June 28 Vladimir was already able to declare *Lolita* a commercial success; he did not think he would need to teach anymore. He could not help adding a regret that Véra felt even more keenly, and repeated nearly verbatim: It should all have happened thirty years earlier. Presumably "in the advance light of a great event" she picked up the diary again, in Montana, toward the middle of July. When she did so an early copy of the Putnam's edition had reached the couple, and Conrad Brenner's glowing and brilliant appraisal of Vladimir had appeared in *The New Republic,* "finally giving V. a long-overdue recognition of true greatness," as Véra saw it. The long essay would prove as prescient as it was astute; Brenner predicted years on the syllabi, but neither a Nobel nor a Pulitzer. From the outset *Lolita*'s author had two things going against him: "He is wildly and liquidly sophisticated, and he writes as well as any man alive." Brenner grasped early on that reading Nabokov is essentially a private experience; that the beauty of the work was not in its metaphors but in the magic of its language; that the Russian-American writer defied all categories, formulae, schools (and most critics); that he was a master of the perverse, in support of which claim Brenner cited as evidence *The Real Life of Sebastian Knight.**

---

* Brenner's appreciative words were vitiated by a lead editorial in *The New Republic,* calling the book obscene, and begging to differ from its own reviewer.

Nabokov vowed to write a history of *Lolita*'s travails—he thought he could squeeze an amusing tale out of it for *The New Yorker*—to which end Véra's entries for the latter part of the year would have been a significant help. At some indeterminate time after his wife's failed shopping expedition, he labeled those pages "Hurricane Lolita." It is unlikely that Véra kept this record for her husband's consultation, or for any but her own reasons, however. She seems simply to have realized that events were about to overwhelm them, to have sensed that momentarily their life would undergo a vast and magnificent change, and to have wanted to linger at the vantage point. Twenty-six years earlier her husband had been the toast of the town in émigré Paris; she had not been on hand to witness the commotion, which had proved a false alarm. In the datebook she wrote in English, less guardedly than she would elsewhere. For the first and only time she proves a trustworthy narrator. At the end of the summer she boasted that she had driven Vladimir over 8,000 miles in seven weeks. (Appropriately, the author of *Lolita* was calling for his mail at AAAs that summer; his first copy of the Putnam's edition reached him this way, probably in Glacier National Park.) In the diary Véra documented some of those excursions, in northern Montana and southern British Columbia: 248 miles through dismal landscape in search of *ferniensis*; 120 miles for three *nielithea*. The delight in her husband's triumphs is the same, but a hint of impatience catches in her voice with the butterflies. It had not helped that the weather was miserable, with gale-force winds and buckets of hail. Moreover there was a lively disagreement between the two Nabokovs over which direction to head. In a housekeeping cabin just south of the American border the two read *War and Peace* to each other in midsummer, Vladimir concluding that the novel "is really a very childish piece of writing." The weather did Tolstoy no favors. Outside the primitive cabin the wind howled through Glacier National Park with such force that Vladimir had trouble hearing his wife read.

Véra permitted herself the opportunity to describe some of the summer's accommodations, which seemed only fair; she was the woman who slept in all of Humbert Humbert's motel rooms. She did full justice to the "horrid dirty little hut" they rented—briefly—in northern Wyoming, at an exhausted Vladimir's insistence; she would have preferred to forge ahead. Which is what the couple did after their encounter with the landlord, who—upon hearing that his new guests hailed from upstate New York—declared, "Good enough so long [as] you are not from the Big City. All sorts of folks come from there trying to jew you." What is wrong with the Jews? the Nabokovs asked their landlord, who was happy to enlighten his guests, advising them that Jews "always try to knife you, get the better of you." "Well, I am Jewish, and I have no intention of swindling you," Véra retorted. The landlord fell all over himself with apologies. After a quick inspection of the local restaurant, the Nabokovs fell into the Buick, "abandoning the rent to our righteous host." Véra allowed her indignation full voice too when writing of the Sheridan, Wyoming, rodeo; she would nearly came to blows with the translator of *The Gift* when he defended bullfighting. "Is it fun for *anyone in the world* to see a frightened calf thrown over and roped?" she asked, reserving for this activity the scorn she generally heaped on the Nabokov nonenthusiast. Three days after *Lolita*'s publication, she set down a full chronology of the first eighteen years in America. She went back to fill in the past, the kind of gesture one makes at a critical juncture, when those years are about to be redeemed, when the future is about to detach itself from what has preceded it, when the need for a new dress announces itself.

The Nabokovs arranged to return from the Rockies by early August so as to attend what Véra alternately billed as *Lolita*'s and Vladimir's coming-out party, a press cocktail Minton had scheduled at the Harvard Club. Véra was impressed by Minton's nimble handling of the critics in attendance, enough so to wonder if the slower-moving, owlish publisher she had met earlier in the year had been the same person. She and Vladimir—better attuned to such possibilities than most people—speculated that Minton had earlier sent "an older and rather obtuse cousin" to Ithaca. She was equally impressed by her husband's Harvard Club performance on August 4: This was the occasion on which she observed that he had managed not to skewer a single contemporary. The press was amused less by the names he failed to sully than by those he failed to recognize. In the course of conversation someone mentioned *Peyton Place* to the professor of literature, who drew a blank. " 'What is it?' he inquired. 'A novel? Who wrote it?' " And of course none of the twenty-five reporters was nearly as interested in what the author of *Lolita* had managed to read than whom he might have shared it with. The *New York Post* took pains to observe that he was accompanied to the reception by "his wife, Véra, a slender fair-skinned, white-haired woman in no way reminiscent of Lolita." At the Harvard Club reception as elsewhere, admirers told Véra that they had not exactly expected the author to show up with his distinguished-looking wife of thirty-three years. "Yes," Véra replied, smiling, unflappable. "It's the main reason why I'm here." At her elbow her husband chuckled, admitting that he had been tempted to hire a child escort for the occasion. But the truth was a potent one: Véra's existence kept the fiction in its place, reassured readers skittish about *Lolita*'s subject that Nabokov's perversities were of a different kind.* Is there a trace of Véra in the novel? No, but her fingerprints are all over it. And some people insisted on searching for her. After Lionel Trilling met the Nabokovs, he told his wife that everything about her gave him the feeling that Véra Nabokov was Lolita.

Even if she had not stepped out from the wings by 1958, her days of living more or less incognito in upstate New York were over. It was important to photograph the author, but especially crucial to include Véra in the frame, the flesh-and-blood—and mercifully middle-aged—woman behind the man behind the man who liked little girls. Once again, "mask" proved the key word. Within the first week back in Ithaca Véra fielded calls from *The New York Times Book Review,* from *Time,* from various book club editors, from Minton. A large and not terribly flattering photo of both Nabokovs appeared in the *Post,* along with a full-page interview with Vladimir. Publication day found *Lolita's* author "serenely indifferent," as Véra repeatedly described him in the blinding light of his success. He was spreading his vast collection of American butterflies at a rate of fifty or so a day, focusing so intently on his winged nymphets it was difficult for his wife to get his attention. She felt she was living with a deaf man; at such times he neither saw nor heard. It took Véra three days to find the time to record the news of publication Monday: There had been three hundred reorders in the morning, a thousand by midafternoon, fourteen hundred by the time Minton finally dispatched his telegram of congratulations to Ithaca, twenty-six hundred more the following day. Even Orville Prescott's lambasting the book in the *Times*—he found it repellent "highbrow pornography"—had assisted sales. In Véra's view Prescott's attack was one of "vicious spite," revenge for what he considered the impossible recall her husband had demonstrated in *Speak, Memory.*

Published on August 18, 1958, *Lolita* began to ascend the bestseller list two weeks later. By early September, eighty thousand copies of the novel were in print. (As the Nabokovs were only too aware, this amounted to all of Vladimir's previous print runs in Russian and English combined.) At the end of the month, the book was number one on the *New York Times* list. Véra was terrifically pleased with Minton, who she felt had published a difficult book "in a subtle and flawlessly tactful way." "Flawlessly tactful" amounted in large part to one thing in the Nabokov household: full-page ads. Minton had begun to publicize the book extensively, to Véra's delight; henceforth it

---

* It was doubtless fortunate for both Nabokovs that the public that sent *Lolita* sailing to the top of the best-seller lists had not yet read the largely untranslated oeuvre that preceded it, full of her prototypes. Vladimir was by no means Humbert, but he was the author of a fair number of works in which middle-aged men fidget under the spells cast by underaged girls.

would be her job to remind editors that her husband thought they should consider ads, big ads, lots of ads. The Nabokovs had too often heard the dull thud fine fiction makes when it lands, which was not what they heard now. The novel was seized by Canadian customs, banned for a second time in France. Movie scouts, reporters, fans, editors, descended on the couple, as did a number of what Véra termed "crackpots." "It becomes increasingly difficult to decide who deserves an answer, and who should be ignored," she noted, the etiquette having changed overnight. She spent her time grappling with admirers like the songwriter who had transformed *Lolita* into a ballad and was intent on securing rights in the title. He insisted on serenading Véra telephonically with the fruits of his labors. After several such calls she was ready to concede that the composer was a perfect crackpot. He had already calculated that the novel would earn its author a tidy profit, a realization to which Véra came more gradually. Only on October 12 did she write Elena Sikorski, "It will apparently bring Volodya a fairly large sum of money."

On September 5 Véra sat upstairs at the brick Colonial on 404 Highland Road writing of *Lolita*'s triumphs while downstairs *Life*'s Paul O'Neil conducted the first of several interviews with her husband. A week later *Life*'s photographer arrived for his two-day blitz.* The journalists found Mrs. Nabokov sophisticated and smart; they were charmed by her, deeply amused by her husband. In his diary, photographer Carl Mydans noted: "They are both delightful people, live together in great respect for each other—happily." He stubbornly clicked away, shooting pictures of Vladimir in front of his books, with his eleven folders of Pushkin, at the chessboard, battering the punching ball in the basement, writing in bed, in the yard, in the car, catching a butterfly, killing it, boxing it, even "in front of an innocent motel." He photographed Véra as well, to her dismay: "I don't like to be photographed (might have enjoyed it if it all had happened some 15 years ago, at least) but it is even more of a nuisance to refuse unless the refusal is accepted at once." If the photographer insisted, she felt she had no choice but to consent, reluctantly but gracefully. She was furthermore wholly taken with Mydans, a modest man of tremendous energy and single-minded concentration. She found his devotion to his work to be an inspiration: "While he is at it nothing else matters—he will stand in the middle of the highway ignoring the traffic until he has obtained the picture he has already created in his mind's eye." It was a skill at which she was an unacknowledged expert, having spent more than thirty-three years doing precisely the same thing.

---

* The *Life* piece did not run until April 13, 1959, in the Nabokovs' opinion because the family magazine feared offending its readers.

2

Lolita spent the fall on the bestseller list, the first novel since *Gone with the Wind* to sell a hundred thousand copies within three weeks of publication. (More meaningfully from Véra's point of view, *Lolita* was the "first representative of true literature on the 'List' " since Thornton Wilder's *Bridge of San Luis Rey,* which she considered "a moderately good book.") Gorgeous full-page ads ran in the major media, into which Minton no longer needed to insert sober endorsements from the academy: In the course of the fall the novel was recognized as a virtuouso performance in *The New York Times Book Review,* in *The Atlantic Monthly,* in *The New Yorker,* by Dorothy Parker in *Esquire.** No day passed without *Lolita* being discussed somewhere in the press.

Only rarely did the couple miss a mention. When the uncle who had settled his enormous, prerevolutionary fortune on Nabokov had died in 1915, Vladimir had had a curious dream: Uncle Vasya reappeared to announce that he would one day return as Harry and Kuvyrkin, in dream terms a team of circus clowns. Harry and Kuvyrkin materialized now, under the aliases Harris and Kubrick. While the Nabokovs lunched on September 13 with Mydans and the *Life* caption writer, the telephone rang. It was Morris Bishop, calling with congratulations. When Véra expressed confusion, Bishop read to her from that morning's *Times.* The Nabokovs had been buying the paper every day—Vladimir was avidly following a Staten Island murder case, in which an eight-year-old Mormon boy claimed he had butchered his parents with a kitchen knife—but had not yet consulted that Saturday's edition. It fell to Bishop to notify Véra that movie rights in the novel had been sold to the directing-producing team of Stanley Kubrick and James Harris for $150,000, or about seventeen times Vladimir's Cornell salary. The couple knew Minton was in negotiations but not that any agreement had been reached. How Véra conveyed Bishop's news to the three at table, who immediately leapt upon the paper in search of the five-paragraph announcement, is unclear. She noted only that "the news was broken in a way *Time*"—but of course not she—"would have called 'dramatic.' "

The film deal made Vladimir popular, or prominent, in a way that was uncomfortable for both Nabokovs. Quickly Véra pointed out that the first half of the money would have to be staggered over several years, for tax reasons; that the second half might never be paid; that the promised 15 percent

---

* Nabokov was one for three with the *Times.* In his October 26 column in the *Book Review,* J. Donald Adams pronounced the book utterly corrupt and revolting.

of producer's profits could prove chimerical, in which prophecy she was correct. Both Nabokovs were clearly embarrassed to be perceived as recipients of
what seemed to all a staggering sum of money. To many on the Cornell campus, even *Lolita*'s five-dollar cover price was prohibitive. When a colleague
observed that Vladimir would surely never have to teach again "having
struck oil in Beverly Hills," Véra countered that they were indeed having a
hectic time, but that the colleague was mistaken. Vladimir could not part
with Cornell; they planned only to take a year's leave. She was particularly
distressed when the interest in her husband appeared to derive from his
Hollywood profits. The secretary of a women's club at the Ithaca Pres-
byterian Church phoned days after the announcement to ask if Professor
Nabokov might address the group. Véra took the call, conveying his regrets.
"Oh, I realize he must be terribly busy *now*," the club secretary had responded. The "now" grated harshly on Véra's nerves. "This is not Lolita's literary merits. It's merely the 150 'grand' mentioned by the *Times*," she carped.
Still, she found some consolation in the secretary's call, vindication of a kind:
"To think that three years ago people like Covici, Laughlin, and also the
Bishops, strongly advised V. *never* to publish Lolita, because, among other
things, 'all the churches, the women's clubs' and so forth would 'crack down
on you.' "

In another kind of conspicuousness she took great delight. *Lolita* instantly made its way into the American vernacular. Véra was particularly
cheered by *The New York Times Book Review*'s "delightful cartoon: Work-
man inside a manhole, absorbed in a book, tells a passer-by, who appears to
be pleading with him: No, no, get your own copy of Lolita." In some magazines *Lolita* could be found once in a humorous sketch, again in a Putnam's
ad. (None of these escaped Véra's notice, certainly not the Martian who demanded, "Take me to your Lolita." Assiduously she compiled a different sort
of *Lolita* diary, volumes of press clippings, great and small.) The Nabokovs
played a good deal of "network roulette" on Highland Road; Véra noted that
Lolita was mentioned between segments on "an idiotic Arthur Godfrey
show." A Steve Allen skit featuring Zorro and a Lolita proved more amusing. In November the couple heard Dean Martin claim that he had nothing
to do in Las Vegas as he did not gamble, so he had sat in his hotel lobby and
read children's books: *Pollyanna, The Bobbsey Twins, Lolita*. (Véra misspelled
two of the three titles.) One Sunday evening Steve Allen caused a little
un-Nabokovian breathlessness in Véra's voice when a doll-girl turned up
in a "scientific skit." Allen concluded, "We should send this doll to Mr.
Nabokov." Exclaimed Véra: "We both heard it distinctly—but could not believe our ears!" Milton Berle opened his first show of 1959 with: "First of all

let me congratulate Lolita: She is thirteen now." He kept up the patter—out-lining the plot of a novel called "Lolita Strikes Back," the story of an eighty-four-year-old woman who falls deeply in love with a twelve-year-old boy—well into the New Year.

Toward the reporters and the exposure they represented Véra was equally accommodating; by and large she found the journalists delightful. After the first gaggle of interviewers had flown off she began to notice a certain set of familiar themes in their questions: "They all hope to find some 'scandalous' angle." She could imagine what they wanted to hear; that Cornell's president, Deane W. Malott, had asked her husband not to set foot on campus unchaperoned. (She seemed unaware of the fact that that was already the case.) In fact reporters found it difficult to locate any controversy whatsoever on campus, where the book was selling beautifully, where graduate students in the English Department played dumb, where the moral issue was nowhere under hot debate. (Some tongues did cluck, but neither the Nabokovs nor the reporters heard them.) President Malott received only the odd letter, to which he replied evenly, probably more evenly than Nabokov would have liked.* Véra saw that from the journalist's perspective this would not do: "They seem disappointed to find Cornell ideally adult and unaffected—although had the situation been different, they would have loved to crusade against censorship!" She knew well that scandal sold books. A decade earlier she had observed that the Boston banning of *Strange Fruit* and *Forever Amber* had worked wonders for both titles.

She did not set down another question no one had bothered to ask until *Lolita* made them do so: Who was Mrs. Nabokov? What was the story behind the silver-haired woman who hung on every word of the man who had written 319 pyrotechnic pages on a cultured European rapist? Visitors drew their own conclusions. The young lawyer who visited to clear up the mess surrounding the unlicensed ballad concluded she was the Department of Recollection. Nabokov conferred with his wife at every step of their discussion. "Now, didn't we . . ." he would begin, and softly Véra would answer, "Well, not exactly," gently correcting his course. A student interviewer learned that Véra filed her husband's random notes in cardboard boxes, producing them on demand for future use, something that Dick Keegan had observed firsthand. The student concluded she was the Department of Con-

---

* And without mention of the offending publication's title. "The book in question was written, of course, not as an academic exercise in connection with professional responsibilities but as a private endeavor. Its author has been on the faculty since 1948 and has done some creditable writing," Malott reassured one riled citizen.

necting Things. Mimicry may well have appealed to Véra but misrepresentation did not; it was at this time that she wrote the *New York Post* with "a correction which is most important to me." This letter to the editor she requested the paper publish, which it did. She was not at all a Russian aristocrat, but proud to report she was Jewish.*

In the course of October the Nabokovs made two weekend trips to New York. On the first occasion Vladimir spoke at *The Herald Tribune*'s Book and Author Luncheon at the Waldorf-Astoria, along with his fellow bestsellers Agnes de Mille and Fannie Hurst. Before a thousand people he read his poem "An Evening of Russian Poetry," mentioning *Lolita* not at all. Véra believed the verse was lost on the audience, which for the most part consisted of elderly women. She felt differently about his first television appearance, a CBC interview conducted at the Rockefeller Center studios. She exclaimed over the makeup person who powdered her husband's head to keep the bald spot from shining; her excitement over the countdown to air time is palpable. As she sat with Dmitri in the darkened auditorium, she was thrilled to watch her husband as she never had before: in duplicate. He performed simultaneously on the studio screen and on the lighted stage, a tidy plagiarism of Professor Nabokov's supposed living room, one Véra heartily approved. She felt he spoke beautifully—he did so very obviously from index cards—and was especially fond of the definition he had provided when asked to elaborate on "philistines." They are, he offered, "ready-made souls in plastic bags."[†] She was equally amused by the ingenuity he displayed in pouring his own small flask of brandy into the onstage teacups. It was ten-thirty at night, and liquor was nowhere available. Presumably not only on account of this sacrifice, he was deemed by the CBC an ideal guest.

Véra's one gripe with *Lolita*'s reception was something a *New York Post* critic had noted early on: "Lolita was attacked as a fearsome moppet, a little monster, a shallow, corrupt, libidinous and singularly unattractive brat." Where the novel's reviewers inclined toward pitying Humbert, she fixed instead on Lolita's vulnerability, stressing that she had been left alone without a single close relative in the world. Had she mentioned her qualms anywhere but in the diary they might have seemed a calculated defense of a difficult-to-

---

* A year later, the *Evening Standard* would prove that to an Anglo-Saxon all Russians look alike: The British paper reported that Nabokov, like his beautiful wife, came from "the rich pre-revolutionary Jewish upper-class of Russia."
† Also interesting is what she did not comment on, presumably because she did not need to. In the course of the program, Lionel Trilling held that all great love affairs, literarily speaking, involve partners separated from each other by social convention. Nabokov hastened to disagree, arguing—in novels as in life—for "passionate love, glamorous love within the terms of normal marriage." He cited Tolstoy's Kitty and Levin. Trilling countered that the novel isn't called *Kitty* or *Levin,* it's called *Anna Karenina.*

defend book, which they were not; she expressed a similar frustration later when reviewers missed the pathos of Hazel's suicide in *Pale Fire*. She lamented the treatment of the nymphet to whom she would owe so much:

> Lolita discussed by the papers from every possible point of view except one: that of its beauty and pathos. Critics prefer to look for moral symbols, justification, condemnation, or explanation of HH's predicament . . . I wish, though, somebody would notice the tender description of the child's helplessness, her pathetic dependence on monstrous HH, and her heartrending courage all along culminating in that squalid but essentially pure and healthy marriage, and her letter, and her dog. And that terrible expression on her face when she had been cheated by HH out of some little pleasure that had been promised. They all miss the fact that "the horrid little brat" Lolita, is essentially very good indeed—or she would not have straightened out after being crushed so terribly, and found a decent life with poor Dick more to her liking than the other kind.

Lolita was a novel but Lolita was also a girl. And this one, Mrs. Nabokov thought, should stand at the center of the story to which she lent her name.

3

F. W. Dupee credited *Lolita* with effecting a volcanic change in America's literary landscape, uniting for once all the brows, high-, middle-, and low-, allowing "the fading smile of the Eisenhower Age to give way to a terrible grin." In an involuted game of After You, Alphonse, she even helped *Hecate County* back into print.* She cleared the way for *Lady Chatterley,* and would work a similarly liberating effect in England; she changed the fortunes of several publishing houses.† But *Lolita,* the book and its heroine, changed no

---

* In a gingerly fashion, Roger Straus reissued the volume, under a defunct imprint, in 1959. The copies carried a warning: "Not for sale in New York State."
† She worked a few soap-operaish effects as well, none of them lost on the diary-keeping Véra, who was not easily shocked, but who was easily amused. Walter Minton had heard of *Lolita,* but read the novel only when he ran into a Copacabana showgirl named Rosemary Ridgewell at a party given by the *New York Mirror's* Lee Mortimer. Ridgewell offered up a copy of the book and, as Minton remembered it, "sat with me one night in her apartment on East 67th Street while I read it." For having put the book in Minton's hands she was offered a finder's fee equivalent to 10 percent of Nabokov's royalties for the first year, plus 10 percent of the Putnam's share of subsidiary rights income for two. Nabokov asked about the arrange-

one's life as much as Véra's. Six days before the novel was published she wrote Goldenweiser, who was preparing her restitution case, that she spent a few hours a day on her husband's work, conducting all of his correspondence, correcting proofs, assisting him with his research. How to value this labor for the Germans she could not begin to say. In September she complained of the new demands of the correspondence. The Japanese had bought the novel; Doubleday had contracted for a book of poems; the British sale of *Lolita* was under discussion; she was correcting the German translation of *Pnin*. By the end of October she could no longer cope with the mail. Thanksgiving hardly qualified as a reprieve, as the Nabokovs were again in New York for meetings. After the holiday Véra wrote Berkman, "We are swamped with work. I never imagined so many letters can rain into one mailbox." She would never have permitted herself the luxury of writing only to announce as much; the purpose of her communication was to ask if Berkman might be interested in taking over Vladimir's classes for the spring term. As it was impossible to imagine his continuing to publicize *Lolita* while teaching, he had applied for a leave of absence. It was granted on the condition that he find a substitute lecturer, no easy feat given his academic range. Véra was particularly concerned that a replacement be found swiftly, as Vladimir had "2 large babies to nurse through publication (Pushkin and a French *Lolita*) and several little ones." Letters went out in all directions, to much the same circle but with a very different urgency as they had in order to locate the Cornell job in the first place. *Lolita* was in its ninth printing in November, when paperback rights were sold to Fawcett for one hundred thousand dollars.

Two matters in addition to the correspondence fell to Véra: access to her husband, and all details concerning contracts and taxes. More than ever, she greeted visitors at the door and manned the phone. (Several years earlier, a group of Nabokov's students had called him at home with an esoteric ques-

---

ment, concerned primarily that Ridgewell's fee not be deducted from his royalties. The situation was more baroque yet: *Time* ran a picture of the striking book scout in its November 17, 1958, issue, along with a description of her as "slithery-blithery onetime Latin Quarter showgirl who wears a gold swizzle stick around her neck and a bubbly smile on her face." Two weeks later, Mrs. Minton told Véra over dinner that she had learned of her husband's involvement with Ridgewell only from reading *Time*. From Minton the same evening Véra learned why the article had assumed the tone it had: He was involved as well with its reporter, who had done her best to portray her rival as a drunken call girl. Véra knew already about the *"petite grue,"* although she was presumably less interested to hear of Minton's domestic troubles than to learn from Jason Epstein that Ridgewell was "gunning" for Vladimir. Mostly she pitied Mrs. Minton, so lovely and so clueless in the suburbs with three children, while her husband—as Mrs. Minton so poignantly phrased it—was "broadening" himself in the city. Fortunately, Véra did not know the half of the tale, Act One of which ended in Paris as Rosemary bludgeoned Minton with a whiskey bottle, while Girodias looked on, in a lesbian nightclub. Ridgewell's scouting efforts probably netted her about $20,000, assuming the commission was paid.

tion. They were initially disappointed to fall on Mrs. Nabokov, flabbergasted when she was able to respond to their query without disturbing her husband.) Another caller met with less gratifying results when he telephoned Ithaca in the fall of 1958. The ensuing contretemps revealed much of what was to make Véra notorious in the years to come. When the phone rang at Highland Road on the evening of November 16, the caller "insisted on talking to V. rather than to me, but since he had not given his name to the telephone operator, and I knew not who was calling, I refused to call V. The operator got rude and I lost my temper . . . ," Véra remembered, blotting out the conclusion of her sentence. "Finally the incognito was cast aside, and then I called V., who had just lain down for a nap." Unwittingly—and with a great deal of embarrassment—she had been shielding her husband from Walter Minton. She was doing so at Vladimir's instruction and for his good, but her behavior would not be construed as such. No one knew how utterly foolish Véra had felt playing the role of tiger at the gate, for which she had in part herself to blame; she suppressed all sign of regret, as she did the telling six words following the wayward temper. Originally the sentence had read: "The operator got rude and I lost my temper, and felt miserable about it afterwards."

It was some time before the routine worked flawlessly; the Nabokovs were molting still from professor and assistant to celebrity author and celebrity wife. On the morning of December 7 a caller from Pennsylvania surprised the couple in mid-metamorphosis. A Lehigh College student phoned to ask if Nabokov would sign his copy of *Lolita*. Véra replied that he did not give autographs. That evening she heard a violent knocking on the front door; the student had driven to Ithaca to plead his case in person. His was not even the insistence of a fan; his fraternity had assigned him the task of procuring the autograph. He was adamant. Would Mrs. Nabokov at least sign the book for him? "Of course not, I did not write it," she replied. Then a revelation occurred. "Suddenly it dawned on me that what he needed was a tangible proof that he had driven to our house and asked for an autograph. And he was almost in tears! I offered to give him a note certifying that Mr. Nabokov gives no autographs. And he was quite consoled, happy and thankful!" she wrote, sounding like the woman who recognized Lolita as the heroine of the piece. And as she was to discover soon enough, her time, like her husband's, had its limits. In January when her sister Lena broke the near-decade of silence, Véra apologized for the tardiness of her reply: "I am swamped by Volodya's enormous correspondence (of which he refuses to take care himself). I am spending hours at the typewriter every single day, but it is a losing battle and I have no hope to catch up with this avalanche of mail." With delight she reported that Dmitri planned to translate *Invitation to a Beheading* into English, for Putnam's.

Lolita was Nabokov's twelfth novel, and its success struck with a particular poignancy. From the publishers' points of view, the situation was almost too delicious; it is not often that a bestselling author steps up to the plate with a neglected, largely untranslated backlist of small masterpieces. It should all have happened well before, and it nearly had: There had been recognitions of Nabokov's genius, and brushes with fame, and an occasional profit, though never all three at once. Without *Lolita,* Véra held, it might all have taken another fifty years. In some opinions, without *Lolita,* it might never have happened at all. But in the immediate, new titles, old titles, even *Eugene Onegin,* which in December Nabokov furiously withdrew from Cornell University Press, which he felt was trying to extort money from him, suddenly became attractive properties. And each of them—along with *Lolita* in her foreign incarnations—required a contract. The Minton call that had caused Véra such anguish had been about the disposition of British rights, which Minton felt should go to George Weidenfeld, who had agreed to defend the book. Véra favored publishing with the Bodley Head, who were offering a lower royalty, but at whose head sat Graham Greene, to whom she felt the couple owed a great debt.* (Given the difficulty of publishing a book like *Lolita* in England, where the law was more strict, the two publishers were essentially vying for the privilege of going to jail for a twelve-year-old girl.) Minton was of the opinion that Greene had made a number of powerful enemies in his early defense of the book, and that that collective animus could undermine his publication. He got through to his author on this call, but it is easy to see why he would do so less often in the future. "V. got so bored with the above-mentioned details," Véra noted disapprovingly of the Weidenfeld-Greene discussion, "that he agreed to Minton's wishes, just so as to get the thing out of the way." Henceforth Vladimir discussed contractual terms with Véra, but this was the last negotiation with which he involved himself.

As early as the first glimmers of *Lolita*'s success, Nabokov had realized that he and the U.S. government were to be in business together; these were the years of the 70 percent tax bracket. (He griped openly of the government's stake in his windfall. When Walter Winchell asked if he had acquired anything new with his Hollywood earnings, the author shrugged. "Yes, a new tax bracket!") Previously Véra had handled their tax preparation, unsystem-

---

* Girodias's interpretation of these events: Suspicious Véra and her husband were persuaded that he had signed a secret agreement with Weidenfeld. In truth Minton was the one lobbying for Weidenfeld, who he felt would defend the book more tenaciously than anyone else in England.

atically. She had admitted to Marc Szeftel that she did all in her power to compile the return as quickly as possible. Szeftel had suggested that her inattention might well be costing the couple income. "Yes, I know that we are losing money but . . . it's so boring!" she had exclaimed. She could not afford this inattention any longer. Money management had always been a treacherous subject for the family; it acquired a wholly different meaning in 1958. Throughout November and December, Véra corresponded with the accountant to whom she had delivered the previous years' tax returns. If her husband were indeed to take a leave of absence from Cornell, if the couple were to spend an itinerant year, would they have any obligations to the State of New York? It was not easy to impress upon her correspondent how perfectly nomadic they intended to be. On December 16 Véra wrote—in strict confidence—that they might never return to Ithaca, the first hint of an idea they admitted to no one. After 1958 these issues claimed an enormous amount of her time. There was every reason why Nabokov now described his wife to a visiting British journalist as his "business manager, chauffeuse, and assistant butterfly catcher all rolled into one." He cited her classroom responsibilities as well, although these came to an abrupt end; Véra traded bluebooks for every imaginable form of contract. In the early years Nabokov had complained legitimately that he had more agents than readers. From 1958 on he was to have countless readers, and one very overworked agent.* In the opinion of those in Doussia Ergaz's office, he could not have asked for a better one.

In addition to December exams, one last bluebook stood between Véra and the end of academic life. Throughout the year the Nabokovs had been in touch with the Swedish publisher Wahlström & Widstrand, whose translations of *Pnin* and *Lolita* were not only poor but seemingly abridged. The publisher had agreed to withdraw the mangled *Lolita* from the stores but— as Véra had been able to establish with the help of a Swedish fan—had not done so. Vladimir insisted the contracts be canceled before the publisher further tortured his prose; he had been advised against litigation, but both Nabokovs were actively fuming. In a Cornell University bluebook Véra assumed the onerous task of comparing the Swedish *Pnin* with the original, which she did with a dictionary at her elbow. With its help, and crossbreeding her Russian and her German, she could squeeze most of the meaning from a sentence. (The exercise may have accounted for her later assertion that if she had the time she would learn two things: Swedish and Spanish.) Whole paragraphs were indeed missing from the Walhström edition, in

---

* Véra handled the agenting alone, except in France, where Doussia Ergaz and her colleague Marie Schebeko represented Nabokov until 1976.

which, more seriously, the political slant of a passage had been subtly modified, its anticommunism tempered.* The feud with the Swedish publisher dragged on throughout the last months at Cornell and the first of Nabokov's leave. Lena Massalsky essentially broke her long silence to chastise her younger sister for having placed her husband's work with Wahlström. It was the worst of Swedish houses, Lena remonstrated, enclosing a host of clippings to bolster her claim. She acknowledged that she had heard a great deal about both *Pnin* and *Lolita* but did not allow her sister the satisfaction of saying she had actually *read* either novel. Which perhaps explains why Véra thanked Lena for the clippings, adding that they were duplicates of those that had been sent on "by a real Swede." Lena was understandably offended by this turn of phrase; for the record, she assured her sister, her Swedish was perfect, as indeed it was. Whatever do you mean, replied Véra, suddenly tone-deaf to the nuances of the English language.

The Wahlström matter was resolved over the summer of 1959, with the assistance of a Stockholm lawyer. In the midst of *Lolita*'s worldwide triumph, the work Nabokov had attempted years before in the East Seneca Street backyard was completed, the flames this time fanned by Véra, six thousand miles away. The Swedes agreed to destroy their stock of both titles; a lawyer served as the Nabokovs' witness. On July 7, 1959, he followed the last of a convoy of trucks from the Stockholm warehouse to a dump two miles outside the city, where the books and unbound pages were unloaded. "Ignition was made and soon the whole stack took fire," he reported. "Tins with petrol were thrown at places where the fire wasn't easily spread. I stayed there for one hour. When I left, the surface of the stack was grey and burnt. I was convinced that no copy in the stack could be sold but it is remarkable how long a time it takes for a heap of books to burn down. It was a beautiful day with a mild wind from the lake, close by. It was indeed dramatic." Véra pronounced the dispatch "charming." This book-burning she could countenance. The destruction of her husband's work was preferable to its bestselling existence in a defective form.

The pitilessness with which she pursued the Wahlström & Widstrand matter speaks forcefully to the question of whether her notion of self changed with *Lolita*'s success. Finally America, and the world, had come around to the conviction on which she had predicated her existence since 1923. Another woman might have found this an occasion to soften her stance;

---

* Véra later instructed Doubleday not to grant interested publishers Serbian, Croatian, or Macedonian translation rights in *Pnin*. Given the political considerations, she did not feel that any such translation could be made faithfully.

thirty-five years as standard-bearer had stiffened Véra into a posture from which she did not easily unbend. Save on the pages of the diary, she did not relax. The world having come finally (and briefly) to pronounce "Nabokov" correctly was, she told friends, a great joy, but the flood of fan mail, the Argentine and Icelandic editions, did not obviate the fact that idiocy, mediocrity, philistinism, and Maurice Girodias still existed. For every discerning Conrad Brenner there was an Orville Prescott; every Jason Epstein had his Swedish counterpart.* The French had banned, unbanned, rebanned *Lolita;* briefly the Belgians did the same. Various American libraries had refused to stock the novel. The book's future in England remained uncertain, the German translation was imperfect, pirated editions were rumored to be on sale in Mexico and Uruguay. For every royalty check there were a thousand memories of instability; the lawyers with whom Véra met in 1959 grew used to the influence of anxiety. A gauge of where the validation of her husband's genius had left Véra can be read in her ardent response to a March fan letter: "We have been running into a number of very young people whose attitude to art is so remarkably adult, detached and penetrating that it warms the cockles of one's heart. How I detest those quacks and hypocrits [*sic*] who pretend that real great art can do anything but ennoble a man's mind!"

And then there was *Doctor Zhivago.* Following upon a history as convoluted as *Lolita*'s, Pasternak's novel was published four weeks after Nabokov's. Its author was awarded the Nobel Prize for Literature on October 23, the first Russian to claim the honor since Bunin. Over the months that followed, the two compatriots' books—both begun in 1948, one published in translation by an author still in the USSR, the other the work of a newly minted American who still contended that his Russian was better than his English— were locked in mortal combat at the top of the bestseller list. *Zhivago* made its first appearance on the list early in October, when *Lolita* assumed the number one position; within six weeks *Zhivago* had overtaken *Lolita.* The success of a book Véra considered aggressively second-rate only proved further that one should not expect too much of the world. She had read the novel before her husband and pronounced it inferior. Vladimir denounced Pasternak's work to Wilson, a reading based, to Wilson's mind, solely on excerpts and, to Roman Grynberg's mind, solely on Véra's appraisal. Grynberg urged his friend: "Really do read it! Otherwise you're making judgments based on the words of dear Véra, who has read a wonderful Russian book in a horrible

---

* Two weeks after publication *The New York Times*'s Lewis Nichols compiled an inventory. Of the first nineteen reviewers weighing in on *Lolita,* eleven had praised the book, five had damned it, three had settled comfortably on the fence.

and hurried translation."* Vladimir agreed wholeheartedly that the translation should be distinguished from the novel. "It's a good translation," he assured a reporter. "It's the book that's bad." He restrained himself as much as possible but still could not resist snorting when told that the waiting list for *Zhivago* in the Ithaca library was longer than that for *Lolita*.† (While he did not admire the novel he did admire Pantheon's efforts on its behalf. "The Zhivago gang is doing its best to prop up the sagging doctor. Should we not do something in regard to our nymphet?" he nudged Minton in May, when the books were numbers one and four respectively on the list.) Véra thought little of the book, and its admirers, for different reasons. "The communists have succeeded in pushing this mediocre concoction into the 'Nobel prize winners' club—merely by pretending that it had been 'smuggled' out of USSR! A stampede of fools, led by the pro-commie knaves," she inveighed in the diary. She crossed out the paragraph later, almost as if she regretted having wasted her energy on such a piece of goods, as if its mention marred the pages on *Lolita*'s conquests. She could not have been embarrassed by the force of her sentiment, about which she was perfectly vocal. Both Nabokovs believed that the Soviet Union approved of the novel and was only putting on a show to the contrary. Véra remained always doctrinaire in her literary standards: If you were a fine writer and your politics were lousy, or questionable (Tsvetaeva), you were a bad writer. If you were a less fine writer, and your politics were laudatory (Solzhenitsyn), you were still a bad writer.

In light of the winter bestseller lists, on which Lolita hung precariously to Lara's feet, the Nabokovs' dismissal of Pasternak looked like sour grapes. Bitterly Véra had observed at the end of October that *Lolita* was still on the list, everywhere, "although she'll probably soon be squeezed out by that pitiful and miserable 'book' by the lowly Pasternak, whom V. is reluctant to badmouth, so as not to be misunderstood." There was every indication he was already misunderstood. Two days later Wilson asserted that Vladimir was "behaving rather badly about Pasternak. I have talked to him on the telephone three times lately about other matters and he did nothing but rave

---

* He did read the novel. In August he alerted Epstein, "I am reading DR. ZHIVAGO—dreary, conventional stuff." How to unravel a friendship in twenty words or fewer: Wilson declared of Pasternak's work in the November 15 *New Yorker*: "*Doctor Zhivago* will, I believe, come to stand as one of the great events in man's literary and moral history." He too criticized Max Hayward's translation, although the two men became friends, in time for Hayward to assist Wilson in his assault on Nabokov's *Onegin*.

† Elsewhere he was happy to be more forthcoming on the subject, speaking of Pasternak's novel as a "sorry thing, clumsy and melodramatic, with stock situations, rambling robbers and trite coincidences." Among the insults he hurled at the book was the accusation that Pasternak's mistress had written the novel for him, the worst that could be said, not because Pasternak might have delegated the responsibility, but because the thing *read* as if written by a woman.

about how awful *Zhivago* was. He wants to be the only Russian novelist in existence. It amuses me to see *Zhivago* just behind Lolita on the bestseller list, and I am wondering whether Pasternak—as they say about horse-races—may not nose her out." (It could not have been easy for the author of the doomed *Hecate County*—the book had been removed from sale after selling fifty thousand copies, Wilson's first substantial earnings—to watch *Lolita* sell many thousand more.) Nabokov was aware of how the *Zhivago* denouncing sounded but could not help himself, except to condemn more generously. "Compared to Pasternak, Mr. Steinbeck is a genius," he edified a reporter in January. He said as much to friends at a dinner on Highland Road that winter, as a rubber-band-powered butterfly sent by Wilson flapped its way around the room. One wing was labeled "Lolita," the other "Zhivago." To his handful of guests, Nabokov protested that his disdain was in no way fueled by professional jealousy.*

Véra was not mistaken to remain on the alert. While Nabokov had not been pilloried as Bishop had feared, his success proved as objectionable as his choice of subject. Many in Ithaca saw *Lolita* as a cunning act of currency conversion; even the Highland Road landlord felt Nabokov was thumbing his nose at America in order to get out of the country. Colleagues quibbled with the novel on artistic grounds. As if to return Véra's parry, Goethe scholar Eric Blackhall held that the book would have been stronger if limited to its first half. The analyses of *Doctor Zhivago*—the language of which cannot even invite a comparison with that of *Lolita*—invited further ill will. With friends like Wilson, Nabokov did not exactly need enemies, but he had them: He had maintained his distance from the Russian community in New York, who now spoke of the two compatriots on the bestseller list as "the saint and the pornographer." Against these naysayers—and the thousand people who demanded her husband's time in the last Cornell months—Véra remained on guard. Four decades of virtual anonymity had not been as fatiguing as was bestsellerdom; the diary entries are shot through with concern for poor, exhausted Vladimir. Before a New York trip in the fall she warned the Hessens that they preferred to dine quietly with them and the Grynbergs: "V. is very tired and when there are a lot of people around he wanes," she explained. At

---

* In an equally memorable moment, Dorothy Gilbert, the former student whose eye trouble had resulted in the withering exchange with Véra, found herself in conversation before dinner with Marc Szeftel, on the Nabokovs' sofa. "Have you read *Pnin?*" asked one of the oldest assistant professors on campus, the man widely believed to have been the model for the addlepated scholar with the endearingly approximate grasp of the English language. The two agreed it was a wonderful book, Gilbert biting her tongue as she did so.

Harvard she had been thought to treat her husband like a work of art that needed to be protected. There was now cause for greater vigilance.

At the same time, events were moving so quickly she barely found time to record them. The novelist Herbert Gold accepted Nabokov's Cornell position, inheriting with it an annotated copy of *Zhivago*. The couple made plans to head west, then east to Europe for several months. Vladimir was so weary that Véra began counting the days. His teaching career came to an end—officially he was on a year's leave—as of February 1, 1959. Henceforth he would devote himself to what he had always done most passionately: writing and collecting. Véra's second career was just beginning. J. G. Smith sent out her last letter as Nabokov's secretary, a near-satire of a recommendation letter for a graduate student. Mrs. Vladimir Nabokov negotiated a series of foreign contracts. Véra packed up the family's worldly possessions—for the forty-three suitcases with which she and her mother and sisters had left Petersburg there were now thirty-four carefully inventoried cartons (chess problems, model airplanes, old reviews, entomological correspondences, stamp collections, Christmas tree decorations, *Lolita* reviews, pistol), all of them entrusted to storage. In the course of the packing she unearthed a draft of "The Enchanter," which she triumphantly presented to her husband, who had thought the dried bud from which *Lolita* had miraculously blossomed to have been lost. The same day he wrote Minton, proposing a translation.* John Updike has written that Nabokov "had ample reason for artistic exhaustion" on his arrival in Ithaca; Véra had ample reason for exhaustion on the departure. In the last weeks at Cornell she whimpered just a little to Sylvia Berkman: "I meant to write you this much sooner but I am simply losing track of things because of the impossible pressure of work. Vladimir refuses to take the least interest in his own business matters, and I do not feel equipped to handle them properly. Besides, I am by no means a Sévigné, and writing ten to fifteen letters in one day leaves me limp."

On Tuesday, February 24, 1959, the Nabokovs left Cornell for New York. The road from Ithaca was less the "thread of gold" which Pnin follows from Waindell College than a thread of silver; the highways were slick with ice. The sheriff's office advised a day's wait, but Véra resolved to battle the frozen roads all the same. They had already once postponed the trip and were eager to leave. Free at last, the couple disappeared—after a bad skid, and an unscheduled overnight near Schenectady—into the frame of the fu-

---

* "The Enchanter" would have to wait until 1986, when it appeared in Dmitri's translation. Véra did not think the story a success.

ture, leaving behind a model airplane and a butterfly net in the Highland Avenue basement, a Goldwin Smith office full of furniture, but no forwarding address.

4

Nabokov had lost his inherited fortune the Old World way—through revolution—and replaced it the American way—by dint of brains and industry.* The New York stay had been expected to last a few days and to be followed by a restorative trip west—Véra informed Filippa Rolf, the "real Swede" who had lent a hand in the Wahlström & Widstrand fiasco, that butterfly collecting was the best respite for her husband—but innumerable business matters and a case of influenza kept the couple at the overheated Hotel Windermere for nearly two months. On all sides they were assailed, by reporters, publishers, television producers. The first New York morning began with a call from a Cincinnati, Ohio, newspaper. What did Mr. Nabokov think of the fact that the city's main library had banned *Lolita?* (Mr. Nabokov felt that if people liked to make fools of themselves they were well within their rights doing so.) The call was followed by those from *Time, Life, The New York Times, The Daily Mail,* and a string of publishers. On Sunday evening, March 1, the Nabokovs met George Weidenfeld, *Lolita's* British publisher, for the first time.[†] He found Véra frosty at the outset, immensely cordial once he had earned her confidence, which he did only slowly. If they had not already done so, the couple observed now that their every move was being followed. The first call on Monday morning was from a reporter for the London *Evening Standard.* What had they talked about with Mr. Weidenfeld at their dinner at Le Voisin? Doubtless they had discussed Weidenfeld's strategy for publishing *Lolita* without incurring a prison sentence. Without having yet appeared there, *Lolita* had occasioned a furor in England, as was reported in that week's issue of *Time.* British publication was delayed pending the new obscenity bill; if that bill failed to pass, Weidenfeld and his partner Nigel Nicolson, a Member of Parliament, risked convictions. As it was, Weidenfeld found it nearly impossible to have the book manufac-

---

* As always, he has the last word in the matter. " 'This is the only known case in history when a European pauper ever became his own American uncle,' " quips a character in *Look at the Harlequins!*
[†] Weidenfeld felt Véra was a Giacometti drawing come to life. For her part, she thought the British publisher a sort of cross between Edmund Wilson and Winston Churchill, a description that could only have pleased.

tured in England, collecting exponentially more letters of regret from printers than Nabokov had from publishers.* *Lolita* had that March sold nearly a
quarter of a million copies in America.

While in New York Véra began to grapple seriously with the tax implications of their new incarnation. At Epstein's suggestion, she consulted with
attorney Joseph Iseman and his colleagues at Paul, Weiss, Rifkind, Wharton &
Garrison; at the same time she drafted a copy of a will. On April 11 her sister
Sonia—now a simultaneous interpreter at the United Nations—gave a
farewell dinner in her West Side apartment for the Nabokovs. The following
evening Anna Feigin did the same. Still it was a few days before the couple
managed to leave town, largely because of the flood of mail. Only two months
later did Véra discover that a bundle of unacknowledged letters had made
their way into a trunk of papers to be filed. She enjoyed the whirlwind all the
same, reveling in her husband's ascension. "We have seen hundreds of people
here and have had a wonderful time," she wrote after the farewell dinners, all
the necessary meetings having been concluded, as well as a brilliant Epstein-
orchestrated coup: The Bollingen Press, which had once passed on the project,
signed up the *Onegin* translation in March. Only on April 18 did Véra at last
ferry Vladimir west, through Tennessee, Alabama, and Louisiana, two butterfly nets on the backseat, her contracts file in the Buick trunk.

At a leisurely pace they picked their way toward Arizona, Véra keeping
up a lively correspondence about translations, jacket changes, contractual
terms, as they did so. She profited from a stop in southern Texas to confer
with Doubleday about Italian rights in *Nabokov's Dozen,* to nudge *Lolita*'s
Dutch publisher about *Laughter in the Dark.* (The Cornell University sta-
tionery still served, but the return address on all of these missives was Putnam's.) As they headed toward the southwestern corner of the state the
weather disintegrated; Véra found the driving treacherous, on one occasion
nearly losing control of the wheel. The raging tornadoes and roaring
thunderstorms could have served as pathetic fallacy for *Lolita*'s European
fates: For a book that concerned itself solely with art, the novel's early fortunes were intensely political. In April Gallimard had brought out Eric Kahane's fine translation, freely sold in a country in which the English edition
was considered under partial ban. (The logic was more Cartesian than it appeared: Gallimard was General de Gaulle's publisher.) Véra grumbled that
Madame Ergaz did little to keep her apprised of *Lolita*'s situation in Paris,
but the fault was not entirely the agent's; the booksellers were not much bet-

---

* More than thirty British printers walked away from the job. Even if the novel was not pornographic
they believed it was certain to be prosecuted.

ter informed. Some believed the interdiction still in place. Others quietly sold the novel, which could be found "huddling shamefully" with Frank Harris and Henry Miller in bookshop corners. At the same time the work was banned from importation into Australia, New Zealand, and South Africa, where its specter kept the vice squads busy.

But *Lolita*'s political repercussions made themselves felt most strongly in England, where an unpublished volume had rarely caused such a sensation. In January Weidenfeld & Nicolson arranged for a list of twenty-one eminent writers to sign a letter deploring government prosecution of literature in the *Times;* it would have been remarkable if as many as half had actually read the book. A Labour-sponsored piece of legislation that might reasonably define obscenity on the page, the Obscene Publications bill had meanwhile been languishing for four years. In essence it established that a work must be judged as a whole—and therefore on its literary merits—not on the basis of potentially objectionable passages read out of context. The debate was reinvigorated by the news of *Lolita*'s imminent arrival on British shores, with Nicolson arguing eloquently—and against his own deep misgivings—that the book could not corrupt, "because it shows depravity coming to such tragic and unenviable ends." Nicolson had made himself unpopular with his constituency in his opposition to the British invasion of Suez; his championing of *Lolita* further eroded confidence in the forty-two-year-old MP.* It hardly mattered how he argued the case; his constituents concluded he was Humbert Humbert in disguise. Nicolson lost his seat in February, eight months before *Lolita* finally arrived in England.

From Texas Véra wrote Laughlin, who was reissuing *The Real Life of Sebastian Knight* and *Gogol,* that they planned to continue on to Arizona, where they might well stay "long enough to evolve a mailing address." By the time they did so, a week later, they were in a pine cabin in Oak Creek Canyon, a red and green oasis twenty miles south of Flagstaff. Véra sounded as enchanted with this canyon as she ever was with any place; by pure chance they had stumbled upon the small resort, above a mountain stream and amid a cool forest of oak, laurel, fir, and pine a few miles from the desert. It was an exquisite landscape, in which, relentlessly, she worked. Morris Bishop felt that the western excursions afforded Véra some well-deserved vacation; this one did not. On May 24 Vladimir reported that his wife was typing his final

---

* "A Naughty Girl Smooths the Way for Randy Churchill's Comeback," read one hopeful February headline.

translation and notes to *The Song of Igor's Campaign,* an epic poem that holds a place in Russian literature analogous to that of *Beowulf* in English literature, and a project he had begun years before. He felt Russia should one day bow at his feet for all he had done for her literature. Véra described the *Igor* project differently:

> My summer so far has not been very restful: I have scores of letters to write in answering the over-voluminous business and fan mail that keeps pursuing us all over the States. V. has just finished a new little book, the translation of the *Slovo,* that Russian 12th-century epic on which he has been working for almost a year. I vow that this is the *last* translation I shall agree to let him do as long as *I* live!

(It would be far from the last, although Véra could have consoled herself that after the five years' work that remained to be done on *Onegin,* Nabokov almost exclusively translated Nabokov.) She checked the proofs of the German translation of *Lolita,* which she thought in many instances substandard. Mostly she found the tale of the *nymphchen* overly delicate, not gruesome enough. She did not shy from proposing a better word for "haunches." And a spade very much needed to be called a spade, however unfelicitous that spade might be: " '*Liebesdingen*' [matters of love] is a polite and unfortunate euphemism substituted by a continental lady-translator for 'matters of sex'. Let us remember that Humbert is neither polite, nor a lady: he is very much a male, and moreover a sex maniac."

She looked east, to the trip to Europe, as her husband had looked west; only on board the steamer where no business mail could be forwarded could she expect any rest. She was working day and night on the correspondence and for Vladimir "on some other matters in which he needs me," as well as cooking meals, which she always considered a burden. She had at least a little reading time: Probably in Arizona she read Robbe-Grillet's *La Jalousie,* which she could not recommend highly enough, although she would do an interesting dance when formulating that opinion publicly. She deferred always to her husband's admiration for Robbe-Grillet, while he repeatedly indicated that she had been the one to discover his work. She raved about the 1957 novel, which she found beautifully compact and tragic, but most of all original, "which is, probably, a quality that counts highest with us." Years later an acquaintance asked Véra if she also wrote. "Oh, she writes all the time," Vladimir cut in, truthfully, but begging the question.

On June 2 a reporter from *Sports Illustrated*—perhaps the only publication in America not yet to have run a piece on *Lolita* or her author—arrived to document Nabokov and his collecting. He endeared himself immediately to Véra by displaying, and making her a gift of, an old photo of her husband he had found in a secondhand bookstore. The next morning Vladimir emerged from the cabin and announced, "It is now 9 o'clock." The reporter could not help noticing that it was only 8:30, but that "Nabokov keeps moving all clocks and watches within his reach ahead to make Mrs. Nabokov move faster so he can get to his butterflies all the sooner." Nor could he help noticing that the designated driver failed to rise to the bait, calling her husband to breakfast instead. Later in the morning Véra emerged from a bout of letter-writing to chauffeur her husband and their visitor several miles north. In the afternoon she joined the chase with her own net. "You should see my wife catch butterflies," Nabokov boasted. "One little movement and they're in the net." The following morning an exuberant Vladimir coaxed his wife along again: "Come on, darling, the sun is wasting away!" Imperturbable Véra did nothing to quicken her pace, confiding in the reporter, "He doesn't know that everyone is wise to him." She was able to put off her husband for all of twenty-five minutes.

As did much else, the spectacular landscape paled in comparison with that husband's triumph. *Lolita* was an explosive success in France and Italy and had done well in Holland; the book was out in Denmark, Spain, Japan, Israel, Poland, Norway, and Argentina; it was about to be released in Portugal, Brazil, Finland, and Germany; Véra was negotiating offers in Greece and Iceland. But what pleased her most was the emergence of a group of young readers who were now taking the trouble—along with publishers everywhere—to hunt down her husband's early volumes. Her fear of fauna manifested itself as fear for her husband as well. In Texas's spectacular Big Bend National Park a ranger had cautioned the Nabokovs about rattlesnakes and mountain lions. Véra was displeased by Vladimir's cavalier response: "V. discounts both statements—which is annoying because he gets careless and may step on a rattler (or, for that matter, on a mountain lion, since he *has* managed to step on a slumbering bear in Yosemite.)" Nabokov's philosophy on the subject was clear; he believed God looks after entomologists as he does drunkards. The Browning slumbered quietly a few thousand miles away, in an Ithaca carton.

Apart from two hurried entries made in August and September, Véra ended the diary in Texas, on or just after May 10. The promise and expectation with which she had begun the account had been fulfilled; the novelty of celebrity may have worn off. Poised to begin her second year on the bestseller list, *Lolita* could clearly fend for herself, at least in America. For all her love of precision Véra was not particularly methodical; she felt no mandate to fill the remaining pages of the book. She may have been overwhelmed by the sheer volume of work. For whatever reason, about two months before the date on which John Shade picks up his pen to begin his 999 lines of *Pale Fire,* Véra made the last complete entries in her short-lived journal, her single act of non-ventriloquism. It is impossible to imagine her having begun such an exercise solely on her own account, just as it is impossible to imagine she was composing this narrative for anyone other than her husband and herself. The pages are all the more revealing because she did so. This was Véra as she was, not as she saw herself, a trick *Lolita* had inveigled. Even so she continued to efface herself. The diary pages include Vladimir's cancer scare of 1948 but not Véra's equally alarming misdiagnosis of 1954. She made no note of the May 15 death in Ithaca of seventy-one-year-old Ilya Feigin, bedridden since the stroke that had paralyzed him several years earlier. She was chagrined not to have been able to help with funeral arrangements, which Anna Feigin had handled alone. As she began the 1958 diary, and over the years that followed, Véra had ample cause to outline the bare facts of her own history for her reparations claim. She proved hopelessly vague, amnesiac, wrong.

5

———

Appropriately, the 1959 road trip ended in Hollywood. The Nabokovs spent the last week of July in a Beverly Hills Hotel bungalow, at Harris and Kubrick's invitation. The press swiftly caught up with them; Vladimir spoke not of *Lolita* but of *Invitation to a Beheading,* a novel he described as a story of Russia in the year 3000. He was polishing Dmitri's fine translation, which Putnam's planned to publish—the idea must have made both Nabokovs chuckle with glee—the day of Khrushchev's arrival in America. Less chortling went on with Harris and Kubrick. The filmmakers hoped to persuade Vladimir to write the screenplay for their *Lolita,* offering him forty thousand dollars to do so. Together the Nabokovs decided to turn down the tempting offer, preferring their freedom to the money. Doubtless it helped that Europe was calling; Vladimir's foreign publishers were politely but firmly clamoring for his presence. Véra was charged with the task of conveying her husband's decision to the moviemakers. She explained his reasoning, referring to Harris and Kubrick's vision: Her husband found the idea of Lolita and Humbert marrying in the end—with a relative's blessing—so repellent that he could not wrap his mind around it.* The more the matter was discussed, the less able he felt to devise a screen solution that would prove compatible with the work. That August *Lolita* headed into her second year on the bestseller list in the number twelve position, seven irritating rungs below *Zhivago*.

In midmonth the Nabokovs began to drift eastward, stopping first in Ithaca, where they called on the Bishops. "Both the Vs looked uncommonly well, brown, western," observed Morris Bishop, who found them in high spirits even at the end of their long drive, and who refrained from pointing out "in the midst of their cheer that living off Lolita's earnings is assez mal vu in some countries." Bishop noted that the couple were traveling separately from, but in tandem with, Dmitri, who planned to pursue his vocal training in Italy, where it was felt that he might most comfortably make the transition from learning to performing. In fact the Nabokovs' itinerary was more fluid even than Bishop suspected. In early September, Véra met several times in New York with the lawyers at Paul, Weiss. In her role as family Exchequer, she discussed tax implications of the banner year and explained the tangled and highly vexing Olympia stranglehold. She also explored the tax advantage in establishing residence in Europe, where the Nabokovs planned to spend a year, and where she suggested they might well stay considerably longer. She guessed they would settle in France, Italy, or Switzerland. Cornell learned as much soon enough. On September 22 Vladimir submitted a letter of resignation, news of which made its way into the national papers. The same day Véra explained to Bishop that she had long felt the combination of teaching and writing was too much for her husband.[†] The following day, from a cluttered desk at the Hotel Park Crescent on Riverside Drive, she sighed, with what sounds like qualified relief: "What the future holds, and how everything will settle, we can only guess." It had been over twenty years since Nabokov had written Altagracia de Jannelli from the south of France—the landscape which was to shape Humbert Humbert—that America's intellectual future appeared to him blindingly bright, brighter even than her so-called avant-gardists imagined. He had looked forward to finding in America the readers that he knew were waiting for him there.

---

* Concerned about their code-seal, James Harris had run this idea past the head of the MPAA censorship committee, which had already indicated they would have trouble with the project. What if we chose to have Humbert and Lolita marry? asked Harris. He had done his research; he pointed out that this would have been possible in several states. Was it immoral if it was legal? Reluctantly Jeffrey Sherlock agreed that under those circumstances, the committee would have to grant the film its code-seal.

[†] An unsurprised and ever-graceful Bishop wrote back, resorting again to the dual-purpose second person: "Dear V & V, . . . Your drudgery should be a writer's drudgery."

The future had been no less certain, but of an entirely different hue. Again displaced persons, the couple asked Walter Minton if they might borrow the Putnam's mailing address a little longer.

Dmitri inherited the Buick. As mail drops, Véra suggested to her husband's correspondents Mondadori, *Lolita*'s Italian publisher, or her sister-in-law Elena, a UN librarian, at her Geneva address. She was heading toward familiar territory but away from most of what remained of her relatives. Only Lena, with whom the correspondence was now more regular, remained in Europe. The two had not seen each other since 1937; Lena was eager for a reunion, having built an entirely new life in Sweden. She prided herself on the fact that her son, Michaël, spoke not a word of Russian. With a certain incredulity Sonia asked Véra that winter: "Are you planning on visiting Lena (our Lena)?" She was not in touch with their eldest sister, and did not realize Véra was. She wondered if Lena knew that Véra was in Europe, a fact Lena could not have ignored had she wanted to; the amount of press generated by the Nabokovs across the Continent over the next months would be impossible to overestimate. Even aboard the *Liberté*, Vladimir was surrounded by admirers. The ship's library boasted an elaborate display of his works. The head of Bobbs-Merrill happened to be sailing as well; he made every effort to cozy up to the author his firm had brought to America and whom another firm was now triumphantly sending forth. The captain interrogated the celebrated passenger about his choice of subject, although he had not read the sensational novel. In between answering his questions, Vladimir fashioned a structure, in miniature, of what would at last become *Pale Fire*.

The Nabokovs had expected to spend a few days in France before heading off to meet Elena Sikorski but found to their consternation that Paris was "undergoing a new occupation," as Véra put it. With the Salon d'Auto in full swing, there was not a hotel room to be found. They took the night train to Geneva, inadvertently retaliating for the ill-fated Gallimard meeting of 1937: Nabokov's French publisher waited in vain at his office for his bestselling author. In Geneva, one of the few cities in which *Lolita* could be purchased in three languages, the couple settled into a lakefront apartment at the Hôtel Beau-Rivage, a far cry from Riverside Drive's Hotel Park Crescent. With satisfaction Véra noted that the novel was prominently displayed in every bookshop window. An emotional reunion with Elena Sikorski on October 7—her brother was so much *larger,* and yet so much the same—was followed by a series of editorial meetings. The Nabokovs met Ledig Rowohlt and his French-born, Oxford-educated wife, Jane, for the first time now; Véra felt it was "friendship at first sight." George Weidenfeld paid a visit, as did representatives of Nabokov's other publishers, and a small herd of reporters.

Perhaps because the Geneva address was known only to a few, the pace of Véra's correspondence slowed here. She wrote Epstein about editorial matters, she conferred with Doussia Ergaz's office about arrangements in Paris, where Gallimard expected the Nabokovs on the twenty-first. She had other worries as well: She was in dire need of evening wear, something of which there appeared to be a great dearth in Geneva.

It was very much the calm before the storm. On the return to Paris two weeks later every one of the couple's moves was documented. The press was waiting at the station, vying for the attention of the "most controversial writer since D. H. Lawrence and Henry Miller." The Nabokovs did their best to be polite while they and their ten suitcases piled into a car for the Hotel Continental, where Ergaz had at last and with some difficulty found them a room, a frantic search Vladimir later contorted into a dulcet memory. His datebook for the sixteen days that followed is more crowded than it would ever be again; in the course of the first day, four interviewers called at the hotel. Eric Kahane, the novel's nimble translator, stopped by as well. All eyes were on Vladimir but the headlines were about someone else altogether; the real news appeared to be that Mr. Nabokov was not escorting a luscious twelve-year-old around Paris. "Madame Nabokov is 38 Years Older than the Nymphet Lolita," screeched one front-page headline. Véra was observed to be "blonde, distinguished, discreet," a statement which was two-thirds true, a fairly good average where the Nabokovs and the press were concerned. (She was forty-five years older than Lolita.) In a mink stole and a light-gray suit, she looked every bit the proper Continental wife. Had she wanted to remain outside the limelight she would not have been able to; if you were truly interested in camouflage, traveling with the author of *Lolita* was the wrong place to be in 1959.

She enjoyed herself immensely. In every account of the Paris-London whirlwind she speaks of how the crush of admirers tired Vladimir, but concludes ebulliently that the adventure was "great fun." Sonia Slonim was not far off when she guessed that the European return must have felt like a brilliant ball. When Parisian reporters could not lure Vladimir to the phone to pose the questions they were burning to ask, they clamored for Véra, who expertly deflected their queries. In a headline two days after their arrival, she was quoted as saying her husband had never known Lolita. She denied having edited, or so much as offered an opinion on, the novel. "When a masterpiece like *Lolita* enters the world, the only problem is finding a publisher," she parried, although she did take credit for having submitted the novel for publication in Paris. She ducked the assault of leading (and absurd) questions deftly. Did it shock her to be the wife of a scandalous author, she was asked, to which she replied that the opinion of those who saw a scandal in *Lolita* counted not an iota with her. Only the opinion of those who saw a masterpiece did. During most of the scheduled talks she sat at her husband's side, occasionally interjecting a comment. When Nabokov told one of the first interviewers that—like Flaubert writing of the death of Emma Bovary—he had cried when composing *Lolita*'s last scene with Humbert, Véra added her usual plea for the heroine's humanity: "She cries every night, and the critics are deaf to her sobs." Afterward Madame Ergaz thanked the Nabokovs—both Nabokovs—for all their hard work in Paris.* Everyone had been charmed by the simplicity with which they had acquitted themselves of a punishing task, and above all by their cordial treatment of all concerned.

On Friday evening, October 23, the Parisian literary world gathered in the sanctum sanctorum of French publishing, the gilded Gallimard salon on the rue Sebastien-Bottin. The Nabokovs arrived by taxi; Vladimir disappeared quickly into the crowd of well-wishers, which was immense. (In an interesting turn of phrase, Véra observed that "Everybody and his wife was invited.") The journalists tore her husband away from each other; they jockeyed for position; they hung on his every word. Véra's pleasure in the sight is nearly palpable. In photographs she looks radiant, vibrant, a poised, porcelain beauty. The shopping had decidedly proved successful: She appeared at Gallimard resplendent in a black moiré dress, a tasteful mink stole, a double strand of pearls. The rain of questions fell on her, too. She profited from the attention to settle a score of her own, telling an amusing Khrushchev anecdote. Natalie and Nicholas Nabokov's son Ivan, a Parisian editor, was in attendance; he found his cousin ill at ease, overwhelmed. Ivan did not see Véra at her husband's side but felt she would have come in very handy indeed. Knowing too well how her brother's distraction manifested itself at such public moments, Elena Sikorski, who remained in Geneva, offered, "he was a little lost in that kind of scene."

Among the luminaries packed into the round reception hall were two people who were especially eager to present themselves to the author of *Lolita* and who felt they did so this evening. Zinaida Shakhovskoy, Ivan Nabokov's aunt and Vladimir's early champion, was nonplussed when the man she had so often assisted twenty years before looked her straight in the eye and uttered a perfunctory *"Bonjour, Madame."* (Véra, who witnessed the greeting from a distance, was equally puzzled.) Shakhovskoy felt the

---

* The novel's sales increased sixfold during the couple's Parisian visit.

slight was intentional, whereas it was most likely a symptom of the same distraction Nabokov had manifested on campus when Véra's cues had so often saved him from social disasters. (When producer James Harris had stepped backstage at the Waldorf-Astoria luncheon the previous fall, he introduced himself as "the man who just bought *Lolita*." Nabokov showed no sign of distinguishing him from any of the other eighty thousand people who had done so, though Harris alone had purchased the book for $150,000. Blankly Nabokov had replied: "I hope you will enjoy reading it.") Maurice Girodias also attended the Parisian reception although he had not been officially invited, Gallimard having been caught in the crossfire between their author and *Lolita*'s original publisher. As Girodias remembered it, Doussia Ergaz introduced him to Nabokov, who looked up from his coterie of admirers and around for his wife, "as if responding to a telepathic message." A few glasses of champagne later, Girodias waded through the crowd to Véra. She had no entourage but needed none to make her point; she offered up the silent treatment to the man standing directly before her. "I did not exist; I was no more than an epistolary fiction, and I had no business wearing a body and disturbing people in a literary cocktail party given in honor of her husband Vladimir Nabokov," recalled the spurned publisher, who coaxed an enormous amount of mileage out of these near- and nonencounters. Véra reported that she had met—and disliked—Girodias on that occasion, but implied that her husband had not.

Both Girodias and Shakhovskoy aired their grievances loudly over the next years. If they could not manage to disconcert Vladimir with their offensives they happily lunged at Véra. It was she who was to spend a decade attempting to extricate her husband from an agreement with a man she only reluctantly admitted existed. She pursued every possible means of annulling the Olympia agreement until 1969, when the third lawyer on the case at last succeeded in separating the parties. For his part, Girodias saw Véra's long, lovely arm everywhere. She was the dragon lady, the decisive partner, "the anti-nymphet." When Paul O'Neil's *Life* profile finally ran in 1959, Girodias disputed various passages of the account. *Life* published his objections to their article, along with a long editorial comment, which—according to Girodias—"although signed with the initials of our mysterious friend ED., seems to carry on its forehead the beautiful aura of Véra Nabokov's distinguished scalp."

Paris proved only a dress rehearsal for the tempest that enveloped the Nabokovs in London, where *Lolita* had been printed but where its distribution remained in jeopardy. The crucial legislation had finally passed, but the Attorney General had not changed; he had estimated the chances of prosecution at 99 percent. On all sides Nigel Nicolson was pressured to abandon his defense of the work; Edward Heath, Chief Whip, implored him to do so for the sake of the Conservative Party.* Before the summer recess, in the House of Commons lobby, the Attorney General had jabbed a finger in Nicolson's chest and warned him that publication would land him directly in jail. Nicolson had been standing at the time with Harold Macmillan, the Prime Minister. The matter constituted a national obsession; Weidenfeld and Nicolson appeared daily in the press, their lives examined for the kind of scurrilous behavior that could be expected of *Lolita* defenders. In October, at Nicolson's suggestion, a few copies of the book were circulated and one was submitted to the Director of Public Prosecutions. If he approved it, the novel would be published officially on November 6. If he did not, Weidenfeld and Nicolson would at least be spared the charge of having distributed licentious matter throughout the British Isles. Twenty thousand copies of *Lolita* meanwhile sat meekly in a warehouse, to be destroyed in the event of prosecution. Into this maelstrom sailed the Nabokovs, landing in Dover on October 28. Two bodyguards whisked them away from the pier in a limousine; the phalanx increased to five at their West End hotel. One frustrated reporter submitted a picture of Vladimir being fitted into the Stafford Hotel elevator that the author of *Lolita* would have appreciated. The security detail frantically rang for the lift, into which they hurried the eminent writer. The journalist caught "a last glimpse of him peering out through the bars."

For months Véra had joked that she hoped to spend Christmas in Italy if Vladimir did not end up in Old Bailey first. George Weidenfeld and Nigel Nicolson found that possibility real enough that they spent an uncomfortable first afternoon with the Nabokovs, unable even to mention the title of the book they were about to publish. After what felt an interminable forty-five minutes of small talk, their author finally broke the ice. He proved less willing to mention the novel when he lectured at Cambridge on censorship on November 4, which he did without once pronouncing the name "Lolita,"

---

* The decision to pursue publication all the same strained a number of relations. Harold Nicolson could not fathom why his son had sacrificed his seat in Commons to a tasteless novel, which he found without literary merit and entirely "corrupting"; he and George Weidenfeld remained permanently estranged as a consequence. By the time the elder Nicolson had begun to write his son about his distaste for *Lolita* he had doubtless forgotten his own 1951 appraisal of the author of *Speak, Memory*: "Mr. Nabokov does not strike me as possessing an integrated character. It seems strange to me that a man of his sensibility should have been so bored at Cambridge and so happy in the United States. He is obviously a poor mixer, since he prefers to eat his meals on the sofa and in silence."

For different reasons others shared his distaste. To the list of *Lolita*'s British detractors could be added Evelyn Waugh, who thought it "smut" (but highly exciting smut); E. M. Forster, who thought the erotic parts "rather a bore"; and Rebecca West, who saw the book as a ploy for attention, and had the ill grace to suggest in the *Sunday Times* that its author had been deeply influenced by Dostoyevsky.

a performance that earned him a standing ovation. The lecture, a magnificent television appearance, and a luncheon with a group of England's prominent opinion-makers were part of Weidenfeld & Nicolson's campaign to establish its author as an impeccably credentialed scholar rather than some kind of demented émigré diarist. It was a great strategic advantage that Professor Nabokov's next book happened to be a two-thousand-page treatise on Pushkin.

With equal parts panache and apprehension, Weidenfeld and Nicolson threw a party for three hundred influential well-wishers at the Ritz on publication eve, Thursday, November 5. They were nervous enough that they billed the event as a party to meet Mr. and Mrs. Nabokov; no books were mentioned. They had every expectation of being prosecuted in the morning. The excitement ran high at that glittering evening, as Véra reported to Minton, miffed that he seemed to underestimate how very frightening was the situation at this crucial juncture. If Vladimir was worried he did not indicate as much; he claimed to be enjoying himself tremendously, although a favored cousin was struck by his shyness in the eye of the storm. At least one reporter noted the distraction that had seemed to plague him in Paris. In the midst of the festivities, observed *Time & Tide*'s correspondent, Nabokov "wore the bemused air of a man who wasn't quite sure what the party was all about." He confused some of those around him too. In one breath, he lamented that his English was still not on a par with his Russian. To Sir Isaiah Berlin he announced "in a very loud voice so that everyone turned round, 'People say that I am a Russian writer. I am not. I am an American writer.' "

Véra was herself too much besieged by reporters to have come to her husband's social rescue. She told one reporter, "Your English accents are still beyond me," by which he assumed she meant that very special bark of the aristocracy. Surely she had no difficulty understanding the news that arrived via an anonymous supporter in the Home Office, who telephoned in the midst of the festivities. Quietly Weidenfeld passed on the message to his partner; Nicolson climbed on a table to announce that the government had decided against prosecution. The cheers could be heard blocks away. As Weidenfeld remembered it, the decision left Véra swabbing tears from her eyes with a batiste handkerchief. It also left Weidenfeld & Nicolson with a sterling future, and British publishers with ampler legroom. There was now the problem of where to spend Christmas.

The next few days in a brilliantly sunny London disappeared in a mad whirl of appointments. The couple sat for a series of portraits, visited with cousins. Both Nabokovs replenished their wardrobes. But mostly they devoted themselves to the press. Every reporter in England appeared to interview Vladimir. (He had no illusions why, telling one journalist that he knew the search was on for the diaries that would prove *Lolita* to be a work of nonfiction.) He had said that if he had foreseen the scandal that it would cause he would have left *Lolita* in his desk drawer. But without that sensation—and in Europe without the danger—the triumphant reception would not have had the intensity it did. Véra knew as much. After the drama she announced, "Lolita is every inch of a cause célèbre." She felt that while several individuals were still snapping at the novel's heels, the ground swell of support had been admirable and invigorating. She sounded all the more excited on account of the heel-snappers, who had no doubt had a hand in selling one hundred thousand books in four weeks. She was, on the other hand, aware that Mondadori lay ahead, and that Vladimir was tired and unable to work. "I hope we can find the peace he needs for this some day soon," she added, in a perfectly married locution.

In Rome, in mid-November, she attempted to catch up on her weeks of neglected correspondence. She felt her husband's various publishers would forgive her if they knew what she had had to contend with. Given all the moving about, she explained, "I have to stuff all the letters into a trunk in the hope of finding them at the next stop, and sometimes I get confused as to which have been answered and which not." Rome proved disappointingly cold, and not nearly as relaxing for Vladimir as she had hoped; the journalists and photographers had besieged them since their arrival. One had been ejected bodily from the hotel. They visited the tourist sites they could; Véra vowed they would return incognito in the spring. Again the reporters pressed for both Nabokovs; Véra consented to one talk at the hotel, during which she was happy to inform her interviewer how deeply unpleasant she was finding the experience. Vladimir settled gleefully into his chair with a drink; the idea that his wife was under interrogation in his stead seemed to put him in a good mood. The reporter managed to coax a few things out of Mrs. Nabokov. She admitted she was her husband's first reader; that she had saved *Lolita*; that she had been the one to insist on its publication. Otherwise she did her best to turn the tables, interviewing the interviewer as to where they might find a villa. Concluded Vladimir: "Hasn't this been a pleasant conversation? Isn't it true that my wife is a marvelous person?"

After ten days they moved south, to Sicily in search of sun. They hoped they might settle in Taormina for the winter, but managed to find only thunderstorms, hail, and a brace of reporters. Even Véra was unprepared for the reception in sleepy Taormina, where the local newsstand exhibited framed photos of the couple. (The pictures were unflattering, to boot. And in the text she was described as a "platinum blonde.") Nor was that the only attention. "The local Germans, very numerous and the only tourists here, whisper and stare after us," she wailed. In search of the ideal proportions of sun and shade, the Nabokovs made the twenty-hour trip north to Genoa, no mean feat given the fact that they had bought a large number of books, which no longer fit into their luggage. "Decent people fly, but you can't fly with our kind of baggage, even if V. would agree to," Véra moaned, in part explaining their itinerary, or lack thereof, of the next eighteen years. In her next breath she reported that her husband was the most renowned author in Italy, where his name appeared in the paper daily.

Genoa, and the Hotel Columbia-Excelsior, proved more congenial. Véra found the rose-colored city itself enchanting, with its "buildings covered in half-erased frescoes and steep staircase-streets." Much of the northern port was in a state of disrepair from the war, but she felt there were enough gems left for a dozen marvels. One early December evening the Nabokovs ventured up a corkscrew street behind their lodgings, where they found themselves strolling among prostitutes and whispered solicitations from alleyway hotels. Véra was amused to hear the author of *Lolita* suggest they had best turn around; she had thought of doing nothing of the kind. With equal amusement she reported on the state of her Italian, in which a request for news ("*actualités*") elicited directions to the lavatory ("*toletta*"). Even the charms of Genoa could not lure her entirely from her desk, however. The Columbia-Excelsior proved the perfect perch from which to report on the commotion of the previous weeks, and from which to direct the search for a house for the winter. The first exercise proved more fruitful. Véra reported as the many triumphs of *Lolita*, whose bestselling claims were matched by pirated editions around the world. She described the critics who suddenly claimed to have been early advocates of Vladimir's work, the old friends who crept out from the woodwork. (She denounced both breeds.) She summed up the second half of 1959: "We have travelled thousands of miles, have met lots of people (some of them very nice), have made the acquaintance of various writers, from Graham Greene (entertaining) to Moravia (very much less so), and seen lots of enchanting things. Among them the delightful little old Italian ladies toting large bags of raw fish to feed stray cats, in Rome." She wondered if the little old ladies were doing this out of the goodness of their hearts, or to earn their way to heaven. The observation sounds as if it was hers, and probably was; Véra was rarely able to overlook a cat, and in Genoa too marveled over the ancient women scurrying up the perfectly vertical staircases with ease. But the impression served double duty. In illustrating his point that the artist's gaze will often settle on the seeming trifle, Vladimir had remarked to a reporter a few weeks earlier: "In Rome, for example, the things which seemed to me more vivid are the old ladies who feed stray cats."

Véra thought she alone, or the two of them together, might push on to Sweden, although she had no intention of doing so before the warm weather. From Genoa she wrote Lena for the first time since the arrival in Europe. Long distance may well have a bracing effect, as Véra had noted before Hurricane Lolita swept in, but proximity can also be jarring. She acknowledged that she would like to make the trip north, possibly with Sonia, who was considering a visit to Europe. "In this connection I have one question to ask you," she wrote her sister. "Does Michaël know that you are Jewish, and that consequently he is half-Jewish himself?" She set forth her concerns with a certain asperity:

> Can one talk to him frankly abut this and all that goes with it? Mind you, my question has nothing to do with your Catholicism, or the religious education you may have given your son. All this is beside the point, and I am not discussing it. The only thing that does interest me is the one I ask. I must admit that if M. does not know who he is there would be no sense in my coming to see you, since for me no relationship would be possible unless based on complete truth and sincerity. Moreover, I have repeatedly told reporters in various countries who I was, and once even wrote a letter to the editor of a newspaper in New York to set that paper right, so that it is pretty well known by now that I *am* 100% Jewish. I have never named you to anyone, and if your feelings in this question differ from mine, we need not meet at all. You must realize that when and if I come to Sweden, I shall probably have to meet reporters (LOLITA is coming out in a new translation, in a paperback edition), and, of course, I shall tell them what I have been telling others, anyway. Please answer my question quite frankly. It is a very important one for me.

The correspondence had always been ticklish, obliquely so from Véra's side, more pointedly so from Lena's. This time Véra lunged toward something close to the heart of the matter. For other reasons the spring reunion never came to pass, but Véra's battle cry did nothing to enhance the relationship. She alerted Sonia to the position she had taken on their nephew, a position Sonia wholeheartedly approved.

The Nabokovs had hoped to spend the winter in Italy, ideally near Genoa, but found it next to impossible to rent a home on a short-term basis. As Fawcett distributed two million paperback copies of *Lolita,* they cast

about in Lugano, in Rappalo, in Nervi, and briefly considered a house in
Positano. The difficulty may have been greater still in that they were looking
for something that existed only in fiction; Vladimir grumbled that there were
no villas in Italy that proved equal to those inhabited by the characters
in Turgenev and Tolstoy. (It should be said that the couple's migratory
habits were culturally ingrained. Nervi, San Remo, Rapallo, were the prerevolutionary watering holes in Italy, as the shores of Lake Geneva and the
Riviera had been the Swiss and French meccas. Not every French city has a
boulevard Tsarévitch and a magnificent, onion-domed Orthodox church, as
does Nice.) After Lugano, the Nabokovs gave Mondadori the ten days they
had promised, putting in a luminous performance at a reception in mid-
December. Véra met with her husband's editors and translators twice the following week; she eased his burden by arranging for him to meet journalists
in groups. On Christmas Day, a half hour before leaving for the station, she
wrote Arnoldo Mondadori to confirm the agreement she and he had sealed
with a handshake. All of her husband's works, past, present, and future,
would be published by his firm. Christmas 1959 found the Nabokovs in San
Remo with the newly installed Dmitri. Even his arrival had been written up
in the papers; a photographer was planning a visit. Véra was pleased to note
that her son took the attention in stride. Mondadori having offered to help
Dmitri settle in Milan, Véra devoted much of December to seeing that a second career began to flourish, even while she still cast about for a "quiet *nook*
where V. could go on with his new *book*." She set her post-Christmas sights
on Menton, on the French Riviera. They were in search of a little kingdom of
their own, where—as he had done so successfully for thirty-six years—
Vladimir might labor in obscurity, the kind of world out of this world in
which his characters so often find bliss.

❋ 8 ❋

AUTRES RIVAGES

Windows, as well known, have been the solace of first-person literature throughout the ages.

— NABOKOV, *PALE FIRE*

1

On New Year's Eve, 1959, Véra wrote Stanley Kubrick, whose second attempt to lure Nabokov to Hollywood had reached him in San Remo. Vladimir had just begun to regret having declined Kubrick's initial offer. Assuming his conditions could be met, Véra explained, her husband would be willing to put his new work aside, for *Lolita*'s sake. He could be in Hollywood by mid-March.* On New Year's Day 1960—having been sick through the night, as were Dmitri and Vladimir, from the Hotel Excelsior-Bellevue's holiday pheasant—she wrote Jean-Jacques Demorest, at Cornell, about a few remnants of their American life. Demorest had inherited Nabokov's office: What to do with the armchairs, the table, the rug, the skis? "If nobody wants them, give them to the custodian, or the Salvation Army," she directed, apologizing for the inconvenience. A great deal of jettisoning went on over these months, when the one thing that seemed perpetually to elude the Nabokovs was an address. On January 6, the day after Véra's fifty-eighth birthday, they settled into a small apartment with an ocean terrace in Menton. Even as they did so they knew that the search for a European "refuge" was likely to be in-

---

* One difference between having accepted Kubrick's invitation in December and not in August was an additional $35,000, or nearly double the original offer.

terrupted by the Hollywood trip. "We do not seem to have any permanent address at the present time," Véra wrote Victor Thaller at Putnam's, who was compiling material for their 1959 taxes. "My husband suggests that you say 'vagrant,' but I think that you might just as well use the one [the address] the Treasury Department has been using up till now: Goldwin Smith Hall." The Ithaca Post Office forwarded everything to Putnam's, she reminded the indulgent Thaller. She sounded contrite: "All this is a little fuzzy but it is the best I can suggest."

The next years were about nothing so much as the luxury of fuzziness, of dislocation, of the domestic arrangement that allows one to abstract oneself from daily life. As the Nabokovs reacquainted themselves with the Riviera, Dmitri was settling in Milan, where a fine voice instructor had been found for him. Véra's letters to the young artist are all of them reminders to put art above comfort. He was to disregard street noise, unsightly lavatories, cockroaches (an inevitable fixture of life, Véra reminded her son), and focus exclusively on his work. It alone mattered. She knew well which facts should be kept at bay so that the fictions might flourish. Dmitri had been commissioned to translate *The Gift* for Putnam's, and his progress was slower than his parents might have liked. "Do tell me your deadline," Véra advised Minton in January. "Don't tell Dmitri." In the end Dmitri translated the first chapter, and Michael Scammell, then a Columbia graduate student, the remaining four.

The dispossession was not entirely spatial. Véra's December challenge to Lena elicited a shrill four-page reply, in French. Lena had been long with her sister's letter: "To be perfectly frank, I was thoroughly disgusted by it." Did Véra think that twenty-one-year-old Michaël believed in the stork? He knew by heart the names of every one of his grandparents and great-grandparents. Surely she could not think it possible that Lena had been decorated as she had—Véra's older sister was very attached to her decorations, as to her title—while making a secret of her ancestry? Lena seemed to think her sister's assumptions were based on reports she had heard from Russian friends, which launched her into a vituperative screed about the behavior of their compatriots in Berlin. Did her sister have any idea how thoroughly the Russian emigration had embraced Hitler, of the difficulty of raising a child alone, of the Nazis' attempt to blacken her husband's name? (The husband, from whom she had separated in 1938, had taken refuge in a Hungarian monastery, bombed in the war. Lena had had word from him in 1945 but never heard from or saw him again.) Where Véra reproached her elder sister for having renounced her Judaism, Lena was happy to provide a litany of reasons why she had entirely shrugged off the past, neglecting to distinguish between religion and nationality. She questioned her younger sister's affiliations, having heard—erroneously—that Véra corresponded with a Russian Nazi in England. Moreover and most objectionably, Lena applied a generous dose of sibling rivalry to the hardships of the previous years. Véra had not suffered sufficiently. Did she remember Lena was a widow? She would not be surprised if Véra had forgotten:

> Your life seems to have been easy and simple compared to mine. You were not involved in the war. [*Tu n'as pas fait la guerre.*] You didn't see people die, or be tortured; you didn't see prisoners. You don't understand what it is to barely escape a violent death. I did that twice. You don't know what it is to, alone, build a life for two: for myself and for the child, and to protect him against the physical dangers as well as the others, more serious than the first. Since his birth, I have been both mother and father.

If she had discarded the past, she had done so with ample reason, whether Véra understood her reasons or not.* (She could have carried the inventory further: Several of Lena's close friends had ended their lives in suicide; she herself had twice been imprisoned, once with her three-month-old son. Her books and papers had been confiscated. She had nearly been deported.) Her postscript was doubtless a high-handed gesture toward conciliation, but could not have been read that way. Lena advised her younger sister on the steps necessary to put Vladimir in contention for the Nobel Prize.

Writing from Menton, in measured tones and in English, Véra failed to rise to the bait. "I am glad your son knows who he is which means that he and we can meet on frank terms of friendship. I do not think the rest of your letter has anything to do with my question," she replied. She was astonished by the explosive letter, a long-winded, nonexplanation of the question she had wanted to ask and had herself posed in a rather roundabout fashion: Why *was* her Jewish sister a practicing Catholic? This was the stumbling block, although it was not discussed; on all levels the sisters were speaking different languages. Véra forwarded Lena's answer to Sonia. The youngest Slonim sister claimed not to be surprised by the letter, which says a good deal about Sonia's continued feelings about Lena, from whom she had now been es-

---

* There was some irony in Lena's argument. It would seem that anti-Semitism had accounted for at least some of the difficulties the Russian emigration had caused her, a factor she never recognized, as if her 1930 conversion had inoculated her against that particular disease. Although she had worked in Berlin as a Jesuit resistant, she had nearly been deported as a "Polish Jew."

tranged for nearly forty years, and who she believed was generally unbalanced. Coolly Véra chided Lena, "I am sorry you did not write me sooner since now we are taking the boat for the States on February 19th." She sounded not at all unhappy to be putting six thousand miles between herself and her elder sister. For the record, she denied that she corresponded with a Nazi, or a former Nazi, in England or elsewhere. And as for the Nobel, she was pleased to report that her husband cared so little for such distinctions that he had only the week before declined membership in the National Institute of Arts and Letters. That was an honorable institution. "The Nobel Prize Committee, on the other hand, has lately become a political racket which keeps dropping curtseys in the direction of the Kremlin. Who wants to be lumped together with Quasimodo [the 1959 laureate] and Dr. Zhivago? I think I have answered your questions," she closed, informing Lena that her next address would be the Beverly Hills Hotel, Beverly Hills, California.

Véra signed the letter "with love," as Lena had done as well, but appears to have had as little inclination to embrace her sister as she did her sister's version of the past. Certain baggage was under no circumstances to be shed, and the Jewish trunk was one such piece, all the more indispensable for being battered. Véra held on to it for moral rather than religious reasons, in much the same way that her husband had once articulated his entire political philosophy: "When in doubt choose that course which annoys the Reds most." What had once been a healthy sibling rivalry—Véra's handwriting is nowhere more polished than in her missives to Lena—displayed itself over the next years in a series of subtle and less subtle digs on Lena's part, a series of lofty but biting acknowledgments on Véra's. The two never got past the religion issue, into which they channeled their differences. Lena felt Véra made too much of her Judaism; Véra failed to grasp why her sister had—as one family member so perfectly expressed it—"gone whole hog into Catholicism." The relationship was not strengthened by the fact that Lena had raised her son alone and felt her disconnection profoundly. She was continually astonished by Swedish mores; she found the world outside Russia to be a barren landscape. Having devoted her life to a single, highly personal cause, Véra, especially in 1960, felt her isolation represented a luxury.

This did not prevent the two sisters from exchanging pleasantries, from sharing photos of their sons, from a short, agreeable visit at the end of 1962. (Véra was startled by how ancient her sister looked, especially since Lena was only eighteen months her elder. The reunion was followed by a two-year silence, which Véra found mystifying but made no effort to break.) Much that she felt about her hard-won statelessness—and much that she felt about her sister—was loaded into a pronouncement she delivered to Lena in 1962, when Véra was still without a permanent address. Lena could reach her by writing any major newspaper, magazine, or library. "Or practically any big publisher—especially, of course, any one of those that publish V's books," she added, grandiosely. While the effort to recapture the past was clear in the couple's itinerary it did not extend overly to family. The Nabokovs left Europe for Hollywood without seeing Lena, or meeting her son. Nor did they manage a second visit with Vladimir's brother Kirill, a travel agent in Brussels, who had attended the Weidenfeld reception. Véra wrote him from California, apologizing for the quick change in continents, and wondering why Kirill—a very talented poet—did not consider working as a translator. She had hopes he might tackle the Russian version of *Lolita.*

Loaded down with gifts for Anna Feigin and Sonia, uneasy about leaving Dmitri on his own in Milan, Véra set off with Vladimir on February 18, 1960. It took *Lolita*'s screenwriter twelve days to travel from Menton to Beverly Hills, to trade European palms for North American ones. Photographers met the couple in Cherbourg and in New York, where after a rough passage—Véra spent one night clinging to the side of the bed, while the armchairs and table in their parlor sashayed into the suite door—they made a forty-eight-hour stop. She met with the Paul, Weiss lawyers; the first item on the agenda was termed "Escape from Olympia." These chains would prove more difficult to slip than had most of the familial and geographic ones. At the end of the year Véra discreetly (and unsuccessfully) appealed to her husband's foreign publishers to withhold Olympia's share of the royalties until their differences with *Lolita*'s original editor were settled; the Nabokovs were never convinced Girodias had respected any terms of their contract. Walter Minton advised Véra to drop the matter, aware that Girodias would not allow himself to be so easily thrown overboard. Minton did not believe in moral victories; Véra did. She conceded only that her husband had lost interest in the dispute. "Girodias bores him, and he would like to drop the fight, which I think would be a pity," she replied.*

In the immediate, and through Irving Lazar, she negotiated a comfortable arrangement with Kubrick. Her husband was to be granted every creative freedom in his work; he was not to be paid for fewer than twenty-six weeks or detained in Hollywood for longer than thirty-four; he was to be entitled to a vacation. In exchange he guaranteed Kubrick his exclusive atten-

---

* Minton had an additional reason to dissuade Véra from pursuing the Girodias matter. "Always at the back of my mind," he admitted, "was the fact that at some point somebody would establish that their copyright was invalid because too many copies of the original Olympia edition had been imported." Nabokov had been paid royalties on one thousand imported copies but suspected that closer to four to five thousand had been sold in the United States.

tion and agreed to participate in the film's publicity. By rail the couple traveled from New York to Los Angeles; having spent a decade in upstate New York, Véra was exhilarated to emerge from the snowbound Rockies into the brilliant California sunshine. Upon arrival Vladimir met with Kubrick at his Universal Studios bungalow, after which he began devoting eight-hour days to the screenplay. On March 11 the Nabokovs moved into a lovely hillside house on Mandeville Canyon Road, a home that came with avocado, tangerine, lemon, and hibiscus trees and, best of all, with Klara, an excellent six-day-a-week, live-in housekeeper. At the same time Véra rented a car with which to ferry her husband to story meetings. He was more enthralled by the vehicle than was its driver. "Papa says 'it's an amazing white Impala,' " Véra told Dmitri. "I say it's an 'enormous thing from which I can't see my own wings.' " She was unaccustomed to no-glare glass; as ever, she drew a certain comfort from reflections. Moreover, something seemed off in the Impala's proportions. Véra could discuss neither the car nor the California roadways without recourse to the word "hypertrophied." She found Los Angeles's sprawl daunting, New York driving simple by comparison, the Impala both unfashionable and almost impossible to park. "We don't go anywhere," she wrote Elena Levin, "and we live quite far from downtown, too, so it takes hours to get to the studio for conferences." It was about a forty-minute drive.

For the most part she settled into the land of perfect rootlessness happily. To a great extent what pleased her in California life was its resemblance to something else: It was, she felt, "an illusion of European life as reflected in a—not crooked, but—unusual mirror." She made the trip to the studio (which was by no measure downtown) only every two to three weeks. While Vladimir sat in the Mandeville Canyon yard with his index cards, she communed with her typewriter. In the letters that issued from it—even the one asking Mondadori to procure a "Lolita doll" for their inspection, as her husband suspected copyright infringement; or the one chastising Dmitri for his disrespect for deadlines—she sounds sunny, casual, at ease, often positively giddy. Didn't Walter Minton think he needed a California vacation? The Nabokovs were playing tennis three times a week with an excellent coach; Véra had made great progress with her backhand. Marvelous reviews continued to pour in from all over the world. Dmitri had already begun to sing on provincial Italian stages with much success; proudly Véra compiled scrapbooks on both of her men. Vladimir expected to finish his script before the six months were out. They rubbed elbows with their share of celebrities: They dined with James Mason and Sue Lyon, who were cast in the film; they

talked with David Selznick and Ira Gershwin.* At a party they were introduced to Marilyn Monroe.† Later Vladimir joked that they did their best to
avoid these gatherings, at which he inevitably offended someone. He asked
John Wayne what he did for a living. ("I'm in pictures," Wayne replied.) He
asked a woman he vaguely recognized if she was French; it was Gina Lollobrigida. While friends were now addressing the Nabokovs as "Dear Rock
Hudson and Greta Garbo," Véra proved as resistant to this brush with
celebrity as she was to the Impala. Her day-to-day life was far from glamorous. In mid-June she apologized for her silence to Filippa Rolf, Nabokov's
fan in Sweden, who had turned out to be a poet, and a better correspondent
than Véra:

> We have been extraordinarily busy since we came here, even for us. I
> have to carry on the whole business side—not only the enormous corre-
> spondence with publishers and agent (we only have one agent, in Paris,
> and I handle most of the other rights myself), but also investments,
> banks, planning future moves, etc. etc. And since I have had very little
> experience in business matters before, everything is far from smooth.
> But my husband has neither experience nor time for all this, so there is
> no choice for me but try to do my best, on a general "hit-and-miss"
> basis.

The Hollywood interlude was twice prolonged, once at Kubrick's request, a second time because Vladimir was happily researching the new book
in a local library and did not want his progress interrupted. This was one of
several periods in which Véra explained that various matters would have to
wait until he was again "movable." The fall itinerary remained undecided;
the Mandeville Canyon lease was extended until October 10. September was
devoted to *Pale Fire,* for which Véra undertook various arcane research assignments: She compiled a catalogue of tree descriptions—"a hoar-leaved
willow," "a cloven pine," "a knotty-entrailed oak"—in Shakespeare. She set
the "word golf" records of which Kinbote brags—from "hate" to "love,"

---

* Mason was Harris and Kubrick's first choice for Humbert. He had a previous commitment which he
was unwilling to cancel, however; the moviemakers pitched the role to Laurence Olivier. Olivier agreed
at once, then changed his mind, presumably dissuaded by his agent. Miraculously, Mason called later to
ask if the part was still available.
† In Vladimir's recollection, "She was gloriously pretty, all bosom and rose"—and holding the hand of
Yves Montand. Monroe took a liking to Vladimir, inviting the couple to a dinner, which they did not
attend.

from "lass" to "male" in three moves—working out the solutions on index cards. By the time the Nabokovs boarded the Super Chief, on October 12, the East had begun to seem entirely unreal to Véra. She had hoped to revisit old haunts and old friends before continuing to Europe but managed only to fly, by herself—it was her first trip by air—to Ithaca, to rearrange the personal effects there. (On her return, as if obliging a theme of the life, the keys to the Nabokovs' trunk challenged their owners to a protracted game of hide-and-seek.) During the two weeks in New York the couple saw only close friends and relatives, save for the occasional chance encounter. On Fifth Avenue one afternoon they ran into German-born Jenni Moulton, whose husband had left Cornell for Princeton. Mrs. Moulton was not the first to notice a change in Véra, with whom celebrity seemed to agree; she was radiant in a silver mink stole. "I thought of you every day in California," Véra informed the younger woman. "Mrs. Nabokov, I cannot think of a single reason why you should think of me," replied the startled professor's wife. "But my dear, in Hollywood we had a German maid," came the icy response.

The *Queen Elizabeth* carried the Nabokovs back to Europe on the afternoon of November 2, 1960. They made their way circuitously to the south of France, never much out of the sight of reporters, settling temporarily at Nice's sumptuous Hotel Negresco. They picked up the housing search where they had left off, renting a spacious apartment in an ornate, mustard-yellow building well past its splendid prime, directly on the Promenade. The place was sober but well-appointed; the pale greenish sea lay just beyond its windows. To the fourth-floor doorjamb Véra tacked a visiting card, on which she printed "Mr. and Mrs. Nabokov." Vladimir found the sea—and even the rain—highly conducive to his work; he began writing the minute they brought their bags into the place. Véra especially appreciated the proximity to Milan and Dmitri, whom they had never before left alone for so long, and who had a more liberal interpretation of a budget than his parents would have liked. Nothing would budge the nomads now; it took a fiction to tie them to earth. Véra was hugely relieved. Her husband had had no real peace since the publication of *Lolita,* and the embryonic *Pale Fire* had nearly died for the screenwriting interruption. She vowed that they were not leaving Nice until the novel was out of danger. All the same the couple's foothold on the planet remained a tentative one. When Nabokov alerted Wilson in 1964 that they were heading for America, he had some difficulty with his phrasing. It was unclear to him whether they were "going to America" or "sailing home." He settled on the latter.

On Véra's part, there appears to have been little temptation to return. The couple's protests that they intended one day to do so, in a month, a season, a year—as serious as they may have seemed in 1961—largely amounted to a polite formality, the exile's abstract idea of return. They did not want to be perceived as disloyal, or ungrateful, or—worst of all—tax exiles, none of which they were. Nor did they want to jeopardize their American citizenship. The party line for the first years was that they were abroad only provisionally; the idea of splitting their time between America and Europe seemed appealing. After the 1960 Hollywood stint Vladimir spent a total of six weeks in America, Véra—who was willing to fly—slightly more. It was not so much that they were avoiding America as that they were embracing a state of semi-permanence; while they were neither light nor leisurely packers, the Nabokovs enjoyed their freedom of movement. Or did for the most part. In the last Cornell year Vladimir had asked where a prized student and her husband expected to settle and was informed they expected "to be in motion for some time to come." "That's a nice town," he had chuckled approvingly. Véra had long written to friends that their plans were vague, the itinerary negotiable, with a hint of triumph. She was after all the daughter of a man whose life had been predicated on residency permits. At the end of the year, in Lugano, she complained of fatigue to Lisbet Thompson, her old Berlin friend, who noticed she looked worn down. She had every reason to feel, with Pnin, "battered and stunned by thirty-five years of homelessness," but claimed to revel in the undecided future. Two more years would elapse before finally she conceded: "Nomadic life is a wonderful thing—for a time. Then it becomes something of a strain. I am well qualified to say so after some 45 years of it. However, we still remain 'homeless.' " At the end of 1961 the Nabokovs were advised to settle on a fixed address for the most paradoxical of reasons: As the Paul, Weiss lawyers demonstrated, a taxpayer cannot be said to be away from home if his only home is wherever he happens to be working. In order to deduct their traveling expenses from their taxes, the couple needed to maintain a permanent residence from which they could be said to be away.

Vladimir's editors routinely located the Nabokovs by reading of them in the paper; often enough they received mail from one publisher at another publisher's offices. They were on the one hand immovable and on the other unrooted, just as the work that had liberated them from Ithaca was so savagely, pitch-perfectly American and so fiercely exotic. August 1961, when Véra had expected to be packing for a New York winter, found the couple in Montreux, Switzerland, at the Hotel Belmont. The woman who had changed flat tires by the side of the road in the dead of an upstate New York night, who had driven through hailstorms and dodged tornadoes, had become so accustomed to staying put in the evenings that she found it an adventure to go out for dinner that month, when she drove the twenty miles from Villars to Montreux in the dark. "We would like to get settled, go out as little as possible, and devote our lives to V.'s and Dmitri's work," she announced. At the same time she luxuriated in the idea that, at least in his reputation, her husband's hold on the planet was an aterrestrial one. Quite literally, he was at large. "A really spectacular achievement on the part of the international mail service was when they delivered to my husband in Montreux a letter that had been addressed to 'Vladimir Nabokov, New Orleans'—one of the few big American cities which we never visited," she marveled, a few years after the couple had taken their lawyers' advice and established a base in Montreux.

2

For the most part visitors to Nice were discouraged, save—as Vladimir described them—for the thoughtful and intelligent ones whose presence proved a tonic after a full day's work. Relatives, even those living nearby, were dissuaded from calling. Just after Christmas, he advised a cousin that he had come to the Riviera expressly to write without interruption. He went nowhere and saw no one. Four days later, Véra replied to Filippa Rolf, whom she had cordially invited to visit in a Christmas card. The Swedish poet had proposed a mid-January trip, assuring Véra, "I hope you know I am eminently and supernaturally able to take care of myself." Véra assured her that even with Vladimir's schedule, an hour or two a day could surely be found for socializing. They had only just begun to realize that Nice was not quite as isolated as they had expected it to be. "Gallimard is about to release *Autres Rivages* (Conclusive Evidence, alias Speak, Memory) and reporters are descending on Vladimir from Paris, Cologne, Israel etc.," she noted, sounding pleased, especially as the intrusions were not preventing her husband from writing assiduously. She invited Rolf for dinner on Saturday evening, January 14.

A measure of the couple's social isolation in Nice could be taken in their hot-potato handling of an invitation that arrived, at George Weidenfeld's urging, from the eccentric Daisy Fellowes, a Weidenfeld author living amidst her leopard-skin prints in a baronial villa in Roquebrune. She invited the Nabokovs to dine in mid-month; Vladimir, not recognizing her name and concluding her cable was from a brash stranger, had opted to ignore it. (Fellowes had attended Weidenfeld's *Lolita* party, but so had everyone in London.) Véra did not think this would be right and telephoned; a very awkward conversation—and a long and charming lunch—ensued. Véra felt dreadful about the near-gaffe, confessing it immediately to Weidenfeld. That winter afternoon they lunched with a British newspaper magnate, Prince Pierre Grimaldi, and Marcel Pagnol, whose work they did not know, but who evidently fared better than had John Wayne; the Nabokovs pronounced the French novelist charming. It was the taxi driver who carried them to Roquebrune who won their hearts, however. He had so beautifully recounted the story of his dead wife that both passengers found themselves on the verge of tears in the backseat. Handing over carfare at the end of the trip struck them as entirely the wrong gesture.

On January 13 Filippa Rolf settled in Nice for a fortnight, unaware that hers was a longer stay than the Nabokovs had anticipated. She telephoned the couple the following morning. Hearing that she had arrived the previous afternoon, Véra exclaimed, "But you missed half a day!" She expected Rolf for lunch in an hour. However imposed upon they may have felt, the Nabokovs were perfectly gracious to their thirty-six-year-old visitor, who revealed herself to be a brilliant, widely read poet and a superbly talented linguist, comfortable in fifteen languages. This emissary from a northern land had an advantage over the about-to-be-invented Charles Kinbote: There was no pulling down of shades before her. Rolf was no less sensitive to the subtexts, as is clear in her description of the first meeting with Véra. Having met her at the door, Vladimir seated the newly arrived guest in a living-room armchair, where he began to interrogate her. What was blue wine made of? he demanded. Rolf was interrupted midway through her response when:

> Here something happened to the sun—vanquished the rain and drizzle, and we must have got up and pirouetted around, for when I came to, I am standing with my back towards the study wall, where there is a fireplace surmounted by a mantelpiece and mirror I now clearly remember, and I am facing at some distance a woman of great beauty, tall and skinny, who is standing freely in the middle of the floor, in a rectangle of sunlight. A moment of speechlessness on my part. She says, "How do you do?" so clearly and slowly that it literally means "How do you go about living? I am curious to know."

As soon as a few preliminary tests were administered—What *was* the riddle of the blue wine? (Juniper berries, Rolf accurately replied) Did Rolf know Mrs. Nabokov was Jewish? Did she dream in color? Did she see patterns in stained ceilings and wall coverings? (She wasn't a *complete* idiot, the young woman assured Vladimir)—as soon as it was established that Rolf was a devoted and discerning reader of Nabokov, all formalities were abandoned. (Véra had made discreet inquiries about the visitor before her arrival. She was reassured that the statuesque chestnut-haired Swede hailed from a fine family. She may or may not have been told what she learned during the visit: that Rolf's childhood had been an unhappy one, that she had lost her father and was estranged from her aristocratic mother.) As Rolf described it in her first letter home, after a few witticisms, and an occasional declaration of love, "Véra positively melted, so now we are not so terribly high society any more." The couple relaxed; both Nabokovs felt free to gossip. Vladimir managed as much instruction to a young poet as he could muster. Their primary lesson for Rolf was *strictness,* the same lesson Véra was attempting to impress upon Dmitri at the time. To the artistic lessons she added a few surprising ones in comportment. When Rolf expressed her chagrin at not being able to treat her hosts to anything, Véra stopped her short: "You just don't do that sort of thing when there is a man around." The woman who had written Rolf that she admired Robbe-Grillet because of his intense originality revealed herself to be a hidebound traditionalist in matters of social convention. Men kiss the hands of married women only. One does not comment on a gentleman's attire. Nor did one wear bright yellow shoes to dinner at the Negresco, especially with a dark suit and a pince-nez, as the author of a most original masterpiece attempted to do that January. He was sent back to the bedroom, from which he sheepishly emerged in standard-issue black footwear.

Presumably not only out of a sense of decorum, the Nabokovs persuaded Filippa Rolf to stay from four that afternoon until after midnight, at which time they escorted her home, through the narrow streets of Nice. She protested that she was a seasoned traveler, entirely capable of making the trip herself. "It is not a matter of how old you *are,*" Véra objected, "it is a matter of how old you *look.*" (Rolf always looked exceedingly young for her age.) And for the next two weeks Véra looked like nothing other than the perfectly obliging hostess, especially to someone who felt she had come to the Riviera for an afternoon tea and instead remained in the near-constant company of her hosts for two weeks, Véra peeling her after-dinner fruit for her. Neither Nabokov communicated any irritation to their visitor, whom they prevailed upon to move to a less modest hotel close to their apartment, doubtless because they knew they would never allow themselves to let Rolf walk home alone and wanted to spare themselves the nightly jaunts across Nice. Eyeing the potted plants in front of the establishment, Véra revealed another reason for her affection for the Hotel Marina. "Do you know why I like this hotel? Because it has those palm trees. They are just like toys, you see, those little feet they are standing on, exactly like toys."

Rolf had published three volumes of verse with Sweden's most prestigious publisher; both Nabokovs immediately took a parental interest in her
career, urging her to trade Swedish poetry for English prose. By the end of
the stay Véra would be slamming a fist into the table to make her point that
Rolf must move to America for the sake of her talent. The existence of this
striking, quirky, beautifully spoken Swede forced her to confront head-on
the idea that women could write, did write, and had written; if only by virtue
of her age and her intelligence, Rolf appears at the outset to have reminded
Véra of herself. From her remarks it is easy to see why Véra had abandoned
any literary aspirations of her own, had chosen to speak to the world through
another's genius. She was a tough grader. She professed antipathy for
Austen. She thought Colette not a writer at all. She detested George Eliot.
She could not shake her sense that Mary McCarthy was the incarnation of
evil; she was convinced that Virginia Woolf was wholly insane. Emily Brontë
and Katherine Mansfield passed the test, though not with flying colors. Natalie Sarraute was a nonentity.* The depths of Véra's passion for those works
she admired—both Nabokovs were particularly smitten with Salinger's
Raise High the Roof Beam, Carpenters at the time—astonished Rolf even
more. On the poets in particular the three were unexpectedly agreed. They
chattered energetically about the merits of Coleridge, Wordsworth, Browning. At her husband's request and with perfect elocution, Véra read Browning's "Memorabilia." Rolf was struck by a quality Nabokov had fixed on
years before: "I had not known that every word in a poem could be given its
entire burden of meaning, its full value," she concluded, feeling dizzy, indulged, exalted, anointed, as if in the company of "royalty of the spirit." Rolf
spoke of her admiration for a scene in *Lolita;* Véra proceeded to quote the
passage from memory. Merrily she volunteered that she knew all the books
by heart. Cornell friends had long before discovered that if they picked out a
phrase from a novel, Véra could recite the paragraph that followed. At least
one of Vladimir's publishers was convinced that she knew her husband's
lines better than did their author.

For the rest of January, Rolf saw the couple nearly every day, often for six
to eight hours at a stretch. Until the biographers came to call, by which time
the Nabokovs had made an art form of their dealings with the world, she
spent more concentrated time with them than anyone outside the family.
She arrived when the celebrity was still fresh, the answers unrehearsed,

---

* Her husband was an equal-opportunity denouncer. Nabokov's list of prominent mediocrities stretched
from Voltaire, Stendhal, and Balzac to Faulkner, Lawrence, Mann, and Bellow by way of James, Dreiser,
and Camus, to name but a few.

the protective, mythologizing camouflage not yet in place. She discovered what Véra had long known—that Vladimir did not like to be alone with interviewers—and she was a shadow in the background when the French, the German, and the Israeli journalists arrived. She discovered what Vladimir had long known—that Véra would sooner offend every person in a movie theater than tamely sit through a newsreel on bullfighting. ("Why do they have to show this rubbish?" she cried aloud, attempting unsuccessfully to whistle through her fingers.) She heard about Dmitri, soon to make his debut "as a real artist," as Véra put it, in *La Bohème*. He was ready for a major performance after only a year's training, although the preparation had been expected to take twice as long. As was natural for a young poet, the more so one whose parents had largely disappeared, Rolf fell quite deeply in love with the couple, who alternately asked after her work and whether she had anything to be ironed. What impressed itself upon her most, and what would preoccupy her later, was the electric current, the brain-bridge, that ran between the Nabokovs, who appeared so agile at catching the sound and shape of the other's approaching thought. So great was the proximity that she told Véra she knew it was she who wrote the books. Véra disavowed all contribution.

Initially Rolf was struck by Véra's fresh-cheeked, straight-spined beauty, "that of the little girl in the bow of a boat with the wind in her hair." She made for a fine decoration in an armchair. But little about either Nabokov was at rest. Rolf felt like a tennis ball in the air, being bashed back and forth between them, "for they were heavily in love with each other, and I didn't truly exist except as a toy making their mutual communicative game possible." She noted that they reveled in the exercise, especially as "the ball sometimes watches." Her English was excellent, but Rolf found herself exhausted by these strenuous workouts. She felt that the Nabokovs had in common a refusal to grow up; she was not the first to observe that this may be precisely what constitutes genius. "Their combined speed is that of lightning multiplied by proximity," she marveled, noting the swift, assured movements, the small intimacies: the two reciting a poem of Chenier in unison, Vladimir elaborating on Véra's elaboration on Vladimir's anecdote, Vladimir catching Véra's hand for a moment as she passed him a candy in the movie theater. The subject of a debate was quickly forgotten but the image of husband and wife volleying back and forth from their respective Louis XV armchairs, across the fake Aubusson, was not. The triumphant Nabokov was not allowed to rest on his laurels. "Poets are never mad—everybody else is," he declared one evening, to be challenged by Véra, in a clearly modulated, musical voice, "And Coleridge?" There was something balletic about their manner, from the condemnation of the work of St. John Perse to the clearing of the dinner plates. (Rolf's stay coincided with the cook's sickness.) Arguably Rolf described the couple in action better than anyone. "They are mating like butterflies behind any bush right in the middle of the conversation, and they separate so quickly that one doesn't notice until later," she wrote home.* It was hardly the portrait of a sedate, middle-aged marriage.

Toward the end of her stay Rolf asked her hostess if she was were familiar with *The Marriage of Figaro*. She had heard strains of the opera in Véra's voice since her arrival; she saw a great deal of the long-suffering Countess, her serenity and shrewdness, in Véra. There was nothing on the order of martyrdom, just the poignant price of constancy, the fervent, lofty sighs of "*Dove sono.*" Véra did make Vladimir behave, in several respects. When she suggested which of his novels he might most easily adapt to the screen, he conceded "with a little despairing moan, like a boy who doesn't want to eat his porridge, but will anyway, open and soft as a mussel before her." And the care someone like Vladimir needed was staggering. (Véra acknowledged as much herself in March, when she hoped to travel to Mantua to hear Dmitri sing, "but we discovered that it would take three days for me to fly to Milan, then go to Mantua, then back to Milan and Nice—and I could not leave V. for so long.") This was not only true in the practical arena. On Sunday the fifteenth the Nabokovs invited their visitor to the deserted Hotel Negresco for a hot chocolate. Vladimir was working well, and had put in a good day's work. Véra looked astonishing in a brown suit and fur cape, which, she explained, had been a *Lolita* gift from her husband. Together the three set off along the Promenade for the hotel. On the way they met a disheveled old Russian, who embraced Vladimir warmly and kept him for a few minutes. Afterward Vladimir wailed. He had been to school in Petersburg with the man forty-five years earlier and found the encounter deeply unsettling. Véra rebuked him sharply: "You'll meet him once every month. It's no tragedy!" On Wednesday the *Onegin* proofs arrived; Vladimir was all aflutter. "Now what do you suggest?" he quizzed Véra, midway through *Pale Fire*'s verse. "Do you think I should finish the poem first and read this later?" He did not want the proofs to accumulate. "Finish your poem!" Véra commanded, carrying the tea tray to the kitchen, while in the living room Vladimir offered Rolf a smell of the proofs. They reeked deliciously of printer's ink.

With the unfinished poem in the house, Rolf felt awed, as if in the pres-

---

* The comment is strangely similar to that of a critic. In *The Rhetoric of Fiction*, Wayne Booth discusses the "secret communion of the author and reader behind the narrator's back" in the work of Nabokov.

ence of a newborn babe. (She was not far off: Véra had begun to refer to those lines as the book's soul.) Toward the end of the first week, after teas, dinners, movies, after Véra had shared her scrapbooks and spoken candidly about their finances, Vladimir wondered if Rolf would like him to read from the work. He had been complaining that he was trying to make the thing obscure, a difficult task as he was by nature so eminently lucid. Véra and Rolf sat together on the couch as Vladimir, from his armchair, recited the first two cantos of *Pale Fire,* his voice swelling "like a happy church organ." Was it moving? he asked when he had finished. It was very much meant to be. The three were nearly drunk on his poetry; Véra's face was wet afterward, glistening with sweat and tears. Out into the street they spilled after discussing the work, Rolf singing, Vladimir shouting, "What a *delightful* evening, what a perfectly *wonderful* evening!"

Until that point, the best thing of all, Rolf noted, had been when Véra called her husband, "not by raising her voice, but by making it broader, warmer, deeper: 'Volodya,' with a very thick 'l.' " She was otherwise undemonstrative, but then her entire life constituted a demonstration. Vladimir's equivalent of this verbal caress was a simple and perpetual "Darling." There was no question of who was being solicitous of whom. At the same time, Véra was not a woman in any danger of being taken for granted. They were in the market for a car that January, when Véra developed a weakness for Alfa Romeos. As the three walked along the Promenade one evening, she vanished abruptly from between her two poets. She had darted across the boulevard, through multiple lanes of traffic, for a closer look at a red Alfa Romeo. Vladimir was faint with horror. He paled, then turned green, as his wife blithely recrossed against the light. As Rolf observed, Véra returned "to our sidewalk in a fine mood, having risked her life, in her little black suit and high-heeled shoes, very innocent and merry, out of a froth of passing cars. She sure knew how to keep her man alive." Rolf had never seen anyone suffer as Vladimir had in that moment. Most poignant of all was the bulk of stiff, smudged index cards loosely held together by a rubber band, the top card bearing the words "To Véra" in its upper right-hand corner.

On January 25, the Nabokovs walked Rolf to her hotel, continuing their conversation about female authors and proposing alternate openings to their works, allusions Rolf felt were carefully served up so as not to go over her head. With great respect Vladimir hummed the American national anthem. When asked to supply the words he offered, "Véra will do that. Véra!" At his request, Véra sang "The Star-Spangled Banner" for the visitor, fitting her gloves to her hands as she did so. Nabokov had allowed their guest to win at chess. She wrote home immediately upon leaving the couple, near midnight:

"Maybe they were themselves. I don't know." It is difficult to believe that at that precise moment, strolling through the deserted winter streets of Nice just after eleven—discouraged by the news that Kubrick had filmed a Charlotte-Humbert bed scene not in Vladimir's script and by the fact that the kitchen help was still irregular, Nabokov a little stuck with *Pale Fire,* Véra preoccupied by the sore throat Dmitri complained of in Milan—they were anyone else. They were much more concerned with who Rolf was, or could be, and dispatched her with all kinds of pressing advice. She was far too talented to remain in a country with a limited readership. She had an obligation to what they repeatedly termed her "genius." They insisted she go to America in the fall, recommending her as a special student in Comparative Literature at Harvard. And when they heard that Rolf was involved in a lesbian relationship they made their disapproval known, strongly advising her to reconsider the friendship. They protested that they did not normally lavish this kind of attention on an acolyte. Nor—Véra seconded this one—did Vladimir ever autograph his books, as he did several times for Rolf in the course of her stay. Her head spinning from the Polonian assault, loaded down with beautifully signed copies of the work, granted carte blanche to write about the visit, Rolf left Nice on January 27.

There was no question that the visit had been exhausting for Véra. At the end of it she described the Swedish visitor to Dmitri: "And what a Swede! 1) a lesbian, 2) she lives with such a tense inner life that just standing next to her is exhausting. Two weeks! Uff!" Nor was there any question that Rolf had failed to pick up on the occasional hint to make herself scarce. The Nabokovs had tried to send her off in the Cologne journalist's taxi, but she had declined. On another afternoon she had stopped by uninvited and clearly half welcome. Seven days into the stay Véra grumbled that Rolf was sweet and talented, but that a fortnight was a bit much: "We save ourselves by taking her to the cinema." From America Anna Feigin wrote apprehensively: "Have you yet broken free from the fantastic lady? Volodya does like that type, after all." Véra calmed these concerns. There was no hint that the visit would have calamitous consequences, however. It coincided with a burst of inspiration on the part of Vladimir, who had found the composition of *Pale Fire*'s verse excruciatingly difficult. Véra wrote cordially and helpfully to Rolf throughout the year, assisting her with the Harvard application and enlisting her as a translator.* Between the two Swedes in her life there was no contest: She energetically defended Rolf to Lena when her sister protested

---

* Along with Harvard, Véra suggested that Rolf write to Berkeley, Columbia, or Cornell, the last-named "a rather boring, out-of-the-way place, but eager to enroll first-rate graduates."

she had never heard of Véra's talented new friend. She let on nothing of her fatigue. The trouble would begin only when, in America, very much under the Nabokovs' spell, Rolf began to read between the lines of their conversations for meanings no author had intended.

3

Initially Véra had been disappointed by Nice, mostly for its having joined the modern world. Just after Rolf's departure she wrote Michael Scammell, the British doctoral student to whom the bulk of the translation of *The Gift* had been entrusted, who asked if the ghost of Henry James still lurked nearby:

> Alas, no shades of Victorian England, or any other Shades, walk the Promenade nowadays. The "Vespas" keep shooting back and forth noisily, and on Sunday afternoons the bottlenecks in the traffic immobilize long queues of car[s] the way they do on Fifth Avenue. On weekday mornings, before going to their respective offices, *les Français moyens* walk their dogs along the wide sidewalks, and this is supposed to be a mark of "*standing*" (which is the French variety of the American "status").

All the same Vladimir was writing furiously, and the Riviera proved sunny and warm; in mid-February, the Nabokovs extended their lease to April, having—despite the elegaic taxi drivers—rented a Peugeot 403. The Peugeot represented Véra's first encounter with a standard transmission; in this sense she was a full-fledged American. On the afternoon of its acquisition she wrote Rolf: "I have been limping around for about an hour today, alone, before I dared drive my husband to the tennis courts. Drive it, I will; but if we buy a car, it will be something more substantial and, at least, without clutch—I hope." She still lusted after an Alfa Romeo Giulietta and inquired if it, or any other Italian car, was available as an automatic. (The automotive gene proved dominant. Dmitri was that winter zipping around Milan in the Triumph TR3 he had acquired in the fall and would modify for racing, a habit his mother thought expensive and an unfortunate distraction from his singing. Privately she spoke of her distress—"We're always in a panic until he informs us that he's whole"—while publicly she boasted of the mantel of trophies.) She soon discovered another unhappy feature of the Peugeot: It looked like every other car on the Riviera. She could identify it only by its license plate.

February passed in a happy blur of work. Vladimir finished *Pale Fire*'s poem in midmonth—"It is a fantastically beautiful thing," he assured Minton—and was finding the prose section far easier to compose. Véra complained he was working too hard but was not setting a much better example herself. She was buried in mail, which she avoided as long as she could "out of sheer distaste." She managed some reading late that winter, not all of it as rewarding as she had hoped. Ledig Rowohlt, Vladimir's German publisher, had sent on the work of Robert Musil, for whom he expected Nabokov to share his admiration. Véra found Musil ponderous in the extreme, because of which Vladimir never read him. Proust fared better. "I cannot even begin to tell you how much pleasure we both derive from the mere presence of LA RECHERCHE in our dwelling," Véra thanked her husband's Gallimard editor, but this before she had begun the Maurois-edited volume, into which she was appalled to see that a great number of slips and misprints had crept. She could not help it; hers was the kind of eye to which typos positively leapt. Michael Scammell was the beneficiary of her perspicacity with his *Gift* translation, as he would be later with *The Defense*. The proofs of the latter constitute a neat summary of the life. Véra penciled a number of suggested rewordings in the typescript's margins, many of which Vladimir incorporated into the text. The comments were then erased. The manuscript is labeled, "Translation by Michael Scammell, corrected by The Author," in Véra's hand.

Late in March the Nabokovs took a break, driving to Geneva for an Easter visit with Vladimir's brother and sister and their families. Véra described these reunions as perfectly chaotic—"They all talk at the same time and just as loudly"—but clearly enjoyed them. They stayed in Geneva longer than expected, originally so as to celebrate Elena's March 31 birthday. The next day Véra fell in the street and tore a ligament in her foot, a misadventure she described as "the stupidest accident you can imagine." The couple had to be chauffered back to Nice, in their own car. The foot bothered Véra throughout April, when she packed their personal effects into two trunks, to be stored in France, and into May, when she drove her husband to Stresa, a lovely, lakeside resort in northern Italy. By mid-June she experienced only a slight discomfort after a long walk. She proved as stoic over these months, and the next years, with the inept royalty departments, the geographically challenged rights people, the nonreading jacket designers. It was well worth the trouble. As she was dismantling the Nice apartment, the April 7, 1961, *Times Literary Supplement* arrived on the Riviera. In Véra's paraphrasing, a British reviewer "flatly declared V. to be the most talented *English* writer, adding that they doubted he had any 'peers,' and congratulated itself and En-

glish literature for his having made the switch from Russian to English."
Vladimir was as indifferent to praise as he was to abuse in the press. "I am not
when it is about him," she noted parenthetically, as close as she could come to
sounding self-congratulatory.

The summer itinerary was dictated by Vladimir's collecting needs, by
Dmitri's performing schedule, peripherally by the search for a place to settle
for the winter. Stresa was enchanting—although, Véra had to admit, they
had arrived positively exhilarated after attending five stellar performances of
Dmitri's, in *La Bohème* and in act-length extracts from *Lucia di Lammermoor.*
They had had a marvelous time. Their luggage overwhelmed their one small
room, but Vladimir was writing happily, in their quarters and in the hotel
garden, dictating his pages to Véra. At a point when her husband's various
European editors left her almost no time for her personal correspondence,
she managed to answer Rolf's frequent missives discursively, recalling with
pleasure the fine time they had had together in Nice. The weather took a
turn for the worse, which, as Véra as always quick to observe, was bad for the
butterflies and good for the book. The Stresa cold and rain suited her plans
as well, or at least insofar as she was able to admit:

> I, too, have been working—at a job for which I am entirely unqualified
> but which I had to take on: V.'s poems, both Russian and English, are
> being translated into Italian; both translators (neither of them entirely
> familiar with the languages of the originals) keep sending queries and
> drafts; and here I was poring over dictionaries, checking every word
> and eradicating blunders. Fortunately I have mastered the rudiments of
> the Italian grammar (a complicated thing), but what a weary job! On
> top of my (actually: V's) voluminous correspondence it took all my time.

The woman whose request for a newspaper had yielded directions to "*la
toletta*" eighteen months earlier checked every word of the translation, providing numerous suggestions. She hoped she had eliminated all the bad blunders. (She had learned her Italian from the newspaper, which she scanned
without difficulty within a matter of months, and from the Italian poets,
whose work she read and reread.) But even she had her limits. No, she wrote
her husband's Bombay publisher, she did not have the time to vet the Hindi
translation of *Lolita.*

As the work expanded the disclaimers multiplied. Véra never tired of
protesting that she was inadequate to the task—an artless translator, a hit-or-
miss mathematician, a poor reader of legal language, slow-witted, absent-
minded, without imagination—just as she—who conducted a quadrilingual

correspondence—despaired that she was an ungifted letter-writer. To those around her there was no question that she enjoyed the work, even in a lakeside resort in northern Italy; her sister-in-law felt that she positively lived for it. A degree of modesty was at issue, as was a certain utilitarianism. The professions of inadequacy allowed her to appear a draftee. And they allowed her to make mistakes. She carried out the Italian translation over her customary protests: "I deeply regret that my complete ignorance of Italian prevents me from being of any help to you in your work," she recused herself, in French, early on in the project. To her letter she attached two pages of queries. The job required a command of four languages—and a grasp of what her husband meant in the first place. After several months of painstaking corrections, she wrote again to say she regretted she did not know Italian. (She similarly quailed when one of the Italian translators referred to something she had said in her rendition. She had not provided a *translation*, had only offered a kind of working gloss.) The protests proved disarming as well. "We are very dumb," the Nabokovs cautioned their lawyers. Véra protested that she was inept in contractual matters. So much was the opposite the case that when it was suggested later that an agreement might be annulled on the basis that Véra had been unfairly exploited, the idea was rejected by her own counsel. She was too notorious as a savvy negotiator.

The disclaimers came from always holding herself to a higher standard, as much a function of her upbringing as of her marriage. Next to Nabokov most people appear ungifted on the page; even in the letters she composed for him, Véra made no effort to make her prose compete with her husband's. (When she did allow herself to wax poetic in a letter to an editor, he posed the obvious question: Had she ever considered writing herself? She did not deign to answer.) She knew she could not compete; to try to do so would have been insulting, and inefficient. The higher standard traveled everywhere. "Sumptuous, my foot!" she exclaimed on reading a newspaper description of the Nice apartment. She who had spent so long in Berlin boardinghouses could not have understood that to some eyes, the eight-room apartment with views over the Mediterranean—even with the cracked portraits, the imitation Louis XV furniture—would have looked sumptuous indeed. Nor was Véra the first woman to relax into the comfortable, casual camouflage of ineptitude. The rain of excuses allowed her to shrink from ambition, made it possible to muddle her very clear sense of self. It was protective coloring of a kind; it did nothing to infringe on her husband's talent. Véra was perfectly capable of self-aggrandizement—the letters to Lena are ample proof—but it did not come naturally, and in her line of work it hardly served her purposes.

Vladimir's search for a special butterfly took all three Nabokovs to

Champex, in southern Switzerland, from which Véra twice drove her husband up the majestic road clinging to the edge of the mountainside, to the
Simplon Pass, to continue his hunting. She was less enamored even of the
Lepontine Alps than of the work on her desk; she was deep in the Proust, but
dearly hoping that Vladimir would capture all of the specimens he needed
quickly so that they could move on, to some place both less desolate and
touristed, to a more comfortable hotel, or at least one with hot water in the
bathrooms. In Simplon-Kulm she prepared letters of recommendation for
Filippa Rolf, addressed to Harvard and Cornell, which went out over
Vladimir's signature. In August she was able to warm up on the shores of
Lake Léman, where the Nabokovs settled in at a Montreux hotel, renting a
furnished apartment at the Montreux Palace for the six months beginning
October 1. From her balcony, Véra wrote Elena Levin, sounding relaxed and
happy: "In front of me is a lake of silk, and there is a small flock of sparrows
scrambling about my feet, which we feed breakfast, and which have become
wholly domesticated and impudent." (She also warned Elena that the brilliant Rolf—whom she had recommended in sparkling terms, and who matriculated at Harvard in the fall—was not "indifferent to girls.") Her
childhood memories had guided them to this mild resort town on the shore
of Lake Léman, as she happily told reporters. She did not add that when she
had visited the area at the age of twelve her family had stayed at the nearby
Hotel Excelsior. The Montreux Palace was considered nouveau riche.

The Palace has been called an Edwardian heap so many times it seems
churlish to insult it further; it is a stately old dean of hotels, a confection of
mile-long hallways, glittering chandeliers, and gilded salons. Its position on
the lake is glorious, allowing for a fairy-tale view of the snow-capped mountains beyond; the air in Montreux is clear, the light silvery-soft, the sunsets
spectacular. The Nabokovs' immediate plans remained fluid—they were
hoping to be summoned to London momentarily for a preview of Kubrick's
work—but they had begun to toy with the idea of establishing permanent
residency in Switzerland, an idea Véra grew more fond of as the fall wore on.
She offered up the Montreux address at first as an interim one, and then only
at the urging of the Geneva post office, which by September had exhausted
itself forwarding the couple's mail in a multitude of directions. She could not
resist disclosing that their wanderings had very much hindered Vladimir's
work, but had all been his idea. By the end of the year Montreux had begun
to make sense for all kinds of reasons. The suit against Girodias continued,
and the Nabokovs liked the idea of being near the French courts, which were
expected to render a decision in February or March. Vladimir hoped to
attend—and his publishers very much hoped he might attend—the Euro-

pean premieres of Kubrick's film. Montreux was close to Dmitri, and to
Elena Sikorski; as an additional lure, the Nabokovs discovered that establishing residency in a Swiss canton would save tax dollars. It was haunted by
the right ghosts: Tolstoy and Chekhov had visited; *Dead Souls* was begun
nearby. But the primary reason remained the one that had dictated nearly
every one of the couple's moves since 1925. Montreux was the first place they
had found where noise did not interfere with Vladimir's work. "In the 4
months we spent here he has been able to complete a portion of his new book
it would have taken him double the time elsewhere," Véra noted approvingly. In mid-November the couple applied for residency permits. To the
lawyer arranging the papers Véra submitted her husband's résumé, drafting
an explanation for the Swiss stay that proved an accomplished fiction in itself:
He would like to settle in Montreux as he intended to work less and less, and
establish a peaceful retirement.

She was not as forthcoming about the nature of the new work itself.
"It . . . is not like anything either he or anyone else has ever written before. It
is absolutely fascinating. I wish I were permitted to say more about it" was
the description she offered the Bishops. She was no less cryptic with Elena
Levin, or with Filippa Rolf, who had already heard the first two cantos.
(For his part, Vladimir told reporters little beyond the fact that the word
"shadow" figured in the title.) The sprint to the finish of *Pale Fire* was, as
friends were well aware, a strain. Véra acknowledged that Vladimir was less
available than ever, apologizing to various correspondents that their questions would have to wait until she could claim his full attention. It was impossible for him to "switch channels." For the first time she was not typing
the new opus; the director of the Palace had put the couple in touch with
Jacqueline Callier, a cheerful bilingual secretary in her early fifties, who transcribed the novel from Nabokov's cards on her machine at home. This left
Véra free to tend to a thousand other matters. Could Minton mail them the
June *Playboy,* in which Vladimir's riposte to Girodias—the feud was now
being fought in the American press as much as in the French courts—had
appeared? Could Doussia Ergaz send on a few good novels? She would return them after reading.

Mostly she was preoccupied by the financial details of their life, especially as the Nabokovs expected the income of the *Lolita* years to prove an
anomaly. There was some disagreement over the Harris and Kubrick
arrangements, which were baroque, and which became more so. Nor was
Véra convinced that the Paul, Weiss lawyering was sufficiently imaginative.
She asked Minton to hint—it was important to her that he not reveal the
source of the query, which says a great deal about a great number of questions

asked of a great number of other publishers over the years—to Iseman that very real and very legal methods of minimizing U.S. taxes *did* exist. Doubtless she had in mind a strategy she had heard Robert Graves had adopted. "Would you know, by any chance, or could you find out who is Robert Graves' lawyer who turned him into a Liechtenstein corporation?" she queried Weidenfeld that fall.* She looked upon the creative interpretation of the U.S. tax code as a kind of magic, to which she applied herself energetically, with various advisers. (Iseman, who was extremely fond of Véra, marveled over her intuition and grasp of detail. He was also well acquainted with her very active concerns. "There never was an emotional tie between Véra and me which would transcend a tax benefit," he commented later.) That brand of sorcery took up a great deal of her time, while in the next room Vladimir fabricated an intricate, nonlinear code of his own. On November 20 Véra predicted that her husband would "reach the blessed shore" in another two weeks, after which he would need only two additional weeks to put the finishing touches on the manuscript. Vladimir surprised even his wife; *Pale Fire* went to Putnam's on December 6.

"Don't work too much, both of you," Filippa Rolf cautioned the Nabokovs a week before Christmas, sounding herself under more end-of-semester strain than was healthy. Véra responded to a flurry of mail—six letters from Rolf in the space of three weeks—a month later. She advised Filippa (still "Miss Rolf" as far as Mrs. Nabokov was concerned) that she must not allow overwork to do her in. That said, she had herself found the pressure of work twice as great in the preceding months. She was well aware of the gift *Lolita* had bestowed: "For me one result of his [Vladimir's] fame is that I can never stop answering his business and fan mail which consumes most of my time." She could say as much, but disagreed heartily when a friend suggested she needed a rest. "V. is the one who works very hard (I do write an enormous number of letters, also an occasional contract, and I read proofs and translations, but this is nothing compared to his work)," she demurred, backpedaling from all prior declarations. There was ample proof in that fall and winter's correspondence—with Lisbet Thompson, with Filippa Rolf, with Dmitri—that self-command was her middle name. Lisbet had just received her chilling medical diagnosis; Véra now shared the philosophy that had helped her through the Taos cancer scare. Most essential was that Lisbet not indulge her worst fears. As for Rolf, she hoped that in Cambridge she might

---

* Probably she had heard of the idea from Peter Ustinov, who had made his way to a Montreux Palace suite before the Nabokovs. Ustinov had moved to Switzerland just after *Spartacus,* Kubrick being partly responsible for both Russians' exiles.

fully realize her tremendous talent. "Don't let anything upset you, just go your own way and write," Véra exhorted, acutely sensitive to but not saddled with the artistic temperament. She was sorry to have to say so, but she could not countenance Rolf's Swedish housemate visiting her in America. It is unclear if she disapproved because she assumed the relationship to be homosexual, or because she assumed it would not be beneficial to the work. She suggested to the young opera singer in Milan that he work eight-and-a-half-hour days, as both she and his father did. By definition an artistic career entailed steps forward and back; Dmitri must take the injustices in his stride. No artist saw his own work clearly, particularly at close range. His father had been no different.

She could perhaps be faulted for having held the rest of the world to the measure of her husband, who had written eight novels under less than idyllic circumstances in Berlin. Much about those years still remained at the forefront of her mind. In February 1962, she began to feel sheepish about her reparations claim. Her husband's books were being translated into German and enjoying a huge success there. At the end of the year, she learned that she was to receive a modest monthly pension for her loss of income, as well as a onetime sum for loss of property. She was pleased with the results, though Goldenweiser felt he could press the case further, and proceeded to do so. Véra returned one of her last affidavits in November 1965, along with a note: "I am unable honestly to bear witness to the loss of my ability to work: never in my life have I worked as much as I do now." Fortune and misfortune met; as she feared the Palace Hotel address might sound too lavish to the Germans, she directed her monthly checks to a borrowed address.

4

In March 1961 Nabokov had attempted to interest *Esquire* in an excerpt of *Pale Fire*. "It is a narrative poem of 999 lines in four cantos supposed to be written by an American poet and scholar, one of the characters in my new novel, where it will be reproduced and annotated by a madman," he had written from Nice.* He warned that the work was "rather racy and tricky, and unpleasant, and bizarre" but hoped *Esquire* might take it. The honor fell to

---

* The novel had evolved significantly from the one Nabokov had described to Jason Epstein almost exactly four years earlier. What it resembled more closely was an indignant letter he had fired off to the publisher of his *Three Poets* when the volume appeared in England in 1958 without a mention of him on the jacket. "A Mr. Stefan Schimanski is named as 'editor'—who the deuce is Mr. Schimanski and what has he been 'editing' in my book?" wailed Vladimir, sounding like a resurrected John Shade.

Harper's, who ran the novel's foreword in their May 1962 issue, on American newsstands just as full-page ads announcing Kubrick's *Lolita* appeared in the papers. Vladimir had said he would travel to Antarctica if necessary to see the film; he had only to sail to New York, which much to Minton's delight, the Nabokovs prepared to do. Véra funneled some of her anxiety about the return into her wardrobe; her seamstress, from whom she had ordered a new coat and dress, took the brunt of it. Explaining that Vladimir had squawked when she tried on the new traveling clothes—"But they're horrible! I would never let you wear that. Send them back"—she did so, regretfully:

> I apologize for causing you such troubles, but mine are far worse: after three weeks' wait, having lost hours to countless fittings, here I am twelve days before my departure without the clothes which are absolutely indispensable for my trip. I cannot risk ordering anything else, I cannot risk another failure, and I don't have time to try things on six or seven times. I have a great deal of work. My only option now is to find something off-the-rack in Geneva or Lausanne which will require only minor alterations.

Madame Cherix admitted that the garments seemed jinxed. All apologies, she made some minor adjustments to an old gray skirt and two black dresses. Véra was distracted from the fashion fiasco by proof pages of *Onegin* and *Pale Fire,* the French translation of *Pnin,* and the English translation of *The Gift.*

The Nabokovs set sail on the *Queen Elizabeth* on the evening of May 31, 1961, Vladimir correcting *Onegin* proofs throughout the crossing. Six journalists met them on the gangway of the ship in New York; a barrage of interviews coincided with the stay, at the St. Regis. Véra was thrilled to see her husband positively "lionized"—photographed, sought after, recognized on the street and in stores. (The exception was the Nabokovs' arrival at Loews for the June 13 premiere of *Lolita.* As they emerged from their limousine, the photographers lowered their cameras, failing to recognize the man who had begun all the commotion.) To his immense relief Vladimir found the Kubrick film extremely good, in no way offensive, vulgar, or unartistic. While he was happy to defend the film publicly, he had no illusions about what had become of his screenplay. It had been almost entirely revised, replaced in large parts by a pre-existing script, again reworked in Kubrick's London attic days before shooting began. Véra was more candid on this point than Vladimir, allowing that "in general the picture would have been much more brilliant" had the producers followed her husband's script more closely. For all the obvious reasons Nabokov received sole credit for the screenplay, the result of which was an Academy Award nomination for an adaptation he had not written.* Proudly he showed off the Hollywood citation to visitors. Only in 1969 did he at last admit that he resented that his script had not been used.

To the work he *had* written, the critics responded as had his Cornell students. Half were seduced, half peevishly puzzled. Orville Prescott was this time joined in his dismissal of the book by the *Times*'s Sunday reviewer, who found *Pale Fire* refreshing but suspected it had been more fun to write than it was to read. Mary McCarthy proved one of the most articulate admirers, concluding in her *New Republic* review:

> In any case, this centaur-work of Nabokov's, half poem, half prose, this merman of the deep, is a creation of perfect beauty, symmetry, strangeness, originality, and moral truth. Pretending to be a curio, it cannot disguise the fact that it is one of the very great works of art of this century, the modern novel that everyone thought dead and that was only playing possum.[†]

Véra acknowledged that the majority of the symbols McCarthy had found in the book were of her own making, but could only have revised her opinion of "that evil woman" at this time. Her personal favorite was Donald Malcolm's glowing piece in *The New Yorker,* a more general reading of the novel, and a more general embrace of its author.

Vladimir himself had little use for the commotion. The man who had sworn nearly a decade earlier that no Switzerlands could lure him away from the canyons of Arizona was now impatient with the fanfare, dreaming of the Swiss Alps. "In general the atmosphere, heady and exhilarating though it is, reflects on his nerves, and I will be glad to set sail on the 20th," Véra declared

---

* The experience did not entirely sour him on Hollywood, on which he had had his eye since the early 1930s. In November 1961 the *Times* announced that he would adapt *Swann's Way* for the screen. There was talk as well of a *Day of the Locust* screenplay. The following year he agreed to write an 8,000- to 10,000-word treatment for a film to be made by Rowohlt's brother-in-law. Véra specifically asked Minton not to "frighten away potential producers" who inquired after her husband's ability to adapt a work in 1962; he discussed offers for various novels, *Laughter in the Dark* foremost among them. Alfred Hitchcock was immensely eager to collaborate with Nabokov; the two volleyed ideas back and forth for several weeks at the end of 1964. None of these projects ever came to fruition.

† Behind the scenes her former husband continued in the opinions that would put him on a collision course with his old friend. Edmund Wilson correctly guessed that the book was in some part inspired by the *Onegin* commentary, of which it was a parody, but failed to succumb to *Pale Fire*'s charm. "I read it with amusement, but it seems to me rather silly," he professed. Another nonadmirer was Gore Vidal, a National Book Award judge with Harry Levin and Elizabeth Hardwick that year. Loyal as ever, Harry Levin argued loudly for *Pale Fire*. The prize went to Walker Percy.

a few days into the stay, sounding as short as she ever would with the nerve-frayed celebrity. (She could have pressed the case further. Recalled one friend, "VN could be like a cornered rhino when he was in a bad mood.") He was spared the sight of his likeness on the cover of *Newsweek,* which appeared on newsstands as the couple sailed back to Europe, and similarly escaped France just as a *Paris-Match* cover story went on sale. Reporters trailed the couple through their summer wanderings, in Zermatt, and later in the hills a few miles above Cannes. They caused quite a commotion in sedate, traffic-free Zermatt, where a six-man team arrived from the BBC to film an interview. Gleefully Véra observed that they followed Vladimir all over, "mostly in cabs, unpacking, putting up cameras and mikes, repacking, moving to another location, and all the time shooting pictures of V. catching butterflies or talking, this occasion, I am afraid, became for many tourists the highlight of their stay here. They followed in droves! And one little old lady (not this one) did her best trying to get into the picture." While not being pursued by the press the couple spent long hours correcting the French page proofs of *Pnin,* which they pronounced the worst translation with which they had ever wrestled.

After New York, and Zermatt, and France, the return to Montreux felt to Véra like coming home, but she lived still in a state of semiflux. She began to talk of a long stay, as opposed to a return to the United States, admitting that she was out of touch with most everyone she had known in Cambridge. A year later she described the perch on Lake Léman—it consisted then of two small apartments and an extra room—more in terms of default than affection: "It still is not a 'home' where one could be completely *'chez soi.'* But it has so many advantages that we hesitate to change." She was perfectly happy to concede that the lodgings were ideal, that hotel life was awfully convenient, that Montreux was "one of the most beautiful places on Earth," but not that they had made a permanent commitment to the place. "Where we'll settle permanently we haven't yet decided. Maybe in Palm Springs, California," she suggested as the years slipped by, and well after she had advised Paul, Weiss to base all financial plans on their remaining Swiss residents.

There would be only one additional joint trip to America, in the spring of 1964. After a decade's work, *Eugene Onegin* was nearing publication; *The Harvard Advocate* prevailed upon Nabokov to speak in Cambridge, at the university. Or had done so before suddenly falling silent: In March Vladimir nearly canceled the engagement when his hosts failed to convey the specifics of the visit. Véra appealed to him to be patient. For all her rigorousness she proved more and more the voice of moderation, signaling to her husband when she thought his words might offend, softening them for public consumption. (In 1961 a Cornellian, then working at Simon & Schuster, had sent her former professor an advance copy of *Catch-22*. Véra was delegated to transmit Nabokov's response. "This book is a torrent of trash, the automatic produce of a prolix typewriter," she proclaimed, although she had been asked to deem it "dialogical diarrhea.") She had other concerns throughout the 1964 American stay, a one-month visit that began with a public reading at the Ninety-second Street YMHA in New York. The Nabokovs lunched on March 25 with the head of the Poetry Center and his assistant, for whom Vladimir performed his analysis of *Anna Karenin(a),* speaking in his customary fully rounded paragraphs. He was nervous about the upcoming evening, but expansive. He described his writing process: He handed on to Véra his cards to be typed and critiqued; she provided her analyses over dinner. If she thought something did not work, he explained, he would revise it, and she would retype it. "I do a lot of typing," Véra offered quietly. At her request, a chair was set up in the wings, from which she observed her husband's splendid performance. The audience was his from the moment he opened his mouth.

The mink Véra wore throughout that trip seemed so inconsistent with the Véra Nabokov of the black cloth overcoats that few friends noticed that the woman inside the fur coat was not entirely herself either. In Cambridge Filippa Rolf, whom the Nabokovs met for tea, caught on immediately. Véra held herself so stiffly she seemed on the verge of toppling over. Elena Levin observed as much that evening, when she threw a small party for the Nabokovs' before the reading. She saw that Véra was ashen, lacking in all vivacity. Since the arrival she had been suffering severe abdominal pains, discomfort she admitted to no one apart from Sonia, which left her some explaining to do afterward; she finally allowed that she had been ill continually since November 1963. In New York the doctors had found nothing amiss and prescribed tranquilizers; she had been heavily sedated in Cambridge. Elena Levin—who sat next to Véra in the ideally uncomfortable Sanders Theater while onstage Levin introduced Nabokov at what was to be his last public reading—thought her behavior heroic, although she, too, had no explanation until later. Véra spent her thirty-ninth wedding anniversary in bed, at Hampshire House, in New York, from which she thanked the Levins for all they had done. She was well enough on April 20 to smoke out the political leanings of a visitor: Arthur Luce Klein picked up the Nabokovs on Central Park South early that rainy Monday to drive them to the sound studio where Vladimir was to make a *Lolita* recording. Véra profited from the rush hour traffic to interview Klein, a former Berkeley professor, about his politics. Why had he not signed the university's loyalty oath? She drilled him mercilessly, the three of them wedged tightly together in the front seat of Klein's beat-up car, the rain pelting down, the traffic going nowhere.

On April 21, in New York, she managed to stand tall at the Bollingen reception, looking, it was remembered, sensationally beautiful; it was after this event that she memorably produced her pistol for Saul Steinberg. After five years of hairsplitting, second-guessing, triple-checking, the 1,945-page, four-volume *Onegin* book was at last scheduled for late June publication. To the dismay of many readers, Nabokov had rendered the most sacred work of Russian literature into English in loose iambic form, preserving Pushkin's fourteen-line stanzas but sacrificing rhyme to meaning. Observing that others had wrongheadedly sacrificed meaning to rhyme, Véra stood familiar ground. To an interested foreign publisher, she billed the work as the first actual *translation* of *Onegin* into English.

Several weeks before the Bollingen reception the Nabokovs had made their last trip to Ithaca, by train, where they spent three days rummaging through the items in storage. Much about the portrayals of their arrival at Owego station speaks to Véra's vocation of the next years. In Field's 1977 account the regal couple emerge from the dingy Erie-Lackawanna, Véra more magnificent than ever. Her husband instantly claps for a porter; of which, needless to say, there is none for hundreds of miles. Boyd pulls the camera back to reveal that it was Morris Bishop who—meeting the couple at the station—observed this grand-ducal gesture, so wholly incongruent with the surroundings, proof that the Nabokovs and America were no longer speaking the same language. Told of this interpretation later, both Nabokovs collapsed in fits of laughter. Dollying the camera back still farther, they maintained that the porter-summoning had been performed solely for Bishop's benefit.* It was, claimed Vladimir, an entirely self-conscious gesture, calculated to raise the eyebrows of their closest American friends. They were this time players on their own stage. The performance paralleled the

---

* In a similar incident in or just before 1950, Bishop, calling for Nabokov one winter night, caught a glimpse through the living-room window of Vladimir on bended knee, wringing his hands before a stern-looking Véra. He did not mention the inadvertent indiscretion; Nabokov did not mention a drama that would have reduced him to the supplicant position. It had been a snowy night; footsteps crunch on sidewalks. Vladimir may well have been begging something of Véra—would she please tell him he did not have to attend that dreaded meeting?—although it does not seem likely that he ever had to reduce himself to bended knee to obtain anything from his wife. More probably he was performing for the picture window. They are slippery subjects, these people always so conscious of the pathetic trespasser at the casement. Or perhaps it genuinely happened, as it would for the mature Van in *Ada*: "An overwhelming tenderness impelled him to kneel suddenly at her feet in dramatic, yet utterly sincere attitudes, puzzling to anyone who might enter with a vacuum cleaner."

couple's general attitude to America, a country on which they had set their
sights since 1923, for which they had held out such great expectations, which
Nabokov had so lovingly, cunningly, dissected, and from which they now
distanced themselves, all the better to work their special effects. Optically
the relationship corresponded to the study Lewis Carroll's Guard makes of
Alice, "first through a telescope, then through a microscope, and then
through an opera glass." The remarks, elucidations, magnifications of the
next years were delivered always with an eye on the full house.

Two days after the 1964 Bollingen reception the Nabokovs sailed home.
Véra was ill on the boat, in bed most of the day on her return. A long series
of tests and diets depleted what remained of her energy; she spent much of
May in a diagnostic clinic, where it was determined her problem was not
parasites, as she had suspected, and where she was operated on early in June.
Her physician, who billed the surgery as exploratory, took the liberty of performing a hysterectomy without prior permission. Véra was livid, but no less
discreet for her anger. She told everyone—Anna Feigin and Sonia included—that the doctors had found nothing of interest, settling finally on an
appendectomy. In this respect she was fortunate there was no medical personnel in the family. "Don't you dare work," Sonia ordered from New York,
but from the Geneva clinic, in longhand, Véra managed a steady stream of
correspondence. Sonia could not understand why neither Dmitri nor
Vladimir had written her *before* the operation; as Véra observed with only a
trace of resentment later, "When I am ill nobody writes any letters in this
house." She spent the summer recovering. It had all been, she announced finally, inaccurately, "Much ado about (practically) nothing."

After the 1964 trip, a coda to a prior life, Nabokov never again set foot in
America. Nor would the author of *Pnin* and *Lolita* ever again set a novel in
America, or at least in a recognizable America. An America trip was planned
for the spring of 1969—"What we won't do for Ada's sake," grumbled
Véra—but ill health intervened again. The lens of her left eye detached
slightly, putting pressure on the retina. She spent a week of April flat on her
back in a Geneva clinic, miserable not only about her condition, for which
complete immobility was prescribed, but about the canceled trip. (Vladimir
was to be honored by the American Academy of Arts and Letters, in which
he had refused membership years before.) "It was unpleasant," she admitted,
with the understatement she always reserved for such matters, "because
there were constant lightning flashes in my eye." From the clinic she apologized for not having been able to prevail upon her husband to make the trip
without her. She felt terrible about having spoiled the visit for everyone, her-

self included.* The recovery was protracted, not much hurried by the fact that Véra was back at her typewriter by mid-May. She spent the summer correcting the German translation of *Invitation to a Beheading* for Rowohlt's August deadline, which she met, although the eye bothered her throughout. Vladimir reported on Véra's condition to the publisher eagerly awaiting a visit from him—*Ada* was the first new novel since *Pale Fire*—concluding, "And of course I would never dream of going alone." Dmitri typed the letter, which very well could have been phrased, "And of course I would never dream of leaving Véra," but was not. Nor would Véra have expected it to be.

The protestations that they intended to return to America grew no quieter; editors were asked to specify in their press materials that their author was traveling, not living, in Europe. Véra requested that an interviewer revise his text accordingly. "He does not intend to perpetuate his stay in Europe and would not like it to appear that he does," she wrote, speaking for their mutual subject. The temporary address remained in force for the rest of their lives; the Montreux Palace lent a whole new meaning to "émigré literature." It was a luxurious address, though as those few who ascended from the palatial salons below to the Nabokovs' sixth-floor quarters observed, the rabbit warren of rooms in the old wing resembled nothing so much as a Berlin boardinghouse, if one with a glorious view of Lake Léman. All looked as if it could be packed in a minute. The effect was something of a mixed metaphor, that of passing from the operatic set of a Visconti film up five flights into the Victorian quarters of Sherlock Holmes. The metaphor was muddled further by the couple's habits: In their luxury hotel, along working-class hours, the Nabokovs essentially lived the bohemian life Vladimir had craved since 1924, when he claimed to need nothing more than a spot of sunshine on the floor, a bottle of ink, and Véra.

Véra spoke more often than did her husband of acquiring a home but—short of some tours of inspection, including one of a small Swiss château—did very little about it. At the end of 1963 the Nabokovs purchased a thousand-square-meter parcel of land, forty minutes from Montreux; they planned to build a small chalet on the village property, but never did so. All the same they continually cast about—in Italy, on the Riviera, in Corsica—for villas. As late as 1970, Véra considered a property in the south of France. She could never seem to find something that was both large enough to entice her and modest enough to feel manageable. Nabokov continued to tease his

---

* One person who was particularly disappointed was *The New Yorker*'s William Maxwell, always very fond of his author's wife. Regarding the missed ceremony, he wrote the couple that "he had planned to manoeuvre myself into a seat next to Véra at luncheon." He accepted the award for Nabokov.

publishers—to his lists of dislikes could be added that bane of all authors: editorial thrift—that he would be happy to accept an advance in the form of a
modest villa in the south of Spain. Hotel life had its attractions however, especially when the party who would customarily have occupied herself with
wallpapers and gardens was too busy to do so. As Anna Feigin regularly reminded Véra, why did she need the burden of a house when she had a job
that claimed twenty-four hours of her day?

The comforts of European life were much closer to Véra's heart than was
America; she understood Europe better, and doubtless Europe understood
her. But *Lolita,* and the experience leading up to the novel, had made of the
Nabokovs English-language Europeans. They spoke Russian when together,
but Vladimir finally, by 1962, was ready to admit that his English was his
stronger tongue. He felt that his written French—the language in which he
lived in Montreux—had become "rusty and unwieldy." English was also the
language Véra claimed to write most rapidly; it was the language in which
she answered her Russian correspondents. On paper she felt more at ease,
more precise, in English than in French, although at times it seemed as if no
language was exact enough for Véra Nabokov. (She allowed Jacqueline Callier to correct her French, whereas Callier was allowed no such liberties with
her English, even when it was ungrammatical.) She conducted the Ergaz
correspondence—throughout the 1960s she wrote the French agent an average of three times a week—in a piquant mixture of tongues, moving from
French to English to French in the course of one sentence, sometimes by way
of Russian. ("We have hit a snag *avec ce contrat . . . C'est un* slip-up *très embe-
tant*" was but the tip of the trilingual iceberg.) English always won out when
a delicate matter, or delicate feelings, were at issue. Vladimir maintained too
that he preferred life in an English-speaking country. As late as 1973 he
protested that America was his favorite country, that he was counting on seeing California the following year. It was his intellectual home; he felt happier
there than anywhere else. (Véra ministered to the bruised feelings. It would
be inexact, she assured a Swiss reporter, to say that her husband felt well *only*
in the United States, as he was happy in Switzerland. But he felt wholly *at
home* only in the United States.)

Without ever having admitted they had done so, then, they settled in
Montreux, wandering farther afield when the tourists alighted in summer
and the butterflies flew elsewhere. June and July generally found them lake-
or mountain-side, in Switzerland or Italy, exiled from their exile. The shores
of Lake Léman proved the perfect ones for the émigré thrice buffeted by history; the country does not rush to claim its new arrivals. For the ultimate
nonjoiner, for the Russian-born American writer who felt enough wrapped

in flags, it must have been a relief to set up shop under a rubric that corresponded so beautifully to his own sense of aesthetics: foreigner not exercising
a gainful occupation. The Montreux Palace afforded Vladimir a luxury the
villas the couple regularly considered did not. The condition of permanent
transience, the address in the professionally neutral country, allowed him to
melt into his prose, to amount to nothing more than the sum of his style.

5

When business required that Vladimir or his representative put in an appearance in New York, Véra made the trip. She did so in 1966, 1967, and
1968, focusing exclusively on the matters at hand. Much as she loved New
York, she turned down all invitations to the theater, the opera, the ballet so
that she could concentrate fully on her husband's affairs. "I was five days in
New York recently but what is 5 days if one has to attend to 1,000,000 business matters?" she grumbled in 1967. She begged friends' indulgence, limit-
ing her social engagements to those with immediate family. Vladimir's
publishers and lawyers saw the most of her. In his mind Vladimir saw her
too: "I have been imagining the entire time how you are winging in your new
black boots across the sky over the ocean, after a stopover in foggy Paris. I
love you, my angel in a mink coat!" he wrote her the day after the 1967
departure. (In her absence he was entrusted to the care of his sister, who referred to her stint at the Palace as "baby-sitting.") He missed Véra unbearably, as he made clear in letters as tender, perhaps more tender than those he
had composed in his twenties. "I was dealt a hellish blow by your departure,"
he proclaimed when she left for eight days in 1967. The returns were a cause
for elation. For a man who spent many of the Montreux years writing on
time and space, it was entirely appropriate that when Véra traveled to New
York he should convert her appointments to Swiss time, synchronizing their
calendars.

The renewed correspondence was a delight at both ends. Véra kept these
missives in her top desk drawer until her death; after one separation, her husband lamented that their reunion would put an end to his letter-writing
spree. It posed its problems, too. Vladimir discovered that he had forgotten
how to write in ink, in Russian, on anything other than an index card.
Doubtless his gratitude to the person who had made that obliviousness possible had something to do with the depth of his devotion. At the end of an aero-
gramme he scribbled a frustrated postscript: "I don't know how this thing is
supposed to fold." Throughout the 1960s he continued as well to write to

Véra in the form of little Russian poems, all of them dedicated to her, most of them signed "V. Sirin." Her desk drawer was littered with these. In December 1964 he dedicated to Véra a five-line composition in which the poet addresses his muse. It ends, "Oh, you mustn't cry so . . ." Véra scribbled her response on the card, one that speaks to so much of the borrowing and lending that went on in Montreux, as earlier: "I wouldn't even think of crying. But for the sake of such a rhyme, you can say as much." As it happened, the letter to her husband's Italian publisher contending that all the previous translators of *Eugene Onegin* had erred in hewing to rhyme at the expense of meaning went out the next day.

With *Onegin*'s publication, Vladimir acknowledged Véra's enormous help; he attested that she had slaved alongside him on the scholarly work for twelve years. Such pronouncements could not have been easy for a man who exploded when asked by the Bollingen editors to include a formulaic acknowledgment to the poem's previous translators. Do I have to say this? he roared. "To *whom* am I grateful? 'Grateful' is a big word." He was never to go half the distance of the deeply reverential J. S. Mill, who credited the woman who was his wife for seven years and his love for much longer as being a full collaborator, "the inspirer of my best thoughts." But in his more relaxed moments he came close. Véra earned a promotion in 1965, when her husband described her more expansively: "She is my collaborator. We work together in the warmest and most candid friendship." And beginning with the interviews of the mid-1960s, he routinely referred to her as his first, his best, his only reader, the person for whom he wrote.* The love, or the closeness, or the mutual respect, was more palpable even than it had been at Cornell, where Dick Keegan had noted that Vladimir lit up instantly in Véra's presence, where Carl Mydans had observed that the couple lived happily in great respect for each other. Saul Steinberg saw an almost insistent physical contact between the two, Vladimir reaching regularly for his wife's sleeve: "I felt he was in constant touch with her, either through looks, or with his fingers, or watching for her reaction." He felt Véra was to Vladimir as the earth to Antaeus. The attachment intensified with time. Even the family members who believed Svetlana Siewert to have been the great love of Vladimir's life had to admit that the couple whom Hurricane Lolita had gusted to Montreux in the 1960s were not only inseparable but deeply in love. In 1973, Véra checked into a Geneva hospital with two slipped discs. A few months shy of the fiftieth anniversary of their first meeting, Vladimir noted in his diary:

---

* Only once, in a 1964 talk, did he use the word "muse."

"The feeling of distress, désarroi, utter panic and dreadful presentiment every time that Véra is away in the hospital, is one of the greatest torments of my life."

The fear of separation manifested itself earlier, in his dream life. "It has been suggested by doctors that we sometimes pooled our minds when we dreamed," proclaims the narrator of "Scenes from the Life of a Double Monster." Save for one very large, common vision, the Nabokovs went their separate way in dreamland, in their separate beds, in what were in Montreux adjoining rooms. For a few months of 1964, however, Vladimir kept a dream journal, partly to support his conviction that we dream prognostically, that the morning's headlines can confirm the previous evening's reveries. Each morning he did his best to retrieve the half-buried images, which often eluded him. On one such occasion he borrowed Véra's metaphor, citing his difficulty: "Tried in vain to pull one of them out by the end of the thread." He enlisted Véra in the project as well, although while he categorized his own dreams (professional, precognitive, erotic, catastrophic, tales of Russia; some of the classifying went into *Ada*), he stopped short of categorizing hers. The past proved a not so foreign country in Véra's unconscious life. Thanks to her husband's notes, we know that she dreamed regularly of escape; of border-crossing; of bribing authorities (in one scenario she did so on Dmitri's behalf, so as to assume the blame); of the floorboards separating underfoot; of being released from a (Portuguese) prison, barefoot, a baby Dmitri in her arms, in the midst of what appeared to be the Inquisition. On November 20, 1964, the Nabokovs had "matching" dreams of the Revolution, with shooting all around.*

The dreamlife proved constant in other ways. Also in November Vladimir dreamed he was lying on a couch, slowly dictating—without cards, and spontaneously—a continuation of *The Gift* in which Fyodor speaks of having fulfilled his ambitions. He was conscious as he did so of impressing Véra. He knew it would "please and surprise" her that he was for once able to compose orally with such eloquence. Exactly forty years earlier he had recorded a dream in which he sat at a piano, Véra at his side, turning the pages of the score. Of the less enchanting visions, a running feature in the calamities category was losing Véra—to another man, in the chaos of travel, into thin air. From these disasters he woke limp with relief. (It seems only fair to note that—at least in 1964—Véra did not suffer the corresponding night-

---

* A similar vision qualifies in *Pnin* as "one of those dreams that still haunt Russian fugitives, even when a third of a century has elapsed since their escape from the Bolsheviks."

mare of losing her husband.) At two in the morning on December 6, 1964, Nabokov visualized that loss in the dimension closest to his heart: "Awoke with a pang. An abstract, terrible accident sliced apart our life's monogram, instantly separating us. A nightmare blazon, Vé and Vn with profiles in opposite directions." The previous day he had written the poem to Véra for which she gave him license to distort the truth for the sake of a rhyme. He blamed the fright on the previous evening's dinner, which had been wild boar. The experiment in "reverse memory" came to an end just after the New Year, but four years later Vladimir recorded a variation on one of the notebook's themes in his diary. "Dream of the hotel in flames. I saved Véra, my glasses, the Ada typescript, my dentures, my passport—in that order!"

For many years he had been a national treasure in search of a nation; Véra was a little bit the country in which he lived. She, and Dmitri, allowed Nabokov what the world had tried to cheat him of: stability, privacy, an atmosphere of Old World taste and original humor, of strong opinion and exquisite, uncorrupted Russian. And it was Véra, more than anyone, who permitted her husband to dissolve into an abstract entity, to live at a full remove from himself. "Perfection," the 1932 short story in which Nabokov executes a perfect half gainer of perspectival shift, was one of her favorites. So the change in perspective colored the Montreux years. Having done all she could to put her husband on the map, she now conspired in his disappearance.

LOOK AT THE MASKS

*He stopped and pointed, with the handle of his net, to a butterfly clinging to
the underside of a leaf. "Disruptive coloration," he said, noting white spots
on the wings. "A bird comes and wonders for a second. Is it two bugs? Where
is the head? Which side is which? In that split second the butterfly is gone.
That second saves that individual and that species."*

—ROBERT H. BOYLE ON NABOKOV, *SPORTS
ILLUSTRATED,* SEPTEMBER 14, 1959

1

Vermeer was her favorite painter; he could have been her patron saint. Véra
Nabokov's life in Montreux had about it all the stilled intensity of the Dutch
master's canvases. The drama was interior; it was private; it was passionate;
it was hushed. And to a great extent it consisted—aside from meals and a
regular walk with her husband, an evening chess or Scrabble game, more
television than was generally acknowledged, a skeletal social life—of the
drama of a woman intently alone in a room with a piece of paper.* Moreover,
there was a certain correlation between Véra's deft compositions of the 1960s
and Vermeer's masterly ones of the 1660s. The reverence with which Vermeer could invest any scene was hers. No one would have agreed more

---

* One of her early run-ins with Jenni Moulton occurred when she failed to recognize a reproduction of
Vermeer's *View of Delft* that hung on the Moultons' Ithaca wall. She refused to believe the work was by
Vermeer, who to her mind painted only interiors.

quickly that whole worlds balanced on the microscopic detail, that shadows may opt not to follow the laws of nature. She shared the Dutch master's obsession with perspective, with the crucial angle from which the exterior world approaches the private realm. Had the alpine chough on the balcony pressed his yellow beak to the Nabokov's sixth-floor windowpanes on a given nonsummer morning, he would have found them breakfasting together; Véra reading the mail to Vladimir; or at work, Véra at the desk in the living room, or in her blue-and-white bedroom. Before lunch the couple walked together; afterward, Vladimir might nap, Véra returned to her desk. Madame Furrer came to cook; as of 1962 Jacqueline Callier spent several afternoons a week typing and filing. Dinner was preceded by the "exchange of impressions"; Vladimir read passages to his wife. After dinner, even with the infrequent guest who was entertained in the suite and not below in the formal dining rooms, Véra excused herself to write a few more letters. It was the impression of most visitors that she worked from the time she woke to the time she went to bed. Her labor alone culminated in a delusional mirror trick worthy of *Despair*: So wed was she to the desk, and so seldom was Vladimir—who wrote in bed, or standing at his lectern, or in the bath—at his, that word went out via the Montreux tradespeople that Mrs. Nabokov was her husband's ghostwriter.

Her intention was less to conceal herself than her husband. She was complicit in this sleight of hand, but the engineer rather than the prime architect of it. (As an astute friend put it, Vladimir had more important things to do than to poison himself with business.) "I don't know why but VN's literary affairs seem always to be so dreadfully complicated," Véra asserted, apologetic for having buried an editor in a flurry of contradictory letters. The affairs *were* complicated and always had been; even Nabokov's short reviewing histories were fraught. His copyright situations were often nightmarish. The couple's expectations made matters worse. Their demands were nearly too much for the international publishing community. (Vladimir blithely referred to his "gay tussles with publishers" but could well afford to; Véra was the one who tussled.) The aggravations were often familiar ones. While Nabokov wrangled publicly with Girodias, Véra continued, undaunted, to explore the legal channels behind the scene. To Louba Schirman, her new Russian-born, Paris-based lawyer for the case, she outlined in late 1964 the long and rocky road with Girodias, whom she remained intent on discarding. She felt he and his lawyers had cleverly "managed to turn the tables on us on two occasions when Olympia was quite obviously at fault." She did not like to be outwitted; she was furious that they had temporarily dropped their case and intent on the agreement's being annulled. It was settled at last in

April 1967, by which time Véra had been tangling with Girodias almost exactly as long as her father had battled the St. Petersburg authorities on his
residency case, but with more satisfactory results.*

Not all of the predicaments were of such long standing. At the end of
1962, George Weidenfeld proposed to Vladimir that he prepare a picture
book of European butterflies, to which Vladimir readily consented. Three
years later, despite the many hours he had devoted to the project, little had
come of it. In September 1965 Véra was charged with conveying to Weidenfeld her husband's irritation with the volume, which "had remained constantly in his thoughts greatly interfering with his other projects." He
wanted nothing more to do with the nonbook; he also expected payment for
the hours he had invested in it. As she finished her peremptory letter, Weidenfeld called from London. Vladimir asked her to explain the matter by
phone, and to mail the document, so that the publisher might have his position in writing. To Weidenfeld Véra appealed regularly, as she had in the
past appealed to Epstein and Minton, and as her husband had once appealed
to Wilson, with all kinds of literary SOS's. Plaintively she went to him with a
most vexing matter in 1968:

> Vladimir has been discovered by the Hindus. They shower us with let-
> ters pleading for an immediate reply about translating LOLITA or
> LAUGHTER IN THE DARK into Bengali, Hindi or Malayalam.
> They publish unauthorized editions of his books. Someone has just fin-
> ished serializing LAUGHTER in a Malayalam newspaper. . . . Is it bet-
> ter to sign some kind of paper and keep these editions on a legal basis or
> wash the hands of them?

She became something of an accidental expert on copyright law.

In large part the appalling (monstrous, disastrous) correspondence
stemmed from Vladimir's thundering international success, as a result of
which the work was misread, pirated, appropriated. Copies of *Lolita* pur-
portedly appeared in Frankfurt with dirty pictures inserted in the book. Véra
ran interference with Mexican lawyers, Greek lawyers, Israeli lawyers, Swiss
lawyers. The letters to Ergaz sound often like military dispatches; in a paragraph, Véra would veer from the Bengalese to the Lebanese front. She corresponded with the interviewers; she replied to those who sent chess problems;

---

* Girodias's take on this persistence: He had worked diligently to give Nabokov the "first real chance of
his life," in exchange for which "I was treated with the most squalid ingratitude by my master, and tram-
pled like a drunken coachman, and whipped to shreds like an impertinent serf."

she answered the admirers, the dissertation writers, the autograph seekers, the courageous friends of Soviet admirers, the would-be translators, the critics, the synesthetics. She composed the thousands of letters saying sorry, no, he is much too busy, he doesn't remember, he would love to write the article but can't, the book was planned but never written, he never takes a political position, he believes the symbols you have identified are your own. In exchange for her efforts she secured the lasting resentment of those who had written the husband but received a response—very often not the one they hoped for—from the wife. Even Katharine White took the arrangement amiss, concluding that Véra was not only answering her husband's mail but imitating his butterfly-signatures as well. (White was mistaken.) And, too, Véra performed her share of about-faces on Vladimir's account. A cookbook compiler was informed that Vladimir had nothing to add to her volume, as his interest in food was limited to its consumption. Something moved him to change his mind, and to set to paper his winning recipe for soft-boiled eggs.* Véra dutifully sent it on. Nabokov poked fun at those writers who left behind prolix correspondences, seemingly without realizing he was one of them, the only difference being that his letters consisted principally of someone else's words.

Her facility for languages was in many respects a curse. Who else would have been bothered to translate a Dutch review of *The Gift* for her 1965 scrapbook? To read her husband in Italian was to discover that he was mistranslated in Italian. It was her job to make sure that the pink clouds described by her husband as "flamingoes" did not mutate into Flemish-painted ones, as they did in one French rendering. She did not find these missteps as amusing as she had found those in the Cornell bluebooks. As the early books were translated—and reworked—in English, as the newer titles were published abroad, as the original Russian works were reissued, the proofs rained down from every direction. Nabokov began *Ada* in February 1965; both Nabokovs felt that anything that took him from the new work qualified as a distraction. Work on the 1969 German *Invitation to a Beheading* was complicated not only by Véra's eye trouble that summer, but by her fear that—while her German was strong enough to detect deviations, inaccuracies, infelicities—it was not rich enough for her to suggest alternate phrasings. None of these editions consumed as much time and mental energy as the Russian ver-

---

* The recipe for "Eggs à la Nabocoque" begins with directions for submerging two eggs in boiling water. It continues: "Stand over them with a spoon preventing them (they are apt to roll) from knocking against the damned side of the pan. If, however, an egg cracks in the water (now bubbling like mad) and starts to disgorge a cloud of white stuff like a medium at an old-fashioned séance, fish it out and throw it away. Take another and be more careful."

sion of *Lolita,* a work Nabokov prepared not for Soviet publication but as a defensive check against his future mistranslator. The tennis player who had spent his glory years on a squash court protesting that his tennis was stronger still, he was shocked in the early 1960s to discover that squash was now his game. Véra contributed a great deal to the Russian language manuscripts, as her husband acknowledged. He found her heavy corrections disillusioning.

The couple spent their 1964 Christmas vacation in rainy Italy, coaxing *Lolita* into Russian. Vladimir's ear was better, and lustier; Véra's Russian was by now deeply infiltrated by English and no longer, strictly speaking, Russian, much less Soviet Russian, in the same way that her husband's English was not English but a divine version thereof. (The modern world posed a difficulty to both Nabokovs in their native language. They struggled valiantly over terms like "glove compartment," or "hitchhiker," for which there is a perfectly good Russian word, but had not been when Véra and Vladimir learned their Russian.)* Work continued, intermittently, through the fall of 1965, Nabokov concluding from the exercise that the English language could be trusted to do things the Russian language could not, and that the converse was equally true. The care taken with these reworkings was not underestimated by close and bilingual readers, of which there were a few: When *Lolita* made her Russian-language debut, Clarence Brown noted that the difference between Nabokov's recasting of his works into other languages and ordinary translation was "like the little abyss between zero and one."[†] When the Library of Congress asked Nabokov if he might render the Gettysburg Address into Russian he practically responded with his own rendition of "The Star-Spangled Banner," adding that he had always thought Lincoln's speech a work of art. The result is in Véra's hand; Vladimir put *Ada* aside to tackle the most difficult turns of phrase, entrusting the rest of the job to his wife. "Incidentally, not having a Russian typewriter here, I wrote the translation in longhand," he explained to the library, sending on the page in Véra's hand. He waived the honorarium but requested translating credit.

Every few months a new Nabokov edition appeared in one major market or another, which meant that every few months a new typo materialized

---

* Nabokov thought the Russian language better translated "from" than "into"; his native tongue offered none of the happy, concise equivalents of English, and was particularly unaccommodating of technical terms. "Windshield wipers," he complained after the *Lolita* experience, could be rendered either in a forty-letter phrase or by a series of vulgar Sovietisms.

[†] The book nearly bankrupted the small American publisher who took it on in 1967, and who appeared to speak publishing as a second language. He failed to endear himself to the Nabokovs for many reasons, not least because he continually lobbed the epistolary ball over Véra's head, after having been instructed numerous times, over the course of years, that that was not how the game was played.

somewhere in the world. (Between the 1962 publication of *Pale Fire* and the
1974 publication of *Look at the Harlequins!* a new Nabokov title appeared in
America every year but one.) When an unfortunate misprint crept into a
British edition of *Speak, Memory* in 1967 Véra wrote of her husband's distress:
"He says that the criminal printer should be made to set MEA CULPA in
italic diamond a thousand and one times." He could not get over the tenacity
of these creatures, sprouting in one edition after another, "like a tenacious ancestral wart." Both Vladimir and Dmitri remembered Véra's consoling them
on the appearance of these indignities as among her greatest acts of humanity. The misprints were to life in Montreux as the rattlers had been to the
American West; Véra wielded only her typewriter in self-defense. At times
she appeared to be struggling single-handedly to keep the world from tumbling into a state of "glossological disarray."

Generally she held people—herself especially—to the standards of her
husband's literature, standards to which few of us, and even fewer publishers, rise. It was her fervent and unreasonable conviction that books should be
accurately translated, properly printed, appropriately jacketed, aggressively
marketed, energetically advertised. Was it really too much to ask of the publishers who acquired her husband's titles that they *read* the books in question? To her fell the futile job of deciphering royalty statements; she seemed
to believe that these should be intelligible and should arrive punctually. Her
volumes on this subject are as poignant as they are pointed. In desperation
she appealed to George Weidenfeld himself when no one else in his firm
could provide satisfaction regarding what she considered his firm's highly
approximate accounting. "My dear George," she concluded her petition,
"would it not be possible for you to get somehow organized in this respect?"
Three years later Weidenfeld's accounting continued to mystify; Véra was
still composing treatises on the subject. At last in 1970 she handed on the
baton. "It irks me to irk you with this as I am aware that ordinarily you can't
be expected to look into bookkeeping matters but I really don't know what
course to follow since Véra has given up in despair," pleaded Vladimir. It has
been noted that women are accustomed to tending to chores that are repetitive in nature, tasks that are undone almost as soon as they are accomplished.
The pursuit of the accurate royalty statement, of the carefully proofread
manuscript, were not the Sisyphean labors those who first observed this phenomenon had in mind. But they constituted the dusting and vacuuming of
Véra Nabokov's life.

Probably much to her regret, the details mattered. She was of the school
that recognized the comma as a point of honor. This was not something universally understood. In November 1962, she wrote Minton with the tri-

umphant news that Mondadori were going back to press for their twentieth printing of *Lolita*. *Pale Fire* was a bestseller in America. On the other hand, shouldn't the book charged to VN's *Lolita* statement be charged instead against his *Pale Fire* earnings? A problematic translation immediately qualified as "hopeless" or "a disaster." One such fiasco was the rendering into French by Elena Sikorski's son, Vladimir, of *Strong Opinions*. The "disaster" was redeemed in the course of two weekends' work. These missteps might have appeared as so many tempests in teapots, but as another keen-eyed miniaturist observed, "If you live in a teapot, a tempest may be a very uncomfortable thing."

Repeatedly Véra trumpeted her husband's battle cry: He was supremely indifferent to criticism but cared deeply, fervently, about his publishers' commitments to his volumes.* Few writers have carped so eloquently, or have had the luxury of doing so symphonically. When Véra deplored Putnam's thrift during her 1966 visit to New York, Minton reprimanded her, "Véra, this amounts to an author telling his publisher how to publish his works." She did not disagree with that analysis. Nor did she believe that Minton had knocked himself out advertising *Despair*. She was convinced that in many cases she herself could sell foreign or subsidiary rights in a work more advantageously than could a publisher's languid rights department; she spent a great deal of time negotiating for the return of these rights. Only occasionally did she prove the publishers wrong. Nothing more came of *Pnin*'s television and movie rights in Véra's hands than in Doubleday's, though she could easily envision Peter Sellers, or Jacques Tati, in the title role.

She too made mistakes, and was the first to admit as much. (Sometimes she did so in perfect slang: "Oh dear, I think I made a boo-boo," she informed an associate when in her eighties.) She made no secret of the fact that her files were not in the best of order; Jacqueline Callier did her best with the collections of agreements and statements that had been traveling about in cartons, some on and off for decades. And Véra remained a master at begging indulgence for her husband's dilatoriness. "I must again apologize to you for my husband's casual approach to correspondence," wrote the woman who must have been most mortified to have to do so. He had promised to read his correspondent's letter as soon as he could. Three months had elapsed in the meantime. Véra extended the customary round of excuses to the publisher

---

* To the small American firm that published *The Eye* in paperback Véra explained her husband's position. "He wants me to forewarn you that there will be many reviews, and some are sure to be vicious, since my husband has many enemies. He asks you not to let this disturb you. Vicious reviews sometimes do more for the book than bland praise."

who was reissuing Nabokov in Russian, for covert distribution behind the Iron Curtain. (The couple relished the image of the books sailing down from the heavens, each with its own miniature parachute.) Every time she broached the subject of which title the firm might issue next, Vladimir responded, "Yes, of course. But let me think which," and then failed to make a decision.

As early as 1963 Véra reported that her husband was working at a frantic clip, perennially in the shadow of a new deadline. But no one in the household felt the pressure of time quite as acutely as did she, who in Dmitri's estimation could not bear for a minute to be wasted. A 1969 reporter engaged the Nabokovs in a conversation about their favorite comic strips, which they read religiously. Vladimir's favorites were *Buzz Sawyer* and *Rex Morgan, M.D.* The couple found *Peanuts* "coy" and skipped *Li'l Abner.* Véra professed her admiration for *Dennis the Menace,* because it had only one frame. The reporter concluded this was because she was so keenly efficient. On a later occasion her husband groused about his interminable voyage on the slow train from Lausanne to Montreux, usually no more than a twenty-minute trip. "That is the difference between you and me. I would wait for the next express train, while you'll take the local just because it's there," Véra interjected.*

2

The dance of the pronouns evolved, on the page, from a proficient Ithaca one-step to an adroit international quickstep. It allowed more latitude in needling publishers. I don't remember if I wrote you that I should like such-and-such, Vladimir could state, genuinely; Véra had been the one to make the demand in the first place. The two voices allowed Nabokov to comport himself—Dr. Jekyll arrived at the same conclusion—as if "man is not truly one, but truly two." Véra could voice her husband's strident opinion, adding reasonably that she was sorry he felt so strongly on the subject, but he did. Or she could render a remark twice as cutting, appending her outrage to her husband's. There was ample reason why Nabokov's correspondents began to imagine the Russian master hurling thunderbolts down from his aerie on a Swiss mountaintop, when actually he lived in a valley. In 1967 Alfred Appel published a two-part review of *Speak, Memory* in *The New Republic.* Véra al-

---

* The situation was reminiscent of the wail emitted by that creative reader of train timetables, Timofey Pnin: "I was thinking I gained twelve minutes, and now I have lost nearly two whole hours."

lowed that if ever Vladimir were to break his rule against thanking critics, Appel's brilliant essay would surely provide the occasion. "This is cheating a little, as you may notice," she added parenthetically. Together the Nabokovs were able to work a dynamic that was familiar from the fictions, the unsettling dance of the seemingly omniscient narrator and the character caught in his drama who begs us not to believe a word he says. (It should be said that Nabokov was equally adept at playing both roles himself. Friends had long complained that he winked at his interlocutor on the rare occasion when he spoke the truth.) In 1966 Véra conveyed her husband's comments to Andrew Field, who two years later became Nabokov's first biographer: "But he adds that 'generally speaking' his 'memory is poor and faulty.' (I disagree.)"

With his wife at his side, Nabokov could speak in the first person plural. And because so frequently the correspondence is not *with* Nabokov but *about* Nabokov, a whole other being was created in the mid-1960s—a monument called VN, someone who is not even Nabokov. In large part this distant, unapproachable VN was Véra Nabokov's construct. How else could Nabokov have established his statuesque other self? "VN does not admire the novel in question" sounds different from the same statement expressed in the first person. Vladimir himself delighted in explaining that the living, breathing, breakfasting Nabokov was but the poor relation of the writer, only too happy to refer to himself as "the person I usually impersonate in Montreux." (Others agreed. When his likeness loomed large at newsstands in 1969, Wilson complained to a mutual friend: "Have you seen Volodya Nabokov on the cover of *Newsweek*? He looks like some model who had been hired to pose as Volodya Vladimir Nabokov." Having witnessed the posing over the years, Jason Epstein concluded: "It is a false idea to imagine a real Nabokov.") The editor replying to Véra's letter about her eminent husband had little choice but to refer to "VN"—or to stumble over his second-person pronouns. Vladimir might compose a letter in the first person about the proliferation of typos in a British edition; quoting him precisely, Véra conveyed his distress in the third person, essentially allowing the sovereign presence to melt into the background. With her assistance, the real Vladimir Nabokov disappeared into Swiss air; it was as if Thomas Pynchon were to enter the federal witness-protection program. Vladimir was the person, VN the author. One came to visit VN, as Alfred Appel did in 1970, but one attended to all of Vladimir's whims, as Véra thanked Appel for doing after the visit.

Initially the disappearing act was devised for efficiency's sake. By the 1960s, Nabokov risked drowning twice: in the business of publishing, and in the admiration of the fans and scholars. Once again the couple were on the lam. Summer addresses were imparted, confidentially, to the few who needed them. Véra explained that for literature's sake, they were doing their utmost to go into hiding. When traveling she felt it necessary "to dissimulate our presence from amiable strangers who might be *de passage* and want to have a look at V." She groaned that there was no place to hide. Fan mail turned up under the doors to their rooms. The Montreux Palace was mentioned in a 1967 piece; the result was droves of strangers on the doorstep. "It's just like some miserable Yasnaya Polyana [Tolstoy's estate] around here," she sighed. (One reporter agreed. It seemed Nabokov drew more people to Switzerland than the banks and the Alps combined.) She felt that photographers and interviewers tore him away from his work at every juncture. Worse yet, she had to convince him to see them. Or at least those of them he should see; the requests were incessant. "If he had the time he would never be given a chance to stop talking," Véra grumbled. A steady stream of "strangers and half-strangers" arrived on the doorstep.*

Nabokov delighted in the smoke and mirrors, informing his publishers when they might best reach his wife by phone, drafting "her" letters in the first person. "He made a great show of hiding behind Véra," remembers a nephew, who observed the routine extended to the most mundane matters. From behind his oversized menu, protectively angled as a shield, Nabokov appealed, "Véra, what am I going to eat?" He had long thought of himself in the third person, or as a collection of splintered selves; Véra's collusion allowed him to live that way. The arrangement was as convoluted as it was cumbersome. Louba Schirman communicated solely with Véra but understood the decisions to be joint. "She does the arguing, and he does the deciding," inferred one visitor. A prickly exchange resulted when Véra questioned the agent Swifty Lazar's ability to extricate Vladimir from a contract, adding that she was inquiring on his behalf. "I think it's almost amusing that you resort to saying 'this is what my husband asks' when you think you're going to be a little harsh with me. Frankly I love both of you very much and admire you very much so it doesn't matter which of the Nabokovs have [*sic*] a complaint," Lazar rebuked her affectionately. Véra headed straight for the bush. Starchly she informed the agent that she was not in the habit of using her husband's name when she needed to be harsh: "Far from it. Vladimir detests

---

* Few made it past the impeccable Palace concierge, Carlo Barozzi, before whose desk a great number of distinguished knees trembled. Barozzi saw to it that no one knew the Nabokovs' room number; that the phone messages piled up at the switchboard; that the telexes made their way upstairs only when welcome.

to go into details and would rather have me do whatever I can without consulting him, but when things take a serious turn, he takes time out to consider a business matter, arrives at a decision, and withdraws again, and then I have nothing to do but carry out his decision." She fell victim to a kind of Carrollian paradox, laboring with all her might to efface herself, managing only to appear larger as a result. A 1968 letter to George Weidenfeld went out in two parts, the first ostensibly composed by Véra. "From here on, the letter is dictated by Vladimir," she wrote partway through the jointly signed document. She had typed most but not all of her husband's contribution, which included the line, "As my husband has no agent who would stand up for him, I must play that role."

It was no wonder that Véra appeared to have some trouble discerning where she ended and her husband began. "While they keep us informed of the new developments, there are a number of permissions they gave before we put our foot (feet?) down," she wrote Field uncertainly. Nearly forty years after her husband had defined true love to his sister with the Siamese twin analogy, Véra wrote, "We have runny noses and blow them (in unison) but decided to go out today." A few years later they had merged more directly: "We have been ill with a cold ever since Christmas," Véra reported in 1968. By the end of the decade the matter appeared settled: "I ask you to bear in mind that we have a poor mind for legal expressions," she contended, sounding like a reconfigured (and delusional) hero of "Scenes from the Life of a Double Monster." Given the speed with which she was writing and the volume of paper that crossed her desk, it comes as no surprise that she blundered occasionally in her correspondence. And given the nature of the beast, it was logical that she should trip most often over the pronouns.* A letter ostensibly written and clearly signed by Vladimir carried this postscript: "Would you please order 10 copies of the Nabokov issue on my husband's account?" So accustomed was Véra to disassociating herself from her text that she might write of VN: "He has asked his son to work on this." A payment could be sent to her husband at "his address," wrote a woman named Mrs. Vladimir Nabokov, who appeared to share that domicile. She almost seemed to forget who she was, although she was not so inconspicuous in the eyes of her correspondents. In a richly Nabokovian double twist of identities, Vladimir complained to Rowohlt. In his previous letter—"signed by my wife"—he had

---

* Together the two blurred into one animated ball. "I rolled over him. We rolled over me. They rolled over him, we rolled over us," Nabokov had written in *Lolita*.

specifically requested his payment for a television adaptation. "Today I receive a check from the Hamburger Sparkasse for $1393.61 made out to my wife's name. This won't do," he admonished, returning the payment.

"It is hard to be happy when one's husband is a mirage, a peripatetic legerdemain of a man, a deception of all five senses," Nabokov had written of another conjurer's less loyal wife. Véra seemed to have no difficulty with the idea. She was happy to sit at VN's side while he protested that he had no real existence, that he was a mirage, an illusion, a masked performer, a mere shadow of his writing self, a "lone wolf," a "lone lamb." She had more difficulty orchestrating her own disappearance. No one who has written so much has ever been as eager to deny responsibility for so many lines. VN declared that his books alone were his identity papers; Véra repudiated the letters she both wrote and signed. She distanced herself even from her own prose style. When Doussia Ergaz took umbrage at two dispatches by which her feelings had been badly hurt, Véra asked the agent if her husband's frank style of expressing himself in English was perhaps to blame. The prose—as well as the frankness—was hers. And the track-covering continued off the page. The journalist who noted that something had been accomplished after consultation between the two Nabokovs—the observation mirrored the "flurry of confabulation between the Shades" in *Pale Fire*—was asked by Véra to delete the remark. She found it embarrassing. The same fate befell George Feifer, when he submitted his 1974 *Daily Express* interview text. From the list of predicate nominatives following his wife's name Nabokov struck "typist" and "editor," claiming that she had not typed for him since 1960 nor edited anything, statements that were both untrue. Elsewhere he requested that Feifer change "she says" to "he says," reattributing to himself a remark his wife had made. It may have been the most profitable appropriation of a partner's voice since *The Autobiography of Alice B. Toklas* had made its author famous, landing Gertrude Stein on the bestseller lists.

Véra was intent on having it both ways. She raised Being Mrs. Nabokov to a science and an art and then pretended that such a person did not exist. Even her husband realized the futility, and the fallaciousness, of her effort. With Field they discussed Véra's place in her husband's story. "Darling, why don't you say something? Why?" implored Vladimir. "I don't think I should be represented," replied the woman whose first literary efforts had been renderings of someone else's prose. "You can't help but be represented! We're too far gone! It's too late!" exploded her husband, tears of laughter raining down his face. Over the next decade, as the focus on the woman at Nabokov's side intensified, Véra scurried for cover, comporting herself like a reverse sphinx: This one seemed poised to tear limbs from those who might guess her riddle. This proved true in the smallest instance as well as in the bigger picture. For Rowohlt she checked every word of the German translations made by the highly meticulous Dieter Zimmer. In 1965 Zimmer submitted a draft of "An Affair of Honor"; Véra made several corrections in the handling of the guns in the story. "So I was surprised to learn that you have done quite a bit of pistol shooting," Zimmer deduced gratefully. Véra did nothing to indulge his curiosity, maintaining that she had altered his text for accuracy's sake. This was the same woman who had written the Swiss Police Ministry months earlier to inquire about pistol permits for Spain. Her husband intended to collect butterflies in isolated regions, which she had heard could be dangerous. What papers would she need to travel internationally with a firearm?

Vladimir made a sensational discovery in 1965: We do not speak as we write. After a highly amusing, very forthcoming few days with Channel Thirteen's Robert Hughes, he had this to say about the transcript of their talk:

> I am greatly distressed and disgusted by my unprepared answers—by the appalling style, slipshod vocabulary, offensive, embarrassing statements and muddled facts. These answers are dull, flat, repetitive, vulgarly phrased and in every way shockingly different from the style of my written prose. . . . I always knew I was an abominably bad speaker, I now deeply regret my rashness.

In future there would be no "spontaneous rot." Questions would be written out and submitted in advance, answers composed on paper and revised only with VN's consent. This elaborate stage management allowed the "real" Nabokov to retreat even further. It also created a good deal of homework in the Nabokov household.* Véra, who sat by her husband's side through each interview—in most cases she had already played the role of the host, reading through the questions and timing her husband's answers—had to convince Vladimir to submit to the inquisitions. She found them exhausting herself but knew their value; some version of her husband needed to be presented to the world.

The face Nabokov put on that individual was not necessarily the real one. Nor was the face he put on Véra. He was equally capable of boasting

---

* It was enough to induce journalists to leave their tape recorders running after the sanctioned interview had ended, as did two intrepid souls, making pleasant conversation with the Nabokovs while praying that the flap-flap-flap of a tape reaching its end would not betray them.

that his wife had the best sense of humor of any woman he had ever met as he was of lamenting that she had none. Was it not a terrible pity that a great clown like himself should be married to someone who never laughed, he asked a journalist? His wife was his memory; his wife was incapable of keeping figures and dates in her head. She did not seem to care; the perfect magician's assistant, she could be sawed in half with no loss of dignity or composure. She refused only to concede that the magician *had* an assistant. To admit that he did so was to admit that some kind of sleight of hand was being worked. She was not going to reveal her husband's tricks. Every artist is a great deceiver, Nabokov reminds us. And Nabokov was a very great artist.

3

How, insofar as she recognized her expanded role, did Véra feel about it? She had difficulty admitting to the weight of her responsibilities. Nowhere is the coyness more evident than in her correspondence with Lisbet Thompson, her oldest friend—the two couples had met in Berlin in 1926—and one of the closest. Temperamentally the two women had a good deal in common: A German Jew several years Véra's elder, Lisbet described herself as a pessimist who had often been proved right. The Thompson marriage fell out along lines similar to the Nabokovs': Lisbet felt that her husband was perfectly sanguine, and that that essential optimism was the reason he had achieved so much in his life. Hers too had been an itinerant life with a brilliant man. A great favorite of Vladimir's, Bertrand Thompson was polymathic even by Nabokovian standards. Having earned a law degree before he was old enough to practice in his native California, he started all over again with a Harvard economics degree. He taught at Harvard Business School in its early years, then moved on to an illustrious, international career in consulting. He made a fortune, most of which he lost in 1929; in 1937 the Thompsons were chauffeuring the Nabokovs around the Riviera in their aging Studebaker. Having worked with the French Air Ministry before the fall of France, Thompson returned to the United States, to study biochemistry. By the 1960s, he was conducting cancer research in a Uruguyan lab. Begun on the Nestorstrasse in Berlin, the friendship with the Thompsons had been renewed in Paris, Nice, New York, Palo Alto, Lugano—Vladimir referred to it as "a kind of rich and varicoloured archipelago"—but by the 1960s consisted almost exclusively of letters.

With other friends Véra might apologize for her delay in writing but rarely allowed apology to veer into complaint. With Lisbet she was more expansive. Here she is in 1963, as close to the edge as she appears to have ventured:

> I am completely exhausted by Vladimir's letters (I mean those he received and *I* have to answer), and it is not merely physical work but he also wants me to make all the decisions which I find more time-consuming than the actual typing. Even when Dmitri was very young and I had no help, I still had more leisure than I do now. Mind you, I do not complain, but I do not want you to think that I am merely lax.

At the end of the same letter she suggested the Thompsons consider a move to Switzerland: "In a way it is such a quiet restful life." Lisbet responded to this quiet rebellion as promptly as the Uruguyan mails allowed. She had so often in the past seen Véra overburdened and so often wished that her fortunes might change. Now at last they had, and she was only working harder as a result. This distressed Lisbet. Why did she not hire more help? She said all of this out of love, as Véra well knew. Lisbet was the kind of friend who most admired in Vladimir's *Eugene Onegin* the line in which he thanked his wife. Instantly Véra retreated; the subject was dropped for a year or so. In 1964 Véra reported only, as she had done before, that her attempts to use a secretary had not been much good. (Jacqueline Callier was in place but Véra was naturally slow to delegate. She found she could type faster than she could dictate, and believed that most of her letters could not be written by anyone else. "But I still hope to get better organized one day," she vowed.) She was more at her ease singing the praises of the mud treatments to which she had submitted in Italy at the end of the year than she was dwelling on the wrist pains that had sent her to Abano in the first place. She highly recommended the treatments to Lisbet, at least initially. A year later, the pains returned. She was deeply solicitous of her friend's health and tight-lipped about her own, admitting only that her wrists ached, that she felt unwell, that medical tests were inconclusive. Finally in March 1966 she proved more forthcoming:

> I am better, on the whole. Still not quite well. My Geneva doctor wants me to do a complete check-up now, but I do not have the time. Have a terrible amount of work to do. Many things for Vladimir, reading proof, checking things, transcribing (the long things that need typing are done by someone else); but also V.'s correspondence which has outgrown the size which can be handled by a single person.

Things only got worse. The next letter was delayed by a "madhouse" of interviewers, publishers, TV reporters, who had followed the Nabokovs all over Italy, something of a feat on the part of the press. In the course of their wanderings, Véra negotiated a clause in a Putnam's contract from each town. Summer had been taxing enough, "but since our return to Montreux it has been really too much for both of us," she confessed in the fall, exhausted, unwell, and dreading the trip she was about to make to New York. In January, 1967 she was hospitalized, a misadventure on which she reported foggily. Lisbet chastised her, about her vagueness regarding her health, as about her stubbornness in rising to publishers' impatient demands. Of course they all looked forward to a new book of Vladimir's, but surely Véra's health did not need to be compromised in the process?

Véra issued an immediate retraction. It was important to her that Lisbet understand how minimal was her own contribution, how utterly mechanical was her work. There was no further mention of messy business decisions sloughed off by demanding husbands:

> Please do not think that we work so hard because of the impatient publishers, or readers, or money. Far from that. Writing is Vladimir's life work, and he has many things he wants to say. As for me, I am trying to help him. The correspondence is overwhelming. Business letters must be answered, but also many others which unfortunately I do not get around to answer any more.

To make matters worse, she was again typing a manuscript herself. Having felt that the original sagged in the middle, Vladimir had reworked too much of *King, Queen, Knave* to have it transcribed by a secretary. He had written the novel twice; Véra was now typing it for the second time. She went out of her way to specify that her involvement fell short of that of Clare in *Sebastian Knight:* "I am not 'working on it' as you so nicely put it, only typing as he dictates," she chided Lisbet, who wisely let the matter rest there. The behavior was consistent with her stressing how unqualified she was for the job. Twenty-five years after protesting that she was by no means a Sévigné, she told Sylvia Berkman that she was a very poor letter-writer, had been all her life, and had done little else for three or four decades.

Did she in truth resent the work? Most friends and visitors never saw a hint that she felt it anything but a privilege to assist VN; the honor of serving him seemed to obliterate the thousand inconveniences. Even Jacqueline Callier recognized that Véra had a firm sense of self-importance, in which she delighted. Véra was always surprised when she learned that someone did not work. She felt she had been raised to. And Vladimir was a man as supremely difficult to resist as VN was an honor to serve. Véra was dispatched on a Montreux errand with these lines: "Ah, sweet socks! So tenderly woolly! Nothing in a nylon blend (so *nasty,* and which irritate the leg)! Size 46, and the usual length, i.e., not to the knee, but not too short. Ah, socks! 2 pairs." Dmitri felt that his mother was disgruntled only by the nonsense chores, by the constant struggle to thwart the incompetents. He felt she would have much preferred to read, and "to [make] little jottings of her own," than to tend to business matters. She had begun an independent project in the early 1950s, having in Ithaca researched a connection between La Motte-Fouqué and Pushkin, to which she returned only in her eighties. Her literary instinct, if not her aspiration, had clearly survived. In 1963 she composed a rather melodramatic piece of Russian poetry; it may have been in response to a challenge issued by her husband. Either because there was a story behind the verse or because she treasured the composition on its own merits, she held on to it. As always the practical backbone shines through. Véra wrote her middling lines on the back of the 1963 McDonnell Aircraft Report to Shareholders.

She continued to read widely. Nabokov boasted of her uncanny instinct for fishing the sole worthwhile title from a voluminous carton of publisher's freebies. She took the *Saturday Review*'s 1962 test, "Your Literary I.Q.," and outscored VN by a long shot; she had no difficulty recognizing the work of Giraudoux or Disraeli or Walpole. Her reading was less canonical, even while she believed James Bond to be the creation of a man named "Fletcher." She was a great fan of Michael Arlen's *The Green Hat* and of his son's limpid memoir, *Exiles.* In 1965 she agreed to keep an eye out for English-language works that might be of interest to Ledig Rowohlt, who could not have realized how recondite were her tastes. The sole title she appears to have proposed to him was Richard Hakluyt's *Voyages,* the volume of explorers' logbooks thought to have inspired *The Rime of the Ancient Mariner.* (It had been republished that year.) She continued to serve as a clearinghouse for her husband, recommending to him Nadezhda Mandelstam's *Hope Against Hope,* which she read shortly after its 1970 translation into English. Both Nabokovs admired Edmund White's first novel, *Forgetting Elena*; Véra astonished its author when she met him years later and recited whole passages by heart.* Not everything merited this much attention. She found Bellow's

---

* Encouraged by her enthusiasm and out of admiration for VN, White began to visualize Véra as his muse. When he formulated his definition of his ideal reader—"a cultivated heterosexual woman in her sixties who knows English perfectly but is not an American"—it was Véra he had in mind.

Herzog "a disaster," boring in the extreme. Moreover she found it anti-Semitic, providing a novel definition of that term. "I know many Jews, including my own family, and never saw anybody or anything even remotely like his Jews and his 'Jewish' atmosphere," she huffed. An Italian friend recommended Pratolini, Soldati, and Gadda, all of whom Véra deemed mediocre, unimportant. "Where are the worth while books?" she asked. She was perhaps fortunate not to have found more of them; she did not often have time to indulge her tastes. "I'm sending Volodya three Russian newspapers," Anna Feigin wrote from New York in the early 1960s, "and for you I'm sending the Steel Report. *Read it.*" She did, though not with any abiding passion. Friends teased her about her interest in the market, but the lists of the Nabokovs' securities are in Vladimir's hand, not Véra's.

A few people teased her about the long hours at her desk. "You mustn't apologize for being behind in VN's correspondence," Alfred Appel assured Véra in the early seventies. "There is only one solution. Go on strike for better working conditions and hours. Walk in front of the Montreux Palace with a picket sign, something along the order of 'VN unfair to auxiliary services.' It would certainly have one kind of effect or another."

4
———

Véra never tired of informing those who requested his presence that her husband was unavailable, but that were he to consider their invitation, his honorarium would be ten times as high as that they proposed.* This was part of the assignment; she was a good sport; she played her part to perfection. One need not strain to hear VN chuckling in the background. Still, when the man who claimed to have no interest in prizes save for those with cash purses attached got wind of the fact that Minton felt he was in no need of money, the Putnam's relationship began to falter. Véra was detailed to settle the matter. In explaining her husband's discontent she went out of her way to be clear about the authorship of her letter to Minton. Vladimir had dictated various demands; from a certain point in the document, he had proposed what he wanted said but not how to say it. What both Nabokovs were saying was that

---

* The invective was nearly formulaic. Occasionally Véra took it a step further, as she did when Case Western University informed Nabokov they were considering him as a candidate for a 1973 visiting scholar position. Could he travel to Cleveland, at their expense, to interview? Véra replied that her husband did not plan to be in the United States in 1973. "And in any case in Mr. Nabokov's opinion, he is sufficiently known for his work to make a preliminary meeting superfluous, and a 14,000-mile round trip for this purpose absurd, whether you pay or do not pay his travelling expenses."

they wanted more money and better publicity for Vladimir's books; Minton countered with a thinly veiled threat to undermine the tax plan they had so diligently worked out. Briefly Véra put herself—and her husband—in the hands of a William Morris agent, who was to exact an improved offer from Minton, and simultaneously, to pursue an unsolicited offer. An English-language edition of the revamped *King, Queen, Knave* was the book immediately in question. Next was *Ada,* of which Nabokov would say only, confidentially, that it was highly erotic, and that "it does not belong in any category though roughly it is the story of three people, two sisters and their halfbrother, with two love stories, one of which lasts from pubescence to happy old age."

By 1967 it was clear to the Nabokovs that the relationship with Putnam's was not destined to endure to any sort of old age. Of the many suitors who presented themselves McGraw-Hill distinguished itself in its devotion—a young editor of whom the couple thought highly was dispatched to Genoa in April to handle the advance work with Véra—and in its clever tax planning. Véra could be a little cloak-and-daggerish about the business arrangements: In October 1967 she advised Weidenfeld, "The project of which you know seems to be developing well, and in complete secrecy." Her approach to this negotiation was in all ways telling; she was most herself when representing someone else. McGraw-Hill made its offer—$250,000 for eleven books, past and future, with a plump 17½ percent royalty—in a letter addressed to both Nabokovs in July.* Véra responded to the generous offer with an unorthodox demand, as shocking to the Paul, Weiss lawyers as it was to McGraw-Hill. She insisted that a cost-of-living provision be inserted into the contract. Iseman outlined the traditional wisdom on the subject for Véra at least nine times: With inflation, book prices rise, and royalties with them. Mrs. Nabokov, however, explained herself in a confidential letter to her distinguished counsel:

> We have lived through two inflations during which the amount of money that would buy half-a-dozen pairs of stockings in the morning would not buy one needle in the evening of the same day. . . . My husband would like some insurance against a RUN-AWAY inflation—the kind of automatic protection that the big workers' unions get—not against the slow kind we are having now.

---

* A quarter of a million dollars in 1967 was the equivalent of $1,250,000 in 1999 dollars.

She was adamant on the subject. Her husband's lawyers had not been in Petersburg in the nineteen-tens or Berlin in the twenties. Véra had. She was accustomed to the bottom falling out of her world. For Nabokov, this left a mark on the fiction; for his wife the trapdoors were very real. She had made the same request of Irving Lazar, who claimed he had had to consult an economics text to fathom her meaning. She was felt to be bracing herself for the wildly improbable.

The lawyers who believed Véra bizarrely preoccupied with her cost-of-living increases in 1967 thought her positively clairvoyant several years later. "It goes without saying that McGraw-Hill—unlike Mrs. Nabokov—never dreamed in 1968 that the United States would suddenly be in a double-digit inflation situation," they chortled in the mid-1970s. They pitied McGraw's CFO, dressed down by Harold McGraw for having agreed to such an outlandish provision. Véra knew she had been ridiculed, and felt vindicated when she learned that her husband's publisher was laughing less loudly. The language proved highly lucrative, all the more so because McGraw-Hill inadvertently based their calculations on the 1967 price index instead of the 1968 index. Nor was this the only odd request that past misadventures induced her to make. "This is a *very private question* from VN to you," she wrote Iseman. Could there be an escape clause somewhere in the contract, in the event that the relationship proved unsatisfactory? She, or both Nabokovs, felt skittish about making such a long-term commitment. Not that Véra was willing to admit as much. "If you see your way of broaching this subject without offending McGraw-Hill, please do so. But, of course, it should come *from you* rather than from VN," she directed Iseman.

By late fall it became clear that someone would need to travel to New York to finalize the McGraw-Hill arrangements.* Vladimir was devoting twelve-hour days to *Ada,* working at what Véra estimated was three times his usual speed. It was clear she would travel alone; Elena Sikorski filled in at the Palace. Véra booked a room at the Pierre Hotel, which put her a block from Natalie Nabokov's old apartment, where she had arrived, with an uncertain grasp of American decimal points, twenty-seven years earlier. That address

---

* The discussions did not prevent the Nabokovs from receiving a mid-November visit from Harper publisher Cass Canfield, who attempted over lunch to lure Vladimir to his firm with a generous and creative offer. Confidentially, Véra asked Iseman if, in good faith, such a proposal could be used as a negotiating tool with McGraw-Hill. She does not appear to have done so, but can only have felt more confident in her dealings with the Harper offer in her back pocket. She wisely waited until the day after the McGraw-Hill contract was sealed to send her regrets to Canfield, noting that "VN was practically committed at the time you arrived in Montreux."

was in some ways closer to the negotiation at hand than was the Pierre's. On December 1, she met for a drink in the hotel bar with Iseman; McGraw-Hill's Edward Booher, the president of the book company; and John Cady, the senior vice president of the overall corporation. A number of details remained to be worked out at the table, where Iseman found himself pushing further than he would have dared, stiffened by Véra's gaze. At one juncture he asked that they step outside together; he wanted to make it at least *appear* that they were conferring. It seemed to him that his client knew better than he how far he could go. From the experience Iseman concluded that Véra was one of the finest natural negotiators he had ever known. To his colleagues he described the extraordinary experience a few days later:

> In the dimly-lit Hotel Pierre bar, at 6:00 PM, on December 1, publishing agreements (including a last-minute supplemental letter) were signed, and carefully left undated, by Edward Booher, President of McGraw-Hill, and Véra Nabokov, as President of the non-existent Coramen, Inc. For a consideration, I will recount to you how Mrs. Nabokov made me scrounge for a few extra percentage points on some of the subsidiary rights (over and above the figures which had been agreed upon at Montreux), while she sat silently, her head arched and her white mane flying, aloofly disdaining the whole shoddy proceeding.

Under the new agreement all three Nabokovs were to receive an annual salary as employees of Coramen, a Delaware corporation. Cady was the wizard behind the ingenious arrangement; he had set up the corporation well before, knowing he would use it when the right author came along.* He was tickled finally to have found his man. In the process Véra acquired a title for the first time. She was president of Coramen, a company whose name was consistent with its utility. Nabokov had cited the word in *Pale Fire* as an example of "choral and sculptured"—and near-meaningless—beauty.

The news that Nabokov had defected from Putnam's for a quarter million dollars—in a deal sealed by a handshake between Mrs. Nabokov and the publisher's executives—appeared in the papers only on January 12, by which time Véra was long back in Montreux. She offered no comment on the negotiation that had so impressed the others at the table. When congratulated on the terms of the deal she did what any half-discreet person would have done: She protested that the numbers had been greatly exaggerated by the press,

---

* The right author was by definition a European-based one, for whom a fixed amount of salary income was exempt from tax.

which they were not. Her delight can be read only in her comments about Minton. With glee she reported that he was "in a state of mourning," "in a rage," "nearly hysterical," about her husband's defection. (Minton was none of these things, being an astute businessman, and having made less money with each subsequent Nabokov title since *Lolita*. Vladimir nonetheless took to calling him "Badminton." Véra's correspondence with Minton ended with teeth clenched on both sides.)

There was no time for prolonged celebration in any event. The Nabokovs succumbed to their mutual flu just after Christmas and, still suffering from it, braced themselves for a small army of January visitors. Alfred Appel and his wife visited in midmonth. Sonia Slonim followed, after which a team of Rowohlt translators descended with their dictionaries on the Palace. Over the course of a week the Nabokovs vetted the German translation of *Pale Fire*. The hotel put a small, spartan salon at their disposal, in which everyone sat with a copy of the original work on his lap as a Rowohlt secretary read slowly through the German text, line by line.* Véra signaled often that something was amiss. A spirited discussion would follow, Véra speaking German when she needed to suggest an alternate phrasing, otherwise confining herself to English. It was clear to the translators that she had been designated to speak for her husband, who would often tease her at the outset of these marathon sessions, as if coaxing her out of her corner, priming her to talk. Afterward he entertained the visitors with garbled French and Italian translations. The strain of the long days on the Nabokovs was clear to the Rowohlt team, who returned in 1973 and 1974 to devote a series of ten-day sessions to *Ada*. The drill was more complicated yet when the Italians came, as they did in November 1969 for their *Ada*. Mondadori's general director knew no English, nor Vladimir any Italian. "Everything," reported Véra, "went over a French bridge."

It would have been easy for someone in that Palace salon to conclude that the two Nabokovs constituted the same sort of "twinned genius-ego" Vladimir had described in *Ada,* a rollicking meditation on time and space, richly allusive, swarming with slights, all of it braided through a particularly happy, particularly long-lived, and perfectly incestuous love affair. Blinding in its mirror-play, the novel is ostensibly written by Van Veen, acrobat-aesthete-philosopher, with textual interpolations by Ada Veen, his sister, his

---

* The process resembled Nabokov's description of reading from his lecturing days: "Literature must be taken and broken to bits, pulled apart, squashed—then its lovely reek will be smelt in the hollow of the palm, it will be munched and rolled upon the tongue with relish; then, and only then, its rare flavor will be appreciated at its true worth and the broken and crushed parts will again come together in your mind and disclose the beauty of a unity to which you have contributed something of your own blood."

peer, and the perpetual if not permanent object of his affection. It did not help that Ada was her own Department of Recollection, playing on the page the role Véra played in the life, questioning the accuracy of Van's recall, appending Russian-speckled comments of her own, laboring to keep their history pure. Nor did it help that the Nabokovs, as much married as Kitty and Levin, seemed to conduct their marriage with the furtiveness of Anna and Vronsky. It is no great surprise that the novel tangled itself up with the reality; it was generally difficult to ignore Véra's presence in light of Ada, described by Appel—who knew them both well—as "not only Veen's muse, desire, tormentor and alter ego, but his severest critic and collaborator as well." The overlapping, intergrading entity termed "Vaniada" in the novel was not so far from the real-life "Vervolodya," the most intimate of VN's doubles, one that delighted in its own brand of "sun-and-shade games." Ada and Van rework a translation of John Shade's verse just as Véra and Vladimir reworked that of Shade's maker. One reviewer read the work as an alchemical conflation of the Tamara of *Speak, Memory* and Nabokov's famously long and happy marriage. If nothing else, what was true of Van was true of Vladimir: All temptations aside, he could not live one day without this particular woman. Nor was there any question that the Nabokovs were engaged in their own trilingual game of total recall. The temptation to see Véra in the novel was irresistible, especially for those who had not found her in *Lolita,* especially given the name on the dedication page, especially given the supremely self-referential character of the work itself.

Of course Ada is not Véra, but the ferocity with which Vladimir charged at the reviewer—even the friendly reviewer—who found traces of her in the work seemed suspect. He tackled the critic who said as much in *The New York Review of Books.* "What the hell, Sir, do you know about my married life?" he challenged Matthew Hodgart, who had the good grace to issue the demanded apology.* John Updike saw more than art and ardor in Ada: "She is also, in a dimension or two, Nabokov's wife Véra, his constant collaboratrice and the invariable dedicatee of his works. . . . I suspect that many of the details in this novel double as personal communication between husband and wife; some of the bothersomely exact dates, for instance, must be, to use a favorite word of our author, 'fatidic.' " Updike's wrist was lightly slapped. He was hitting a nail upon its head in his last observation, although it would be Brian Boyd who, palpating the tender ground later, learned to parse the denials. Speaking after her husband's death, Véra voiced her discomfort with an observation Boyd made regarding dates in the novel, which she suggested

---

* A Cornell professor, Matthew Hodgart had surely heard something of the Nabokov marriage.

he omit. "But there are many birthdays commemorated in *Ada,*" he objected. "I know," she replied, waltzing neatly around the fact that her birthday figures prominently and meaningfully in the novel. No one ever dared ask her if there was something in the twinned genius motif, what she made of the novel-as-dialogue, the woman who claims her ideas to be the "mimotypes" of another's. Had they done so they would doubtless have been rewarded with another of Véra's dazzling non sequiturs. But Ada likes snakes, she might have responded—as she had noted that Zina was only half-Jewish—therefore, she is not I. Earlier she had listened carefully as VN described to a journalist her intercepting him on his way to the incinerator with the partial manuscript of *Lolita.* "I don't remember that. Did I?" she asked vaguely. She could not possibly have forgotten. Of course, as Nabokov reminds us in *Ada,* if people remembered the same things, they would not be different people.

A long-awaited novel, *Ada* was greeted in 1969 mostly with extravagant praise from reviewers, more than some of them later wished they had showered on the novel. Appel reviewed the book glowingly on the cover of *The New York Times Book Review,* although he had disliked it on his first reading, finding it overly precious. He came around to the belief that he had written his review in a state of starstruck intoxication, from which he later awoke—to the conviction that Nabokov in his *Ada* period was but a step away from Joyce in the period of *Finnegans Wake,* a novel Nabokov dismissed as a "petrified superpun." British reviewers came more directly to a negative appraisal, referring to the seven-hundred-page volume as Nabokov's Waterloo, alleging that language had perhaps too facilely triumphed over imagination. *Ada* is a ravishingly beautiful piece of writing; it can also fairly be said to be a flabby novel, in which the acrobatic commingling of centuries and nationalities works less well than that of the human limbs. All the same the May 1969 publication landed Nabokov on the cover of *Time,* a place where the magazine's editor had long hoped to see him; VN was hailed as "the greatest living American novelist." Briefly *Ada* battled *The Love Machine, Portnoy's Complaint,* and *The Godfather* on the summer bestseller lists, where it remained for five months, an overweight and off-putting tome selling, to McGraw-Hill's relief and delight, "like six-packs of Budweiser in July."

5

Véra was less willing to underwrite the fictions that leapt out of her husband's mouth than those he committed to the page. One interviewer noted that nothing—least of all the truth—could stand between VN and a good story. He vaulted at a good pun, or a fertile coincidence, from a mile away. The interviewer did not reckon on Véra, a one-woman Department of Corrections, who—at the risk of inviting back the specter of *Ada*—assisted Vladimir as much in his efforts to order and reorder the past. Nabokov had been happy to inform Filippa Rolf that he had played at the magnificent, mirrored halls of the Hotel Negresco as a child in 1905—at least until Véra pointed out that the hotel had not yet been built. He summoned the same synthetic nostalgia for the Continental in Paris, the only establishment at which the couple had been able to find a room in 1959, but which VN jovially declared he had chosen for sentimental reasons, having visited the hotel in 1906, which was perhaps true as well. For the ninety-ninth time Véra might listen to his lurid tale of the Belgian cannibal, rolling her eyes. She reserved a half-bemused smile for her husband at such moments, as if astonished that he could still be trotting out this outrageous repertoire. The cannibal story was no more true today than it had been in the 1930s, she objected. When Vladimir began to discourse on Mozart, she reminded him he knew nothing about the subject. Quietly and with good humor she corrected him in front of an interviewer: He did not weigh eighty-five kilos, but eighty-nine. And when he bragged that his Russian Scrabble scores hovered between four hundred and five hundred points, Véra pointed out that "five hundred is barely possible," a statement with which Vladimir heartily agreed, being the first to confess to a hyperbole addiction.

He was as eager to make use of his wife's credibility as he was, for the sake of a good story, to steamroll past it. In Cambridge he had had a habit of spinning a yarn that was patently false, then bolstering its veracity by insisting that he had told Véra all about it, as if his having done so constituted irrefutable proof. Véra could not always have been pleased to squash these tall tales. In front of Nina and Alfred Appel she did so reluctantly. At the Palace her husband shared with an acquaintance the story of the Appels having met in his class, edging their way closer to each other as the semester progressed until—by *Anna Karenina,* and under his spell—they had practically emerged as Mr. and Mrs. Appel. Sadly, Appel demurred. The future Mrs. Appel had taken the course in 1954–55, while he had done so the previous year. Vladimir looked helplessly to Véra for corroboration. Slowly and solemnly, like an Old Testament judge, she shook her head no. Vladimir shrugged, and slumped a bit. "Well, it's a beautiful story anyway," he concluded. It should have happened that way, just as there should have been a charity ball on May 8, 1923, when he had met an enchanting masked woman for the first time.

"Véra has a much better memory than I do," Nabokov boasted, trusting

himself to it completely. He lived in manifest if occasionally ill-humored deference to his wife's ability to summon details from the past. As the man who
had now revisited his own autobiography—one hundred pages of new material, photographs, and an index were added to the book in 1966—well knew,
his recall was faulty.* He wished Véra had made him write more down when
he was younger, a statement that made his wife growl, with what sounds to
have been the foot-stamping frustration of someone who had tried to do precisely that. William Buckley Jr., who met the Nabokovs in the 1970s, found
the corroborating almost a tic. Vladimir's conversation was studded with
regular "Isn't that right, Véra?"s. As often as not, the answer was "Almost."
Not for a second would she have failed to reply honestly, so long as the question was impersonal. Nor would she hesitate to intrude on the narratives. In
the course of a dinner with the Appels the Nabokovs wound up in a hearty
disagreement about the definition of "*ananas*" in Russian. Was it pineapple or
banana? As soon as her table manners allowed, Véra bolted upstairs to settle
the matter. After a few moments she returned from her consultation with the
dictionary; she did not have time to open her mouth before her husband
boomed, "Defeat. I recognize the posture of defeat." Véra smiled. "I can always tell when she knows she's wrong," he trilled in jolly triumph. These
miniature intellectual tournaments were standard fare, the good-natured
rivalry between a man who thought his wife's Russian stupendous and a
woman who thought her husband's without equal. Nabokov folded this
minor contest into *Ada*.

Véra was graceful in her defeats, though often visibly vexed with her
husband. Along with the fact-keeping and fiction-quashing came a fair
amount of straightforward conversational disciplining. As the stream of visitors to Montreux observed, the act came to consist of Vladimir verging into
the off-color, the provocative, Véra reining him in, Vladimir complying like
the errant schoolboy. He seemed to be playing not so much to his visitor as to
his wife's amused—or not so amused—tolerance. Late in the 1960s, Jason
Epstein was walking north across the Place de la Concorde in Paris when he
heard a familiar Harry Truman twang, a booming midwestern laugh. It was
Vladimir. Over a drink at the Meurice, Vladimir went on to relate to his liberal friend and former editor his deep affection for Nixon. Véra interceded,
clearly embarrassed. Vladimir glowed as she did so, the naughty boy who en-
joys the mess being swabbed up around him. When he announced to a visi-

---

* Some preferred the more impressionistic volume. Updike felt the new version of Nabokov's past paled
in comparison to the old version of his past; to his mind the corrected sentences hobbled "under their new
loads of accuracy."

tor that he had decided to return to Russian prose for good, he was dismayed
to see that his wife did not flinch. That was the point of the exercise. On some
occasions when he made inflammatory remarks but could not coax Véra out
of her corner he still obtained the reaction he was after. The 1969 *Time* researcher noted that after one particularly tasteless comment she looked as if
she would like to choke her husband. It was certainly one way to tease her
out.

Filippa Rolf found another. The Cambridge-based poet had engaged in
a steady correspondence with Véra since the Nice visit that had so changed
her life; Véra had hardly been able to keep up with the torrent of letters. Generally she waded her way past the more personal comments but was at times
provoked into taking a stand. In early 1962 when she had written about the
visit of Rolf's Swedish friend she took a very firm stand indeed. She believed
the relationship "imprudent and unwise," adding that Vladimir was in full
agreement with her. "Do you *always* do *exactly* what is expected from you?
You are the best actress any director could dream of," Rolf remonstrated, a
legitimate question phrased less delicately than it might have been. Véra ignored the outburst. A month earlier she had asked Rolf if she might see her
way clear to translating *Pale Fire,* a request she did not rescind even after
these insolent comments. She could not have been pleased to hear later that
Rolf had "smuggled" both Nabokovs into a short story but gracefully assured
the self-appointed protégée that "we trust completely in your discretion and
good taste." Equally she continued to dispense professional advice, encouraging Rolf to focus on the drama on the page instead of that in Harvard
Square, not to brood about Life and Love. In response to that brief and cordial statement she received, late in April 1963, a suicide note: "Goodbye. You
are the only one I have ever loved or ever will love."

The communication may have been unexpected but Rolf's fixation
on both Nabokovs, her mental unrest, and her difficulty in acclimating to
America had long been obvious. Véra and Elena Levin had exchanged numerous letters on the subject. Véra treated the April missive as she did most
threats that did not offend her honor: she gave it a wide berth. In October she
was writing sympathetically about Rolf's new book of verse, which her publisher had rejected, and about the Nabokovs' abiding confidence that Rolf
should undertake the *Pale Fire* translation. That Véra, in her eminent, stiff-
upper-lip sanity, would have preferred to have waltzed past the suicide note
and its personal overtures makes sense. That she felt the proper therapy for
someone on the brink of mental illness might be to lock her up with a fictional madman's fantasies would seem either a lapse of logic or an overdose
of the stuff. She did all she could to limit her contact with Rolf during the

1964 Cambridge visit and claimed to do so again in December of that year, when Rolf traveled to Europe for a quiet visit with the couple, in the course of which they reviewed her translating progress. They also bought her a coat, an act that would not have impressed on Rolf any burgeoning rift in the relationship. Véra could not seem to wean herself from the idea that she had found, for all the complications, the ideal Swedish translator for her husband's work. And Rolf could not seem to get past the idea that the Nabokovs had banished her to an inhospitable place, which they had made all the more inhospitable by writing the Levins in advance of her very private sexual habits. Véra appeared—hers had been the fist that pounded the table for emphasis—the prime culprit. Her assuredness, her invincibility, seemed to egg Rolf on.

By 1965 she was bombarding the couple with drafts of the story she had written about them, "an act of vandalism," she confessed, but one she labored obsessively to perfect. The Nabokovs did not flinch. At the time Vladimir wrote glowingly on Rolf's behalf to *The New Yorker*. Véra defended her energetically to Lena, in Sweden, with "She is one of the most gifted women we have ever met." Of another draft she wrote that Rolf could indeed publish the story if she liked, with two minor changes. She went out of her way to make it clear that the request was Vladimir's, although the lines in question concerned her. She herself was wholly indifferent.* Of course nothing could have been further from the truth, as the highly perceptive Rolf would have known. She seems to have been incited by Véra's protests, determined to force her to drop the mask. At times the correspondence reads like a feral attempt to scare Mrs. Nabokov out of the bushes; in May 1966 Rolf taunted Véra by saying that she knew Nabokov's works were, all of them, letters to his dream of a wife, from whom she expected an autobiography. A hint of exasperation crept into the correspondence only a year later, when Véra sidestepped again, deferring to Vladimir in her communication. "My husband has been terribly busy and simply could not keep track of the revisions of your story and the story of your revisions," she wrote stiffly. A whole collection of rambling letters had arrived in the interim. Increasingly these proved to be sardonic, half-lucid documents penned in a spidery script that wound itself around the page, in and out of several languages en route. For all of the madness in the fictions, Véra's encounters with mental illness were few. She continued to describe the demands of her life to Rolf—the Rowohlt transla-

---

* She adopted the same strategy later with Field, when it came to the Guadanini affair. "I would rather keep this out of the book, mainly because I know VN would not want it published. As for me, I do not really care whether it will be published or not."

tors had just left, dissecting *Pale Fire* line by line had been debilitating, the correspondence only grew and grew—as if she could somehow will the correspondence back on to neutral, rational ground.

In 1969, when the letters, postcards, and telegrams amounted to some twenty communications a month and when Rolf's insolence had devolved into brute obscenity, Véra turned to Paul, Weiss for help. She was obviously rattled; her June letter to the firm is a jumble of pronouns. She did not seem to know if she was writing as herself, her husband ("In the middle 60s I surrendered to her eager desire of translating into Swedish one of my longest and most difficult novels . . ."), or both of them. Since November of the previous year they had chosen not to answer Rolf's unsettling letters, about her obsessive adoration of, or her ripening hatred for, them; Rolf continued to insist the Nabokovs were characters in her own work. Véra read and approved the Paul, Weiss missive, to which Rolf contemptuously replied that she could not and would not discontinue her correspondence with the couple. The rain of mail in Montreux tripled. Véra issued her own ultimatum at the end of July, setting out her version of the relationship in a document that makes clear that the meticulous, too, can disfigure history. Her summary was supremely lucid, perfectly truthful, highly inaccurate. Véra failed to acknowledge that the Nice invitation had been anything but casual; that Rolf had clipped Swedish reviews at her request and been a great help in the Wahlström fiasco; that the Nabokovs had in any way enjoyed what Véra now termed her "endless visit"; that they had in large part set the agenda. Rolf was not, and never had been, a friend. Her habit of advertising her lesbianism was shameless. She was abusing the considerable talent with which she had been born. Furthermore, and in perhaps the worst instance of impertinence, she had never been granted permission to address either Nabokov by his or her given name.

Only toward the spring of 1970 did Rolf's Cambridge friends discover what she had been up to; the Nabokovs were not the only recipients of the aberrant spiralgrams. A devoted friend saw that she was taken to a hospital, where she spent a much-needed month. She was later diagnosed as having suffered a psychotic episode of paranoid megalomania, for which therapy and complete rest were prescribed. She recovered, and published her first English prose in *Partisan Review* soon after. The Nabokovs continued to receive two communications from her a day. In 1978, she was mailing regular letters and compositions to Véra, along with poems through which she laced references to the Nabokovs, a theme with which she never finished. In August of that year Rolf was diagnosed with advanced kidney cancer and died within weeks; word of her death must have reached Switzerland but left no

record there. The entire episode proved a drain on the already taxed resources in Montreux, where such a premium was placed on the rational that
Véra was able to say of a brilliant, temperate summer day that "the weather
has finally come to its senses."* Rolf had been one of the few to challenge her
to drop her mask, to speak, as herself, with a near-stranger. Véra tried to
claim the whole saga was a madman's fantasy, which was not true. Having
long evaded the credit, in this case she dodged all personal responsibility as
well. The strategy worked less well with people than with literature.

6

At the beginning of October 1967, Phyllis and Ken Christiansen, Vladimir's
Museum of Comparative Zoology assistant and her entomologist husband,
passed through Montreux. They were delighted to see the boy for whom
Phyllis (then Phyllis Smith) had occasionally baby-sat in Cambridge, now a
dashing six-foot-five-inch professional singer. To their astonishment they
found Véra virtually unchanged. They were all the more taken aback when
she asked about the cocker spaniel Phyllis had owned twenty years before,
by name. The Nabokovs had forgotten nothing, and over Sunday lunch
(tournedos, strawberries) plied Phyllis with questions about her family,
whom they had known through the museum. In particular they expressed
concern for her thirty-six-year-old sister, with whom Phyllis had had a troubled relationship, and who had since been diagnosed as mentally ill. Vladimir
returned persistently to the subject, probing for the cause of the disorder.
Phyllis was so startled by the interest, and by the line of direct questioning,
that she felt she fumbled the answers. It is unlikely that the close interrogation of 1967 had anything to do with the flurry of mail then arriving from
Filippa Rolf. But it was abundantly clear that the Nabokovs did understand—and could summon compassion for—those grappling with their
balance. The visit was an altogether charmed one, from both sides. The
Christiansens remarked especially on the continued adoration of husband
and wife. Vladimir still called Véra "Darling"; as another visitor observed,
there was nothing remotely casual about his use of the appellation. In the
lounge after lunch he spooned sugar into his coffee but missed the cup. A
small mountain of crystal balanced neatly on his loafer. Impishly Véra broke

---

* Don't be angry with the rain, her husband had begged in 1926; it simply does not know how to fall
upward.

the news: "Darling, you have just sweetened your shoe." Her husband roared with laughter.

Filippa Rolf was not the only visitor who thought the Nabokovs lonely in their European exile, which she assumed was the reason she had been invited to Nice. Martha Duffy, the *Time* researcher who flew to Montreux for the 1969 cover story, found them constantly on the brink of loneliness as well. Nina Appel felt the loneliness seeping out of them at all times. Philippe Halsman, who had photographed VN in 1966, asked as much directly. "No, we do not feel lonesome. We have the run of the hotel, and peace," Véra assured him, grousing instead about the weather, more intractable even than the worst of her husband's publishers. She seems to have had a point. The Nabokovs were, after all, a couple who could have a rollicking good time alone with a couple of dictionaries. Vladimir's sister Elena, widowed in 1958, visited biweekly from Geneva; she agreed that Véra would have been entirely happy on a desert island with Vladimir. Which she for the most part was. Off-season the 350-room Palace was empty—some twenty guests flitted among its hallways and salons—with a kind of *Last Year at Marienbad* feel to it. Regular visits from Dmitri, to whom Véra spoke by telephone several times a week, were equally vital. Asked about his social circle, Vladimir provided a short list, beginning with tufted ducks, crested grebes, and the characters in his new novel. He told Wilson, who visited Montreux for the first time and the Nabokovs for the last time in 1964, that they saw almost no one in the winter, which kept his mind uncluttered.

A steady stream of intellectuals—the first Nabokovians—came to call, as, less formally, did old and new fans. Screwing up his courage, a Cornellian ambushed Véra one spring morning in Montreux in 1964. Positioning himself near a favored Montreux newsstand, he reminded her of the 1958 conversation in which her evangelical husband had advised him that if he was going to become a writer he had better memorize the names of everything. Véra beamed and assured the former student, "We tell that story *all* the time." She was unfailingly gracious with these visitors, though many saw the public game Rolf had described, Véra playing net to VN's unfailing ground strokes. In the fall of 1968 Leonard Lyons was very nearly accurate in reporting that "every major studio is sending a man to Vladimir Nabokov's home in Switzerland to read his new novel," because he refused to let the manuscript—which boasted two nymphets—leave the house. Lazar was behind the unprecedented arrangement, having stipulated that only heads of studios need apply. Paramount's Robert Evans was the first on the scene. The Nabokovs balked when they met him, subjecting him to a cross-examination. "You're a child," VN asserted. "You can't be more than twenty," alleged

Véra. "You're really head of Paramount?" (Evans wound up trading his passport for the 881-page *Ada* manuscript, which he read in a day, with amphetamines. And did not buy.) Andrew Field, who at twenty-nine had already published a trailblazing study of Nabokov's work, arrived for a week's stay in January 1969. He returned later in the year, and spent all of January 1971 with the Nabokovs. The admiration, and the conversation, must have been welcome, but Véra remained ever mindful that anything that escaped either Nabokov's lips might end up on a library shelf one day. Her philosophy on the subject was crystal clear: Under the circumstances one said only congenial things.

With other scholars she loosened up considerably, most often doing her impressive best to fade into the background, even if she had to lunge forward to keep herself there. Ellendea and Carl Proffer paid their first visit call on the Nabokovs in Lugano, late in July 1969, on the return from Moscow. Proffer was then a young professor with a deep love of Russian literature; the two couples enjoyed a spirited three-hour lunch, in the course of which Ellendea was struck by Véra's deep curiosity about people. She appeared especially appreciative of the twenty-four-year-old miniskirted graduate student who asked good questions and showed no particular deference to the man whose picture had just graced the cover of *Time*; generally Véra smiled on those women who stood up to her husband. On a subsequent visit, having navigated a number of difficult subjects, Ellendea mentioned the informal study she was making of how couples met. Vladimir began willingly to talk. It was at this time that Véra cut in with her quip about the KGB. What *were* all these questions? She had a half-smile on her face when she did so, but proved a master of the conversationally spilled ink. A half hour later she turned the question around, almost shyly. "And when did you find *your* happiness?" she asked the Proffers. She could be warm and welcoming—Stephen Parker and his French-born wife Marie-Luce, the Appels, Berkeley's Simon Karlinsky, the scholar Gennady Barabtarlo and his wife, all saw the twinkle in the eye, enjoyed the sprightly turns of phrase—without giving away anything of herself.* Nina Appel noted that it was almost impossible to prompt Véra into talking about herself. Parker learned to disguise his questions as ones about VN if he expected Véra to answer. Those who got beyond, or around, the wariness found something of the Véra her husband knew. An agent who worked with her in her eighties believed her the most interesting person she

---

* Karlinksy was an especially welcome visitor. In January 1969, he nominated VN for the Nobel Prize, as he would again, an honor VN decidedly coveted. "Even if Borges and I split it, it would still amount to $500,000," he reminded one visitor.

had ever met, echoing a comment Alison Bishop had made about the two Nabokovs at Cornell. Jane Rowohlt perhaps put it best. The Montreux rooms were declared a nonsmoking zone; Jane was a committed smoker. It hardly mattered, she shrugged. One smoked when one tended to be bored, and with Véra one was never bored.

These, though, were friendships as bibliography. A few relationships reached beyond art. Véra and Sonia grew closer in middle age than they had been previously, although they remained capable of the full-fledged blow-out, the kind that could send one party hurtling out of a hotel in a self-righteous huff. After Sonia moved from New York to Geneva in mid-1968 the sisters managed to see each other with some regularity. Together they had arranged for Véra to fly to New York earlier in the year so as to relocate the ailing and disoriented Anna Feigin to Montreux. Sonia was happy to assist with the move, but the responsibility for Feigin's care necessarily fell to her older sister; Anna and Sonia feuded on alternate days of the week and had been on and off speaking terms for years. Feigin thought Sonia selfish in the extreme; she trusted only Véra. By the time Véra arrived in New York in March 1968, the seventy-eight-year-old Feigin had begun to talk of traveling to Switzerland by taxi. She was frail but combative. Véra remained calm, in a gray suit and pearls, throughout the ordeal. She installed her cousin with a *dame de compagnie* in a Montreux apartment, visiting her every other day. The arrangement placed new burdens on her time. She resorted even to a form letter, attributing her silence to her cousin's deteriorating health.

She spent considerably less time with Lena, whose manner she found irritating even at nearly a thousand miles' distance. She disapproved of the emotional tone of her sister's letters; of Lena's relationship with her son, Michaël; of her vaunted sense of self-importance. The nondiscussion of the matter that lay between them continued. After Lena alluded to the religion issue in 1966, Véra suggested crisply that they agree to disagree: "It is no use raking up that past of which you write. You know what I think about it, and you have explained your own viewpoint. So why call up memories which are distracting to you?" Lena did not endear herself to her sister by warning— she would have known this numbered among Véra's greatest fears—that she was letting herself be duped in Sweden, where Vladimir's books were execrably translated. She was evidently as put off by her sister's not having consulted her on the subject as Véra must have been by the reprimand. It says a good deal that Véra rarely appealed to Lena, a translator among a tight-knit community of such experts—she knew, and boasted of knowing, most of

Sweden's foremost translators—for so much as a newspaper clipping. In her own way each sister made a play for sounding superior. Véra's manner of doing so was to sound detached, serene, utterly unflappable.

Relations deteriorated in early 1967, when Lena described her first grandson, born nine weeks premature and three months after his parents' marriage, in less than tender terms. Véra found her choice of words offensive and indignantly said as much, adding: "And thank God that we live at a time when at least some of the medieval prejudices have been abandoned—who cares whether a child was born outside of wedlock insofar as the child itself is concerned?!" By midyear the two had moved the battle to the arena where they clearly felt most comfortable. " '*Avorton*' is a French word to designate any animal, plant, or person that appears prematurely. The word is derogatory only when it is applied outside of this definition or to an adult. As I have this poor child with me one week out of two, I know what I'm talking about," Lena insisted, describing her two-pound, fourteen-ounce grandson. (He proved entirely healthy.) She concluded with an exasperated: "You don't understand a thing!" After she saw photos, Véra backed down, though not without a parting shot: "Of course, I did not understand anything—but then you never explained anything in an intelligible way." She professed shock to hear in 1968 that Lena, who was not well-off, had neither known of nor applied for reparations payments. Her own case had been successfully resolved, Goldenweiser having secured monthly payments for his client that exceeded even his expectations. The amount seemed like a princely sum to Lena. Even in her ostensibly helpful letter Véra managed to include a little gibe about Jews and non-Jews; she could not forgive her sister for hiding behind a faith not her own. Nor did she forgive her when, inadvertently or not, Lena managed to insult Goldenweiser, with whom Véra put her in touch to file a claim.*

She was more at ease with a few well-chosen friends. She met Vivian Crespi in 1964 through James Mason, Kubrick's Humbert Humbert and a Swiss neighbor. Crespi endeared herself immediately to Véra, who found the new divorcée's personal life a source of continual fascination and who took a maternal interest in it. Worldly, effervescent, politically conservative, irreverent, Crespi more than held up her end of the deal. She proved the kind of woman whom Vladimir could interview over dinner about her views on incest. "What would you think of a relationship between a brother and sister?"

---

* Vladimir had a less-favorite sister too. He supported but had no interest in meeting his sister Olga, who was living in Prague during these years, and whom he had not seen since 1937.

he inquired. "Well, I've never *had* a brother," replied Crespi.* She could testify to Véra's gift for friendship—Véra counseled her on her liaison with Mason, whose exit she applauded, as she did the entrance of Luigi Barzini; Véra confided in Crespi her concerns about Dmitri's future—but felt too that Véra had little need for others. Crespi's ribald humor was much appreciated; Véra howled when she explained the allure of a mutual friend's new wife, a retired contortionist. Véra also admired her younger friend's taste in clothing and recruited her for visits to a Vevey dress shop, where she bought much of her understated wardrobe. She had a limited tolerance for such endeavors, and told Crespi it bored her terribly to go alone. Doubtless it did, but the vivacious Crespi thought she was asked to go for an additional reason: She found Véra painfully, cripplingly shy. With Crespi Véra was as much at her ease as she ever allowed Mrs. Nabokov to be. Informed that Mason's daughter was dating a member of the band Blood, Sweat and Tears, she quipped, "I trust it isn't the second." Asked her opinion of a portrait Mason had painted, she offered, "It looks just like that little creature in *Mad* magazine."

Crespi was somewhere at, or near, the ambiguous center of the Nabokovs' limited social life in Montreux. "I could always get them out for Americans," she noted, and she did. She had less luck coaxing them farther afield. Come to Rome, she insisted in 1973, shortly after the Paul Getty III kidnapping and its gruesome ransom note. "No thank you," Véra demurred, "Vladimir prefers to keep his ears." It was Crespi whom the Nabokovs included in their evenings when Saul Steinberg or George Weidenfeld visited; it was she who introduced the couple to William Buckley, one of the few Americans of her acquaintance whom Véra found politically enlightened. They did not often consent to an outing, nor were they easy to invite.† Topazia Markevitch, the Italian ex-wife of the Russian conductor, discovered as much when she entertained the Nabokovs one evening in her delightful Vevey apartment. She racked her brains for someone else to invite with the couple, whom she had met soon after their move to Montreux. It must be

---

* Véra had been at the other side of the table. "What did you say to Vladimir last night?" she phoned Crespi to ask the next morning; suddenly her husband was writing in a white heat. While composing *Ada* Vladimir examined Crespi's teenaged son about his sexual activities. A budding poet, Marcantonio Crespi quizzed him back about verse and meter; Vladimir kept returning the conversation to the lower ground. He had to do his research somewhere.
† It fell to Crespi to tell Nabokov that Charlie Chaplin should like to meet him, an invitation VN had no trouble resisting. "A man of Chaplin's talent and intelligence can not be excused his politics," he thundered. The two comedians, great admirers of each other's work, neighbors for years, never met. Nor did the Nabokovs meet another neighbor on the hill, Noël Coward, who had claimed never to have been able to finish *Lolita*.

someone intelligent, it must be someone who knew how to read, it must be someone who was anticommunist. She settled on the Swiss writer Denis de Rougemont, whom she briefed before the meal. He was not to speak of left-wing causes, half seriously or otherwise. The dinner began swimmingly, de Rougemont following his instructions to the letter. Midway through the meal he made an anti-Zionist comment. The air turned arctic. Markevitch tried her best but could do nothing to salvage the evening.

Crespi came to know the frustrations of Véra's life. She bestowed on the Nabokovs a Cyrillic Scrabble board she had bought in New York, on which the couple fought well-matched duels in the evening. (Véra's game was often ingenious, strong rather than truly great. Vladimir focused more on the brilliant *trouvaille*.) It counted among the best gifts they had ever received, but was a source of some aggravation as well: "You've been a bad influence," Véra informed Crespi with a chuckle. "Vladimir is cheating. He's inventing words I know don't exist." It was probably the first time she had complained of this particular phenomeon, on which she had after all staked her life. Buckley observed that Vladimir preferred for Véra to put the brakes on; the responsibilities extended well beyond keeping the Scrabble scores in check. In his diary, Nabokov kept careful track of his liquor consumption, which he rationed, as his weight was of some concern. Véra's concerns were different. As early as the 1950s, when the jug of Tokay lounged on the kitchen counters in Ithaca, she had warned that alcohol destroys brain cells. Mary McCarthy had found her positively prohibitionist. Occasional skirmishes resulted. Horst Tappé arrived to photograph Nabokov in 1971, at about two in the afternoon. His subject kept him waiting. Véra asked the photographer to make himself comfortable and offered him a glass of wine; the bottle was nowhere to be found. "The wine is gone," announced Vladimir on his return. But what had happened to it? "I dropped it off the balcony," he replied, as if doing so were the most natural thing in the world.

Montreux made of them fervent Americans. Véra lost no time in canceling the 1967 Chamonix vacation to protest France's military withdrawal from NATO. She was perfectly happy to explain her disgust with de Gaulle's belligerence toward the United States to the Hotel Savoy, which forwarded the letter to *Le Figaro,* where it appeared in print. She did the same to the real estate agent who had located a Corsican property for the Nabokovs and who was informed in late 1967 that they were doing everything in their power to boycott French goods. "We simply *could* not buy anything in France or from France at this time!" she explained forcefully. Their patriotism increased the distance between the Nabokovs and many of their Stateside friends. "We are not with you on Viet Nam," Véra alerted the Bishops, who were of the opinion that the U.S. government was acting abominably. "Perhaps living abroad gives us a different perspective. Nothing could be worse than this war, but we honestly do not see what the President or any one else can do about it. Leave the country and the entire Far East to the Communists? People do not want to see that it is Russia that is fighting against the U.S. in Viet Nam. Without Russia the North would have been beaten ages ago. This is a life and death struggle against Communism, not just a little war somewhere at the other end of the world, alas." It had long been her conviction that Communists responded only to extreme measures; many of the Americans who visited Montreux—scholars, editors, and journalists, they were almost by definition liberals—felt her to be of the Bomb Hanoi school. (These were what Vladimir referred to as "dumb intellectuals," of which he counted more than a few among their friends.) The Nabokovs were delighted by the Russian-Chinese border skirmish in 1969; they would heartily approve a war between those two countries. They were all for Nixon in 1972, convinced that McGovern was "an irresponsible demagogue," in a position to do infinite harm to America. Nothing quite incited Véra's wrath as much as the student demonstrations. Most of her anger on this front she directed to Elena Levin who, in Cambridge, was in the thick of events, and whom Véra must have assumed to be of a similar mind; Elena too knew that the Russian Revolution had rumbled first through the universities. Véra was outraged that the Harvard faculty had not been more severe with its protestors. She was all for civil rights, but "hooligans" should be arrested—for good. The 1969 Cornell commencement exercises were led by Morris Bishop, who used his gold-and-silver mace to whack a disrupting protestor in the ribs and off the platform.* From the sidelines, three thousand miles away, Véra cheered.

She attributed most of America's troubles to an ill-advised liberalism. "Oh, dear Lena, if only there had never been that 'progressive education' fad; if only they hadn't laughed off the Communist plot to destroy the American educational system and pervert the younger generation, but taken it seriously when they should have; if only Timothy O'Leary had been prosecuted as a criminal," read one 1969 Levin dispatch. Were the letter not in Russian—and in prerevolutionary orthography—its sentiments would have read very dif-

---

* To the press Bishop explained that the mace was a medieval weapon: "Richard the Lion Hearted always had one by his side. I merely put it to the use for which it was intended." To his daughter he sounded a more poignant note regarding his heroics: "I thus achieved in a few seconds more fame than I have earned in 77 years of sober academic output."

ferently. Vladimir had just declined an invitation to return to Cornell; the
day after doing so the newspaper had arrived with a photo of student protestors leaving the Ithaca administration building, where they had pressed their
demands at gunpoint. "We didn't regret that we declined," Véra reported.
She was immovable in these convictions, not that she often encountered anyone willing to argue with her. Jason Epstein might have; his *New York
Review* pieces had so offended the Nabokovs that they had removed him
from his post as literary trustee.* "We are the senior authorities in judging
the Communist utopia, and nobody is going to tell us anything new," Véra
swore to Elena Levin, who all the same remained a more open-minded
senior authority. Vladimir too was more subtle in his thinking, but did not
entirely live in this world. He routinely asked after the fuss over Wintergate.
What had "that Mr. Watergate fellow" done to get himself into such a
scrape? As Arthur Schlesinger Jr. saw it, VN simply did not have a political
mind at all.

Véra's politics continued as ever to color her literary judgments. She responded as would be expected to a bestselling work by a violent black Marx-
ist radical, otherwise known as *Soul on Ice*: "When I see a cute young woman,
a tourist from America, dressed in the latest fashion, sitting on the train and
reading (with awe) that rapist Cleaver's book, I feel compelled to ask her
whether she is capable of thinking, capable of thinking at all, and why she is
reading that garbage." Her historical judgments hewed to the same unbend-
ing principles. Even the wise Simon Karlinsky could not make her see the
merits of Marina Tsvetaeva, one of the greatest poets of the emigration, and
for that matter, a woman who had combined marriage, motherhood, and a
literary career. Tsvetaeva had been no worse off than the rest of the émigrés
and had been as well published as anyone, argued Véra, speaking for both
Nabokovs. "In her letters there is a constantly recurring whining note which
is not exactly endearing," she added. More importantly, Tsvetaeva was an
artist, and therefore perceptive. How could she not have known, in the
cramped quarters in which they lived, that her husband was a Soviet agent?
Later Véra cited a more serious offense, when Karlinsky himself began to
sound a little tired of the poet:

> Some day, I hope, you will agree with me that she maltreats the Russian
> language by knocking the words on their little heads with a hammer
> until she can make them stay in, quite oblivious of their comfort, no

---

* He was replaced by William McGuire, about whose politics the couple fortunately never inquired. They
were indistinguishable from Epstein's, but McGuire did not broadcast his position in a national journal.

matter that here and there a damaged leg or arm may stick out. In Russian poetry Pushkin's way to treat the words is the kindest, no wonder they sound so happy in his verse.

Neither Nabokov would brook any criticism of America. "The Germans are usually quite right when they hate Germany," Véra proclaimed unapologetically, persuaded history was on her side. "The Americans are *never* right when they hate America." It was she who conveyed her husband's disapproval of Gallimard's cover design for their edition of *Pnin,* which stood Professor Pnin on an American flag:

> Without being enthusiastic about it [the design], VN does not object to it except for one detail: Being an American he objects to the Stars and Stripes being used as a floor covering or a road surfacing material. He simply finds it in bad taste after all the American-flag-burning and other insults inflicted on the flag by the so-called "protesters."

The America Véra so valiantly defended—from their Montreux perch both Nabokovs held it to be the center of the world—had about as much relation to the real America as it did to the America of *Ada,* in which there is a nonstop Geneva–Phoenix flight. Reports of racial unrest from Anna Feigin, from Sonia, from other correspondents, summoned up a too-familiar set of images. As the Nabokovs saw it, New York was burning. They were afraid to return, claiming that it was too dangerous to do so in the late 1960s. "I keep receiving warnings from friends that under no circumstances should one venture out in the evening alone," Véra wrote Crespi, who had reported that New York was no longer what it once had been. They remained intently focused on America, plying emissaries for the latest news, the latest scuttlebutt—Was Jason Epstein corrupting American youth? Was the eminent scholar who had visited earlier gay? What was Mr. Pynch-ON like? Was it true about Joyce Maynard and J. D. Salinger?—and yet wholly out of touch with the country, separated by a set of preconceptions formed decades earlier.

In Switzerland Véra's sense of propriety functioned as a final moat, after politics and geography. (In the contest with politics, propriety won out. Mason bestowed upon Nabokov a red, white, and blue tie, featuring Uncle Sam. On the inside it said "Fuck Communism." Véra was not amused.) When Minton visited with the woman who became his second wife, Véra arranged for separate bedrooms for the two at opposite ends of the hotel. She nearly fainted when Irving Lazar, on a Montreux visit, embraced her warmly, addressing her by her first name; the two had corresponded for more than a decade. She was similarly long in recovering from the effrontery of the unknown woman in the hotel elevator who had wished her a good evening. She expected people to know their stations and admired those who did. She made exceptions for those whose devotion to her husband's work was so great it presumably clouded their grasp of etiquette or their good taste. "I don't like your shirts at all," she advised a biographer, whose style was less formal than hers. He only guffawed. Véra seemed pleased by his nonreaction. She had herself no gift for, nor any inclination toward, ingratiating herself.

Nor had she any expectation of being understood. She insisted she had no part in the story, no stake in how it was told. This was more a diminished expectation of the world than of herself. She knew well that the transparency was a pose, that some of the most arresting canvases ever painted, seemingly crystalline worlds, are rich in deceptions. Using the husband for whom she was meant to be fronting as cover, she engaged in her own game of hide-and-seek. This did not mean she was not there. There is no swelling of pride when Véra noted that her husband would like a particular volume—after the move to Switzerland, this was true of every volume—to carry, as a dedication, "To Véra." But as Dmitri understood, those two words meant the world to her. She banished herself with the resolve of someone who knows how very present she is. "The more you leave me out, Mr. Boyd, the closer to truth you will be," Véra insisted. In the course of the same conversation, she conceded, despite Boyd's taste in shirts and without deigning to elaborate, "I am always there, but well hidden."

❊ 10 ❊

THE LAND
BEYOND THE VEIL

He lies like an eyewitness. —Russian saying

1

As her seventieth birthday approached, Véra had the distinct sense that time—the medium outside of which she allowed her husband to live, so that he might tame, cheat, abolish, deny it in his art—had suddenly accelerated. There were so many new editions of his work that she had lost track; she could not answer the question when Lazar asked if *Despair* had been published in paperback. Two days after Christmas, 1971, she mailed Andrew Field her corrections to the bibliography he was preparing: "I apologize for this disjointed bit of work. I cannot convey to you the atmosphere of incessant interruptions in which I have to work, the condition of my desk flooded with unanswered and half-answered mail etc. etc." All her holiday's were now busman's holidays. It was fortunate that, as Dmitri observed, "her attention span for pure amusement was quite limited." The industrious Goldenweiser professed envy of her "phenomenal capacity for work." Nabokov said that his pencils outlasted his erasers but Véra's were sorry little two-inch stubs, worn down to the ferrules, keeling under the weight of their add-on erasers.

Primarily because of Anna Feigin, the two Nabokovs occasionally traveled separately from Montreux, Vladimir decamping first, Véra following once she had seen to her cousin's needs. In early April 1970, just before their forty-fifth wedding anniversary, they were separated for a week. Vladimir traveled alone to Taormina, where Véra was to meet him. He was in search of butterflies, sun, and salvation from American tourists, who considered him their property. From Sicily he picked up the correspondence where he had left it years earlier, writing his wife daily, reprising his themes of the 1920s. Had she found the note he had slipped into her suitcase? He had found their restaurant, the one they remembered with such affection from the 1960 visit. He was utterly in love with Taormina, and had nearly bought a villa ("8 rooms, 3 baths, 20 olives"). He was bored without her. He could not resist the old temptation of coining a new endearment with each letter. She was his "golden-voiced angel." A *New York Times* reporter called about a visit; Vladimir put him off until Véra's arrival, when the three could explore the local lepidoptera together. He had bought her a present. He held tenaciously to her being with him on their anniversary, a sentiment he expressed in a trilingual sentence, days before her arrival on the fifteenth, when her favorite orchids were delivered to her room. He was sorry to see the correspondence end. By August he was composing love poems to her again.

Nineteen-seventy was the year of translating mercilessly. It began with Vladimir reworking Michael Glenny's version of *Mary*, Nabokov's first novel, to which he did not feel Glenny had done justice. (For his part, Glenny concluded the author to be "some kind of lexicomaniac.") The couple spent Easter week in Rome, during which time Véra was in constant touch with Mondadori, who had brought out and hastily withdrawn an Italian *Ada*. If the Milan-based editor would consent to travel to Rome with the book's translator and a fat English-Italian dictionary, the Nabokovs would be willing to consecrate several evenings to all three of them, Véra offered, in French. She took careful notes of the phone conversation that followed this proposal. The Mondadori editor assured her that "it did not matter for Italian readers if [the] translation has some howlers." Véra rejoined that it did for the author. Although there was no further contact with Mondadori, the Nabokovs occasionally attempted to rework the text themselves over the summer. They made minimal progress, as Vladimir threw up his arms in despair each time they sat down to check a passage or two. (As well he should have: Five years later the original defective translation was back on sale in Italy.) At the end of the year he noted in his diary that Dmitri had reworked some two-thirds of *Glory* into English. "The rest heroically translated by Véra, the entire thing corrected by me, an excruciating task that took 3 months to complete with a few interruptions. Last Russian novel, thank God," he added, a sentiment his wife could only have shared. Not that that was her salvation. Two years later she was badgering Mondadori again, this time on *Glory*'s account. She had discovered thirteen serious errors in the first twelve pages of the Italian edition. These tribulations led VN to an inevitable conclusion: "All writers should write in English."

Not unrelatedly, 1970 proved something of a banner year financially. The taxes about which Vladimir carped so vocally were considerable; he pronounced them "shocking." Véra assumed all blame for the situation. She had made provisions for only about half the amount her husband actually earned that year. "Lack of imagination on my part," she quipped in a letter to Paul, Weiss, inquiring as to how, if at all, the damage might be minimized after the fact. She proposed a rather novel interpretation of foreign rights income, one, alas, that counsel was not convinced would be acceptable to the IRS. There was nothing whatever lacking in her imagination. She was moreover befuddled by Putnam's accounting. "I wonder what other writers (or their wives) do to keep these things in order. I feel sadly incompetent," she lamented.

The paper threatened to bury her—the folders and files cluttered most surfaces of the Montreux apartment, where the overflow of office files occupied her bedroom—but the intrusions she most resisted, or most attempted to resist, were the human ones. In 1970 she counseled Dmitri that a crucial lesson in life was learning to push people away without offending them. There were simply not enough hours in a day. She had additional reason to have resisted the callers; no one who knew her well thought her extroverted. In the spring of 1970, after a trip to London, McGraw-Hill's executive editor and director of subsidiary rights, Beverly Jane Loo, stopped in at the Montreux Palace. A poised and tough negotiator, Loo was not known in the industry as a shrinking violet. All the same she changed her clothes four times before the initial meeting, settling finally on a classic glen plaid suit, in which she paced nervously by the lake. In the lounge a half hour before the appointed time she found Vladimir, who greeted her warmly; he may have been told she was Chinese, as he recognized her immediately. Explained Nabokov to the woman with whom his wife had been corresponding and speaking regularly: "Oh Miss Loo, it's so good to meet you at last. I'm sorry Véra isn't here, but she's very nervous about meeting you. She thinks of you as *la Formidable*." When Véra came down she ordered a whiskey, neat. Loo was stunned, and said as much. "I thought all Americans drank whiskey," Véra explained quietly. The two *formidables* became fast friends, joking later about their mutual apprehension. Véra had already requested that all McGraw-Hill paper—she had been writing various members of the firm as often as four letters a day—be channeled through Loo, who took to visiting once or twice a year, and who became one of the two New York publishers to whom Véra signed her letters with love.

Beverly Loo kept a small menagerie in and near New York: a dog, four cats, and a horse. Véra displayed photos of them in the Montreux apartment and sent warm regards to them in her letters. Asked why the Nabokovs did not keep an animal, Vladimir told Loo he was unwilling to share Véra with anyone, even a pet. (Given that response and the couple's general demeanor, she was surprised to discover they had a son.) Loo lunched one day with the Nabokovs in early 1976, after which the three moved to the salon for coffee. Between courses, Vladimir excused himself. He was not feeling well, and promised to rejoin the two women in the lounge. He had brought down his wooden box of notecards to impress his progress on their visitor, lunching with the cards on the floor beside his chair. Uncharacteristically, he forgot the box when he left the table. The maître d' came running into the lounge to return the cards to Véra, who smiled at Loo. "Let's play a little joke," she suggested, wedging the box behind the visitor on her plush armchair. By the time Vladimir returned the cards had vanished. "Oh, VN, you took the box upstairs with you, didn't you?" Véra asked off-handedly. Her husband flashed red and and began to sputter. He seemed on the verge of a heart attack. The panic was contagious; Véra and Loo scrambled to produce the box, waving it excitedly in the air. The genial conjurer rebounded splendidly. Slyly he assured his wife, "I was just trying to scare you."

The select few for whom she might have cooked scrambled eggs in the apartment—the other half of the repertoire remained a family secret—came too seldom. She missed neither America nor campus life, but did long for a few friends. Véra protested regularly that she did not hear from Elena Levin as often as she would like, sounding slightly hurt. "I don't know if you ever remember us but we do remember you—affectionately," she wrote on her 1970 Christmas card. Wistfulness crept into her voice as the decade wore on, not enough to move her to revise her opinion of Solzhenitsyn, whom Elena admired and Véra dismissed as third-rate, but enough to make clear her affection: "How sadly we regret that you do not come to Europe; or if you do, never to Switzerland; or, if you do, never to Montreux! Please *do* do it!" she implored the Levins. More stunning was the concession she made in early 1975 to Barbara Epstein, who had written from *The New York Review* to see if she might tempt Vladimir into a review. "We still have not given up hope that at some time in a not too distant future we may have the pleasure of seeing you and Jason again. We shall not discuss Viet Nam or anything political, and shall have a wonderful time together," Véra promised, having delivered the news that her husband was far too busy to consider Epstein's assignment. She was at once deeply concerned, and deeply serious, about friends' children. Were they happy? Were they in love? Were they in good schools, i.e., those with old-fashioned curricula?

The Véra of the tender emotions did not for a minute disagree with the assertion that she was charged with representing her husband's anger. The letters to Ergaz are strung together with protests that VN was distressed, furious, enervated, perplexed, resentful, offended, incensed. *"Le doux M. Nabokov' n'est pas toujours doux,"* Véra warned the French agent on one occasion. If she first performed a little jig of do-I-have-to-Volodya? it has been lost to posterity. It seems unlikely; she was generally as angry as he, often more so. As early as January 1971, Andrew Field began to notice resistance on the part of his subject; he and Vladimir exchanged no unpleasant words. That dialogue was entrusted to Véra, "acting as plenipotentiary," in a phone call between hotels. A good year later she sounded still a reluctant (or naïve) plenipotentiary. Surely Field could not resent her for having typed what her husband dictated.

There was of course a certain disingenuousness in the don't-shoot-the-messenger-missives. Her husband's words were immortal, hers were to be thrown away. "I don't think about my letters, write them anyhow and they are not fit to be quoted. Incidental information that I impart is not meant to be treated as anything absolute. Not fit for footnotes," she cautioned Boyd. When her words were taken at face value, when she was cited, she availed herself of a ferocious instinct to disavow. No one, it seemed, could get his facts straight. In 1971 she denied every remark ascribed to her in a scrupulously researched *New York Times Magazine* piece. She engaged in a veritable cult of denials. She swore up and down that she had never said a single word Boyd quoted her as saying; she abjured all marginal notes, even those in her firm hand; she went so far as to deny to a reporter that she was proud of Dmitri. Appel watched her renounce statements he had heard with his own ears. She asked him to delete a comment she had made about Gina Lollobrigida from his manuscript of *Nabokov's Dark Cinema*: "I am sorry to bother you with this but I really hate to appear to be insulting poor Lollobrigida and I never, ever, ever made the remark ascribed to me!"* The objections were all the more heated the closer they approached truth, as Boyd noted when Véra attempted to wriggle free of Zina Mertz. She attempted to refute the entire Irina Guadanini affair and had gone so far as drafting a letter to that effect— until, wrangling with his conscience, Boyd broke the news that the love letters had survived. She remained elusive even after having admitted to him

---

* She had asserted that the actress looked "shopworn." And on the very outside chance that she had not said as much to Appel, it should be noted that she had used the same adjective in describing Lollobrigida in a letter to the Bishops.

that she was well hidden. He felt she would have denied she was the "you" of *Speak, Memory* if she could have.

At Cornell the Polish princess who had accompanied Nabokov to class had been silent. In Montreux the woman over whose patronymic her Russian correspondents routinely stumbled was anything but.* This only allowed greater room for misunderstanding. She went blithely on her way, letting the counterfeit versions of Véra Nabokov pile up while the original remained unknown. She seemed to feel she could will someone to believe she cast no shadow, or, if he noticed an angular black shape trailing behind her, that that shadow was not hers. She remained a bafflement to the biographer. Having given him next to nothing to go on, she rebuked Boyd, sounding a little wounded, that she "was surprised by my reflection in your mirror." Nabokov wanted what every writer wants: to exist solely in his prose. This was to be their mutual fate. It was Vladimir's blessing, Véra's misfortune. In any language her letters were terse; they arrived in place of her husband's; she haggled over money where he did not; her eyes never left her husband in interviews; she would not deign to explain herself. In short she was a shrewish, controlling, dragon lady, and she was holding her husband hostage in Montreux. The biographer abhors a vacuum.

For many years she was unaware of the ill will. It took her some time to see that a shy, overworked, morbidly private, highly principled woman could appear prickly, humorless, aloof, and instransigent. For the most part she did not care. She laughed with Sonia at the assertion that she was "sharp-witted." Doubtless this read to her as a compliment. Less flattering was the description Edmund Wilson provided in *Upstate,* published in 1971. Before the book of recollections was published Wilson had written Vladimir to say that he trusted the account would do nothing to "again impair our personal relations." Since the two had been feuding publicly since 1965 over matters Vladimir considered as much personal as professional, it is unlikely anything could have done so.† Véra's charms had always been lost on Wilson, who now

---

* The fault was not entirely theirs. Because Véra signed always "Mrs. Vladimir Nabokov," she reduced her Russian correspondents to asking awkwardly after her patronymic, which she rarely supplied. As a result she often became "Véra Pavlovna" or "Véra Nikolaevna."

† The relationship had always balanced on provocation and finally foundered on *Eugene Onegin,* the translation of which Wilson denounced—as Nabokov knew he would—in the July 1965 *New York Review of Books.* More amazing than its demise is the fact that the friendship survived as long as it did. Wilson never read *The Gift,* was disappointed in *Bend Sinister,* did not like *Despair* as much as *Laughter,* which he did not like as much as *Sebastian Knight,* cared even less for *Lolita,* could not finish *Ada.* The first of his own books he had inscribed for his Russian friend had been *To the Finland Station,* which he hoped would persuade Vladimir to reconsider his opinion of Lenin. A faculty wife who stopped by the Nabokovs, on the happy weekend immortalized in *Upstate,* felt the two men were in the process of tearing each other limb from limb.

published an uncharitable account of his May 1957 Ithaca visit, in which she appeared prudish, disobliging, belligerent, blinded in her devotion to her own live-in juggernaut. She knew that she was not one of Wilson's favorites but was taken aback all the same to find herself portrayed so unflatteringly. Each Nabokov wrote off the attack as fiction, in his and her own way. Vladimir bellowed that Wilson's words verged perilously on libel, that the Nabokov of which his former friend wrote was but a fiction. Among much else, his wife's begrudging special attention to anyone other than himself was a matter of pure invention. Véra shrugged the matter off, or at least did a year later, when there was no longer any Edmund Wilson left with whom to spar. "For my part I did not mind at all the silly things he ascribed to me in UPSTATE," she wrote Elena Levin. "I was not very close to him. He could not have any idea of my feelings or moods, and never showed particular interest, so that those petty insinuations were like so many signals from a distant and alien planet. There were many things I valued highly in him, and V. was genuinely fond of him. He was nonetheless angry at the silly attack on me." Her composure would be sorely tried over the next years. She knew as well as anyone that there are stock characters in literature, and that writers' wives—and writers' widows—are among them.

2

After forty-eight years of marriage, Countess Tolstoy drafted a press release from Yasnaya Polyana announcing that having devoted her entire life to him, she was leaving her husband. (She did not get far. Several months later it was Tolstoy who fled; the story of his defection consumed the front pages.) The same year in her marriage found Véra Nabokov tangling with Andrew Field on her husband's behalf. Field's manuscript arrived in mid-January 1973, poor timing in the extreme. On January 6, the day after Véra's seventy-first birthday, Anna Feigin had died of a sudden heart attack in the Montreux hospital. She was legally blind and practically deaf; the Nabokovs had been caring for her for exactly five years. The emotional loss was rivaled by physical pain for Véra, who was suffering from two slipped discs. She was uncharacteristically vocal about the discomfort, which had plagued her since Christmas and would continue through February, admitting that the French phrase "*deux vertèbres écrasés*" much better conveyed the torture of her condition than the English. (The Nabokovs' illnesses were by and large occupational hazards. Vladimir twisted his thumb picking up a dictionary; he pulled out his back lifting a case of books—"second-rate books," more insultingly. Véra's eyes, wrists, right arm, and back caused her the most trouble. Cribbing from his own lectures, VN held in the 1972 *Transparent Things* that the spine is "the true reader's main organ"; it was almost too appropriate that Véra's should crumple.) The discomfort was such that she was barely able to fold herself into a taxi—with Anna Feigin's *dame de compagnie,* in imitation ermine, and with Vladimir carrying Véra's handbag—to attend to the formalities. Véra was too ill to attend the cremation, at which Sonia joined Vladimir. The loss of the relative with whom the family's fortunes and misfortunes had been so much entwined for nearly a half century was deeply unsettling. Vladimir woke from his sleep the night before the funeral in an "angry panic," having dreamed that he and Véra had been separated at an Italian railway station. He had lost her to a departing train. Two nights later he sat up in bed and saw a set of guillotines in the shadows under the window in his room. He had just enough time before the image faded to wonder if Véra was being "prepared" next door.

Field's manuscript arrived the following week. The original plan had been for Véra to read through the pages first, but she returned from a hospital stay only at the end of January, by which time Vladimir had already begun his review. He pronounced the manuscript "cretinous." In discomfort of all kinds, Véra annotated the chronicle as she read; between them the Nabokovs produced 181 pages of comments on a 670-page manuscript, a process that consumed the better part of a month. Husband and wife submitted their general comments to the biographer in separate letters, along with a long list of matters of fact to which they expected him to attend. Véra's six-page missive went out on March 10. She was primarily disturbed by the flattened image of her husband she found on the page:

> You have written a book about a man whose life *is* creation and cannot be separated from its creative substance, and you have managed to write it without ever allowing this creative substance to show. Your subject is as creative when he speaks of last night's dinner as of his new work in progress. After close to 48 years of life together I can swear that I never once heard him utter a cliché or a banality. This is the *central* point of his life, and you have managed to miss it completely.

Vladimir made the same point differently. He existed only on the pre-prepared page. He disassociated himself from the lame words he may—or may not—have let fall in conversation. A monumental ego doing his best to obliterate the self, he had long contested he was a dreary character, of uninteresting habits and few friends. These assertions sounded different when they came from Véra, as did the account of her husband's Parisian affair, which she was assigned to address as well. A husband's infidelity always sounds different in a wife's retelling; this wife essentially shrugged off the events of 1937.

The review made for an arduous and infuriating exercise, and the opening skirmish in what became a protracted war. Ever the obscurantist, Véra did herself no favors. Field attempted to deny she was "a guardian harpy" and was asked to excise the reference. He was not allowed to assert that she loved her husband. (As Vivian Crespi observed of Véra, "She so often put her worst foot forward due to shyness.") At the end of May Field delivered a revised manuscript, which did nothing to pacify Vladimir; by December biographer and subject were off speaking terms. In Véra's view a hideous year's labor had yielded a biography "which teems with factual errors, snide insinuations and blunders that Field refuses to correct after having promised, when starting the job, to publish nothing that VN would not approve." A full-dress legal battle ensued, the manuscript hurtling back and forth between publisher and lawyer over the course of four years. Véra read the final version upon its 1977 publication. By page two she had disputed Field's physical description of her husband, of the sitting room of the apartment, his report on how VN took his coffee. With his statement that the marriage was as intricate and as essential as the work she had no quibble.

She was well enough to travel by the end of May, when the couple set off for Italy, on a vacation that disappeared under a deluge of letters and tax forms. Moreover, the McGraw-Hill contract had been good for five years and was up for renewal; Véra was under some pressure to set her thoughts on the matter to paper. "This still is not the long letter on the McGraw-Hill employment agreement which I am slowly composing but cannot complete because of the ever more baffling monetary situation and also because the complexities and diversity of the details to be tackled leave me breathless whenever I try to look at them all at once. So I write down something different every now and then but know that I still do not have a proper picture of the entire situation," she apologized to the lawyers. She was weary, and gave up ground in the negotiation. Her personal correspondence came to a halt. At the end of the summer she was was moving at a reduced speed, and felt miserably behind in everything. Two weeks later the Rowohlt translators arrived for their last weeklong *Ada* session; they conferred every evening until seven. As ever Véra's concern was for her husband, who was working flat-out on a new novel—it was to be *Look at the Harlequins!*—from which he could not be separated. She was practically beside herself. "I know that he doesn't need to work so much, that it's bad for him, but I don't know what to do," she wrote

Dmitri, adding that she felt herself impossibly beleaguered. Even the letters she most wanted to answer sat sometimes for four months. "We can only plead the appalling pressure of work that obliterated all sense of time," she apologized to Simon Karlinsky, who had attempted to intervene with Field.

Field was the most conspicuous of the shadowgraphers in 1973 but not the only one. In Paris Irina Guadanini continued to pine for Nabokov, as she had since 1937. She kept a file on him nearly until her death in 1976, clipping even Véra's photos from the paper. Less fond of Véra, and more vocal, was Zinaida Shakhovskoy, still licking her wounds from the near-encounter at the Gallimard party in 1959. Shakhovskoy had known the Nabokovs since the early 1930s and was happy to distort most of the intervening years to her own uses. Slowly it came out that the two women had had an unpleasant conversation in Paris, before the war. But in Shakhovskoy's eyes Véra's offenses were legion. First and foremost, the Nabokovs appeared intolerably happy. "It has not been an unhappy marriage then?" an interviewer inquired. Vladimir won no new friends by replying, "That is the understatement of the century." This was clearly a hoax. How could it be otherwise when Véra so effectively shooed visitors away, when her husband had been renowned in the emigration for his amorous conquests? Among their countrymen the trouble went beyond jealousy. The sense was that Véra did not want Russians around. And as Rosalind Wilson, Edmund's daughter, observed of Véra's profile in a certain community: "High-born Russian ladies of Tsarist times are hopeless snobs about Russian ladies they consider bourgeoise." That Véra was celebrated and supreme in Montreux was all the more unpardonable, in the eyes of an ex-aristocrat, for her not having been born so.

She was of course something far more objectionable still. It was Véra who paid the price for Vladimir's exogamy. Old friends still wrote to say that while they were enthralled by *Pnin, Lolita, Ada,* they could not help mourning the fact that Vladimir had parted with Russian prose. Véra was held responsible for his defection, just as, biographically speaking, she often took the bullet meant for her husband. Nabokov's early readers, the old family friends, waited in vain for him to return to his real themes, to their passions, to novels of the heart and not the mind. For him to have escaped all the schools who liked to claim him was one thing, but this was the Homeland calling. Quite obviously, the "foreign influence" was to blame. Shakhovskoy saw Véra where *Pale Fire*'s Kinbote saw Sibyl Shade, reviewing her husband's pages and artfully excising everything connected with his luscious Zemblan theme from the manuscript. If it were not for Véra, Vladimir would be jolly and forthcoming and gregarious and spiritual, and most important, he would write in Russian. That he was by nature discerning in the company he kept, and jealous with his time, and bored by most of the polemics that consumed émigré society, and a champion grudge-holder*— that he *enjoyed* playing cat-and-mouse games with his reader—meant nothing if there was a Jewish wife in the picture. In a word, he had been "Jewified."

In Paris Shakhovskoy made herself an active clearinghouse for all the noxious comments occasioned by envy, linguistic resentment, and unsettled scores. Véra's cardinal sins began with the 1932 morning in Kolbsheim, when she had reminded Shakhovskoy's mother that she did not celebrate a saint's day. She had answered correspondence in her husband's stead; she had suggested her husband write *Lolita* for commercial gain; she had coddled Dmitri; she had sent back her hot consommé in the Palace dining room; she was a mythmaker. Shakhovskoy went so far as to assert that Véra had nearly been her husband's coauthor, acknowledging that in her efforts she had outstripped all the other Russian literary wives. As the pantheon included Sonya Tolstoy and Anna Dostoyevsky, this was some feat. The taller pedestal only made her more vulnerable to attack. Into this mix of admiration and resentment Shakhovskoy stirred a fair, and potent, quantity of prejudice.[†] The charges were the usual ones, this side of well-poisoning: The Nabokovs surrounded themselves with Jews. Véra was tightfisted, and made her husband miserly. They were cunning. They were ambitious. They were rich. Asked if he would ever travel to Russia, Vladimir had replied, to the Soviet Union, no, to Israel, yes. Generally this is the wrong thing to say within earshot of someone who subscribes to racial stereotype.

Even as Vladimir published *Strong Opinions,* a volume of comments and crotchets meant to brick up any chinks in the walls of his fortress reputation, Shakhovskoy began quietly sandblasting away. In 1973 Véra believed Field to be her greatest headache, but that was only because she had not read a Paris-based Russian periodical called *The New Review.* Its June issue carried Shakhovskoy's "The Desert," a short story about the acclaimed writer Walden, a name the Russian reader recognizes immediately as a variation on "Volodya." Celebrated as much for his genius as for his arrogance, Walden has lived for years in temporary accommodations and resides finally in a luxury hotel. His daughter is beautiful and spoiled and an amateur actress, mak-

---

* "One has to know how to loathe," he had declared in 1927. Forty-six years later, Joyce Carol Oates observed of his work: "Nabokov exhibits the most amazing capacity for loathing that one is likely to find in serious literature, a genius for dehumanizing that seems to me more frightening, because it is more intelligent, than Celine's or even than Swift's."
† To an interviewer she responded immediately, on hearing Véra Evseevna's name, "She had many complexes." Asked to elaborate, she did, very clearly, "Of course—she was Jewish."

ing a film in Italy. For years Walden's wife has done everything for him, from ordering his meals in restaurants to arranging his interviews. Now he is to face a young scholar alone for the first time; his wife has died six weeks earlier. Her photo sits on the table in the apartment: "Her blue eyes seemed transparent, her thin lips were compressed, and her thin-nosed sharp face bore the mask of the refined arrogance which she considered the mark of aristocracy specifically because she did not belong to the aristocracy." Walden's thoughts drift back to a great love, a fiancée of his youth, the perfect embodiment of all Slavic ideals, a simple-hearted girl whose father had advised against the marriage. And he is overwhelmed by emotion, by the sudden realization that he has lost his entire empire, that the dead wife, "under the pretense of caring for him and liberating him from his cares," has instead sapped him of his strengths:

> It was only to her that he read his manuscripts, it was her advice alone that he followed. She signed his contracts, corrected the proofs, drove him in an automobile, ordered his clothing and plane tickets, decided whom he might see and whom he should not. She was his cashier and manager and besides her, he had nothing except that which he imagined and about which he wrote.

His works were soulless. He has turned to ice, in person and on the page.* Overwhelmed by his memories of the past, by the realization that once, long before, he had been alive, in love, radiant, surrounded by friends, "he suddenly felt like removing the forcibly placed mask that had already overgrown his actual face." Rising from his chair he defies the pale eyes that stare out at him from their frame. Fearfully but decisively, he relegates the photo to a drawer. He is flooded with relief.

Only when the story found its way into an anthology later did "The Desert" come to Véra's attention. So transparent were its references that a reviewer referred to the "Swiss hotel" in which Walden lives, although the country of his residence appears nowhere in the story. Elena Sikorski read the story in 1978 and lost no time in firing off an outraged letter to its author. She predicted that Véra Evseevna—"like a true aristocrat in spirit, if not in estate"—would not even dignify the Princess's screed with her attention. She underestimated the force of Véra's inattention. She was livid that her sister-in-law had leapt into the fray, all the more so after reading her letter. "Why

---

* Shakhovskoy argued the same point nonfictionally, writing in a 1981 book review that Nabokov's universe had become increasingly glacial, "a frozen desert."

did you find it necessary to defend me?" she reprimanded her. A birthday plant arrived from Elena the same week; petulantly Véra informed her that she would not even thank her for the present. She was less certain of how to proceed in 1979, when Shakhovskoy published a Russian-language biography of Nabokov, a work that offered up a similar effigy of Véra, this time as nonfiction.*

"Without drawing a portrait of Véra Evseevna myself I will say only that virtually all the printed descriptions I have read of her strike me as wholly or seriously wanting," conceded Field, in a line that provoked no marginal eruptions. Véra doubtless agreed, with one possible exception. Throughout the latter half of 1973 Nabokov was at work on the new novel for which McGraw-Hill was waiting impatiently, having scheduled the book for the fall of the following year. He finished *Look at the Harlequins!* in April 1974, days after his seventy-fifth birthday, which the couple celebrated quietly in Montreux with George Weidenfeld. The forced march left both Nabokovs winded. Véra did all she could to put off visitors until May, to allow her husband a chance to catch his breath; the weather was damp, aggravating his neuralgia and the rheumatism in her neck and shoulders. Pressured for a description from which he might draft catalogue copy, editor Fred Hills was informed that the book was a love story, spanning fifty years and several continents. It is in fact another novel masquerading as a memoir, in which a latticework of truth occasionally flashes provocatively from beneath the luscious overgrowth of a thousand fragrant fictions. Vadim Vadimovich is an émigré novelist with whom Vladimir Vladimirovich shares a birthday and a backlist, as well as a taste for soft-boiled eggs. He is thought by his compatriots to be arrogant, unsocial, a traitor to the Russian language. He has great success with women, four of whom consent to marry him. The most succulent bloom of his variegated love life is a prepubescent girl; this time the

---

* The biographical misadventures spawned fictions of their own, one of which serves as an apt counterpoint to "The Desert." An aging Russian émigré novelist celebrated for a scandalous volume, a conflicted biographer, and an alabaster-skinned, white-haired Jewish wife all appeared in 1985 in Roberta Smoodin's *Inventing Ivanov.* The occasional line jumps energetically off the page: "Sometimes when she [the glorious, flirtatious, Garbo-like, white-haired wife-of-writer] looks at her face in the mirror and marvels at her appearance, at the fact that she looks to be not much past forty, when in fact she is over sixty, she thinks that the secret, really, is living entirely for someone else, giving one's life away as one gives coins to mendicants, old clothes to Goodwill." Mrs. Ivanov's husband predeceases her; having had for so long no life separate from his, she wonders how she might possibly proceed. "How," she asks herself, "can a character exist without her novelist?" Véra would face neither this particular dilemma nor Smoodin's novel for a few more years. But Smoodin's conclusions provide a sort of accidental answer to Shakhovskoy's. At the end of the day Mrs. Ivanov walks out from under her husband's shadow—she pauses briefly in the arms of the waiting biographer—and into the real world, which bursts into Technicolor. Death has liberated her from her days of forced servitude.

nymphet is his biological daughter. If ever a book was written to confound a "matter-of-fact, father-of-muck, mucking biograffitist," this is it; Nabokov seems to have set out to prove that no one could travesty his life as elaborately as the man inside that life.

Vladimir had enjoyed pulling Field's leg about his previous wives and now gave full rein to the idea, providing a familiar catalogue of Nabokovian women. Wife number one speaks no Russian, is cruel, and disloyal; wife number two is dismally stupid, prudish, forgetful, and a poor typist. Both die before their time, freakishly sacrificed to the plot. Wife number three is a willing sexual partner but volatile, an inattentive reader, a lover of middle-brow literature, and ultimately faithless. The twenty-seven-year-old whom Vadim Vadimovich meets when he is seventy proves the "ultimate and im-mortal one." She is again "You," as was Véra in *Speak, Memory*. As in that memoir, she appears well before her entrance into the novel. That entrance is made in a fashion far more appropriate to the relationship it calls to mind than was the evening encounter on a Berlin bridge: On an American college campus "You" comes upon Vadim Vadimovich as gravity conspires against him and the folder under his arm spills its contents onto the campus walk-way. She helps him to order his papers. She knows the whole radiant oeuvre, having studied the early work in photocopies. She disapproves of the smell of liquor on his breath. She addresses a sheet of paper as if it were an animate object. She identifies a butterfly, in gorgeous Russian. And she does this nim-bly, animatedly, decisively, all at once, exactly as Véra did everything.

A "turquoise temple-vein" glistens under the late arrival's translucent skin; Vladimir had nuzzled a blue one in a letter to Véra. Zina's is alternately blue or turquoise in *The Gift*. When asked to read a manuscript attentively, You snaps—sounding almost too much like Véra—"I read everything atten-tively." This VV decides retroactively to dedicate his early works in their En-glish editions to You.* He slams the door shut in the face of the prying biographer in precisely the words he used in *Speak, Memory,* when writing of the other "You," the real-life Mrs. Nabokov; we are not to know what she, what he, what the two of them, know. "Your delicate fingers" of *Speak, Mem-ory* are here "your dear delicate hand." Her mask is a fictionally inspired one, a pair of harlequin sunglasses, a *Lolita* legacy Véra had modeled for a pho-tographer in Montreux. In a gratifying case of life imitating art imitating life, You makes faint crosses in the margins of Vadim's manuscript cards, ostensi-bly the book we hold in our hands. What should appear on the manuscript

---

* According to Shakhovskoy's circle, these dedications were added later at Véra's bidding, so as "to present to the world the image of a 'loving couple.' "

pages of *Look at the Harlequins!* but Véra's faint little querying crosses. You turns everything in Vadim's life around, quite an achievement, given his particular spatial disability. It is a peculiar tribute to someone who has deprived the book's author of a language and a life and was holding him hostage in a foreign country.

When pressed to name her favorites among her husband's works, Véra generally cited *Pale Fire.** Whether she felt exposed or not, she allowed herself the rare luxury of an extravagant opinion about *Look at the Harlequins!* Where *Transparent Things* had been "adorable" and *Ada* had been "wonderful," she raved about the new novel, which she positively loved. Vladimir suspected that reviewers of *Harlequins* might fail to share that rapture. On October 1 he composed a Russian poem, dedicated to Véra. His harlequins would be ill appreciated, he predicted, "dubbed jesterly and deceptive." Véra alone would properly grasp and appreciate their—and his—kaleidoscopic virtues. He was right; the book struck many as self-indulgent, as if Nabokov had penned a Festschrift to himself. It seemed a kind of dead-end novel, a work in which a high-octane writer was noisily spinning his wheels. The general sense was that VN should, well, get out more. "To say it plainly, the book strikes me as the production of an imagination paralyzed by vanity," opined Anatole Broyard in the *Times.* Where Shakhovskoy had credited Véra with having stifled her husband, reviewers began to suspect Switzerland. Even some of Nabokov's best readers believed the isolation was taking a toll on the work. They had a point. Where the rest of the oeuvre is involute, the last works feel ingrown, *Harlequins* perhaps most of all. "This is the novel to end all of Nabokov's novels—or at least one hopes so," declared a less-than-smitten Peter Ackroyd in London. He could not have known his statement to be to some measure prophetic.

3

"Here we are at last my darling," Vladimir wrote Véra in Russian, illustrating the dates April 15, 1925, and April 15, 1975, with a splendid, shimmering butterfly. For years he had reminded himself of his wedding date by posting the prepared agenda book sticker *"Aujourd'hui, c'est notre anniversaire de*

---

* The biographical account she would have found most acceptable would doubtless have resembled Mrs. Shade's entry in the *Pale Fire* index: "*Shade, Sybil, S's* wife, *passim.*" She would have shuddered at Véra Evseevna Nabokov's lengthy index entry in Boyd's second volume, which begins with "advises N not to burn *Lolita,*" and ends with "as writer of N's letters."

mariage" in his datebook. (Generally he was sensitive to anniversaries. On May 8, 1963, he had scrawled, "40 years since Véra and I met." On the same day he noted that the tailor was to mark up her fur coat.)* The April date must have been particularly significant to the author of *Ada,* to the writer who has been called America's great artist in nostalgia. Véra was aware of the fifteenth of April as well, although she usually forgot her birthday, which Vladimir very touchingly remembered. The extent to which the life and the work were inseparable in her mind—and the extent to which she was ill equipped to discuss the former—is clear in the only mention she made of that golden date in her correspondence. Just after the anniversary she wrote the Paris lawyer Louba Schirman, who was exploring possibilities of a film adaptation of *Mary.* Véra was pleased with the idea, as she was particularly fond of that novel. "Incidentally, *Mashen'ka* [*Mary*] was written in the first year of our marriage of which we celebrated the 50th anniversary this April 15. That makes the book fifty years old," she extrapolated. It was an odd way of putting it: That also made the marriage fifty years old. She spent at least part of that anniversary at her desk. On April 15, 1975, she replied to an admirer who confessed to having relieved the Schlesinger Library at Radcliffe of their copy of *The Real Life of Sebastian Knight,* having found an inscribed volume in the stacks. She had removed it to her home for better care, replacing the library gem with a fresh copy. On her husband's behalf, a chuckle in her voice, Véra wrote: "Though basically a law-abiding citizen he cannot help condoning your little crime."

The Nabokovs celebrated *Ada's* French publication more elaborately, traveling to Paris at the end of May for four days. It was more of a dislocation than it sounded. Vladimir had taken to joking that a trip to Lausanne had become the equivalent to a trip to Hawaii. Geneva was solar systems away. The effort paid off: *Ada* made an early showing on the French bestseller lists. On their return they set off for the mountain resort of Davos, where, Véra dearly hoped, they might spend a relaxing six weeks, assuming of course—the language of tempests in teapots again—there was no "noisy construction in the proximity or some similar horror." At least on some level she intended to refrain from work. "Rather incredibly," she did not pack her address book. (Despite herself, she was back at her desk within a matter of days. She reconciled herself to sending her mail out registered, in case she mangled the addresses she now plucked from memory.) So many urgent matters competed for her attention that Madame Callier was summoned to join the couple for

---

* The diary was a shared one. VN was not above doctoring the preprinted birthday sticker by one letter so that it read: *"Aujourd'hui c'est l'anniversaire de ton mari."*

two weeks. Vladimir continued energetically to collect mountain butterflies, but he did so now without Véra, who felt she could no longer keep up with him. He was alone, then, late on the cool morning of June 13 when he took a terrible fall, tumbling 150 feet down a steep slope, his net clinging to a fir tree well above him. He was not far from a funicular and waved his arms in the air, to no avail; it was five hours before he was rescued by professionals. A "horrible shock," as Vladimir wrote later, the fall proved the first in a series of painful misadventures.

In mid-October he endured what he considered one of life's greatest tortures: For prostate surgery he submitted to general anesthesia. Véra was her usual unforthcoming self about the procedure, telling her sister-in-law that Vladimir was to undergo a minor operation but refusing to name body parts. She was less cryptic afterward, a small tumor having been removed and found to be benign. The recovery was agonizing, for both Nabokovs; Vladimir's insomnia was more acute than ever, and Véra found him nervous and edgy, easily annoyed. At the end of November her patience showed signs of wearing thin. She felt he would be completely recovered if only he could be persuaded not to work for a few more weeks. But that, she concluded, "is a hopeless undertaking in which I feel completely defeated." Moreover, she was again experiencing trouble with her vision. Rowohlt patiently awaited her approved pages of *Glory*; three weeks after Vladimir's surgery she found that the translation was not giving her any trouble, but that her eyes were, the more so because of the number of matters competing for her attention. Before the year was out Beverly Loo arrived for a short stay. As she had recently had surgery herself, the conversation turned to hospital visits. Vladimir insisted he did not really mind the stays. With a laugh Véra corrected him, reminding him that he did nothing but complain. "Only because you're not there. I would never mind a hospital stay if I could take you, wrap you up in my top pocket and take you with me," he countered, effectively ending the discussion.

She was, and she began to sound, defeated by the tasks at hand. With Loo she investigated the possibility of appointing an agent for several foreign countries, an enormous concession on her part, given her pride in having avoided representation. The returns were not spectacular, she advised Loo, but the paperwork was. Similarly she complied with some unusual demands for documentation made by the IRS, but had to admit to the New York accountant: "As for me, I am just getting too old to spend days rummaging in trunks and bookcases, etc." At the same time she learned that Marie Schebeko—whom she had been writing several times a week for over a

decade—planned to retire. Schebeko offered to suggest a possible replacement, but did not think it necessary: "I have always thought—and proclaimed—that you are a far better agent than any I know." At the time the
compliment probably did not go far. The demons with which she battled
continued to be the McGraw-Hill accounting statements; the political convictions of those eager to adapt her husband's novels (Rainer Fassbinder had
proposed a film of *Despair,* but the Nabokovs had heard he was anti-Semitic);
the perceived transgressions of Andrew Field, a dialogue still conducted primarily, and very expensively, through lawyers.

   Of grave concern too was Dmitri, whose finances Véra continued to
manage. ("I am sorry that my son is such an elusive individual!" she apologized to their mutual accountant, evidently not realizing how easy she made
it to be elusive.) Dmitri was again happily single, having parted ways with a
girlfriend of whom Véra had been particularly fond. As allergic as she was to
drama, she appealed to him solemnly to consider the consequences of his decision. She worried that he might find himself alone in the world in some not
too distant future. He would soon be forty-two, she reminded him; he was
laying the ground for his own unhappiness. She implored him to turn his
imagination to this essential matter. The letter reads like an advertisement
for the safe harbor that marriage can provide and which it clearly had, for
Véra as well as for Vladimir, for fifty years. She regretted that her son might
not experience the same gratifications. Would she have counseled a daughter
any differently? It does not sound so. There was no question in her mind that
the enterprise was a perfectly reciprocal one, that the compromises and sacri-
fices extended in both directions, or, for that matter, that the looking-after
was any less a marvel than the being looked after. (One of Dmitri's public explanations years later for not having married was in essence the very luxury
his mother outlined now. He knew how uncommon was the rapport his parents had enjoyed, what an elusive rarity is the "twin soul.") Véra professed
relief that Dmitri had not married—she claimed she was horrified by the results when most young people attempted the sport—but she worried a great
deal about him, increasingly so as the years wore on.

   By April 1976 Vladimir had completed the first hundred pages of the
new novel, *The Original of Laura,* to which he referred as "TOOL." "He does
not know, he says, what is more brilliant, the novel itself or its acronym—this
is as much as he can disclose at the moment," Véra reported to Fred Hills,
three days before the couple celebrated Vladimir's seventy-seventh birthday
privately, with champagne and caviar. Both Nabokovs worked at a reduced
tempo through the spring, when Vladimir suffered a second fall, closer to

home but more serious. Having caught his foot on something in his bedroom, he tripped and fell backward, hitting the back of his head on the floor. The resulting concussion kept him in the hospital for ten days. Véra consequently met alone with the associate of Fassbinder's who traveled to Montreux to plead the director's case. She was convinced by his arguments, and successful in exacting an agreement that would allow her husband to vet the finished *Despair* screenplay.* Meanwhile the siege of ill health continued. On June 16 Vladimir returned by ambulance to the hospital for a third time, having developed an infection that mystified his doctors. He spent much of the summer in various clinics, weak and feverish, while in Montreux Véra labored on, alerting McGraw-Hill to the fact that TOOL would be delayed, probably until Easter 1977. She found the convalescence disturbingly slow, the doctors frustratingly unforthcoming. Those who saw VN at this time felt a shiver of sadness.

In November Véra wrote, as Vladimir, to report that *Laura* was practically complete in his head but that its transcription was taking some time. Three months later she wrote, as herself, to concede that little progress had been made. "I am writing you on my husband's request. He would not like you to believe either that he is not working on the novel or that he will finish it within a few weeks," she warned Hills. That month a team of BBC interviewers descended on Montreux, where they found both Nabokovs slow-moving, Vladimir a hunched and diminished version of himself, Véra walking stiffly with a cane. In some ways nothing had changed. Softly Véra asked the interviewer if he was nervous; he jumped out of his seat with fright to deny as much. The BBC dialogue had been prepared in advance, but the producers were a few minutes short of their twenty-five-minute program. It was decided that Vladimir would supplement the talk with the reading of a poem, fifteen strophes at so many seconds a strophe, he began to calculate, interrupted by Véra, who reminded him that the verse in question consisted of twelve. Weeks later the Nabokovs shared their last flu, which developed in Vladimir's case into pneumonia, and took him back to the hospital. He stayed for seven weeks. Véra found distraction where she could. "My husband wants me to say he is very much disturbed by the complete lack of publicity for his book," she cautioned Loo. He returned home in early May, but was back at the hospital a month later with a persistent fever. The Proffers

---

* She was displeased with the finished product, which she thought "rather dreadful" and untrue to the spirit of the book.

were shocked by the change in the normally robust writer when they visited in the spring; the tenderness with which Véra observed her husband combined now with fear. The conversation moved at a full and invigorating gallop all the same.

It is unclear at what point it would have occurred to Véra, or Vladimir, that this was the end. Anna Feigin's death had unsettled the couple; Lena Massalsky had died in the spring of 1975, having spent the previous year in a nursing home. The morning before his seventy-seventh birthday Vladimir had been woken at one by raw terror of the " 'this-is-it' sort." He had screamed—discreetly. He hoped to wake Véra and at the same time feared he might actually succeed in doing so; he had not felt entirely unwell. A year later Dmitri sensed the attitude to be one of resignation. In defiance of all antibiotics Vladimir's temperature again began to climb; Nicholas Nabokov suggested to Véra that his cousin be moved to the United States, an idea she could not even begin to consider seriously as she felt Vladimir was too weak to make the trip. When Field's *Nabokov: His Life in Part* arrived on June 16, its subject did not have the strength to read the volume. Véra had a cursory glance at the first pages. Throughout these months her tone—even, self-assured, uninflected—did not falter.

At the end of June Vladimir appeared rapidly to be losing what remained of his strength. His doctor nonetheless declared himself optimistic about a recovery; he was visibly angered when Véra disagreed, stating that in her opinion her husband seemed to be in the process of dying. Dmitri returned to Italy shortly after this conversation, to be called back to Lausanne almost immediately. His father was breathing with difficulty, expelling pus. His temperature had climbed to 107 degrees; bronchial pneumonia had set in. Dmitri noted that "the physicians' manner was changing from bedside to graveside." We are as far from knowing the last meaningful words Véra and Vladimir exchanged as we are from knowing those that had been imparted on a Berlin sidewalk fifty-four years earlier. A few days before the last Véra remarked that she did not believe everything finished with death, one matter she and her husband had plainly discussed in the first flush of their courtship, and a statement with which he still agreed. A different veil now descended: The heart that had been racing from one abyss toward another at a rate of about forty-five hundred heartbeats an hour reached its final destination. As Véra and Dmitri stood watch, it stopped at 6:50 on Saturday evening, July 2.

Seconds after it did so a Lausanne nurse precipitated herself bodily upon Véra, with condolences. Véra pushed her away with an acid, *"S'il vous plait, Madame."* She had no patience for clichés and did not intend to play the grieving widow. When she saw her sister-in-law that month she issued equally stern (and unnecessary) instructions for the visit: "But please, no tears, no wails, none of that." She had a similar request to make regarding the quiet ceremony in nearby Clarens that followed the cremation on July 7: She asked a family member not to embrace her. She appeared in perfect command of herself on that occasion, as the forty or so friends and relatives who gathered at the hillside cemetery—Sonia, Topazia Markevitch, the Rowohlts, Beverly Loo, the numerous Nabokov cousins—expected she would. The mask had served her well for over half a century; there was no reason to drop it now. Nor was there any reason to assume that the mask and the face were one. As soon as she heard the news, Beverly Loo had called to ask if Véra would like her to fly to Switzerland. Sounding grateful and relieved, Véra said she would, very much. She was in tears when Loo next saw her. Dmitri had driven his mother back to Montreux from the Lausanne hospital at dusk on July 2, in his blue Ferrari, on the last day of his father's life. Véra had sat silently for a few minutes and then uttered the one desperate line Dmitri ever heard escape her lips: "Let's rent an airplane and crash."

Generally Dmitri stayed close to his mother's side, attending to the few calls that had to be answered. On July 4 she had managed to compose a note to Marie Schebeko, whom she felt would understand her loss: "I am writing to inform you that my husband died on July 2nd. I know that it will touch you deeply. I do not want to add anything today, I just wanted you to know." On the same day she and Dmitri had disclosed the news of VN's death to the papers. If there was relief of any kind it was only that a protracted struggle was over, that Vladimir need not suffer further. The last weeks had been grueling. Véra later contradicted a niece who remarked that her husband's death had been a shame. He had gone when he should have, Véra insisted. He had not been able to think, or write, as he liked. (Elena Sikorski had sensed that something was radically wrong when she managed to defeat her brother at Scrabble that spring.) There was otherwise no hint of a character having been liberated from a novelist's iron grip; there were no thwarted ambitions, no deep, slumbering regrets. If anything there was bewilderment of the opposite kind. There was no longer a VN behind which to hide. Of Véra's emotional state there was no question. Two years later a childhood friend was widowed in Paris. Véra offered keenly felt condolences, "because it is so much more grim for those who remain than for those who have gone on." Boyd was in Montreux on the fifth anniversary of Nabokov's death. "It doesn't feel like five years," he commented to Véra, with whom he had been working since 1979. "It feels like fifty to me," she replied.

4

The remarkable thing about Véra Nabokov's life after Nabokov was not how much but how little it changed. Since 1923 she had not posited herself at the center of her own existence. She showed no sign of doing so now. "A book lives longer than a girl," Vladimir had noted, speaking of the two Madame Bovarys. His widow took comfort in the fact that a book also outlives its author. A month after his death she was back at her desk, soliciting publishing advice, asking Schirman what course of action she should pursue against a public appraisal of Vladimir's work that he had found objectionable. She was still not up to receiving guests. At the end of the month she packed Dmitri off for a vacation in San Remo. She knew he was cruelly wounded by their loss. The previous year when Vladimir had fallen in his room she had attempted to break his fall but proved no match for his weight; her spine had been injured as a result, and was now crooked in two places, giving her a biggish hump. Her right arm refused to function properly—it was "half an invalid in its own right," she declared—which made the letter-writing more of an ordeal than ever. She had no choice but to dictate her words to Madame Callier. She avoided social calls as much out of self-consciousness as out of any kind of emotional frailty. Over and over she explained that she had grown hunchbacked. Ultimately she would be as bent over as a question mark.

While she was indifferent to how the world perceived her, she was not without her vanity. In March 1978 Alison Bishop traveled to Europe, where her daughter, now Alison Jolly, was living. The one thing she wanted to do before returning to Ithaca was to see Véra again. Véra was oddly reluctant to see the surviving member of the couple who had been their intimates at Cornell; Alison was left with the feeling that she was inflicting herself on an old friend. Ultimately it was agreed that the three would meet for a quiet dinner in the Montreux apartment. Alison Bishop was herself eighty-one and crippled by knee trouble; it required some effort on her part to wade through the vast hotel lobby and down the corridors leading to the elevator to the sixth floor. Véra received the two Bishop women in the apartment all in black. The curtains were drawn, and the lights turned down low; her radiant face and the sweep of white hair appeared to float magically, a semi-shimmer in the darkness. The twisted back was barely visible. Dinner was wheeled in quickly, evidently so that the visit could be brief. Any fears she may have had about the reunion were quickly dispelled. The conversation sparkled, and Véra's joy was evident. There was much laughter. When the younger Alison asked if she had fallen, Véra shrugged and replied that it been her husband who fell. The shoulder had hurt a great deal, but no longer gave her any pain.* As they rose to leave, one of the Alisons could not help but tell Véra how extraordinarily beautiful she was. "Oh, you don't find me so ugly then?" she asked, touched and surprised, and alluding to the hump. It could only have weighed all the heavier on a woman whose carriage had been for decades so utterly exemplary. The deformation made no difference; Véra remained in the mind of Alison Bishop Jolly the most beautiful woman she had ever known.

For the most part and with few exceptions, she resisted callers. She was as always inundated with work. In the first year without VN she checked the French translation of *Look at the Harlequins!*—she was quite happy with the results—and devoted her time to polishing a collection of Russian poems, to be published by the Proffers' Ardis Publishers. She contributed a brief, dispassionate preface to the collection as well, one line of which, stressing the presence of the otherworldly in VN's work, would set Nabokov studies off in a new direction. The regular housekeeping affairs proved as complex as ever: VN had five publishers in France alone. On top of this came the estate-related details. The complications were the usual ones. "I have received from the I.R.S. an answer to a letter I never sent them," Véra complained at the beginning of 1978. She felt she was living under the sword of Damocles in the perennial anticipation of staggering legal and tax bills.† The evaluation of the estate was complicated by the volume of paper with which she lived; she nearly begged Iseman not to ask her to provide a detailed inventory. "We have been living here for almost 17 years, in a very small apartment, and every drawer, every trunk and lots of cases are filled with papers, most of which have no value at all and have not been destroyed for the only reason that the task of taking everything out and sorting it was too much for me." The bulk of it was of little value, she added, having been written by her.

For leisure she read about the Old Masters, primarily Vermeer and Georges de La Tour; this was one of her favorite pastimes. She was at her desk no fewer than six hours a day, as prosaic as ever in her reports. But a note of pathos sounds just beneath the lacquer-hard surface. She thanked Loo for having come all the way to Montreux to see her in the spring of 1978; she was deeply touched by the publishers who offered to visit. She

---

* Having observed the couple in action for a decade, Alison Bishop instinctively divined the truth. "She tried to catch him when he fell," she whispered to her daughter as they left.
† The former were especially hefty because her lawyers—accustomed to Véra's creative whittling—adjusted their computations accordingly.

sounded almost surprised when someone from the distant past wrote her. She seemed to live in expectation of being forgotten, was pleased when she discovered that was not. (At their ends, friends like the Christiansens hesitated to write, worried they were presuming, and were just as taken aback by Véra's heartfelt responses. Somehow it never seemed to occur to anyone that she actually enjoyed receiving mail, which she did.) There was almost a note of entreaty to the letters, thought Elena Levin. "Don't forget me," Véra implored the Appels. She remained as plainspoken as ever. In 1983 she wrote Alfred Appel, "I do hope you will visit Europe some day before I leave it for good."

She never tired of telling friends that the work kept her sane, healthy, happy. At the same time she continued in her quiet protests. At eighty-one, still spending full days at her desk (her writing desk had become her writing armchair), she was still insisting she lacked all epistolary gifts. Sylvia Berkman asked if Véra might write something about Vladimir, a question she was not alone in posing; Véra replied that neither her Russian nor her English was strong enough. She was not to be a writing widow, like Fanny Stevenson or Anna Dostoyevsky, not even a faux writing widow, like Florence Hardy, whose name went on the so-called biography her husband had written of himself, and dictated to his wife, before his death. She did not care to have the last word. While she admired Nadezhda Mandelstam's memoir of a marriage that was in many respects similar to her own under radically different circumstances, she expressed no desire to emulate Mrs. Mandelstam. Nor did she subscribe to any kind of widows' network. There was no being tigresses together; there was no consulting on publishing procedures, as there had been between Countess Tolstoy and Mrs. Dostoyevsky. She would read Carl Proffer's 1987 *The Widows of Russia,* a work on the women who upheld and fostered and transmitted a literature, but if she saw anything familiar in the text, or in its cast of committed, culture-preserving characters, she offered no reflections on it. She had always held herself apart, insisted, as much as her husband, on the supremacy of the individual. Given the work in which she had so deeply immersed herself for five decades, that sense was understandable. Less easy to grasp was the diffidence, which had for so many years been read as arrogance. She was inundated with requests for meetings, interviews, opinions, by those who wanted to talk about literature, or just talk: "Since they cannot talk to V. they ask if they can talk to me (*faute de mieux*)." And this, she added, after she had done everything in her power, all her life, to avoid meeting new people.

Much of the late 1970s were consumed by yet another translation effort. Having corrected *Speak, Memory* in German, *Look at the Harlequins!* in

French, her husband's poetry in Italian, she undertook a translation of *Pale Fire* into Russian. She backed into the project accidentally, having agreed to check the work of a young poet, commissioned by the Proffers. The task was arduous—William Buckley remarked that he would have thought such a rendering impossible, but had long known "that nothing is impossible for you"—but not as arduous as were the battles with the original translator. To her horror Véra determined that he had no sense of her husband's work, little grasp of English, and a disastrous conception of Russian, especially literary Russian. After a number of rounds she gave up on his version, retranslating the novel herself from beginning to end, finishing only in 1982. Years into the project, with only about seventy pages to go, she felt no great sense of triumph. If she compared her work with the original she was maddeningly disheartened. "But at least it is all exact," she consoled herself.

The manner in which credit was negotiated for the work is instructive. Initially, Véra had no intention of lending her name to the project. Given the amount of time she dedicated to the task, she later agreed to a line indicating that the translation had been made under her supervision. When the Russian *Pale Fire* was inadvertently announced without any mention of her contribution, she felt honor-bound to assert herself. She had proposed a shared credit so as to spare the poet's feelings; now her own had been badly hurt. She regretted having been so "stupidly generous" in the first place. Having spent years correcting someone else's "illiteracies and errors," she insisted on sole credit. It was as if she were willing to step forward only out of spite. "I have now decided to be ruthless," she warned the Proffers. She was adamant about this formulation, as a bibliographer who later stumbled discovered. He was duly notified that all mention of the poet must disappear. "This is very important to me," Véra stressed.

The *Pale Fire* translation was but one of many projects competing for her attention. More so than ever before, she was her husband's representative, the quicksilver mediator between a divine sensibility and its earthly interpreters. It had long been her job to set translators, cover artists, royalty departments, journalists, on the straight and narrow. She did so all the more stringently now. She admitted that she was perhaps a bit more pious than was necessary, but did not see how she could act differently. Only Vladimir could have granted special dispensations, and he was not around to do so. She doubted he would want a poem of his to appear in an anthology alongside a mystical salute to Lenin. And when in doubt, she explained to the volume's editor, her rule was to abstain. She apologized to an editor for her punctiliousness: "You may find my corrections to be only details," she explained, "but style consists of details." VN had held that style alone should constitute a writer's biography; only in this respect was Véra writing her husband's story. In preparing his Cornell lectures for publication she subscribed to a simple rule, citing a case her father had spoken about that had clearly much impressed her. A Roman author had requested in his will that nothing whatever be added to his work. On the other hand, his heirs should feel free to eliminate whatever they liked. She remained as always alert to the misprint, the slight, the inaccuracy, the mangled line, the lapse of logic. Nothing escaped her vigilance, as John Updike discovered when he submitted his introduction to the first volume of lectures. It was returned to him with Véra's three incisive pages of notes. (Her seventeenth point: "A personal request: Could you please take me out of the article?") "What an impressively clear mind and style she has," Updike commented, revising his pages.

With her directness and literalism, Véra labored to preserve the poetry and mystery—to her mind the two essential aspects—of her husband's work. The indignities piled up, as they always had, but now she faced them alone, or with the help of Dmitri, who spent part of the year in Montreux, and who since the mid-1970s had been translating his father's work into Italian. How could *The Defense*'s British paperbacker even dream of putting such a pseudomodern abomination on the cover? She agreed the work of a young Russian writer was promising but wished he did not imitate her husband quite so much. She battled as ferociously, as directly, on the page as she had a half century earlier; if she had not been the original Zina Mertz, she had certainly inherited her idiosyncratic directness. "No one else—not students, colleagues here, Nabokov scholars elsewhere—returns a critical serve with such force," Boyd wrote, thanking Véra for her comments on his pages. When George Hessen published his memoirs she commented that she had always known of his deep affection for Vladimir but had been touched to see it in print. What she had not known was what a dreadful writer Hessen was. In 1979 Harry Levin reviewed *The Nabokov-Wilson Letters* in *The New York Review of Books*. "I was not going to say anything about Harry's article about *The Letters,* but I like to be quite frank, and so perhaps I had better say that the article distressed me very much," Véra wrote Elena. It was a year and a half before she explained her indignation.

On top of this affront arrived Shakhovskoy's 1979 *In Search of Nabokov,* published in Paris. Véra was willing to overlook the personal attacks, what she read as flagrant anti-Semitism, even the insinuation that she had participated in the writing of her husband's books. What she could not stomach were the charges leveled against Vladimir. As she saw it, Shakhovskoy—to whom she referred by her married name, Malévitch—had two objectives: "1) to prove my hatred (entirely imagined by her) for Russia and the Russian people; 2) my having brought about VN's estrangement from a) Russia and b) Christianity and God (and the Maleviches)."* This was beneath contempt, where Véra intended to leave it. But as Madame Malévitch seemed intent on a second objective—to "connect him [VN] with pedophilia, and insinuate that VN had commerce, if not with the devil himself, then at least with some of his representatives"—she contemplated legal action.† (The matter was complicated by the fact that the two women shared a lawyer. Louba Schirman, who had so ingeniously freed the Nabokovs from Girodias, was also a close friend of Shakhovskoy's.) In a meeting in Montreux with Dmitri, Schirman counseled Véra against taking action; a suit would only focus attention on the book. She cannot have had an easy time doing so, but Véra turned the other cheek. The issue flared up again two years later, when Ullstein brought out the volume in Germany. Véra felt this publication more acutely. She believed that Russian readers would recognize Shakhovskoy's charges for what they were but that the German public would not. Schirman hesitated to pursue the matter, which Ledig Rowohlt advised Véra to drop as well. In his opinion the book was boring and would go unread. Generally friends agreed that the biography amounted to character assassination, but a few relations suffered. How could you have failed to notice the baseness, the villainy, all the vulgarity, Véra rebuked one Parisian friend? Shyly she asked Natalie Nabokov, who had been so kind to her in America, if she had joined her sister's faction. "I shall not love you less," wrote the woman who knew one could judge a man as much by his enemies as by his friends, "but I shall not write you anymore." The correspondence ended there.

All of these battle cries went out from a woman who continued to profess that she was alternately too lazy or too tired to attend properly to her work. She was suffering from Parkinson's disease; when the tremor was strong and she was obliged to receive visitors, she hid her hands under a shawl. She avoided dinner invitations; she did not dare attempt a cup of tea. After 1980, she no longer ventured into the hotel restaurant, telling visitors she was not fit to sit out a whole meal. Her health never constituted an excuse, despite the obstacles it presented: She had attempted to use a tape recorder for her *Pale Fire* corrections but found that her fingers were too weak to manipulate the controls of the machine. Her hearing had faded to the point that a scholar's taped translation proved useless. Her right arm con-

---

* As Dmitri saw it, Shakhovskoy's volume "was not so much about Vladimir Nabokov as against Véra Nabokov, mainly because she could not stomach my parents' long and blissful marriage."
† Shakhovskoy held out hope that Véra might sue, begging a mutual friend to encourage her to do so.

tinued to hang limp. There remained a vast discrepancy between the woman and her words. At one point she received a sixteen-page memo from a German authors' guild, a right-minded organization. She appealed to Ledig Rowohlt to intervene. "I loathe organizations. I am suspicious of all questionnaires, detest unnecessary paperwork—in a word I would not like to have anything to do with VG Wort." It was difficult to believe that the woman behind this letter was a frail and decorous seventy-eight-year-old who described herself as an invalid. A Lausanne-based scholar who worked with Véra on VN's poetry was taken aback by the contrast "between her physical frailty on the one hand and, on the other, her calm sense of purpose, her firm will, and the remarkable clarity of her mind and intellect."

She proved a gold mine to scholars, having committed to memory not only what was in the books but what was no longer in them. For Véra as for Zina, the word combinations amounted to archaeological ruins that "stood for a long time on the golden horizon, reluctant to disappear." She occasionally astonished a scholar by letting slip a palimpsestic truth, some telling tidbit that had failed to make the final cut. She was a kind of walking key to the works. She regularly identified Cornell colleagues in *Pnin*; she could authenticate a text; she could suggest a liberty the honest translator would not otherwise have hazarded. Boyd confronted her with an anonymous literary parody of 1940, from a Russian newspaper published in New York. Was the piece Nabokov's? "Could be," nodded Véra, taking it from him. "Beyond a doubt," she asserted after a few paragraphs. "Absolutely," she concluded at the end of the column, with a laugh. Was a particular meaning accidentally embedded in a line in *Invitation to a Beheading*? she was asked. "My husband would never commit a coincidence," came the reply. Were it not for all the archival and editorial work, concluded one friend, she would have been a prominent Nabokov critic. Dmitri found her omniscient.

Omniscience has a price; like any oracle she inspired fear. Even members of the immediate family were terrified of her, as were most of her husband's editors. She ruled by cordial but distant fiat. As the Lausanne scholar quickly discovered, she knew all of her husband's verse—from 1921 on—by heart. When a journalist mentioned Paul Bowles in her presence, she immediately demonstrated that she knew and understood Bowles's work better than he. She remained as adamantine as ever in her judgments. You ask, she wrote the Paris friend whom she had rebuked for having misread the Shakhovskoy volume, why there are no worthwhile new Russian poets and writers. They did exist. The problem was that most of them were illiterate. She gave voice to only one warmhearted regret: that her grandchildren were all of them literary.

5

On September 26, 1980, Dmitri called his mother to say that he would not be home for lunch, as expected. He had had a little accident. That was something of an understatement, as Véra discovered before the afternoon was out. Between Montreux and Lausanne, his Ferrari had spun out of control, bouncing between guardrails and bursting into flames. As he forced himself from the burning car, Dmitri's back, hands, and hair had caught fire. Minutes after speaking with his mother that Friday, he lapsed into a coma. He had suffered third-degree burns over 40 percent of his body. He had also broken his neck. It would be three and a half months—and six skin grafts—before Véra saw her son again up close. When she visited him in the hospital burn unit she would be brought outside the glass-walled room, in a wheelchair. Dmitri turned the lights down low. He could feel her gaze; she seemed to regard him "like a rare animal." She passed on Dmitri's understatement—she wrote the family accountant that Dmitri was under the weather—but nonetheless focused much of her energy on his recovery. Those who saw her at this time easily glimpsed the fragile woman beneath the steely exterior; she was nearly out of her mind with worry. This was not conveyed by the voice on the page. "The car was wholly burned to a crisp," she informed one relative. "Dmitri has seen a wonderful return from the other side of the Styx," she assured another. She apologized to Carl Proffer for her inability to vet a *Pnin* translation. Between the final pages of the *Pale Fire* manuscript and her calls and visits to the hospital she was insanely busy.

Dmitri spent a total of forty-two weeks in intensive care and rehabilitation. Martin Amis was on hand shortly after the worst was over, having secured Véra's consent to an interview about her life with VN for the London *Observer*. Amis found Mrs. Nabokov's humor and warmth much on display, though he was himself largely "frozen with deference." Dmitri was still living at the Lausanne hospital but joined his mother; his scorched fingers made an impression. Véra observed the striated skin on her son's arms and asked solicitously when the "purple lace" was likely to disappear. She hoped Amis could reassure her that he drove with immaculate care. Stephen and Marie-Luce Parker also visited Montreux at the time. When Dmitri stepped out of the room at one point Véra turned to the couple: "Don't ever let your children get burned."

One bargain she did not make with the gods in the course of Dmitri's recovery was to be more forgiving. The Amis piece was edited like any other; Véra recoiled when she saw that Amis intended to repeat her observation that VN "was as a young man extremely beautiful," a remark she categorically denied having made. (And that Amis vividly remembered having heard. It remained in the piece.) Simon Karlinsky's draft introduction to Nabokov's *Lectures on Russian Literature* arrived during Dmitri's convalescence; it was shot through with admiration for VN's work, but Véra deemed it unacceptable, on the grounds that Karlinsky's approach to literature did not accord with her husband's. An erudite scholar in his sixties, Karlinsky had been a discerning reader of Nabokov since the age of twelve. He rallied eloquently to his own defense; Véra had misread the piece, which was not intended to diminish her husband in any way. Véra proved in equal parts thick-skinned and hypersensitive. She could not impress upon Karlinsky how much his essay had upset her. (She most resisted Karlinsky's persuasive attempts to locate Nabokov within a historical continuum, where she felt he neither belonged nor aspired to belong. To her mind her husband had neither peers nor equals.) The little victories in the verbal skirmishes still mattered. To the editor of the volume, who agreed to forgo Karlinsky's pages, she wrote with unusual fervor: "You are not a publisher, you are an angel."

Much of the last decade of her life was dedicated to the fine art of perfecting the past, an activity that in some views teetered on the brink of censorship. In the late 1970s Karlinsky edited the Nabokov-Wilson letters; he testifies that there was no tension between the two widows, aside from the fact that Mrs. Wilson wanted to put everything in and Véra wanted to take everything out. A scholar researching Nabokov's fiancées was free to publish his work—so long as he did not mention Véra. She persisted not in correcting references to herself, to the marriage, to her past, but in deleting them from texts. She swore she had never said anything Boyd had quoted her as saying. She was gnomic in her pronouncements. Was it not unusual that most of her husband's books were dedicated to her? Amis asked. "What should I answer? We had a very unusual relationship," she offered. "You were very different from your husband," Boyd insisted, leadingly. "Yes, but everyone was different from VN," Véra parried. Have you ever written fiction yourself? she was asked. "No," she replied. Her favorite VN work? "Unanswerable." On the publication of *Selected Letters* in Milan, she consented to a talk, accompanied by Dmitri, with an Italian journalist. She proved the world's worst interview subject. "Madame Nabokov, I am told you were a passionate equestrienne, that you fired a pistol, that you went up on acrobatic flights. What do you believe has been the most important thing in your life?" the journalist asked. "My life, it has been full of important things," replied Véra, slipping deftly through the net.

It would be difficult to say that she had come into her own since Vladimir's death; she had never really left herself. But she spoke now for and as herself. There was no more Vladimir wants me to say, asks me to say, insists I say. For some time she used the line that her husband would have agreed, or railed, or expected as a weapon; she knew as well as anyone that it is difficult to argue with a memory. As time went on she found that saying that she, Mrs. Vladimir Nabokov, was insulted, or unhappy, was potent enough, perhaps even more so. As Karlinsky observed, people became more attentive to Véra after VN's death, for the right and the wrong reasons. The quiet humor, too, was more on display, at least for those who had an ear for it. Gennady Barabtarlo, whose Russian *Pnin* translation Véra reviewed, perhaps put it best: "Suffice it to say that she possessed a wonderful humor for which not all people had a sense." He found her delightfully droll. "For once," Véra wrote Beverly Loo, well acquainted with how unlikely was the scenario, "you have overpaid me." She hoped that the insane printer Carl Proffer had located proved every bit as good as the sane one. Her nephew Michaël Massalsky reminded her of Halley's Comet, with his infrequent visits, advertised long in advance. (She had warm feelings for him, whatever her differences with his mother.) She thanked the director of the Palace for the orchids he sent on her eighty-seventh birthday, informing him that she had decided now to start counting backwards on her birthdays, toward takeoff. She stretched against every instinct in her body to accommodate the prying biographer. She shared with Boyd all her memories of a family he had asked about, including their light-brown poodle, Dolly, finishing her account with a sly "I don't know her patronymic."

Increasingly the difficulty was one of communicating. She heard uncertainly, which meant one spoke to her uncertainly. A long pause might follow a question, as if to indicate that she had not heard, or grasped, the issue at hand. Then suddenly, swiftly, an exact, often very clever response would follow, accompanied by a beaming smile. Although she had been advised against typing she still, on a day that Madame Callier was not at hand and she felt she had something urgent to communicate, made her way to the machine. She was immensely frustrated by her pace at the best of times; dictating was a cumbersome procedure. Moreover, Madame Callier was often overburdened. In 1986, when the manuscript of Andrew Field's *The Life and Art of Vladimir Nabokov* arrived, Véra did her best to annotate what she considered an error-filled text but was hampered in her efforts; Callier was busy with the tax returns, and the employment agencies who had provided help sent "young women who knew neither the grammar nor the orthography, nor half of the words I was using." A proofreader hired to look over Barabtarlo's *Pnin* "made a great number of idiotic suggestions." She had difficulty hearing on the telephone. Her letters, often staccato and spare, began to sound like telexese.

At the end of 1984 her pulse dropped precipitously; Dmitri arranged for her to be taken by ambulance to the emergency room at the Lausanne hospital, where a pacemaker was installed. Véra delighted in telling friends that her heart was now connected to a battery, ticking away like a little electric clock. The incident did little to impress upon her her fragility. A 1985 letter went out: "Sorry to be so long in answering your letter. I had a pacemaker installed last week. I do not think your article is worth publishing . . ." The body's betrayals continued, however. Having recovered from a bad flu, in February 1986, she fell in the apartment, "like a fool," breaking a chair, and a rib. Her correspondence eased, especially as she suffered pains in her side for months afterward. She was eighty-four when she and Dmitri decided that an agent would be necessary; Ledig Rowohlt put the Nabokovs in touch with Nikki Smith in New York, who assumed the bulk of the correspondence and the negotiating. In 1988, encouraged by Gennady Barabtarlo, Véra went back to the La Motte Fouqué research she had begun in the mid-1950s, at Cornell. She had established a link between the German writer's *Pique-Dame* and Pushkin's *Queen of Spades*; having retrieved a rare copy of the 1826 novel from Germany, she had begun a scholarly essay on the subject. (Nabokov mentions the connection in an *Onegin* footnote without crediting Véra, adding that he will pursue the matter elsewhere.) Véra had already pursued the matter thoroughly. Barabtarlo cemented together her notecards and draft pages, publishing the research with Véra in a 1991 journal. It was quite a performance for someone who had been thought too frail to attend university.

For the most part her spirits remained good, although she was the first to admit that being old was very difficult. "You speak of depression. It's something I'm not familiar with; I always keep myself busy," she wrote a friend from the 1930s. She still enjoyed, and was keen to discuss, synesthesia, which had proved such a powerful part of her imagination; her grasp of images remained as sure as ever. In her eighties, she considered translating *Ada* into Italian. She was delighted when Nabokov appeared in print for the first time in 1986 in his—in their—native country. An excerpt from *Speak, Memory* had been published in a chess magazine; a one-volume anthology was in the works. Véra asked Karlinsky, whose tolerance and scholarly excellence allowed the relationship to weather its occasional storms, if he was planning a European trip that summer. "Though very old I am still alive, and 'kicking,' " she assured him. He sent his 1985 biography of Tsvetaeva in response. Véra was no more approving of the woman or her marriage than she had been, but could not put Karlinsky's work down once she had begun it. She was equally enchanted by a bibliography of VN's work prepared by Michael Juliar, in which she made all kinds of gratifying new discoveries. It read to her like a novel. Her pleasure now was reading about her husband, as it had once been reading her husband. The friends were now friends of his memory.

On the first day of November 1987, she fell again, in her bedroom, breaking her left hip. Surgery was scheduled, but postponed due to a circulatory problem. For the next week and a half she was in what she described as "exquisite pain." She and Dmitri twice said their good-byes while she waited for a synthetic ball joint to be implanted. The operation was followed by a five-month hospital stay, during which she worried incessantly about Dmitri, who she felt had been buried under the still-massive business correspondence. The piles of paper that greeted her on the return from the hospital were nearly enough to send her back. She spent most of the spring in bed. She was in no shape to check a translation of any kind; she did not have the strength to hold two texts before her. She was all apologies with Boyd, whose biography chapters arrived with regularity: "For half a year I have been out of circulation, out of life I should say. The correspondence accumulated unanswered and I did not have the courage to make a fresh start." The hip never entirely healed; her future walks were awkward, shuffling affairs. Soon enough she reported that moving from one room to the next was a major journey for her. Writing a letter constituted a vast enterprise. She could hold a hardcover book upright only with difficulty. She was extremely displeased to learn at the end of 1989 that she would have to move from the Palace because of renovations, especially as apartments in Montreux were difficult to come by. As usual the world proved less lucid than she. After much searching, Dmitri managed to find an apartment, although, as Véra put it, the seller did not seem to understand he had sold.

"I live in Montreux. I'm 87 years old, but soon I'll be 88. I'm a hunchbacked old woman and I'm very hard of hearing. . . . This year slipped away from me somehow unnoticed," Véra wrote Elena Levin in the fall of 1989. The birthday that felt so imminent was still four months in the future. She was virtually immobile; she did not go out. All that was left to her, she claimed, was to read and reread. Elena Levin was herself seventy-seven, but could not imagine Véra as "a hunchbacked old woman." Twenty-five years had elapsed since the two had seen each other, but the quarter century was of little consequence. "In my memory you're a marble-white beauty with animated facial expressions," replied Elena, by return mail. The letter evidently meant a great deal to Véra. She did not give it up to be filed, but relegated it to the empty chocolate box in her desk drawer that held various scribblings from Vladimir. Time had done to her what neither exile nor indigence nor inept royalty departments had managed to: It had bent her to its own designs. She was grateful that someone knew to peer beneath the mask that she thought so deforming. The move to the new apartment in the spring of 1990 proved a wrench after nearly three decades at the Palace. She worried about security, that someone would break into the glass-walled dining room from the garden, where she repeatedly pointed out a black cat, an animal no one else ever saw, and which Dmitri assumed it to be a fanciful version of the barbecue. She spent her time parsing the newspapers, checking Boyd's every word, reading aloud the work of Pushkin, Blok, Tyutchev, Nabokov with Dmitri in the evenings, attempting to teach the Italian cook English. She was less and less stable when attempting to cross a room, even fully assisted. Dmitri admitted she was not having much fun. Stephen Parker saw her late in the summer of 1990. Tears began to roll out of her still-radiant eyes when the subject turned to Vladimir.

Ellendea Proffer asked Véra in her last year if she got bored. "No, never" was the answer. A distant relative on the Feigin side spoke with her by telephone in mid-1990. "Aunt Véra, how do you feel yourself?" she inquired. "Very bad," replied Véra, with laughter. Vivian Crespi visited her that fall, in the bedroom of the new apartment. Véra was in a wheelchair, in a black-and-white shantung shirt and black pants, perfectly coiffed, ravishingly beautiful. There was still a very real shimmer about her. The clear eyes sparkled; the wit was lambent. The two talked while Crespi drank a cup of tea. "Is there anything I can do for you?" she asked before leaving. The wheelchair bothered her; it seemed to her that Véra—so accustomed to being active—must have felt trapped. "Vivi dear, just pray that I have a quick death," Véra whispered into her ear.

That she had, six months later. On April 6, 1991, she was taken to the Vevey hospital when she began to suffer respiratory trouble. She was unconscious when Dmitri joined her late the following afternoon. He spent several hours talking to her, stroking her hair; in tiny, subtle flutters she seemed to be attempting to express something. She died quietly that evening at ten. "Véra Nabokov, 89, Wife, Muse, and Agent," read the *New York Times* headline to her obituary. Her ashes were joined, as she had requested they be, with her husband's. A line was added to the blue-gray tombstone in Clarens so that it now reads:

VLADIMIR NABOKOV
ECRIVAIN
VERA NABOKOV

It was an appropriate wording. As Alfred Appel wrote when he heard the news, it seemed that "the monument called 'Nabokov' (his collected work) is really the variegated work of two, that if he had indeed been a sculptor she would have written her name at the base, in very tiny print so that no one could have read it, and then stood back and flashed her best small, enigmatic smile, her Mona Lisa smile, really." He had no idea how tiny her print had actually become. In her last days Véra was at work on a rough translation of the most intricate passages of "Gods," an unpublished story Vladimir had written in the first days of their relationship. Her vocal cords were going, her eyesight had dimmed, she was nearly deaf, her memory was failing. She was determined to finish the work. Her handwriting, once so full-bodied and regal, was cramped and shriveled. She had begun to write over her own lines. It was as if she were dissolving into the text as, for so much of her life, she had chosen to do.

Not for a second had she believed you could go home again, but she understood that patience prevails, that, as her husband had remarked, "the movements of stars may seem crazy to the simpleton, but the wise men know that the comets come back." So did the black cat, a fat, fluffy animal who put in a single appearance the afternoon of the funeral, as if to pay his respects, and then disappeared for good. Six months after Véra's death Leningrad became St. Petersburg again. After 1987, you could even buy a copy of *Lolita* there. In 1959 Véra had predicted that the critics had not even begun to write about that book. Finally, around the world, they had. A vast number of things went with her—we know now but a fraction of what he and she knew—which was exactly as she had wanted it. Her name survived her, on those pages that so perfectly recapitulate the theme of the life, near but keeping a respectful distance from the works that follow, proffered by her husband, in a line as straightforward as any Nabokov ever wrote. Surrounded by a deep and comfortable sea of blank space, she is right there—one end of a luminous brain-bridge—plain as day, front and center, hidden in full view.

ACKNOWLEDGMENTS

"The unravelling of a riddle is the purest and most basic act of the human mind," proclaimed Nabokov. For assistance with riddles, mysteries, and enigmas of all kinds, I should like to thank: Robert M. Adams, M. H. Abrams, Martin Amis, Svetlana Andrault de Langeron, Alfred Appel, Jr., Nina Appel, Dr. Bernard Asher, Gennady and Alla Barabtarlo, Carlo Barozzi, Marie Schebeko Biche, Patricia Blake, Robert H. Boyle, Norma Brailow, Abraham Bromberg, Josef Bromberg, Matthew J. Bruccoli, Jean Bruneau, Cyril Bryner, William F. Buckley, Jr., Richard M. Buxbaum, Jacqueline Callier, Allegra Markevitch Chapuis, Ken and Phyllis Christiansen, Gardner and Florence Clark, Gerald Clarke, Dr. Bruce Cowan, Marcantonio Crespi, Vivian Crespi, Harold and Gert Croghan, Constance Darkey, Jean-Jacques Demorest, Galya Diment, Alexander Dolinin, John C. Downey, Martha Duffy, Barbara Epstein, Jason Epstein, Lazar Feygin, John G. Franclemont, Helen French, Natalie Markevitch Frieden, Helmut Frielinghaus, George Gibian, Christopher F. Givan, Herbert Gold, Henry A. Grunwald, Albert Guerard, Moussa Gucassoff, Lillian Habinowski, Evan Harrar, James B. Harris, Fred Hills, Nat Hoffman, Robert C. Howes, Margaret Stephens Humpstone, Joseph S. Iseman, D. Barton Johnson, Alison Bishop Jolly, Eric Kahane, Morris and Audrey Kahn, Peter Kahn, Simon Karlinsky, Serge Karpovich, Steve Katz, Alfred Kazin, Robin Kemball, Arthur Luce Klein, Vera Kliatchkine, Jill Krementz, Mati Laanso, Dan Lacy, Robert Langbaum, Frances Lange, Sophie Lannes, James Laughlin, Dmitri Ledkovsky, Marina Ledkovsky, Richard L. Leed, Maria Leiper, Elena Levin, Alan Levy, Beverly Jane Loo, Peter Lubin, Irina Morozova Lynch, Joan Macmillan, Princess Zinaida Malewsky-Malévitch, Prince Michaël Massalsky, Niclas Massalsky, William Maxwell, Joseph Mazzeo, Beatrice MacLeod, James McConkey, William McGuire, Polly Minton, Walter and Marion Minton, Tatiana Morozoff, Jenni Moulton, Helen Muchnic,

Anne Dyer Murphy, Carl Mydans, Dominique Nabokov, Ivan Nabokoff, Peter Nabokov, Benjamin Nathans, Michael Naumann, Nigel Nicolson, Ivan Obolensky, J. D. O'Hara, William Orndorff, Stephen Jan and Marie-Luce Parker, Louise Parry, Willa Petschek, Joan de Peterson, Rodney Phillips, Otto M. Pitcher, Ellendea Proffer, Robert M. Pyle, Charles Remington, Jean Remington, Kay Rice, Oleg Rodzianko, William W. and Eleanor Rowe, Dorothy Rudo, Robert Ruebman, Joanna Russ, Michael Scammell, Louba Schirman, Arthur Schlesinger, Jr., Ruth Schorer, Lore Segal, Christine Semenenko, Alain Seznec, Ruth Sharp, Ron Sheppard, Nilly and Vladimir Sikorsky, Roberta Silman, David R. Slavitt, Dorothy Staller, Saul Steinberg, Dave Stephens, Roger W. Straus, Mary Struve, Ronald Sukenick, Kitty Szeftel, Marc Szeftel, Horst Tappé, Frank Taylor, Victor Thaller, Diana Trilling, Aileen Ward, Lord George Weidenfeld, Edmund White, Herbert and Jane Wiegandt, Richard Wilbur, Galen Williams, Reuel Wilson, Rosalind Baker Wilson, Miriam Worms, Helen Yakobson, Isabella Yanovsky, Dieter Zimmer. To this list should be added Nabokov's Wellesley, Harvard, and Cornell students, as well as his Harvard section men, who I hope will accept a collective expression of gratitude here. They are named individually in footnotes. I have relied especially heavily on several former students, among them Jane E. Curtis, Tanya Clyman, Edouard C. Emmet, Dorothy Gilbert, Dick Keegan, Dr. Peter Klem, Katherine Reese Peebles, Harriet Dorothy Rothschild, Pedro Sanjuan, Ross Wetzsteon.

The tiles from which Véra Nabokov's life can be reconstructed are small and my debts proportionately great, especially to the individuals who supplied correspondences, memoirs, and documents of various kinds: Dimitri Andrault de Langeron, Norma Brailow, Natalie Barosin, Mary Bellino, Lewis Dabney, Brian Gross, Lillian Habinowski, Hans Georg Heepe at Rowohlt, Glenn Horowitz, Alan Jolis, Ron Kohls at the Jüdische Gemeinde zu Berlin, Michael Juliar, Polly Kemp, Elena Levin, Lilla Lyon, Prince Michaël Massalsky, Dr. Doris Nagel, Inger Nielsen at the Wellesley College Alumnae Association, Albert N. Podell, Ellendea Proffer, Terry Quinn, Helene Sikorski, Susan Strunk at the Office of Public & Congressional Affairs, FOIA Section, Lidia Tanguy, Tompkins County Clerk Aurora Valenti, William Vesterman.

The bulk of the Nabokovs' papers make their home at the Berg Collection of The New York Public Library, a researcher's heaven. In addition I am indebted to the following institutions for access to, and in many cases permission to quote from, their collections: the Amherst Center for Russian Culture, Amherst College, and in particular Stanley J. Rabinowitz and Tanya Chebotarev; the Bibliothèque Littéraire Jacques Doucet, Paris; Kathy

Whalen, Manuscripts Librarian at the Bryn Mawr College Library; the CBC Radio Archives; the Central State Historical Archive of the City of St. Petersburg; the Bakhmeteff Archive, Columbia University Library; Division of Rare and Manuscript Collections, Cornell University Library, and above all to the peerless Phil McCray; the Rare Book, Manuscript, and Special Collections Library at Duke University, in particular Janie C. Morris; the Hoover Institution Archives, Stanford University; the Houghton Library, Harvard University; the Institut Mémoires de l'Edition Contemporaine, Paris; the Library of Congress; Slavic and East European Library, University of Illinois at Urbana-Champaign; Saundra Taylor, Curator of Manuscripts, and the Lilly Library, Indiana University, Bloomington, Indiana; the Special Collections Library, University of Michigan, and curator Kathryn Beam; the archives of the Ministère des Affaires Etrangères, Quai d'Orsay, Paris; the archives of Paul, Weiss, Rifkind, Wharton & Garrison; Rare Books and Special Collections, Princeton University Libraries; the Russian State Historical Archive, St. Petersburg; the Russian National Library, St. Petersburg; Nathalie Auerbach at the Stanford University Archives; the Harry Ransom Humanities Research Center at the University of Texas at Austin; the Tolstoy Foundation, especially Cyril Galitzin; the University of Toronto archives; the Washington University Libraries, St. Louis, Missouri; the Wellesley College Archives, where I plagued Wilma R. Slaight; the Beinecke Rare Book and Manuscript Library, Yale University. At the Nabokov family archive in Montreux, Switzerland, Oxana Chkolnik and Béatrice Chiaradia were unfailingly helpful.

Anatolij Chayesh and Dmitri Elyashevich provided invaluable research assistance in St. Petersburg, as did Robert E. Lee, who doubled as translator.

This book could neither have been researched nor written without generous fellowships from the John Simon Guggenheim Memorial Foundation and the National Endowment for the Humanities. I owe personal thanks to many people, chief among them Harold Augenbraum, Marc de La Bruyère, David Colbert, Mary Deschamps, Dr. Orli Etinger, Joshua Karant, Mameve Medwed, Philip Milito, Gavriel Shapiro, Nikki Smith, and Peter Straus.

Brian Boyd strongly discouraged me from attempting this biography, then proceeded to assist generously with its research. For both acts of humanity he has my gratitude. His footsteps are large, and I have done my best to avoid attempting to fill them. Stephen Crook at the Berg Collection of the New York Public Library should know already of my admiration and if he does not, can read of it here. He is a prince among men, which makes him emperor of archivists. I am indebted to Bob Loomis for many things, but especially for his consummate skill with a pencil. He should be grateful to two individuals who read before him, and took half the calls that might have been rerouted in his direction: Lois Wallace, incomparable agent, and Elinor Lipman, steadfast and superior friend.

My most considerable debt is to Dmitri Nabokov, who—above and beyond opening the archives—afforded me the biographer's greatest luxury: He allowed me to torture him with questions without ever reversing the equation. From the beginning he understood perfectly why I needed not only his parents' correspondence but that 1943 grocery list, the one on which his father suggested his mother acquire a "monster pineapple."

NOTES

Notes for primary sources follow; a list of select secondary sources appears in the Bibliography, page 433. Except where indicated, all archival materials can be found at the Berg Collection of English and American Literature, The New York Public Library. Some of Nabokov's letters remain in private collections, abbreviated as PC.

Family names have been rendered as follows: VN (Vladimir Nabokov), VéN (Véra Nabokov), DN (Dmitri Nabokov), HS (Nabokov's sister Elena [Hélène] Sikorski).

Translations from the Russian are by Robert E. Lee; from the Swedish by Scott A. Mellor and Susan Brantly; from the Italian by Karina Attar; from the French by the author. Russian translations may vary slightly from previously published texts.

Nabokov's texts, and the collections in which his papers or related documents can be found, have been abbreviated as follows (unabbreviated Nabokov titles appear in all caps):

ANL	Annotated Lolita
BEND	Bend Sinister
CE	Conclusive Evidence
EO	Eugene Onegin
GIFT	The Gift
IB	Invitation to a Beheading
KQK	King, Queen, Knave
LD	Laughter in the Dark
LL	Lectures on Literature
LO	Lolita
LRL	Lectures on Russian Literature
LATH	Look at the Harlequins!
NWL	The Nabokov-Wilson Letters
GOGOL	Nikolai Gogol
PF	Pale Fire
RLSK	The Real Life of Sebastian Knight
SL	Vladimir Nabokov: Selected Letters
SM	Speak, Memory
STORIES	The Stories of Vladimir Nabokov
SO	Strong Opinions
TT	Transparent Things
Amherst	Amherst Center for Russian Culture, Amherst College
Bakhm	Bakhmeteff Archive, Columbia University
BMC	Bryn Mawr College Library
Cornell	Carl A. Kroch Library, Cornell University
Hoover	Hoover Institution Archives, Stanford University
LOC	Library of Congress
Lilly	Lilly Library, Indiana University, Bloomington, Indiana

VNA   Nabokov family archive, Montreux
Michigan   Ardis Press Archive, University of Michigan, Special Collections Library
PW   Paul, Weiss, Rifkind, Wharton & Garrison archives
HR   Harry Ransom Humanities Research Center, University of Texas at Austin
TF   Tolstoy Foundation Archives
WCA   Wellesley College Archives
Yale   Beinecke Rare Book and Manuscript Library, Yale University

INTRODUCTION

xi   "There is only one": RLSK, 111.

Other writers: Interview with Frank Taylor, May 17, 1995.

"It was as close": Interview with William Maxwell, May 4, 1995. As Carl Proffer told Brian Boyd, "They seemed as one person." Boyd notes of April 28, 1983, Boyd archive. Similarly, Vivian Crespi, April 5, 1995; Matthew J. Bruccoli, April 18, 1995; Herbert Gold, June 22, 1995.

Even her detractors: Interview with Zinaida Shakhovskoy, October 26, 1995.

Apologizing for the pencil: VN to his mother, January 24, 1928, VNA. VéN to Elena Levin, March 10, 1963, PC.

xii   "She was just": Interview with James Laughlin, July 27, 1995.

"She was the international": Herbert Gold to author, June 19, 1995.

"She was the Saint": Interview with Alfred Appel, April 19, 1995.

lady driver: VéN to DN, July 1, 1960, VNA.

credited cameo: KQK, 232.

"She was a Polish": Interview with Helmut Frielinghaus, May 28, 1996.

Several of her husband's: Interviews with Joanna Russ, May 6, 1996 (a German princess), Marvin Shapiro, October 22, 1996 (a Russian countess), Peter Klem, September 25, 1996. French: Interview with Ivan Obolensky, May 31, 1996.

write around her: "There is a hole at the center of Nabokov's biography, and there always will be; it is part of the romance of his story," concluded Boyd, after twenty-seven chapters and two thousand pages. *The Nabokovian* 27 (Fall 1991), 27. See also Andrew Field, *Nabokov: His Life in Part* (New York: Viking, 1977), 180: "Without drawing a picture of Véra Evseevna myself I will say only that virtually all the printed descriptions I have read of her strike me as wholly or seriously wanting." They could not get closer; both men were writing in her lifetime.

the two projects: VN diary entry, March 10, 1966, VNA.

"He would have been": Interview with William Maxwell, May 4, 1995. Echoed by Beverly Loo, Louba Schirman, HS, Joseph Iseman, Vivian Crespi.

"the only place in America": Alan Nordstrom, *Ivy* magazine (New Haven), February 1959.

lit up around his wife: Interview with Isabel Kleigman, July 27, 1996. Similarly, Dick Keegan, Herbert Gold.

shared a secret: Interview with Carol Levine, September 10, 1996.

"He was the most": Interview with Joseph Mazzeo, January 7, 1997.

xiii   "Mr. Keegan": Interview with Keegan, January 15, 1998.

An American admirer: Interview with Evan Harrar, August 26, 1996.

"Portrait of the Artist": DESPAIR, 201.

"refined their marriage": Gerald Clarke, "Checking in with Vladimir Nabokov," *Esquire,* July 1975, 67.

Shaped his work: See Boyd, 1990, 283–85; Boyd, 1991, 627–31.

xiv   "It would be difficult": Interview with Saul Steinberg, January 4, 1996.

1   PETERSBURG 3848

3   "I don't remember": Interview with Alfred Appel, April 19, 1995.

"Who are you": Interview with Ellendea Proffer, May 31, 1995.

"No," shot back: See Boyd, *The Nabokovian* 27 (Fall 1991), 23.

"I met my": SO, 127.

4   "All this is rot": VéN copy of Field, 1977, 179, VNA.

    "While there he": William Vesterman, "Nabokov's Second Fiancée Identified," *American Notes and Queries,* September/October 1985. VéN to Vesterman, April 20, 1984, VNA. VéN amended Vesterman's title ("Nabokov's Second Fiancée Identified") to "Nabokov's Third Fiancée Identified." In a second set of marginal remonstrations, she quibbled with the following of Field's statements in *VN: The Life and Art of Vladimir Nabokov,* VNA: VN did not write "one postcard" to VéN. The two did not meet at a charity ball. They did not meet for the first time at her father's office. They did not meet because her future husband played chess with her father. While acknowledging that her husband correctly recalled the date of their first meeting, she rejected as well Boyd's description of the charity ball encounter, which she swore she would deny if ever she was asked, protesting that the account "is very unlike the truth" (VéN to BB, October 14, 1987, VNA). She doubted moreover that her husband would have been in the mood to attend a ball in May of 1923, VéN to BB, May 1986, VNA. As for the three "untruths" in Vesterman's line, VN wrote VéN more than once during the summer weeks he was away. And it is possible that he did not leave Berlin immediately after meeting her; the two met on either May 8 or May 9, and the first letter dates from several weeks later. Which leaves as a third potential untruth—VN was incontrovertibly in the south of France, and the girl was incontrovertibly named Véra Slonim—only the charity ball.

    " 'reminiscence' ": VéN cited in Boyd, 1990, 202.

    "organized by society": VéN to Field, March 10, 1973.

    "But without these": LECTURES ON DON QUIXOTE, 1.

    confide in a visiting: Interview with Beverly Loo, October 24, 1996.

    "many of whom were": Alexander Brailow to Boyd, October 20, 1983, Boyd archive.

5   "tender lips": "The Encounter," May 1923.

    "He was, as a young": VéN interview with Martin Amis, *Visiting Mrs. Nabokov,* 118. VéN to Amis, September 11, 1981, VNA.

    one to pursue Nabokov: Interview with Svetlana Andrault de Langeron, January 28, 1997. Also HS, interviews of July 11, 1995, January 15, 1997; Vera Kliatchkine, interview of June 16, 1995; Boyd interview with Rene and Evgenia Cannac, March 11, 1983, Boyd archive.

    "certain unusual refinement": Field, 1977, 181.

    "I suppose one could": Ellendea Proffer to author, May 9, 1997.

    "I know practically": VéN to Stephen Jan Parker, January 22, 1981, VNA. The claim that she had followed his career for some time went undisputed in VéN's copy of Field, 1986, 97, VNA.

    "a dear, dear mask": VN to VéN, July 6, 1926, VNA.

6   "linked in my memory" to "settle there forever": VN to Svetlana Siewert, May 25, 1923. Transcribed copy, Shakhovsky papers, Amherst. VN's sister felt he was near-suicidal at the time of the broken engagement, interview with HS, February 26, 1995.

    "I won't hide it" and "I desperately: VN to VéN, May 27, 1923, VNA.

7   "He was a poet" to the removal of the rings: Interview with Svetlana Andrault de Langeron, January 28, 1997.

    "a youth of energetic": Boyd, 1990, 4.

    "a rejected suitor's": EO, III, 200.

    allowed that it had: VéN to Vesterman, June 15, 1981, VNA.

    "But sorrow not": Nabokov, "The Encounter."

8   "rickety" soul: Untitled poem, "You entered airborne."

    "My happiness": VN to VéN, January 8, 1924, VNA.

    "And night flowed" to "are to be my fate": Nabokov, "The Encounter." A draft of the poem, more vulnerable-sounding in an early version, bears the dedication "To Véra Slonim."

    On her Bulgarian: VéN to Natalya Tolstoy, December 18, 1985, VNA. The *Rul* translations appeared between June 6 and September 16, 1923.

    "Is there a place": Iosef Hessen, unpublished memoir, chapter 16, page 11, Hoover.

9   "Song": "Pesnia," composed July 19, 1923 in Toulon.

    "witches' sabbath": Stefan Zweig, *The World of Yesterday* (Lincoln: University of Nebraska Press, 1964), 311.

10   two Russian soccer teams: Otto Friedrich, *Before the Deluge* (New York: Harper & Row, 1972), 86. For the most comprehensive portrait of Russian Berlin, see Robert C. Williams, *Culture in Exile* (Ithaca: Cornell University Press, 1972). I have drawn as well on John Glad, ed., *Conver-*

sations in Exile: Russian Writers Abroad (Durham: Duke University Press, 1993); Simon Karlinsky, *Marina Tsvetaeva: The Woman, Her World and Her Poetry* (Cambridge: Cambridge University Press, 1985); Fritz Mierau, ed., *Russen in Berlin,* 1918–33 (Leipzig, Reclam-Verlag,
1991); Nicolas Nabokov, *Bagazh* (New York: Atheneum, 1975); Marc Vishniak, *"Sovremennye
Zapiski": Vospominaniya redaktora.* (Bloomington: Indiana University, School of Slavonic and
East European Studies, 1957).

horseback riding: VéN to Field, March 10, 1973.

"All of us sleepless": Nina Berberova, *Italics Are Mine,* 165.

"clinging couples": Khodasevich, cited in Ilya Ehrenburg, *Memoirs, 1921–1941,* 22.

surprised with the precipitate: Interview with HS, February 26, 1995.

"Divining, you notice": STIKHI, 115–16, dated September 25, 1923. In the original the poem is
signed "Nabokoff," not "Sirin."

"amazingly" and "inept endearment": VN to VéN, November 8, 1923, VNA.

11   "With her for a reader": Filippa Rolf, "January," 70, PC.

"You came into my": VN to VéN, November 8, 1923, VNA.

"Have you ever": VN to VéN, December 3, 1923, VNA.

"entered his life": RLSK, 79–80.

12   "They became lovers": RLSK ms., LOC.

"Despite the complexity": GIFT, 185.

"They're all Picassos": James Lord, *Picasso and Dora: A Personal Memoir* (New York: Fromm International, 1994), 123.

"What was it about": GIFT, 177.

"You and I are": VN to VéN, July 15, 1924, VNA.

autobiographical results: GIFT, 364. VN was not quite so easily swayed as his hero. After a portion
of the book appeared he wrote Mark Aldanov unapologetically (February 3, 1938, Bakhm) defending himself against charges of having appropriated characteristics of various recognizable
individuals: "Smile, Mark Alexandrovich! You say that *The Gift* can count on a very long life.
If so, then it is all the more polite on my part to have taken along on this journey for free the
images of certain of my contemporaries who would otherwise remain at home forever." VN
applauded this practice in the Master, noting: "There is something very pleasing in Pushkin's
device of having his best friends entertain his favorite characters" (EO, iii, 120).

13   the amorous conversations: HS to VN, August 28, 1956, PC.

"as if gliding" and "airborne": "You," dated November 25, 1923, and untitled, November 1923,
VNA.

"Is 'mask' " and "delight in the semitranslucent": LO, 53.

"a little obscurity": VN to Katharine White, undated note, "Gardens and Parks," LOC.

"My sweet, today": VN to VéN, July 4, 1926, VNA.

"the little silk mask": Cited in Alden Whitman's obituary of VN, *The New York Times,* July 5, 1977.

14   "You are *my* mask": VN to VéN, January 8, 1924, VNA.

VéN's birthdate: Old style, December 23, 1901. She shared a birthday with *Ada*'s Demon and Daniel
Veen, Aqua and Marina. Marina and Demon begin their affair on January 5 as well. See Boyd
in *The Nabokovian* 31 (Fall 1993), 13.

The late marriage: The average ages among Jewish businessmen and intellectuals marrying in 1899
was twenty-nine for men, twenty-three for women.

Slonim background: Much of the information on Evsei Slonim comes from the archives of the Imperial University of St. Petersburg, synagogue archives, and the lists of barristers of the St. Petersburg Judicial Chamber, Central State Historical Archive of the City of St. Petersburg; the
Russian State Historical Archive, St. Petersburg (RGIA); and from the Russian National Library (RNB). I am hugely indebted to Prince Michaël Massalsky as well, for sharing materials
from his family archive. For a sense of the Feigin family, I am grateful to Abraham and Josef
Bromberg, interviews of May 20, 1997. Home addresses are from *All St. Petersburg, 1894–1913,
All Petrograd,* 1917, or from RGIA. Birth certificate, RGIA, Fond 14, opis 3, delo 24224, document 2.

15   For a sense of the Furstadtskaya neighborhood, see Mikhail Beizer, *The Jews of Saint Petersburg*
(New York: Jewish Publication Society, 1989). Furstadtskaya is today Petra Lavrova Street,
and the address of the American Consulate in Petersburg.

16 "the little boy": GIFT, 213.

the precocious newspaper reading: Brian Boyd very generously shared the text of his talks with VéN. VéN to Boyd, February 25, 1982. Boyd interview with VéN, August 29, 1982, Boyd archive. See also Boyd, 1990, 213.

"completely disregarding: Berberova, *Italics Are Mine,* 14.

educational statistics: I. A. Kurganoff, *Women in the USSR* (London [Ontario]: S.B.O.N.R. Publishing, 1971).

17 On the texture of life in prerevolutionary Petersburg: E. M. Almedingen, *My St. Petersburg* (New York: Norton, 1970); James H. Billington, *The Icon and the Axe* (New York: Knopf, 1966); William Barnes Steveni, *Petrograd Past and Present* (London: Grant Richards, 1915); Zinaida Shakhovskoy, *La vie quotidienne à Saint-Petersbourg à l'époque romantique* (Paris: Hachette, 1967). And generally on Petersburg: Katerina Clark, *Petersburg: Crucible of Cultural Revolution* (Cambridge: Harvard University Press, 1995), and Solomon Volkov, *St. Petersburg: A Cultural History* (New York: Free Press, 1995).

VéN and her German: VéN to Boyd, May 1986, VNA. On the girls' linguistic education, interviews with Massalsky, February 17, 1996, and June 16, 1997.

telepathy: DN to author, May 16, 1997.

VéN's Obolensky record: VNA.

special permission: VéN to Alexis Goldenweiser, June 8, 1957, Bakhm.

"When you are married": Field, 1977, 179.

Dickens, Byron: Interviews with Massalsky, September 21, 1996, and June 16, 1997.

18 walkways at Terioki: Filippa Rolf, "January," 57, PC. For a similar childhood see Osip Mandelstam, *The Noise of Time.*

relative later reminded: Anna Feigin to VéN, October 6, 1962, Berg.

Evsei Lazarevich raised: Interviews with Massalsky, February 17, 1996, and November 14, 1997.

splendid stage set: For a sense of the city, see James H. Bater, *St. Petersburg: Industrialization and Change* (London: Edward Arnold, 1976); Marshall Berman, *All That Is Solid Melts into Air* (New York: Simon & Schuster, 1982); Volkov, *St. Petersburg.*

19 scratch-scratch: Boyd interview with VéN, February 25, 1982, Boyd archive.

"One cannon shot": VéN to Boyd, June 6, 1987, VNA. See also DEFENSE, 21.

the words "Russian" and "Jew": The summary is Benjamin Ira Nathans's, from his doctoral dissertation, "Beyond the Pale: The Jewish Encounter with Russia, 1840–1900," UCLA, Berkeley, 1995, 290. "Beyond the Pale" proved a singularly valuable source of information on the Jews of Petersburg. Equally indispensable was Robert Melvin Seltzer's "Simon Dubnow: A Critical Biography of His Early Years," Ph.D. dissertation, Columbia University, 1970. The following histories of Jewish life and its restrictions in prerevolutionary times have proved especially helpful, Dubnow perhaps most of all: Salo W. Baron, *The Russian Jew under Tsars and Soviets* (New York: Macmillan, 1976); Mikhail Beizer, *Jews of St. Petersburg;* S. M. Dubnow, *History of the Jews in Russia and Poland,* vols. II and III (Philadelphia, Jewish Publication Society of America, 1918); Leo Errera, *The Russian Jews: Extermination or Emancipation* (Westport, Conn.: Greenwood Press, 1975, repr. of 1894 edition); Harold Frederic, *The New Exodus* (New York: Arno Press, 1970, repr. of 1892 edition); Jacob Frumkin et al., eds., *Russian Jewry (1860–1917)* (New York: Thomas Yoseloff, 1966); Louis Greenberg, *The Jews in Russia* (New Haven: Yale University Press, 1965); Avrahm Yarmolinsky, *The Jews and Other Minor Nationalities under the Soviets* (New York: Vanguard Press, 1928).

"I would rather be": Cited in Errera, *The Russian Jews,* 108.

20 greatest historian: The historian was Simon Dubnow; the president Zalman Shazar.

Simon Poliakov: Greenberg, *Jews in Russia,* 173.

Gamshey Leizerovich: Russian State Historical Archives [TSGIA]. His name appears as such in all official correspondence until 1905.

21 admitted to the bar: Greenberg, *Jews in Russia* II, 38.

kitchen tile company: Russian National Library [RNB]; Merchant Directories. RGIA.

Véra Nabokov remembered, to "skilled peasants": VéN to Field, March 10, 1973.

Leo Peltenburg: I owe much of the information on the Peltenburg family to Alphonse Roebroek, interview of December 6, 1996.

22 On the Jewish timber trade: Frumkin et al., *Russian Jewry,* 131–37.

"system wherein a second": VN to Katharine White, March 17, 1951, SL, 117.

The Rodzianko work: Oleg Rodzianko kindly assisted in the untangling of the Rodzianko history, interview of June 7, 1998. RGIA files.

Slonim's political leanings: VéN to Boyd, December 13, 1981, VéN corrections to Field 1986, 94, VNA.

23   longest-running legal concern: State Historical Archives (RGIA), Collection 23, Collection 1330. The case is highly unusual for its longevity.

"specific gravity": Field, 1977, 89.

Speaking for Martin: GLORY, 54, SM, 25.

"An average Russian": VéN diary, VNA.

24   "Both of our sets": Interview with Evan Harrar, August 26, 1996.

turn the key: Lena Massalsky to VéN, December 19, 1967.

"Judging by your letter": Anna Feigin to VéN, 1964.

"They were raised," the sense of noblesse oblige, and the seating arrangements: Interview with Prince Michaël Massalsky, April 6, 1997.

"One is always": SM, 116.

25   "A few years": VéN to Field, March 10, 1973. Slonim was able to buy the land with two guards officers as partners.

"calm, but uninteresting": Leonid Feygin, Moya Zhizn' (Moscow: Materik, 1993).

slandered in a newspaper: Boyd interview with VéN December 2, 1986, Boyd archive.

"As a little bit": O. Mandelstam, 77.

"traced his descent": VéN to Field, March 10, 1973.

the Jewish tutor: O. Mandelstam, 78.

throwing down a glove: Interview with Vivian Crespi, June 20, 1997. Filippa Rolf to Estrid Tenggren, January 15, 1961, PC. Rolf, "January," 45, PC.

26   "My father often": O. Mandelstam, 86.

"since for me no": VéN to Lena Massalsky, December 4, 1959.

"In your article": VéN to New York Post, August 22, 1958.

"Yes, Russian and Jewish": Roberto Cantini, "Nabokov tra i cigni di Montreux," in Epoca, July 10, 1973.

"I loathe people": VéN diary, VNA.

27   supplementary coaching: Nicolas Berdyaev, The Russian Idea (London: G. Bles, 1947), 27.

"intellectual arrogance": Diana Trilling, The Beginning of the Journey (New York: Harcourt Brace, 1993), 20.

breadlines: For a sense of the Revolution and day-to-day life, see especially Iosef Hessen, unpublished memoir, Hoover; and Miriam Kochan, The Last Days of Imperial Russia (New York: Macmillan, 1976). For the history of the Revolution, I have drawn almost exclusively on the work of Richard Pipes: Russia under the Old Regime, The Russian Revolution, and Russia Under the Bolshevik Regime.

28   member of the intelligentsia: Interview with DN, May 23, 1997.

"the spirit of self-sacrifice": VN to Edmund Wilson, February 23, 1948, NWL 194–96.

"syphilis": Pipes, Russian Revolution, 60.

could not object strenuously: Her marginal reaction to the assertion in Williams, Culture in Exile, is "nonsense." Also VéN to Boyd, December 13, 1981, VNA.

A wrong step: Hessen, unpublished memoirs, chap. 16, p. 32, Hoover.

29   "I remember vividly": VéN to Anastasia Rodzianko, May 9, 1984, VNA. The original is in French.

all the cars: Karlinsky, Marina Tsvetaeva, 81.

"not so much decided": VéN to Boyd, May 1986, VNA. Sonia's recollections, Anna Feigin to VéN, December 7, 1964. Lena's recollections, interview with Massalsky, June 16, 1997.

The train ride to Odessa, through the arrival in the Crimea: I have based this account on Boyd's notes of his conversation with VéN, June 13, 1982, and December 13, 1981. Also on P. J. Capelotti, ed., Our Man in the Crimea (Columbia: University of South Carolina Press, 1991).

the rail ties: Interview with DN, May 23, 1997; interview with Massalsky, June 16, 1997.

31   She could sing: Interviews with DN, November 1, 1996, May 23, 1997.

"No one knew": Ilya Ehrenburg, People and Life, 1891–1921 (New York: Knopf, 1962), 313. Or as VN described Yalta in GLORY, 2: "the town kept trying on now one regime, now another, and could not make up its finicky mind."

"sailing as if by chance" and rest of Martin's departure: GLORY, 24–28. By some reports the family left Yalta in March 1920. VéN remembered the Red Army pushing past the isthmus's fortifications and reported that the family stayed as long as Wrangel held the peninsula, which would place the departure in or slightly before November 1920. Lena Slonim put the departure in 1918, presumably borrowing the date on which the family had left Petersburg.

filthy vessel: See VN's description, to Cécile Miauton, n.d.

32 Véra on Vienna: To HS, December 1, 1967. The bulk of this account is again via Boyd's interview notes, especially those of June 13, 1982. Also, see Slonimsky, below.

sight of white bread: Nicolas Slonimsky, oral history of March 15, 1977, University of California at Los Angeles, Dept. of Special Collections, No. 300/169.

"made much money" to the charity balls: VéN to Field, March 10, 1973. Also, Boyd interview with VéN, June 5, 1982, Boyd archive.

"everybody was going": VéN to Field, March 10, 1973.

She talked, and argued: Boyd interview with VéN, December 20, 1981, Boyd archive.

"deprived of its high" through "Scala": VéN to Field, March 10, 1973.

"welter of vodka": Friedrich, *Before the Deluge,* 21.

33 discouraged in her plans: Boyd interview with VéN, November 11, 1982, Boyd archive. The architectural engineering degree: Filippa Rolf, "January," 22, PC.

import-export firm: Goldenweiser archives, Bakhm.

teaching herself to type: VN to Kirill Nabokov, n.d.

On Orbis: VéN to Goldenweiser, March 6, 1967, Bakhm.

the Dostoyevsky translation: Field, 1977, 178.

34 strolled by their governesses: Interview with Alfred Appel, October 20, 1995.

"They could have met": Penelope Gilliatt, "Nabokov," *Vogue,* March 1967.

"directed the searchlight": ADA, 153.

What would have to "as we are now": Field, 1977, 34.

Fate was ill-inclined: VN to VéN, November 1923, and August 24, 1924, VNA.

whole catalogue: Fate finds a way from the earliest stories ("Doorbell," 192) to the later novels (ADA, 152).

Nabokov at work in the background: W. W. Rowe, *Nabokov's Spectral Dimension*, 120ff.

Fate's devious ways: VéN to Boyd, May 1986, VNA.

35 "If you look carefully": Interview with Matthew J. Bruccoli, April 18, 1995.

"Oh, I have a thousand": GIFT, 193–94.

"the upper hand": RLSK, 7

He was bored: VN to VéN, December 30, 1923, VNA.

dreaming prophetically: VN to VéN, January 12, 1924, VNA.

"Something has happened": VN to VéN, January 24, 1924.

2   THE ROMANTIC AGE

36 "Don't you think": VéN to Boyd, May 1986, VNA.

37 "I've had many more": VN to Field, October 2, 1970, VNA.

regretted, though: SM, 240. "How many there had been already of these silk rags, and how he had tried to hang them across the gaping black gap!" laments the hero of one of VN's first stories, five months after VN had met VéN. "Wingstroke," STORIES, 28.

"hardly an ordinary": VN to VéN, November 8, 1923, VNA.

negative side of things: Boyd, 1990, 215.

"tiny sharp arrows": VN to VéN, December 3, 1923, VNA.

"At first I" to "sharp corners": VN to VéN, undated, 1924, VNA.

"I feel pain": Poem beginning, "Your face between palms," VNA. The "sharp corners" were again *ostrye ugly,* as in VN's letter.

38 "You see," he averred: VN to VéN, August 24, 1924, VNA.

value for posterity: Interview with DN, November 12, 1997.

Boyd feels: Boyd to author, June 21, 1997.

"Austen is a kitten": Interview with Joanna Russ, May 6, 1996.

the usual preconceptions: To which he readily confessed, VN to Wilson, May 5, 1950, NWL, 240–41.

"family disease": HS to VN, April 19, 1938, VNA. Selections from the Sikorski correspondence have been published, in Russian, as *Vladimir Nabokov: Perepiska s sestroi* (Ann Arbor: Ardis, 1985).

a symptom of provincial literature: VN to Aldanov, May 6, 1942, Bakhm.

"stellar" communication through "many other ways": VN to VéN, January 8, 1924, VNA.

synesthesia: See especially A. R. Luria, *The Mind of a Mnemonist* (New York: Basic Books, 1968), and Gladys A. Reichard, Roman Jakobson, and Elizabeth Werth's "Language and Synesthesia" in *Word* 5, no. 2 (August 1949).

39   pink flannel: VN to HS, November 26, 1945, PC. Also, BBC interview with VN, November 22, 1962. Nabokov lent some features of his palette to Fyodor, GIFT, 74.

"She spoils everything": Gerald Clarke, September 17, 1974, interview notes for *Esquire* profile.

"must convey the colour": RLSK, 70.

delighted in the luminosity: VN to VéN, January 17, 1924, VNA.

"She has different": Field, 1977, 179.

"possessed, too": RLSK, 81. The images are again conjoined in PF, 165.

40   "Véra says that the top": VN diary, January 15, 1951, VNA.

"capacity to wonder": VN, "The Creative Writer," *NEMLA Bulletin,* January 1942. LL, 374.

sitting under the dryer: Rolf, "January," PC.

general strike, to "everything then seemed": The offender was Friedrich, *Before the Deluge,* VéN copy.

acknowledged privately: VéN to DN, June 28, 1961, VNA.

coddled him: Iosef Hessen, *Gody izgnania* (Paris: YMCA Press, 1979), 94–95. Interview with HS, February 26, 1995.

"the smallest and oldest": SM, 41.

"All Nabokovs": Interview with HS, March 4, 1995.

"He loved himself": GIFT, 190.

41   "When we were last": VN to VéN, July 15, 1924, VNA. An unrelated character in "Terror," STORIES, 175, does too.

a number of critics: Boyd, 1991, 639. See also the work of W. W. Rowe, Gennady Barabtarlo, among others. VéN on "potustoronnost": STIKHI, 3.

soul is transferred: VN to VéN, May 12, 1930, VNA.

"I am so certain": VN to his mother, March 27, 1925, VNA.

afflicted by total recall: Richard Wilbur to author, May 21, 1997. Boyd, 1990, 278.

space may be finite: Boyd, 1990, 253.

"ex-mortals": "Lance," STORIES, 635.

"serene superknowledge": DN, in George Gibian and Stephen Jan Parker, eds., *The Achievements of Vladimir Nabokov,* 176.

42   small miracles: VN to VéN, January 24, 1924, VNA. To one elder he did thank for his kind words, Sirin confessed: "I write much and mindlessly." VN to Potresov (S. V. Yablonovsky), September 28, 1921.

"Now I truly" and "In winding ways": VN to VéN, January 24, 1924, VNA.

"circumlocutions": "THE WALTZ INVENTION," 10.

"Writing is all": VN to Svetlana Siewert, May 25, 1923, Amherst.

"I am prepared": VN to VéN, January 24, 1924, VNA.

among the three people: VN to VéN, December 3, 1923, VNA.

This was the winter: VéN remembered 1924 as the year she rendered Harold Nicolson's *Some People* into Russian for her father, possibly with an eye toward an Orbis edition. The volume counted as well among VN's favorites. (Nicolson's "Miss Plimsoll" does seem to cast a spell on "Mademoiselle O," which became the first installment of *Speak, Memory.* And which was reviewed in its British edition by Harold Nicolson.) She must have done so later, however, as Nicolson published the volume only in 1927. In a lovely interpenetration of time and generations, years later, on one of the most emotional days of her life, VéN would discuss another of her husband's favorite books, in London, with Harold Nicolson's son.

"savagely," and "to the point": VN to VéN, January 17, 1924, July 17, 1924, VNA.

Evsei Slonim's domestic arrangements: Interview with HS, July 11, 1995. Similarly, Ellendea Proffer, Michaël Massalsky.

43   "has always had": Anna Feigin to VéN, January 20, 1966.

"Anna Feigin was my cousin": VéN to G. Shapiro, January 16, 1985, VNA.

pleased to report: VN to his mother, probably July 1924, VNA.

44 recopying the enclosed: VN to VéN, July 17, 1924, VNA.
    "The sharpest jealousy": VN to his mother, probably July 1924, VNA.
    "We were ridiculously": SO, 191–92.
    "By the way": Boyd, 1990, 239.
    not to have been told: Gleb Struve on Nabokov, Box 50, Folder 54, Hoover.
45 "a predatory campaign": VN to VéN, August 24, 1924, VNA.
    embraced Véra warmly: Interview with HS, June 30, 1997.
    "Of what religion": Field, 1977, 78. VéN raised no marginal objection to the line.
    "I'm sorry he told": DEFENSE, 115. Mrs. Luzhin has no name prior to her marriage, just as Luzhin
        has no name and patronymic prior to his disappearing into his passion, on the last page of the
        novel.
    "Marry me, or": Interview with Vera Kliatchkine, June 16, 1995.
    "*imariable*": Zinaida Shakhovskoy, quoting Eugenia Cannac, October 26, 1995.
    "idiosyncratic form": GIFT, 185.
    "The one who finally": Alexander Brailow, unpublished memoirs, 88, PC.
46 "The most important": VN to HS, undated but probably 1926, PC.
    "the brain-bridge": LRL, 175.
    "Things that are precious": VéN to DN, November 16, 1975, VNA.
47 "We think that is": Rolf, "January," 51, PC.
    "understands so well," and the farms: VN to his mother, October 13, 1925, VNA.
    "My pet, I am": VN to VéN, June 29, 1926, VNA.
    attempts to commit: VN to VéN, June 7, 1926, VNA.
    miserable, homesick: VN to his mother, July 10, 1926, VNA.
48 the Binz trip: Interview with Abraham Bromberg, June 30, 1997.
    "a hook on the man's jaw": Cited in Boyd, 1990, 274. See also Field, 1986, 102.
    They appear lost and "The foreign girl": KQK, viii, 254. Leona Toker has pointed out that the cou-
        ple's appearance is briefer but more substantial in the Russian novel, in which they register as
        a sort of ambulatory emblem of true love. See *Nabokov: The Mystery of Literary Structures*
        (Ithaca: Cornell University Press, 1989), 63.
    "Her open dress": VN diary, October 16, 1964, VNA.
    "VN splashed the man's": VéN copy of Field, 1977, marginal note, 152.
49 Emma Bovary nomenclature: LL, 132.
    union of Marian Evans: Phyllis Rose, *Parallel Lives* (New York: Vintage, 1984), 210.
    reading an obituary: VN to VéN, January 17, 1924, VNA.
    Valentina as typist: The detective work on Valentina is not mine but Dieter Zimmer's. See Alexan-
        drov, ed., *The Garland Companion*, 352.
    watershed year: Field, 1986, 83. See also Marina Turkevich Naumann, *Blue Evenings in Berlin*.
50 "soon after my marriage": MARY, xiii.
    new Turgenev: Eugenia Cannac, *Russkaya Mysl* 3184 (December 29, 1977). VN was not pleased by
        the comparison. See also Aikhenvald review, *Rul,* March 3, 1926.
    oblivious to his lessons: VN to his mother, January 13, 1925, VNA.
    eight-hour marathon: VN to his mother, October 30, 1927, VNA.
    Véra contributed to this: VN to Field, October 2, 1970.
51 "He [Vladimir] never": VéN notes on Field's 1977 ms., VNA.
    The primer has survived: See Dieter Zimmer, *The Nabokovian* 27 (Fall 1991), 37–40.
    "After all, I'm afraid": VN to VéN, January 24, 1924, VNA.
    "everything connected": October 1964, unpublished VN interview notes.
    Telephone numbers: RLSK, 113. TT, 27.
    Newark as in New York: VN to Zenzinov, May 28, 1944, Bakhm.
    Auden and Aiken: VN to Edmund Wilson, February 16, 1946, NWL, 163.
    "The obstructive behavior": ADA, 571. He admitted to lending *Pale Fire*'s John Shade his litany of
        loathings, SO, 18.
    "Stupid, inimical things": Nurit Beretzky interview, *Ma'Ariv* (Israel), January 5, 1970.
    "the uncouth manuscript": RLSK, 34.
52 "She presided as adviser": Interview with Herbert Gold, *The Paris Review,* October 1967. Repr., SO,
        105. Elsewhere this was, "then my wife corrects the slips of my pencil," Gerald Clarke inter-
        view notes, September 17, 1974.

"still warm and wet": Robert Robinson, "The Last Interview," repr. in Peter Quennell, ed., *Vladimir Nabokov,* 123.

shrugged off: See for example Alfred Appel to VN, October 17, 1970; VéN to Appel, October 30, 1970.

"was very absent-minded": VéN to Simon Karlinsky, February 27, 1978, VNA. Cf. unpublished last chapter of SM, LOC, in which VN writes of a Mr. Nabokov who "seems to combine a good deal of absentmindedness with his pedantism."

"No, my dear": RLSK, 83.

"Wonderful, but I'm not" and "as a regulator": GIFT, 204–5.

This would have mandated: Hessen, *Gody izgnania,* 205.

"Well, after that my very": Robert Hughes interview tape, December 28, 1965.

53   "Most of my works": SO, 191.

radiant, delicate, thin-wristed: Gennady Barabtarlo reminds me that a similar presence, erect and slender and white, with a "pale conflagration" of golden hair, appears in VN's spring 1924 story "Revenge." See Barabtarlo, *Aerial View,* 6–19.

some of the shimmer: For a discussion of the shimmer semantically encoded in Zina's surname, see D. Barton Johnson, *Worlds in Regression,* 98ff. In 1968 VN inscribed a book, with a butterfly, to Véra. "Here's an iridescent butterfly for my iridescent darling," he offered, using a word related to *mertsat'.*

"And Clare, who": RLSK, 82.

"She and I are": Hughes interview, December 28, 1965.

Friends felt: Stephen Jan Parker to author, November 25, 1996.

54   "To get into" and "And once inside": G. Ivanov, cited in V. S. Yanovsky, *Elysian Fields,* 12.

"Reviews were considered": Yanovsky, 11–12. I have drawn here especially on Berberova, Williams, and Yanovsky.

one writer calculated: Volkov, *St. Petersburg,* 227.

"almost idyllic isolation": VN to Vladislav Khodasevich, July 24, 1934, Berberova papers, Yale.

Emily Dickinson: Rolf to Tenggren, January 15, 1961, PC.

essentially congratulated: VéN to Morris Bishop, May 23, 1973.

55   "The people I invite": Nantas Salvalaggio interview, *Il Giorno,* n.d.

"She had imagination": RLSK, 81.

erotic poems: VéN to Boyd, May 1986, VNA.

"Were you really": Interview with Ellendea Proffer, May 9, 1997.

a Berlin champion: Boyd interview with VéN, November 11, 1982, Boyd archive.

assassination plot: Interview with Vladimir Sikorsky, March 5, 1997. VéN denied all involvement in such a scheme in a *Washington Times* response to Andrew Field, December 22, 1986. But her affirmations tend to outweigh that protest to a biographer with whom she had fallen out: She told Ellendea and Carl Proffer, Serge Karpovich, Boyd, and her son of the Trotsky plan (HS heard of it from her brother), and others more generally of the revolver. With a laugh she admitted to Ellendea Proffer that "she had been quite carried away" (EP to author, May 9, 1997). Nor did she cavil with Field's allusions to the assassination attempt in the margins of his 1977 and 1986 volumes, which she marked up freely.

56   "I know, with certainty" and "all these, my idle": "Teddy," November 1, 1923, VNA. The "seven deaths" became "seven compressed deaths" in LD, 283.

"Fragile, tender": "Véra," unpublished Aikhenvald poem, LOC.

"Everyone in the Russian": Interview with Isabella Yanovsky, May 31, 1996.

"in the full bloom" and "the typewriter": VN to his mother, April 4, 1928, VNA.

57   death records: I am grateful to the Jüdische Gemeinde zu Berlin for documents relating to both Slonims' deaths.

"his readiness to ignore": *Rul,* June 30, 1928.

clerical position: There is no indication the position was anything but. Archives of the Ministère des Affaires Étrangères, Quai d'Orsay, Personnel, Berlin; Nantes, Berlin ambassade, série B, série C.

"How to Organize": Helen Yakobson, *Crossing Borders,* 157.

58   "hysterical over all sorts": VN to VéN, July 12, 1926, VNA.

Even he admitted: VN to Struve, January 25, 1929, Hoover.

claimed to have read: Hessen, *Gody izgnania,* 250.

"was nothing more": VN Memoriam to I. V. Hessen.

59   "only the squirrels": SM, 303.

deep orange: VN to Aikhenvald, July 15, 1927.

exercised with the windows: VN to mother, November 28, 1925, VNA.

"Personally, my husband": VéN to Robert C. Williams, February 23, 1965, VNA.

VN's German: Interviews with Josef and Abraham Bromberg, May 20, 1997. Struve was convinced VN knew the language, "Vladimir Nabokov as I Knew Him and as I See Him," 8, Hoover. Reading of DEFENSE, VéN to Ledig Rowohlt, March 8, 1960, VNA.

mangling it: VN to Roman Grynberg, February 18, 1967.

In a 1932 interview: "Meeting with V. Sirin," *Sevodnya* (Riga), November 4, 1932.

long disliked: VN to VéN, July 4, 1926, and draft of SM, LOC.

he could read but not write: VN to Princeton University Press, March 29, 1975.

60   "Who wanted assimilation": VéN copy of Williams, *Culture in Exile,* 282.

"Nansen-sical" passports: DESPAIR, 128. By LO, 27 they had become Nonsense passports. Anyone doubting the impression these sickly green papers made on the Nabokovs has only to inventory the references to them in the later work. The indignities bring to mind "the funnels and pulleys of the Holy Inquisition," " 'That in Aleppo Once . . .'," STORIES, 561.

"rat-whiskered": SM, 276–77.

"criminals on parole": SM, 276. In PNIN, 46, the passport is "a kind of parolee's card." Small wonder VN claimed to dote on his sacred blue American papers. As he told a French journalist in 1967: "J'éprouve une sensation de chaleur et d'orgueil lorsque je montre mon passeport américain aux frontières en Europe." Pierre Dommergues, *Le Monde,* November 22, 1967.

61   "Russian literature": VéN to her mother-in-law, July 26, 1929, VNA.

relinquished the land: VéN note in Field, 1986, 155.

French and German stenography: VéN to Goldenweiser, March 6, 1967, Bakhm. Most of VéN's employment history has been pieced together from her protracted reparations claim. Also PW archives, vol. 18.

Nabokov resented: VN to VéN, from Prague, probably 1930, VNA.

"my morning blind": VN to VéN, June 20, 1926, VNA.

62   employment statistics: Detlev J. K. Peukert, *The Weimar Republic* (New York: Hill & Wang, 1992), 96ff. Equally helpful as background for this chapter were Alix de Jonge, *The Weimar Chronicle* (New York: Paddington Press, 1978); Walter Laqueur, *Weimar: A Cultural History, 1918–1933* (New York: Putnam's, 1974); Otto Friedrich, *Before the Deluge.*

"we always had": VéN to Field, March 10, 1973.

proud assertion of 1935: VN to Ellen Rydelius, December 6, 1935.

"having developed his": VéN to Field, March 10, 1973.

Anna Dostoyevsky: see Anna Dostoyevsky, *Reminiscences* (New York, Liveright, 1975).

63   one of his then-admirers: Zinaida Saranna (Shakhovskoy), *Le Rouge et Le Noir* (Brussels), November 16, 1932. His detractors went further, accusing him of repackaging foreign literature in an appropriated style. See Georgy Ivanov in *Chisla,* February 1930.

"As a young author": VéN to Stephen A. Canada, March 4, 1966.

64   "in a German paraphrase": GIFT, 189.

On Weil, Gans: VéN told Boyd that the law firm had made the transition to fiction intact, down to the last detail, February 26, 1983, Boyd archive. Goldenweiser attested to the same, to VN, July 29, 1938, Bakhm.

"high adventure": VéN to Field, March 10, 1973.

his happiest work, Field, 1977, 158.

a third of what she had been earning: On his April 10, 1935, declaration of income, VN reported RM 1156 as compared to VéN's 3300 of the previous years, LOC.

she flatly denied: VéN to Robert MacGregor, New Directions, July 29, 1960.

one visitor's opinion: Rolf, "January," 26. VéN was responding to Helen Lawrenson's "The Man Who Scandalized the World," *Esquire,* August 1960, 70–74.

answered that they could not: Brailow, unpublished memoir, 88, PC.

65   "When are you fleeing": Mikhail Osorgin to VN, April 28, 1933; A. Kaun to VN, December 24, 1936, LOC.

"in somewhat of a": VN to Anna Shakhovskoy, November 22, 1932, LOC.

"I'm Jewish": See the accounts of Zinaida Shakhovskaya, Amherst.

"lives in two rooms": Galina Kuznetsova, diary entry of March 19, 1931, reprinted in *Novyj zhurnal,* 76 (1964).

66   On VN as houseguest: See VN, in memory of Amalia Osipovna Fondaminsky, Bakhm. Also Zenzinov correspondence, LOC.

crossing the streets: VN to VéN, October 17, 1932, VNA.

"I said to Aldanov": VN to VéN, October 24, 1932, VNA. Others did not joke about VéN's assistance. Asked later if she had felt professional envy for Khodasevich, Berberova protested, "There was nothing to envy there." She then added forcefully, with a near-tragic frown, "Now Sirin was really envied by all. Because he had such a wife." Omry Ronen to author, September 19, 1998.

survive otherwise: VN to VéN, November 5, 1932, VNA.

67   Jewish emigration: See Saul Friedländer, *Nazi Germany and the Jews,* vol. I, 62. For a sense of the last Russians in Berlin, I have leaned as well on Brailow, unpublished memoir; on Zinaida Shakhovskoy, *Une manière de vivre* (Paris: Presses de la Cité, 1965); and on Williams, *Culture in Exile.*

"I said, 'they won't' ": VéN to Field, March 10, 1973.

she got the job: VéN to Goldenweiser, May 22, 1958, Bakhm.

they were said to resemble: Christopher Isherwood, *Goodbye to Berlin* (London: Folio Society, 1975), 252.

their bonfire: Boyd interview with VéN, November 19, 1982, Boyd archive.

miserable dead end: VN to VéN, August 24, 1924, VNA.

provincial outpost: VN to VéN, July 4, 1926, VNA.

"He did not have enough": VéN interviewed by D. Barton Johnson and Ellendea Proffer, *Russian Literature Triquarterly* 24 (January 1991), 79.

"thrice-damned Germany": VN to Magda Nachman-Achariya, December 16, 1937.

Véra had admired: Field, 1977, 198.

68   "On the map of Europe": Berberova, *Italics Are Mine,* 223.

She pointed out: Shakhovskoy, *Une manière de vivre,* 240.

"occupy themselves" VN to Khodasevich, July 24, 1934.

"We were always": Field notes, PW.

laziness: *Sevodnya* (Riga), November 4, 1932.

Sirin call: Albert Parry acknowledged his work in *The American Mercury,* July 1939. For the background to Parry's having named VN as a Russian writer of promise—he had been counseled by editor Mencken, "Just pick two or three dark horses and ride 'em"—see Parry, "Introducing Nabokov to America," *The Texas Quarterly* (Spring 1971), 16–26. In Russian, Parry, *Novoe Russkoye Slovo,* July 9, 1978.

"the kike": Hessen, *Gody izgnania,* 70.

69   eleven A.M.: VN remembered that he had taken VéN to the hospital himself, a few hours before DN was born. As Hessen's daughter heard a different account, and as DN was born at eleven A.M.—not before five A.M. as VN recalls in SM—I have deferred to the Hessen account. VéN appears to support that version; she quibbled with Field's statement that VN had played chess until three A.M., "when it was time." VéN copy of Field, 1977, 200, VNA. Interview with Natalie Barosin, August 28, 1997.

"ein kleiner" and after some deliberation: Interview with DN, July 21, 1997.

"I've been somewhat": VN to Struve, July 30, 1934, LOC.

She took some pleasure: Displaying her own grasp of logic, she challenged Field's assertion that she was "very pregnant" in January, at the time of the Bunin festivities. (She was in her sixth month.) "Not enough for this to have been noticed by anyone," she scrawled in Field's margin, Field, 1986, 159, VNA.

another pregnancy: VN to VéN, June 10, 1936, and June 11, 1936, VNA.

emotional reserve: VéN pages on DN childhood.

"postlactic all-clear": SM, 299.

70   "This extraordinary and": Richard Holmes, *Footsteps: Adventures of a Romantic Biographer* (New York: Viking, 1985), 120.

"That was pure Véra": Interview with HS, February 26, 1995.

"heavenly labor": VN to his mother, September 4, 1934.

husband's silence: VéN to Grasset, June 10, 1934.

exhausted Véra: VN to Vadim Rudnev, November 25, 1934, Slavic and East European Library, University of Illinois.

"we heard Hitler's": Simon Karlinsky and Alfred Appel, eds., *The Bitter Air of Exile*, 249.

3   THROUGH THE LOOKING GLASS

71   "Véra was a pale" and Véra reported with pride: Alan Levy, "Understanding Vladimir Nabokov," *The New York Times Magazine,* October 31, 1971, 28. See also Levy, *Vladimir Nabokov: The Velvet Butterfly.* The word "iridule"—defined by VN as "a mother-of-pearl cloudlet in *Pale Fire*"—comes to mind, but is not in the dictionary. SO, 179.

as wan as she reportedly: VN to his mother, October 3, 1935, VNA.

Lena Massalsky: LM to VéN, undated, probably 1948.

"I wish" to "Not if they look": Interview with Keegan, November 14, 1997.

air of divinity: Interview with Saul Steinberg, January 17, 1996.

72   one hairdresser's amazement: Rolf to Tenggren, January 17, 1961, PC. For those who need to know, the preferred shampoo was Helena Rubenstein's "Silvertone."

"The camera and I": Interview with Simon Karlinsky, May 3, 1995.

"People of the writing": VN to Gleb Struve, August 17, 1931, LOC.

On VN's impenetrability: See *Sevodnya,* November 4, 1932. Also Aleksey Gibson, *Russian Poetry and Criticism in Paris, 1920–1940* (The Hague: Leuxenhoff Publishing, 1990), 161–62; Yanovsky, 207 (from which comes "The thoughts and feelings"), and H. Jakovlev recollections, VNA.

"the mirrory quality": Draft of *Conclusive Evidence,* LOC.

Aldanov held: VN to VéN, January 30, 1936, VNA. One can only wonder what would have happened had Christopher Isherwood—as adept as VN in slipping from the first to the third person in the course of a sentence—been added to the equation.

his Russian colleagues: Diment, *Pniniad,* 132. VN to Grynberg, December 16, 1944, Bakhm.

73   "who would be an experienced": Field, 1977, 206. See also Boyd, 1990, 419.

panicked every time: VéN to Boyd, June 6, 1987, VNA.

"Back in Berlin": Vera Peltenburg to VéN, May 6, 1978, VNA.

"V[éra] says that": VN diary, April 9, 1951, VNA.

"their work": Dominique Desanti, *Vladimir Nabokov,* 120.

"My wife and I": VN to Struve, October 26, 1930, Hoover.

74   claimed in August: VN to Mikhail Karpovich, August 21, 1933, Bakhm.

"from the moment": VéN to Rowohlt, July 5, 1987.

design to Packard: Interview with DN, November 22, 1996.

"As before, Véra": VN to his mother, December 6, 1934, VNA.

her freelance efforts: VéN to Goldenweiser, May 22, 1958, Bakhm. The control of the Ruthspeicher firm was transferred to its head engineer, a Nazi.

"I'm rather sick": VN to his mother, May 1, 1935, VNA. The line is in English in the original.

names of plants: VN to his mother, March 23, 1935, VNA.

transfer of the pistol: Boyd interviews with VéN, November 19, 1982, January 5, 1985, Boyd archive.

75   "The point of émigré": VéN to Field, March 10, 1973.

"I, you understand": VN to VéN, December 3, 1923, VNA.

"our age has been": VN to his mother, August 8, 1935, VNA.

work permit was revoked: VN to Alexandra Tolstoy, August 27, 1939, TF.

"I appeal": SM, 85.

mistaken in a photo: VN to VéN, January 20, 1936, VNA.

76   "my feet hurting": VéN pages on DN childhood.

"and the fervency": SM, 302.

"He was always" to "armful of a baby": VéN pages on DN childhood.

He wrote a little: VN to VéN, June 10, 1936, VNA.

77   "You would really": VN to VéN, February 17, 1936, VNA.

suitcase-dusting: VN to Struve, August 17, 1931, Hoover.

the tussle over *Despair*: VN to VéN, February 4, 1936, June 11, 1936, VNA.

"I am not afraid": VN to Karpovich, May 24, 1936, Bakhm.

"desperate in the extreme": VN to Sir Bernard Pares, November 16, 1936. Similarly, to George Ver-
nadsky, December 9, 1936, Bakhm; to Mikhail Rostovzeff, December 9, 1936.

"there were decent people": VéN to Rowohlt, July 5, 1987, VNA.

"ferreting out Russian": Field, 1977, 82–83, quoting VéN. Taboritsky had been sentenced to but did
not serve a fourteen-year prison term.

78   "We're slowly dying": VN to Z. Shakhovskoy, c. 1937, LOC.

"my husband was abroad": VN to Goldenweiser, June 8, 1957, Bakhm. VéN's concern had melted
into moral indignation by 1939, when VN wrote that it had become ethically impossible for
him to remain in Germany when the Biskupsky committee controlled the fate of the Russian
émigrés, and the undersecretary of that committee was none other than his father's assassin,
VN to Tolstoy, August 27, 1939, TF.

Biskupsky's treachery: Lena Massalsky to VéN, February 6, 1960, Onya Fasolt to VN, December 14,
1951. Fasolt to Shakhovskoy, November 13, 1979, Amherst.

79   all of them artists: *Vozrozhdenie,* January 30, 1967. Also on the reading, VN to VéN, January 25,
1937, VNA.

"I will refrain from": Aldanov, *Poslednie novosti,* Paris, January 28, 1937.

"I'm the toast": VN to VéN, February 4, 1937, VNA.

VN and Joyce, and Gallimard visit: VN to VéN, February 12, 1937, VNA.

a very un-Nabokovian: VN to VéN, February 27, 1937, VNA.

80   "I am rather fed": VN to VéN, February 27, 1937, VNA. In English in the original.

"I have never loved": VN to VéN, January 27, 1937, VNA. In English, in the original.

felt he would burst, and "My hat": VN to VéN, February 22, 1937, VNA.

"I have been encountering": VN to VéN, March 10, 1937, VNA.

81   "His eyes were not": VéN to Edward Weeks, February 27, 1978, VNA.

"Tell yourself that our": VN to VéN, February 10, 1937, VNA.

"that after your letter": VN to VéN, February 20, 1937, VNA. See also SL, 19.

"The Eastern side": VN to VéN, February 28, 1937, VNA.

82   "helpmeet, on the": "Véra," unpublished Aikhenvald poem, LOC.

"What is the problem" and "Without the air": VN to VéN, April 6, 1937, VNA.

83   tongue-wagging: VN to VéN, April 20, 1937, and May 1, 1937, VNA.

Nobelist into a fit: Berberova, *Italics Are Mine,* 257.

"Of course" to "gossip rewards me": VN to VéN, May 11, 1937, VNA.

He always told her: VN to VéN, April 20, 1937, VNA.

Shakhovskoy's visit: Boyd interview with VéN, November 16, 1982, Boyd archive.

"among the rascals": VN to VéN, April 21, 1937, VNA.

84   "I lack the strength": VN to VéN, April 27, 1937, VNA.

commas and all: VN to VéN, May 1, 1937, VNA.

sigh of relief: Boyd, 1990, 437.

begged her to arrange: VN to VéN, May 14, 1937, VNA.

"a series of petty": VN to VéN, May 14, 1937, VNA.

"to which we journeyed": SM, 306.

85   "Sunlight is good": GIFT, 338.

"delicious daze": LL, 166–67.

He could not shake: VN to Irina Guadanini, July 28, 1937, PC.

"I suggested that": VéN corrections to Field, 1977, VNA.

"You should never": Rolf, "January," PC.

wrote his mistress: Vera Kokoshkin diary entry, July 17, 1937. VN to Guadanini, July 15, 1937, PC.

"She was not more": Geoffrey Scott, *The Portrait of Zélide* (New York: Scribners, 1926), 1.

86   "clear but weirdly": SM, 288.

the anonymous letter: There were a number of possible candidates for authorship, including at least
one person who knew both women, and had known VéN since her childhood.

"a pretty woman": VN to Guadanini, June 21, 1937, PC.

"20th century miracle": Kokoshkin diary, PC. Madame Kokoshkin was citing Khodasevich.

three times: Kokoshkin to her son, February 10, 1937, PC.

Her laugh: I am indebted to Tatiana Morozoff for much of the background on Irina Guadanini.

When a twenty-one-year-old to "How beautiful!": Desanti, 34–40. For the most part I have steered clear of Desanti's *Vladimir Nabokov,* billed as an *"essai fantasme."* I have made an exception for these few moments, at which Desanti was actually present. The Fondaminsky report rings true for a second reason: VN wrote precisely the lines Desanti cites, earlier, in a letter to his mother.

"Anna Karenin!": Boyd interview with Elizabeth Marinel Allan, March 29, 1983, Boyd archive.

87   With tears streaming: Kokoshkin diary, August 3, 1937, PC.

Games of hangman: Guadanini diary, PC.

"Were his hands": Desanti, 35.

A week later, he: VN to Guadanini, June 21, 1937, PC.

beyond his strength: Guadanini diary, PC.

The strain was such: VN to Guadanini, June 14, 1937, PC.

88   a lovely ruse: VN to Guadanini, June 19, 1937, PC.

"indescribable, unprecedented": VN to Guadanini, June 22, 1937, PC.

"around like a bomb": VN to Guadanini, June 14, 1937, PC.

"You always have": VN to Guadanini, June 22, 1937, PC.

tormenting her lover: Guadanini diary, June 25, 1937, PC.

Adultery was a perfectly: LL, 133.

89   "I love you more than": Guadanini diary; also Kokoshkin to Guadanini, July 3, 1937.

yearned for Irina: VN to Guadanini, July 15, 1937, PC.

He promised: VN to Guadanini, July 23, 1937, PC.

"Her smile kills" to "hallucination": VN to Guadanini, July 28, 1937, PC.

"bamboozle her husband": Kokoshkin diary, July 23, 1937, PC.

felt so madly sorry: VN to Guadanini, August 2, 1937, PC.

promised to terminate: VéN corrections to Field, 1977, VNA.

90   prove under oath: VéN to Boyd, June 6, 1987, VNA.

powerful evidence: In Kokoshkin's and Guadanini's diaries. Both were replying to VN's reports from the Riviera.

The Guadanini-VN encounter: Guadanini's diary.

learned later that her rival: Boyd interview with VéN, December 5, 1986, Boyd archive.

hoodwinked Vladimir: Kokoshkin to Guadanini, September 13, 1937, PC.

She predicted that he would: Guadanini's diary.

"If he loves you": Kokoshkin to Guadanini, September 13, 1937, PC.

91   "The Tunnel" to "penetrate his letters": Aletrus, "The Tunnel," *Sovremennik* 3 (1961), 6–23.

ode to fidelity: Boyd, 1990, 444.

single most appealing: Defending VN against Field's charge that the work provided few moral heroines, VéN countered with Zina and Mme. Luzhin. VéN copy of Field, 1986, 165, VNA.

In June he told: VN to Guadanini, June 21, 1937, PC.

Later he reported: VN to Guadanini, August 2, 1937, PC.

92   "light, popular fiction": undated Bobbs-Merrill report, Mariam Lyman, Lilly.

series of fleeting affairs: VN to Guadanini, June 19, 1937, PC.

bristled visibly: Interview with George Weidenfeld, April 21, 1997. Eva had studied chemistry under Madame Curie in Paris; she was cultured, cosmopolitan, and beautiful.

ready to deny: Interview with Boyd, November 21, 1996; VéN to Boyd, June 6, 1987, VNA.

hints of philandering: VN to Struve, May 26, 1930, LOC; VN to Khodasevich, April 26, 1934, Berberova papers, Yale.

93   lent his hero: VN to Aldanov, February 3, 1938.

"autobiography thinly": Spender, *The New York Times Book Review,* May 26, 1963. "Please do not look for V.'s or my biography in *The Gift*. Apart from some absolutely external circumstances (very few even of those) there is nothing of V. in Fyodor. He gets quite vexed when people try to find it there," VéN wrote Lisbet Thompson on October 29, 1964. It never helped that Berberova and Shakhovskoy, among those who knew VN best in the 1930s, found the novel to be closer to the truth than his autobiography. Or that VN cited *The Gift* as one of his three most autobiographical works, Field, 1986, 52.

Vladimir's favorites: VéN to Barley Alison, Weidenfeld & Nicolson, May 15, 1963.

write off *Orlando*: VN to Shakhovskoy, July 25, 1933, LOC.

It has been read: Boyd, 1990, 463.
"hopeless desire": GIFT, 392.
ask that she return: Kokoshkin diary, December 29, 1937, PC.
"fragments of a novel": LO, 96.
a long protest: VéN to Boyd, October 7, 1985, VNA.
"alien, sullen" and "looked down": GIFT, 185, 195.
"Everyone lived": Cannac, cited by Shakhovskoy; interview of October 26, 1995.

94   The last letter: Kokoshkin diary, February 7, 1938, PC.
"I want this": Jannelli to VN, June 26, 1937.
author's questionnaire: November 1937, Bobbs-Merrill archive, Lilly.
"Our situation is": VN to Shakhovskoy, n.d., LOC.
Sergei Rachmaninoff: Rachmaninoff to VN, May 28, 1938, LOC.

95   "The smooth bits": VéN pages on DN's childhood.
"And among the candy-like": SM, 308.
nude sunbathing: VN to Raisa Tatarinov, November 12, 1937.
"and now it is my wife's": VN to Jannelli, January 31, 1938.
She was delighted: VéN to Shakhovskoy, 1938 postcard, LOC.

96   major French writer: Field, 1977, 141, 209. Despite what her husband said in jest, in VéN's opin-
     ion, "his French was as excellent as his English." VéN to Boyd, June 6, 1987, VNA. She re-
     called that VN had cast about, uncertain what language to write in. January 9, 1985, Boyd
     archive.
     article on Pushkin: "Pouchkine, ou le vrai et le vraisemblable," NRF, March 1, 1937. "Mademoiselle
     O," Mesures, 1936.
     "both men might have chosen": Unpublished last chapter of SM, LOC.
     fantastic congealing: LL, 182–84.
     convoluted copyright: Jannelli to VN, April 23, 1938, Lilly.
     before the outbreak: VéN to Rowohlt, July 5, 1987, VNA.
     "dazzlingly brilliant": A. I. Nazaroff's report, Bobbs-Merrill ms., Lilly.
     "threaded on my hero's: VN to Jannelli, July 14, 1938, Lilly.
     an editor's suggestion: Putnam to VN, March 17, 1937.
     "I schall [sic] never": VN to Jannelli, May 18, 1938.

97   high cinematic hopes: It had been conceived for the screen, VN to Walter Minton, November 4, 1958.
     "Eiffel Tower": VN to VéN, February 19, 1936, VNA.
     "because there is nowhere": VN to Struve, December 23, 1938, LOC.
     "the residence of most": VéN to Rowohlt, August 5, 1960, VNA.
     a lucrative market: As Newsweek had it in VN's obituary, "He might as well have been writing in
     Icelandic," July 18, 1977, 42.
     one reliable witness: Interview with Irina Morozova Lynch, December 6, 1996.
     handwriting can be found: Ms. of RLSK, LOC.
     "a champion figure": VN to Roman Grynberg, January 29, 1963.
     "switched from" to "VN's and my marriage": VéN to Field, March 10, 1973, VNA.

98   suitcase balanced: VN was fond of drawing historical radii between writing desks—he was keen to
     say exactly where Flaubert had been in the composition of Madame Bovary when Dickens was
     composing Bleak House, one hundred miles away—but remained scornful of the idea that
     Joyce had had any influence on him. At the same time, he admitted in the early 1960s that he
     reread Ulysses annually. VN to Grynberg, December 11, 1950. (He had done so at least since
     1931, when he told Struve he had reread the novel. Struve, "Vladimir Nabokov as I Knew and
     as I Saw Him," 11, Hoover.)
     Boyd has located: Boyd, 1990, 496.
     Viennese delegation: DEFENSE, 10.

99   "pages slipped": RLSK, 81.
     poetry of Donne: VéN translated Donne, and Marvell, into French. Interview with DN, January 16,
     1997. (She has this in common with Sibyl Shade, PF, 58.) The immensely astute Mary Bellino,
     recognizing VN's inscription in a 1937 Chatto edition, supplied the information about Christ-
     mas 1938.
     great deal of squabbling: HS to author, January 5, 1997, April 16, 1997.
     "Thank God": Sergei Nabokov to HS, January 18, 1939, PC.

his brother's conversion: VN to his mother, June 15, 1926, VNA. For a decoding of the name, see Barabtarlo, *Aerial View,* 213–17.

"Why couldn't you": Interview with Svetlana Andrault de Langeron, January 28, 1997. Similarly, Sergei Nabokov to HS, January 18, 1939, PC.

perfectly charming or: Interview with Moussa Gucassoff, July 29, 1996. Interview with HS, January 15, 1997.

"always a good dresser:" VéN to Lena Massalsky, February 10, 1959.

100 also proved unhappy: VN to Shakhovskoy, November 1938, LOC.

twice been interrogated: Massalsky family archives.

"Now I feel like going": VéN to Shakhovskoy, November 16, 1938, LOC.

Could the Tolstoy: VN to Tolstoy, March 19, 1939, TF.

a cramped room: VéN to Berberova, March 14, 1939, Yale. Also, VN to Berberova, January 29, 1939, Hoover.

Bitterly he complained: VN to VéN, April 11 and April 13, 1939, VNA.

101 "No—emphatically": VN to VéN, April 17, 1939, VNA.

vexed by her dark hints: He also disapproved of some of her ideas. She should not insist on planning their summer around a weekend with the Churches—Henry Church was the wealthy American-born publisher of *Mesures*; VN had described Mrs. Church as "literature-addicted"—as there were no new connections to be made there. VN to VéN, June 19, 1939, VNA.

"criminally absent-minded": VN to Berberova, July 4, 1938, Hoover.

"yield to the male": Trilling, *The Beginning of the Journey,* 353.

"our love, and everything": VN to VéN, April 12, 1939, VNA.

"old and fat": VN to VéN, April 13, 1939, VNA.

on Eva Luytens: VN to VéN, April 16, 1939, VNA.

102 the funeral: Sergei Nabokov managed to attend the funeral only by securing Gestapo permission.

" 'telephone' + 'armadas' ": VN to VéN, June 1, 1939, VNA.

painfully aware: VN to VéN, June 7, 1939, VNA.

"What do you expect": Jannelli to VN, March 14, 1939.

first of several letters: Karpovich to VN, June 3, 1939.

lost all the charm: VéN to Topazia Markevitch, August 24, 1972, VNA.

103 They missed him: VN to Berberova, September 1939, Yale.

He fretted: VN to Tolstoy, November 2, 1939, TF.

"And, please, make it": VN to Jannelli, September 30, 1939, Lilly.

affidavit for domestic: Tolstoy to American Friends Service Committee, October 23, 1939, TF.

most miserable: The impression was confirmed by friends. See Lucie Léon Noel, "Playback," Alfred Appel, Jr. and Charles Newman, eds., *Nabokov,* 214.

On the mobilization: Boyd interviews with VéN, December 19, 1981, June 4, 1982, Boyd archive.

"the nightmarish feeling": VN to Marinel sisters, April 26, 1942, PC.

offered a portrait: Boyd interview with Elisaveta Marinel Allan, March 29, 1983, Boyd archive.

104 Berberova provided: VéN emphasized later that Berberova had stopped by uninvited, as if to press the point that they had not *asked* for the chicken, VéN to Elena Levin, August 19, 1969, PC. Boyd interview with VéN, May 16, 1982, Boyd archive.

"We have a very hard": Marinel sisters to the Nabokovs, March 31, 1940.

"Tonight my son": Boyd interview with E. Allan, Boyd archive.

delivering it to the walls: VN to Karpovich, April 20, 1940, Bakhm.

purely "metaphysical": VN to Tolstoy, September 28, 1939, TF.

Nicholas Nabokov: Tolstoy to VN, April 24, 1940, TF. Karpovich made the same suggestion, to VN, June 3, 1939, Bakhm. The anti-Semites had a field day later with VN's hesitation. See Nathalie Dombre letter, Amherst.

105 200-franc bribe: She was certain she would be arrested for the offer, Boyd interviews with VéN, December 19, 1981, June 4, 1982, Boyd archive.

"I have sound reasons": VN to Tolstoy, December 6, 1939, TF.

"to stutter his astonishment": SM, 258.

application for immigration: U.S. Department of Justice, Immigration & Naturalization Service, No. 707. Special thanks to Brian Gross.

"slithering down": Isherwood, *Christopher and His Kind, 1929–1939* (New York: Farrar, Straus & Giroux, 1976), 337.

106 first-class cabin: VéN to Goldenweiser, December 28, 1957, Bakhm. Much of the account of the departure is drawn from the Goldenweiser files, those of the TF, and the Marinel correspondence, thanks to Michael Juliar.
"but you, Véra": E. Marinel to VéN, May 31, 1940.
visibly pulsing: Isherwood, *Christopher,* 338.
The trunk: Interview with DN, October 24, 1996.
looked miserably lost: VN to Robert Hughes, interview text, 10.
honest driver: VéN read Field's 1986 account, 203, without disputing it. If he was not the one to fumble, VN nonetheless appropriated the misstep, Harvey Breit, *The New York Times Book Review,* February 18, 1951. On his visa application he stated that he had savings of $600, but there is every reason in the world to believe he inflated the number.
"out of the cell": Boyd, 1990, 211.
a refugee: Mary McCarthy parsed these meanings beautifully in *The New York Review of Books,* March 9, 1972, 4: "If a group of Greek writers draws up a manifesto, they are writers-in-exile, but if we are trying to raise money to help them, they are refugees."

4   THE PERSON IN QUESTION

107 "I speak fluently": VéN curriculum vitae, July 23, 1939, TF. The TF materials prove the most complete of documentation for the first American year. As background, Anthony Heilbut, *Exiled in Paradise* (New York: Viking, 1983).
"I find it difficult": VéN diary, VNA.
when he first invited her: VN to VéN, December 3, 1923, VNA.
108 "the panic-stricken": VN to Marinels, August 25, 1940, SL, 33.
"A miracle has occurred": VN to Rostovzeff, summer 1940, Duke University.
Natalie Nabokov: Interview with Ivan Nabokov, October 24, 1995.
Vladimir concluded: VN to Karpovich, summer 1940, Bakhm.
a Russian friend: Goldenweiser to Mikhail Kantor, August 14, 1940, Bakhm.
"genteel book" to "satisfy her": VN to Marinels, August 25, 1940, SL, 34.
"so that his wife": Jannelli to Bobbs-Merrill, October 1, 1940, Lilly.
a perfect nuisance: VN to Karpovich, October 7, 1940, Bakhm.
109 "a ram-chakal farmhouse": VN to Edmund Wilson, June 16, 1942, NWL, 66.
the Karpovich estate: Interviews with Serge Karpovich, April 4, 1996, Mary Struve, August 11, 1995; Elena Levin, June 6, 1995. See also Yakobson, 127–28.
"with a certain horror": VN to Tolstoy, July 29, 1940, TF.
"Vladimir Vladimirovich": Interview with Serge Karpovich, April 4, 1996.
"would be glad to take": VN to Tolstoy, August 12, 1940, TF.
On Wreden: Interview with Peter Wreden, September 29, 1997.
110 "One of the few things": VN to Karpovich, September 15, 1940, Bakhm.
"a dreadful little flat": VéN diary, VNA.
"promoted": VéN diary, VNA.
"brilliantly debunk": VN to Karpovich, November 11, 1940, Bakhm.
"Dear Mr. Wilson": VN to Wilson, October 7, 1940, Yale.
Mozart and Salieri: Wilson to VN, December 27, 1940. The translation appeared in the April 21, 1941, issue. On the two scholars, see as well Gleb Struve in the *Times Literary Supplement,* May 2, 1980, 509–10.
111 "a man named Ross": Wilson's plea on his friend's behalf is reproduced in Wilson, *Letters on Literature and Politics,* 409.
Free French newspaper: VéN to Goldenweiser, July 1, 1958, Bakhm.
wore better than her gaunt: Ellendea Proffer, *Vladimir Nabokov,* v–vi.
"We are going to put": VN to VéN, March 20, 1940, VNA. The line is in English.
In the eyes: Interview with Margaret Stephens Humpstone, August 20, 1996.
Statue of Liberty: Interview with DN, November 22, 1996.
"American" in which he was: VN to Hessen, May 25, 1941, PC.
112 bundled in fur: Interview with Constance Darkey, October 16, 1997.
indelible impression: Interview with Janet Lewis (Mrs. Yvor Winters), November 6, 1997.

"*Stranger* always": LL, 372.

"On walks through": VéN pages on DN childhood.

113   retired blazer: Interview with Elena Levin, June 6, 1995. Elena Levin was eleven years VéN's junior, and already much in awe of VN's work.

"play the real American": VN to George Hessen, May 25, 1941, PC.

"rapid acculturation": Nathans, "Beyond the Pale," 91.

"pathetic attempt of a very small": VéN pages on DN's childhood.

"Everything looked elegant": Interview with E. Levin, November 9, 1997.

"He just had to walk": Cited in Boyd, 1991, 26.

crippling case of sciatica: VN to Hessen, May 25, 1941, PC.

114   "I'll be so bold" and filling the blackboard: VN to VéN, March 25, 1941, VNA.

She failed to place: VéN to VN, March 17, 1941, VNA.

took care to specify: VN to VéN, March 31, 1941, VNA.

"It's true, it is": VN to VéN, March 28, 1941, VNA. His impracticality took other forms; earlier in the month he had written so stridently political a book review for *The New Republic* that the magazine had had no choice but to reject it.

She had not recovered: VN to Hessen, May 25, 1941, PC.

"an interdepartmental visitor": Mildred H. McAfee to VN, June 30, 1941.

115   "Yes, Russia is *en vogue*": VéN to Goldenweiser, May 27, 1942, Bakhm.

"Funny—to know Russian": VN to Wilson, June 16, 1942, NWL, 66.

"illness which resulted": VéN to Goldenweiser, July 1, 1958, Bakhm. She was filing her reparations claim, but even there steered well clear of exaggeration.

south rim of the Grand: Field, 1977, 238.

"that right beside": Boyd, 1991, 29. For "A Discovery," See POEMS AND PROBLEMS, 155.

"I've had wonderful" to "into the air": Field, 1977, 179.

116   "I am not a trained": VéN to Stephen Jan Parker, October 15, 1984, VNA.

"I bungled my family's": SO, 315.

"a cultured country": VN to Hessen, May 25, 1941, PC.

"Because you have" to "Holmes?": Nikolai All., *Novoe Russkoye Slovo,* June 23, 1940.

"I don't have" to "by the road": VéN pages on DN's childhood.

"It was a real drifter's": Interview with DN, November 10, 1997.

"On a slope near Togwotee": SO, 325.

"I also caught a white female": VéN to Epsteins, January 19, 1953.

On Stanford: See Polly Kemp, *Stanford Magazine,* September 1992. I am grateful to Polly Kemp for her assistance, as well as to the magazine.

117   "My husband is working": VéN to Goldenweiser, August 26, 1941, Bakhm.

"The existing translation is vileness": VN to Karpovich, 1941, Bakhm.

the Stanford routine: I have drawn here on Glen Holland's letter of October 9, 1992, to *Stanford Magazine.* The samovar was Holland's recollection.

"very 'formal' ": VéN diary.

"He kept score": VN to Hessen, n.d., PC.

forfeited his own summer salary: Interview with Janet Lewis, October 21, 1997.

"I wonder where": Field, 1986, 210, VéN copy, VNA.

"Nabokov lost as many": Cyril Bryner to Polly Kemp, September 23, 1992. Interview with Bryner, August 21, 1997.

118   their chagrin at having had: VN to the Marinels, January 26, 1941, SL, 35–36; VéN to Choura Barbetti, October 23, 1945; VN to Karpovich, summer 1940, Bakhm. The "Neanderthal hardships" figures in the first, SL, 36.

barely detach himself: VN to Wilson, July 18, 1941, NWL, 46.

"Despite this, we're very": VéN to Goldenweiser, July 26, 1941, Bakhm.

"interesting in a Walt": *The New York Times Book Review,* January 11, 1942, 14.

openly admitted: In the *Wellesley College News,* April 26, 1945. And SL, 42.

And still not on a par: VN to James Laughlin, August 8, 1942, SL, 42.

"I don't know what language": Vita Sackville-West to Nigel Nicolson, cited in Nigel Nicolson, ed., *The Later Years, 1945–62* (New York: Atheneum, 1968), 357.

"a delight to read": *The New Republic,* January 26, 1942.

119   "a dewy multitude": VN to Wilson, August 1944, NWL, 139.

"a very long and very badly": Katharine White to E. B. White, April 28, 1945, Cornell. White felt Nabokov was still very much *learning* to compose in English (note to file, BMC) and urged him to tone down his impressive vocabulary. "Mr. Ross says that he would feel self-conscious and embarrassed to use all of your big words," she wrote. White to VN, March 1, 1949. See also Linda H. Davis, *Onward and Upward,* 146–51.

professed great sympathy: Boyd interview with VéN, January 13, 1980, Boyd archive.

Harold Ross swore: Ross to Katharine White, BMC, undated. In a note on Ross's memo, White allowed that Wilson had been the one to suggest that his friend VN had learned his English from the unabridged *OED.*

"splendid solitude" and "At night I have": VN to Aldanov, October 20, 1941, Bakhm.

"I am not a good cook": VéN to Judith Matlack, October 29, 1951. She used the word "heroism."

general feeling: Katharine White to VN, March 1, 1949, BMC.

direct from *Webster's*: John G. Hayman, *Twentieth Century,* December 1959, 444–50.

scrambled eggs: Interview with Alfred Appel, June 2, 1995.

"All of my time": VéN to HS, December 17, 1945, and "As a housekeeper," VéN to HS, January 21, 1946, PC.

120 "Why is no one taking you": Interview with DN, October 25, 1997. Dmitri felt his mother was a little sad not to have known of the holiday.

series of letters: VN to Rostovzeff, December 16, 1941. On the same day he wrote Boris Stanfield regarding a position at Columbia University; Stanfield later grumbled to VéN that he felt it necessary to refresh her husband's "phenomenal memory," June 14, 1969.

"Marketing, washing, ironing": Stephens file, WCA.

commanding a squadron: VN to Aldanov, May 20, 1942, Bakhm.

prospect of being drafted: VN to Marinels, April 26, 1942, Juliar collection.

"To talk with him": VéN to HS, August 20, 1958, PC.

121 "We're hoping that he'll": VéN to Goldenweiser, July 9, 1942, Bakhm.

"Why is it so difficult": GLORY, 185.

dollop of refugee: As she explained to the couple's lawyers decades later: "No one can predict the rate at which the inflation will progress. But we are conditioned by personal experience to fear it very much. I remember days when an hotel bill presented in the morning was no longer valid in the afternoon because the price of money had decreased so much in the intervening hours." VéN to Joan Daly, February 22, 1971, PW.

122 "Véra Evseevna, you will": Maria Marinel to VéN, October 5, 1940.

"depressed that everyone": DEFENSE, 195.

"As before, we have no": VéN to Goldenweiser, May 27, 1942, Bakhm.

"Vinteuil is accepted": LL, 231.

"the insufficiency": ADA, 579.

"the boomerang variety": VN to Wilson, June 16, 1942, NWL, 66.

"Try to be cheerful": VN to VéN, November 10, 1942, VNA.

"little economic wailings": VN to VéN, October 13, 1942, VNA.

enjoyed less: VéN diary, VNA.

"was so kind": VN to Wilson, June 16, 1942, NWL, 66.

under strict instructions: VN to VéN, August 3, 1942, VNA.

On the furniture: Boyd interview with Mary McCarthy, January 12, 1985, Boyd archive.

123 cramped headquarters: VN to John Finley, August 29, 1951. In BEND it is a "dingy little flat," xi.

strewn with index: Interview with Phyllis Christiansen, August 10, 1996.

Isabel Stephens: Stephens interview, WCA.

"Now this gigantic": VN to Hessen, December 1942, PC.

"Good Girl": VN to VéN, October 20, 1942, VNA.

"dilly-dallying": VN to Griselda Ohannessian, New Directions, January 29, 1942.

"not the best-looking": VN to VéN, October 5, 1942, VNA.

"expecting a gentleman": VN to VéN, October 5, 1942.

"Then again, only *humans*": ENCHANTER, 11.

124 would have disappeared: VN to Hessen, December 1942, PC. VN to Aldanov, December 8, 1942, Bakhm.

"She still cannot manage": VN to Laughlin, January 12, 1943.

"It is a very pleasant": VN to Laughlin, April 9, 1942, SL, 40.

"presided as adviser": SO, 105.

125 grind every one: Karpovich to VN, October 18, 1943, Bakhm.

overindulged in puns: VN to Roman Grynberg, October 10, 1944, Bakhm.

his own reflection: He had done so before and would be accused of doing so again, taken to task for "simply telling a tale of Nabokov in the mirror of Gogol." Marc Slonim, *Novoe Russkoye Slovo,* November 12, 1944.

"Gogol was a strange": GOGOL, 140.

"Artists are unusual": VéN to Lisbet Thompson, October 29, 1964.

"I invent my own": VN to Hessen, March 7, 1943, PC.

126 "as if it's not myself ": VN to Hessen, December 1942, PC. See also *The Last Word* (Wellesley College), April 19, 1943, 19–21.

"Wars pass": VN to Wilson, December 13, 1943, Yale. Discussing Hitler's designs on Russia, he enlightened a *Stanford Daily* reporter (July 1, 1941): "Of course I'm not much interested in politics."

The MCZ: Charles Klaus to author, March 7, 1996. Interview with Charles Remington, July 10, 1996.

"I love to play": VN to his mother, April 29, 1921, VNA. This took some doing at the MCZ, which was filled with colorful characters. For Hessen VN described the eleven A.M. scene at the museum, where four scholars gathered on the steps for a cigarette, "a paleontologist, the curator of mollusks, the curator of reptiles, and Dr. [*sic*] Nabokov, all old men, except the doctor." VN to Hessen, March 30, 1943, PC.

"An eccentric": SO, 132.

hallway greetings: Interview with Kenneth Christiansen, August 11, 1996.

"Is this really": Interview with Phyllis Smith Christiansen, August 10, 1996.

127 "not quite normal": VN to Hessen, December 1942, PC.

glacial charms: Interview with Laughlin, July 27, 1995; interview with E. Levin, November 10, 1997.

edge of a cliff: Interview with Laughlin. See also "Ezra Pound Said Be a Publisher," *The New York Times Book Review,* August 23, 1981, 13.

systematically defeating: VN to Hessen, July 1943, PC.

The John Downey encounters: Interview with John Downey, November 11, 1997.

"he really let himself ": GOGOL, 140.

128 "knowing that if I did": Gerald Clarke, *Esquire,* July 1975, 69.

"Véra has had a serious": VN to Wilson, January 3, 1944, NWL, 121.

"I, or rather Vera": VN to Wilson, January 7, 1944, NWL, 123.

"acclimated": VN to Jan Priel, March 17, 1946.

"I am devoting": VN to Wilson, May 8, 1944, NWL, 134–35. Also VN to Grynberg, May 8, 1944, Bakhm.

"It's Sunday today": VN to Hessen, May 8, 1944, PC.

"I have long since": VN to Hessen, December 10, 1943, PC.

129 less willing victims: Interview with Margaret Stephens Humpstone.

portion of his tuition: VéN to Goldenweiser, July 1, 1958, Bakhm; to Barbetti, January 28, 1946.

returned from leave: Affidavit for Goldenweiser, Bakhm.

"was incompatible": VéN to HS, December 17, 1945, PC. She received some compensation from the Department of Foreign Languages in 1947 as well.

Harvard library position: VéN to HS, April 6, 1947, PC.

promising to write: See J. D. O'Hara, "Fondling the Details," *The Nation,* November 8, 1980. O'Hara to VéN, February 9, 1980, VNA.

Sparing her husband: Boyd interview with VéN, February 25, 1982, Boyd archive.

Together the two: VN to Wilson, January 25, 1947, NWL, 182.

"Volodia, would it be": Cited in Boyd, 1991, 109.

"A little tartly": Interview with J. D. O'Hara, September 11, 1996.

"My husband wishes": VéN to Mavis McIntosh, October 27, 1947.

130 remembered him fulminating: Interview with C. C. Sprague, May 20, 1997.

allegedly on the grounds: See Parry, *The Texas Quarterly,* Spring 1971.

Vladimir's ill humor: Interview with Kay Rice, August 13, 1996.

"I think he would have": VéN to Miss Henneberger, February 5, 1944.

Rumor around the VOA: Interview with Helen Yakobson, November 29, 1996.

"Since you are asking": VN to Vaudrin, November 6, 1947, VNA.

love to "Sonya": Wilson to VN, October 26, 1944, Yale.

131 "Tell it to Véra": Boyd interview with Sylvia Berkman, April 9, 1983, Boyd archive.

"Véra sends you": VN to the Hessens, May 1944, PC.

"My husband has turned": VéN to Emily Morison, Knopf, February 12, 1945, HR.

Vladimir accidentally: VéN to Max Pfeffer, March 20, 1947, VNA.

"Véra is wonderful": Wilson to Elena Thornton, October 4, 1946, Yale. Lewis Dabney unearthed this letter.

Anglicisms were creeping: VéN to Barbetti, May 13, 1947.

crowded faculty party: James McConkey to author, August 12, 1996.

132 similar tastes from the beginning: Boyd to author, December 14, 1997.

"Now why did I marry": Rolf to Tenggren, c. January 21, 1961, PC.

"Good Heavens": Interview with DN, November 12, 1997.

psoriasis on his elbow: VN to Hessen, October 10, 1944, PC.

she would forgive him: Wilson to VN, January 25, 1947, Yale.

what Stalin thought: See *Wellesley Magazine,* February 1948, 179–80. For a portrait of VN at Wellesley, see also Barbara Breasted and Noëlle Jordan, "Vladimir Nabokov at Wellesley," *Wellesley Magazine,* Summer 1971, 22–26.

fought like cocks: VN to Hessen, October 10, 1944, PC.

Nabokov divided the Russian: VN to Vladimir Zenzinov, March 17, 1945, Bakhm.

133 difficult even for Wilson: See Jeffrey Meyers, "The Bulldog and the Butterfly," *The American Scholar,* Summer 1994, 379–402.

"When I have to choose": VN to Rev. Gardiner Day, December 21, 1945.

"even more catastrophic": VN to Marinels, May 22, 1946, SL, 68.

hate for the Germans: VN to HS, October 25, 1945, PC.

"I don't understand": VéN to Barbetti, January 1, 1947.

"knowing the Germans": VéN to Col. Joseph I. Greene, January 14, 1948, SL, 80.

134 call a duel: Boyd interview with E. Allan, March 29, 1983, Boyd archive.

charges of racism: VN to Aldanov, January 21, 1942, Bakhm. In 1953, he refused even to review her biography of her father. VN to *The Yale Review,* September 22, 1953, VNA.

The accommodations: VN to Phyllis Smith Christiansen, July 18, 1946.

"And what would happen": VN to Hessen, n.d. In VN's letter to Wilson of July 18, 1946, NWL, 170, the "nervous exhaustion" became "practically a 'nervous breakdown.' " For a later, enhanced version of what was presumably the same New Hampshire episode, see ANL, 436.

"We had a few": VéN to Field, September 20, 1968.

work precluded any: VéN to Barbetti, January 1, 1947.

"She treated him like": Verna Irwin Marceau to author, December 7, 1995. Interview of May 1, 1996.

135 FBI investigation: FBI file number 121-10141, report of June 26, 1948.

"Véra and I watch": VN to HS, November 26, 1945, SL, 58.

"She had so": Boyd interview with Berkman, April 9, 1983, Boyd archive.

Isabel Stephens assumed: Interviews with M. S. Humpstone, August 20, 1996, Dave Stephens, August 19, 1996.

"She was much too busy": Interview with E. Levin, June 6, 1995.

"slice, chop, twist": VN to Laughlin, August 8, 1942, SL, 42.

"intervestibular connecting": SM, 144. The word for which he was searching was "diaphragm," according to Sue Pasccucci, New York Transit Museum.

136 "I hope this helps": VéN to Charles R. Timmer, December 20, 1949.

she was disappointed: VéN to Barbetti, January 1, 1947.

strongly recommended: VéN to Barbetti, May 13, 1947.

Evelyn Waugh: VéN to Barbetti, January 1, 1947.

"She won't let her": Wilson to Elena Thornton, October 4, 1946, Yale.

to inhale his scent, and "We shall fight": VN to Hessen, July 17, 1945, PC.

137 felt wretched: VN to Zenzinov, June 17, 1945, Bakhm.

"Nothing like it": VN to Wilson, June 17, 1945, NWL, 154.

torment her: VN to Wilson, June 9, 1944, Yale.

"In fact he does not": VéN to Betty Cage, *View,* March 24, 1946, Ford papers, Yale.

"I am afraid" and "He also thinks": VéN to Edith E. Dana, March 19, 1947.

"Incidentally I vomited": VN to Wilson, June 9, 1944, Yale.

138 "devices of shadography": BEND, 120. Gradus proves by contrast an uncertain "shadowgrapher," PF, 180. Lolita makes "shadowgraphs" at camp, LO, 114. In the 1970s VN warned an interviewer that he could expect little from their talk but a "shadowgraph," SL, 551.

grew taller: VéN to HS, April 6, 1947, PC.

"Volodya is always": VéN to the Hessens, December 29, 1945, PC.

"shrunken dwarf apartment": VN to Grynberg, September 1, 1948, Bakhm.

"At least I know": Lewis Carroll, *Alice's Adventures in Wonderland* (New York: Signet, 1960), 47.

"literally born again": Amy Kelly to the Nabokovs, October 30, 1945.

"generally inspirational": Karpovich to Ernest J. Simmons, April 20, 1942, Bakhm.

"I spent most of ": Interview with Harriet Dorothy Rothschild, March 11, 1997.

"I know I always": Interview with Jocelyn Rogers Jerry, July 1997.

"We were all": Interview with Jean H. Proctor, August 8, 1997.

139 being taken care of: Interview with Rosemary Farkas Meyerson. Also H. D. Rothschild.

"they noticed a face": *Wellesley College News,* October 17, 1946.

"He was the only man": Interview with Mary Pryor Black Lindley, February 1997. For a colorful account of VN at Wellesley, see Naomi B. Pascal, "A Reminiscence of Nabokov at Wellesley," *The Nabokovian,* Fall 1995, 7–10.

Could he trouble: Interview with Jane Sharp, March 1997.

Merrily he informed: Interview with Jeannie Rudolph Pechin, July 20, 1997.

the butterfly visit: Interview with Jane E. Curtis, March 7, 1997.

Few of the girls: Pechin, Betty Comtois. Also Caroline C. Hendrickson, interview of July 10, 1996, Ruth D. Stoddard, August 13, 1997, Jane E. Curtis.

watched him adoringly: Interview with Marian McC. Kuhns, April 8, 1997. Also Sharp, Pechin.

best-looking girls: Interviews with Kitty Helm Hartnett, Alma Weisburg, Rothschild, Comtois. "He always needed to have his harem around," quipped one.

"Ah, Miss Rogers": Interview with Jocelyn Rogers Jerry, July 1997.

"He definitely flirted": Interview with Rothschild. Similarly, Comtois, Pologe, Weisberg, interview with Nancy Ignatius, July 7, 1997.

"Do you have any idea": Wellesley alumna to author, November 13, 1995.

140 "I took a course": Interviews with Katherine Reese Peebles, December 6, 1996, February 7, 1997. See her fine portrait of the professor in *We,* December 1943, 5. Interview with Priscilla Rasmussen, February 10, 1997.

"He did like young": Interview with Peebles, February 7, 1997.

"I was a perceptive": Interview with Peebles, November 12, 1997.

"avid eavesdropping": Dr. Glen Holland, cited in Polly Kemp, "It Is Lolita Who Is Famous, Not I," *Stanford Magazine,* September 1992, 52.

"Then can you read": Interview with Peebles, December 6, 1996.

141 apparent helplessness: Interview with Grace Pologe, February 26, 1997. Similarly, interview with Aileen Ward, November 1, 1995.

"Do you realize": Interview with Nancy W. Ignatius.

"with long, thick" and "I could see": Hannah Green, "Mister Nabokov," *The New Yorker,* February 14, 1977. Repr. in Quennell, *Vladimir Nabokov,* 34–41.

general swooning: Interview with Sally Luten Morse, August 25, 1997.

"I have given": VN to Hessen, March 14, 1947, PC.

"gentle dismay": Green, "Mister Nabokov," 41.

denied all: VéN corrections to Field, 1977, n.d. She insisted too that he was always in a hurry to return to Cambridge, to his work, VéN to Barbara Breasted, December 28, 1970, VNA.

142 "I like small-breasted": Interview with Peebles, December 6, 1996.

"No, never!": VéN copy of Field, 1984, 224, VNA.

frank anticommunism: VéN diary, VNA.

"quite a wrench": Boyd interview with Berkman, Boyd archive.

terrified that the Cornell: VN to White, May 30, 1948, BMC.

"I didn't receive any": VéN to Goldenweiser, August 12, 1958, Bakhm.

Mrs. Horton later: Interview of Winter 1970, WCA.

rather frightened the dean: Boyd interview with Berkman, Boyd archive. Also Berkman interview, WCA.

"the safe drabness": ADA, 472.

"I did not take it": Wilson to Grynberg, November 19, 1948, LOC.

foreglimmers: Ernest J. Simmons to Karpovich, April 15, 1942, Bakhm. For a full account of the events that brought VN to Cornell, see Galya Diment, *Pniniad.*

143   better teacher: Interviews with Ignatius, Curtis. Also Ruth Stokes, August 1996. VéN quibbled with the assessment of her talent, which she thought inferior to her husband's.

"my head is spinning": VéN to Marinels, April 25, 1948, PC.

"had been compelled": VéN to Eric Bergh, April 5, 1948, VNA.

His mood: VN to Hessen, June 13, 1948, PC.

"It will be a sequence": VN to Kenneth McCormick, September 22, 1946.

had been irritated: VéN to *The Saturday Review,* December 29, 1947.

"a short novel about": VN to Wilson, April 7, 1947, Yale.

original employment proposal: Bishop to VN, September 13, 1947, PC.

144   "Possibly my wife": VN to Milton Cowan, June 1948. Draft, VNA.

"scrubbing was Mrs.": Bishop to VN, May 21, 1948. The house belonged to a professor of electrical engineering, who Bishop reported was "off to Brookhaven to make bombs for the summer."

"The horrible packing": VN to Hessen, June 13, 1948, PC.

"I will never," and the Ithaca anti-sesame: Boyd interview with Berkman, Boyd archive.

5   NABOKOV 101

147   "always so kind": Burton Jacoby to the Nabokovs, June 24, 1969. Interview with Bill Pritchard, February 7, 1997.

bought a car: VN to Wilson, September 3, 1948, NWL, 205.

"One of us had better": Interview with Dick Keegan, April 9, 1997.

or an obsolete one: VéN to Sonia Slonim, May 17, 1947.

worry about his health: VéN to HS, November 30, 1948.

"It's not very hard": Interview with Keegan, April 9, 1997.

He distrusted cars: Arthur Mizener, *Cornell Alumni News,* September 1977.

electric pencil sharpeners: Interview with Jill Krementz, March 1973.

Keegan noticed: Interview with Keegan, March 25, 1997. Keegan had the firm sense that the Plymouth had a very great deal to do with the relationship, at least initially.

"carts around her": VN to Karpovich, September 28, 1948, Bakhm.

148   wonder mischievously: VN to Harry Levin, May 31, 1949, Houghton Library, Harvard University.

a pinch-hitting driver: Interview with Frank Tretter, September 26, 1996.

Salt Lake City: Interview with Richard Buxbaum, May 6, 1996. Boyd notes of Buxbaum interview, May 3, 1983, Boyd archive.

East Seneca Street: See William R. Orndorff, *Cornell Alumni News,* February 1984, 20–21.

"Why don't you call": Interview with Harold Croghan, November 23, 1996.

"an elderly man": FBI File 105-11456, serials 1, 4, 5, 6, 8, 9.

149   A neighbor on East Seneca: Robert Ruebman to author, April 22, 1996.

"And pray, find me": Cited in GOGOL, 111.

"minus my teeth": VN to Wilson, June 3, 1950, Yale.

She had not understood: Interview with DN, November 15, 1996.

"Iso-Rivolta is not": VéN to Walter Minton, February 18, 1966.

asserted proudly: Taped conversation following CBC interview with Mati Laanso, March 20, 1973.

"I *loved* driving": Rodney Phillips to author, January 1997. Boyd interview with VéN, January 16, 1982, Boyd archive.

"my heroic wife": VN to Wilson, September 1951, NWL, 265.

150   "I have upwards": VéN to Eugenia Cannac, February 14, 1962.
      "My Oldsmobile" to "Oh, the sunlight": VN 1951 diary. For the last, see LO, 95.
      she compiled an inventory: LOC. The results can be read in LO, 208.
      "and a few 'dust devils' ": VéN to the Bishops, summer, 1959.
      "apocaliptic [sic]": VéN to D. Lindsay, December 17, 1965.
      "The most exciting": VéN to Elena Levin, June 24, 1956, PC. Also, Boyd interview with VéN, December 22, 1981, Boyd archive.
      "through the grey wall": VN to the Hessens, November 27, 1950, PC.
151   to the liquor store: Interview with Keegan, December 15, 1997.
      "Inseparable, self-sufficient": Alfred Appel, Jr., "Nabokov: A Portrait," The Atlantic, September 1971, 85. Repr. in J. E. Rivers and Charles Nicol, eds., Nabokov's Fifth Arc, 12.
      immobile, oblivious: Interview with Frances Halperin, January 15, 1996. Similarly, interviews with Gardner and Florence Clark, September 1, 1996, Dorothy Staller. See also Diment, Pniniad, 162.
      husband's galoshes: Interview with Marcia Elwitt, August 20, 1996.
      "Wives, Mr. Shade": PF, 22.
      "Did you grade" to "brute strength": Interview with Keegan, November 14, 1997.
152   "This is a genuine": VN to Grynberg, September 1, 1948, Bakhm.
      "We miss him": VN to HS, winter 1948.
      his last priority: VN to Zenzinov, January 21, 1949.
      "You must go": Interview with Keegan, January 12, 1997.
      "Everything has its limits": Cited in Diment, Pniniad, 35.
      "Will you tell me": Interview with Anna Balakian, September 2, 1995.
      "I am the new professor": Interview with Aileen Ward, November 1, 1995.
153   "I envy you": VN to Mrs. Victor Lowe, May 24, 1949.
      braced himself: Victor Lange, Michigan Quarterly Review, October 1986, 479–92. Also, David Daiches, "Nabokov à Cornell," L'Arc 24 (Spring 1964), 65–66.
      "I want to warn you": VN to Dean C. W. de Kiewit, March 21, 1948. The line is from the unedited text, penciled in the margin of de Kiewit's letter. For amended version see SL, 83.
      "was deemed 'too literary' ": Diment, Pniniad, 34. Also, VN to Grynberg, March 31, 1949, Bakhm. The letter appears to have been written by VéN.
      no respect: Interview with Dr. Bruce Cowan, March 14, 1997.
      "You just wait": Diment, 34.
      poisoned her husband's mind: Alice Colby-Hall to author, April 9, 1997. Interview with George Gibian, August 29, 1996. Leonard Blorenge, Chairman of French Literature and Language at Pnin's Waindell College, distinguishes himself on two counts: "he disliked Literature and he had no French" (PNIN, 140). In the Nabokovs' opinions, Fairbanks had no Russian. VN shivered to think what havoc Fairbanks's graduates would wreak at the State Department (SL, 263). As late as 1958, he was writing the Cornell Daily Sun to protest the poor language instruction at the university.
154   "the French gave her": VéN corrections to Field, 1977.
      "used whoever was": Boyd interview with VéN, December 12, 1982, Boyd archive. Blorenge brags that an instructor of French "is required to be only one lesson ahead of his students," PNIN, 142.
      do his laundry: Interview with E. Levin, June 6, 1995.
      "Nabokov never scraped": VéN corrections to Boyd's Chapter 29, n.d. Interview with Harold Croghan, November 23, 1996.
      the eighteen-year-old English major: Robert Ruebman to author, "Snacking at the Nabokovs," April 10, 1996.
155   "Sonst noch was": Ruebman to author, March 14, 1997.
      "If he had office hours": Interview with Rona Schneider, September 1996.
      The few who delved: Interviews with Stanley Komaroff, April 29, 1996, Dick Wimmer, December 1, 1997.
      chief of a fire brigade: VN to Aldanov, February 2, 1951, Bakhm.
      "he worked for the wages": VéN corrections to Field, 1977, ms. p. 271.
      essentially parked: Demorest, (Cornell) Arts and Sciences Newsletter, Spring 1983. VN lent a similar administrative limbo to Pnin, PNIN, 139.
      "a touch of almost": Lange, Michigan Quarterly Review, October 1986, 482.

156   He assured Keegan: Keegan recollections of VN, February 4, 1997.
       "It is fine": Laughlin to VéN, November 30, 1948.
       "As you have probably": VN to White, "Gardens and Parks" ms., LOC.
       "Avatar" to "Touché": Interview with Keegan, January 15, 1998.
       "I wouldn't want to see": *La Notte,* April 26/7, 1962.
       "It is foolish": VéN to HS, October 25, 1949, PC.
157   "1) that he was very": VéN to Zinaida Shakhovskoy, January 9, 1949, Amherst.
       "Volodya has still": Natalie Nabokov to VéN, c. 1956.
       "Dear Véra and Volodya": Grynberg to the Nabokovs, March 30, 1949.
       Wilson simply glided: Wilson to VN, July 15, 1949, Yale. The letter is addressed, "Dear Véra."
158   "I am afraid": VN to Croghans, November 7, 1948.
       "unsolicited sounds": VéN to Geoffrey Hughes, July 26, 1963.
       "husband and wife serfs": Interviews with the Croghans, November 22, 1996, November 26, 1997.
       "slamming doors": VN to Katharine and Andy [E. B.] White, October 25, 1950, Cornell.
       "There is nothing louder": LO, 129.
       "I have no illusions": VN to Katharine and E. B. White, October 25, 1950, Cornell.
       Jane Carlyle: See Rose, *Parallel Lives,* 247.
159   fixing a flat tire: On a similar occasion on the 1949 trip with Buxbaum, VN excused himself at this
           juncture, setting off with his butterfly net.
       "What can I do?": Interview with Bea McCloud, April 3, 1996.
       wooden cart of blocks: Edward C. Sampson to author, October 10, 1995. Interview with Frances
           Halperin, January 15, 1996.
       He confessed to: ANL, xliv.
       notebook in hand: Interviews with Shari Hathaway, Mrs. Orval French, May 3, 1996.
       "Oh yes, I know": Interview with Milton Konvitz, August 9, 1996.
       "book clubs, bridge clubs": "Conversation Piece," STORIES, 586.
160   "autobiographical thingamabob": VN to Edward Weeks, September 9, 1948.
       she testified that working: White to Cass Canfield, November 29, 1948, HR.
       "pessimistically thought that": Unpublished last chapter of SM, LOC.
       "so carefully mutilated": VN to White, March 1948.
       a "beginning" writer: John Fischer to VN, February 17, 1949, HR.
       alarm bells: Handwritten note on John Fischer to VN, April 28, 1949, HR.
       "If anybody again ever": Allen Tate to VN, November 6, 1946.
       all evidence points: DN felt his mother was the contract reader from the earliest days. Interview of
           December 1, 1997.
161   familiar-seeming woman: Interview with HS, January 15, 1997.
       "amiable feelings": VN to HS, May 22, 1949, PC.
       addressed to Véra: VN to White, November 27, 1949, SL, 95. He had used the device before, in
           GIFT, and in BEND, in which Krug addresses his dead wife. See also Johnson, *Worlds in Re-
           gression,* 97.
       shrugged it off: Interview with Appel, April 24, 1995.
162   "the year I married": CE, 183. And in that edition she was "my wife" sleeping in the next room, not
           yet the abstract "you." CE, 222. Nor does she make appearances as frequently; she joins her
           husband on his mid-book lepping excursion (SM, 129) but does not do so in *The New Yorker* of
           June 12, 1948, or in Chapter VI of CE.
       Madame Chateaubriand: See Dan Hofstadter, *The Love Affair as a Work of Art* (New York: Farrar,
           Straus & Giroux, 1996), 83ff.
       Dorothy Wordsworth: Elizabeth Hardwick, *Seduction and Betrayal* (New York: Random House,
           1974), 148.
       On reading the first half: Guadanini letter of July 27, 1959, probably to her mother, PC.
       "this exquisite": Draft pages, SM, LOC. "That slow-motion, silent explosion of love" (SM, 297) is in
           " 'That in Aleppo Once . . .' " "that vast silent explosion," STORIES, 557.
163   "In the hush of pure": SM, 309.
       "doing an amazing" and "Seen and approved": VN to Hessen, April 17, 1950, PC. VN made the
           same report to Wilson, on the same date.
       "absolute lucidity": Enclosed with VN to John Fischer, March 16, 1950, HR.

164   "With one thing and": VN to John Selby, Rinehart, January 17, 1951.
      the Hemingway translation: VN to Chekhov Publishing, November 10, 1954.
      "Why don't you translate": Alvin Toffler, *Playboy,* March, 1964, 44.
      "Could you not send": VéN to Hessen, September 24, 1950, PC.
      "but the author found": VéN to HS, January 1, 1951, PC.
165   "Fluorescent Tears": SM material, LOC.
      The two buried "v"s: VN to H. Levin, February 18, 1951. Also to Grynberg, December 11, 1950,
         Bakhm.
      "It Is Me": VN to VéN, February 2, 1936, VNA.
      "He is not interested": *The New York Times,* February 23, 1951. Nicholas Nabokov's *Old Friends and
         New Music* had been published in January.
      "In the course of ": VN to Hessen, February, 1951, PC.
      "But you did": Boyd interview with VéN, January 13, 1980, Boyd archive.
      "Incidentally, I glanced": H. Levin to VN, March 5, 1951.
      "The icicles": VN diary, February 3, 1951, VNA. (The line is in Russian.) Rarely have melting ici-
         cles been put to such imaginative—and, to White, such abstruse—effect.
166   "dismal financial": VN to White, January 28, 1950, SL, 96.
      precarious monetary state: Interview with DN, December 4, 1997.
      "Moreover, I am engaged": VN to Pat Covici, Viking, November 12, 1951.
167   "Get away" and "We are keeping": Interview with Keegan, November 14, 1997.
      She did so again to "She was responsible": SO, 20, 105. VéN could sound foggy on this subject, al-
         though she never cavilled with written accounts, even when she quibbled with all else on those
         pages. VN did not include his wife in the first account of the attempted ignition, written in
         1956. ("On a Book Entitled Lolita," ANL, 312.) There appear to have been multiple rescues;
         there was certainly no incinerator on Seneca Street.
      She feared that: "Sono stata io a salvare Lolita," *Epoca,* November 22, 1959.
      "No, you're not": Field, 1986, 287. Also Arthur Mizener, *Cornell Alumni News,* September 1977, 56.
      one uncomfortable colleague: Interview with Alison Jolly, May 20, 1995.
      "Right now there's": VéN to HS, March 7, 1948, PC.
      "intellectual visa checkpoint": Field, 1977, 34.
      "My wife, of course": *Radcliffe News,* November 21, 1947.
168   "Go to sleep": Cannac, *Russkaya Mysl,* December 29, 1977.
      "We had no close": VéN to Field, October 20, 1968.
      boasted regularly: Jean Bruneau to author, February 8, 1996; interview of July 27, 1996.
      "dreadfully drafty": SO, 230.
      "One was a professor": VéN to HS, May 18, 1951.
      "Remember, it is not": Marc Szeftel, *Cornell Alumni News,* November 1980.
169   "You know, Véra": Interview with Elena Levin, June 16, 1995.
      "Véra always sides": Wilson, *Upstate* (New York: Farrar, Straus & Giroux, 1971), 160–61. In Wil-
         son's *The Fifties,* Edel, ed., 425 the line reads: "Vera invariably sides with him [VN] and be-
         comes slightly vindictive against people who argue with him."
170   Generally she had little: Interview with DN, December 5, 1997.
      a long, "newsy" letter: VéN to Lena Massalsky, February 10, 1959.
      "I would like to call": L. Massalsky to VéN, January 29, 1959.
      one student thought: Edouard C. Emmet to author, March 6, 1997.
171   "There are two great": Interview with Anthony Winner, n.d. For additional memories of the Har-
         vard year I am indebted to Robert J. Blattner, Edouard C. Emmet, John B. Forbes, Norman
         Friedman, Stephen P. Gibert, William Hedges, Herbert Howard, Saul Magram, Arthur
         Nebolsine, David Osnos, Ivan Pouchine, Pedro Sanjuan, Franklin D. Thompson, Gregory
         Troubetzkoy.
      did not universally charm: Interview with Franklin D. Thompson, February 1997. Similarly,
         Gregg, Massey, Winner.
      how he would have written: Interview with Irving Massey, March 2, 1997. VN later recalled with
         delight having dismembered the book before hundreds of students in Memorial Hall, SO, 103.
      Another disapproved: Interview with Winner.
      And was it truly necessary: Interview with Richard Gregg, March 4, 1997.

revealing only late: Interview with Myron Laseron, March 15, 1957.

"V. is giving *grandiose*": VéN to Hessen, March 22, 1952, PC.

"he is obviously taking": VéN to HS, April 13, 1952.

official enrollment: Harvard University archives.

172   "a gutter cat": Boyd interview with VéN, June 19, 1982, Boyd archive.

"When V. reads and writes": VéN to HS, April 13, 1952.

"He was much thinner": VéN to May Sarton, June 19, 1952.

"But you must": Interview with E. Emmet, May 9, 1997.

made him repeat: Arthur Mizener, *Cornell Alumni News*, September 1977, 56.

Langer was a punctual: Interview with DN, November 1, 1996.

173   Reasons for attendance: VN to Wilson, January 16, 1952, NWL 268. Boyd interview with VéN, December 2, 1979, Boyd archive; Karpovich to VN, February 21, 1954.

"the double-dotted": VN to Bart Winer, Bollingen Press, 1963, LOC.

"Now without Russian": VN to Hessen, June 2, 1951, PC.

As early as: Interview with Buxbaum, May 6, 1996.

The Cornell recollections were a tidy echo chamber of overlapping memories, a comfort to the biographer but difficult to acknowledge properly. Where possible I have separated out individual quotes but am indebted as well to the following Cornellians for their descriptions of the Nabokovs' routine: Laura T. Almquist, Arlene Alpert, Robert Bamberg, Leland Beck, Dr. Martin Blinder, Harry Bliss, Doris Nagel, Donald R. Brewer, Joe Buttino, Karin Cattarulla, Tanya Clyman, Peter Czap, William Elder Doll, Edwin Eigner, Marcia Elwitt, Elisavietta Ritchie Farnsworth, Stephen Fineman, Roberta Foy, Barton Friedman, Richard Isaac, Harry Gelman, Dorothy Gilbert, Roslyn Bakst Goldman, Ronald Goodison, Ted Heine, Renie Adler Hirsch, Steve Hochman, Richard Isaac, Isabel Kleigman, Peter Klem, Leighton Klevana, Stanley Komaroff, Edward L. Krawitt, M. Travis Lane, Dr. David C. Levin (of the "Gray Eagle" school), Carol Levine, Joan Macmillan (from whom comes the chalk dust allergy), Joseph F. Martino, Jr., Hilda Minkoff, Bill and Myra Orth, Joanna Russ, Kirk Sale, Rona Schneider, Robert Scholes, Marvin Shapiro, Roberta Silman, Penny Sindell (especially for the ventriloquism theory), Janet Sperber, Ron Sukenick, Bob Tapert, Robert G. Tischler, Frank Tretter, Darryl R. Turgeon, Marty Washburn, Ross Wetzsteon, Dick Wimmer, Marjorie and Stefan Winkler, Sandra Wittow (for the Seeing Eye dog hypothesis), Richard Wortman. See also Robert M. Adams, "Nabokov's Show," *The New York Review of Books*, December 18, 1980; Elizabeth Welt Trahan, "Laughter from the Dark: A Memory of Vladimir Nabokov," *The Antioch Review*, Spring 1985; Appel, "Remembering Nabokov," in Quennell, 11–33; Ross Wetzsteon, *The Village Voice*, November 30, 1967; Peter Klem, "Prejudices and Particularities," *Bloomsbury Review*, January 1981.

Her eyes: Interview with Charles Klaus, April 1996.

She lingered: Interviews with Peter Czap, August 28, 1996, Ross Wetzsteon, August 10, 1995.

administrative affairs: Interview with Tanya Clyman, July 1996.

"Oh, yes, yes, yes": Interview with Dorothy Gilbert, March 15, 1996.

174   sophisticated diagrams: See Trahan, *The Antioch Review*, Spring 1985, 175–82.

"rubberized tweed": Interview with Klem, September 25, 1996. In the published version the outfit is "waterproof tweed," LRL, 219.

"This monogrammatic": LRL, 175.

the mask dropped: Interview with Robert Tischler, September 1, 1996.

In some courses: Interview with Roslyn Bakst Goldman, August 22, 1996.

175   proved more memorable: Interview with Wetzsteon, August 10, 1995.

"quite a performance": Interview with Henry Steck, November 27, 1995. Similarly, Peter Czap.

as legendary: Wetzsteon, *The Village Voice*, November 30, 1967. Repr. in Appel and Newman, 240–46.

"Everybody was fascinated": Alison Bishop, in Gibian and Parker, eds., *The Achievements of Vladimir Nabokov*, 217.

One student winced: Trahan, *The Antioch Review*, Spring 1985, 179. Similarly, interview with Anthony Winner, February 1996. (Winner observed the act at Harvard.)

Gray Eagle: David C. Levin to author, October 10, 1995.

the Countess: Interview with Keegan, January 12, 1997.

"the most beautiful": Interview with Alison Bishop Jolly, May 20, 1995.

a countess: Interview with Marvin Shapiro, October 22, 1996. The German princess is from Joanna
Russ, interview of May 6, 1996.
"subtly endowed": RLSK, 80.
"But who is going": Appel to VéN, December 20, 1984, VNA.
176   geniality might register: Interview with Wetzsteon, August 10, 1995.
Initially she waded: Interview with Keegan, November 14, 1997.
adding a panegyric: Interview with Dick Wimmer, December 1, 1997.
"I estimate that I shall": VN to William Sale, October 26, 1953.
"my assistant, Mrs. V": VN to Diane Adams, June 14, 1954.
complaining that he had: VN to Grynberg, November 6, 1953, LOC.
He spent five days: Henry Steck to author, October 9, 1995. Interview with Steck, November 27,
1995.
177   "What was the pattern": M. Travis Lane to author, May 16, 1996. Interview with Lane, July 25, 1996.
"*We* thought you": Interview with Russ, May 6, 1996.
"I have written" to "some difficulty": Interview with Dorothy Gilbert, March 29, 1996.
"he leaned over": Interview with Steve Katz, October 24, 1996. See also Katz, *Contemporary Authors
Autobiography,* vol. 14, 165–66.
"way, way over": Franklin D. Thompson to author, March 3, 1997.
"I write you while": VN to Hessen, October 22, 1956, PC.
beneath his dignity: Interview with Carol Levine.
He grumbled: VN to Hessen, May 3, 1957, PC.
"I am too little": LRL, 98
178   "a woman full of ": Lecture drafts. The words "Dostoyevsky was proclaimed a great writer mainly
by philosophers or philosophizing critics whose opinions on literature should never be quite
trusted" were, among others, hers.
"not literature but": Osip Mandelstam, 114.
"He savored words": Justice Ruth Bader Ginsburg to author, September 3, 1996.
appeared superficial: Interview with Charles Klaus. Roberta Silman (interview of May 6, 1996) was
discouraged from taking the course. Similarly, Rona Schneider, Marcia Elwitt. Interviews
with Kirk Sale, October 21, 1996; Doug Fowler, August 1996; Edwin Eigner, July 31, 1998.
179   how to read: Some students knew this. interview with Myra Orth, October 29, 1996. Similarly, Dr.
Doris Nagel.
"on willingness for": LRL, 147.
lit up a cigarette: Interview with Matthew J. Bruccoli, April 18, 1995.
"as good a piece": VéN copy of Lange, *Michigan Quarterly Review,* October 1986, 482, VNA.
he was unable: Interview with Gold, June 22, 1995.
turning on a light: Interview with Wimmer.
nervous little dance: Interview with Donald R. Brewer, January 25, 1998. Stephen Fineman remembered VN appealing to VéN to work her magic on the dais light, which resisted him. Interview of September 20, 1998. To another student he explained that all went technologically
awry if he turned on a television himself. Interview with Nagel.
"Of course you remember": Interview with Robert Ruebman, April 9, 1996. James McConkey to author, August 12, 1996.
amphitheater lights: Appel, "Remembering Nabokov," Quennell, 18.
180   "We did not know": Interview with Robert Tischler, September 1, 1996.
"Véra Nabokov was": Roberta Silman, letter to editor, *The Los Angeles Times,* August 7, 1977, 2.
The Subnormal Adolescent Girl: LO cards, LOC.
"ruffled by a too robust": LATH, 234.
pushed the envelope: Schimmel to author, November 28, 1996.
an attractive favorite student: Interview with Nagel.
the fugitive information: Interview with Stephen Jan Parker, November 13, 1996.
When his classes were: Interview with Ted Heine, January 23, 1996.
181   "No, Volodya" to "absolutely right": Interview with Robert C. Howes, May 5, 1997.
intellectual partner: Interview with Dr. Zygmunt M. Tomkiewicz, August 27, 1996.
to jot it down: Trahan, 179. Appel, in Quennell, 17.
One student looked: Interview with Robert Howes. Also, Grynberg to VN, December 20, 1948.
tribute to his delivery: Interviews with Michael Rubenstein, December 8, 1997, Klem.

laughing so hard: Interview with Wetzsteon. Hughes, interview text, 47.
182   switched to the page: Interview with Joanna Russ.
       "rabbits out of textual": Robert M. Adams, "Nabokov's Show," *The New York Review of Books,* December 18, 1980, 61–63.
       The pink shirt: Klem, "Prejudices and Particularities," *The Bloomsbury Review,* January 1981. Similarly, interview with Joseph F. Martino, Jr., September 18, 1998. Klem interview.
       Did he dress: Interview with Russ.
       Nabokov's apparel: Schimmel to author, November 28, 1996. Similarly, Gould P. Colman to author (via Phil Macrae), September 12, 1996. Interview with Gregory Troubetzkoy (Harvard), February 1997.
       "Once she smiled": Klem, *Bloomsbury Review.*
       three reasons why: Interview with DN, October 29, 1996.
       "very straight, smooth-haired": "Bachmann," STORIES, 118.
       "It was as if ": Interview with Dr. Martin Blinder, July 1996.
183   illiterate bootstraps: Interview with Blinder.
       the most visible: Many testified to VN's having been supremely conscious of VéN's presence. Interview with E. Levin, October 7, 1996; similarly, Bruccoli, Carol Levine.
       "Who is Sirin" to "his work": Interview with Tanya Clyman.
       Harvard students: Interview with Pedro Sanjuan, April 15, 1996. Also Trahan, 181.
       eyes lit up: Interview with Isabel Kleigman, July 27, 1996.
       "Ladies and gentlemen": Interview with Kleigman, April 15, 1996.
       "Do you have any": Interview with Appel, August 28, 1996.
       "But one is inclined": Unpublished chapter of SM, LOC. See also PF, 28.
184   an oil well: VéN to Joan Daly, September 22, 1971, PW.
       uneasy in the classroom: Interviews with Keegan, Richard Gregg, March 4, 1997. See also Harry Levin in Alexandrov, *Garland Companion,* 228.
       Nabokov regularly dreamed: VéN to Darryl R. Turgeon, March 13, 1966.
       "likes to be able": Field, 1977, 247. "Nabokov likes to be able": Viking corrections to Field, 411, VNA. As David Slavitt noted when he interviewed him for *Newsweek* in 1962, VN looked to VéN repeatedly as he spoke. To Slavitt the reason seemed clear: "It was as if even if I weren't getting some of these jokes, she was." Interview with Slavitt, August 14, 1998.
       "Mrs. Vladimir Nabokov": VéN to Tischler, February 21, 1967.
       "being destroyed by emperors": LRL, 10.
185   "radiant presence": LL, 97.
       "cannot be discarded": LRL, 43; GOGOL, 119.
       as far as can be ascertained: Interview with DN, December 13, 1997.

                      6   N A B O K O V   1 0 2

186   "No one ever had to": Interview with Elena Levin, June 6, 1995.
       "with a certain deadliness": Wilson, *Upstate,* 160. In *The Fifties,* 426, Wilson used the phrase to describe the tone in which VéN addressed the two men of letters giggling helplessly over *Histoire d'O,* which Wilson had brought along for VN.
       intrusive moonlight: Interviews with Herbert and Jane Wiegandt, November 21, 1997; Lester Eastman, November 21, 1997.
       "We never used": VN to Wiegandt, February 13, 1953.
       "I am not interested": VN to Wiegandt, draft.
187   "Goethe" to "ever written": Interview with Jenni Moulton, March 2, 1997.
       how he could possibly: Interview with Alain Seznec, January 28, 1998.
       "To your knowledge" to "Chateaubriand": Demorest, *Arts and Sciences* 4, no. 2 (Spring 1983). "You know, there are no German translations of world literature of any value whatever," VN challenged another colleague, needless to say a German-born literature professor. See Lange, *Michigan Quarterly Review,* October 1986, 489.
       "irritate the intelligent": VN to Shakhovskoy, May 23, 1935, LOC.
       Not only was Auden: Interview with James McConkey.

Jane Austen: Daiches, in *L'Arc* 24, 65–66.

"Spousal censorship": Carl R. Proffer, *The Widows of Russia,* 70.

188 "and therefore was amusing": VéN diary.

counseled a little mercy: Interview with Dick Wimmer, December 1, 1997.

the home botany exam: Interview with Dmitri Ledkovsky, July 1996.

censoring the censoring: Willa Petschek, *The Observer* (London), May 30, 1976.

London theatre: RLSK, 85

" '*Volodya!* '": Appel, in Quennell, 20. Similarly, Roberta Silman.

"teetered always": Adams, *The New York Review of Books,* December 18, 1980. "For all of his famil-
     iarity with American mores, he often misread American manners," concluded another col-
     league. Interview with M. H. Abrams, October 18, 1998.

"I am sorry to disappoint": VéN to Howard S. Cresswell, March 20, 1953.

189 "show off her family": VéN to Lena Massalsky, August 28, 1950, Massalsky family archive.

in speaking with Sonia: L. Massalsky to VéN, September 9, 1950.

"in another selfless": Szeftel November 8, 1971, journal entry, cited in *Pniniad,* 128.

"Don't bother hiring him": Interview with Ruth Schorer, August 25, 1996.

"Well all right": Interview with Peter Kahn, August 29, 1996.

It was felt: Interviews with Frances Lange, September 12, 1996, Kitty Szeftel, August 15, 1996. Also
     Elena Levin.

respected but not universally liked: Interviews with Silman, Elwitt, Fowler, Kahn. Richard L. Leed
     to author, April 8, 1997; Steck to author, November 27, 1995.

shared Sonia's low opinion: VN to Shakhovskoy, c. 1938, LOC.

190 tucked rather inaccessibly: See Robert M. Adams, *The New York Review of Books,* January 30, 1992.

"Our only airline": VéN to Peter de Peterson, May 25, 1958.

end in his expulsion: Bruneau to author, February 8, 1996.

playacting: Schimmel to author, November 1, 1996.

As for American schools: VéN to L. Massalsky, May 15, 1950, Massalsky family archive.

"I think Vera": Blanche Peltenburg to VéN, November 1955.

"prosperous usurers": See Frederic, *The New Exodus,* 19. In a letter to the *Cornell Daily Sun,* Octo-
     ber 20, 1958, 4, VN insisted he was "strictly a Goldwin Smith man."

191 "lyrical plaintiveness": VN to Grynberg, December 16, 1944, Bakhm. He was speaking in particu-
     lar, and privately, of Wilson. Earlier it had been "the spiritual tempest, the pulsing, the shining,
     dancing savagery, that evil and tenderness that drive us to God knows what heavens and
     depths." VN in *Rul,* October 28, 1921.

"Amazing Americans!": VéN diary, VNA.

"It's dangerous": Interview with Keegan, January 15, 1998.

Vladimir never voted: Boyd interview with VéN, September 3, 1982, Boyd archive.

192 "the two McSenators" to "Dewey": VéN to the *Cornell Daily Sun,* December 12, 1952.

"She also says": VN diary entry, January 14, 1951, VNA.

"We both loved": VN to Katharine White, January 4, 1953.

saw only propaganda: Alice Colby-Hall to author, April 9, 1997.

Fairbanks did not speak: VéN copy of Field, 1977, VNA.

impassioned defense: Interview with Arthur Schlesinger, Jr., October 9, 1996.

193 "I suppose that McCarthy": VéN to Mark Vishniak, February 19, 1955, Hoover.

firm measures were the only: VéN to Berkman, October 25, 1962.

"After all": VéN to Vishniak, February 19, 1955, Hoover.

194 He reminded her that: Vishniak to VéN, February 23, 1955, VNA.

"I continue to consider" and "Enough": VéN to Vishniak, February 27, 1955, Hoover.

principle informed all: VéN to Anna Feigin, February 14, 1963. Also, Boyd interview with VéN,
     March 16, 1982, Boyd archive; Boyd to author, June 14, 1997.

tore her check: Interview with DN, November 12, 1997.

"We spent two months": VéN to HS, March 29, 1953.

printsipialnost: cited in Abram Tertz cited in Seltzer, "Simon Dubnow: A Critical Biography of His
     Early Years," 60.

195 cut-up liver: May Sarton, *The Fur Person* (New York: Norton, 1978), 7–9.

"on the verge": VN to Wilson, May 3, 1953, NWL, 280.

a fat rattlesnake: VéN to Hessen, May 23, 1953, PC. Boyd interview with VéN, February 2, 1982, Boyd archive. See also, Levy, *The New York Times Magazine,* October 31, 1971, 20–41.

"St. George-Vladimir": VéN to Rosemary Mizener, May 12, 1953.

"Moreover, Vladimir": VéN to Alice James, May 17, 1953.

"mellow academic townlet": LO, 179.

far preferred the green: VéN to Karpovich, June 17, 1953, Bakhm.

196   on Lance and Dmitri: In her letter to HS, February 23, 1952, PC, VéN noted that the old Bokes' only son shares some of DN's idiosyncrasies. DN is "Lance" in VN to Aldanov, 1940 from Palo Alto, Bakhm.

"of melting light": "Lance," STORIES, 631.

offshore racing: His first boat was called *Vera I,* the second *Vera II.* "You could have called it 'Lolita,' " commented VN wistfully, lips pursed. Interview with DN, September 30, 1997.

"A parent's job": VéN to HS, July 16, 1966.

"We like it much": VéN to HS, July 31, 1953.

horror: Interview with Boyd, November 23, 1996.

no snakes in the neighborhood: VéN to HS, May 19, 1960.

"She liked guns": Interview with DN, February 10, 1996.

"My wife has some": VN to Alexander B. Klots, May 16, 1949. D. Barton Johnson sent on this letter.

197   "For protection while": Tompkins County Courthouse records.

After the meal: Interviews with Jean-Jacques Demorest, Joseph Mazzeo, January 7, 1997. Bayonet Bob Ruebman served as general firearms consultant. I had more questions for him than I thought I would.

Nestled in the glove: Clarke, *Esquire,* July 1975.

a viewing of the gun and "She really had": Interviews with Jason Epstein, September 24, 1996, and May 11, 1998. Interview with Barbara Epstein, September 17, 1996.

198   wholly unsurprised: Interview with Elena Levin, January 12, 1998.

"Véra, show him": Interview with Saul Steinberg, January 17, 1996.

ripe with symbolism: Steinberg was not the only one; Humbert Humbert, too, evokes a comparison between a woman's purse and her genitals, LO, 62. See also LO, 216, for the original anti-Freudian's take on such symbolism.

Anna Karenina's handbag: *Cornell Magazine,* July-August 1997.

"You will perhaps": VéN to Collete Duhamel, La Table Ronde, November 18, 1953.

December 1953: Nabokov slipped slightly in his afterword, "On a Book Entitled Lolita." He remembered that he "finished copying the thing out in longhand in the spring of 1954, and at once began casting around for a publisher." The search for a publisher continued through that year, when revisions continued, but an early typescript had been ready as of December 1953.

199   a final draft: VN wrote his sister of the translation "Véra and I made of *Conclusive Evidence.*" VN to HS, September 29, 1953, PC.

"V. asks me to jot": VéN to the Hessens, December 6, 1954, PC.

"that his incognito be": VéN to White, December 23, 1953, SL, 142–43.

"a time bomb": VN to Laughlin, February 3, 1954, SL, 144.

"In an atmosphere of ": VN to Wilson, June 20, 1953, NWL, 282.

five granddaughters: White read the novel only in March 1957, while one of the "potential nymphets" was visiting. It made her shudder. (White to VN, March 25, 1957, BMC.) She did not read the manuscript when VéN delivered it for two reasons: She was given only the weekend to do so, during which she was entertaining; she did not feel she could in good faith conceal the material from Shawn. In light of Covici's opinion that the book was pornographic, she had already warned VéN that she did not feel qualified to offer an opinion on U.S. publication as she was personally unacquainted with the laws governing obscenity. Nor did she feel comfortable guaranteeing VN total anonymity, at home or at the office. Note to files, White archive; White to VN, February 1, 1954, BMC.

"I can't believe": VéN to HS, February 28, 1957.

"Would we like": VN to White, April 4, 1957, SL, 215.

200   "unpleasantness" and "In any case": VéN to HS, November 12, 1955, PC. The Nabokovs were slow to send copies of LO to both HS and Kirill Nabokov, VN's brother. Neither knew even the name of the volume's publisher in January of 1956; both were clamoring to read the book. As

for Sikorski's son, HS reassured VéN that she had nothing to fear: His English was not yet good enough. HS to VéN, January 13, 1956, Cornell.

"reality always lies" and "in her mind": Proffer, *Widows of Russia,* 47.

"V is afraid that Lolita": VéN to HS, January 12, 1956.

"I am very fond": VéN addition to VN to Wilson, March 8, 1946, NWL, 165.

had not yet met him: Richard Wilbur to author, February 20, 1998.

left her indifferent: VéN to A. Barbetti, May 13, 1947.

"But it is a great": VéN to HS, January 12, 1956.

"legally binding": VN to Pat Covici, October 14, 1952.

201 "up to his chin": VéN to Wilson, April 24, 1955, NWL, 293.

"the novel about H.H.": VéN to Wallace Brockway, June 5, 1954.

"My husband has": VéN to Doussia Ergaz, Clarouin Agency, August 6, 1954.

202 even more alarmed: VéN to HS, August 5, 1954.

"fiasco": VN to Wilson, July 30, 1954, NWL, 285.

"never found" to "try and stay": VéN to Gordon Lacy, August 23, 1954.

"a second-rate": VéN to Laughlin, July 20, 1954. Similarly, to HS, August 5, 1954.

"is a dismal hole": VN to Wilson, July 30, 1954, NWL, 285.

203 "She's a dreadful": Interview with Otto Pitcher, August 29, 1995.

"hurtling in pursuit": DN to Boyd, August 20, 1987, VNA.

"How can you say": Interview with DN, January 28, 1998.

Mount Sinai Hospital: Interview with Mrs. Arthur Dallos, February 6, 1998. VN diary.

"Keep track" to "these thoughts": VéN to Lisbet Thompson, October 1, 1961.

204 black magic: VéN to HS, January 10, 1949.

liver trouble: Among others, VN to H. Levin, September 5, 1954, Houghton Library.

"in a pitiful state": VN to Wilson, September 9, 1954, NWL, 287.

Roger Straus: Straus remembers the manuscript having come to him directly from Wilson, although the correspondence suggests otherwise. Interview with Roger W. Straus, January 30, 1998.

"in his right mind" and "from various": Straus to VN, November 11, 1954. See also, Straus letter to the editor, *The New York Times Book Review,* July 3, 1988.

205 He admitted: Straus to VéN, November 29, 1954.

"The poor darling": Interview with Bowden Broadwater, September 1996.

"It's repulsive": Interview with Jason Epstein, May 11, 1998.

"Did you read his": Wilson to Grynberg, September 28, 1955, LOC.

Elena Levin suspected, and the Levins' reading: Interviews with Elena Levin, June 6, 1995, February 20, 1998. The Levins' daughter was born in 1941; Helen Wilson in 1948.

a Dorothy Parker: Diment was the first to note the coincidence, *Pniniad,* 60–61.

"a yelp": VN to Maxwell, August 26, 1955.

firmly reassured him: White to VN, August 31, 1955.

failed tribute to *Fanny*: Wilson to Louise Bogan, March 22, 1946, *Letters on Literature and Politics,* 437. Wilson says the same: Field, 1986, 300.

"That the passion" to "Without suggesting": Epstein reader's report, PC.

206 "The four American": LO, 313.

Nabokov later claimed: LO, 314. There is no evidence whatever for the claim.

"If only everything": VéN to HS, January 29, 1955.

"Just think of all": VéN to Berkman, September 7, 1956.

"I suppose it will": VN to Wilson, February 19, 1955, Yale.

"one would not dare": Ergaz to VN, August 24, 1954, Glenn Horowitz collection.

207 Even the Karpoviches: Karpovich to Anna Feigin, January 26, 1955.

"I do have": VN to Chekhov Publishing, May 6, 1952.

The agent of providence: See John de St. Jorre's delightful *Venus Bound: The Erotic Voyage of the Olympia Press and Its Writers.*

"I felt I had" to "respectable": Maurice Girodias, *Une journée sur la terre,* Vol. II, *Les Jardins d'eros,* 294. The first volume of the memoir (*Une journée sur la terre,* Vol. I, *L'Arrivée*) appeared in different form as *The Frog Prince* (New York: Crown, 1980). Also unpublished Girodias memoir pages, Gelfman Schneider Literary Agents, Inc; Girodias, "Pornologist on Mt. Olympus," *Playboy,* April 1961.

second and third readers: Interviews with Muffie Wainhouse, January 29, 1998; Miriam Worms, June 18, 1996; Eric Kahane, June 12, 1996.

"If the publisher": VN to Ergaz, May 6, 1955. Having agreed to attach his name to the work, VN got cold feet several weeks later, as the contract was negotiated. "J'aurais, comme je vous le disais, certainement préféré de publier sous mon nom de plume. N'accordez donc l'usage de mon nom que si l'éditeur en fait une condition absolue," he advised Ergaz on May 24. The matter was settled when Girodias advised that he held absolutely to VN's signing the work with his own name.

208   "I queried him": Morris Bishop to Alison Bishop, May 18, 1955, Bishop family papers. Interviews with Alison Bishop Jolly, May 20, 1995, Louise Boyle, September 10, 1996, Robert M. Adams, October 13, 1996.

Neither author nor publisher: See Girodias, *Une journée,* II, 297.

one's idiot child: Interview with Robert Langbaum, June 24, 1997.

"It's full of pepper": VN to DN, April 23, 1957, VNA.

shared her fears: Boyd interview with Alison Bishop, April 14, 1983, Boyd archive.

same vehemence: Caryn James, "Their Most Regrettable Character," *The New York Times Book Review,* May 6, 1984, 34–37.

209   "moral turpitude": Edmund Wilson to Helen Muchnic, August 18, 1955, in Wilson, *Letters on Literature and Politics,* 577. The words were most likely Morris Bishop's. White also remembered that VN worried he would lose his job, 1977 note to file, BMC.

"He was happy": VéN to HS, July 5, 1955.

Ithaca Public Library: Boyd interview with Alison Bishop, April 14, 1983, Boyd archive.

"nostalgic longing": VéN to Berkman, summer 1955.

"which you will need" to "*by mail*": VéN to DN, July 1, 1955.

210   "If anyone wants": Berkman to VéN, June 27, 1955. Also, Boyd interview with Augusta Jaryc, April 14, 1983; Boyd interview with Berkman, April 9, 1983, Boyd archive. Berkman to VéN, October 1, 1954.

"has assisted Véra": VN to Wilson, August 14, 1956, NWL, 300. Negotiated by Véra, the contract was between Doubleday and Dmitri.

"I have finished": VN to H. Levin, September 14, 1956, Houghton.

"Last year": VéN to Amy Kelly, September 18, 1956.

"We have just": VéN to Elena Levin, June 24, 1956, PC.

"Instead of taking": VéN to DN, June 8, 1956.

"each of which is really": VN to Natalia Peterson, December 18, 1955.

211   stimulating effect: Wilson to Muchnic, in Wilson, *Letters on Literature and Politics,* August 18, 1955. Cf. the account of a later visit, *Upstate,* 159. Wilson remained flabbergasted that Vladimir considered LO his best book in any language, Wilson to Struve, June 21, 1957.

Wilson happily confided: Wilson to Grynberg, September 28, 1955, LOC. "I was glad to have an opportunity to renew my good relations with him and get to like him again" were the actual words.

"My mistake": VéN copy of Harry Levin, *Memories of the Moderns* (New York: New Directions, 1980), 215, VNA.

"The only thing": VéN to Berkman, summer 1955.

212   "As one of us": Epstein to VN, July 13, 1956.

213   "Sheer unrestrained pornography": John Gordon, *The Sunday Express,* January 29, 1956.

He had himself: Edward de Grazia, *Girls Lean Back Everywhere* (New York: Random House, 1992), 257. De Grazia's is an eminently lucid guide to the publishing difficulties surrounding LO, among other volumes.

"lewd and libertine": VN to Covici, March 29, 1956, SL, 185.

"V & V Inc.": VéN to DN, March 30, 1967, VNA.

lovely cottage: Alison Bishop had located the rental, though she worried it might be too isolated for the Nabokovs. "No fear of solitude; the only question is whether food is obtainable in Mt. Carmel. Véra doesn't want to live on canned goods," Morris Bishop advised his wife. Bishop to Alison Bishop, May 14, 1955, Cornell.

"Another busy" to "three months": VéN to Kelly, September 18, 1956.

washing machine repairman: Boyd interview with VéN, January 9, 1985, Boyd archive.

214   "Since he is working": VéN to HS, December 31, 1956.
      "Yes, of course": VéN to HS, February 28, 1957.
      she grumbled: VéN to HS, February 11, 1958.
      "a lovely row": VéN to Berkman, February 20, 1957.
      "How persistently": PF, 79.
      "loves to lose": Bishop, cited in Michael Scammell unpublished pages, PC.
      The Anchor Review: The excerpt was chosen in consultation with Doubleday's lawyers. VN and
          VéN were thrilled with the presentation.
      about little girls: Interview with Barbara Epstein, September 17, 1996. See also Tom Turley, *Niagara
          Falls Gazette,* January 11, 1959. At the same time a very proper German academic, Dr. Freder-
          ick Kohner, wrote a novel about a teenage girl that America embraced as wholesome and
          amusing. To capture the patois of the bikini-and-bobby-sox set for *Gidget* (1958), he eaves-
          dropped on his daughter's phone conversations, taking notes from the extension in the kitchen.
215   neat carbonic tribute: VéN to Doubleday, March 31/April 1, 1957.
      "I wonder if you": VéN to Epstein, January 16, 1957.
      "albino camels": VN to White, April 4, 1957, SL, 216.
      Véra heard only: VéN to HS, February 11, 1958.
      Siamese cat: Interview with Ruth Sharp, January 23, 1998.
      mouse-tennis and "Do you think": Doris Nagel to parents, February 27, 1957, PC.
216   distasteful subject: See for example William James to VN, June 22, 1956.
      fretted over the subject: Interview with Alison Jolly, May 20, 1995; Jolly to author, November 6, 1996.
      "I would not like": Szeftel, *Cornell Magazine,* November 1980.
      on Pnin and Szeftel: See Galya Diment, *Pniniad.* Also Boyd interview with Appel, April 23, 1983,
          Boyd archive. Field, 1986, 29.
      Even Mrs. Szeftel: Interview with Kitty Szeftel, August 15, 1996.
      "Nabokov's *Pnin*": Bishop to Alison Bishop, April 28, 1957, cited in Diment, *Pniniad,* 63.
      "Oh, well, every Russian": Parry, *The Texas Quarterly,* Spring 1971.
      "Lolita is young": VN to Epstein, March 5, 1957.
217   Having robbed a bank: Ken McCormick note to Doubleday files, LOC.
      She was startled, and "repulsive": Interview with Maria Leiper, February 8, 1998.
      shunning *Lolita*: James, *The New York Times Book Review,* May 6, 1984.
      reselling copies: A little bookstore in Ithaca obtained a few copies, marked them $10 each, and sold
          them out in the course of a half hour. VéN to Ergaz, September 10, 1957.
      tempted to publish privately: William Styron, "The Book on Lolita," *The New Yorker,* September 4,
          1995, 33.
      "revolted to the point": Hiram Haydn, *Words and Faces* (New York: Harcourt Brace Jovanovich,
          1974), 264–66. None of Nabokov's other works went over any better with Haydn, who never
          made it past page 22 of *Pale Fire* and had the decency to admit as much.
      devoted nearly as much: *Time,* March 18, 1957.
      twilight games: VN to Hessen, April 22, 1957. It was also the house in which VN read his way
          through the resident anthropologist's personal library. Interview with Ruth Sharp.
      "Well then, if that": VéN to Goldenweiser, June 3, 1957, Bakhm.
218   "The question of " to "your man": VéN to Houghton Mifflin, July 24, 1952. The editor happened to
          be Wilson's daughter, Rosalind.
      "nightly roamings" and "I have finally": VéN to Chekhov Publishing, January 28, 1953.
219   "about those magic": GIFT, 110.
      "is as sketchy": VéN to Edgar S. Pitkin, February 13, 1959.
      more gently suggested: VéN to Robert Sigman, November 29, 1957, VNA.
      "On August 6 of that year": SO, 270.
220   "Allow me to clear up": VéN to Mrs. Sherwood, June 30, 1969.
      "I have no way": VN to Michael Mohrt, Gallimard, c. 1959.
      "Personally I would appreciate": VéN to Prins & Prins, April 10, 1968.
      "He simply does not": VéN to HS, November 20, 1952.
      "a bad letter-writer": VéN to Berkman, October 25, 1962.
      "fiercely protective": VéN copy of Alan Levy, *The Velvet Butterfly,* 13.
      a sensational, book: VéN to Irving Lazar, September 9, 1968, VNA.

221   "And, as you can well": VéN to William Lamont, July 5, 1952.
      "your talented boy friend's": Lamont to VéN, November 4, 1952.
      "In doing so": VéN to Lamont, November 22, 1952.
      "V. was asked" to "push now": VéN to Berkman, October 10, 1956, SL, 188–89.
      "I'm sorry" and "repeat it": VéN to HS, April 9, 1959.
      "Dear V. & V." to "at will": Bishop to the Nabokovs, April 17, 1959.
      "My husband asks": VéN to Jack Dalton, October 15, 1963, SL 350.
222   The situation was complicated: Interviews with Walter Minton, June 5, 1995; Ivan Obolensky, May
           31, 1996.
      "Vladimir started this letter": VéN to Minton, December 22, 1957.
      "space spooks": LO, 235.
223   instantly forgot: VN to Frank Taylor, McGraw-Hill, December 13, 1969.
      "V hates the telephone": VéN diary, VNA.
      "communicatory neurosis": VéN to William Maxwell, January 16, 1964.
      conferred with her: Interview with Obolensky, May 31, 1996.
      "making one last appeal": Minton to VN, December 27, 1957.
      "I just lied my head": Interview with Minton, June 5, 1995.
224   Véra was to blame: Minton to Girodias, November 29, 1958, cited in Girodias, "Lolita, Nabokov,
           and I," Evergreen, September 1965, 47.
      "Mama is angry": VN to DN, December 3, 1959, VNA.
      "beneath the word": PF, 68.

7   PAST PERFECT

225   "Long distance" to "handling the MS" and all subsequent diary entries: VéN 1958 diary, VNA.
226   "Should they send": VN to Levin, May 22, 1958.
      "The very thought": VéN to Agnes Perkins, April 29, 1958.
227   "Some days I barely": Eric Kahane to VN, February 2, 1958.
      "That's a beautiful" to "Alcatraz," Gallimard's low expectations: Interview with Kahane, June 12,
           1996.
      "in the advance light": LATH, 6.
      "finally giving": VéN diary, VNA.
      "He is wildly": Brenner, The New Republic, June 23, 1958, 18–21.
      master of the perverse: The word "perverse" had a habit of attaching itself to the work. When fi-
           nally she read and failed to admire the novel, White begged Nabokov: "Please try to forgive
           my perversity on your perversity." Brenner offered: "Perverse. Of all the words one should em-
           ploy to tag Nabokov's art, this now seems to me by far the most accurate." He was astute
           enough to apply the adjective equally to the earlier works and sophisticated enough to recog-
           nize it as a virtue. Two months later, Orville Prescott, Lolita's most visible non-admirer, wrote
           in The New York Times: "To describe such a perversion with the pervert's enthusiasm without
           being disgusting is impossible." Doussia Ergaz used the same word in pitching the novel to
           Girodias.
228   vowed to write: VéN to Kelly, February 7, 1960. VN told Italian journalists as much as well.
      It is unlikely: Boyd concurs, interview of November 21, 1996.
      she boasted: VéN to Filippa Rolf, September 25, 1958.
      "is really a very childish": Unpublished interview with Phyllis Méras, May 13, 1962.
      Humbert's motel rooms: She found motor courts tolerable, motels less so.
229   coming-out party: VéN to Berkman, August 25, 1958.
      "What is it?" to "It's the main": The New York Post, August 6, 1958, 10.
230   Lionel Trilling met: Diana Trilling to author, September 13, 1995.
      "serenely indifferent": VéN diary, VNA.
      "highbrow pornography": Prescott, The New York Times, August 18, 1958.
      "vicious spite": VéN diary, VNA. Prescott was not the only one to balk at VN's memory; Katharine
           White's colleagues at The New Yorker were convinced he was inventing details in 1948, when
           the magazine rejected an early section of his memoirs. White to VN, September 6, 1948, BMC.
      "in a subtle": VéN to Berkman, August 25, 1958.

231 "It will apparently": VéN to HS, October 12, 1958, PC.
     the *Life* team: Interviews with Carl Mydans, March 24, 1998, Betty Ajemian, April 5, 1998.
     "They are both": Mydans diary, PC.
     "in front of " to "moderately good book": VéN diary, VNA.
232 No day passed: VéN to HS, December 8, 1958, PC.
     Harry and Kuvyrkin, Harris and Kubrick: VéN diary, VNA.
     Mormon boy: Melvin A. Nimer, Jr., age 8, asserted he had killed both parents.
     utterly corrupt: *The New York Times Book Review,* October 26, 1958, 2.
233 "having struck oil": Arthur Mizener to VN, October 11, 1958.
     the Women's Club conversation: VéN diary, VNA.
     press clippings: She also compiled a "not-for-file" file, of the related but off-color clippings, the bra
          ads, the personals. The non-file expanded greatly with *Ada*'s publication.
     "network roulette": PF, 45.
     the television routines, "They all hope": VéN diary, VNA.
234 tongues did cluck: Interviews with Peter Czap; Roberta Silman; Barton Friedman, July 1996. I have
          relied here on David Slavitt's recollections of his *Newsweek* interview, posted on NABOKV-L,
          July 10, 1994. See also *Newsweek,* November 24, 1958, 114.
     "They seem disappointed": VéN diary, VNA.
     "The book in question": Malott to C. B. Kelley, January 27, 1959, Cornell. See also, Bishop, in Appel
          and Newman, eds., *Nabokov,* 238.
     Strange Fruit: VéN to Barbetti, May 13, 1937.
     "Now, didn't we": Interview with Ellis Duell, September 12, 1997. Similarly, Jean-Jacques Demor-
          est.
     producing them on demand: Interview with Albert Podell, October 21, 1996. Similarly, Keegan,
          January 15, 1998.
235 "a correction which is": VéN to *The New York Post,* August 22, 1958.
     "the rich pre-revolutionary": *Evening Standard* (London), November 5, 1959.
     excitement over the countdown: VéN diary, VNA. VéN to HS, December 8, 1958. VéN to Jason
          Epstein, December 7, 1958.
     "ready-made souls": CBC, November 26, 1958, interview with Pierre Bertin.
     "Lolita was attacked": *The New York Post,* August 31, 1958.
     she fixed instead: *Syracuse Post-Standard,* September 14, 1958; VéN diary, VNA; Szeftel, *Cornell
          Magazine,* November 1980.
236 Lolita discussed: Hazel's suicide struck her as one of the most affecting passages in all of her hus-
          band's work. To Filippa Rolf, March 22, 1966.
     "the fading smile": F. W. Dupee, "Lolita in America," *Columbia University Forum,* Winter 1959, 39.
     "sat with me one night": Minton to author, August 12, 1995.
237 *"petite grue":* VéN diary, VNA. See also Girodias, *Une journée,* II, 429–30, and *L'Express,* January 8,
          1959.
     Six days before: VéN to Goldenweiser, August 12, 1958, Bakhm.
     could no longer cope: VéN to Elena Levin, October 30, 1958, PC.
     "We are swamped": VéN to Berkman, November 30, 1958.
238 the Minton call, the Lehigh student: VéN diary, VNA.
     "I am swamped": VéN to Lena Massalsky, January 1959, VNA.
239 another fifty years: VéN to Berkman, April 19, 1961.
     to extort money: VéN to Jason Epstein, January 18, 1958.
     "V. got so bored" through "put back": VéN diary, VNA.
     "Yes, a new tax": Walter Winchell, *New York Mirror,* October 14, 1962. Also, John Coleman, *The
          Spectator* (London), November 3, 1959.
     Suspicious Véra: Girodias, *Une journée,* II, 455.
240 "Yes, I know": Cited in Diment, *Pniniad,* 134.
     "business manager, chauffeuse": Jeffrey Blyth *The Daily Mail* (London), March 16, 1959 (first of a
          two-part article).
     could not have asked: Interview with Marie Schebeko Biche, February 10, 1997.
     crossbreeding her Russian: *Arts* (Paris), November 3, 1959.
     learn two things: Rolf to Tenggren, January 21, 1961, PC. "January," 29, PC.
241 "by a real Swede": VéN to Lena Massalsky, April 12, 1959.

"Ignition was made": B. B. Ribbing to Mina Turner, Doubleday, July 9, 1959. In all some four thousand *Lolitas* and two thousand *Pnins* went up in smoke. The Wahlström relationship had got
off to an awkward start. Having published *Camera Obscura* many years earlier, the firm did not
discover that Sirin and Nabokov were one and the same until six months after they had acquired LO.

"charming": VéN to Pyke Johnson, Jr., Doubleday, July 20, 1959.

242   a great joy: Interview with Dorothy Gilbert, March 29, 1996.

Lewis Nichols: *The New York Times Book Review,* August 31, 1958.

"We have been running": VéN to Mrs. J. P. Ashmore, March 25, 1959, VNA.

to Wilson's mind: Wilson to Grynberg, August 23, 1958, LOC.

"Really do read it!": Grynberg to VN, probably January 19, 1958.

243   "I am reading DR.": VN to Epstein, August 26, 1958. Max Hayward: See Patricia Blake introduction to Max Hayward, *Writers in Russia 1917–78.*

"It's a good translation": Blyth, *The Daily Mail* (London), March 17, 1959.

"The Zhivago gang": VN to Minton, May 18, 1959.

"The communists": VéN diary, VNA.

"sorry thing, clumsy": *Niagara Falls Gazette,* January 11, 1959.

Pasternak's mistress: VéN to David Slavitt, to Filippa Rolf. A decade later: SO, 206. See also Szeftel,
Cornell Magazine, November 1980; *Russkaya Mysl,* February 7, 1961.

"although she'll probably": VéN to Elena Levin, October 30, 1958, PC.

"behaving rather badly": Wilson to Grynberg, November 1, 1958, LOC. The phrase was indecipherable to me but not to Lewis Dabney.

244   "Compared to Pasternak": Alan Nordstrom, *Ivy* Magazine (New Haven), February 1959, 28.

felt Nabokov was thumbing: Interview with Mrs. Orval French, May 3, 1996.

"Have you read *Pnin*": Interview with Dorothy Gilbert, March 15, 1996.

"the saint and the": Szeftel, *Cornell Magazine,* November 1980.

"V. is very tired": VéN to Hessen, October 9, 1958, PC.

245   work of art that needed: Interview with Pedro Sanjuan, April 15, 1996.

"had ample reason": John Updike, preface to LL, xxvi.

"I meant to write": VéN to Berkman, February 2, 1959.

246   no forwarding address: Interview with Mrs. Orval French.

best respite: VéN to Filippa Rolf, April 4, 1959.

On Sunday evening: VéN diary, VNA. Interview with George Weidenfeld, April 21, 1997. See
Weidenfeld, *Remembering My Good Friends* (New York: HarperCollins, 1994), 248.

"This is the only": LATH, 129.

247   "We have seen": VéN to the Bishops, April 15, 1959.

More than thirty: Weidenfeld files, Berg Collection.

248   "huddling shamefully": *The Tatler* (London), March 25, 1959, 594.

sign a letter: *The Times* (London), January 23, 1959.

"because it shows depravity": Interview with Nigel Nicolson, August 8, 1996. See Nigel Nicolson,
Long Life (New York: G.P. Putnam's, 1998), 186–93.

"A Naughty Girl": *New York World-Telegram & Sun,* February 27, 1959.

Humbert in disguise: Interview with Nicolson.

"long enough to evolve": VéN to Laughlin, May 12, 1959.

249   *The Song of Igor's Campaign*: The epic poem had never been properly translated into English. VN
was interested in working on it even before 1952, when VéN queried Harper about the idea.
That year he agreed to collaborate on a Bollingen edition of the poem, with Szeftel and Harvard's Roman Jakobson, the country's most eminent Slavist. On April 14, 1957, VN bowed out
of the project. He curtly informed Jakobson that his conscience would not stand for a collaboration, as he was "unable to stomach your little trips to totalitarian countries" (VNA). At the
same time he requested that Jakobson refrain from making use of his translations in his Harvard classes. (The Nabokovs were convinced that Jakobson was a political agent.) As Diment
has made clear in her *Pniniad,* VN had additional cause for fury. Harry Levin had proposed
him for a position at Harvard that year, an appointment opposed by Jakobson, who deemed his
then-collaborator "unscholarly." Elena Levin told VéN privately of the slight (March 3, 1957,
PC). As it was, VéN believed her husband had been far too kind to Jakobson already. Mikhail

Karpovich did not rise to VN's defense regarding the appointment; their relationship never recovered.

felt Russia should: VN to HS, May 24, 1959.

"My summer so far": VéN to Bishops, summer 1959.

" *'Liebesdingen'* is a polite": VéN to Rowohlt, May 21, 1959.

"needs me": VéN to Amy Kelly, June 11, 1959.

"which is, probably": VéN to Filippa Rolf, June 16, 1960.

"Oh, she writes all": Interview with Galen Williams, December 4, 1996.

Sports Illustrated: All quotations drawn from Robert H. Boyle, "An Absence of Wood Nymphs," *Sports Illustrated,* September 14, 1959, 5–8. A longer version of the article appears in Robert H. Boyle, *At the Top of Their Game* (New York, Nick Lyons, 1987), 123–33. Interview with Boyle, October 7, 1998.

250   what pleased her most: VéN to L. Thompson, June 3, 1959.

"V. discounts both": VéN diary, VNA.

251   in the year 3000: *Los Angeles Evening Mirror News,* July 31, 1959.

252   "Both the Vs looked" to "in some countries": Morris Bishop to his daughter Alison Bishop, August 30, 1959, Cornell.

Was it immoral: Interview with James B. Harris, September 12, 1996.

suggested they might well stay: S. L. Posel to J. B. Lewis, September 15, 1959, PW.

"What the future holds": VéN to E. Levin, September 23, 1959, PC.

"Dear V & V": Bishop to the Nabokovs, September 24, 1959.

253   prided herself on the fact: Lena Massalsky to VéN, January 29, 1959.

"Are you planning": Sonia Slonim to VéN, December 15, 1959.

"undergoing a new": VéN to the Bishops, October 12, 1959, SL, 300.

Gallimard meeting: *Paris Presse L'Intransigeant,* October 8, 1959.

"friendship at first": VéN to Rowohlt, March 12, 1978, VNA.

254   dire need of evening wear: Anna Feigin to VéN, October 18, 1959.

"most controversial writer": *France-Soir,* October 21, 1959.

"Madame Nabokov" and "blonde": *Paris Presse L'Intransigeant,* October 21, 1959.

"When a masterpiece": *Paris Presse L'Intransigeant,* October 22, 1959.

255   "She cries every night": *Les Nouvelles Littéraires,* October 29, 1959.

"Everybody and his wife": Boyd interview with VéN, June 29, 1982, Boyd archive.

Véra's pleasure: VéN to HS, October 26, 1959.

amusing Khruschchev anecdote: *Le Figaro,* October 24, 1959.

ill at ease: Interview with Ivan Nabokov. Interview with HS, February 26, 1995.

equally puzzled: Boyd interview with VéN, June 29, 1982, Boyd archive. Interview with Zinaida Shakhovskoy, October 26, 1995.

256   "the man who just": Interview with Harris, September 12, 1996.

"as if responding": Girodias, *Une journée,* II, 459. See also "Pornologist on Mount Olympus," *Playboy,* April 1961, in which the account is slightly different, and in which VN, after exchanging a few words with Girodias, moves "with the easy grace of a dolphin" toward VéN. The story continued, with zoological variation, in *Evergreen,* September 1965, 91: At the introduction, "Vladimir Nabokov pivoted on himself with the graceful ease of a circus seal, throwing a glance in the direction of his wife . . ."

"I did not exist": *Evergreen,* September 1965, 91.

met—and disliked: VéN to Minton, November 9, 1959. Oddly she wrote, "Did I tell you that in Paris we met . . . ," then substituted "I" for "we." Her recollection was that she said, "Hello," and then walked away. Boyd interview with VéN, June 29, 1982, Boyd archive. VN insisted he had never met Girodias in his *Evergreen* rejoinder, February 1967, 37–41. Interview with Miriam Worms, June 18, 1996.

"the anti-nymphet": Girodias, *Une journée,* II, 301.

"although signed with": Girodias, *Evergreen,* September 1965, 90. Both Nabokovs believed the piece ran late, in *Life*'s international edition only, for one reason—"thus protecting domestic farmers and their daughters from bad influence." VéN to Bishops, April 15, 1959.

257   Nigel Nicolson was pressured: Interview with Nicolson, August 8, 1996. See Nicolson, *Long Life,* 190–93. On Harold Nicolson's distaste for LO, see Stanley Olson, ed., *Diaries and Letters,*

1930–1964 (New York: Atheneum, 1980), and Nigel Nicolson, ed., *Harold Nicolson: The Later Years, 1945–1962* (New York: Atheneum, 1962).

"Mr. Nabokov does not strike": Harold Nicolson, *The Observer,* November 4, 1951, 7. Evelyn Waugh: Waugh to Nancy Mitford, June 29, 1959, in Charlotte Mosley, ed. *The Letters of Nancy Mitford and Evelyn Waugh* (London: Hodder & Stoughton, 1996). E. M. Forster: Cited in Mollie Panter-Downes, *The New Yorker,* September 19, 1954. Rebecca West: *The Sunday Times* (London), November 8, 1959.

"a last glimpse": William Hickey, *Wellington Evening Post* (New Zealand), November 6, 1959.

felt an interminable: Interview with Nicolson, August 8, 1996.

258   every expectation: Weidenfeld, *Remembering My Good Friends,* 251.

miffed that he seemed: VéN to Minton, November 26, 1959.

shyness in the eye: Interview with Joan de Peterson, October 25, 1995.

"wore the bemused": *Time & Tide,* November 14, 1959.

"in a very loud voice": Sir Isaiah Berlin to author, September 10, 1997.

"Your English": *Evening Standard* (London), November 6, 1959.

batiste handkerchief: Weidenfeld, 252. Interviews with Weidenfeld, Nicolson.

259   He had no illusions: *Daily Sketch* (London), October 30, 1959.

"cause célèbre": VéN to Minton, November 26, 1959.

all the more excited: VéN to L. Thompson, December 1, 1959.

"I hope we can find": VéN to Minton, November 9, 1959.

"I have to stuff ": VéN to L. Thompson, February 7, 1960. Similarly to Ergaz, January 6, 1960.

"Hasn't this been": Giorgio Salvioni, "Sono stata io a salvare Lolita," *Epoca,* November 22, 1959, 77–81.

260   "platinum blonde" to "stare after us": *Gazzetta del Sud,* November 21, 1959. VéN to Joan de Peterson, November 25, 1959.

"Decent people fly": VéN to Sonia Slonim, December 24, 1959.

"buildings covered" and prostitutes: VéN to Elena Levin, December 7, 1959, PC.

she denounced: To L. Thompson, December 1, 1959. In the same letter she complained that in a recent interview VN's words had been put in her mouth.

"We have travelled": VéN to Berkman, December 4, 1959.

261   "In Rome, for example": Ugo Naldi, November 14, 1959, no source, VNA.

"Can one talk": VéN to Lena Massalsky, December 4, 1959.

262   Vladimir grumbled that: VN to Hessen, January 28, 1960, PC.

pleased to note: VéN to Sonia Slonim, December 24, 1959.

"quiet *nook* where": VéN to Bishop, December 7, 1959, SL, 303.

8   AUTRES RIVAGES

263   "If nobody wants them": VéN to Demorest, January 1, 1960.

264   "We do not" to "I can suggest": VéN to Victor C. Thaller, February 6, 1960.

"Do tell me your": VéN to Minton, January 16, 1960.

"To be perfectly" to "mother and father": L. Massalsky to VéN, February 6, 1960.

265   twice been imprisoned: Massalsky to VéN, September 9, 1960, April 29, 1966.

"Polish Jew": Massalsky to VéN, April 29, 1966.

"I am glad your son" to "your questions": VéN to Massalsky, February 12, 1960.

266   "When in doubt choose": VN diary, June 25, 1966, VNA.

"gone whole hog": Interview with DN, October 29, 1967.

Véra was startled: Sonia Slonim to VéN, November 30, 1962.

267   "Or practically any big": VéN to Massalsky, November 19, 1961.

"Girodias bores him": VéN to Minton, December 28, 1960.

"Always at the back": Minton, cited in St. Jorre, *Venus Bound,* 153.

268   "Papa says": VéN to DN, March 8, 1960, VNA.

She found Los Angeles's sprawl: VéN to Joan de Peterson, September 3, 1960.

"We don't go": VéN to E. Levin, May 10, 1960, PC.

great progress: VN to Hessen, September 15, 1960, PC.

269 inevitably offended someone: *Weekly Tribune* (Geneva), January 28, 1966.

"I'm in pictures": Appel, *Nabokov's Dark Cinema,* 58. VéN's .38 made another discreet appearance in a Hollywood powder room, where she opened her bag, on the vanity, alongside that of a film star's wife. News of the "gleaming pearl handle" circulated rapidly.

he vaguely recognized: Rolf to Tenggren, January 15, 1961, PC. "January," 25, PC.

"We have been": VéN to Rolf, June 16, 1960.

Olivier agreed at once: Interview with James B. Harris, September 12, 1996.

"She was gloriously": VN to Field, June 12, 1970. Cf. "She was all rose and honey," LO, 111. VéN to the Bishops, June 21, 1960.

catalogue of tree descriptions: PF cards, LOC. See PF, 262.

270 East had begun to seem: VéN to Amy Kelly, July 24, 1960.

"I thought of " to "German maid": Interview with Jenni Moulton, March 26, 1998.

he began writing: VéN to Mohrt, Gallimard, December 18, 1960.

vowed that they were not leaving: VéN to HS, January 1, 1961.

he had some difficulty: VN to Wilson, March 18, 1964, Yale.

271 "to be in motion" and "That's a nice": Doris Nagel to her family, August 24, 1958, PC.

"battered and stunned": PNIN, 144.

"Nomadic life": VéN to Berkman, October 25, 1962.

an adventure, and "We would like": VéN to Lisbet Thompson, August 21, 1961.

272 "A really spectacular": VéN to Carl Proffer, August 24, 1966, Michigan.

the thoughtful and intelligent: VéN to Gallimard, January 19, 1961.

"I hope you know": Rolf to VéN, December 27, 1960, PC.

"Gallimard is about": VéN to Minton, January 12, 1961.

sounding pleased: VéN to Ergaz, January 20, 1961.

273 Handing over carfare: Rolf to Tenggren, January 26, 1961, PC.

"But you missed": Rolf, "January," 12. The Rolf visit has been reconstructed from Rolf's letters and her subsequent writings, especially her short story, "January," as from supplementary details provided by Lillian Habinowski and Elena Levin. The visit with the Nabokovs represented Rolf's first in-depth encounter with spoken American English; a great number of expressions she had never before heard flew past her. And as often happens with foreign idioms, these expressions instantly imprinted themselves on her linguistically nimble mind; she was able to recall whole conversations verbatim. Or at least changed them not at all between her letters home, written in the January 1961 evenings, and her pages on the Nabokovs, composed years later, in Cambridge.

"Here something happened": Rolf, "January," 17–18, PC.

274 "Véra positively" to "It is not a matter": Rolf to Tenggren, January 15, 1961, PC.

"You know why": Rolf to Tenggren, January 17, 1961, PC.

275 "I had not known": Rolf, "January," 70, 76, PC.

"royalty of the spirit": *Ibid.,* 76.

On VéN's familiarity with the work: See David Slavitt, *Newsweek,* June 25, 1962, 53. Interviews with George Weidenfeld, April 21, 1997, DN, January 1997.

276 "Why do they have to": Rolf to Tenggren, January 21, 1961, PC.

"that of the little girl": Rolf to Tenggren, January 15, 1961, PC.

"for they were heavily": Rolf, "January," 23. The passage begins: "I felt like a tennis ball in the air, being bashed back and forth between their two hard, sensitive and hence impatient rackets. In my mind's eye I could see their knees bending, their tendons straining, their faces glazed in a smile of absorption and deep enjoyment, for they were heavily in love. . . ."

"the ball sometimes watches" to "speed": Rolf to Tenggren, January 15, 1961, PC.

"Poets are never" and "And Coleridge?": "January," 23, PC. Rolf to Tenggren, January 18, 1961, PC. Rolf to VéN, December 15, 1961.

277 "They are mating like": Rolf to Tenggren, January 16, 1961, PC.

"with a little despairing": Rolf to Tenggren, January 17, 1961, PC.

"but we discovered that": VéN to Lisbet Thompson, March 11, 1961.

"secret communion of ": Wayne Booth, *The Rhetoric of Fiction* (Chicago: University of Chicago Press, 1961), 300.

"You'll meet him": Rolf to Tenggren, January 16, 1961, PC. See Luzhin's encounter with his old schoolmate, DEFENSE, 198–200.

"Now what do" to "your poem!": Rolf to Tenggren, January 17, 1961, PC.
278 book's soul: VéN to HS, February 11, 1961, PC.
"like a happy" to "*wonderful* evening!": Rolf to Tenggren, January 18, 1961, PC.
"not by raising": Rolf to Tenggren, January 15, 1961, PC.
"to our sidewalk": Rolf, "January," 68, PC.
"Véra will do" to "I don't know": Rolf to Tenggren, January 25, 1961, PC. Also, "January," 43.
279 "And what a Swede": VéN to DN, January 30, 1961, VNA.
"We save ourselves": VéN to HS, January 24, 1961.
"Have you yet": Feigin to VéN, January 25, 1961.
"a rather boring, out-of-the-way": VéN to Rolf, June 10, 1961, PC.
280 "Alas, no shades": VéN to Michael Scammell, January 30, 1961.
"I have been limping": VéN to Rolf, February 11, 1961.
unfortunate distraction: VéN to DN, December 5, 1962, VNA. VéN to Lisbet Thompson, November 11, 1962.
"We're always in a panic": VéN to Elena Levin, June 4, 1964, PC.
281 "It is a fantastically": VN to Minton, February 18, 1961.
"out of sheer distaste": VéN to Rolf, February 9, 1961.
"I cannot even begin": VéN to Mohrt, Gallimard, February 9, 1961.
"they all talk at the same": Rolf to Tenggren, January 26, 1961, PC.
"the stupidest accident": VéN to Lisbet Thompson, April 7, 1961.
"flatly declared V." and "I am not": VéN to Amy Kelly, April 19, 1961. See *Times Literary Supplement,* April 7, 1961, 218.
282 "I, too, have been working": VéN to Lisbet Thompson, June 12, 1961.
283 "I deeply regret": VéN to Alberta Pescetto, June 26, 1961, VNA.
"We are very dumb": VN to McGraw-Hill, January 31, 1973, SL, 509.
in contractual matters: VéN to Joseph Iseman, July 14, 1971, PW.
rejected by her own counsel: Joan Daly to files, August 22, 1988, PW.
posed the obvious question: Robert MacGregor, New Directions, to VéN, July 11, 1963.
"Sumptuous, my foot!": Rolf, "January," 16, PC.
284 "In front of me" and "indifferent": VéN to E. Levin, September 8, 1961, PC.
considered nouveau riche: Boyd interview with VéN, December 24, 1984, Boyd archive.
She could not resist: VéN to Anna Feigin, September 18, 1961.
285 "In the 4 months": VéN to Don Wallace, Jr., December 9, 1961, PW.
"It . . . is not like": VéN to the Bishops, November 4, 1961, SL 331.
a strain, and "switch channels": H. Hirschman to VéN, March 8, 1961. VéN to Grynberg, September 14, 1961.
286 "Would you know": VéN to Weidenfeld, October 19, 1961.
"There never was an emotional": Joseph Iseman to author, May 2, 1996.
"reach the blessed shore": VéN to Minton, November 20, 1961.
"Don't work too much": Rolf to the Nabokovs, December 17, 1961.
"For me one result of his": VéN to Alison Bishop, March 29, 1963.
"V. is the one": VéN to L. Thompson, October 1, 1961.
287 "Don't let anything upset": VéN to Rolf, March 7, 1962.
in his stride: VéN to DN, June 28, 1961, VNA.
began to feel sheepish: VéN to Goldenweiser, February 11, 1962, Bakhm.
"I am unable honestly": VéN to Goldenweiser, November 29, 1965, Bakhm.
"It is a narrative" to "bizarre": VN to Rust Hills, *Esquire,* March 23, 1961, SL 329.
evolved significantly: See VN to Epstein, March 24, 1957, SL, 212–13. "A Mr. Stefan Schimanski": VN to David Higham, March 24, 1958.
288 "But they're horrible!": VéN to Mme. Cherix, May 7, 1962.
in no way offensive: VéN to Lisbet Thompson, July 16, 1962.
It had been almost: Interview with Harris, September 12, 1996.
"in general the picture": VéN to L. Thompson, December 17, 1962.
289 Proudly he showed: *La Tribune de Lausanne,* September 1, 1963.
Only in 1969: Interview with Martha Duffy, November 14, 1995. See also Harris and Kubrick in *Newsweek,* January 3, 1972, 30.
more fun to write: George Cloyne, *The New York Times Book Review,* May 27, 1962.

"In any case": McCarthy, *The New Republic,* June 4, 1962, 21–27. The two approaches to the *Pale Fire* coin are perfectly represented in Mary McCarthy and Hannah Arendt's correspondence on the subject. McCarthy wrote of her joy in the book, of the sheer delight she had had reviewing it. To her it seemed as if Nabokov had turned "this weird new civilization into a work of art, as though he'd engraved it all on the head of a pin, like the Lord's Prayer." Arendt had not read the novel but greatly disliked Nabokov; he seemed always so eager to prove his superior intelligence. "There is something vulgar in his refinement," she replied, promising to read the novel all the same. Carol Brightman, ed., *Between Friends: The Correspondence of Hannah Arendt and Mary McCarthy, 1949–1975* (New York: Harcourt Brace Jovanovich, 1995), 133–36.

"I read it with amusement": Wilson to Grynberg, May 20, 1962, Bakhm. On the other side of the ocean, Evelyn Waugh arrived at a different conclusion: "Too clever by half. But a pleasure." See Mosley, ed., *Letters of Nancy Mitford and Evelyn Waugh,* 468.

"that evil woman": Rolf to Tenggren, January 25, 1961, PC. VéN told William Maxwell that McCarthy had found far more in the novel than the author had intended, but that VN was pleased with the review. Maxwell to Katharine White, n.d., BMC.

"In general the atmosphere": VéN to HS, June 8, 1962, PC.

290   "VN could be like": Interview with Appel, June 2, 1995. Then again, VéN was a woman who could, and did, summon compassion for a panicked rhinoceros—in this case one filmed from the air, for television. See Dmitri Nabokov in *The Nabokovian* 26 (Spring 1991), ii.

"mostly in cabs": VéN to the de Petersons, July 24, 1962, SL, 338–39.

like coming home: VéN to Berkman, October 25, 1962.

"It is still not a 'home' ": VéN to Lisbet Thompson, November 8, 1963.

"Where we'll settle": VéN to Elena Levin, March 10, 1963, PC.

291   "This book is a torrent" and "dialogical": VN and VéN to Karin Hartell, October 1, 1961.

"I do a lot of typing": Interview with Galen Williams, December 4, 1996.

opened his mouth: His first words at the April 5 reading: "I shall begin by reciting 'The Ballad of Longwood Glen,' which is a short poem composed in Wyoming, one of my favorite states of existence."

Why had he not signed: Interview with Arthur Luce Klein, October 30, 1996.

292   sensationally beautiful: Aileen Ward to author, May 25, 1996; interview with William McGuire, October 16, 1995.

she billed the work: VéN to Mondadori, December 7, 1964. Russian scholars felt differently about the brilliant, petulant, outsized *Onegin.* Elizabeth Hardwick conveyed their position perfectly in one line: The volume "was a folly of such earnest magnitude that it might have been conceived in *Bouvard and Pécuchet.*" *Sight Readings* (New York: Random House, 1998), 207. See also William McGuire, *Bollingen: An Adventure in Collecting the Past,* 264.

The Ithaca return: Field, 1977, 278–79. Boyd, 1991, 482. VéN to Boyd, March 11, 1989, VNA. Interview with Appel, August 7, 1996. It was Appel who knew of Bishop's inadvertent espionage mission of about 1950, and who first connected the two incidents. "An overwhelming tenderness": ADA, 574.

293   "first through a telescope": Carroll, *Through the Looking Glass* (Signet: New York, 1960), 149.

Véra was livid: Interview with DN, November 1, 1996.

"Don't you dare work": Sonia Slonim to VéN, June 13, 1964.

"When I am ill nobody": VéN to Marcantonio Crespi, May 22, 1969, VNA.

"Much ado about": VéN to Berkman, March 19, 1965.

"What we won't do": VéN to Elena Levin, April 1, 1969, PC.

"It was unpleasant": VéN to E. Levin, June 3, 1969, PC.

294   "And of course I would": VN to Frank Taylor, April 7, 1969, Lilly.

editors were asked: VéN to Minton, March 15, 1963.

"He does not intend": VéN to Martin J. Esslin, February 28, 1968, SL, 429. VéN's concern may have been with citizenship. At the time, naturalized Americans were required to return to the United States periodically.

All looked as if: Interview with Appel, April 19, 1995.

"he had planned": Maxwell to the Nabokovs, April 1969.

to feel manageable: Martha Duffy notes for *Time,* PC.

295   modest villa in the south: VN to Minton, February 16, 1965.

The comforts of European: VéN to the Bishops, November 4, 1961, SL, 331.

"rusty and unwieldy": VéN to Ergaz, November 13, 1962.

Callier to correct: Interview with Jacqueline Callier, March 29, 1998.

"We have hit a snag": VéN to Ergaz, January 8, 1962.

America was his favorite: *Le Figaro,* January 13, 1973. Also, *Le Monde,* November 22, 1967.

It would be inexact: VéN to Drago Arsenijevic, *La Tribune de Genève,* October 17, 1967.

296   "I was five days": VéN to Elena Levin, 1967 postcard, PC.

"I have been imagining" and "I was dealt": VN to VéN, November 28, 1967, VNA.

"I don't know how": VN to VéN, October 2, 1966, VNA.

297   "Oh, you mustn't" to "think of crying": Untitled poem, December 6, 1964, VNA.

Véra's enormous help: *La Tribune de Lausanne,* September 1, 1963.

"To *whom* am I": VN to McGuire, June 14, 1963, LOC, SL, 346. In the end he extended his thanks to his wife, his son, and the Bollingen editors. The translation is dedicated, "To Véra."

"the inspirer of my": J. S. Mill, *Autobiography of John Stuart Mill* (New York: Columbia University Press, 1948), 184.

earned a promotion: Dostoyevsky referred to Anna Grigoryevna as his "collaborator" from the start. She more accurately spoke of their work as "our joint publishing activity"; like Countess Tolstoy, she doubled as her husband's publisher. Anna Dostoyevsky, *Dostoyevsky Reminiscences* (New York, Liveright, 1975).

"She is my collaborator": Guy de Velleval, *Journal de Genève,* March 13, 1965.

"I felt he was": Interview with Steinberg, January 4, 1996.

Even the family members: Interview with HS, July 20, 1997.

298   "The feeling of distress": VN diary, January 18, 1973, VNA.

"It has been suggested": "Scenes," STORIES, 613.

For VN on prophetic dreaming, see Herbert Gold, "The Artist in Pursuit of Butterflies," *The Saturday Evening Post,* February 11, 1967, 81–85.

"Tried in vain" to "please and surprise": VN journal, 1964.

"one of those dreams that still": PNIN, 109.

299   "Awoke with a pang": VN journal, 1964.

"Dream of the hotel": VN 1968 diary, VNA.

9   LOOK AT THE MASKS

300   early run-ins: Interview with Jenni Moulton.

301   "exchange of impressions": VN to HS, November 1967, SL, 418.

read passages: Interview with Jacqueline Callier, July 11, 1995.

impression of most visitors: Interview with Stephen Jan Parker, November 13, 1996.

the Montreux tradespeople: Levy, *The Velvet Butterfly,* 14.

poison himself: Interview with Louba Schirman, June 17, 1996.

"I don't know why": VéN to Parker, November 4, 1967.

"gay tussles": Simona Morini, *Vogue,* April 15, 1972, 74–79.

"managed to turn": VéN to Louba Schirman, September 7, 1964, VNA.

302   "had remained constantly": VéN to Weidenfeld, September 9, 1965.

"first real" to "impertinent serf ": Girodias notes for unfinished volume, May 20, 1969. Gelfman Schneider Agency.

"Vladimir has been discovered": VéN to Weidenfeld, September 21, 1968.

303   Even Katharine White: White comment on VéN note of 1967, BMC.

poked fun at those writers: Clarke, *Esquire,* July 1975.

"flamingoes": Duffy notes, PC.

it was not rich enough: VéN to Rowohlt, February 11, 1969, VNA. It flourished as the translations multiplied. Dieter Zimmer to author, March 6, 1996.

"Stand over them with a spoon": VNA. See also LATH, 116, for the "ectoplasmic swell in the dancing water."

304   He found her heavy: Hughes interview text, December 28, 1965, 32. As is clear from the pages each Nabokov reworked of the 1933 story "The Leonardo," when moving from Russian to English VéN's language tended toward the more fluid and literal, VN's toward the more neologistic.

Where VéN has "those crackling vertebrae," VN has "that crumpy backbone"—which took the day. STORIES, 361.

"like the little abyss": Clarence Brown, *The New Republic,* January 20, 1968, 19.

"Incidentally, not having a Russian": VN to Library of Congress. In his diary (April 11, 1966, VNA), VN noted: "With Véra's suggestions, finished Lincoln."

305   "He says that the": VéN to Barley Alison, Weidenfeld, February 11, 1967.

"like a tenacious ancestral": National Medal acceptance speech, 1975, courtesy of Fred Hills.

"glossological disarray": VN to the editors, *The New York Review of Books,* July 8, 1965, SL, 375. Elsewhere he termed the battles that stood at the center of his wife's existence "the poignant demands of pedantic purity." VN to Taylor, December 9, 1969.

Was it really too: VéN to Prins & Prins, May 17, 1966.

"My dear George": VéN to Weidenfeld, June 13, 1966.

"It irks me": VN to Weidenfeld, June 10, 1970.

chores that are repetitive: Mary Catherine Bateson, *Composing a Life* (New York: Plume, 1990), 213.

306   shouldn't the book charged: VéN to Minton, November 26, 1962.

The "disaster": Interview with Vladimir Sikorsky, March 5, 1997.

"If you live in a teapot": Jane Austen, cited in John Lukacs, *The Hitler of History* (New York, Knopf, 1997), 32.

"Véra, this amounts": VéN to Minton, May 3, 1967.

"He wants me to forewarn": VéN to Oscar de Liso, Phaedra, September 16, 1965.

"Oh dear, I think": Interview with Nikki Smith, September 24, 1998.

"I must again apologize": VéN to D. Lindsey, March 13, 1966.

307   relished the image: Interview with Evan Harrar, August 26, 1996.

"Yes, of course": VéN to Robert Shankland, International Book Exchange, January 14, 1967.

A 1969 reporter: Interview with Martha Duffy, November 14, 1995.

"That is the difference": Levy, *The Velvet Butterfly,* 30.

"man is not truly one": Stevenson, cited in LL, 199.

"I was thinking": PNIN, 17.

308   "This is cheating": VéN to Appel, January 24, 1967. See Appel, "Nabokov's Puppet Show," *The New Republic,* January 14 and 21, 1967.

seemingly omniscient narrator: See especially Wood, *The Magician's Doubts,* 164.

Friends had long: As Wilson observed in Slavitt's June 25, 1962, *Newsweek* cover story on Nabokov, 54: "He loves to tell you something which is not true, and have you believe it; but even more, he loves to tell you something which *is* true, and have you think he is lying."

"But he adds that": VéN to Field, March 1966.

"the person I usually": SO, 298.

"Have you seen Volodya": Wilson to Sonya Grynberg, May 9, 1969, Bakhm. Harry Levin acknowledged as much in his 1964 Cambridge introduction, Levin, *Grounds for Comparison* (Cambridge: Harvard University Press, 1972), 376.

"It is a false idea": Interview with Jason Epstein, September 24, 1996.

309   go into hiding: VéN to Schirman, April 11, 1966, VNA.

"to dissimulate our presence": VéN to Sonia Slonim, August 4, 1966.

"It's just like some miserable": VéN to Elena Levin, July 21, 1967, PC; to Anna Feigin, July 18, 1967.

Worse yet, she had to: VéN to the Hessens, October 18, 1965, PC.

"If he had the time": VéN to Irving Lazar, March 5, 1972, VNA.

Barozzi saw it: Interview with Carlo Barozzi, July 10, 1995.

"strangers and half-strangers": VéN to Nat Hoffman, April 8, 1975, VNA.

"He made a" and "Véra, what am": Interview with Ivan Nabokov, October 24, 1995.

"She does the arguing": Levy, *The New York Times Magazine,* October 31, 1971, 24. "She was his secret weapon," concluded another. Interview with Willa Petschek, October 9, 1998.

"I think it's almost": Lazar to VéN, November 19, 1963, VNA.

"Far from it": VéN to Lazar, December 2, 1963, VNA.

310   "From here on": VéN to Weidenfeld, October 7, 1968.

"While they keep us informed": VéN to Field, March 1966.

"We have runny noses": VéN to HS, January 20, 1965, PC.

"We have been ill": VéN to De Liso, January 28, 1968.

"I ask you to bear": VéN to Joan Daly, April 8, 1971, PW.

"Would you please": VéN to René Micha, *L'Arc,* March 4, 1964.

"I rolled over him": LO, 316.

"He has asked his son": VéN to Bud MacLennan, Weidenfeld, May 3, 1965.

"signed by" and "Today I receive": VN to Rowohlt, October 30, 1970.

311   "It is hard to be happy": "The Potato Elf," STORIES, 232.

"lone wolf ": VéN to Rex Stout, c. June 23, 1965.

"lone lamb": *Vogue,* December 1969, 191; SO, 156.

"flurry of confabulation": PF, 259. Also LATH, 87.

She found it embarrassing: VéN to Esslin, February 28, 1968, SL, 429.

"Darling, why" to "It's too late": Field, 1977, 176–77.

312   "So I was surprised": Dieter Zimmer to VéN, November 3, 1965. VéN to Zimmer, November 8, 1965.

Swiss Police Ministry: VéN to Département de Justice et Police, February 7, 1965, VNA.

"I am greatly distressed" and "spontaneous rot": VN to Hughes, November 9, 1965. SL, 381.

equally capable of boasting: Field, 1977, 180, vs. James Salter, *People,* March 17, 1975, 64.

It was enough: Interviews with Sophie Lannes, June 11, 1996; Mati Laanso, March 26, 1997.

313   His wife was his memory: Interview with Appel, April 24, 1995, vs. Laanso, CBC interview of VN, March 20, 1973.

"a kind of rich and varicoloured": VN to Bertrand Thompson, April 4, 1962.

314   "I am completely exhausted": VéN to Lisbet Thompson, April 12, 1963.

"But I still hope": VéN to L. Thompson, November 8, 1963. She appears to have been discouraged too by Callier's occasional missteps in English. On a Bristol card VN prepared for their secretary a little primer: "their" and "*leur*" behaved differently in their respective languages, so that "They cleared their throats," unless of course "they were Siamese twins with two bodies but one head and one throat!"

"I am better": VéN to L. Thompson, March 9, 1966.

315   "but since our return": VéN to L. Thompson, October 25, 1966.

"Please do not" and "I am not": VéN to L. Thompson, March 11, 1967.

firm sense of self-importance: Interview with Callier, March 29, 1998.

316   "Ah, sweet socks": VN to VéN, October 25, 1974, VNA.

"to have made little jottings": Interview with DN, June 23, 1996.

Véra astonished its author: Interview with Edmund White, January 23, 1995.

White began to visualize: Interview with White. White continues: "Reaching her, despite our differences, is a project that for some reason excites my imagination; I picture her as the 'interior paramour.' " See *States of Desire: Travels in Gay America* (New York: Dutton, 1980), 255.

317   "a disaster," "I know many," and "Where are the": VéN to Topazia Markevitch, June 5, 1965.

"I'm sending Volodya": Anna Feigin to VéN, September 26, 1963.

"You mustn't apologize": Appel to VéN, September 22, 1968.

she went out of her way: VéN to Minton, May 3, 1967.

"And in any case": VéN to Flora Stone Mather College, December 8, 1971, VNA.

318   "it does not belong": VN to William Morris, January 10, 1967, VNA.

"The project of which": VéN to Weidenfeld, October 25, 1967. The young McGraw-Hill editor was Peter Kemeny, of whom VéN was very fond, but who left the firm just as VN was arriving.

Paul, Weiss lawyers: Interview with Joseph Iseman, May 19, 1995.

"We have lived": VéN to Iseman, August 20, 1967, PW.

319   consult an economics text: Irving Lazar, with Annette Tapert, *Swifty: My Life and Good Times* (New York: Simon & Schuster, 1995), 203.

"It goes without saying": Daly to Iseman, October 23, 1975, PW.

knew she had been ridiculed: Boyd interview with VéN, January 9, 1985, Boyd archive.

"This is a *very private*" to "from VN": VéN to Iseman, September 14, 1967, PW.

"VN was practically": VéN to Canfield, December 2, 1967.

320   the Pierre meeting: Interview with Iseman, May 19, 1995. Boyd interview with VéN, January 9, 1985, Boyd archive. Interview with Dan Lacy, April 27, 1998.

"In the dimly-lit": Iseman to Alan Cohen, December 4, 1967, PW.

"choral and sculptured": PF, 136.

321　"in a rage": VéN to Iseman, December 21, 1967.

Minton was none: Interview with Minton, June 5, 1995.

"Badminton": VéN to Louba Schirman, May 22, 1968, VNA.

The Rowohlt sessions: Interview with Helmut Frielinghaus, May 28, 1996.

the marathons session were: VN to Rowohlt, April 17, 1974, VNA.

"Everything," reported Vera: VéN to DN, November 10, 1969, VNA.

"Literature must be taken": LRL, 105.

322　"not only Veen's muse:" Appel, *The New York Times Book Review,* May 14, 1969.

"sun-and-shade games": ADA, 579.

One reviewer read: Matthew Hodgart, *The New York Review of Books,* May 22, 1969, 3–4.

could not live: ADA, 575.

"What the hell, Sir": VN to Hodgart, May 12, 1969, SL, 450–51. Hodgart's elegant apology, *The New York Review of Books,* July 10, 1969.

"She is also, in a dimension": Updike, *The New Yorker,* August 2, 1969, 67–73. Alfred Kazin arrived at the same conclusion, expressing great enthusiasm for VN but mustering only partial admiration for ADA. "It is too much about himself, his wife, his Russia-America, rather than an extension of the art that bears his name," he declared. VN howled; an enterprising editor had the good sense to change—with Kazin's permission—the "w" to an "l" in the eighth word. See Kazin, *Bright Book of Life* (Boston: Little Brown, 1971), 317. Interview with Alfred Kazin, November 10, 1996.

Updike's wrist: James Mossman, *The Listener,* October 23, 1969, 560, repr. in SO, 146. Boyd circumvented the problem by concluding that VN's "married love for Véra Nabokov inspired" a number of works, *Ada* among them. In Alexandrov, ed., *Garland Companion to Vladimir Nabokov,* 6. Karlinsky explains the matter differently in "Nabokov's Russian Games," *The New York Times Book Review,* April 18, 1971.

323　"But there are many": Boyd interview with VéN, December 8, 1984, Boyd archive.

Zina was only half-Jewish: VéN to Simon Karlinsky, December 10, 1986, VNA.

Appel's reaction: Interview with Appel, April 24, 1995.

"petrified superpun": LL, 122.

Nabokov's Waterloo: Martin Seymour-Smith, *The Times Literary Supplement,* October 2, 1969.

"the greatest living": Ron Sheppard, *Time,* May 23, 1969, 49.

"like six-packs": Taylor, McGraw-Hill to VN, June 6, 1969, VNA.

"I don't remember that": Gilliatt, *Vogue,* March 1967.

324　the same synthetic nostalgia: *L'Espresso,* November 1, 1959, 1.

a half-bemused smile: Boyd interview with Appel, May 1, 1983, Boyd archive.

knew nothing about Mozart: Interview with Fred Hills, April 7, 1995. Nor did she herself pad ignorance with eloquence. William Buckley once began a conversation about the New Testament; VéN bowed out with "I am not informed on that subject." Interview with Buckley, December 12, 1996.

spinning a yarn: Boyd interview with Berkman, Boyd archive. The Negresco opened for business in 1913.

the story of the future Appels, and "Well, it's a beautiful": Interview with Appel, May 8, 1998.

"Véra has a much better": Interview with Appel, April 24, 1995.

325　conversation was studded: William F. Buckley Jr., *Buckley: The Right Word* (New York: Random House, 1996), 380.

"Defeat" to "she's wrong": Interview with Appel, April 19, 1995. ADA, 557.

"under their new loads": Updike, *Life,* January 13, 1967.

deep affection for Nixon: Interview with Jason Epstein, May 11, 1998.

326　wife did not flinch: Field, 1977, 24.

like to choke her husband: Duffy notes, *Time,* PC.

"imprudent and unwise": VéN to Rolf, April 20, 1962.

"Do you *always*": Rolf to VéN, April 26, 1962.

"we trust completely": VéN to Rolf, February 1, 1963.

"Goodbye. You are the only": Rolf to VéN, Easter Sunday, 1963.

327　banished her to an inhospitable: Interviews with Lillian Habinowski, March 25, 1998, E. Levin, September 1997.

"an act of vandalism": Rolf to the Nabokovs, September 1965, PC.

"She is one of the most": VéN to L. Massalsky, October 1, 1965.

"My husband has been terribly": VéN to Rolf, March 21, 1967.

"I would rather keep": VéN to Field, regarding his ms. page 176, 1973.

328   "In the middle 60s": VéN to Joan Daly, June 7, 1969, PW.

perfectly truthful, highly inaccurate: VéN to Rolf, July 29, 1969.

much-needed month: Interview with L. Habinowski. Rolf's "As It Is Written" appeared in *The Partisan Review* 37, no. 2, 1970.

329   "the weather has finally": VéN to Topazia Markevitch, June 19, 1965, VNA.

Don't be angry: VN to VéN, June 15, 1926, VNA.

over Sunday lunch, and "Darling, you have": Interview with Phyllis Christiansen, August 10, 1996.

nothing remotely casual: Ellendea Proffer to author, May 9, 1997.

330   constantly on the brink: Interview with Martha Duffy, November 14, 1995.

loneliness seeping out: Interview with Nina Appel, August 7, 1996.

"No, we do not feel": VéN to Philippe Halsmann, February 9, 1969, VNA. Dieter Zimmer saw the situation differently. "My impression was that the problem was not loneliness but rather the necessity to fend off intruders." To author, March 12, 1996.

entirely happy on a desert: Interview with HS, July 11, 1995.

provided a short list: Esslin, *The New York Times Book Review,* May 12, 1968, 4. To an Italian journalist, VN quipped: "When I really need people, I paint them on the walls of my cave," Gaetano Tumiati, *La Stampa,* October 30, 1969.

"We tell that story": Interview with Dick Wimmer, December 1, 1997.

many saw the public game: Interview with Christopher F. Givan, February 7, 1997. Two of VN's American tennis opponents testified that he could not be lured from the baseline. *Sports Illustrated*'s Robert H. Boyle resorted to the same metaphor in recalling the couple's relationship. "It was almost as if they played verbal tennis with each other—he hit the ball, and back it flew." Interview with Boyle, October 7, 1998.

"every major studio": Lyons, *The New York Post,* September 27, 1968, 51.

"You're a child" to "head of Paramount": Robert Evans, *The Kid Stays in the Picture* (New York: Hyperion, 1994), 128.

331   all of January 1971: "He walks about the acropolises of my past with a tape recorder. It is sometimes difficult for the tourist; much is closed," VN sighed, January 4, 1971, VN to Hessen.

On the Proffer visit: Interview with Ellendea Proffer, May 31, 1995; E. Proffer to author, May 9, 1997.

She could be warm: Interviews with Marie-Luce Parker, April 17, 1997; Nina Appel, August 7, 1996; Gennady and Alla Barabtarlo, May 26, 1996.

believed her the most interesting, and It hardly mattered: Interview with Nikki Smith, April 9, 1997. See also Alison Bishop in Gibian and Parker, eds., *Achievements,* 216–17.

VN for the Nobel: McGraw-Hill correspondence, January 6, 1969, Lilly; Karlinsky to VéN, October 16, 1980, VNA.

332   in a gray suit: Interview with Michael Bergman, May 17, 1996.

"It is no use raking up": VéN to Lena Massalsky, May 19, 1966.

333   "And thank God that": VéN to L. Massalsky, February 22, 1967.

" '*Avorton*' is a French" and "You don't": L. Massalsky to VéN, June 22, 1967.

"Of course, I did not understand": VéN to L. Massalsky, June 27, 1967.

managed to insult: VéN to Goldenweiser, June 15, 1968. She apologized for the behavior of her sister, whom she called a sick individual. Lena had mixed feelings about the reparations payments and may have said as much, Interview with Michaël Massalsky, September 12, 1996; also L. Massalsky to VéN, March 14, 1968.

source of continual: Interview with V. Crespi, January 25, 1995.

"What would you" and "What did you say": Interview with V. Crespi, July 4, 1998.

334   examined Crespi's teenaged: Interview with Marcantonio Crespi, May 5, 1998.

painfully, cripplingly shy: Interview with V. Crespi, April 16, 1998. Rolf had noted the same.

"I trust it isn't the second" and "It looks like": Interview with V. Crespi, October 24, 1996.

"I could always" and "No thank you": Interview with V. Crespi, January 25, 1995.

"A man of Chaplin's": Interview with V. Crespi, July 4, 1998.

335 The de Rougemont dinner: Interviews with Allegra Markevitch Chapuis, Natalie Markevitch Frieden. Topazia Markevitch, *Le Matin des Livres,* May 15, 1981.

"You've been a bad influence": Interview with V. Crespi, October 21, 1996.

alcohol destroys: Robert Ruebman to author, April 22, 1996. McCarthy made the prohibitionist remark to Boyd, Boyd interview of January 12, 1983, Boyd archive. This was something VéN shared with Sibyl Shade.

"The wine is gone" to "off the balcony": Interview with Horst Tappé, February 10, 1997.

"We simply *could* not": VéN to Mr. Westbrook, December 13, 1967.

336 "We are not with you": VéN to Alison Bishop, March 13, 1968.

"dumb intellectuals": Levy, *The New York Times Magazine,* 36.

Russian-Chinese border skirmish: Duffy notes, *Time.*

"an irresponsible demagogue": VéN to E. Levin, July 27, 1972, PC.

"Oh, dear Lena, if only": VéN to E. Levin, August 19, 1969, PC.

"Richard the Lion" and "I thus achieved": Alison Jolly to author, June 21, 1998.

337 "We didn't regret": VéN to E. Levin, June 3, 1969, PC.

"We are the senior authorities": VéN to E. Levin, March 12, 1971, PC.

"that Mr. Watergate fellow": George Feifer, "Vladimir Nabokov," *Saturday Review,* November 27, 1976, 21.

did not have a political mind: Interview with Arthur Schlesinger, Jr., October 9, 1996. In VéN's analysis, her husband's world was built entirely on daydreaming, art, and scientific schemas. "These components simply left no room for political and economic notions." VéN to Karlinsky, November 20, 1978, VNA. See also Gold, in Gibian and Parker, *Achievements,* 53–54.

"When I see a cute young woman": VéN to Elena Levin, June 3, 1969.

"In her letters there is": VéN to Karlinsky, February 28, 1968, VNA.

"Some day, I hope": VéN to Karlinsky, September 21, 1987, VNA.

338 "The Germans" and "The Americans": Clarke, *Esquire,* July 1975, 132–33.

"Without being enthusiastic": VéN to Schebeko, March 16, 1973.

center of the world: Interview with Evan Harrar, August 26, 1996.

They were afraid: Boyd interview with Appel, April 30, 1983, Boyd archive; interview with Ellendea Proffer.

"I keep receiving warnings": VéN to V. Crespi, November 15, 1967.

the latest scuttlebutt: Interviews with Crespi; Loo; Anne Dyer Murphy, June 2, 1995 (for Mr. Pynchon); Jill Krementz (Joyce Maynard); George Weidenfeld, April 21, 1997 (for Jason Epstein); Mati Laanso, March 26, 1997.

"Fuck Communism": Duffy notes, *Time.*

separate bedrooms: Interview with Minton, June 5, 1995.

339 "I don't like your shirts": Interview with Boyd, November 21, 1996.

"The more you leave me out" and "I am always": Boyd interview with VéN, January 14, 1980, Boyd archive.

10   THE LAND BEYOND THE VEIL

340 had the distinct sense: VéN to Berkman, March 19, 1965.

could not answer: VéN to Lazar, September 9, 1968, VNA.

"I apologize for this": VéN to Field, December 27, 1971.

"her attention span": Interview with DN, November 1, 1996.

"phenomonal capacity": Goldenweiser to VéN, December 13, 1969, Bakhm.

341 sun, and salvation: VéN to Goldenweiser, April 12, 1970, Bakhm.

"8 rooms, 3 baths" and "golden-voiced": VN to VéN, April 8, 1970, VNA.

"some kind of lexicomaniac": *Publishers Weekly,* September 25, 1972.

"it did not matter": VéN to Mondadori, March 26, 1970, VNA.

threw up his arms: VéN to Mondadori, August 28, 1970, VNA.

"The rest heroically": VN diary, December 3, 1970, VNA.

342 "All writers should": Duffy notes for *Time,* PC.

"Lack of imagination": VéN to Daly, November 1, 1971, PW.

"I wonder what other writers": VéN to Joan Daly, June 29, 1970, PW.

folders and files: As early as 1963, VéN felt the Montreux apartment too small. VéN to Anna Feigin, May 16, 1963.

"Oh Miss Loo" to "just trying to scare you": Interviews with Beverly Jane Loo, June 2, 1995, November 1995, May 9, 1998. The other New York publisher to whom she sent love was Epstein.

343   "I don't know": VéN to the Levins, Christmas 1970, PC.

"How sadly:": VéN to E. Levin, Christmas, c. 1972, PC. As for Solzhenitsyn, he wrote like a shoemaker. Interview with E. Levin, June 6, 1995.

"We still have not": VéN to Barbara Epstein, February 26, 1975, VNA.

344   *"Le doux M. Nabokov"*: VéN to Ergaz, February 3, 1959.

"acting as plenipotentiary": Field, 1977, 9.

"I don't think about my letters": VéN to Boyd, May 2, 1986, VNA.

denied every remark: VéN to Field, December 5, 1971. She chastised Boyd: "You see how unreliable [an] 'interview' can be? I can swear that I never said any of what is on this page." VéN to Boyd, notes to his Chapter 9, VNA.

"I am sorry": VéN to Appel, November 8, 1974.

"shopworn": VéN to the Bishops, June 21, 1960.

345   He felt she would have denied: Interview with Boyd, November 23, 1996.

"was surprised by my reflection": VéN to Boyd, March 19, 1989, VNA.

her eyes never left: Interview with Sophie Lannes, Lannes in *L'Express,* June 30, 1975.

"sharp-witted": VéN to Sonia Slonim, January 20, 1967.

"again impair our personal": Wilson to VN, March 8, 1971, NWL, 333. VN's animus toward Wilson was already quite clear to a 1969 visitor, Duffy interview. After the May 1957 visit VéN reported on the gout which had disabled Wilson, revealing no ill will. She had been surprised, however, that what Wilson felt he needed to recover was "a glass of whisky, undefiled by water" (VéN to Epstein, June 1, 1957). In his *American Scholar* piece, Meyers suggests that VéN had been offended by Wilson and had urged her husband to retaliate, a supposition for which there is no basis. See also Wilson, *Upstate,* 156–63.

A faculty wife: Interview with Frances Lange, September 12, 1996.

346   bellowed that: SO, 218–19.

"For my part": VéN to E. Levin, July 27, 1972, PC.

better conveyed the torture: VéN to Goldenweiser, January 15, 1973, Bakhm., VéN to Schebeko, February 19, 1973, VéN to Elena Levin, May 9, 1973, PC.

"second-rate books": Philip Oakes, *The Sunday Times* (London), June 22, 1969.

347   "the true reader's main": TT, 75.

"angry panic" and "prepared": VN diary, January 9 and 11, 1973, VNA.

"cretinous": VN to Samuel Rosoff, March 23, 1973, SL, 513.

"You have written": VéN to Field, March 10, 1973.

348   "She so often put": Interview with V. Crespi, May 3, 1998.

"which teems with factual": VéN to Parker, December 12, 1973. Field had his work cut out for him. For Paul, Weiss (May 25, 1973, PW) VN annotated the list of people to whom the biographer had spoken: "Dislikes me personally, I hardly know him, an enemy, knew him very little, unknown to me, knew him slightly, not sure ever met him, never met him, unknown to me, a cousin, a man of great imagination, saw me last in 1916, almost certainly a figment of AF's imagination."

By page two: VéN copy of Field, 1977, VNA.

"This still is not the long": VéN to Joan Daly, August 29, 1973, PW.

"I know that he doesn't": VéN to DN, January 14, 1974, VNA.

349   "We can only plead": VéN to Karlinsky, February 22, 1974, VNA.

"It has not been" to "of the century": Salter, *People,* March 17, 1975. The difficulty in accepting a happy marriage at face value is not new; VN could nearly have added it to his short list of taboo topics in the afterword to LO, 314. Writing of another hugely productive couple, Leonard and Virginia Woolf, Carolyn G. Heilbrun has observed: "The marriage of a woman and man of talent must constantly be reinvented; its failure has already been predicted by conventional society, and its success is usually . . . disbelieved or denied." Heilbrun, *Writing a Woman's Life* (New York: Ballantine, 1988), 81.

"High-born Russian ladies": Rosalind Baker Wilson to author, September 28, 1994.

parted with Russian: Nadezhda Mandelstam conveyed this very message to Montreux in 1975, via the Proffers (Carl Proffer to the Nabokovs, November 12, 1975, Michigan). Solzhenitsyn too lamented VN's having abandoned Russia and her themes. E. Stein, "Reminiscences of Nabokov," *Russkaya Mysl,* July 13, 1978, 11.

350   "Jewified": Krivoshein to Z. Shakhovskoy, Amherst.

for commercial gain: Jeanne Vronskaya, *The Independent,* April 16, 1991. For a catalogue of VéN's offenses, see Shakhovskoy's addendum to "In Search of Nabokov," Amherst.

"One has to know how": VN, "The Anniversary," *Rul,* November 18, 1927.

"Nabokov exhibits the most": Joyce Carol Oates, "A Personal View of Nabokov," *Saturday Review of the Arts,* January 1973, 37.

Asked if he would ever travel: Interview with Schirman, June 17, 1996.

"She had many" to "was Jewish": Interview with Z. Shakhovskoy, October 25, 1995.

351   "Her blue eyes" to "his actual face": "Pustynia," *Novyj zhurnal,* June 1973, 27–33.

"like a true aristocrat": HS to Shakhovskoy, January 7, 1979 (transcribed copy of original), Amherst.

"a frozen desert": *Le Matin des Livres,* May 15, 1981.

"Why did you find it necessary": Interview with HS, February 26, 1995.

352   "Sometimes when": Roberta Smoodin, *Inventing Ivanov* (New York: Atheneum, 1985), 31.

"How," she asks herself: Smoodin, 293.

"Without drawing a portrait": Field, 1977, 180.

Pressured for a description: Interview with Fred Hills, April 7, 1995.

353   "matter-of-fact, father of muck": LATH, 226.

"ultimate and immortal one": LATH, 122.

"turquoise temple-vein": LATH, 233.

"I read everything attentively": LATH, 231.

slams the door shut: LATH, 226; SM, 295.

"your dear delicate hand": LATH, 227.

"to present to the world": Vronskaya, *The Independent,* April 16, 1991.

354   "dubbed jesterly": Untitled poem, October 1, 1974, VNA.

"*Shade, Sybil*": PF, 313.

"advises N" to "N's letters": Boyd, 1991, 769–70.

"To say it plainly": Broyard, *The New York Times,* October 10, 1974.

a toll on the work: The collective disappointment brings to mind Braque's dismissal of Picasso. "He used to be a great artist, but now he's only a genius."

"This is the novel": Peter Ackroyd, "Soi-disant," *The Spectator* (London), April 19, 1975, 476.

"Here we are at last": VN to VéN, April 15, 1975, SL, 546.

355   "40 years since": VN diary, May 8, 1963, VNA.

great artist in nostalgia: Julian Moynahan, *Vladimir Nabokov,* Pamphlets on American Writers 96 (Minneapolis: University of Minnesota Press, 1971), 5.

"Incidentally, *Mashen'ka*": VéN to Schirman, April 21, 1975, VNA.

"Though basically a law-abiding": VéN to ML, April 15, 1975, PC.

"noisy construction": VéN to Weidenfeld, June 7, 1975, VNA.

"Rather incredibly": VéN to the Proffers, June 27, 1975, VNA.

356   nervous and edgy: VéN to E. Levin, April 24, 1976, PC.

"is a hopeless undertaking": VéN to Daly, November 24, 1975, PW.

"Only because you're not": Cited in Boyd, 1991, 658. Interview with Loo, May 9, 1998.

"As for me, I am just": VéN to Nat Hoffman, February 24, 1976, VNA.

357   "I have always thought": Schebeko to VéN, February 12, 1976, Interview with Marie Schebeko Biche, February 10, 1997.

"I am sorry that my son": VéN to Hoffman, August 5, 1975, VNA.

she appealed to him: VéN to DN, November 16, 1975, VNA.

"twin soul": Nicoletta Pallini interview with VéN and DN, "Una vita segreta," *Gioia,* October 16, 1989. Also "Così traduco mio padre," *Il Secolo,* October 11, 1987.

horrified by the results: VéN to Helen Jakovlev, June 3, 1983, VNA; interview with Nilly Sikorsky, March 4, 1995.

"He does not know": VéN to Hills, McGraw-Hill, April 20, 1976, VNA.

358   shiver of sadness: Interview with Christine Semenenko, January 27, 1998.

"I am writing you on": VéN to Hills, McGraw-Hill, February 5, 1977, VNA.

hunched and diminished: See also Buckley, *The Right Word,* 379–81.

The BBC dialogue: The account is Robert Robinson's, "The Last Interview," in Quennell, *Vladimir Nabokov,* 119–20.

"My husband wants me to say": VéN to Loo, McGraw-Hill, April 4, 1977, VNA.

359   full and invigorating: Ellendea Proffer to author, May 9, 1997.

He had screamed: VN diary entry, April 24, 1976, VNA.

not even begin to consider: VéN to Nicholas Nabokov, June 27, 1977, VNA.

"the physicians' manner": DN, "On Revisiting Father's Room," *The New York Times Book Review,* March 2, 1980, repr. Quennell, 136. Interview with DN, February 27, 1995.

A few days before the last: VéN to Carl Proffer, June 15, 1983, Michigan.

"S'il vous plaît, Madame": Interview with DN, January 1997.

360   "But please, no tears": Interview with HS, February 26, 1995.

similar request: Interview with Nilly Sikorsky, March 4, 1995.

On the funeral: Interviews with HS; Loo; Marina Ledkovsky, May 19, 1997.

"Let's rent an airplane": Interviews with DN, February 27, 1995, January 1997.

"I am writing to inform": VéN to Schebeko, July 4, 1977, VNA.

contradicted a niece: Interview with Marina Ledkovsky, May 16, 1998.

something was radically wrong: Interview with HS, January 15, 1997.

"it is so much more grim": VéN to Anastasia Rodzianko, July 26, 1979, VNA.

"It doesn't feel": Interview with Boyd, November 23, 1996.

361   "A book lives longer": LL, 125.

packed Dmitri off: VéN to Mrs. Timm, August 30, 1977, VNA.

"half an invalid": VéN to E. Levin, August 7, 1979, VNA.

a question mark: Interview with Ivan Nabokov. VéN wrote Ivan's mother, Natalie Nabokov, that she was bent nearly in two, September 3, 1980, VNA.

the Bishop reunion: Interview with Alison Bishop Jolly, May 20, 1995.

362   the most beautiful woman: A. B. Jolly to DN, April 11, 1991, VNA.

"I have received from": VéN to Nat Hoffman, November 23, 1978, VNA.

"We have been living": VéN to Iseman, January 31, 1978, PW.

"She tried to catch him": A. B. Jolly to author, July 7, 1998.

creative whittling: Interview with Iseman, October 3, 1995.

one of her favorite pastimes: VéN to Vera Peltenburg, June 5, 1978, VNA.

deeply touched: Interview with Matthew J. Bruccoli, April 18, 1995.

363   a note of entreaty: Interview with E. Levin, June 16, 1995.

"Don't forget me": VéN to the Appels, July 3, 1980, VNA.

"I do hope you will visit": VéN to Appel, October 30, 1983, VNA.

still insisting she lacked: VéN to Berkman, April 20, 1983.

neither her Russian nor her English: Boyd to author, June 14, 1997.

"Since they cannot talk": VéN to Elena Jakovlev, September 1984.

364   "that nothing is impossible": Buckley to VéN, February 17, 1980, VNA.

"But at least it is": VéN to Barabtarlo, September 5, 1980, VNA.

"stupidly generous" and "illiteracies": VéN to Parker, December 29, 1982, VNA.

"I have now decided": VéN to the Proffers, November 29, 1982, Michigan. In some card catalogues, she appears as the author of the Russian *Pale Fire.*

"This is very important": VéN to Michael Juliar, January 22, 1986, PC.

And when in doubt: VéN to Kathryn Medina, Doubleday, July 19, 1978, VNA.

"You may find": VéN to Bruccoli, April 8, 1980, VNA.

365   A Roman author: VéN to Bruccoli, August 27, 1979, VNA.

"What an impressively": Cited in Bruccoli to VéN, February 25, 1980, VNA.

the two essential aspects: VéN to Boyd, June 21, 1985, VNA.

wished he did not imitate: VéN to Carl Proffer, August 1, 1978, Michigan. The writer in question was Andrei Bitov.

"No one else—not students": Boyd to VéN, July 6, 1985, VNA.

"I was not going": VéN to E. Levin, December 21, 1979, VNA. See *The New York Review of Books,* July 19, 1979.

"1) to prove my hatred" to "representatives": VéN to Schirman, July 20, 1979, VNA.

366 "was not so much about": DN, *The Nabokovian* 29 (Fall 1992), 15.
begging a mutual friend: Interview with Karlinsky, September 10, 1997.
rebuked one Parisian: VéN to Evgenia Cannac, February 11, 1980, VNA.
"I shall not love you less": VéN to Natalie Nabokov, July 18, 1980, VNA.
she hid her hands: Interview with Karlinsky, May 25, 1998.
367 "I loathe organizations": VéN to Rowohlt, December 5, 1980, VNA.
"between her physical": Robin Kemball to author, March 6, 1997.
"stood for a long time": GIFT, 205.
astonished a scholar: Interview with Barabtarlo, December 27, 1995.
suggest a liberty: Barabtarlo to author, June 30, 1998.
"Could be" to "Absolutely": Boyd to author, December 14, 1997.
"My husband would never": Interview with Barabtarlo.
prominent Nabokov critic: E. Tolstoy, *Smena* (St. Petersburg), April 11, 1991.
terrified of her: Interview with Vladimir Sikorsky; Interviews with Frank Taylor, May 17, 1995;
     Herbert Gold, June 22, 1995.
Paul Bowles: Interview with Bruccoli, April 18, 1995.
most of them were illiterate: VéN to Cannac, June 20, 1980, VNA.
warmhearted regret: VéN to Alison Bishop, May 6, 1983; interview with V. Crespi, January 26,
     1996.
368 a little accident: See DN, "Close Calls and Fulfilled Dreams," *Antaeus* (Autumn 1988), 299–323.
"like a rare animal": Interview with DN, February 27, 1995.
under the weather: Interview with Nat Hoffman, January 23, 1997.
Those who saw her: Interview with E. Proffer, May 15, 1996.
"The car was wholly": VéN to Joan de Peterson, May 13, 1981, VNA.
"Dmitri has seen": VéN to Serge Nabokov, September 25, 1981, VNA.
about her life: Martin Amis to VéN, April 15, 1981, VNA.
"frozen with deference": Interview with Amis, March 10, 1997. The *Observer* piece, from which
     "purple lace" comes, is reprinted in *Visiting Mrs. Nabokov,* 113–21.
"Don't ever let": Interview with Parker, March 2, 1995.
"was as a young man," and the denial: Amis, 118. Interview with Amis; VéN to Amis, September
     11, 1981, VNA.
369 could not impress: VéN to Karlinsky, June 17, 1981, VNA. Karlinsky's piece ran in an abridged
     form in *The Partisan Review* 50, no. 1 (1983). It places VN within an historical context but in no
     way diminishes his work, in or out of the classroom. It does suggest an occasional grudging ad-
     miration for Dostoyevsky.
"You are not a publisher": VéN to Bruccoli, May 18, 1981, VNA.
He testifies that there: Interview with Karlinsky, September 10, 1997.
so long as he did not mention: VéN to Parker, February 4, 1984, VNA.
deleting them: She explained her rationale to Boyd: "There are several reasons why I wish to be kept
     out of the book as much as possible. 1) I am a private person, and would like to stay so. 2) I don't
     think about my letters, write them anyhow and they are not fit to be quoted. Incidental infor-
     mation that I impart is not meant to be treated as anything absolute. Not fit for footnotes" VéN
     to Boyd, May 2, 1986, VNA. She had her wish in some respects: The correspondence that con-
     stitutes SL is so carefully selected as to be misleading. As one critic concluded of VN on pars-
     ing the collection, "He usually served as his own agent." John M. Kopper, in Alexandrov,
     Garland Companion, 62.
"What should I": Amis, *Visiting Mrs. Nabokov,* 119. Interview with Amis.
"You were very" to "from VN": Interview with Boyd, November 21, 1996.
"No" to "Unanswerable": D. Barton Johnson, Ellendea Proffer interview with VéN and DN, *Rus-
     sian Literary Triquarterly* 24 (January 1991), 73–85.
"Madame Nabokov" and "My life": Pallini, *Gioia,* October 16, 1989.
370 people became more attentive: Interview with Karlinsky, September 10, 1997.
"Suffice it to say": Barabtarlo to author, February 15, 1997.
"For once," Véra wrote: VéN to Loo, McGraw-Hill, May 16, 1979, VNA.
"I don't know her patronymic": Boyd interview with VéN, December 19, 1981, Boyd archive.
a beaming smile: Interview with Barabtarlo.

"young women who knew": VéN to Daly, April 17, 1986, VNA.

"made a great number": VéN to Carl Proffer, August 26, 1983, VNA.

371   "like a fool": VéN to Alfred and Nina Appel, March 5, 1986, VNA.

On the "Queen of Spades" research: Interview with Barabtarlo. VN to Gleb Struve, April 15, 1971, LOC; VéN to Barabtarlo, May 6, 1988. See "A Possible Source for Pushkin's 'Queen of Spades,' " *Russian Literary Triquarterly* 24 (January 1991), 43–62. VN's note promising more on the La Motte-Fouqué connection appears in EO, vol. 3, 97.

"You speak of depression": VéN to Cannac, August 25, 1980, VNA.

"Though very old": VéN to Karlinsky, April 9, 1986, VNA.

372   "exquisite pain": VéN to E. Levin, April 19, 1988, VNA.

twice said their good-byes: Interview with DN, October 24, 1996.

which went unread: VéN to Michael Juliar, November 7, 1988, VNA.

"For half a year": VéN to Boyd, May 4, 1988, VNA.

seller did not seem: VéN to Robin Kemball, February 13, 1990, VNA.

"I live in Montreux": VéN to E. Levin, October 5, 1989, VNA.

"a hunchbacked" to "facial expressions": E. Levin to VéN, October 20, 1989, VNA.

373   not having much fun: Interviews with DN, May 26, 1998, Nikki Smith, September 24, 1998.

Tears began to roll: Interview with Parker, March 2, 1995.

"No, never": Interview with E. Proffer, May 15, 1996.

"Aunt Vera" and "very bad": Irina Korsunsky conversation, cited by Lazar Feygin to author, September 14, 1995.

"Is there anything" to "quick death": Interview with V. Crespi, May 20, 1998.

"Véra Nabokov, 89": *The New York Times,* April 11, 1991. For other tributes, see *The Nabokovian* 26 (Spring 1991), i–x.

374   "the monument called 'Nabokov' ": Appel to DN, April 8, 1991, VNA. The sentiment was shared by family members. In her condolence letter to VéN of August 28, 1977 (VNA), Nilly Sikorsky had written, "je suis convaincue que cette oeuvre est vraiment votre oeuvre commune à tous les deux."

"the movements of stars": VN to Jannelli, July 14, 1938, Lilly.

the black cat: Interviews with DN, February 26, 1995, Morris Kahn, July 6, 1998.

ACKNOWLEDGMENTS

375   "The unravelling of a riddle": Unpublished last chapter to SM, LOC. Nabokov worked on the pages for about two months, revising them innumerable times. In the end he decided the fictional premise of the chapter conflicted with the tone of the rest of the memoir. VN to Katharine White, August 2, 1950, BMC.

SELECTED BIBLIOGRAPHY

For a complete Nabokov bibliography, see Michael Juliar's *Vladimir Nabokov: A Descriptive Bibliography* (New York: Garland, 1986), regularly updated in *The Nabokovian*.

Alexandrov, Vladimir E., ed. *The Garland Companion to Vladimir Nabokov.* New York: Garland, 1995.

Amis, Martin. *Visiting Mrs. Nabokov.* New York: Harmony Books, 1993.

Appel, Alfred, Jr., ed. *The Annotated Lolita.* New York: Vintage, 1991.

Appel, Alfred, Jr., and Charles Newman, eds. *Triquarterly* 17 (1970). Reprinted as *Nabokov: Criticism, Reminiscences, Translations and Tributes.* Evanston, Il.: Northwestern University Press, 1970.

Appel, Alfred. *Nabokov's Dark Cinema.* New York: Oxford University Press, 1974.

———. "Nabokov's Puppet Show." *The New Republic,* January 14 and 21, 1967.

L'Arc 24 (Spring 1964). Special Nabokov issue. Aix-en-Provence.

Barabtarlo, Gennady. *Aerial View: Essays on Nabokov's Art and Metaphysics.* New York: Peter Lang, 1993.

Berberova, Nina. *The Italics Are Mine.* New York: Knopf, 1992.

Billington, James H. *The Icon and the Axe.* New York: Vintage, 1970.

Blake, Patricia. Introduction to *Writers in Russia 1917–78,* by Max Hayward. New York: Harcourt Brace Jovanovich, 1983.

Boyd, Brian. *Vladimir Nabokov: The American Years.* Princeton: Princeton University Press, 1991.

———. *Vladimir Nabokov: The Russian Years.* Princeton: Princeton University Press, 1990.

Brenner, Conrad. "Nabokov: The Art of the Perverse." *The New Republic,* June 23, 1958, 18–21.

Buhks, Nora, ed. *Vladimir Nabokov et l'emigration.* Cahiers de l'emigration russe, 2. Paris: L'Institut d'études slaves, 1993.

Davis, Linda H. *Onward and Upward: A Biography of Katharine S. White.* New York: Harper & Row, 1987.

Desanti, Dominique. *Vladimir Nabokov: essais et reves.* Paris: Julliard, 1994.

Diment, Galya. *Pniniad: Vladimir Nabokov and Marc Szeftel.* Seattle: University of Washington Press, 1997.

Ehrenburg, Ilya. *Memoirs 1921–1941.* Translated by Tatiana Shebunina. Cleveland: World Publishing, 1964.

———. *People and Life, 1891–1921.* Translated by Anna Bostock and Yvonne Knapp. New York: Knopf, 1962.

Europe 791 (March 1995). Special Nabokov issue. Paris.

Field, Andrew. *Nabokov: His Life in Art.* Boston: Little Brown, 1967.

———. *Nabokov: His Life in Part.* New York: Viking, 1977.

———. *VN: The Life and Art of Vladimir Nabokov.* New York: Crown, 1986.

Fraser, Kennedy. *Ornament and Silence.* New York: Knopf, 1996.

Gibian, George, and Stephen Jan Parker, eds. *The Achievements of Vladimir Nabokov.* Ithaca: Cornell Center for International Studies, 1984.

Girodias, Maurice. *Une journée sur la terre.* Vol. I, *L'Arrivée.* Paris: Éditions de la Difference, 1990.

———. *Une journée sur la terre.* Vol. II, *Les Jardins d'eros.* Paris: Éditions de la Difference, 1990.

———, ed. *L'Affaire Lolita.* Paris: Olympia Press, 1957.

Heilbrun, Carolyn G. *Writing a Woman's Life.* New York: Ballantine, 1988.

Johnson, D. Barton. *Worlds in Regression: Some Novels of Vladimir Nabokov*. Ann Arbor: Ardis, 1985.

Karlinsky, Simon, ed. *The Nabokov-Wilson Letters*. New York: Harper & Row, 1979.

Karlinsky, Simon, and Alfred Appel, Jr., eds. *The Bitter Air of Exile: Russian Writers in the West, 1922–1972*. Berkeley: University of California Press, 1977.

Levy, Alan. *Vladimir Nabokov: The Velvet Butterfly*. Sag Harbor, N.Y.: Permanent Press, 1984.

Maddox, Brenda. *Nora: A Biography of Nora Joyce*. New York: Fawcett, 1989.

Mandelstam, Nadezhda. *Hope Against Hope*. New York: Atheneum, 1970.

Mandelstam, Osip. *The Noise of Time*. New York: Penguin, 1993.

McGuire, William. *Bollingen: An Adventure in Collecting the Past*. Princeton: Princeton University Press, 1989.

Nabokov, Dmitri. "Close Calls and Fulfilled Dreams: Selected Entries from a Private Journal." *Antaeus*, Autumn 1988, 299–323.

Nabokov, Dmitri, and Matthew J. Bruccoli, eds. *Vladimir Nabokov: Selected Letters, 1940–1977*. New York: Harcourt Brace Jovanovich, 1989.

Nabokov, Vladimir. *Ada or Ardor: A Family Chronicle*. New York: Vintage, 1990.

———. *Bend Sinister*. New York: Vintage, 1990.

———. *Conclusive Evidence*. New York: Harper & Bros., 1951.

———. *The Defense*. New York: Vintage, 1990.

———. *Despair*. New York, Vintage, 1989.

———. *The Enchanter*. New York: Vintage, 1991.

———. *The Eye*. New York: Vintage, 1990.

———. *The Gift*. New York: Vintage, 1991.

———. *Glory*. New York: Vintage, 1991.

———. *Invitation to a Beheading*. New York: Vintage, 1989.

———. *King, Queen, Knave*. New York: Vintage, 1989.

———. *Laughter in the Dark*. New York: Vintage, 1989.

———. *Lectures on Don Quixote*. New York: Harcourt Brace Jovanovich, 1983.

———. *Lectures on Literature*. New York: Harcourt Brace Jovanovich, 1980.

———. *Lectures on Russian Literature*. New York: Harcourt Brace Jovanovich, 1981.

———. *Lolita*. New York: Vintage, 1987.

———. *Lolita: A Screenplay*. New York: Vintage, 1997.

———. *Look at the Harlequins!* New York: Vintage, 1990.

———. *The Man from the U.S.S.R. & Other Plays*. New York: Harcourt Brace Jovanovich, 1985.

———. *Mary*. New York: Vintage, 1989.

———. *Nikolai Gogol*. New York: New Directions, 1961.

———. *Pale Fire*. New York, Vintage, 1989.

———. *Pnin*. New York: Vintage, 1989.

———. *Poems and Problems*. New York: McGraw-Hill, 1970.

———. *The Real Life of Sebastian Knight*. New York: Vintage, 1992.

———. *Speak, Memory: An Autobiography Revisited*. New York: Vintage, 1989.

———. *Stikhi*. Ann Arbor: Ardis, 1979.

———. *The Stories of Vladimir Nabokov*. New York: Knopf, 1995.

———. *Strong Opinions*. New York: Vintage, 1990.

———. *Transparent Things*. New York: Vintage, 1989.

———. *The Waltz Invention*. New York: Phaedra, 1966.

———, trans. *The Song of Igor's Campaign: An Epic of the Twelfth Century*. New York: Vintage, 1960.

———, trans. *Three Russian Poets*. Norfolk, Conn.: New Directions, 1944.

Naumann, Marina Turkevich. *Blue Evenings in Berlin: Nabokov's Short Stories of the 1920s*. New York: New York University Press, 1978.

Nicolson, Nigel. *Portrait of a Marriage*. New York: Atheneum, 1973.

Nosik, Boris. *Mir i dar Vladimira Nabokova: pervaia russkaia biografiia*. Moscow: Penaty, 1995.

Parker, Stephen Jan, ed. *The Nabokovian*. Lawrence: University of Kansas, 1984–. Previously *The Vladimir Nabokov Research Newsletter*, 1978–84.

Perry, Ruth, and Martine Watson Brownley, eds. *Mothering the Mind*. New York: Holmes & Meier, 1984.

Pipes, Richard. *Russia Under the Bolshevik Regime*. New York: Knopf, 1993.

———. *Russia under the Old Regime*. New York: Penguin, 1995.

———. *The Russian Revolution*. New York: Vintage, 1990.

Proffer, Ellendea, ed. *Vladimir Nabokov: A Pictorial Biography.* Ann Arbor: Ardis, 1991.

Proffer, Carl R. *The Widows of Russia.* Ann Arbor: Ardis, 1992.

Pushkin, Alexander. *Eugene Onegin.* Translation and commentary by Vladimir Nabokov. 4 vols. Princeton: Princeton University Press, 1975.

Quennell, Peter, ed. *Vladimir Nabokov, His Life, His Work, His World: A Tribute.* New York: William Morrow, 1980.

Rivers, J. E., and Charles Nicol, eds. *Nabokov's Fifth Arc: Nabokov and Others on His Life's Work.* Austin: University of Texas Press, 1982.

Rose, Phyllis. *Parallel Lives: Five Victorian Marriages.* New York: Knopf, 1983.

Rowe, W. W. *Nabokov's Spectral Dimension.* Ann Arbor: Ardis, 1981.

Russian Literary Triquarterly 24. Special Nabokov issue. Ann Arbor: Ardis, 1991.

St. Jorre, John de. *Venus Bound: The Erotic Voyage of the Olympia Press and Its Writers.* New York: Random House, 1994.

Shakhovskoy, Zinaida. *V poiskakh Nabokova.* Paris: La Presse Libre, 1979.

Shirer, William L. *Love and Hatred: The Troubled Marriage of Leo and Sonya Tolstoy.* New York: Simon & Schuster, 1994.

Sikorski, Hélène, ed. *Vladimir Nabokov: Perepiska s sestroi.* Ann Arbor: Ardis, 1985.

Trahan, Elizabeth Welt. "Laughter from the Dark: A Memory of Vladimir Nabokov." *The Antioch Review,* Spring 1985.

Vesterman, William. "Nabokov's Second Fiancée Identified." *American Notes and Queries,* September/October 1985.

Vishniak, Mark. *Sovremennye zapiski: vospominaniia redaktora.* Bloomington: Indiana University Publications, 1957.

Volkov, Solomon. *St. Petersburg: A Cultural History.* New York: Free Press, 1995.

White, Edmund. *The Burning Library.* New York: Knopf, 1994.

Williams, Robert C. *Culture in Exile: Russian Emigrés in Germany, 1881–1941.* Ithaca: Cornell University Press, 1972.

Wilson, Edmund. *Letters on Literature and Politics, 1912–1972.* Edited by Elena Wilson. New York: Farrar, Straus & Giroux, 1977.

———. *The Fifties.* Edited by Leon Edel. New York: Farrar, Straus & Giroux, 1986.

———. *Upstate.* Syracuse: Syracuse University Press, 1990.

Wood, Michael. *The Magician's Doubts: Nabokov and the Risks of Fiction.* Princeton: Princeton University Press, 1995.

Yakobson, Helen. *Crossing Borders.* Tenafly, N.J.: Hermitage Publishers, 1994.

Yanovsky, V. S. *Elysian Fields.* De Kalb, Ill.: Northern Illinois University Press, 1987.

INDEX

PHOTO CREDITS

With the exception of the following, all photos are from the Nabokov family archive.

Title-page spread: Philippe Halsman, © Yvonne Halsman, 1991
Svetlana Siewert: private collection
Irini Guadanini: private collection
Lena Slonim Massalsky: private collection
Zinaida Shakhovskoy: Shakhovskoy archive, Amherst Center for Russian Culture
Wellesley tea: Wellesley College Archives
Katherine Reese Peebles: Katherine Merle Reese Peebles
Véra at the typewriter: Carl Mydans/LIFE Magazine, © Time Inc.
Butterfly hunting: Carl Mydans/LIFE Magazine, © Time Inc.
Parisian arrival: Bibliothèque Historique de la Ville de Paris
In London: Colin Sherborne
In Milan: Frederico Patellani
Filippa Rolf: Lillian Habinowski
The couple photographed by Rolf: private collection
Villars, 1961, Véra alone, and with Dmitri: Topazia Markevitch
Véra as makeup artist: Henry Grossman
With tennis racquets: Topazia Markevitch
Véra poolside: Philippe Halsman, © Yvonne Halsman, 1991
Véra in 1976: Topazia Markevitch
Montreux Palace, 1964: Henry Grossman

ABOUT THE AUTHOR

STACY SCHIFF was educated at Phillips Academy and Williams College. A recipient of fellowships from the Guggenheim Foundation and the National Endowment for the Humanities, she is the author of *Saint-Exupéry: A Biography*. Her essays and articles have appeared in *The New Yorker, The New York Times Book Review, The Times Literary Supplement,* and *The Washington Post,* among other publications.

A B O U T   T H E   T Y P E

This book was set in Granjon, a modern recutting of a typeface produced under the direction of George W. Jones, who based Granjon's design upon the letter forms of Claude Garamond (1480–1561). The name was given to the typeface as a tribute to the typographic designer Robert Granjon.